The Official

Identification and P

ROC
AND ROLL

The Official®

Identification and Price Guide to

ROCK AND ROLL

Magazines, Posters

and Memorabilia

DAVID K. HENKEL

FIRST EDITION

House of Collectibles • New York

Important Notice. All of the information, including valuations, in this book has been compiled from the most reliable sources, and every effort has been made to eliminate errors and questionable data. Nevertheless, the possibility of error, in a work of such immense scope, always exists. The publisher will not be held responsible for losses which may occur in the purchase, sale, or other transaction of items because of information contained herein. Readers who feel they have discovered errors are invited to *write* and inform us, so they may be corrected in subsequent editions. Those seeking further information on the topics covered in this book are advised to refer to the complete line of *Official Price Guides* published by the House of Collectibles.

©1992 by David K. Henkel

This is a registered trademark of Random House, Inc.

All rights reserved under International and Pan-American Copyright Conventions.

Published by: House of Collectibles
201 East 50th Street
New York, New York 10022

Distributed by Ballantine Books, a division of Random House, Inc., New York, and simultaneously in Canada by Random House of Canada Limited, Toronto.

Text design by Holly Johnson

Cover photo by George Kerrigan

Manufactured in the United States of America

ISBN: 0-876-37851-3

First Edition: June 1992

10 9 8 7 6 5 4 3 2 1

This book is dedicated to the ones I love

Judy Lang
my father Robert Henkel
my sister Pat
my wife Diane
my sons Keith and Matthew
and to all
the lovers of rock 'n' roll

Contents

Acknowledgments

I would like to thank the following for helping me put this guide together:

Toni Brown: *Relix Magazine*, P.O. Box 94, Brooklyn, NY 11229.

Philip Cushway: *Art Rock*, 1153 Mission St., San Francisco, CA 94903.

Sandi Kreml and Annette Funicello: P.O. Box 26610-313, Sacramento, CA 95826.

Susan Ratkis and Carl Giammarese: *The Buckinghams*, P.O. Box 32137, Chicago, IL 60632-2137.

Bill Griggs (Buddy Holly): 3022 56th St., Lubbock, TX 79413.

Bruce Harrah-Conforth and the Rock-and-Roll Hall of Fame and Museum, 520 Terminal Tower, Cleveland, OH 44113.

Shanlee Johnson: *Smiler*, Box 433, Postal Station A, Winnipeg, Manitoba R3K 2C2, Canada.

Karen and John Lesniewski: New England Kiss Collectors' Network, 168 Oakland Ave., Providence, RI 02908.

Rainer Moddeman: *Doors Quarterly*, AM Oelvebach 5, D.4150 Krefeld-Stratum 12, West Germany.

Ann Morgan: *Rumours*, P.O. Box 7210, Virginia Beach, VA 23458.

Charles F. Rosenay: *Good Day Sunshine*, 397 Edgewood Ave., New Haven, CT 06511-4013.

George Schwartz: Celebrity Photos, R.D. 1, Box 1419, Freeland, PA 18224.

Lou Schwartz (Jimi Hendrix): 24 Hillside, Ansonia, CT 06401.

The Back Issue (rock 'n' roll magazines): 24 Orchard St., Ridgefield Park, NJ 07660.

The National Association of Fan Clubs, P.O. Box 4559, Pueblo, CO 81003.

ROCK
AND TEEN
MAGAZINES

Introduction

Teen and rock magazines have always played an important role in America's youth culture. Since the mid-fifties, teenagers and young adults have been drawn to pop music magazines with their eye-catching full-color covers, pin-ups, posters, and inside facts on the most current pop personalities.

In the fifties, it was Elvis Presley, Buddy Holly, Annette Funicello, and others who stirred the emotions of the young. In the sixties, it was the likes of the Beatles, the Rolling Stones, the Monkees, and many others. Today, these magazines appeal to teenagers and adults as well. Unlike many other publications, back-issue teen/rock magazines have not faded into obscurity, but are highly prized by their owners. Teens of today find themselves listening and rocking to many of the same pop performers that their parents enjoyed in past decades and continue to enjoy today.

With the increased popularity of pop music during the past four decades, thousands of radio stations and record shops throughout the modern world service these fans daily. This is one indication of how important music and music stars are in the lives of the fans. They want to know more about their favorites, and they have a need to obtain pin-ups and posters. Their prime source for the past forty years has been the rock/teen magazine.

WHAT MAKES A ROCK/TEEN MAGAZINE VALUABLE?

The primary element in determining the value of a rock or teen magazine is its contents—who is on the cover; what or on whom the feature articles are about; how long, interesting or unusual the articles are and do they include interviews; how many and how rare are the photos; and whether or not color posters or pin-ups are included.

If a group has or is currently enjoying some measure of success, the demand for rock magazines and related memorabilia on that group or personality increases. In short, the greater the star (or stars), the greater the demand for memorabilia on that star, thus increasing the value of the magazine, poster, etc. The exceptions are magazines that were overly mass produced (for example, Elvis Presley and Beatles magazines of 1977–1981).

3

Also, when an older group makes a comeback through touring or new albums, values of magazines featuring them can double or even triple in a very short time. Tribute films and movies also play a major role in determining who is currently popular.

Condition also determines a rock/teen magazine's value. Due to the very nature of pop music fans, few early music magazines survive today in complete mint condition. That is, most enthusiastic fans, after picking up a copy of their favorite issue, would have spent an enjoyable couple of hours pulling out posters and pin-ups, and clipping photos or articles for their cherished scrapbooks. For a magazine to have any value at all, therefore, it must, in most cases, be complete.

After completeness, physical condition of the magazine is next in importance. Unlike comics, coins, and many other collectibles, however, rock and teen magazines are not held to such a strict form of grading. A very good and a very fine copy of an older issue will usually have the same value. Truly mint copies from the fifties and sixties are rare and considerably more valuable.

BUYING AND SELLING ROCK/TEEN MAGAZINES

Current issues of magazines can be found on newsstands or purchased directly by subscription, and many back issues can be ordered through a magazine publisher's back-issue department. When back issues are no longer available from the publisher, however, it is necessary to find other sources.

Record dealers are increasingly including pop music magazines with their inventory, and quite often they offer the latest hard-to-find specialty and foreign rock magazines. When visiting a record shop, it is best to advise the manager of your magazine needs. If he does not have your particular magazine in stock, he will, at least, be conscious of your needs the next time he purchases a magazine collection.

Flea markets and garage sales are also prime collecting sources, and, best of all, the unexpected goodies you find there can usually be purchased at a fraction of their real value. Trade papers that specialize in pop records, magazines, and memorabilia, however, will be your most reliable sources. Dealers and collectors from the United States and many foreign countries regularly offer a continuing supply of back-issue pop magazines. These publications are also excellent for the collector to advertise his or her needs when attempting to add to a collection or when it is time to sell a collection.

Comic book stores, used book shops, and record shows and conventions are also places to acquire back issues. A collector of Kiss magazines, for example, would be wise to attend a Kiss convention. Hundreds of pop music conventions are held in the United States annually. These conventions are not only fine sources for adding to your collection, but are doubly rewarding as places to meet other enthusiasts. Joining a fan club should also be seriously considered as a positive source for acquiring back issues, and also for the additional benefit of being kept informed of upcoming events relating to your fave.

In the recent past, mail-order dealers specializing in rock and teen magazines have become the most reliable means of acquiring magazines on a steady basis. Many mail-order dealerships, such as The Back Issue (24 Orchard St., Ridgefield Park, NJ 07660), purchase magazine collections on a daily basis and maintain active inventories of tens of thousands of issues. If a mail-order dealer does not currently have your back issue in stock, many times he will keep your want list on file and inform you at a later date of its availability.

Before purchasing any rock or teen magazine, however, it is extremely important that you inspect each page for missing pin-ups and clippings. Furthermore, when posters are included in an issue, examine the issue closely to see if they are all there and are reasonably intact. Many magazines with glossy shining covers will appear to be in fine condition. Be cautious, however—it is easy to assume that the entire magazine is this way, but you cannot always judge a book by its cover. When buying through the mail, ask for return privileges if an issue is not complete.

Selling pop music magazines involves basically using the same sources that you used in acquiring issues. Highest prices will be attained when marketing your collection to collectors of your particular group or personality. Trade papers, fan-club newsletters, and conventions are where these collectors are found. In the trade papers and newsletters, an inexpensive classified ad will tell thousands of collectors that your collection is up for sale.

When offering your collection through an ad, you may state your asking price outright for each individual issue or for the entire collection. Another way is to ask for bids. Probably the best way, however, is to sell to a dealer who specializes in rock and teen magazines. When selling to a record shop dealer or your local back-issue magazine and comic book store, don't be shocked to be offered 10–20% of its listed value. In attempting to get your best price, be patient and be willing to negotiate. Most dealers are operating with high overhead and must buy in volume in order to be able to supply a collector's single want. Thus, many purchased issues will remain in inventory for the sake of satisfying an individual customer.

MAGAZINE GRADES

Poor: Any copy that has been clipped and/or has pages or cover missing.

Good: A good condition magazine is a copy that has been well read and handled often, and shows the wear. Color from the cover may be fading. There may be some light water staining, minor tears, and chipping from its cover and pages. Cover may be separated or separating from spine.

Fine: Magazines in fine condition will show sharp covers with no fading of color photos, and no stains, marks, tears or chipping. Cover will be firmly attached to spine. Some very light wear may exist. A subscription label may be on cover but does not affect cover subject.

Mint: Mint copies are issues that are nearly flawless and are as first printed and received by newsstands. A subscription copy can be mint if it is received in a mailing envelope and does not have a subscription label attached to its cover.

PROTECTING MAGAZINES

The best way to preserve the condition of your magazines is to place them individually in specially designed mylar bags backed by acid-free cardboard inserts, and then store them collectively in acid-free boxes. Magazine bags and acid-free boxes can be purchased through the mail, at comic shops, and at back-issue magazine stores. Mail-order dealers supplying bags and boxes regularly advertise in comic books, magazines, and trade publications.

USING THE PRICE GUIDE SECTION

All magazines in this guide are listed alphabetically by title. Each title is then listed by year and issue date or issue number—when applicable, both issue date and number are listed. A detailed listing of contents follows with cover subject(s) appearing first, followed by feature personalities and articles. Finally, prices listed in this guide represent a retail price range based upon actual dealer and auction sales throughout the United States, Canada, and Europe. Prices apply to items in very good to mint condition.

Since it is impossible to list all the rock/teen magazines of the past thirty-five years in this guide, a Collectors' Hotline is available for information on magazines not listed. Also, any other information regarding buying, selling or any other aspect of collecting magazines will be made available to you, the collector, upon request. The Collectors' Hotline number is (201) 641-7212. The hours of availability are 9:00 A.M. to 9:00 P.M. (EST), Monday through Saturday (no collect calls, please).

Rock and Teen Magazines Listing

A

AARDSCHOK AMERICA
1986
Spring #1 Metallica Special Issue with color wall poster, Yngwie Malmsteen, Ozzy Osbourne, Kiss, Savage Death, Death Angel, Queensryche..$4–8
All other issues $2–4

AFTER DARK
1976
Sept. Nona Hendryx & Sarah Dash, Patti Labelle, Special Musicmania Issue, Neil Sedaka: A Song in Two Keys, Mick Jagger, Patti Smith, Peter Frampton, David Bowie, Paul McCartney, The Who..$2–4

AMERICAN CINEMATOGRAPHER
1970
Oct. Special Woodstock Issue, The Film Happening at Woodstock, *Woodstock*: The Acid Test, Getting it All Together..$10–20

1982
Sept. Dolly Parton cover & feature story: *The Best Little Whorehouse in Texas*.........$2–4

AMERICAN PHOTOGRAPHER
1984
June Cher cover & feature story $2–4

ANABAS

1987

#1 Issue is devoted entirely to U2, U2: In the Beginning, The War Tour, Conquering America, Live Aid, U2 Discography, U2: From Strength to Strength $3–6
#2 Issue is devoted entirely to Bon Jovi, Bon Jovi: A Fresh, Exciting New Sound, The Tour of '86, Discography, Bon Jovi: Slippery When Wet, Lending a Hand, Reaching New Heights $3–6
#3 Issue is devoted entirely to Motley Crue, The Theatrics of Rock, The Motley Crue Creation, Monsters of Rock at Donnington, Discography, Motley Crue: Girls, Girls, Girls.....$3–6
#4 Issue is devoted entirely to Kiss, It Started With a Kiss, Sealed With a Kiss, Kiss Discography $4–8
#5 Issue is devoted entirely to Madonna, From Michigan to the Big Apple, Paris–New York Return, Madonna: Video Star, Like a Virgin, Solo Manhattan, Madonna Discography $3–6

1988

#6 Issue is devoted entirely to Michael Jackson, The Michael Jackson Profile, "Victory," The Jacksons, Discography, The Main Men..$3–6
#7 Issue is devoted entirely to George Michael, How it All Began, Birth of Wham, George Michael's School Days, The End, George's Private Life, Solo Artist, Discography $2–4

AQUARIAN WEEKLY (New Jersey Tabloid)

1970

Mar. 11 Rod Stewart..$6–12
Dec. 2 The Beatles, Badfinger...$6–12

1971

Jan. 27 John Lennon & Yoko Ono, George Harrison, Grand Funk Railroad...........$10–20
Feb. 17 Capt. Beefheart, Janis Joplin $15–30

1972

Jan. 31 Frank Zappa movie review: Zapped by Zappa $5–10
Aug. 17 Strawberry Lake: After Woodstock, The Rolling Stones, The Grateful Dead....$5–10
Nov. The Kinks...$5–10
Dec. Old Fillmore Issue $5–10

1973

Apr. Joe Cocker, West, Bruce & Laing, Edgar Winter..$5–10
May Procol Harum, Foghat, John Hammond...$5–10
June Robin Trower, Wishbone Ash $5–10
July The Persuasions, Roger Daltry, Joan Baez, Rare Bird, Paul Simon...................$5–10
Sept. Climax Blues Band interview, McCoy Tyner...$5–10
Oct. 1 The Allmans: A Day at the Track, Eagles interview $5–10
Oct. 30 Mahavishnu Orchestra at the Capital, Chris Jagger, Mike Oldfield...............$5–10

1974

July 18 Argent: Rock Band at the Crossroads, Climax Blues Band interview $4–8
#78 Lou Reed interview, Labelle at the Metropolitan Opera House, Joe Cocker........$3–6
#79 Keith Richards: Stoned Again, Raspberries, Bruce Springsteen...........................$5–10
#82 ELO: Band on the Move, The Miracles: Still Smokin', Jerry Garcia, Bonnie Raitt ..$3–6

1975

#84 Bob Dylan, Alvin Lee, Joe Walsh, Linda Ronstadt $4–8
#86 The New Bette Midler, Al Green, Jackson..$3–6
#87 New York Dolls, Led Zeppelin, Bonnie Bramlett, Harry Chapin, David Lindley interview...$3–6
#90 Janis Joplin: A Love Affair With Janis, Phoebe Snow, David Bowie $5–10
#91 Lou Reed: The Last Great, Ray Davies...$3–6
#94 Brian Jones: Ghost of Rolling Stones' Tours Past, On the Road With the Rolling Stones, Elton John, The Eagles $5–10

#95 Pink Floyd, Renaissance, Dave Bromberg $3–6
#96 Women in Rock, Dana Gillespie, Deadly Nightshade............................$3–6
#99 Punk Rock, Grateful Dead, Jefferson Starship.................................$3–6
#104 Kiss Hath Come: Kiss special—cover, centerfold & feature story, Lou Reed, ELO, The Tubes, Rod Stewart, Bay City Rollers, Abba, Jimmy Cliff $10–20
#105 Frank Zappa, ZZ Top, Bea Flatte $3–6

1976

#106 Disco '75, Patti Smith: Ladies & the Tramp, The Who: Pete Townshend Confronts Himself, Rockin' With Roxy Music, Paul Simon......................................$3–6
#107 John Prine, Talking Heads, Patti Smith, Dr. John, The Osmonds $3–6
#108 Rolling Thunder, Aretha Franklin at Carnegie Hall, Queen, Fleetwood Mac, The Bay City Rollers $3–6
#109 Deep Purple: Party & Interview With Patti Smith & Doc Watson, The Dolls, The Bay City Rollers, Brian Jones $3–6
#110 David Bowie: The Diamond Dog, Lou Reed, Paul McCartney, Jodi Foster $3–6
#111 Bob Dylan, Cher, Greg Allman..$3–6
#112 Pete Seger, Dr. John, Roger Glover/Deep Purple $3–6
#113 Roger Daltry, Patti Smith, Rachel Sweet, Steeleye Span, Poco.....................$3–6
#114 Mick Jagger & Keith Richards, Melanie, Dave Mason Special...........................$4–8
#115 Marijuana Issue, Lynyrd Skynyrd, David Bowie, Genesis...........................$3–6
#116 Punk Rock in the 70s, The Tubes, The Asbury Jukes, The Ramones, Jackson Browne $3–6
#117 Disco: Is it Dead Yet?, Eric Anderson, Abba, Nektar............................$3–6
#118 Wings, Talking Heads, Feelgoods, David Bowie, Flamin' Groovies, Angels of N.Y. $3–6
#119 Fans of the Grateful Dead, The Runaways, Jethro Tull, Elvis Presley, Patti Labelle, Beach Boys...$4–8
#120 Steve Miller, Uriah Heep...$3–6
#121 Kiss cover & Exclusive Interview, Asbury Jukes..................................$5–10
#123 Boz Scaggs interview, Tiny Tim, Patti Smith, Rory Gallagher & Donovan........$3–6
#124 Godspeed & The Beach Boys interviews...$3–6
#125 Blue Oyster Cult, Brian Ferry, Grand Funk, Robbie Benton $3–6
#126 Steve Miller at the Capital, Edgar Winter, Nona Hendryx.........................$3–6
#127 Bee Gees, Arlo Guthrie, John Mayall, Herman's Hermits, Christine McVie.......$3–6
#129 Strawbs, Blue Oyster Cult, Flamin' Groovies, Gangster, Steve Miller $3–6
#130 The Peter Frampton Party: cover & story, The Frankie Valli Party, Bonnie Bramlett Invades Manhattan, John Mayall, Cherry Vanilla......................................$4–8
#132 Punk Rock, Tower of Power, Hot Tuna, Steeleye Span $3–6
#133 The Saga of Punk Rock, Bruce Springsteen, Nektar, Robin Trower, Peter Tosh, Steve Stills $4–8
#134 Southside Johnny, Steeleye Span, Be-bop Deluxe...............................$3–6
#135 Phoebe Snow, Sparks, Ry Cooder, Melanie, Don McLean, The Heartbreakers...$3–6
#136 Hall & Oates, Mad Oates, Charley Mingus, Dave Mason $3–6
#137 Robert Palmer, Ruby & the Rednecks, Neil Young, Chicago $3–6
#138 Patti Smith Returns to the Apple: cover & story, Elvin Jones, Uncle Floyd......$3–6
#139 Bee Gees, Leo Sayer, Tim Hardin, Ray Charles, Atlantics, Ted Nugent.............$3–6

1977

#140 Linda Ronstadt: Lowbrow Tease or Best Female Singer Around?, Flo & Eddie, Graham Parker...$3–6
#141 The Ramones, Tom Petty $3–6
#143 The Kinks: The Greatest Rock Band of the Decade, Melba Moore, The Good Rats, Boston...$4–8
#145 Jethro Tull: The Minstrel at Radio City, Marshall Tucker, Charlie Daniels, The Outlaws, Chuck Berry $3–6
#147 Debbie Harry/Blondie Laughing All the Way to the Sack—cover & story, UFO, Muddy Waters, Gentle Giant, Boston..$4–8
#149 Queen: The Boys are Back in Town, Thin Lizzy, Blue Oyster Cult $3–6

#150 George Benson Interviewed, Santana, New Riders of the Purple Sage, The Leather & Heart of Bruce Springsteen $4–8
#151 Genesis, Dave Mason, Fleetwood Mac, Manfred Mann, Roy Buchanan, The Hit Man $3–6
#152 Dr. Hook, ELO, Jethro Tull, Santana, Maynard Ferguson, Niecey.................$3–6
#153 Martin Mull, Mighty Clouds of Joy, Tangerine Dream, Charlie Daniels, At the Top With Iggy Pop & David Bowie $3–6
#154 Gregg Allman, Bonnie Raitt, Papa John, America.................................$3–6
#155 Two Ghosts: James Morrison & Lee Harvey Oswald, Peter Gabriel $3–6
#156 The Grateful Dead Special $3–6
#157 Nils Lofgren, The Four Seasons $3–6
#158 David Bromberg, Bay City Rollers, Southside Johnny in London, Garland Jeffreys $3–6
#159 Lenny Kaye Interviewed, Joan Baez, Roger McQuinn, The Outlaws, Hit Man..$3–6
#160 Mike Nesmith Interviewed, Renaissance $4–8
#161 Asbury Park Music, The Angels, The Shirts, Godspeed $3–6
#162 *Star Wars*, The Damned in London, Asleep at the Wheel $3–6
#163 Phil Spector, Olivia Newton-John, Led Zeppelin at the Garden....................$3–6
#164 Chick Corea & Stanley Clarke...$3–6
#165 Pegasus, Dave Mason interview, Television & Blondie in London, Herbie Hancock Interviewed...$4–8
#167 Tommy James, Lester Bangs..$3–6
#169 Liza Minnelli, Bo Diddley, Nektar, Hit Man $3–6
#171 Leonard Nimoy, The Kinks, Crosby, Stills & Nash..................................$3–6
#173 Woodstock Comes to New Jersey, Joey Ramone, The Dictators, Renaissance....$3–6
#174 Yes & Wakeman Reunite, Hit Man, Pink Floyd......................................$3–6
#175 James Taylor, The Asbury Jukes, Keith Richards, The Moody Blues, The Beatles..$3–6
#176 Complete Coverage of the Grateful Dead Concert, *Hair* $3–6
#178 The Return of Bruce Springsteen, The Climax Blues Band............................$4–8
#179 Elvis Costello, Todd Rundgren Interviewed...$4–8
#180 Leo Sayer, Lenny Bruce, Foghat, Rolling Stones, Jackson Browne $3–6
#181 Linda Ronstadt, James Talley & the Woodstock Mountain Review $3–6
#182 Jane Fonda, Carly Simon: Rock Star as Mother, Ultravox $3–6
#183 Playmate Sondra, Bad Company, Backstage at *The Wiz*, The Doobie Brothers, Pete Townshend $3–6
#184 Bruce Springsteen, Mick Jagger, Meat Loaf, The Cream, Bad Company Part II...$3–6
#185 Jack Bruce...$3–6
#186 Tom Waits: The In-crowd's Prophet, The Babys Break Out, Jake Bruce, Chicago ..$3–6
#187 Iggy Pop: Punk Gone Astray, Roger Daltry, Lofgren, Linda Ronstadt, Edgar Winter, Yes, Sex Pistol Madness...$3–6
#188 Rick Nelson: Wonder in His Eyes, Marshall Tucker Band: Southern Rock Survives $3–6
#189 Graham Parker: Rock's Hottest Find, Eddie Money $3–6
#190 Andy Gibb: All the Girls are Star Struck, Simon & Garfunkel, Rod Stewart....$3–6
#191 John Travolta: Disco's Newest Darling, Todd Rundgren on Tour, Ted Nugent: Wild Man $4–8

1978

#192 Linda Blair, John Travolta, Capt. Beefheart, Paul Stanley Without Makeup, AC/DC $3–6
#194 Queen: Creative Abdication, Joni Mitchell, Billy Joel.............................$3–6
#195 Clint Eastwood, Kiss Pictorial, Meat Loaf, Johnny Rotten, Ex-Runaway: Jackie Fox $4–8
#198 Peter Allen, Flo & Eddie, Bob Dylan, Bette Midler, Runaway Lita Ford..........$3–6
#198B The Definitive History of Jazz, Roger Daltry......................................$3–6
#199 The Sex Pistols in the Wilds of Texas, Is Cher Fair?, Al Green, Debbie Harry, Iggy Pop $3–6
#200 John Hammond, Crosby, Nash, Ringo Starr, America, Charlie Daniels, Sha Na Na, Foghat $3–6

#201 Lawrence Hilton Jacobs: Super Sweat Hog, The Dollars & Sense of Punk Rock, Good Rats $3–6
#202 Disco, Foghat..$2–4
#203 The Bee Gees, Peter Frampton, Salute to Jersey Music................................$3–6
#204 Jimmy Buffett, Stephanie Mills: *The Wiz*, The Rolling Stones......................$3–6
#205 Bob Weir on Tour, Leon Russell..$3–6
#206 Exclusive Interview With Harry Chapin...$3–6
#207 Harry Chapin Interview, Bruce Springsteen...$3–6
#208 Bruce Springsteen Short..$2–4
#209 John Hall With James Taylor, George Benson $3–6
#210 Melanie: Making Music Without the Mush, Bill Nelson & Be-bop Deluxe $3–6
#211 Carly Simon Comes of Age, The High Art of British Rock 'n' Roll—Elvis Costello & Nick Lowe, Rolling Stones Reviewed...$3–6
#212 Bob Seger: The Rocker's Right Moves, Jackson Browne, Donny Osmond Gets Married $3–6
#214 Bruce Springsteen Storms the Spectrum, A Brief History of Rock 'n' Roll Movies $4–8
#215 Ray Davies & Company: The Kinks Confuse the Issue....................................$3–6
#216 Mick Jagger: Exclusive—The Rolling Stones Story at the Capital, Grace Jones $4–8
#217 Al Dimeola, Tom Petty: Don't Call Him a Punk..$3–6
#218 The Beach Boys interview, Lou Reed $3–6
#219 Kris Kristofferson, The Buddy Holly Story, Alice Cooper: Alive & Well $3–6
#220 Elton John, Lionel Hampton, Al Jarreau...$3–6
#221 Mark Hamill, Woody Guthrie..$3–6
#222 The Bee Gees, Bruce Springsteen: The Second Look $3–6
#223 Stevie Nicks, The Kinks..$3–6
#224 Kenny Rogers, Buddy Holly Story, Aerosmith, Jimi Hendrix short................$3–6
#225 Elvis: One Year Later, Poco, The Grateful Dead..$3–6
#226 Debby Boone, Jan-Michael Vincent...$3–6
#227 Shaun Cassidy: The Teen Screen Dream $3–6
#228 Chicago Sets Sail, Rick Derringer...$2–4
#229 Herbie Mann, Peter, Paul & Mary $2–4
#230 ELO at the Garden, The Day James Dean Died $2–4
#232 Interview With Ian Anderson of Jethro Tull, Cheap Trick Celebrates $2–4
#233 Elton John Breaks Silence: A Major Interview, Jim Morrison short: The Return of Jim Morrison, Steve Hackett, Flamin' Groovies, Sid Vicious Murder Suspect....................$3–6
#234 *The Wiz* $2–4
#235 Dave Brubeck, Prism, Santana...$2–4
#236 Tom Smothers, Elvis Presley Exclusive: The Secret Elvis Tapes, Heart at the Palladium $3–6
#237 Janis Ian: From Finger-pointing to Painting With Words, Little Feat, Chuck Berry $3–6
#238 Richard Dreyfuss, Frank Zappa on Middle Ground, Steppenwolf, Donna Summer $3–6
#239 Rachel Sweet, Lene Lovich, Wreckless Eric $2–4
#240 Aerosmith: Tyler's Gang, The Outlaws, Blondie short, The Pointer Sisters........$3–6
#241 Grace Jones, Beyond *Rocky Horror Picture Show*, Sonny Rollins interview, The Cars, Marshall Tucker $3–6
#242 Stephen Bishop, Mike Bloomfield, Thin Lizzy, The Clash, Lynyrd Skynyrd......$2–4

1979

#243 George Clinton, Hall & Oates Downplay Their Roots $3–6
#244 Tanya Tucker, Weather Report Talks...$3–6
#245 Bruce Springsteen, Jimi Hendrix: Voodoo Child of the Aquarian Age, The Bee Gees, The Rolling Stones $4–8
#246 Jerry Garcia: Dead Come Alive, 10CC...$3–6
#247 Sarah Dash: After Labelle, Alice Cooper short...$2–4
#248 1979 Music Directory $2–4
#249 Richie Havens, Elvis Imitations, The Grateful Dead Feature Interview.............$3–6
#250 Robert Gordon, Pat Travers...$2–4

#251 Bruce Dern, The Clash Takes U.S.A. by Storm, Phoebe Snow, XTC $3–6
#252 The Doors: Jim Morrison's Poetry of the Dispossessed, Dire Straits Turn U.S. Upside Down, Ronee Blakely...$4–8
#253 The Boomtown Rats: Is America Ready?, Sea Level....................................$3–6
#254 Cher photo in see-through blouse, George Thorogood, David Johansen.............$2–4
#255 Sally Field, Good Rats, Salty Dogs..$2–4
#256 Lene Lovich, Howard Devoto, Jim Morrison short...$3–6
#257 Beatlemania: Behind the Scenes, Patti Labelle: The Bluebird of Success, Elvis Presley, John Lennon, Elvis Costello Holds a Press Conference....................................$3–6
#258 Interviewing Roger McGuinn, Cher, Sister Sledge, Joe Jackson Stands Tall, Chuck Berry Keeps Rockin' $3–6
#259 Rickie Lee Jones, The Jam Looks Outward...$3–6
#260 Bruce Springsteen: Easter in Asbury Park, The Allmans at the Capital............$4–8
#261 The Allman Brothers Reclaim Their Roots, The Stones Benefit.......................$3–6
#262 Ian Hunter Faces the Music, Nazareth...$2–4
#263 Bob Dylan Underground, Tavares...$2–4
#264 *Alien*: The Movie, Roxy Music: Re-make, Re-model, Rick James $3–6
#265 Sigourney Weaver, *Alien*, Dion: 60's Rocker, Rick James...............................$3–6
#266 Bobby Benson Comes of Age, Felix Pappalaardi, Donna Summer....................$3–6
#267 Charlie Daniels: A Rebel-rousing Family Man $2–4
#268 Susan Anton, Steve Harley, Barbara Streisand, The Punk Funk of Rick James, Graham Parker...$3–6
#269 Pete Townshend/The Who interview, Margot Kidder, Diana Ross Calming a Caged Tiger...$3–6
#270 Moonraker/007, Lene Lovich, The Damned $3–6
#271 Mick Taylor Becomes His Own Boss, Cheap Trick in the Afternoon, Rockpile ...$3–6
#272 Rachel Sweet Doesn't Have the Time to Fool Around, Johnny Winter: From Blues to Rock-&-Roll Again $3–6
#273 Music Directory Issue...$2–4
#274 Gram Parson's Saga: The Death of the Grievous Angel, Southside Johnny & the Asbury Jukes $3–6
#275 Kansas, Annette Funicello...$3–6
#276 Marlon Brando, Remembering Woodstock, Stephanie Mills, Wings...................$2–4
#277 Dennis Hopper, Herbie Hancock, Dionne Warwick: 17 Years & Still Going Strong, Robert Fripp: On Sound & Silence, Reggae $3–6
#278 Farrah Fawcett interview & cover, Lani Hall..$3–6
#279 Bob Dylan, Neil Young, Alice Cooper, Kiss, Carly Simon $3–6
#280 Michael Caine, Talking Heads: Simplicity Need Not be so Simple, Dave Edmunds, Edgar Winter, Bruce Springsteen..$3–6
#281 *Star Wars*, The Who, John Entwistle interview, The Shirts, Jackson Browne short, Alvin Lee, B-52's, Talking Heads $3–6
#282 Abba cover & interview, Stanley Clarke...$3–6
#283 Robert Palmer Obeys His Own Instincts, Fleetwood Mac short, Elvis Presley ..$3–6
#284 Candice Bergen, A Taste of Honey, The Police..$3–6
#285 Klaus Kinski/Dracula interview, Little River Band, Rick Ocasek of The Cars ...$3–6
#286 Cheap Trick, Bruce Springsteen short, Led Zeppelin.....................................$3–6
#287 Rita Coolidge, Leslie West Exclusive Interview, Debbie Harry, The Eagles.......$3–6
#288 Bette Midler: The Making of *The Rose*, The Motels, The Beat.........................$3–6
#289 Fleetwood Mac, Stevie Nicks...$3–6
#290 Dick Clark Talks About the Birth of the Beatles, Herb Alpert, Pat Benatar, Tom Petty .$3–6
#291 Sally Field interview, Stevie Wonder, Aretha Franklin....................................$3–6
#292 Jefferson Starship Finds "Freedom at Point Zero": interview.........................$3–6
#293 *Star Trek: The Movie*'s Persis Khambatta, Crystal Gale, Graham Nash $3–6
#294 Plasmatics short, John Lennon Returns short, Ellen Foley, J.D. Souther, Flying Lizards...$3–6
#295 Henry Fonda, Jimi Hendrix short, Kiss short, Pat Benatar $3–6

1980

#296 Linda Blair interview, Charles Mingus..$2–4
#297 Melissa Manchester Sizes Up Her Gypsy in Her Soul, The Slits.......................$2–4

#298 Dustin Hoffman, Foreigner Sets the Record Straight, Soupy Sales $2–4
#299 *MASH*, Jimi Hendrix mention, John Mayall interview, Todd Rundgren..............$3–6
#300 Music Directory Issue, Debbie Harry/Blondie $2–4
#301 Robby Benson interview, Ian Hunter...$2–4
#302 John Ritter interview, The Beatles, Melba Moore, Debbie Harry, Tribute Rock.....$3–6
#303 The Pretenders, Taj Mahal, New Riders of the Purple Sage................................$2–4
#304 ....$2–4
#305 Martin Sheen, Joan Armatrading, Iggy Pop on Morals $3–6
#306 Nicolette Larson, Linda Ronstadt, The Pretenders, The Flying Burrito Brothers....$2–4
#307 Gary Numan Ponders the End of the World, The Specials, Bruce Dern, Billy Joel
....$2–4
#308 Karen Allen, Teddy Pendergrass, Pink Floyd $2–4
#309 Alan Bates, Wilson Pickett, Lacy J. Dalton, Bob Geldoff $2–4
#310 Martin Mull, Lacy J. Dalton, The Jam $2–4
#311 Hall & Oates, Kristy McNichol, No More Rock for Patti Smith $2–4
#312 Susan Sarandon, Warren Zevon, Leonard Nimoy, Ted Nugent Tests His Suspension
System..$2–4
#313 Bill Murray, Peter Wolf of J. Geils Band...$2–4
#314 Peter Fonda interview, Grace Slick Follows Her Dreams $2–4
#315 James & Stacy Keach, Robin Trower, Pat Travers, Bobby Bare.......................$2–4
#316 Harrison Ford, Van Halen, Selector, Lene Lovich, Bob Dylan $2–4
#317 Jack Nicholson, Bruce Springsteen, Southside Johnny & the Asbury Jukes $3–6
#318 Ted Nugent, Jan & Dean, The Brothers Johnson, Gang of Four $2–4
#319 Emmylou Harris, Kitty Hawk, Gentle Giant, Nazareth, Spider, The Feelies......$2–4
#320 The Blues Brothers, Genesis, Mickey Gilley, Chris Atkins, Dave Bromberg......$2–4
#321 Robert Redford, John Travolta: *Urban Cowboy*, Debbie Harry/Blondie, Meat Loaf
....$3–6
#322 The Eagles interview, Triumph, John Cale $3–6
#323 Elliot Gould interview, The Grateful Dead's Jerry Garcia: After 15 Years, He's Still
Playing in the Band, The Rolling Stones at Danceteria.......................................$3–6
#324 Susan St. James, Bonnie Raitt $2–4
#325 Wreckless Eric, Dr. John $2–4
#326 Music Directory Issue, Cheech & Chong, Herman's Hermits...........................$2–4
#327 Mark Hamill, James Brown, The Fabulous Thunderbirds, Devo $2–4
#328 ....$2–4
#329 ZZ Top, Lynyrd Skynyrd, Queen Bob Marley, Allman Brothers, John Lennon Returns
....$2–4
#330 Kris Kristofferson, Nancy Allen...$2–4
#331 Yes, Ron Ely, Judas Priest, Blood, Sweat & Tears...$2–4
#332 Eddie Money: Playing for Keeps, Peter Noone..$2–4
#333 Bob Marley, Ex-Kiss Member Peter Criss, The Kink's Dave Davies, Hall & Oates,
Delta 5 ....$3–6
#334 Bruce Springsteen: The Return of the Boss, Journey $3–6
#335 Art Garfunkel, Soupy Sales, Bette Midler, Johnny Paycheck, Ted Nugent, Bruce
Springsteen..$2–4
#336 David Bowie: Musician & Actor Glows on Broadway, Eddie Jobson: Jethro Tull, John
Lennon Speaks, Bruce Springsteen..$4–8
#337 Christopher Reeves, Blue Oyster Cult, Bruce Springsteen, John Lennon, Todd
Rundgren...$2–4
#338 Cher interview, Gary Numan...$2–4
#339 On the Set With Adrienne Barbeau, Billy Burnette, Mickey Hart: The Grateful Dead
....$2–4
#340 Donald Sutherland, Kansas, Kid Creole & the Coconuts, Backstage With Billy Joel
....$2–4
#341 Christopher Walken, Tom Petty, Joni Mitchell $2–4
#342 Badfinger..$2–4
#343 James Colburn, Ray Sharkey, James Brown...$2–4
#344 Stephen Bishop, The Stranglers, Pat Benatar: The First Lady of Rock 'n' Roll....$2–4
#345 ....$2–4

#346 John Lennon Vigil Edition, John Travolta, The Mo-dettes, Rick Springfield interview, Abba, Cheap Trick...$3–6
#347 Rockpile interview, John Lennon Remembered $2–4

1981

#348 Jim Morrison & Why The Doors are Hot in 1981, After John Lennon.............$4–8
#349 The Top Ten in 1980, The Police: Breaking Down All the Established Barriers...$2–4
#350 Cheap Trick interview, Rick Derringer, Abba, Meat Loaf's Exclusive Return....$2–4
#351 Charlie Daniels, Mick Jagger, The Police, The Good Rats.................................$2–4
#352 Music Directory Issue $2–4
#353 Talking With Greg Allman, Marshall Tucker Band, Elvis Costello....................$2–4
#354 Rex Smith Talks: *Pirates of Penzance*, Adam Ant......................................$2–4
#355 John Lennon & Yoko Ono: Here at the Dakota, Bruce Springsteen, Elvis Costello $4–8
#356 Ric Ocasek: The Cars' Driver, Prince: The Next Stevie Wonder........................$3–6
#357 Pat Benatar: Best Rock Performance Female, The Grammys $3–6
#358 Garland Jeffreys, Lenny Kaye, The Rolling Stones $2–4
#359 Jack Nicholson interview, Brian Eno, Pink Floyd interview $2–4
#360 Rick Nelson: The Wine Keeps Getting Better, Rosanne Cash, Remembering the Beatles...$4–8
#361 REO Speedwagon, Bruce Springsteen $2–4
#362 Elvis Presley: Did the Myth Take Over the Man?.......................................$3–6
#363 Cliff Richard, Peter, Paul & Mary interview...$2–4
#364 Susan Sarandon, Ozzy Osbourne, Johnny Lee, U2, Phoebe Snow $2–4
#365 The Knack: Don't Knock It if You Haven't Got It, Dick Clark, Teardrop Explodes, The Dead Kennedys..$2–4
#366 Keith Richards: Ready to Rock, Jimi Hendrix short, Ellen Foley, The Rolling Stones $3–6
#367 AC/DC interview, Hazel O'Connor $2–4
#368 Ringo Starr & Barbara Bach, Bob Marley, Ted Nugent, Blasters, Public Image....$2–4
#369 Styx, Spandau Ballet...$2–4
#370 Kim Carnes: The Eyes Have It, John Cale, Reggae $2–4
#371 Sean Connery, Gary U.S. Bonds, Ritchie Blackmore, Joe Sample, Ian Stewart........$2–4
#372 Exclusive Interviews With—Southside Johnny, Rush & Mick Fleetwood, Brenda Lee, U2, Teardrop Explodes $3–6
#373 Eric Clapton: Rock Retrospective, Oak Ridge Boys, Gary Lewis & the Playboys, Ray Charles $3–6
#374 Roger Moore, Adam Ant, Rick Wakeman, Gloria Gaynor, Jimmy Cliff, Ricky Scaggs $2–4
#375 The Outlaws, Bruce Springsteen, Juice Newton, Warren Zevon, Murray the K, Squeeze $2–4
#376 Kurt Russell, Asbury Park: The Sound is Not the Same, Judas Priest Defends its Image, Little Richard, Chic $2–4
#377 Cicely Tyson, Roger Taylor Steps Out from Queen, Ornette Coleman, Plastics, Blues Project $2–4
#378 Music Directory Issue $2–4
#379 Isaac Hayes interview, Blackfoot interview, Adrienne Barbeau, The Moody Blues $2–4
#380 Brooke Shields, Journey: Finding the Right Formula, The Searchers Battling Back from the 60s, Stiff Little Fingers, REO Speedwagon, Bay City Rollers, The Temptations $2–4
#381 The Saga of Hank Williams Sr. & Jr., Marshall Tucker Band interview, Tom Petty $2–4
#382 Van Halen in Control, Judas Priest..$2–4
#383 Mick Jagger & Stones Fever, Joe Walsh, Richard Thomas, Specials, Killing Joke, ZZ Top $2–4
#384 John Entwistle: Rebels Against His Image, Exclusive Report from Paris: Ceremony at Jim Morrison's Grave...$4–8
#385 Foreigner interview, Psychedelic Furs, The Go-go's, Iggy Pop, The Jackson Five.$3–6
#386 Meat Loaf interview, Pablo Cruise, Tom T. Hall, The Electrics............................$2–4

#387 Stevie Nicks: The Mystic & the Star, Peter Tosh: "I'm Not the Next Bob Marley," The Rolling Stones Concert, Simon & Garfunkel: A Day in the Park $5–10
#388 John Belushi interview, Ray Davies exclusive interview, Squeeze $2–4
#389 Electric Light Orchestra...$1–2
#390 Billy Idol: From Generation X, King Crimson, Pretenders, Kinks, Journey........$2–4
#391 Peter Falk, Lynda Carter interview, Little River Band interview, Bush Tetras interview $2–4
#392 John Densmore: Ex-Doors' Drummer, Siousie Sioux & the Banshees, George Harrison interview, Dan Fogelberg...$2–4
#393 Mick Jagger & the Rolling Stones, Harry Chapin, Bob Dylan $2–4
#394 1981 Rolling Stones Diary, A Look Back in Time With the Rolling Stones—Circa 1965, The Stones in Newark $4–8
#395 Paul Newman $1–2
#396 Pigbag, Hall & Oates, Bebe Buel, The Village People, Killing Joke $2–4
#397 Foreigner's Mick Jones interview, Dexy's Midnight Runners $2–4
#398 Prince, Rod Stewart, Bow Wow Wow, AC/DC, The Knack, Genesis, Greg Lake, Pete Shelley $2–4
#399 Steve Martin, Alabama, The Slits...$1–3

1982

#400 Chevy Chase, Bob Weir, Eddie Murphy $2–4
#401 Blondie's Jimmy Destri Spins His Heart on a Wall, Amy Irving, Foreigner, Joan Jett on Long Island, Natalie Cole..$3–6
#402 Siousie & The Banshees, John Lennon Bootlegs...$2–4
#403 Special Country Pickin' Issue, Dottie West, Juice Newton, The Kinks, J. Geils Band $2–4
#404 Music Directory Issue, Nils Lofgren $1–2
#405 Hall & Oates, The Bloods, Allman Brothers...$2–4
#406 Pia Zadora, J. Geils' Peter Wolf, New Riders of the Purple Sage.....................$2–4
#407 Nick Nolte interview, The Return of Janis Joplin, Todd Rundgren, The Fleshtones $3–6
#408 Waylon Jennings interview, Rosanne Cash $1–3
#409 Depeche Mode, Wayne Kramer, Del Shannon...$2–4
#410 Marianne Faithful, James Mason $2–4
#411 Joan Jett Exclusive Interview $5–10
#412 Michael Caine, Twisted Sister, Pure Prairie League, Blasters $2–4
#413 Christopher Reeve, Merle Haggard, Simon & Garfunkel, Joan Jett, Dolly Parton....$2–4
#414 Lesley Ann Warren $2–4
#415 Paul Schrader & the Cat People $1–2
#416 Ozzy Osbourne interview, Marshall Crenshaw profile $2–4
#417 Jimi Hendrix Reveals Himself at the Other End, The Good Rats......................$4–8
#418 Journey: At the Top, Sonia Braga interview..$2–4
#419 Special Heroin Issue, Rod Steiger $1–2
#420 Sylvester Stallone, John Cougar, Peter Tork $2–4
#421 Arnold Schwarzenegger & Sandahl Bergman $2–4
#422 Joe Jackson, Mamas & Papas interview, Clint Eastwood...................................$2–4
#423 Gilda Radner, The Clash: Two Views, Joe Cocker $2–4
#424 Charlie Daniels: A Symbol of Down Home $2–4
#425 Steve Miller, Uncle Floyd, Tab Hunter, Jobeth Williams...................................$2–4
#426 John Carpenter, Southside Johnny interview...$2–4
#427 Harrison Ford interview, Steve Forbert, Mick Taylor interview, The Asbury Park Sound $3–6
#428 Duran Duran, Steve Miller, Bonnie Raitt...$2–4
#429 Kurt Russel interview..$2–4
#430 David Johansen interview, Echo & the Bunnymen, Smokey Robinson, Chuck Mangione $2–4
#431 Henry Winkler $1–2
#432 Pink Floyd: The Wall, Kristy McNichol, Elton John...$2–4
#433 Christopher Atkins..$1–2
#434 Elvis Costello, Grace Slick...$2–4

#435 Beatlemania in 1982, The Original Beatles $2–4
#436 Tanya Roberts interview, Graham Nash interview, Crosby, Stills & Nash..........$2–4
#437 George Thorogood interview $2–4
#438 Bruce Springsteen, The Rock Industry..$3–6
#439 Matt Dillon interview, Bruce Springsteen $2–4
#440 Linda Ronstadt, Billy Joel, Jimi Hendrix, Billy Squier, Billy Idol, Kenny Loggins, Kim Carnes, Catholic Girls, Peter Gabriel..$3–6
#441 David Lee Roth interview, The Who Farewell..$3–6
#442 Judas Priest: A Talk With Rob Halford, Bellamy Brothers............................$2–4
#443 Jefferson Starship interview, The Go-go's are So Much Fun......................$4–8
#444 The Ramones: Still Makin' Music...$3–6
#445 REO Speedwagon, Nicolette Larson, Psychedelic Furs, George Harrison, Men at Work, Poco, Linda Ronstadt, Jerry Garcia...$2–4
#446 A Conversation With Billy Squire, The Cramps, Kenny Loggins, R.E.M., Tanya Tucker, Eric Anderson, Blue Oyster Cult...$2–4
#447 Iron Maiden interview, Kim Carnes, Peter Gabriel, Stray Cats, Gary Numan, Van Halen, Tom Petty, Rose Tatoo $2–4
#448 Devo: Back to the Womb, Led Zeppelin, The Jam, Keith Jarrett, Altered Images, Nash the Slash $2–4
#449 Pat Benatar: Will Success Still Her Song?, Roches, Squeeze, Steve Forbert, Grace Jones, Human League, Joni Mitchell $4–8
#450 The Plasmatics: Wendy O. Williams Speaks $3–6
#451 Stray Cats interview, Sunrize, Joe Jackson, Robert Plant, Gary U.S. Bonds, Foreigner, Culture Club, Psychedelic Furs..$3–6
#452 Bow Wow Wow, George Thorogood, Thompson Twins, ABC............................$3–6
#453 Billy Joel, Genesis, Thompson Twins, Rod Stewart, John Lennon, Led Zeppelin, The Jam, Musical Youth $3–6
#454 Bongos, Bob Seger, Grandmaster Flash, The Fleshtones, David Johansen, Persuasions $3–6
#455 Ron Wood: Disaster at Town Home, Lydia Lunch, Poco, John Cale..................$3–6
#456 The Rolling Stones: The Party...$3–6
#457 Catholic Girls interview, Waylon Jennings, Dicky Betts, Missing Persons, James Blood Ulmer..$2–4
#458 Aerosmith: An Anterview With Steven Tyler, Dexy's Midnight Runners, John Hall, Chuck Berry, The Outlaws...$3–6
#459 Dave Wakeling of the English Beat interview, Garland Jeffreys, Randy Newman, Todd Rundgren, Otis Blackwell...$3–6

1983

#460 Phil Collins interview, Boy George interview, A Talk With Nina Blackwood of MTV $3–6
#461 The Pretenders' Martin Chambers interview, Eric Clapton, ELO, Simple Minds, Thompson Twins, Berlin...$3–6
#462 Rita Marley interview, Thomas Dolby, Neil Young, Herbie Mann, James Brown, Nona Hendryx, Culture Club, America...$3–6
#463 Greg Kihn, Alvin Lee, Lou Reed, Warren Zevon $2–4
#464 The Tour of Lene Lovich, Nails, Dr. Hook, Robert Fripp, Bongos $3–6
#465 Styx: Tommy Shaw interview, Prince, Scandal, Metallica, Hall & Oates, Blotto...$3–6
#466 Carl Wilson interview, Randy Newman, Billy Squier......................................$3–6
#467 Bob Weir interview, Tom Petty, Nick Lowe, Beach Boys, Blotto, Styx, John Stewart $3–6
#468 Keith Richards in Words & Music, The Brian Jones Story, Nick Lowe, Depeche Mode, Little Steven $3–6
#469 Joey Ramone interview, Modern English, The Shirelles, Greg Kihn, The Grateful Dead $3–6
#470 Peter O'Toole, Blasters, Renaissance...$2–4
#471 Ultravox, Bananarama, Muddy Waters, Man Parish.....................................$2–4
#472 Kinks interview, The Waitresses, Troggs...$3–6
#473 Asbury Park 1983, Marianne Faithful interview, A Talk With Molly Hatchet, The Roches, Modern English..$3–6

#474 Journey: The Hard Journey to Talk, Dave Edmunds, Ellen Foley, The Kingston Trio, Marvin Gaye, Golden Earring..$3–6
#475 In Search of Reggae, The Kinks, Rockats, John Prine...$2–4
#476 Interview With The Edge & Larry Mullen Jr. of U2, Roxy Music, Dead Kennedys, Anthony Perkins interview, Martin Briley $3–6
#477 Roger Moore, Bongos, Bobby & the Midnites...$2–4
#478 Dave Edmunds: A Rock 'n' Roll Survivor, Tubes, Rickie Lee Jones, Duran Duran $2–4
#479 ....$2–4
#480 Hall & Oates interview, Marshall Crenshaw, Robert Palmer, U2, Willie Nelson....$3–6
#481 Steve Ray Vaughan interview, The Animals 1983 interview, The Beach Boys, Rank & File, Peter Tork, Hall & Oates $3–6
#482 Bob Dylan, Talking With Motorhead, Melanie interview, Shirelles, Joni Mitchell..$3–6
#483 The Mystique of Def Leppard, Flamin' Groovies, Marillion, Peter Gabriel, The Animals, Marty Balin, Davie Bowie $3–6
#484 Tears for Fears, Violent Femmes, Meat Loaf, Jackson Browne.............................$3–6
#485 Chevy Chase interview, Krokus, Madness, Dr. Demento, Aztec Camera, King Sunntade, Twisted Sister, Flock of Seagulls, Early Beatles on Film, Tom Cruise........$3–6
#486 Joan Jett interview, The Police at Shea...$5–10
#487 Neal Young, Culture Club interview, David Bowie $3–6
#488 Marshall Crenshaw interview, David Bowie, The Moody Blues, The Beach Boys ..$3–6
#489 Southside Johnny interview, The Spinners...$3–6
#490 An interview with Dave Stewart of Eurythmics, Bruce Springsteen.....................$3–6
#491 Led Zeppelin: They Rocked—Special Rock Giants Series, NRBQ.........................$3–6
#492 Big Country interview, interview with Kevin Dubrow of Quiet Riot $3–6
#493 Carly Simon: Her Sensuality & Psyche, The Bongos...$3–6
#494 Beau Bridges interview, Graham Parker, interview with Michael Been of the Call..$3–6
#495 Jim Morrison: The Influence of the Lizard King Continues, Dennis Quaid interview, Interview With Ian Gillan of Black Sabbath, Miles Davis $5–10
#496 Pat Benatar: Close to Home, Johnny Lyon Thrashes It Up at Montclair State, John Cougar Mellencamp Reclaims His Soul, Jim Morrison & the Doors—Giants of Rock Series, Bob Dylan $4–8
#497 Christopher Walken, The Stones: Raw $3–6
#498 Paul McCartney, Interview With Oingo Boingo...$3–6
#499 Interview With John Doe of X, Paul Simon $3–6
#500 Jack Nicholson, Clarence Clemons, Heavy Metal in New Jersey...........................$2–4
#501 AC/DC interview, The Return of Ginger Baker, Michael Jackson $3–6
#502 Nancy Wilson of Heart interview, Ronnie Lane, Eurythmics.................................$3–6
#503 The Alarm, Billy Idol, Genesis, Yes, Michael Jackson/*Thriller* $3–6

1984

#504 Before Words, There Were the Ramones, Peter Gabriel...$3–6
#505 Cyndi Lauper interview, The Alarm...$3–6
#506 Interview With Martin Fry of ABC, The Everly Brothers $3–6
#507 Buddy Holly: A Miracle Worker $3–6
#508 Interview With Tony Banks of Genesis..$3–6
#509 Fellini, Stray Cats, Pretenders $3–6
#510 The Beatles: It Was Twenty Years Ago Today, Tommy James $3–6
#511 Bruce Springsteen interview, Dave Mason, Jimi Hendrix Reveals Himself at the Other End $4–8
#512 The stars of *Footloose*, Huey Lewis & The News $2–4
#513 Music Directory Issue $2–4
#514 Folk Lives, Cyndi Lauper...$2–4
#515 Grace Slick & Paul Kanter interview..$3–6
#516 Debra Winger, Spyro Gyra, Roger McGuinn..$2–4
#517 David Lee Roth interview $3–6
#518 Tarzan: The New Movie, James Brown, Suzanne Vega $3–6
#519 Jimi Hendrix: Color Him Transcendental, Van Halen, John Cougar, Arlo Guthrie, Echo & the Bunnymen..$4–8
#520 Bill Nelson interview, Talking With Girlschool, Sammy Hagar..............................$3–6

#521 Thomas Dolby interview, Jason & the Scorchers...$3–6
#522 Interview With Martin Chambers of the Pretenders..................................$3–6
#523 Marshall Crenshall interview..$3–6
#524 Jon Bon Jovi: Living Dangerously, Ellen Foley.......................................$3–6
#525 Harrison Ford, XTC..$3–6
#526 Steve Van Zandt: A New Voice of America, Peter Garrett of Midnight Oil $3–6
#527 *Star Trek*, Willie Nelson, Bruce Springsteen, The Jacksons, Elvis Costello $3–6
#528 Confronting Bruce Springsteen..$3–6
#529 Interview With Bob Halford of Judas Priest: Keeping the Faith, David Gilmour, R.E.M...$3–6
#530 Bananarama interview, Black Lace...$3–6
#531 R.E.M.: An Interview With Peter Buck, Bruce Springsteen......................$3–6
#532 Bruce Springsteen in St. Paul, Jimmy Buffett, Lou Reed.........................$3–6
#533 George Thorogood, Bill Bruford of King Crimson......................................$3–6
#534 Prince, Nick Lowe...$3–6
#535 The Cars: Stalled, Little Steve Van Zandt, London Beat.........................$3–6
#536 Michael Jackson: Where There's Hype There's Fire..................................$3–6
#537 Bruce Springsteen: New Jersey's Own Comes Home................................$3–6
#538 Tanya Roberts, Paul Simon, Crosby, Stills & Nash, Livingston Taylor..............$3–6
#539 INXS Interviewed, Gun Club...$3–6
#540 Interview With Ronnie James Dio, Bonnie Raitt..$3–6
#541 Warren Zevon, Fashion...$2–4
#542 John Sayles, John Waite interview, David Knopfler...................................$2–4
#543 Linda Ronstadt: A Bright Victory, Rod Stewart, Maria Mauldaur..............$3–6
#544 Psychedelic Furs: They're Doing Alright, Christopher Reeve...................$3–6
#545 Lou Reed, Diana Ross...$2–4
#546 David Bowie: A Look at King David..$3–6
#547 Theresa Russell, The Night Thousands Gave Southside Johnny the Finger........$2–4
#548 John Lydon interview, The Story of Johnny Rotten....................................$3–6
#549 Lindsay Buckingham: Taking Risks...$3–6
#550 Southside Johnny interview, John Cafferty...$2–4
#551 *Supergirl*: The Movie, Richard Hell, John Cale, Test Dept. $2–4
#552 Vanessa Redgrave interview, Pat Benatar, Lenny Kaye............................$2–4
#553 Dave Wakeling of General Public Interviewed, Madonna's "Virgin".............$2–4
#554 *Dune*: The Movie, Pete Seger...$2–4
#555 Big Country...$2–4

1985

#556 Jim Carrol interview, The Fixx..$2–4
#557 Matt Dillon: The Flamingo Kid, J. Geils Band, Toto.................................$2–4
#558 Bob Geldof, Joan Jett & the Black Hearts, The Skirts.............................$3–6
#559 Tom Robinson interview, Talking With the Triffids....................................$2–4
#560 Roddy Frame & Aztec Camera..$2–4
#561 Phoebe Snow, The Fleshtones, Folk Music...$2–4
#562 Johnny Winter, The Ramones...$2–4
#563 Music Directory Issue..$1–2
#564 The Breakfast Club, London Beat...$1–3
#565 The Ramones: Joey Ramone interview, Bruce Springsteen Wraps Up His Tour $2–4
#566 Interview With Andy Partridge of XTC, REO Speedwagon, Mick Jagger..........$3–6
#567 Hall & Oates: John Oates interview, Breakfast Club.................................$3–6
#568 Deep Purple, Los Lobos...$2–4
#569 Malcolm McLaren interview, Keith Richards...$2–4
#570 Madonna, Talking With Mary Travers, Malcolm McLaren........................$3–6
#571 Billy Bragg interview, The Kinks...$2–4
#572 Richard Thompson interview, Deep Purple, Ramblin Jack interview.............$2–4
#573 Linda Thompson interview, Kiss at the Meadowlands................................$3–6
#574 Del-Lords interview..$2–4
#575 Angry Young Housewives, Dead Kennedys..$2–4
#576 The Bongos, Richie Havens..$2–4
#577 Sylvester Stallone, Eddie & the Cruisers, Southside Johnny Special Interview ..$2–4

#578 Jason & the Scorchers interview...$2–4
#579 John Travolta & Jamie Lee Curtis..$2–4
#580 Todd Rundgren interview, Suzanne Vega $3–6
#581 The Stranglers...$2–4
#582 Madonna & Her Followers..$2–4
#583 *Mad Max*, Alive With DOA, Jody Guthrie, Tom Petty, Fairport Convention $2–4
#584 Bob Dylan, Katrina & The Waves.....................................$2–4
#585 Tina Turner in *Mad Max*, The Return of Dan Fogelberg............$2–4
#586 The Blasters interview, Raven Invades New York $2–4
#587 Carly Simon: Carly Comes Back, New Order......................$2–4
#588 Simon Townshend interview, Bruce Springsteen $2–4
#589 Angus Young & Brian Johnson of AC/DC, Bonnie Raitt.......$2–4
#590 Supertramp, Tina Turner $2–4
#591 Bruce Springsteen, Punk Zombies $2–4
#592 Sandra Bernard, Godzilla, The Searchers, Nina Hagen $2–4
#593 Jane Fonda, Squeeze..$2–4
#594 Godley & Creme, R.E.M...$1–2
#595 Peter Garrett of Midnight Oil, Neil Young, Creator, Genocide, Madonna...........$2–4
#596 John Cafferty interview, Foreigner....................................$2–4
#597 Squeeze, John Cougar, Heavy Metal $2–4
#598 Sting, NRBQ, Cocteau Twins...$2–4
#599 Dire Straits, Heavy Metal $2–4
#600 James Taylor: A Profile, Porn Rock, Frank Zappa $2–4
#601 Scritti Politti...$1–2
#602 Howard Jones, Rosanne Cash $2–4
#603 Nick Lowe, The Cure, Cheap Trick $2–4
#604 Red Hot Chili Peppers, Ratt, Bon Jovi.................................$2–4
#605 Stevie Nicks: The High Priestess of Rock, Little Steven $5–10
#606 Grace Jones, Charlie Daniels, Jason & the Scorchers, Tom Waitts......$2–4
#607 John Cougar Mellancamp, Violent Femmes..........................$2–4

1986

#608 The Replacements...$2–4
#609 Interview With Paddy McAloon of Prefab Sprout, Residents $2–4
#610 The Alarm on the Roll, Todd Rundgren $2–4
#611 Mike Rutherford interview: The Genesis Man, Marshall Crenshaw $2–4
#612 A Profile of Pat Benatar: Rock's Royal Bitch, Simply Red $3–6
#613 Robyn Hitchcock, Pat Benatar Part 2.................................$2–4
#614 The Damned, Twisted Sister, Dokken, Cockrobin..................$2–4
#615 Kate Bush Interview: Forget the Personality Stuff.................$3–6
#616 Music Directory Issue $1–2
#617 Handsome Dick Manitoba, Dictators, John Weton of Asia.......$1–3
#618 10,000 Maniacs, Loverboy, Ozzy Osbourne, The Firm, Dokken $2–4
#619 The Earth, Wind & Fire of Jackson Browne, Long Ryders interviews, Pat Benatar
....$3–6
#620 Lloyd Cole, Tom Rush, The Replacements, Husker Du $2–4
#621 INXS interview, The Fall, The Damned, Wall of Voodoo.........$2–4
#622 Paul Rogers interview, The New Van Halen, Violent Femmes......$2–4
#623 The Rolling Stones: Can Millionaires Really Rock-&-Roll?, Mink Deville interview
....$3–6
#624 Brian Setzer, The Bangles: A Convincing Performance, The Cult, Lloyd Cole, Charlie
Sexton, Vid Times..$2–4
#625 John Lydon interview, Husker Du, Cab Calloway, Julian Lennon.............$2–4
#626 Stan Ridgway, Ministry, Noise Fest....................................$2–4
#627 The Cult, Brian Setzer, Smashed Gladys, Prince $2–4
#628 Lou Reed, Cherry Bombz, Ozzy Osbourne, Thin White Rope............$2–4
#629 Bob Seger: Older & Better, John Hammond, Greg Kihn.............$2–4
#630 Joe Jackson, Stevie Nicks: Somewhat Away from the Center of Herself, Lords of the
New Church..$3–6
#631 Green on Red interview, John Prine, Culture Club $2–4

#632 Husker Du, Madness, Del-Lords, Moody Blues $2–4
#633 Julian Lennon, Jackson Browne, Bo Diddley, Meatmen, Simple Minds..............$3–6
#634 Robert Smith of the Cure, Judas Priest, Richard Lewis $2–4
#635 Mitch Easter, Depeche Mode $2–4
#636 The Fixx, Modern English, Peter Gabriel $2–4
#637 The Church, Modern English, Rod Stewart, Eric Burdon $2–4

AWARD-WINNING KISS EXCLUSIVE

1978

#1 The Girls of Kiss, Monster Kiss Photos, Color Kiss Wall Posters, Giant Color Kiss Photo Album, Diary of a Kiss Photographer, Can Kiss Lick Back?, Led Zeppelin, Peter Frampton, Rolling Stones $10–20

The Beatles

Collecting
THE BEATLES

The Beatles, along with Elvis Presley, are the most collectible and collected artists in the history of rock 'n' roll. From their raw beginnings in Liverpool to their "invasion" of the world, right up through their break-up and solo careers, no musical act ever captured the imagination, ears, and pocketbooks of so many as did John Lennon, Paul McCartney, George Harrison, and Ringo Starr.

While musicologists can debate what elements made the Beatles so successful, there's no debate over the degree to which the Beatles were commercialized at their peak. It's hard to think of an item merchandised in the mid-sixties that didn't boast the Beatle's logo, photo or likeness. Why?—Because it sold! Along with purchasing millions of records, consumers raided department stores for such goods as Beatle wigs, lunchboxes, trays, "Flip Your Wig" board games, trading cards, buttons, dolls, and so much more.

Although there are no exact figures available, one can only speculate how many millions of packs of Beatle gum cards (at only a nickel a pack) were sold in the mid-sixties. In the sixties, your local 5 & 10 shop was a haven for ten-cent items licensed by NEMS (The Beatles Merchandising Company). Today in the nineties, investors scan the international auction houses for autographs, gold records, instruments or original clothing which may cost more than a fine car. The smaller ten-cent items and gum cards have significantly increased in value as well.

Instead of dwelling on the one-of-a-kind items, which cost a king's ransom, the focus here will be on the numerous and less expensive items that graced the shelves of every other shop in the mid-sixties. Thousands upon thousands of enthusiasts brought these items home for a few dollars or less. Today they are highly sought-after collectibles, and often can be found "collecting" dust in your attic or garage.

The following sample list of moderately priced Beatle collectibles is just the tip of the iceberg when it comes to the enormous number of Beatle items that are available. There are several comprehensive price guides, such as Jerry Osborne's *Official Price Guide to Memorabilia of Elvis Presley and The Beatles*, which will more thoroughly detail the many, many Beatle collectibles that may be found.

Beatles loose notebook binder	$40–80
Blue metal lunchbox	$120–200
Blue metal lunchbox, with thermos	$150–250
Bubblegum cards	
1st series; each	$.50–.75
2nd series; each	$.50–.75
3rd series; each	$.40–.60
A Hard Day's Night; each	$.50–.75
Color series; each	$.50–.75
Diary series; each	$.50–.75
Entire sets of any series	$25–50
Coloring book	$30–45
Coloring book, colored in pages	$20–30
"Flip Your Wig" board game	$75–125
Girl's vinyl lunch pail	$100–175
Girl's vinyl lunch pail, with thermos	$225–275
Ice-cream bar wrapper	$45–75
Irish linen wall hanging	$100–175
Model kits by Revell, assembled. For George or John, add $25 to given price range.	$30–50
Model kits by Revell, unassembled in box. Same as above.	$75–125
Pillow	$75–120
Pillow, full-figure pose	$100–175
Richard Avedon Look poster; each	$20–35
Ticket stubs	
Complete unused ticket	$80–120
Complete unused ticket, with Beatles photo	$90–150
Stub without the word Beatles	$10–20
Stub with photo of the Beatles	$50–90
Stub with the word Beatles	$40–60
Tray, set of five	$125–200

Tray, individual...$35–60
Tray, reissue without sticker..$10–20
Wallet $50–90
Wallpaper, panel with complete pattern...$12–30
Yellow Submarine **comic book** $20–40
Yellow Submarine **hanger; each**..$30–50
Yellow Submarine **hangers**, set of four...$125–200

If you are a buyer and can get the items you're looking for at prices below those listed, chances are that you are getting a great deal. If an item is mint (be sure it is original, of course), expect to pay top dollar, because excellent condition always commands premium prices. If you are selling, do not expect dealers or people in the business (fan clubs, convention vendors, antique dealers, etc.) to pay these listed prices. They have to resell these items for these prices, so try to get 40–50% of the value. Dealers would rather purchase entire collections whenever possible, but high-priced items are always in demand.

Experience the Beatles trading marketplace first-hand by attending a convention or joining a Beatles fan club. Through the years, conventions and fan clubs have managed to keep the spirit of the Beatles alive. Collectors, in turn, keep the conventions and fan clubs going strong. One organization, Liverpool Productions, produces Beatles conventions (and "expos") across the country, while publishing one of the foremost Beatles fan club publications, *Good Day Sunshine*. They also package tours to London and Liverpool for the truly die-hard fans and collectors who wish to visit "Beatleland."

To join the Beatles fan club, Good Day Sunshine (or GDS), send check or money order for $10 ($15 Canada/Mexico, $20 elsewhere), payable to Charles F. Rosenay, to: Good Day Sunshine, 397 Edgewood Ave., New Haven, CT 06511-4013.

Fan club benefits include a subscription to the GDS magazine for one year (five issues of 50 or more pages of news, articles, reviews, collectors columns, ads, trade sections, and much more), GDS membership card, invitations to special events, special sales offers, reduced admission to conventions, and other benefits. A sample copy of the GDS magazine is $3. For information on future conventions, Beatle-fan tours to England, or to be added to Liverpool Productions' mailing list, send a self-addressed stamped envelope to the address given previously.

B

BACKSTREETS (Dedicated to Bruce Springsteen)

All issues...$3–7

BASS PLAYER

All issues...$2–4

BEAT INTERNATIONAL AND INTERNATIONAL RECORDING STUDIO MAGAZINE

1971
Apr. #96 The Doors, Pink Floyd, Stud, Yes...$10–20
July #97 The Band, *Jesus Christ Superstar*, Jellybread...........................$5–10
Oct. #102 Humble Pie, The Beach Boys, Grease Band, Rick Wakeman, Sandy Denny...$5–10

1972
Jan. #105 King Crimson, Frank Zappa, Redbone, Fanny, Polly Palmer, Isaac Hayes...$5–10

BEATLEDOM
1964..$10–20

BEATLEMANIA
1964..$15–30

BEATLEMANIA COLLECTOR'S ITEM
1964..$15–30

BEATLES (E-GO Collectors' Series)
1977
May #8 Their Music & Their Lives...$3–6

BEATLES (A Charlton publication)
#1–#6...$7–15

BEATLES (THE)
1964..$10–20

BEATLES ARE BACK (THE)
1964..$10–20

BEATLES ARE HERE (THE)
1964..$15–30

BEATLES AT CARNEGIE HALL
1964..$20–40

BEATLES, BEATLES, BEATLES
1964..$12–25

BEATLES COLOR PIN-UP ALBUM
1964..$10–20

BEATLES COMPLETE LIFE STORIES
1964..$12–25

BEATLES COMPLETE STORY FROM BIRTH TILL NOW
1965..$15–30

BEATLES FILM (THE)
1964..$12–25

BEATLES FROM THE BEGINNING (THE)
1970..$7–15

BEATLES FUN KIT
1964..$25–50

BEATLES IN AMERICA (THE)
1964..$15–30

BEATLES MAKE A MOVIE (THE)
1964..$12–25

BEATLES MEET THE DAVE CLARK FIVE
1964..$15–30

BEATLES MOVIE
1964..$10–20

BEATLES ON BROADWAY
1964..$12–25

BEATLES PERSONALITY ANNUAL (THE)
1964..$10–20

BEATLES 'ROUND THE WORLD
1964
#1 Includes 10″ × 13″ color wall poster $20–40
#2 Includes 10″ × 13″ color wall poster $15–30
#3 Elvis Presley vs. The Beatles..$25–50

BEATLE SONGS (A Charlton publication)
All issues $7–15

BEATLES STARRING IN A HARD DAYS NIGHT (THE)
1964 ....$12–25

BEATLES TALK (THE)
1964 ....$12–25

BEE GEES SPECIAL
1978
The Bee Gees from Hot Rock to Disco, Andy Gibb: The Gibb Family's Fastest Rising Star, The Gibb Family Legend, The Beatles, The Bee Gees & Peter Frampton: Sgt. Pepper, Their Rocky Road to Stardom, The Bee Gees Discography, Peter Frampton Discography & His Struggle for Success, The Beatle Legend, The Beatles Discography $5–10

BEETLE
1973
June The Bee Gees, Rory Gallagher, The Kinks, Silverhead, Wishbone Ash............$5–10
July Jeff Beck, Edward Bear, Canned Heat, Slade, King Crimson, Frank Zappa......$5–10
Aug. Leonard Cohen, Humble Pie, Herman's Hermits, Genya Ravan, Leslie West, Chad Allen..$5–10
Sept. Guess Who, Mac Davis, Robert Klein, Lee Michaels, Robin Trower, Chad Allen..$5–10
Oct. Alice Cooper, Mott the Hoople, John Mayall, Tony Kosinec, Papa John Creach..$10–20
Nov. The Osmonds, David Bowie, Sha Na Na, Bo Diddley, Gilbert O'Sullivan.......$7–15
Dec. New York Dolls, Spencer Davis, Joe Walsh, Ian Thomas, Focus......................$6–12

1974
Jan. Todd Rundgren, Alvin Lee, Electric Light Orchestra, Edgar Winter, Rick Derringer $7–15
Feb. Keith Emerson, Bachman-Turner Overdrive, Genesis, Lighthouse $5–10
Apr. Iggy Pop & The Stooges, Wolfman Jack, Climax Blues Band, War................$10–20
May Pointer Sisters, Hawkwind, Man, Reggae, The Beach Boys, Mott the Hoople.....$5–10
Oct. Bill Wyman: The Silent Stone Speaks, Roxy Music: Men at the Top, Silverhead: Sixteen & Oversexed, Rory Gallagher, Brownsville Station Goes to College, David Bowie, Mahogany Rush, Chuck Mangione, Billy Joel $10–20
Nov. Grace Slick: Cannibalism & the Death of Airplane, Roy Wood, Sharks, New York Dolls, Staus Quo, Golden Earring, Kiss: Year of the Kiss-off, The Kinks, Mike Oldfield, Eric Clapton..$10–20

BERKELEY TRIBE (Bay Area tabloid)
1969
#23 The Rolling Stones Concert Ends It: America Now Up for Grabs $10–20

BEST OF THE BEATLES
1964
The Beatles in Their First Movie, The Girl Who Stopped Paul's Marriage, What It's Like to Love Beatle John, The Two Tragedies That Haunt the Beatles, Hollywood & the Beatle

Invasion, 63 Ways to Meet the Beatles, A Day-by-day Report of the Beatles' American Tour, issue contains a giant three-page Beatle fold-out pin-up, Is Ringo Taken by Ann-Margaret? $15–30

BIG BOPPER

1988

Jan. Special Poster Issue, Contains 12 Huge Color Wall Posters of Kirk Cameron, Alyssa Milano, Corey Haim, The New Monkees, River Phoenix, Jon Bon Jovi, Sean Astin, Corey Feldman, Whil Weaton, Menudo, Larry Saltis of the New Monkees, & Madonna.....$3–6
Feb. Contains 16 Super Color Pin-ups—Alyssa Milano, Corey Haim, Kirk Cameron, Sean Astin, River Phoenix, Tiffany: The Singing Queen of Malls, The Beastie Boys, Madonna, Jon Bon Jovi: He'll Rock You Out, Menudo, INXS, Ralph Macchio.........................$2–4
Mar. Contains 12 Enormous Color Posters—A Special Rare Poster Edition Featuring Alyssa Milano, Kirk Cameron, River Phoenix, Corey Haim, Sean Astin, Corey Feldman, Menudo, Jon Bon Jovi, Mackenzie Astin, Michael Fox, & Madonna, With Rare Stories $3–6
Apr. Special Jam-packed Pin-up Issue, Revealing Stories on Debbie Gibson, River Phoenix, Michael Fox, Johnny Depp, Corey Haim, Alyssa Milano, The New Monkees, Kirk Cameron...$2–4

1989

Feb. Corey Haim Special Collectors' Issue, Jon Bon Jovi Needing Help, Kirk Cameron, Debbi Gibson at Home, Johnny Depp, Alyssa Milano, Kiefer Sutherland....................$2–4
Mar. Johnny Depp, Debbie Gibson's Private Life Revealed in Color Pics, Kirk Cameron, Alyssa Milano, Jon Bon Jovi, New Kids on the Block, issue includes pin-ups & poster ..$2–4
Apr. Twelve Blazing Giant Full-color Wall Posters, An Exclusive Poster Edition, Alyssa Milano, Corey Haim, Johnny Depp, Kirk Cameron, Debbie Gibson, Patrick Swayze, Kiefer Sutherland, Chad Allen, River Phoenix, Corey Feldman, Wil Wheaton, Tiffany $3–6
May The New Kids on the Block: Having the Right Stuff, Johnny Depp, Corey Haim, Def Leppard Exclusive, Debbie Gibson's Bag of Tricks, Alyssa Milano, Kirk Cameron, Chad Allen..$2–4
Dec. The New Kids on the Block: Party After Hours, Alyssa Milano's New Love, Kirk Cameron, Chad Allen, Debbie Gibson, Tiffany, Bon Jovi $2–3

1990

Jan. All New Poster Edition Special, Includes 12 Giant Color Wall Posters—Seven Different New Kids on the Block Posters, Alyssa Milano, Debbie Gibson, Kirk Cameron, Chad Allen, Corey Haim...$3–6

BIG FAT

1970

Feb. #1 Mick Jagger, The Beach Boys, Commander Cody.......................................$20–40
Mar. #2 Buddy Holly cover, Rod Stewart, The Flamin' Groovies, Janis Joplin, MC5, James Taylor...$15–30
Apr. #3 Rock-&-Roll Revived, A Night With Joe Cocker, Jackie Wilson, Neil Young, The Shirelles, The Coasters, Bill Haley & the Comets...$15–30
May #4 Manfred Mann, Festivals 1970 ....$10–20
June #5 John Sinclair interview, Felix Pappallardi, Taj Mahal, Grace Slick, The Rolling Stones...$12–25
July #6 Pete Townshend & the Who, Crosby, Stills, Nash & Young.....................$12–25
Aug. #7 Jimi Hendrix 1945–1970, Woodstock $25–50

BIG TOWN REVIEW

All issues..$3–5

BILLBOARD

All issues..$1–4

BIM BAM BOOM
All issues...$5–10

BLACK BEAT
1989
May Al B. Sure, Karyn White, The New Edition, Ziggy Marley, Tony Toni Tone, Luther Vandross, Cherrelle $2–3
Nov. The Unstopable Bobby Brown, Jody Watley: On & Off Stage, Public Enemy, The New Edition, Prince: The Secret Story Behind His *Batman* Album, De Le Soul.................$2–3
Dec. Guy, Paula Abdul: Exploding on the Pop Scene, New Edition, Salt 'n' Pepa, Chuckii Booker, Chris Williams...$2–3

1990
Mar. MC Hammer Special Feature, New Kids on the Block, Bobby Brown: His Off-stage Lifestyle, Heavy D & the Boyz, LL Cool J $2–3
May Heavy D & the Boyz, Janet Jackson Exclusive, Rob Base, New Kids on the Block, Tyler Collins, Babyface, Shirley Lewis, Prince...$2–3
June Bobby Brown Exclusive, Janet Jackson: She's Bad, Mic Lyte, Big Daddy, Paula Abdul: The Best is Yet to Come, MC Hammer, Maze...$2–3
Aug. Salt 'n' Pepa: Style on the Road, Johnny Gill, Queen Latifah, 3rd Bass, Janet Jackson on Tour Exclusive, Backstage on Soul Train $2–3
All other issues $2–3

BLACK MUSIC
1974
July Britain's Black Underground...$1–2

1975
Feb. Al Green Exclusive, Shirley Brown, Gloria Gaynor, Tavares...............................$1–2

BLACK MUSIC REVIEW
1969
#1 Jimi Hendrix Special Issue...$50–100

BLACK SOUNDS
1989
Dec. Bobby Brown, Jodi Whatley: Grammy Greatness, El Debarge, Kool & the Gang, Neneh Cherry, LL Cool J...$2–3

BLACK STARS
1975
Feb. B.B. King, Billy Preston, Jayne Kennedy...$1–2
Apr. Stevie Wonder: The Joys of Being a Genius..$1–2

BLAST (Fass/Harris Publishers)
1976
Aug. #1 Paul McCartney & Wings: Wings Over America, Patti Smith: Misplaced Joan of Arc in a Bicentennial Blitz, ZZ Top: Torpid Texan Turds, Little Feat's Fan Mail, The Doobie Brothers Take to the Streets, Outlaws, BTO, War, Hudsons, Al Green's Love Music, color pin-ups of—Paul McCartney, Rod Stewart, Van Morrison, Little Feat, Nils Lofgren, ZZ Top, Doobie Brothers, Jackson Browne, Crosby & Nash, America, Greg Allman, Ian Anderson, Peter Frampton, Michael Phillip Jagger, The Tubes, Kiss, Patti Smith, Bruce Springsteen..$10–20
Oct. #2 Mick Jagger: The Stones in Europe, Keef (Keith Richards) Speaks, Exclusive Pix of Mick Jagger in Germany, Jefferson Starship & the Double Platinum Miracle, Jimmy Page

BLAST, 1976, Oct. (#2)

BLAST, 1987, #7

BLAST, 1987, #10

BLAST, 1987, #12

BLAST, 1987, #13

BLAST, 1988, Jan. 2

BLAST, 1988, Jan. 23

BLAST, 1988, Mar. 26

BLAST, 1988, May 28

interview, Kris Kristofferson, Hall & Oates, Emmylou Harris, Jeff Beck, Fleetwood Mac, Kiss, issue contains full-page photo of Iggy Pop nude, Led Zeppelin, America, Patti Smith, Queen, Elton John, David Byrne..$15–30

Dec. #3 The Who: Roger Daltry & the Wheelchair Races, Bryan Ferry: Sticks Together, Rastaman Invasion, Reaping Fortune With Blue Oyster Cult, Janis Ian interview, The Secret Life of Frank Zappa, History of San Francisco Rock, Labelle, Rick Derringer, Ian Hunter, Steve Miller..$7–15

BLAST (Ashley Publishing)

1987

Mar. #1 Motley Crue: On the Prowl Again, Iron Maiden: They Can't be Stopped, Ratt: Talking With Warren Demartini, Van Halen, Ozzy Osbourne, Metallica, Warlock, Bon Jovi, Poison, Gary Moore, Ronnie James Dio, Abbatoir, Heretic, Metal Church, issue includes 16 color pin-ups...$3–7

Apr. #2 Motley Crue's Vince Neil Fighting His Way Back, Ronnie James Dio, Bon Jovi: Too Much, Too Soon, Iron Maiden, Europe, Saxon, Metallica, Vivian Campbell, Keel, Megadeth, Hurricane, Armored Saint, Alcatraz, Flotsam & Jetsam, Yngwie Malmsteen, AC/DC, Paul Stanley, Judas Priest, David Lee Roth, issue includes 16 color pin-ups.......$3–6

June 6 #5 Nikki Sixx: As You've Never Seen Him, Bon Jovi Tells All, Vince Neil: His All New Look, Cinderella, Dokken, Stryper, Ratt, Autograph, Lita Ford, Poison, Guns 'n' Roses, Van Halen, issue includes color poster & pin-ups...$2–5

June 27 #6 Vince Neil, Ratt: Night People, Bon Jovi: Sensationally Sexy, Why Cinderella Rules, Vinnie Vincent's Amazing Stories, Dokken, Lizzy Borden, Alice Cooper, Dio, Poison, Ratt, Europe..$2–5

July 18 #7 Motley Crue on Tour, David Bryan & Bon Jovi, Ratt, Lita Ford, Cinderella, Poison, Sammy Hagar: For the Last Time..$2–5

Aug. 18 #8 Can Tommy Lee be Tamed?, Motley Crue, What It's Like to Live With Poison, Europe: Too Sexy for Rock?, Don Dokken, Ace Frehley, Vanity, Judas Priest, Night Ranger, Bon Jovi, Ozzy Osbourne..$2–5

Aug. 24 #9 Rare Motley Crue Tour Photos, Poison's Outrageous House, The Hidden Side of Bon Jovi, Lita Ford, Tommy Lee Exclusive Interview, Quiet Riot, Cinderella, Ratt, Great White..$2–5

Sept. 19 #10 Motley Crue's Nikki Sixx: No More Satan, Poison, The Ozzy Osbourne You Don't Know, Bon Jovi's Big Turn, Kiss, Def Leppard: The Tragedies are Over, Poison, Loudness, Dio..$2–5

Oct. 10 #11 Exclusive: Bon Jovi's New Adventures, The Amazing Bret Michaels, Motley Crue: Super Night Backstage, The Cult, Whitesnake Strikes Back, Def Leppard, Stryper, Poison, Iron Maiden..$2–5

Oct. 31 #12 Exclusive: Bon Jovi's Final Tour Days, Motley Crue: Still Street Ratts, Stryper, Whitesnake, Twisted Sister, Crazy Nights With Kiss, Poison, Metallica, Def Leppard, Y & T, Ratt, Cinderella..$2–5

Nov. 21 #13 Kiss, Black 'n' Blue, Alice Cooper, Bon Jovi, Dokken, Def Leppard, Poison, Motley Crue, Yngwie Malmsteen, Ratt..$2–5

Dec. 12 #14 Special Backstage Issue: Dressing the Stars, Poison, W.A.S.P., Guns 'n' Roses, Ratt, Richie Sambora, Alice Cooper, Faster Pussycat, Kiss, Def Leppard's Joe Elliot Cinderella..$2–5

1988

Jan. 2 The Real Story of Poison by Bret Michaels, Stryper, E-Z-O, Whitesnake, Aerosmith, Def Leppard, Great White, Motley Crue, Jon Bon Jovi, Guns 'n' Roses, Bret Michaels centerfold $2–5

Jan. 23 Poison's Real Story Concludes by Bret Michaels, Kiss, Bon Jovi, Motley Crue, Vinnie Vincent, Loverboy, Great White, David Lee Roth, Faster Pussycat, Aerosmith, Gene Simmons, Black 'n' Blue..$2–5

Feb. 13 The Year 1987 in Review, Poison, Cinderella, Motley Crue, Ratt, Whitesnake, Bon Jovi, David Lee Roth's Moment of Glory, Black 'n' Blue, Faster Pussycat, Dokken, Helloween, Guns 'n' Roses..$2–5

Mar. 5 First Anniversary Issue Special—A Look Back and a Look Ahead, White Lion, Guns 'n' Roses, Poison, Tesla, Lita Ford, Bon Jovi, David Lee Roth, David Coverdale, Stryper, Steve Vai $2–5
Mar. 26 Kiss, Motley Crue, Cinderella, Ozzy Osbourne, Great White, David Lee Roth, Europe, Guns 'n' Roses, Lizzy Borden, AC/DC, Black 'n' Blue, Whitesnake, Stryper, Gene Simmons $2–5
Apr. 19 Motley Crue: The Story of '87—Nikki Denies Everything, David Lee Roth, Bret Michaels, The Big Interview With Guns 'n' Roses, Stryper's Michael Sweet, Faster Pussycat, Kiss, L.A. Guns $2–5
May 7 Motley Crue in Japan, Introducing Kingdom Come, AC/DC, Ratt, Poison, Dokken, White Lion, Megadeth, Guns 'n' Roses, David Lee Roth, Hurricane, Ted Nugent, The Bissonettes, Billy Sheehan..$2–5
May 28 Nikki Sixx Laughs Last, Axl Answers the Rumors, Ozzy Osbourne, Billy Sheehan, Queensryche, Dokken, Ted Nugent, Stryper, Kingdom Come, White Lion, Joan Jett, Faster Pussycat, Joan Jett $2–5
July 30 Motley Crue's Vince Gets Hitched, Whitesnake, Bon Jovi, Iron Maiden, Judas Priest, Metallica, Poison, Queensryche, Black 'n' Blue $2–5

1989

Jan. Axl Reveals the Truth About Sex, Drugs & Guns 'n' Roses, Bon Jovi, Unexpected Confessions from Poison's Leading Man, Cinderella, L.A. Guns, Ratt, Stryper, Anthrax, Hurricane, Europe $2–5
Feb. Axl Interview: Guns 'n' Roses Sexy Wild Man Special, Bon Jovi Confesses About Success, Bret Michaels Tells Raunchy Truth, Ratt, Winger, White Lion, Motley Crue, L.A. Guns, Europe, Stryper, Cinderella, Hurricane, Dokken Bites Back................................$2–4
Mar. Poison's Sex Computer Exposed, Bon Jovi Unmasked by Richie Sambora, Guns 'n' Roses Exclusive Photo Layout: Thru the Years, Kiss, Vixen, D'Molls, Winger, Megadeth, White Lion, Def Leppard, Ratt, Stryper, Metallica, Bulletboys....................................$2–4
Apr. Guns 'n' Roses & Poison Exclusive, Bon Jovi: More from Inside the Band, Winger, Bulletboys, Ratt, Metallica, Def Leppard..$2–4
June Guns 'n' Roses & Motley Crue interviews & posters, Poison, Bon Jovi, Skid Row, Warrent, Cinderella, Bulletboys, Britney Fox, At Home With Stryper's Michael Sweet, Bon Jovi, Tesla...$2–4
July Poison & Guns 'n' Roses Exclusives: Who are the Real Bad Boys?, Axl Rose New Power Interview, Bon Jovi, Skid Row, Britney Fox, Bobby Dall, White Lion, Bulletboys, Def Leppard..$2–4
Aug. Axl Rose Talks: An Exclusive New Interview, Skid Row, Bon Jovi Makes a Difference in Russia, White Lion, Cinderella, Kingdom Come, Great White, Motley Crue: Unexpected Confessions, Poison Exposed, Bulletboys, Bret Michaels $2–4
Sept. Bon Jovi Exclusive: Jon Tells Everything, L.A. Guns, Motley Crue, Guns 'n' Roses' Axl interview, Poison, Bulletboys, Whitesnake, Winger, White Lion, Skid Row, Sleeze Beez, W.A.S.P..$2–4
Nov. Def Leppard: Joe Elliot Reveals His Band's Shocking Future, The Skid Row Scandal, Bon Jovi interview, Poison, Motley Crue, White Lion, Bulletboys, Lita Ford, Tora Tora, Winger..$2–4
Dec. Def Leppard: Joe Elliot Reveals His Band's Shocking Future, Skid Row Scandal, Poison, Motley Crue, Lita Ford, Guns 'n' Roses, Tora Tora, White Lion, Bon Jovi........$2–4

1990

Jan. Motley Crue interviews, Bret Michaels, Whitesnake, Warrent, Exclusive: Jani Lane's Own Shocking Story, Def Leppard, Skid Row, Poison, Bulletboys, Faster Pussycat, Winger..$ 2–4
Feb. Warrent's Jani Lane Exclusive—Touring With Motley Crue, Kix, Skid Row's Sebastian Bach: "I've Always Been Nuts," Poison, Aerosmith, Faster Pussycat, Tora Tora, L.A. Guns, Bon Jovi...$2–4
Mar. Poison: Two Very Special Interviews, Motley Crue, Guns 'n' Roses, Dangerous Toys, Warrent, Whitesnake, Bon Jovi, Faster Pussycat, Aerosmith, Tora Tora, L.A. Guns, Kix .$2–4
Apr. Jani Lane, Skid Row's Sebastian Bach, Aerosmith, Guns 'n' Roses, L.A. Guns, Tesla, Whitesnake, Bonham, Poison in Vancouver...$2–4

June Skid Row's Rachel Defends Sebastian Bach, Guns 'n' Roses, Poison, Aerosmith, Warrent, L.A. Guns, Jon Bon Jovi, Pretty Boy Floyd, Sleez Beez, The Cult, Whitesnake, Ratt, Def Leppard, The Front..$2–4

July Skid Row, Poison: Out of the Studio & on Tour, The Front, Motley Crue interviews, Aerosmith, Slaughter, D'Molls, Guns 'n' Roses, L.A. Guns, Stryper, Winger, Jon Bon Jovi, Warrent in Hawaii...$2–4

Aug. Poison's Back: Photos & Interviews, Two Skid Row Interviews, Axl Roses' Strange Marriage & Divorce, Warrent, Motley Crue, Ratt, Slaughter Races Their Fans, Faster Pussycat, Aerosmith $2–4

BLAST FROM THE PAST (Tabloid)

All issues..$2–5

BLAST LIVE METAL (Each issue contains 10 giant wall-size, color, high-gloss posters)

1987

Dec. #1 Stephen Pearcy, Bon Jovi, David Coverdale, Joey Tempest, Vince Neil, Tom Keifer, Bret Michaels, Def Leppard, Robert Sweet..$4–8

1988

Feb. #2 Warren DeMartini, Tommy Lee, Riki Rocket, Bobby Dall, C.C. Deville, Vince Neil, Nikki Sixx, Mick Mars, Jon Bon Jovi $3–6

May #4 Whitesnake, Poison, Joey Tempest, Bret Michaels, Ratt, Mick Mars, Michael Sweet, Steve Vai, Robin Crosby..$3–6

June Guns 'n' Roses, Ratt, Axl Rose, Bon Jovi, Poison, Stryper, Anthrax, Cinderella, Metallica, Bulletboys $3–6

Sept. Nikki Sixx, Van Halen, Poison, Dokken, Scorpions, Guns' Duff, Guns' Slash & Izzy, Stryper, Metallica, Mick Mars $3–6

Dec. Guns 'n' Roses, Metallica, Aerosmith, Poison's Bret Micheals, White Lion, Motley Crue, AC/DC, Ratt, Def Leppard, Phil Collen, Cinderella's Tom Keifer......................$3–6

1989

Feb. Jon Bon Jovi, Aerosmith, Motley Crue, Metallica, Lita Ford, Poison, Cinderella, Megadeth, White Lion, Guns 'n' Roses $3–6

Apr. Guns 'n' Roses, Metallica, Bon Jovi, Ratt, Winger, Def Leppard, Don Dokken, Poison, Cinderella...$3–6

Oct. Motley Crue's Joe Elliot, Nikki Sixx, Whitesnake, Axl Rose, Slash, Mike Tramp, Sebastian Bach, Bret Michaels, Marq Torien $3–6

Dec. Skid Row's Sebastian Bach, Motley Crue, Bulletboys, Kip Winger, Nikki Sixx & Mick Mars, Mike Tramp, Bret Michaels, Axl Rose, Slash, Faster Pussycat, Richie Sambora....$3–6

1990

Feb. Poison, Skid Row's Sebastian Bach, Metallica, Winger, Warrent, Bulletboys, Aerosmith, Axl Rose, Tora Tora, Kix, C.C. Deville...$3–6

Aug. Aerosmith's Steven Tyler, Motley Crue, Poison, Skid Row, L.A. Guns, Kiss, Warrent, Guns 'n' Roses, Great White, Alice Cooper $3–6

BLAST METAL SPECTACULAR POSTER MAGAZINE (Each issue contains 10 giant wall-size, color, high-gloss posters)

1987

Jan. #1 Five Motley Crue Posters, David Lee Roth, Poison Metallica, Iron Maiden..$4–8

Aug. #3 Five Motley Crue posters & five Poison posters..$4–8

Sept. #4 Led Zeppelin, Def Leppard, Cinderella, Stryper, Bon Jovi, Poison, Europe, Ratt, Dokken $3–7

Nov. #5 Led Zeppelin, Poison, Great White, Cinderella's Tom Keifer, Motley Crue, Bon Jovi, Kiss, Whitesnake, Ratt, Def Leppard..$3–7

1988

Jan. Bon Jovi, Poison, Kiss' Paul Stanley, Motley Crue, Whitesnake's David Coverdale, Y & T, Dokken, Def Leppard, Ratt, Guns 'n' Roses.....................................$3–7
Feb. Poison, Bon Jovi, Nikki Sixx, Joey Tempest, Richie Sambora, Don Dokken, Stephen Pearcy, Faster Pussycat, Vince Neil, Warren Demartini.....................................$3–7
Mar. Motley Crue, Poison, Stryper, Kiss, Jon Bon Jovi, Guns 'n' Roses, David Lee Roth, Joe Elliot, Faster Pussycat, Steven Pussycat.....................................$3–7
Apr. Poison, Motley Crue, Def Leppard, Robin Crosby, Whitesnake, Steve Vai, Faster Pussycat, Paul Stanley, Axl Rose, Robert Sweet $3–6
May Tesla, Cinderella, Vince Neil, Europe, Whitesnake, Stryper, Bret Michaels, White Lion, Kiss $3–6
June Def Leppard, Aerosmith, Europe, Poison, Great White, Ratt, Dave Roth, Don Dokken, Judas Priest, Nikki Sixx $3–6
July Whitesnake & Poison, Motley Crue, Nikki Sixx, Axl Rose, Mike Tramp, L.A. Guns, Aerosmith, Dave Roth, Faster Pussycat, Kingdom Come $3–6
Aug. Poison, Cinderella's Tom Keifer, Guns 'n' Roses, Dokken, Nikki Sixx, Vince Neil, Mike Tramp, Scorpions, Richie Sambora, Robert Sweet.....................................$3–6
Oct. Ratt, Guns 'n' Roses, White Lion, Bon Jovi, Bret Michaels, Tom Keifer, Faster Pussycat, Michael Tramp, Axl Rose, Robert Sweet, Black 'n' Blue, Motley Crue......$3–6

1989

June Guns 'n' Roses, Motley Crue, Bret Michaels, Skid Row, Tesla, Def Leppard, Bulletboys, Winger, Warrent, Metallica.....................................$3–6
Aug. Axl Rose, Def Leppard, Steven Adler, Richie Sambora, Mike Tramp, Poison, Nikki Sixx, Duff McKagan, Skid Row.....................................$3–6
Dec. Skid Row's Sebastian Bach, Poison, Bon Jovi, Motley Crue, White Lion, Winger, Bulletboys, L.A. Guns, Faster Pussycat, Axl Rose.....................................$3–6

1990

Apr. Poison, Bonham, Nikki Sixx, Slash, Aerosmith, Sebastian Bach, Tesla, Warrent, Kip Winger, Dangerous Toys.....................................$2–5

BLAST VINTAGE METAL POSTER MAGAZINE

1987

#1 Van Halen, Motley Crue, Led Zeppelin, Randy Rhoads, Nikki Sixx, Robert Plant, Jimmy Page, Richie Sambora, AC/DC, ZZ Top, Ratt.....................................$4–8

BOB (THE) (Tabloid)

All issues.....................................$2–6

BOP

1986

Oct. The Guys of Duran Duran, Mitch Gaylord, Ricky Fox, Kirk Cameron, Menudo Exclusive, Ralph Macchio, Madonna, Rob Lowe, Prince at Home, A-Ha, Corey Hart $2–3

1989

Nov. New Kids on the Block 14-Page Exclusive, Alyssa Milano, Debbie Gibson, Bon Jovi.....................................$2–3
Dec. The Final Moments of the New Kids on the Block Party, Debbie Gibson: Behind the Scenes of Her Tour, Kirk Cameron, Alyssa Milano: The Truth About Her Mysteries, pin-ups & posters $2–3

1990

Jan. New Kids on the Block, Chad Allen, Debbie Gibson Tour Pix, Corey Haim, Alyssa Milano, Staci Keanan, Johnny Depp.....................................$2–3
Mar. New Kids on the Block Exclusive, Dancing With Debbie Gibson, Alyssa Milano: Brains & Beauty, Kirk Cameron, Tiffany, Corey Haim, Corey Feldman & Others $2–3

July New Kids on the Block to the Extreme, Alyssa Milano Shares Her Shapely Secrets, Paula Abdul: "I Like to Do Unusual Things" $2–3
Aug. New Kids on the Block Special 20-Page Section, Paula Abdul: The Secret Behind Her Love Life, Alyssa Milano, Debbie Gibson...$2–3

BOSTON ROCK (Boston Area music tabloid)

All issues $3–6

BUZZ
1988
Aug. Patti Smith Has Come Home..$3–6

C

CASHBOX
All issues $1–3

CD REVIEW
All issues $1–2

CELEBRITY SPOTLIGHT SERIES PRESENTS: ELVIS, 10TH ANNIVERSARY SALUTE
1987
#1 The Road to Growing Up: As Told by Elvis, June 1953 a Star is Born & the Legend Begins, A Complete Guide of Every Film Elvis Made, Elvis' Army Days.................$3–6

CHANGES (Tabloid)
1969
#1 Bob Dylan Looks Back, Richie Havens, Eric Clapton, Jeff Beck, Jimmy Page $20–40
#3 The Who: "Try to See it My Way," The Beatles, Yoko Ono.............................$12–25
#5 The Newport Festival, A Rap With the Incredible String Band $10–20
#6 Woodstock, Bob Dylan, Joan Baez Concert, Ian Anderson.................................$10–20
#8 Moondog Muses, Bob Dylan, MC5 & the Stooges, Jeff Beck.............................$10–20
#9 The Band, Lord Buckley, Grace Slick, The Moody Blues...................................$10–20
#11 The Kinks, Jefferson Airplane...$10–20
#12 Rolling Stones Feature & Poster, Charles Mingus $10–20
#13 Mick Jagger & the Rolling Stones: A Five-page Special...................................$15–30
#14 Ian Anderson & Jethro Tull, The Nice $10–20

1970
Mar. 15 Ike & Tina Turner, King Crimson $6–12
Apr. 1 Lenny Bruce, The MC5, Billy Joel...$10–20
Apr. 15 History of the Comics: The Hulk & Others, Rock Music: 10 Years of the Road $5–10
June 1 Costa Gavras, Elvis Presley...$5–10
July 1 The Who, Quicksilver Messenger Service, Jimi Hendrix, Creedence Clearwater Revival $15–30
July 15 Crosby, Stills, Nash & Young..$5–10
Aug. 1 Bob Dylan, Poco, Tony Williams...$10–20
Aug. 15 Traffic, Woodstock, Free, The Rounders $5–10
Sept. 1 Pink Floyd $10–20
Sept. 15 Frank Zappa..$5–10
Nov. 1 Jimi Hendrix...$30–60
Nov. 15 Johnny Winter & Steve Paul, Janis Joplin, Jake & the Family Jewels $12–25

Dec. 1 John Mayall, Jake & the Family Jewels, Elvin Bishop.................................$10–20
Dec. 15 Iggy Stooge, McLaughlin, Derek, Fahey, Ackels..$12–25

1971

Jan. 1 Humble Pie, Grace Slick & Jefferson Airplane..$5–10
Jan. 15 The Angels at Altamont: The Rolling Stones, The Grateful Dead interview ..$15–30
Jan. 31 John Lennon & Yoko Ono...$15–30
Feb. 15 Tom Rush, Cat Mother...$5–10
Mar. 1 Frank Zappa, Cat Stevens...$5–10
May 15 Pink Floyd, Tim Hardin, Lou Reed, Dada, Curtis Mayfield.........................$5–10
Aug. 15 Coming to Terms With Grand Funk Railroad, Dr. Feelgood.......................$10–20
Sept. 1 Rita Coolidge...$5–10
Oct. 1 Bob Dylan Resurrected..$10–20
Oct. 15 John Lennon & Yoko Ono...$10–20
Nov. 1 The Band..$5–10
Dec. 1 Ian Anderson & Jethro Tull...$6–12
Dec. 15 The Grateful Dead...$6–12

1972

Jan. 15 Ravi Shankar, Ike & Tina Turner..$5–10
Feb. 15 Alice Cooper...$10–20
Mar. 15 Charles Mingus..$5–10
Apr. 1 Women Songwriters, Jazz in the 50s..$5–10
May 1 Oz Trial Off-Broadway: John Lennon, Mick Jagger...$10–20
June Bangladesh, The Kinks, Hot Tuna...$6–12
Sept. Mick Jagger & the Rolling Stones: Imitation of Youth.......................................$10–20

CINEMA ODYSSEY
1982
Vol. 2, #1 Olivia Newton-John: Hopelessly Devoted to You $3–6

CIRCUS MAGAZINE
1969
Mar. Jimi Hendrix on Black and White America, The Doors, The Rolling Stones, Steve
Winwood, Steppenwolf, MC5, The Who, The Rascals, Black Music.........................$40–80
May Janis Joplin in Memphis: A Special Five-page Color Section, Women in Rock, The
Doors: Their Music & Their Hassles, 20 Questions With Donovan, Backstage With the
Moody Blues, Experiences With Jimi Hendrix, Johnny Winter, Tim Hardin on Song Writ-
ing $40–80
June Special Zappa Issue, Doors, Johnny Winter, Mothers, O. Redding.................$20–40
July Rock & Revolution: A Symposium With John Kay, Frank Zappa, Phil Ochs & Country
Joe, Johnny Winter Five-page portfolio, Sneak Preview of Mick Jagger's First Flick, John
Mayall, The Nice, Lawrence Welk...$20–40
Aug. Country Pie: Johnny Cash/Bob Dylan/Byrds, Poco, Etc., The Beatles, John & Yoko
Exclusive Interview, Led Zeppelin, The Incredible String Band, Chuck Berry, Sly & the
Family Stone $20–40
Sept. The MC5, Farewell to Brian Jones, Jimi Hendrix: Body & Soul, The Kinks, The
Byrds...$30–60
Oct. The Beatles Splashdown: Is the Split Near?, Scenes from *Hair*, Special Wild
Woodstock Issue, Detroit is Alive: The Stooges & The MC5, Iggy Pop, Eric Clapton/Blind
Faith...$25–50
Nov. Bob Dylan on the Isle of Wight, CSN & Y, The Rolling Stones $20–40
Dec. John Lennon & Yoko Ono, Sha Na Na, Joe Cocker, Led Zeppelin, Jethro Tull, The
Band...$25–50

1970
Feb. Surviving the 70s issue—The Doors: From Demons to Darlings, Ike & Tina Turner,
Elvis Presley, Arlo Guthrie, The Beatles, The Rolling Stones, Lulu, Diana Ross, Grace
Slick, Steve Miller, Janis Joplin, Blind Faith...$25–50

CIRCUS, 1969, Nov.

CIRCUS, 1969, Feb.

CIRCUS, 1970, Dec.

CIRCUS, 1973, Mar.

CIRCUS, 1979, #218

CIRCUS, 1978, #194

CIRCUS, 1978, #190

CIRCUS, 1978, #186

CIRCUS, 1978, #181

Mar. The Grateful Dead, Crosby, Stills, Nash & Young, John & Yoko Lennon, The Who, Quicksilver Messenger Service, Allman Brothers, Robert Plant, Grand Funk Railroad $20–40
Apr. John & Yoko: At Home With the Lennons, Delaney & Bonnie, Eric Clapton, The MC5 Back Again, Tom Rush, Bob Dylan, Grand Funk Railroad, Chicago, Jim Morrison, Stones, Creedence $25–50
May Ten Years After, John Mayall, Joe Cocker, Sebastian, Linda Ronstadt, James Taylor, Leon Russell, Joan Baez, John Hammond, Jim Morrison short, John Lennon $20–40
June Grace Slick/The Jefferson Airplane: Marching to a Different Drum, The Youngbloods, Neil Young: The Only Survivor of CSN & Young, Gordon Lightfoot, Taj Mahal, The Rolling Stones, The Velvet Underground, Paul McCartney $20–40
July Steve Winwood on the Road Again/Traffic Gets the Green Light, Jethro Tull: A Subtle Acceptance, Procol Harum, Manfred Mann, The Small Faces: From Pop to Euphoria, Led Zeppelin, Tone Down, Stooges, Alice Cooper, Creedence Clearwater Revival: A Travelin' Band, Jim Morrison $20–40
Aug. Joe Cocker, Steven Stills Exclusive Interview, Edgar Winter, Todd Rundgren, The Moody Blues, Grateful Dead, Who, Pink Floyd...$20–40
Sept. The Band Plays On, Steve Miller, The Doors are Still Real Cool, Steven Stills, Zappa Reforms the Mothers, Alvin Lee, The Byrds are Amazingly Graceful $20–40
Oct. Janis Joplin's Full-tilt Boogie Band: An Informative & Pictorial Look at Janis' New Group, What Big Brother is Up To, Country Joe & the Fish, Steppenwolf Takes Another Step, An Interview With Eric Clapton, Savoy Brown, Dr. John: The World Tripper, The Doors, Kris Kristofferson $40–80
Nov.
Dec. Jimi Hendrix Dead: 1942–1970, A Special Report, Santana, Country Joe McDonald is Alone Again, Quicksilver, The Isle of Wight: The Last Festival, Led Zeppelin, Johnny Winter, Iggy & the Stooges Play in the Fun House $45–90

1971

Jan. Grand Funk Railroad: Coming of Age Special, Jim Morrison Interview: Catching the Bearded Convict in Los Angeles, Lee Michaels, Eric Burdon, Janis Joplin: Patti Smith Plays Tribute to Janis, Donovan Gets Married: Features Photo of Donovan With Jimi Hendrix, includes 1971 *Circus* calendar $30–60
Feb. Leon Russell: Long Time Coming, The Stones' Altamont Film Special Report, The Jim Morrison Interview Part II: Where Does Jim Go from Here?, Poco, This is Jethro Tull, The Grateful Dead: Breaking the Quality Barrier, George Harrison, Zappa, Elton John, Randy Newman...$30–60
Mar. Jerry Garcia Raps, Sly Stone, Creedence Clearwater, The Kinks....................$20–40
Apr. Riding With Crosby, Stills, Nash & Young, John Sebastian, The Great Jefferson Airplane, Hot Tuna, The Moody Blues, Savoy Brown, Mountain, Buddy Miles..........$20–40
May James Taylor: The Taylors—A Rock Dynasty, Livingston Taylor, Neil Young Comes Home, Captain Beefheart, The Bee Gees: Clean Rock, The Flamin' Groovies, Curtis Mayfield, Mama Cass & Dave Mason, Rod Stewart, Mick Jagger $20–40
June Alice Cooper, Three Dog Night, Beach Boys, B.B. King..............................$20–40
July Cat Stevens: Cosmic Superstar, interview with Rod Stewart & The Faces, John Sebastian, Laura Nyro, The New Rascals, includes full-size Rolling Stones poster, Rick Derringer, Nico, Tim Hardin, Elton John $20–40
Aug. Paul McCartney: The McCartneys—comes with full-size McCartney poster, Emerson, Lake & Palmer, The Black Sabbath Cult, Poco, Jethro Tull, James Gang, Mick Jagger's Wedding, Bob Dylan, Mitch Ryder $20–40
Sept. Jim Morrison Death Issue: 1943–1971—Jim's Death, His Life & the Legend He Left Behind, Carole King, So the Byrds are Still Around, Moby Grape, Grand Funk interview, Rita Coolidge, Elton John After the Hype, John & Yoko Visit New York, Carly Simon, Jackie Lomax, Jeff Beck $45–90
Oct. George Harrison: Helping Bangladesh, The Interstellar Thunder of Pink Floyd, Soft Machine: Ignored When Touring With Jimi Hendrix, Woodstock: A Tin Pan Alley Rip-off, Pete Seger, Joe McDonald interview, Deep Purple, Religious Revival: Pete Townshend, George Harrison $20–40
Nov. Ringo Starr Speaks Out: The Fight With Paul, Ten Years After, Pete Townshend's Vision, Steppenwolf Explains, The Three Faces of Savoy Brown, Mick Jagger & Eric Clapton,

Kris Kristofferson, The Jefferson Airplane Without Marty Balin, The Guess Who, Humble Pie, Leon Russell, Dennis Wilson $20–40

Dec. John Lennon: Crippled Inside, Cornering Led Zeppelin's Jimmy Page, Ringo Gets it Off His Chest Part II, Leon Russell: Lord of His Own Domain, Are the Beach Boys for Real?, Seatrain, New Riders of the Purple Sage, T. Rex, The Doors Revive, Black Sabbath, James Taylor, Melanie, Traffic, Iggy Pop $20–40

1972

Jan. The Doors: Amputated but Alive, Santana, Traffic, The Grateful Dead: Buddy Holly in Reverse, Chicago, Cat Stevens, John Mayall, Van Morrison, B.B. King, Felix Pappalardi, Stones, Alice Cooper $20–40

Feb. Ray Davies/The Kinks Unravel the Muswell Puzzle, Jeff Beck, The Trauma and Triumph of Fleetwood Mac, The Youngbloods, What Makes Alice Cooper Run?, Neil Young: The Gentle Giant at Work, Carly Simon: The Scenic Route to the Top, Alvin Lee, John & Yoko, Bonnie Raitt, Blue Oyster Cult $20–40

Mar. Emerson, Lake & Palmer: The Dagger Does More Than You Think, Yes: Weaving the Fragile Web, Badfinger, McCartney on Apples & Wings, Seals & Crofts, Rod Stewart at the Pub, Simon Without Garfunkel, Jamming with the Stones: It's a Bitch, What Hath Mick Jagger Wrought?, Leon Russell, Gilbert O'Sullivan, Black Oak Arkansas $15–30

Apr. Jethro Tull/Ian Anderson, Special Jimi Hendrix Report, Lee Michaels, King Crimson $15–30

May Humble Pie: Inside Steve Marriot's Head, The Allman Bros. Band: Did They Grieve?, Edgar Winter Kills White Trash, Fairport Convention, Joan Baez, Bobby Whitlock, The Taming of Savoy Brown, T. Rex, Jackson Browne, Harry Chapin $15–30

June Graham Nash's Past: The Inside View, Hot Tuna, The Secret Identity of Harry Nilsson, Loggins & Messina, Why Has Bob Dylan Come Back?, Deep Purple, Grand Funk Railroad: The Fight for the Throttle, Beach Boys, Yes, Elton John $15–30

July The Confessions of Steven ("Manassas") Stills, The New Riders of the Purple Sage Gliding Without the Grateful Dead, Zappa, A Nervous Night With Procol Harum, Elton John & Rod Stewart, Sonny & Cher: Outfoxing Hollywood, Janis Joplin: Backstage With Janis in Concert: Four Small Tales of the Texas Lady, Photo Extra: The Stones Before They Hit the Road, Jack Bruce, ELO $20–40

Aug. Alice Cooper: Inside School's Out, Elton John, Uriah Heep, Roberta Flack, Free, Chuck Berry, Paul & Linda McCartney, ZZ Top, Dr. Hook, Rolling Stones............$15–30

Sept. Leon Russell, The Rolling Stones Tour, ELP, Pink Floyd Kicks a Two-Year Slump, Rod Stewart, Peter Frampton Solo Flight, John Lennon Grabs a New Band, David Bowie, Paul Simon $15–30

Oct. Marc Bolin, T. Rex, Alice Cooper Hatches This Year's Biggest Rock Extravaganza, Black Sabbath, Chicago, Grace Slick Hijacks Jefferson Airplane $15–30

Nov. Cat Stevens: Retreat from the Sting of Applause, A Quiet Pete Townshend Roars to the Surface, The Band, Ray Davies: Head Kink Unbuttons His Mind, The Night J. Geils Fried a "Full House," Grand Funk, Alice Cooper for President, Jethro Tull: The Rise of Ian the Demon, David Bowie, Neil Young, Yoko Ono...$15–30

Dec. Moody Blues, Yes, Bowie, Rod Stewart, Deep Purple, Joe Cocker $15–30

1973

Jan. Behind Carole King, Uriah Heep, Jinx, Cream-West, Bruce & Laing, Alice Cooper, David Bowie, Black Sabbath, Eric Clapton: The Reluctant Superstar Inches Out of Hiding, ELP, Alvin Lee, Chicago, Melanie, Bob Dylan $10–20

Feb. Edgar Winter: What Have They Done to Him?, Why Black Sabbath Hates America, Carly Simon: James Taylor's Leggy Lover, Hurricane Alice Cooper Takes Europe by Storm, Yes, The Legend of Duane Allman, Neil Young, Joni Mitchell, Buffalo Springfield, Grace Slick, The Grateful Dead, Marc Bolan, David Bowie...$10–20

Mar. Carly Simon: You're So Vain, Black Sabbath's Country Hideaway, Yes, Behind Deep Purple, ELP, Stevie Wonder, Mick Jagger, Uriah Heep, Jeff Beck, Pete Townshend $10–20

Apr. Elton John Blesses Marc Bolan, Bette Midler: How a Star is Born, Eric Clapton, David Bowie, Jethro Tull Calendar, Alice Cooper Battles the Billion-Dollar Babys, Mick Jagger Special $10–20

May Steve Marriot/Humble Pie, Led Zeppelin Roars Out of Hiding, The Hollies Hop Over Disaster, Procol Harum, Elton Shows Off, Alice Cooper Tours With Monster Tooth, Deep Purple, Doors, Leon Russell, Bob Dylan, David Bowie $10–20
June Rod Stewart Mellows the Faces, The Beatles are Back, Deep Purple in Japan, Slade: The Underwater Stompers, Arrive, Pink Floyd: The Dark Side of the Moon, Alice Cooper, Byrds Reunion, The Future of Crosby, Stills, Nash & Young, Yoko & John...........$10–20
July David Bowie: The Personal Story Behind "Aladdin Sane," Paul McCartney, Alice Cooper Quits the Stage, Marc Bolan, Uriah Heep, Robert Plant, Seals & Crofts, Rod Stewart, Iggy Pop Strips to the Skin $10–20
Aug. Rick Wakeman/Yes: Their Future, Santana, David Bowie Divines Doom in Moscow, Alice Cooper: How to Start Your Own Rock Band, Alvin Lee, Allman Brothers, Janis Joplin..$10–20
Sept. Ian Anderson/Jethro Tull & Leon Russell, West, Bruce & Laing, Deep Purple Shock, Chicago, Alice Cooper, Foreigner, Grand Funk, George Harrison $10–20
Oct. Robert Plant/Led Zeppelin: Six Reasons Why They're Bigger Than the Beatles, Mott the Hoople Dumps Bowie, Grateful Dead Make Musical History, The Band at Watkins Glen, The Allmans, Sly Stone, David Bowie Scraps Concert Career, Alice Cooper's Neal Smith Tells About the Ordeal of Touring, Greg Allman color calendar, Cheech & Chong, George Harrison $10–20
Nov. Uriah Heep, America: The Magic of Growing Up, Jethro Tull: His Fans Fight Back, Led Zeppelin: They Won't Stop Touring, Mark Farner calendar, Mick Jagger's "Goat's Head Soup": A Jump into Music, Eric Clapton, Rod Stewart, Who, Winter, The Moody Blues $10–20
Dec. Elton John: Goodbye Yellow Brick Road, David Bowie Salutes the Sixties' Stars, Neil Young's Goodbye to the Concert Scene, Grand Funk Railroad, Lou Reed, The Double Life of Alice Cooper, Slade Fights for Their Lives in America, Mott, Stones, Graham Parsons....$10–20

1974

Jan. Alice Cooper: Shocking Course in Pop Sex, Traffic: Caught in a Jam, The Worst of the Allmans, The Rolling Stones: Down & Out in Europe, ELP, J. Geils: Boston's Bad Boy, Paul McCartney, Elvis Presley, Neil Diamond..$10–20
Feb. The Band Out of Hiding, Grand Funk Sneak Preview, Pink Floyd, Mick & Bianca Jagger, Keith & Anita Richards, Roger Daltry, Genesis, Loggins & Messina $10–20
Mar. Johnny Winters Celebrates Life With "Saints & Sinners," Yes Soars, Led Zeppelin: Sires a Kingdom, Alvin Lee & Mylon, Mahavishnu, Keith Emerson, Black Sabbath: Bloody Sabbath, Status Quo, David Essex, Bachman-Turner Overdrive, Deep Purple, Seals & Crofts, Alice Cooper, N.Y. Dolls, Wings...$10–20
Apr. Beck & Bogart, Deep Purple Rises from the Ashes, Bob Dylan & the Band Return With "Planet Waves," Mick Ronson/David Bowie, Alice Cooper Retires Rock Career, Robert Plant's Private Thoughts, Rod Stewart, John Lennon $10–20
May Mark Farner, Grand Funk Surges Skyward With Shin' On, Carly Simon Serves Hot Cakes, Inside Jimmy Page: The Musician & the Man, Lou Reed interview, Black Sabbath Backtalks, Blue Oyster Cult, Yes, Carpenters, Lou Reed..$10–20
June Ian Hunter/Mott: The Struggle to Stay on Top, Todd Rundgren's Last Stab at Stardom, Peter Frampton, Deep Purple interview, Rick Wakeman's Second Solo Plunge, Alice Cooper on Birth Control, ELP's Palmer Exposes Secrets, Roger Daltry Tells Why the Who Will Never Break Up, Roxy Music $10–20
July Edgar Winter & Rick Derringer/The Trio Behind Edgar Winter's "Shock Treatment," Cat Stevens, Grand Funk, Alice Cooper Assaults Brazil, Black Sabbath, Deep Purple, ELP, Black Oak Arkansas, N.Y. Dolls, David Bowie, The Jefferson Airplane's Grace Slick interview, Queen, Elton John, The Rolling Stones...$10–20
Aug. David Byron, Uriah Heep's "Wonderworld," The Eagles, The N.Y. Dolls: "Too Much Too Soon," The Kink's Ray Davies interview, Mott the Hoople, Greg Allman Takes the Plunge in the Nude, Edgar Winter, Rick Nelson, Suzi Quatro, Sharks, Bad Company, Queen, Bill Wyman, Rod Stewart, Eric Clapton, Led Zeppelin, Bob Dylan............$10–20
Sept. Jim Dandy Mangrum/Black Arkansas Raps on Raunch, Rock & Sex: A Special Interview, Bob Dylan Captures Tour '74, Elton John, Kiss, ELP's Greg Lake: His First Solo, The Who's Secret Tour Plans, Sly Stone, Eric Clapton, Genesis, Ron Wood, Uriah Heep, Nektar, Ray Davies, Ronnie Lane, Mick Jagger, Paul McCartney $10–20

Oct. Greg Allman/Dickey Betts, America Revive Their Reputation, Elton John, Alice Cooper's Greatest Hits, Leslie West Mouths on Hustling, Muscling & Mountain: An Interview, Edgar Winter, Loggins & Messina, T. Rex Bombards the USA, Pete Townshend & Todd Rundgren posters, Ozark Mt. Daredevils, Led Zeppelin, The Who, Souther Hillman Furray Band..$10–20

Nov. Peter Wolf, J. Geils Band, Ron Wood: Solo Supersession With Keith Richards, Mick Jagger & Rod Stewart, Todd Rundgren interview, ELP, Edgar Winter Group, Bachman-Turner Overdrive, Rolling Stones, Alice Cooper, N.Y. Dolls, Bryan Ferry, Sparks, Marth Reeves, Eric Clapton, David Bowie/Queen posters $10–20

Dec. The State of Future Rock 1975: A Special Issue—The Who, David Bowie, Mott, Alice Cooper, Grand Funk, Uriah Heep, Led Zeppelin, Suzi Quatro, Aerosmith, Foghat, Sparks, Yes, ZZ Top, Queen, T. Rex, Genesis, Jackson Browne...$10–20

1975

#102 January Issue Elton John's Greatest, Mott the Hoople, Jethro Tull, Chicago VIII, Rick Wakeman, Queen, The Year on Tour With ELP, David Bowie, The Who, Eric Clapton, Bob Dylan, CSN & Y, Genesis, Kiss, Yes, Alice Cooper, Fleetwood Mac $8–16

#104 February Issue Jimmy Page: Led Zeppelin on Tour, Loggins & Messina, Keith Moon interview, Roxy Music Will Take Over the Sonic 70s, Bad Company's Paul Rogers Brings Back Bluesy Basics, BTO, Mott, Mahogany Rush, Kevin Ayers, Black Oak Arkansas, Johnny Winter $8–16

#106 March Issue Peter Gabriel, Genesis: Will America Swallow the Lamb?, Joni Mitchell, Ringo, The Guess Who Battle Obscurity, Kiss: Why the Big Bands Hate Them, Nektar, The Kinks, Ian Anderson, Mark Farner interview, Led Zeppelin, Alvin Lee, The Who, David Bowie, Bad Company, J. Geils...$8–16

#108 April Issue David Bowie, Rod Stewart, Jim Dandy, Queen's Freddie Mercury interview, Mick Ronson, Yes, Labelle, Peter Frampton, Eno, Nico & John Cale, Led Zeppelin, Elton John, The Who, Derringer, Guess Who...$8–16

#110 May Issue Alice Cooper interview: The Lone Vampire is Back With More "Nightmares," Golden Earring, The Who's *Tommy* Film, Faces: How Rod & Rod Survived the Solo Syndrome, America, Jimi Hendrix: The Hunt for His Last Tapes, Queen, Charlie Daniels Band, Cockney Rebel, Led Zeppelin Exclusive: Tales of Touring, The Kinks, Orchestra Luna $10–20

#112 June Issue Rick Derringer, Robert Plant interview, Lynyrd Skynyrd Still Fighting the Civil War, AWB, Jeff Beck, Eric Clapton Happy at Last, Golden Earring, Jack Ford Exclusive, Alex Harvey, Charlie Daniels Sets the South Aflame, Cockney Rebel, Aerosmith's Steven Tyler interview, Alice Cooper $8–16

#114 July Issue Todd Rundgren Strives to Make His Dream a Reality, Wakeman, Trower Tour, Golden Earring, Ace, Lofgren, David Bowie, Mangrum: Black Oak Scrubs Up Their Sound in Europe, Alex Harvey interview, Kiss, Alice Cooper: How They Banned Him in Australia, Clapton, Jerry Garcia, Pink Floyd, Stones, BTO, Lynyrd Skynyrd...........$10–20

#116 August Issue Mick Jagger/The Stones Special: Jagger Talks on Touring: Rare '75 Concert Photos & A Decade of Rare Pix, The Eagles—Kings of the West Coast, Edgar Winter, AWB, Bad Co., The Mick Ronson Interview, The Beach Boys & Chicago, Ian Hunter, Ringo & Moon, Roxy Music, Rod Stewart: Why Rod Deserted Britain.....$10–20

#118 September Issue Ronnie Wood: Ron Goes it Alone, Wings & McCartney, The ZZ Top Interview, Lou Reed, The Stones, Keith & Ronnie are the Best Team Ever, Alice Cooper, Prarie League, Queen, Faces, Mick Jagger & Keith Richards Posters, Ohio Players, Bad Company, Mott, Tomita..$8–16

#120 October Issue Gregg Allman: A Special Report, The BTO Interview, Pink Floyd, Nilsson Exclusive, Roger Daltry, Eric Clapton: The Comeback That Wouldn't Quit, Bob Marley & the Wailers, ELP, Kiss poster, Robert Palmer, Mick Taylor, Tennille & Her Captain, Elton John, Doobie Brothers, Faces...$8–16

#122 November Issue Rod Stewart/Faces Making Up or Breaking Up?, Dandy/Black Oak Arkansas: How They Live & Love, Labelle, Leo Sayer, The Outlaws, Peter Wolf vs. Wolfman Jack interview, Elton John Announces New Band Members, Black Sabbath/Ozzy Osbourne interview, Roger Daltry poster, Bob Dylan, Waylon Jennings & Dolly Parton, Thin Lizzy, Tull, Aerosmith, Edgar Winter, Heep...$8–16

#124 December Issue Ian Anderson/Jethro Tull Exclusive Interview, Jimi Hendrix: How They Harnessed "Midnight Lightning," Jefferson Starship/ Chicago interview, Faces, Carly

Simon poster, Todd Rundgren, David Bowie: The Story He Filmed in the Desert, Bay City Rollers: Hysteria in Britain, Black Oak Arkansas, Edgar Winter, Leo Sayer, Janis Ian, Space 1999 ....$8–16

#125 December 30 Issue Linda Ronstadt: Superstar in Disguise, The Who: Beyond the Breakup Myth, Ritchie Blackmore, Hot Tuna, Smokey Robinson, Bruce Springsteen poster, John & Edgar Winter, Janis Ian: Society's Child Gets Tough, Bill Wyman, Elton's New Sensational Band $5–10

1976

#126 Ray & Dave Davies/The Kinks, Kiss "Alive" Vicious Enough to Survive?, George Harrison: More Hairy Less Krishna?, Jethro Tull, David Essex, Steve Tyler, J. Geils, Faces interview: Kenny Jones & Ian McLagan, Bruce Springsteen: The Tramp Those 60's Sluts Yearned For, Bob Dylan, Neil Sedaka: Golden Oldie Shines Anew $5–10

#127 Bob Dylan Runs Free, Queen: Night at the Opera, Patti Smith: Poet for a New Age, Neil Young & Crazy Horse Ride Again, Earth, Wind & Fire, Black Sabbath, Carmen: Ex-Raspberry Triumphs, Stanley J. Clarke, The Allmans Leap into Politics, Kiss: Gets Keys to Cadillac, Iggy Pop, Led Zeppelin Heads for Munich, Bette Midler, Dave Mason.....$5–10

#128 The Best Raw Talent for '76—Bruce Springsteen, Patti Smith, Sweet, AWB, Bob Marley, Tubes, Bay City Rollers, Charlie Daniels, Roxy Music: Streamline Their Sound for the States, Little Feat, The Band Exclusive, Rory Gallagher, The Who, Bowie Blasts Out of Babylon, Bob Dylan, John Lennon: Smoke Screen Enigma, Leslie West, Joni Mitchell, BTO..$5–10

#129 Lou Reed: Last Exit to Brooklyn, BTO, Deep Purple: Re-made in Japan, Sweet, 10CC, Bryan Ferry/Roxy Music: Bored With Decadence, Angel: Hard Rock Messengers, Elton John: Hairlift in Toronto, Ted Nugent: Beserk on West Coast, Patti Smith, Queen, The Who, David Bowie $5–10

#130 Kiss Special: A Report, Bette Midler, Bad Company, Deep Purple, Jethro Tull, Johnny Winter, The Doobie Brothers $10–20

#131 David Bowie interview, Lynyrd Skynyrd on the Road, Rush: Behind Their Space Odyssey, Black Sabbath, ENO, Nazareth Reveals Why Love Hurts, Rick Derringer: New Band in Studio, Led Zeppelin & Bad Company Cavort in N.J., Rick Wakeman, ELO, Johnny Winter...$5–10

#132 Robert Plant, Led Zeppelin, Rolling Stones, Queen, Genesis, Ted Nugent, Kiss, Kansas, Johnny Winter, Uriah Heep $5–10

#133 Jagger & Richards/The Stones: Black 'n' Blue Controversy, Ritchie Blackmore, Kiss: Bob Ezrin—How He Produced Their Hottest Album, Bad Co., Supertramp, Sailor, Tanya Tucker: No Longer Jailbait, Robin Trower, Fonzie, Foghat: Enjoying the Fruits of Success $5–10

#134 Steven Tyler/Aerosmith: America's Best Young Band, Ian Hunter, Bob Marley, Genesis: Hacket Solos, Sweet: Brian Connolly interview, Paul McCartney: Wings Over America, David Bowie Film Debut, Queen: Mobbed in Japan, Feelgood, The Beatles Exclusive: Bootleg Discography...$5–10

#135 Summer Tours Issue—ELP, Aerosmith, Allmans, Elton John, Alice Cooper, Kiss Jets Off, America, Tubes, Queen interview, Todd Rundgren, Uriah Heep, The Ramones: Bargain of the Year, Santana, The Rolling Stones, ZZ Top...$5–10

#136 Jeff Beck: The Definitive Interview, The Cult, Nazareth, The Stones: How They Rolled Over Europe, Black Oak Arkansas: Rudy Starr Joins, Marriot, The Eagles Celebrate Summer, Kiss Tapes Part I: Ace Frehely Profiled, Aerosmith, Beach Boys, ZZ Top....$5–10

#137 King Kong, Jethro Tull: Ian Anderson Salutes the Rockers of Yesteryear, Rainbow: Blackmore & Dio Interviewed, Kiss Part II: Peter Criss Profiled, Johnny & Edgar Winter Team up Together, Wings: The Tour, Rod Stewart, The Runaways: L.A. Jailbait—The Bad & The Beautiful, Aerosmith, Eagles, Elton John, Beach Boys, Chicago, Yes, ZZ Top......$5–10

#138 Alice Cooper, Robert Plant interview, Kiss Profile, ZZ Top, Heart, Jefferson Starship Gets Down to Love, Eagles, Jethro Tull, Yes, The Beach Boys.................................$5–10

#139 Caroline Kennedy, Zappa, Aerosmith interview: Tom Hamilton Caught Off Bass, Rick Derringer, Kiss Part IV—Blood on the Wax: Gene Simmons Profiled, John Denver's Starland Vocal Band, Yes, The Beach Boys: The Return of Brian Wilson, Rush, Chaka Khan, Eagles, Fleetwood Mac, ZZ Top, Tull, Beck, Starship, Stills & Young...........$5–10

#140 Chevy Chase & the Saturday Night Gang, Kiss/Hell on Wheels: How They Staged Their Summer Tour, Hall & Oates, Chicago, Starz, Uriah Heep, ZZ Top Makes History, Beach Boys, Lynyrd Skynyrd, Stills & Young...$5–10

#141 Lindsay Wagner/The Bionic Woman, John Travolta/Barbarino, Fonz, Starsky & Hutch, Frank Zappa, Ronnie Montrose/Aerosmith's Producer, Reggae: Peter Tosh, Burning Spear, Etc., Deep Purple: Why They Finally Split for Good, Beach Boys, Chicago, Starship, Jimmy Page interview, Aerosmith on the Road to Riches..$5–10

#142 Clint Eastwood, Ted Nugent: The Rock Rebel, Yes/Jon Anderson, Black Sabbath Rises from the Crypt, Beach Boy: Dennis Wilson interview, Aerosmith: Untold Trials & Triumphs of America's Hottest Band, Mackenzie Phillips, BTO, Blue Oyster Cult, Jackson Browne, Outlaws, Chicago, Orleans...$5–10

#143 The Captain & Tennille: Pop Sweethearts, Marc Bolin: Footloose & Lawless, Kiss: New Lustre, Linda Ronstadt: Sad-eyed Lady of the West, Ted Nugent, Bad Co.: Disaster in the Recording Studio, Orleans, Deep Purple, Ringo's Beatle Bingo............................$5–10

#144 Cherie Currie/The Runaways: Foxy Photos of Their Debut Tour Plus Color Poster, Queen: Preparing Their Next LP, Bob Dylan, Yes: The Private Life of Chris Squire, Aerosmith: Part V, Rush, Eric Clapton, Lynyrd Skynyrd: Kings of the New South, The Eagles, Todd Rundgren...$10–20

#145 John Travolta/Barbarino: My Life Beyond Barbarino, Foghat's Torrid Tracks, Stevie Wonder, BOA, Patti Smith: Radioactive Signals from the Princess of Ethiopia, Savannah Band, Jodi Foster/Bugsy Malone, Peter Frampton poster, Kiss, Hall & Oates, Ted Nugent, Rainbow, Starz..$5–10

#146 ZZ Top: Tall Tales from the Band Too Big for Texas, Thin Lizzy, Led Zeppelin/Plant poster, Ted Nugent: Rock's Resident Madman, Boston: The Next Led Zeppelin?, Blue Oyster Cult, Foghat, Hall & Oates $5–10

1977

#147 "Breakouts," Stevie Nicks color poster, Fleetwood Mac, Elton John, Kiss, Richard Pryor, Laverne & Shirley, Space Shuttle Flies...$10–20

#148 Kris Kristofferson: *A Star Is Born*, Queen Exclusive—Freddie Mercury Delivers the News/with poster, The Bee Gees' Hit Story, Hall & Oates: Behind the Veils of the Sultry Philadelphia Soulmates, Lou Reed, Bob Seger: Signals from Detroit, Starz, Kiss..........$5–10

#149 Lindsay Wagner, Rush, George Harrison, Jackson Browne, Nazareth, Blue Oyster Cult, Leo Sayer, Genesis, Elo, Linda Ronstadt poster...$5–10

#150 David Bowie: From Europe With Love, Queen Tapes Part I, Rod Stewart poster/The Crown Prince of Stain Soul, Lofgren & Dwight Twilley, Black Sabbath, Ted Nugent, Jim Morrison/The Doors Resurrected $5–10

#151 Paul Rogers/Bad Company/with poster, Queen Tapes: Freddie Mercury Talks About Life Before Queen, Rush, Foghat, The Ramones: New York's Punk Rollers, Peter Gabriel, Graham Parker: The Boldest British Badboy, Yes, Doobies, Steve Tyler full-page color pin-up $5–10

#152 Christine McVie of Fleetwood Mac: The Truth About Rumors—McVie & Lindsay Buckingham Lay Out the Facts, Genesis: The Survivors, Angel: The Heavenly Music That Sizzles, Bad Co. Part II: The Ralphs interview, Wonder Woman/Lynda Carter poster & story, Ann Wilson of Heart, Queen, Rush, Yes..$8–16

#153 Ian Anderson Exclusive: The Creator of Jethro Tull, Fleetwood Mac Part II, David Bowie poster, Kinks: The Ray Davies Sleepwalker interview, Boston: What's Next?, Rick Derringer Takes Chicago, The Hardy Boys: Shaun Cassidy & Parker Stevenson, Keith Richards, Patti Smith Spins Off Tampa Stage, The Runaways Off to Asia $5–10

#154 Keith Emerson of ELP, Pink Floyd on Stage: The Dark Side of Animal Farm Comes to Life, Cream Alive Again, Kiss Fire Secrets, Starz poster, Queen's Act Stuns New York, Clash, Elton John, Alice Cooper $5–10

#155 Alice Cooper—The Coop Returns: The Story Behind the New Stage Show, Kiss Exclusive Interview—Gene Simmons and Paul Stanley Talk About the Kiss Cult, Deep Purple, Marshall Tucker, Rush poster, Johnny Winters/Muddy Waters.....................................$5–10

#156 Sex & Today's Teenager, ELP 1977 Poster on Stage With—Tull, Queen, Genesis, Utopia, Iggy Pop: Bowie's Favorite Zombie Returns With the "Idiot," Beach Boys: Al Jardine Speaks—The Story of Brotherly Love, Kiss Exclusive Interviews: Ace & Peter Criss, Alice Cooper/Billion-Dollar Babies: Alice's Ex-sidemen Swing Their Own Swords, also "Welcome To My Nightmare" $5–10

#157 Jimmy Page of Led Zeppelin: Special Mid-tour Report, Jeff Beck, Wakeman Exclusive: Framed in Sex Pistols Exit, BTO, Kiki Dee, Boston poster, Rock Wives: The High

Life on the Road & Off With Kiss, Boston, Derringer & The Dolls, Beck Explodes, Beach Boys..$5–10

#158 Ted Nugent: The Long Climb to Number One, Steve Miller, Kiss Rocks the Orient: Japan Will Never be the Same—The Exclusive Story & Pictures, Little Feat, Alice Cooper—The Nightmare Comes True: Jailed in Australia, Jimmy Page poster, *Star Wars*, Bad Co..$5–10

#159 Linda Blair, Ian Hunter Talks About Punk, The Beatles: The Legend Lives, Van Morrison, Steve Winwood, On Tour With Bad Co., Women in Rock—Stevie Nicks, Linda Ronstadt, Chaka Khan, Valerie Carter, Debbie Harry, Kiss in Japan Part II with poster $6–12

#160 Sissy Spacek, Heart: The Wilson Sisters Unwind, 10CC, Outlaws, "Saturday Night Live," Rock Wives Part II, Alice Cooper..$5–10

#161 Kiss Special, Ritchie Blackmore, Rush..$10–20

#162 Peter Frampton: His Fantastic Success, Robby Benson, Kiss Comics, Starship to Saturn, The Grateful Dead Film Feature, ELP Tapes, Ian Gillan, UFO, Neil Young $5–10

#163 Rick Wakeman Rejoins Yes, Ted Nugent poster, Elp/Keith Emerson Tapes, Doobie Bros./Disaster Rock, J. Geils, Alice Cooper: New Tricks Unveiled, William Shatner, Kiss: "Love Gun"..$5–10

#164 The Fonz, Punk Rock Special—TV, Sex Pistols, Erasers, DMZ, Stranglers, Ramones, Talking Heads, Mink Deville, The Damned Dead Boys, Etc., Foghat: What Next?, AWB, Black Oak Arkansas, Johnny Winter: Bringing Back the Basics, *Star Wars* poster, *Star Trek*'s Lt. Uhura, Bob Marley, Brian Wilson, Linda Ronstadt..$5–10

#165 Keith Richard of the Rolling Stones Exclusive Interview, Thin Lizzy, Foreigner, Climax Blues Band, Fireball, Farmer: The One Man, Grand Funk Revival, Jimi Hendrix: A Tribute on the Anniversary of Hendrix's Death, Nugent, Streisand, Rick Wakeman.........$5–10

#166 Hall & Oates: On the Road With the Backstreet Beauties, Rush, Kiss: True Confessions of the Former Press Agent, KC & The Sunshine Band, Andy Gibb: The Fourth Bee Gee Goes it Alone, Suzanne Somers, Elvis Years: Special Color Pull-out, Foghat ...$5–10

#167 Linda Ronstadt, Cheap Trick, Shaun Cassidy, Dennis Wilson, Rush, Yes, Richard Pryor, Sha Na Na, UFO, Styx...$5–10

#168 "Logan's Run"/TV Show, Rush Tapes Part III, Michelle Phillips, Kansas, Rita Coolidge, Lynyrd Skynyrd: The Rowdy Boys Go Straight, Jackson Browne, Crawler, Eric Carmen..$5–10

#169 Nancy Wilson of Heart/Heart & The Canadian Explosion, Rush, April Wine, Rod Stewart: Has He Abandoned His British Roots?, Dwight Twilley, Robin Trower, Billy Squier interview, Ted Nugent poster, Graham Parker, Labelle Goes Solo...................$6–12

#170 Cindy Williams, Fleetwood Mac poster, Behind the Scenes of Blue Oyster Cult, Steely Dan, Leo Sayer, Elton: Rocks' Biggest Hitter, The Ramones, Aerosmith, Foghat.....$5–10

#171 Gene Simmons of Kiss/Kiss Alive Exclusive—In the Studio With Kiss, David Bowie, The Ramones, Edgar Winter: New & Improved, Phoebe Snow, ELP II, Elvis Presley poster, Ted Nugent, Iggy Pop: Hanging from the Rafters With Rock's Master Grotesque, Pete Townshend $10–20

1978

#172 Dolly Parton: The Queen of Country-Crossover Lets Her Curls Down, Rush tour poster, Steve Martin, Kiss II Exclusive Interview—The Never Before Told Story: How Gene Simmons Creates His Stage Image, Genesis, Randy Newman, Sex Pistols: The Meanest Punks Invade America, The Beatles: Love Songs for a Lifetime, Lynyrd Skynyrd.$5–10

#173 Freddie Mercury of Queen/Exclusive Freddie Mercury & Brian May Interview, Kansas color poster, Debby Boone, John Belushi, Rick Wakeman, Alice Cooper, Nazareth, Charlie Daniels...$5–10

#174 The Bee Gees, Aerosmith, Queen, Alice Cooper, Neil Young, Tom Petty, The Kiss Tour...$5–10

#175 Linda Ronstadt & Robert Plant, Special Awards Issue: Kiss, Fleetwood Mac, Yes, Etc., Rod Stewart Exclusive Interview, Boz Scaggs, Elvis Costello Exclusive Interview, Kiss Reviews, Angel $5–10

#176 Jackson Browne/Joni Mitchell, Neil Young, Eagles, CS & N, Stevie Wonder, Starz, Natalie Cole, Pat Travers, Sex Pistols: Reviled & Cheered, Kiss Photo Special, Queen tour poster, Clint Eastwood...$5–10

#177 Ted Nugent, Sex Pistols, Ramones, Leif Garrett: The Kid Grows Up, Emmylou Harris: Country's Next Queen, Sea Level, Aerosmith poster, Rick Wakeman, Kiss for Sale: Behind the Multimillion-Dollar Mail-Order Miracle, *Rocky Horror Picture Show*, Johnny Rotten..$5–10

#178 Barry Gibb/Sgt. Pepper, Bee Gees, Aerosmith, Frampton, Alice Cooper, Ted Nugent, How Kiss Moves Special, Journey, Abba, Kiss Tour Exclusive, Gene Simmons of Kiss poster..$6–12

#179 Peter Criss of Kiss, Chaka Khan, Angel, Barry Manilow, Sweet.....................$10–20

#180 Grace Slick/Jefferson Starship, Ace Frehley interview & poster, Be Bop Deluxe, Manfred Mann, Gordon Lightfoot, Mahogany Rush, Little Feat, Andrew Gold, Blondie: Is There More to Blondie Than Glamour?, Ringo Starr..$6–12

#181 Paul Stanley/Kiss, John Travolta poster, Heart's Nancy Wilson/California Jam Special Report, Stevie Nicks, Aerosmith, Ted Nugent, Zeppelin, Outlaws, AWB, Rush, Emmylou Harris, Starship...$10–20

#182 Paul McCartney & Wings: Paul Speaks, Ted Nugent: "My First Gig," Kiss: Peter Criss poster, Genesis, Atlanta Rhythm, Jerry Garcia: Hanging Out Backstage With the Dead, Van Halen, Peter Frampton..$8–16

#183 Carly Simon Exclusive Profile, Heart: The Truth About "Magazine," Jimmy Buffett, Kiss in Japan poster & story: Kiss Conquers Japan, Isley Bros., Steve Hackett, Beatlemania/ Beatle Crazy, REO, Patti Smith, Roger McQuinn/The Byrds, great full-page Heart color photo...$10–20

#184 The Band's Robbie Robertson, Kiss, Angel-Punky poster, Jethro Tull, Patti Smith: The Goddess of Punk, Todd Rundgren: The Hermit of Mink Hollow Returns, Ritchie Blackmore, Elvis Costello: England's Mysterious New Wave Genius Threatens the World, Neil Diamond, Joni Mitchell...$5–10

#185 John Travolta/Grease/Olivia Newton-John, Bob Marley, Marshall Tucker, Cheap Trick, Bruce Springsteen color poster, Mick Jagger/The Stones Tour, Bee Gees, Climax Blues Band, Joni Mitchell..$5–10

#186 Foghat, Kiss Photo History Exclusive: A Trip Through Time With Guide Paul Stanley—The Masked Madman's History from the Beginning, Hall & Oates, Pure Prairie League, O'Jays, Kiss' Paul Stanley Unmasked, Tom Petty: Back on the Track, Alvin Lee: Ten Years Later..$6–12

#187 Bob Seger, Bruce Springsteen, Barry Gibb, Bonnie Tyler, Bee Gees, *Rocky Horror Picture Show*, Little River Band, Seals & Crofts, Van Halen.......................................$5–10

#188 Andy Gibb: How He Made it Good on His Own, The Kinks: Surviving a Second Decade, Joe Walsh, Dave Mason, Pablo Cruise, Chuck Mangione, Mahogany Rush poster, The Road With the Rolling Stones, Elvis Presley: "The King is Not Dead"......................$5–10

#189 Texas Jam, Aerosmith, Ted Nugent, Heart, Journey, Foreigner, Paul Stanley, Pink Floyd, Moody Blues, Buddy Holly $5–10

#190 Peter Frampton/Bee Gees/Aerosmith: Sgt. Pepper Comes Alive, Cheryl Ladd poster, Bob Dylan on the Road Again, John Lennon/Paul McCartney, ELO, Kenny Loggins, Alan Parsons, The Stones Rise from the Dead...$5–10

#191 Barry Gibb/Kiss/Mick Jagger/Ronstadt/Led Zeppelin: The Rock Aristocracy—An Indepth Look Part I, Peter Gabriel, UFO..$5–10

#192 The Beatles "Get Back," The Who, Meatloaf, Peter Frampton, Foreigner, ELO, Aerosmith, Van Halen, Keith Moon Dead at 31: The Complete Story, Boston..........$5–10

#193 Shaun Cassidy: Can He make it as a Real Rocker?, Lynyrd Skynyrd: One Year After the Crash, Pete Townshend on Rock Aristocracy, Blue Oyster Cult, The Beatles Exclusive Chronology, Van Halen vs. Black Sabbath, Battlestar Galactica, The Ramones, Trower $5–10

#194 Kiss Times Four: Exclusive Interviews With Paul Stanley & Gene Simmons as They Unleash Their Long-Awaited Solo Albums, Rock & Sex: Stevie Nicks/Blondie/Ted Nugent/ Donna Summer/Eddie Money, Rick Wakeman poster, Yes, Bruce Springsteen: How He Builds His Incredible Wall of Sound, K.C. and the Sunshine Band, Lynyrd Skynyrd's Finest Hour...$10–20

#195 25 Years of Rock-&-Roll: The Greats, The Near-Greats—The Full Story, Chuck Berry, Linda Ronstadt, Presley, McCartney, Freddie Mercury, Jimmy Page, Jackson Brown, Buddy Holly, Steven Tyler, Ted Nugent, Dylan, Janis Joplin, Plant, Bill Haley, Jimi Hendrix, Bill Haley to Van Halen, Kiss: Ace Frehley & Peter Criss Continue the Solo Blitz........$6–12

#196 Linda Ronstadt: It's Been a Tough Ten Years, Cheap Trick Exclusive Interview, Al Stewart, Chicago: They're Back, Boston, Elton John...$5–10

#197 Ian Anderson/Jethro Tull: Why They're Bursting Out, Hall & Oates, The Hulk interview, 10CC, Rock on Radio: Aerosmith, Nugent & Others, Blondie & The Ramones: The New Wave, Bowie Poster, Yes $4–8

CIRCUS, 1978, #180

CIRCUS, 1978, #178

CIRCUS, 1978, #175

CIRCUS, 1977, #174

CIRCUS, 1977, #171

CIRCUS, 1977, #167

CIRCUS, 1980, #248

CIRCUS, 1980, #247

CIRCUS, 1981, #258

#198 Billy Joel: His Records Go Platinum, David Bowie: A Behind-the-scenes Look, Neil Young: Entering the Second Decade, Stones' Keith Richards Pleads Guilty in Toronto— Feature Story, Eddie Money, Nancy Wilson, Ann Wilson, Meat Loaf, Cheap Trick, Van Halen, Boston..$4–8

#199 Elton John Speaks Out on Jagger, Bowie, Zappa, Tull & More: An Exclusive Interview, Black Sabbath Together Again, The Beach Boys: The Family That Plays Together, Pat Travers, Fireball, *The Wiz*: Diana Ross, Michael Jackson, Ozzy Osbourne, Mike Lowe of The Beach Boys, Black Sabbath's Lommi Interviewed, Tom Petty, Ace Frehley $4–8

#200 Ted Nugent's Trial by Tube, Van Morrison, Sea Level, Bob Seger poster, Billy Joel, Neil Young, Chicago...$4–8

#201 Steve Tyler/Aerosmith Fights Back, Geddy Lee Interviewed, Rush, Styx & The Cars on the Road, Devo: Taking America by Storm, Toto...$4–8

#202 Freddie Mercury: Queen Cuts Loose, Kansas, Santana, The Outlaws, Chaka Khan, Robin Williams interview, Heart...$4–8

#203 Alice Cooper: Back From His Bout With the Bottle, Eric Clapton poster, Bob Dylan Exclusive Interview, Southside Johnny: The Jersey Juker, Elton John, Elvis Presley/Elvis Costello $4–8

1979

#204 Steve Martin: The Story Behind the Comic, Meat Loaf Exclusive Interview, Steve Miller, The Outlaws, Ted Nugent, Rick Nielsen, Rory Gallagher, Eddie Van Halen, Johnny Ramone—Guitar Heroes...$4–8

#205 Rock-&-Roll's Super People of the Year Issue—David Lee Roth, Ted Nugent, Bruce Springsteen, Anne Wilson of Heart, Steven Tyler & Joe Perry of Aerosmith, Mick Jagger, Queen poster, The Bee Gees, Cheap Trick, Meat Loaf & Many Others.......................$4–8

#206 Marijuana, The Grateful Dead: Passing the Acid Test, ELP Profiled, Kiss, AC/DC: Can the Aussies Make It?, Rod Stewart..$4–8

#207 Rod Stewart's Strange Return, Cheap Trick Gone Disco?, Todd Rundgren: An Era Comes to an End for the Runt, The Doors: Why Forbidden Tapes can be Released Now, Jethro Tull Bursting Out...$4–8

#208 "Mork & Mindy," Cars poster, "Saturday Night Live," Steve Miller special, Cheap Trick, Queen, An American Dream: The Doors $3–6

#209 Robert Plant & Anne Wilson, Jimmy Page, The Cars, Rolling Stones, J. Geils, Jazz '79 ....$4–8

#210 Sex in America, Elvis Costello Attacks, Elvis Presley: The TV Bio, Rod Stewart color Poster, Bee Gees, Donna Summer, Abba...$3–6

#211 Dan Aykroyd & John Belushi: *The Blues Brothers*, Meat Loaf poster, Cat Stevens is Back, Tanya Tucker: Sex Sells, Cheap Trick, Van Halen, Meat Loaf, Cars, Toto, Queen Has no Clothes, Todd Rundgren..$4–8

#212 *Animal House* Exclusive, Rush: A Roadie's Diary—Go Behind the Scenes & Backstage, Meat Loaf/Blondie/Kiss & Others Tell How They First Hooked Up, Sid Vicious, Dead, The Doobie Brothers $3–6

#213 Eddie Money Cashes In, Linda Blair Trials, UFO/Michael Schenker, ELP, Elvis Costello, Elton John, Lesley Ann Down, Loni Anderson $3–6

#214 The Bee Gees Life at the Top, Marie Osmond Tells All: Why She Turned Down Olivia Newton-John's Sexy Role in *Grease*, Supertrain, Peter Frampton: Split & Being Sued by Penny McCall, Roger McQuinn, Elvis Costello centerfold poster.............................$3–6

#215 Cheryl Ladd & Miss Piggy, Jefferson Starship: With Grace Slick Out Will They Go Around?, McCartney's TV Special, George Harrison...$3–6

#216 Elvis Presley: The Selling of Elvis, Lynda Carter, The Warriors, John Denver Takes a Dive, Todd Rundgren, Rex Smith...$3–6

#217 Blondie's Debbie Harry: The New Sex Symbol, *Star Wars*: Han Solo/Harrison Ford Exclusive, Adrienne Barbeau $4–8

#218 Bucky Dent, Sally Field, Ted Nugent's Long Hot Summer, Cheap Trick, Eddie Money, Van Halen...$3–6

#219 Jane Fonda, Cheap Trick: An Exclusive Chat With Bun E. Carlos, Britt Ekland & Rod Stewart, George Harrison is Back Again, Boomtown Rats: A Hot New Irish Band Live on Their Home Turf, Allman Brothers...$3–6

#220 Stockard Channing's Real Life, The Allman Brothers: Greg Allman Tells All, Andy Kaufman, Rush color poster, Bad Company...$3–6

#221 *Hair*'s Donnie Dacus, Elvis Presley Lives: The Men Who Imitate the King, Cheryl Ladd poster, The Babys: How They Finally Scored, Bob Welch, Bob Geldof............$3–6
#222 Patti Hansen: Lynda Carter, Bob Welch: Still Tight With Fleetwood Mac, Van Halen, Graham Parker, Dracula, Toni Tennille...$3–6
#223 Ron Wood & Keith Richards, Jackson Browne, Joni Mitchell, Doobie Brothers Default, Fleetwood Mac Family Follow-up, Supertramp $3–6
#224 Cher: Disco Rocks America—Village People, Donna Summer & Others, The Beatles One-night Stand, The Tubes, Sha Na Na's Denny Green $3–6
#225 Summer Movie Special, Sigourney Weaver/Alien, The Who on Tour, Summer Tours—Kiss, Yes, Van Halen, Cheap Trick, Bad Company, Led Zeppelin, Roxy Music Future Pop
....$3–6
#226 The Most Influential People Issue—John Belushi, John Travolta, Mick Jagger, Etc., The Who in *The Kids Are Alright*, Paul McCartney, Wings Evolve Beyond "Let It Be," Dire Straits Mellows Out...$3–6
#227 Special 10th Anniversary Issue—The Best of Circus, "Saturday Night's" Bill Murray in *Meatballs*, Alice Cooper, David Bowie, Marc Bolan, Kiss, Stones, Janis Joplin, Jimi Hendrix, Led Zeppelin, Black Sabbath, Little Feat's Lowell George Dies on Tour.....$3–6
#228 Woodstock Special—Ten Years On: What Ever Happened to Woodstock Nation?, Bad Co.: Living With Their Families, Dracula, Ringo Starr, Neil Young, Rachel Sweet is Not a Punk Rocker $3–6
#229 Gilda Radner/"Saturday Night Live"—How Outrageous Can They Get?, The Cars: Ric Ocasek Talks, Peter Frampton's Back in Action, Eagles, Stevie Nicks Short: Fleetwood Mac Sound May Go Digital, The Kinks $3–6
#230 Robert Plant/Led Zeppelin: After Personal Tragedy & Two Years of Silence—Talks, Kiss Without Makeup, Roll Over John Travolta, REO Speedwagon: Going for the Spotlight, Stevie Nicks Short—Fleetwood Mac Album Nearly Ready, Mackenzie Phillips: *American Graffitti* $3–6
#231 Ric Ocasek/The Cars, The Knack, Police, Kiss: Have the Masked Marvels Reached the End of the Road?, Stevie Nicks Short—Fleetwood Mac Tour Firmed Up, AC/DC, Foley & Shipley, Blondie...$4–8
#232 Stevie Nicks: "Tusk"—A New Stage in the Mac Success Story, Aerosmith's Steven Tyler: "We're Back to Raw Guts," Cheap Trick's Rick Nielsen: Superstars, The Who's Triumphant Return: with special concert color section, Blondie, Eagles, Zappa.............$5–10
#233 Steve Martin, Foghat, Eagles, Foreigner, Judas Priest, Styx, Blondie..................$3–6
#234 Cheap Trick, *Rocky Horror Picture Show*, Fleetwood Mac....................................$3–6
#235 Styx, Willie Nelson, The Rolling Stones, Tom Petty, Molly Hatchet, Debbie Harry/Blondie...$3–6
#236 Foreigner: Dirty-minded Boys & Hot-blooded Girls, Aerosmith, The Bee Gees: The Truth About the Break-up Rumors, The Police, Bonnie Raitt: Career on the Line, Fabulous Poobles, The Shoes...$3–6

1980

#237 Debbie Harry Special Report—Rock of the 80s, The Cars, Led Zeppelin, Queen, Van Halen, The Eagles Exclusive Interview, Jefferson Starship Flies With a New Crew, Pat Metheny, The Who, Gilda Radner...$4–8
#238 Debbie Harry/Robert Plant, Special Awards Issue—Rock Stars of the Year, Kiss concert poster, The Knack: Best New Group, Zappa, Graham Nash, Pat Benatar, Jackson Browne, Jan & Dean, Derringer..$4–8
#239 Steven Tyler of Aerosmith: Joe Perry Exits, Steve Collapses—Can They Survive?, Tom Petty: New Wave Explosion, The Ramones: Teaming Up With Phil Spector, The Clash: The British Rock Bombers, Pink Floyd: A Peek Behind the Wall, Little Feat, Paul McCartney $4–8
#240 Rush Exclusive Interview, Van Halen: Kings of the Road?, Cheap Trick: Their Elaborate Stage Show, Foreigner, Styx, Steve Forbert, Joe Perry's Instruments, ZZ Top, Rundgren/Adventures With Utopia $4–8
#241 Pink Floyd Exposed: Who Really Built the Wall?, Britt Ekland, UFO, Heart: The Wilson Sisters Emerge Triumphant, Blondie's Boys, Babys, Zeppelin, Nugent, Queen, Judas Priest, Dylan, Zevon $4–8
#242 David Lee Roth/Van Halen, Journey, J. Geils Band, Cheap Trick: The Robin Zander Interview, Kristy McNichol & Tatum O'Neil, Linda Ronstadt, Rachel Sweet.............$4–8

#243 Bob Seger, Ted Nugent, Pretenders, Johnny Rotten, Robin Trower, Joe Perry, Grace Slick, Fantastic Color Photos of—Kiss, Blondie, Priest, Van Halen & Others, Beach Boys at Ebb Tide, Johnny Winter...$4–8

#244 Summer Rock '80 Special, Pat Travers, Linda Ronstadt: Gadfly or Golden Girl?, Genesis, Marshall Tucker: Can They Survive?, England's Heavy Metal Explosion, Cooper, Journey, Van Halen, Kiss, Yes...$3–6

#245 Journey: How They Cope With Platinum, Paranoia, Judas Priest, Ian Hunter, Debbie Harry & Meat Loaf in Roadie, Paul McCartney, The Grateful Dead: 15 Years in Rare Pictures...$4–8

#246 Black Sabbath vs. Ozzy Osbourne, Van Halen Exclusive Color Scrapbook, Kinks, Scorpions, Outlaws, Rolling Stones...$3–6

#247 Freddie Mercury/Queen, *The Blues Brothers*, AC/DC, The Stones: With Keith Richards poster, Hendrix short & photo, Jackson Browne $4–8

#248 Kiss cover & feature story, The Rolling Stones, Queen, Van Halen, Led Zeppelin, Jim Morrison/The Doors, Pink Floyd, Blondie, Rush, Foghat, Special 11th Anniversary Issue With Rare Rock Interviews, Color Posters & Photos..$8–16

#249 Ric Ocasek/The Cars: Too Remote for Their Own Good, Yes, AC/DC, Foghat, Whitesnake, Def Leppard, Slade, Led Zeppelin's John Bonham, David Bowie, Doobie Brothers, Elvis Costello, The Police..$4–8

#250 Special Year-end Issue—15 Rockers Who Shook the Pop World in 1980: Pat Benatar, AC/DC, Bowie, Cheap Trick, Doors, Queen, Who, Stones, Springsteen, Dire Straits, Rockpile, REO Speedwagon, Kansas: Hits from the Heartland, Springsteen poster, Gary Numan, Led Zeppelin, Pink Floyd, Chrissie Hynde, John & Yoko $5–10

1981

#251 Jim Morrison/The Doors: An Exclusive Report, Police, Dire Straits, Kiss/Peter Criss, Blondie, Steve Forbert, John Cougar, John Lennon Memorial $5–10

#252 Special Awards Issue, Pat Benatar & Robert Plant, Def Leppard, Queen, John Lennon, Rockpile, Journey, A Farewell to Zeppelin, Blondie's Debbie Harry Speaks Out: A Special Interview With Debbie, Chris, Clem & Nigel...$4–8

#253 A Frank Talk With Rush, Black Sabbath, Styx, REO Speedwagon, Triumph, Fleetwood Mac, Police, Grace Slick, Kiss/Peter Criss $4–8

#254 Ritchie Blackmore Talks, The Who: Can They Cut It?, Steve Winwood, Elvis Costello Hits the Road, Judas Priest, Scorpions, Riot, April Wine, Rainbow, The Tunes of Jimi Hendrix, Seger & The Doors...$4–8

#255 The New British Invasion, Police, Judas Priest, The Clash, AC/DC, Blue Oyster Cult, Grateful Dead, Jefferson Starship, Cheap Trick, UFO, The Rolling Stones..................$4–8

#256 Ozzy Osbourne Scrapbook & Exclusive Interview, Journey, The Who & Pat Travers, Styx, Van Halen, Ted Nugent, Tom Petty, Rush, The Pretenders, The Stones, REO Speedwagon, Jefferson Starship, The Marshall Tucker Band..$4–8

#257 AC/DC, REO Speedwagon, Van Halen, Pat Travers, Adam & The Ants, 38 Special, Santana & Ritchie Blackmore, Emerson & Wakeman...$4–8

#258 Tom Petty, Rush, Joe Perry, Kim Carnes, Bruce Springsteen, Moody Blues, REO Speedwagon, Van Halen, Meat Loaf, Elton John...$4–8

#259 Moody Blues, Pat Benatar, The Knack, Van Halen's David Lee Roth, Def Leppard $4–8

#260 Special 12th Anniversary Issue—The Biggest Color Issue Ever: The Rolling Stones, Rush, Led Zeppelin, The Who, David Bowie, Billy Squire, Debbie Harry/Blondie, AC/DC, Beatles, Stevie Nicks, Tubes, Elton, Darryl Hall, Alice Cooper, Tom Petty, McCartney $4–8

#261 Special Rolling Stones Tour 1981 Souvenir Issue, The Pretenders: Special Interview, Foghat: The Boogie Band in Action, The Police: Can They Succeed?, Rick Springfield: Reveals His Stormy Past, Stevie Nicks, Kinks, John Lennon $4–8

#262 Special Year-end Issue, Stevie Nicks, Rush, REO Speedwagon, AC/DC, Billy Squire, The Rolling Stones $5–10

1982

#263 Phil Collins/Genesis: Taking Its Biggest Gamble, Queen: What Happened in Switzerland?, Foreigner, Devo, The Go-go's: Is There a Life Beyond 20?, Adam & The Ants, The Who: Special Photo Scrapbook, Little River Band, Journey, Cars, Santana, Police.....$3–6

#264 Pat Benatar: Woman of the Year, Mick Jagger: Man of the Year, The Who: Action Photos & Exclusive Stories, Rolling Stones color poster, Billy Squier, Rod Stewart, J. Geils Band, Beatles, AC/DC...$3–6

#265 Angus Young: Inside AC/DC, Black Sabbath, Kiss: Gene Simmons & Paul Stanley Take Off Their Make-up—A Revealing Interview, Joan Jett: She's Still Dressed in Leather, Rush, Allman Bros./Genesis on the Road, Cars, Ozzy, Trower, J. Geils, Journey, Police.............$3–6

#266 Ozzy Osbourne, Molly Hatchet, Journey, Alice Cooper, Loverboy, Abba, Del Shannon...$3–6

#267 Ritchie Blackmore/Rainbow, J. Geils Band on the Road, The Cars: A Revealing Look, Nick Lowe, Sammy Hagar, Quarterflash, Waitress, Jefferson Airplane 1967, Billy Squire, Black Sabbath, AC/DC, Ozzy Osbourne...$3–6

#268 Special Rock on Tour Issue—Van Halen, Queen, Joan Jett, Asia, Foreigner, Billy Squier, REO Speedwagon, Judas Priest, Rainbow, includes giant 16″ × 21″ Randy Rhoads & Ozzy Osbourne poster...$3–6

#269 Debbie Harry/Blondie: Five Years On, Billy Squier, Led Zeppelin wall poster, A Decade of Stars—Zeppelin, AC/DC, Rod Stewart & Others, Cream '68, Judas Priest, Bob Weir, Asia: Newest Supergroup

#270 REO Speedwagon Exclusive Interview, Cheap Trick, Heart: Why the Wilson Sisters Fired Their Sidemen, Huey Lewis, Journey, AC/DC, Joan Jett & Sammy Hagar, The Go-go's: Tips from Charlotte Caffey, Eddie Van Halen color concert poster, Pat Benatar.....$4–8

#271 David Lee Roth/Van Halen, Robert Plant, Squeeze: The Upscale, Pop, Scorpions, AC/DC, Iron Maiden, Kinks, Foreigner, Loverboy, Billy Idol, Joan Jett short, Debbie Harry short $3–6

#272 Ozzy Osbourne: The Heavy Metal Madman's Exclusive Story, Rush, Robert Plant giant wall poster, Black Sabbath's Bloody Homecoming, Pink Floyd, Journey, AC/DC, Van Halen, Squier, Queen Live...$3–6

#273 Rush, John Cougar, The Go-go's, Aerosmith, Black Sabbath, The Who Farewell ...$3–6

#274 Rock-&-Roll '82—The Year in Review: Van Halen/Exclusive Interviews With Eddie & David, The Who: Never-before-published Concert Photos, Pat Benatar, Ozzy, Iron Maiden, Judas Priest, 38 Special, Journey, John Cougar, Rush.....................................$3–6

1983

#275 Led Zeppelin Exclusive, includes the 1983 rock wall calendar—12-page/12-month color pullout, Journey, Van Halen, Iron Maiden, Pat Travers, Police, Hall & Oates: Rock's Odd Couple, AC/DC, Rush..$3–6

#276 David Lee Roth/Van Halen Backstage Exclusive, Robert Plant, Pat Benatar: Woman of the Year, Asia, Judas Priest, Def Leppard, Ozzy, Rush, Aerosmith, Randy Rhoads...............$3–6

#277 Ozzy Osbourne, David Lee Roth, Van Halen, Rush, Black Sabbath, Kiss, Sammy Hagar, Aerosmith, Loverboy, Who, Zeppelin, Journey.......................................$3–6

#278 Journey's Steve Perry, Van Halen, Judas Priest, Def Leppard, Rush, Kinks, Keith Richards: How He Gets His Sounds, ABC, Led Zeppelin....................................$3–6

#279 David Lee Roth/Van Halen, Billy Squier, Kiss: A Frank Talk With Paul & Gene, Judas Priest, Def Leppard, Ozzy, Iron Maiden, Eddie Van Halen, Scorpions: The German Heavies Break Down the Language...$3–6

#280 Rock on the Road Special—Def Leppard, Van Halen, Ozzy, Judas Priest, Billy Squier, Journey, Loverboy, Stray Cats $3–6

#281 Rock Sounds Off Issue—Def Leppard, Iron Maiden, Judas Priest, Duran Duran, Ozzy, Joan Jett: Rock's Leather Princess Lets it All Out in an In-depth Interview, Van Halen, Scorpions..$4–8

#282 Def Leppard Exclusive: How They Lost Touch With Their Hard-core Fans, Iron Maiden, Journey, Pink Floyd, Judas Priest, Van Halen, Ozzy Osbourne, Scorpions, Triumph, Bowie, U2, Stray Cats, Quiet Riot, Pretenders $3–6

#283 Def Leppard Rocks America Issue, Robert Plant, Iron Maiden, Randy Rhoads, Triumph, Krokus, Van Halen, Judas Priest...$3–6

#284 Special 14th Anniversary Issue/The Biggest Issue Ever—Def Leppard, AC/DC, Duran Duran: A Flash in the Pan, Van Halen: The Start of a Mad Career, Judas Priest, Billy Squier, Ozzy Osbourne, Journey, Joan Jett...$3–6

#285 Kevin Dubrow/Quiet Riot, Def Leppard, AC/DC, Asia, Iron Maiden, Duran Duran, Talking Heads, Elvis Costello, The Police..$3–6

#286 The Year in Rock Issue—Def Leppard, Quiet Riot, Iron Maiden, Judas Priest, AC/DC, Van Halen: David Lee Roth Sounds Off..$3–6

1984

#287 Quiet Riot Special Issue—includes 12-page color souvenir section, Def Leppard, Iron Maiden, Van Halen, Duran Duran Exclusive, AC/DC, Police, McCartney, Kiss, sheet music to "Slick Back Cadillac"...$3–6

#288 Joe Elliot/Def Leppard, Quiet Riot: Kevin Dubrow Looks Ahead, Judas Priest, Van Halen, Black Sabbath, Motley Crue, Ozzy, Jimmy Page, Clapton, Jeff Beck, Dylan, 38 Special, Romantics, Krokus..$3–6

#289 Vince Neil/Motley Crue, Quiet Riot, Def Leppard, Van Halen: David interview, Judas Priest, The Doors: Thirteen Years After Jim Morrison's Death—Some Closed Doors Open Up, Duran Duran, ZZ Top, Blue Oyster Cult, John Cougar, Kiss, Girlschool, Huey Lewis.....$4–8

#290 Marked 289 . . . April 30th . . . Heavy Metal Spectacular, Motley Crue, Van Halen: A One-to-one Interview With David Lee Roth, Judas Priest, Ozzy, Rainbow: Back on Top, Quiet Riot, Billy Idol, The Pretenders...$3–6

#291 David Lee Roth/Van Halen Exclusive, Motley Crue's Nikki & Vince Exclusive Interviews, Ozzy, Duran Duran, Kiss: full-color centerspread, Judas Priest, Scorpions, Queen, Night Ranger, Iron Maiden, Michael Jackson, Sammy Hagar, Who's Hot/Who's Not.....$3–6

#292 Special Rock on the Road Issue—Rush, Ozzy, Krokus, Michael Jackson, Motley Crue, Van Halen, Scorpions, Judas Priest, Iron Maiden, Kiss: Eleven Years On, They're Still Going Strong, Slade, Go-go's, April Wine, Accept, Hagar, Cars, Cheap Trick, Romantics $3–6

#293 Klaus Meine/Scorpions: Story With Color Centerfold, Van Halen Exclusive: Eddie Van Halen Speaks Out, Ozzy: Is He Settling Down?, Rush, Motley Crue, Krokus, Steve Perry, Ted Nugent, Cars, Ratt, Stevie Nicks, Slade, Huey Lewis, Modern English, John Cougar.......$3–6

#294 Motley Crue Blows Away the Foes, Van Halen, Scorpions, Iron Maiden, Leppard, Ozzy: Road Disasters, Rush, Idol, Springsteen...$3–6

#295 Stephen Percy/Ratt, Motley Crue: Nikki Sixx Speaks, Van Halen: What Happened When David Dropped Money on the Audience?, Iron Maiden, Scorpions, Judas Priest, Quiet Riot, Def Leppard, Night Ranger, Bon Jovi: Jail Threats on the Eve of Japanese Tour....................$3–6

#296 Special 15th Anniversary Issue—Ratt, Van Halen, Motley Crue, Def Leppard, Judas Priest, Iron Maiden, Quiet Riot, Twisted Sister, Squier, Cyndi Lauper, Go-go's, Eurythmics, Huey Lewis, Dio..$3–6

#297 Dee Snider/Twisted Sister, Quiet Riot, Billy Squier, Judas Priest, Scorpions: The Bizarre Odyssey, Ratt, Dio, Krokus, Kiss: The Guitars of Paul Stanley, Springsteen, Idol, Lindsay Buckingham...$3–6

#298 Stephen Percy/Ratt: Can They Survive?, Van Halen, Twisted Sister, Iron Maiden: Will They Break Free?, Billy Squier, Dio, Quiet Riot, Rush, Dokken, Queensryche, Tull, Thompson Twins, Buckingham...$3–6

1985

#299 Bruce Dickinson/Iron Maiden: Behind the Iron Curtain, Ratt, Quiet Riot, Krokus, AC/DC, Joan Jett: Joan Opens Up With the Story of Her "Misspent Youth," Sammy Hagar, Twisted Sister, Kiss: A Critic's Eye View of "Animalize"—with color centerfold, Lita Ford, Dokken, Night Ranger, Big Country, Hall & Oates, Honey Drippers, Billy Idol.........$3–6

#300 Paul Stanley/Kiss—Paul Tells How Kiss Made the Biggest Comeback of the Year, Ratt, Lita Ford, Motley Crue, Iron Maiden, W.A.S.P., Billy Squier, Robert Plant: Unfolding the Tale of Zeppelin, Bowie $4–8

#301 Vance Neil/Motley Crue, W.A.S.P., Kiss: Gene Simmons—From Metal Master to Movie Madman Plus a Look at the Kiss Tour, Iron Maiden, Pat Benatar: Hurting Her Homelife, Van Halen, Twisted Sister, Bon Jovi: To Madison Square Garden, Dokken, Y & T, Hall & Oates $4–8

#302 Gene Simmons/Kiss—Eric Carr & Bruce Kulick Stand Their Ground and Kiss Off Their Troubles, Motley Crue, W.A.S.P., Iron Maiden, Deep Purple, Twisted Sister, Judas Priest, Bruce Springsteen, Journey, Pat Benatar, David Lee Roth, Foreigner $4–8

#303 Paul Stanley/Kiss: Have These Metal Godfathers Lost Their Touch With Their Audience?—Paul Says No, Motley Crue, W.A.S.P., Ratt, Van Halen, Twisted Sister, Dokken, Queensrkyche, Tom Petty, Dio, The Firm...$4–8

#304 Rock on Tour Issue—Kiss: Has the Comeback Run Its Course?, A Frank Talk With Ex-master Ace Frehley, Motley Crue, Ratt, Twisted Sister, Krokus, Accept, Bon Jovi, The

Firm, Deep Purple, Dio, Stones, Ozzy, Julian Lennon, John Fogerty, Mountain, Kenny Loggins, REO Speedwagon..$4–8

#305 Hard Rock's Newest Invaders—Queensryche, Metallica, Lita Ford, Keel, Giuffria, Bon Jovi, Motley Crue, W.A.S.P...$3–6

#306 Dokken, Paul Stanley of Kiss full-color centerfold, Motley Crue, Ratt, Twisted Sister, Scorpions, Night Ranger, Robert Plant, Bruce Springsteen, Eric Carr, Tom Petty.......$3–6

#307 Motley Crue, Ratt, Dokken, Robert Plant, Ozzy, AC/DC, Tom Petty, Iron Maiden, Metallica, Jimmy Page, Bon Jovi, Huey Lewis, Grim Reaper...$3–6

#308 Special 16th Anniversary Issue—Motley Crue, Ratt, Van Halen, Dokken, Scorpions, Kiss: Behind the Scenes & The Making of "Destroyer," Robert Plant: Led Zeppelin's Immigrant Songster, Dio, Jeff Beck, Cheap Trick, Y & T, UB40, Night Ranger, Pat Benatar, Dire Straits, Helix...$3–6

#309 Jon Bon Jovi Exclusive: Telling His Story, Ratt, Scorpions, Dokken, Motley Crue, Kiss: Paul Stanley Sounds Off on Kiss & the Making of "Asylum," Keel, Y & T, AC/DC, Armored Saint, Bruce Springsteen, Huey Lewis, Marillion, Dire Straits, Dio, Foreigner.....$3–6

#310 Nikki Sixx/Motley Crue, Bon Jovi: Beating Stage Fright, Dio, Iron Maiden, W.A.S.P., Kiss, Y & T, AC/DC, Scorpions, Triumph..$3–6

1986

#311 Paul Stanley/Kiss—Paul Tells Why the Veteran Metallists Can't Stay Away from the Glory Trail, Bon Jovi: How They Blew Away the Audience, Dokken, Rush/Heaven, Dio, Scorpions, Ratt, Aerosmith, David Lee Roth, Metallica, Van Halen, Y & T, The Cars, Platinum Blondie...$4–8

#312 Vince Neil/Motley Crue, Lita Ford, AC/DC, Kiss: Gene Simmons Recalls How the Band Skirted Disaster, Dio, W.A.S.P., Rush, Twisted Sister, Bruce Springsteen, Marillion, Pat Benatar, INXS, Stevie Ray Vaughan..$3–6

#313 Ratt Exclusive, Kiss Out on the Road With Gene Simmons & the Boys, W.A.S.P., Twisted Sister, AC/DC, Motley Crue, Bon Jovi with centerfold, Dokken, Dio: The A to Z Story, The Who, Pat Benatar, Dire Straits..$3–6

#314 Motley Crue, Ratt, Kiss: Paul Stanley Reveals Why They Hold the Record for the Longest Kiss in History, Dokken, Judas Priest, Ozzy, Twisted Sister: Behind the Scenes, Aerosmith, Asia, Bangles...$3–6

#315 Ozzy Osbourne: The Return of a Madman, Motley Crue, David Lee Roth Exclusive, Van Halen, Dokken, Metallica, Pat Benatar: On the Scene of Her New York Gig, Ratt, Bon Jovi centerfold, Rainbow, King Kobra...$3–6

#316 Eddie Van Halen, W.A.S.P., 12-page tour section, Ozzy, Judas Priest, Rush: Mystic Rhythms, Keel, Twisted Sister, Ratt, The Rolling Stones, Bob Seger..........................$3–6

#317 Judas Priest: Inside the Making of "Turbo," Ozzy: Behind the Scenes of His Tour, Van Halen, Krokus, Dokken, Metallica, Ratt, Bon Jovi, Motley Crue, Def Leppard, Iron Maiden, Heart, Starship...$3–6

#318 Bon Jovi: On Slippery Wet Ground, Judas Priest, Queensryche, Ozzy, Dokken, ZZ Top.$3–6

#319 David Lee Roth vs. Van Halen, Sammy Hagar, Judas Priest, Krokus, Ozzy, Metallica, Dio, Motley Crue, Jimmy Page, Kiss, W.A.S.P..$3–6

#320 Special 17th Anniversary Issue—Motley Crue, Ratt, Bon Jovi, Def Leppard, Kiss, AC/DC, Van Halen, Iron Maiden, Ozzy Osbourne, Scorpions, Rush.............................$3–6

#321 Motley Crue, Bon Jovi, Cinderella, David Lee Roth, Iron Maiden, Ratt, AC/DC, Alice Cooper Returns, Dokken..$3–6

#322 Cinderella Breaks Loose, Bon Jovi: Face to Face with color centerfold, Motley Crue, Ozzy & Jake, Ratt, Metallica, Quiet Riot, Alice Cooper, Cyndi Lauper, Iron Maiden, Idol, John Fogerty...$3–6

1987

#323 The Year in Rock-&-Roll—Motley Crue, Cinderella, Bon Jovi, Iron Maiden, Metallica, David Lee Roth, Ozzy, Ratt, Van Halen, Dokken, Stryper, Twisted Sister, Scorpions, Billy Idol, Kiss/Bruce Kulick..$3–6

#324 17th Annual Readers' Poll Issue—Bon Jovi, Motley Crue, Lita Ford, Cinderella, Iron Maiden, David Lee Roth, Kiss, Metallica, Ozzy, Van Halen, Stryper, Judas Priest, Paul Stanley & Gene Simmons..$3–6

#325 Hottest Rockers of All Time Special—Bon Jovi, Motley Crue, Kiss, Iron Maiden, Jimi Hendrix, Billy Idol, The Doors, Beatles, Led Zeppelin, Rolling Stones, Stryper, Deep Purple, Judas Priest, Metallica, Van Halen..$3–6

CIRCUS, 1981, #252

CIRCUS, 1989, #357

CIRCUS, 1989, #356

CIRCUS, 1989, #354

CIRCUS, 1989, #353

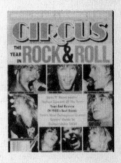

CIRCUS, 1988, #346

CIRCUS, 1988, #339

CIRCUS: SOLID GOLD,
1978

CIRCUS, ROCKING
INTO THE 1990s, 1989,
VOL. 1

#326 Bon Jovi: The Inside Story—A Complete History With Rare Photos of the Early Years, Motley Crue, Iron Maiden, Cinderella, Ratt $3–6

#327 Special Issue—Rock Roars Back, Bon Jovi: Rocking on the Ultimate Tour, Poison, Cinderella, Motley Crue, Europe: Invading the U.S.A., Ratt, Anthrax, Ozzy, Metallica, Tesla, Megadeth..$3–6

#328 Rock on Tour '87—Bon Jovi, Poison, Europe, Motley Crue, Cinderella, Ratt, Dokken, David Bowie, Billy Idol, Armored Saint, Y & T...$3–6

#329 The Motley Crue Story, Bon Jovi: Becoming a Household Name, Poison, Europe, Cinderella, Ozzy Osbourne Tour Burnout, Dokken...$2–4

#330 The 24 Most Intriguing Rockers—Bon Jovi, Dokken, Ace Frehley, Gene Simmons, Paul Stanley, Halford, Ozzy Osbourne, Dickinson, Nikki Sixx, Etc..............................$2–4

#331 Sept. 30 Bon Jovi, Motley Crue, Cinderella, Poison, Ratt, Whitesnake color poster, Ozzy, Keel, Tesla, Megadeth on Stage Exclusive $2–4

#332 Oct. 31 18th Birthday Bash Issue—Bon Jovi: An Exclusive Interview, Motley Crue, Poison, Cinderella, Ratt, Whitesnake, Kiss, Ozzy, Def Leppard, The Original, Ace Frehley, Kiss' Eric Carr $2–4

#333 Nov. 30 Def Leppard Exclusive Interviews With Over 20 Color-packed Pages Including Their Complete History & Joe Elliot Color Poster, Bon Jovi, Kiss, Motley Crue, Poison...$2–4

#334 Dec. 31 The Year in Rock: Special Issue/The Heaviest & Loudest of 1987, Whitesnake, Motley Crue, Bon Jovi, Poison, Def Leppard, Metallica, Dokken, Europe, Kiss Rocket Back, Alice Cooper..$2–4

1988

#335 Jan. 31 Whitesnake Explodes: A Super Whitesnake Special—Up Close With David Coverdale, A Complete History, Photos & Much More, Motley Crue, Aerosmith, Dokken, Poison, Def Leppard, Pink Floyd...$2–4

#336 Feb. 29 Special Rock Awards Issue, Motley Crue, Whitesnake, Bon Jovi, Poison, Def Leppard, Dokken, Guns n Roses, Black Sabbath...$2–4

#337 Mar. 31 Complete Guide to Who's Who in Rock: Motley Crue, Bon Jovi, Whitesnake, Def Leppard, Europe, Poison, Cinderella, Dokken, Kiss, Ozzy, Lita Ford, Guns 'n' Roses, Megadeth, Metallica, Scorpions, Etc..$2–4

#338 Vince Neil's Wild Side interview, Motley Crue, Whitesnake, Dokken, Poison, Guns 'n' Roses, Megadeth, Cinderella: Rags to Riches, Ted Nugent.....................................$2–4

#339 May 31 Bret Michaels/Poison, Def Leppard, Whitesnake: An Exclusive Backstage View, Dokken, Guns 'n' Roses, White Lion, Great White, Megadeth, includes Def Leppard wall poster, Rush, Anthrax...$2–4

#340 June Rockers on Tour, Poison, Def Leppard, Dokken, Metallica, Guns 'n' Roses, White Lion...$2–4

#341 July 31 Don Dokken: Facing the Ultimate Challenge, Poison, Def Leppard, Lita Ford, Guns 'n' Roses, White Lion: Turning Near Disaster Around, Metallica, Megadeth: Will Success Spoil Them?, Nikki poster..$2–4

#342 Aug. 31 Most Exciting Rock Stars Issue: Guns 'n' Roses, Poison, Lita Ford, Iron Maiden, Ratt, L.A. Guns, David Lee Roth, Aerosmith, Metallica, Van Halen, Scorpions & All the Monsters of Rock $2–4

#343 Sept. 30 Guns 'n' Roses Special Rock America Issue: A Special Report, Monsters of Rock/A Special Photo Report, White Lion, Def Leppard, Poison, Metallica color wall poster, Legacy of Hendrix...$2–4

#344 Oct. 31 Big 19th Birthday Issue: A Special Collection of Our Best, Guns 'n' Roses, Def Leppard, Poison, Motley Crue, Jon Bon Jovi, Aerosmith, Van Halen, Ratt, Lita Ford & Others, interviews, pix..$2–4

#345 Nov. 30 Poison Prove Their Metal: A Special Report, Bon Jovi poster, Guns 'n' Roses, Metallica: A Face-to-face Dressing Room Showdown, White Lion, Cinderella, Def Leppard, Europe, Armored Saint...$2–4

#346 Dec. 31 The Year in Rock-&-Roll: Jon Bon Jovi, Def Leppard, Guns 'n' Roses poster, White Lion, Poison, Cinderella, Metallica, G. Simmons..$2–4

1989

#347 Jan. 31 Guns 'n' Roses: The Real Axl Rose Story With an Exclusive Full-color Splash Wall Poster, Up Close With Bon Jovi, Poison, Def Leppard, Metallica, Ozzy Osbourne, Ratt, Aerosmith $2–4

#348 Feb. 28 Def Leppard, Guns 'n' Roses, Bon Jovi, Poison, Lita Ford, Metallica, Motley Crue, Anthrax, White Lion, Axl Rose wall poster $2–4

#349

#353 July 31 Guns 'n' Roses Back on Top/Outrageous Axl Quotes & Special Poster, Skid Row, Poison, Winger, Bon Jovi: Absolutely Live & Screaming, Motley Crue, Metallica, White Lion in Studio Exclusive $2–4

#354 Aug. 31 Most Intriguing Rock Stars Issue: Jon Bon Jovi, Nikki Sixx, Bret Michaels, Skid Row's Sebastian, Axl Rose, Kik, Tesla, The Cult, Badlands, L.A. Guns, Vixen, Winger, Poison, Warrent, Ozzy Osbourne..$2–4

#355 Sept. 30 Skid Row Breaks Big/contains color wall poster, White Lion, Guns 'n' Roses, Mouth Off & Complete History, Motley Crue, The Cult, Aerosmith: Joe Perry Delivers the News, Steve Stevens..$2–4

#356 Oct. 31 Special 20th Birthday Issue—*Circus'* Rock Hall of Fame Issue: Jimi Hendrix Tribute, The Who, Poison, Winger, Warrent, Def Leppard, Stones, Bon Jovi, Motley Crue, Guns 'n' Roses, Skid Row...$2–4

#357 Nov. 30 Skid Row vs. Warrent, Battle of the Bands Issue, Motley Crue, Bon Jovi, Poison, White Lion $2–4

#358 Dec. 31 The Year in Rock-&-Roll: Warrent, Skid Row, Motley Crue, Guns 'n' Roses, Metallica, Aerosmith, Bon Jovi, Gene Simmons/Kiss $2–4

1990

#359 Jan. 31 Skid Row: The Inside Story/Most Outrageous Quotes/Photo History/Sebastian Bach poster, Warrent, Motley Crue, Metallica, Aerosmith...$2–4

#361 Mar. 31 Who's Who in Rock/The 4th Annual Rock 'n' Roll Almanac—Motley Crue, Aerosmith, Skid Row, Warrent, Guns 'n' Roses, Bon Jovi, Def Leppard, Metallica, Whitesnake, Rush, Alice Cooper, Tesla, Kiss..$2–4

#362 Apr. 30 Skid Row: What Really Happened on the Road?, Motley Crue: How Nikki Celebrated His Birthday, Warrent, Metallica, Aerosmith, Whitesnake, Alice Cooper, The Cult, Bonham, Lita Ford, Dangerous Toys, issue includes Skid Row & Guns 'n' Roses posters..$2–4

#363 June 30 Rock's 10 Best Bands: The Facts, The Secrets, The Truth, Guns 'n' Roses, Def Leppard, Warrent, Bon Jovi, Whitesnake, Skid Row, Aerosmith, Metallica, Motley Crue & Poison, issue includes two posters of Skid Row & Slaughter, Grateful Dead, L.A. Guns, Dangerous Toys, Bruce Dickinson, Ozzy Osbourne, Great White, Badlands, Bonham, Faster Pussycat, Tesla, Kiss, Slayer...$2–4

#365 July 30 Metal's Hottest Heroes, Slaughter: Metal's New Kids, Warrent, Tesla, Skid Row, Motley Crue, Faster Pussycat, Slayer, Dangerous Toys, Babylon A.D. Mouths Off, Def Leppard, The Cult, Heaven's Edge, Ozzy Osbourne, White Lion, Bon Jovi, Tora Tora, Poison, Law & Order, Trixter, Bang Tango, Metallica, Pretty Boy Floyd, L.A. Guns, issue includes two giant color Metal wall posters of Motley Crue & Tesla $2–4

All issues to present...$2–4

CIRCUS MAGAZINE'S PIN-UPS

1975

#1 Over 100 Rock 'n' Roll Photographs in Color—Mick Jagger, Rod Stewart, Edgar & Johnny Winter, David Bowie, The Rolling Stones, Keith Emerson, Robert Plant, Alice Cooper, The Who, Carly Simon & Others $15–35

#2 Dedicated Entirely to the Rolling Stones, 70 Pages in Full Color.....................$15–35

#3 The Elvis Years—Elvis Presley: The Idol Revealed in Words and Photos..........$15–30

CIRCUS MAGAZINE'S ROCKING INTO THE 1990S MAGAZINE

1989

Vol. 1 A Special Rock-&-Roll Report—Chaos into Power: The Guns 'n' Roses Story With Wall Posters (three Roses, one Poison poster, one Motley Crue poster, one Warrent poster, one Skid Row poster, one Bon Jovi/Richie Sambora poster) $4–8

CIRCUS PAPERBACK EDITIONS POPULAR LIBRARY

Alice Cooper by Steve Demorest, 1975...$12–25
Elton John by Cathi Stein, 1975 ....$5–10
Robert Plant by Michael Goldman, 1975 ....$10–20

CIRCUS RAVES

1974

#1 Feb. Issue printed March on cover—Johnny Winter Celebrates Life, Yes Sours Back to Earth, Led Zeppelin Sires a Kingdom, Alvin Lee, Mahavishnu, Status Quo, David Essex, Bachman-Turner Overdrive, The Rock-&-Roll Sex Index Exclusive $15–30
#2 Mar. Issue Roger Daltry/The Who Plunge to Madness, Mott, Black Oak Arkansas: Rocks' Bad Boys Celebrate Success, Steve Miller, Bette Midler: What's Behind Her Mystique, Led Zeppelin Exclusive Poster, Ringo/The Beatles: End the Cold War, Mick Jagger $15–30
#3 Apr. Issue Paul McCartney: His Seven Trials With "Band on the Run," Alice Cooper's Jailhouse Rock, Humble Pie, Chicago, Seals & Crofts, Spencer Davis, Aerosmith, Deep Purple, James Montgomery Band, Rock Comedy, Grand Funk: Knight Boils Them in Oil $15–30
#4 June Issue Noddy Holder/Slade: American Triumphant, Joni Mitchell: Search for Satisfaction, Elton John, Jan Akkerman, Dr. John, Mott's Ian Hunter Tells Searing Tales, Barry White, Yes, Leo Sayer...$15–30
#6 Aug. Issue Keith Emerson/ELP, Procol Harum, Deep Purple: The Worldwide Search for David Coverdale, Mott: Their Broadway Smash, Loggins & Messina, Brewer & Shipley, Rick Wakeman poster $10–20
#7 Sept. Issue Bill Wyman: Grab for Stardom, Deep Purple's Jon Lord, Leon Russell Switches Gear, King Crimson, Grand Funk, Edgar Winter & Roxy Music: two color posters, Black Sabbath, Deep Purple...$12–25
#8 Oct. Issue Eric Clapton: After the Drug Peril, James Taylor Strides Out from Carly's Shadow, Uriah Heep, Rick Wakeman Reveals Why He Split Yes, John McLaughlin, Climax Blues Band, David Bowie & Kiss color posters, Edgar Winter, Kiki Dee, Harry Chapin, Todd Rundgren, Keith Emerson, Rod Argent...$12–25
#9 Nov. Issue Ian Anderson/Jethro Tull: Caught Between Love & Hate, David Bowie, Lou Reed, Black Sabbath, Deep Purple, Frank Zappa Spreads the Mothers, Steppenwolf Roars Back, Keith Emerson & Mick Jagger color posters, REO Speedwagon, Weather Report $12–25
#10 Dec. Issue Rod Stewart Talks, Queen, Robin Trower, Dickie Betts, The Moody's Kiss: Boiling Their Tunes, Traffic: Search for Limbo, Mott the Hoople, The Allman Brothers Band, Queen/Gregg Allman posters $12–25

1975

#101 Jan. Issue Ritchie Blackmore/Deep Purple, The Beach Boys: A Surfin' Interview, John Lennon, Elton on Tour, Lou Reed, Suzi Quatro: How She Was Seduced, Marshall Tucker Band, Rod Stewart: Asleep Behind the Eight Ball, Rick Wakeman, Bad Company, ELO, Frank Zappa, John Cale...$10–20
#103 Feb. Issue Mark Farner/Grand Funk Opens Hunting Season, Johnny Winter, ELO Zaps on the Wattage, Santana interview, David Bowie, ELP: The Night the Show Almost Ended, includes 12-page calendar pullout, Jim Dandy, The Stones: Behind the Graffiti Mystery, Todd Rundgren, Little Feat, Tangerine Dream...$12–25
#105 Mar. Issue Freddie Mercury/Queen, The Blue Oyster Cult, Maggie Bell, George Harrison, Deep Purple, Jack Bruce, Special Pullout: The Family of Rock 1955–1975, Elton John Battles the Promoters, Roger Daltry, Rock's Bad Girls—Suzi Quatro, Linda Ronstadt, Fanny, Maria Mauldaur, Labelle, Roxy Music, Black Oak Arkansas, Aerosmith.....$15–30
#107 Apr. Issue Robin Trower Fires Off, Joe Walsh, Mott: What's Next for Ian Hunter & Mick Ronson, Sparks interview, Rod Stewart & Peter Gabriel: two color pullout posters, Average White Band: The Black Soul Sound, Ozark Mountain Daredevils, Lynyrd Skynyrd, Steve Marriot, Billy Cobham, Gentle Giant, The Dictators, The Led Zeppelin Story: A Very Special Report, Joe Walsh...$10–20
#109 May Issue Steve Marriot/Humble Pie: A Farewell Tour, Doobie Brothers, Elton John's Exclusive Backstage Report, Steely Dan, Jethro Tull, Ray Manzarek, Mick Taylor/

CIRCUS RAVES,
1974, Mar. (#2)

CIRCUS RAVES,
1974, Aug. (#6)

CIRCUS RAVES,
1974, Apr. (#3)

CIRCUS RAVES,
1974, June (#4)

CIRCUS RAVES,
1974, Sept. (#7)

CIRCUS RAVES,
1974, Oct. (#8)

CIRCUS RAVES,
1974, Nov. (#9)

CIRCUS RAVES,
1974, Dec. (#10)

CIRCUS RAVES,
1975, Feb. (#103)

CIRCUS RAVES,
1975, #107

CIRCUS RAVES,
1975, #109

CIRCUS RAVES,
1975, #111

CIRCUS RAVES,
1975, #113

CIRCUS RAVES,
1975, #115

CIRCUS RAVES,
1975, #117

CIRCUS RAVES,
1975, #119

CIRCUS RAVES,
1975, #121

CIRCUS RAVES,
1975, #123

Joe Walsh posters, Eric Burdon interview, Black Oak Arkansas, Allman Brothers, Lynyrd Skynyrd, Flo & Eddie $10–20

#111 June Issue David Bowie: Why He Went Disco, ZZ Top, Leslie West, The Who Interview: John Entwistle Goes Ape, Queen's Brian May Tells Secrets, Roxy Music: Ferry & Mackay Declare They Can Rule America, Ian Anderson/Suzi Quatro color posters, Jethro Tull, Faces, Alice Cooper, Led Zeppelin, Aerosmith, Average White Band $10–20

#113 July Issue Paul Rogers/Bad Company, Aerosmith Play With Their Toys, Hunter/Robinson: Will Their Honeymoon Last?, Sadistic Mika Band, Alex Harvey, David Bowie Courts Moviemakers, Yes: Turning Back the Hands of Time, 10CC, Roy Wood, Jim Dandy, The Kiss interview..$7–15

#115 Aug. Issue Elton John: Captain Fantastic, BTO, Kinks, Alice Cooper: How He Escaped His Own Chilling Nightmare, Mangrum/Black Oak, Maggie Bell, Steely Dan, Nektar, The Moodies, Ringo, Ian Hunter interview, Jeff Beck & Ron Wood Posters, Punk Rock: The Two Faces of Lofgren & Derringer, Stones, ZZ Top..$7–15

#117 Sept. Issue David Byron/Uriah Heep: On the Eve of the Tour, Preston, Stones' Piano Man Spins Road Tales, Deep Purple, Queen, The Stones Tapes, David Bowie, Bob Dylan, Grace Slick, Skynyrd interview, Iggy Pop..$7–15

#119 Oct. Issue Ozzy Osbourne/Black Sabbath: A Savage Blue Print for Their U.S. "Sabotage," Rod Stewart Special Report, Climax Blues Band, The Doobie Brothers interview, The Tubes, Yes: Veggies in Vegas, BTO, Bob Dylan Exclusive Bootleg Discography, Led Zeppelin, Alice Cooper color poster, Ronnie Lane..$7–15

#121 Nov. Issue Edgar Winter Exclusive: In the Lab With the Next Frankenstein, Bruce Springsteen: New Hero or Last of a Breed?, Aerosmith, REO Speedwagon, Rush: Canada's Rock Patrol, Yes, Uriah Heep interview, Mott, Elton John color poster, Mick Jagger, Faces, Jethro Tull...$7–15

#123 Dec. Issue Pete Townshend/The Who: A Special Report Plus Exclusive Discography, Deep Purples's Bolin, The Eagles: The Method Behind Their Madness, Baker Gurvitz Army, Rod Stewart: Rock's Royal Tease, Jeff Beck, Elton John, David Bowie: To Film Ziggy Stardust, The Frank Zappa interview, Be-Bop Deluxe: Axe Victims, Edgar Winter, 10CC $7–15

CIRCUS ROCK IMMORTALS MAGAZINE
1980

#1 Jim Morrison: Excerpts From a New Biography, Alice Cooper: The Man Behind the Makeup, Janis Joplin: Why She was Never Understood, David Bowie: His Bisexuality, Black Sabbath: Their Secret Powers, Led Zeppelin: The Historic Robert Plant interview & color wall poster, Marc Bolan, The Beatles, Jimi Hendrix, Grateful Dead, The Who, Elvis Presley, Elton John, Deep Purple, New York Dolls, The Rolling Stones, Blue Oyster Cult, Cream, Traffic, Jefferson Airplane, Jeff Beck $15–25

CIRCUS' SOLID GOLD CIRCUS
1978

Contains 100 Wildest Rock-&-Roll Photos & 100 Best Rock-&-Roll Albums of the Years With Dozens of Full-page Color Glossy Pin-ups—The Gregg Allman Band, Asleep at the Wheel, Beach Boys, Blue Oyster Cult, Chicago, Eric Clapton, Alice Cooper, The Doobie Brothers, Eagles, Fleetwood Mac, Genesis, Grateful Dead, Emmylou Harris, Heart, Janis Ian, Kiss, Jefferson Airplane, Led Zeppelin, Lynyrd Skynyrd, Moody Blues, Queen, Stones, Linda Ronstadt, Bob Seger, Talking Heads, Yardbirds & on & on $15–30

CO-ED
1978

Sept. Donny & Marie, Change Your Image from Dull to Dynamite: Marie Osmond Shows You How, Shaun Cassidy Talks About His Family, His Fans & The Perfect Date, issue includes giant color Shaun Cassidy wall poster...$3–7

CONTEMPORARY MUSIC
1974

Sept. Elton John Interview: He's Only Just Begun, Rock-&-Roll Revisited—Elvis Presley, Paul Anka, Buddy Holly, Coasters $2–5

The Buckinghams

Collecting

THE BUCKINGHAMS

BY THE BUCKINGHAM—CARL GIAMMARESE

When Dave Henkel approached our group about being included in this memorabilia guide, I was delighted, but it brought me to the realization that, though I've been involved with the music business most of my life, I really haven't had much of an opportunity to do much rock 'n' roll collecting.

Back in the sixties, when our records were hitting the charts faster than I could keep track, my life was kept rather hectic with concert tours, radio promos, TV shows, and the like. I pretty much left the collecting of Buckinghams memorabilia in the hands of my mother. I didn't have to put her in charge of collecting, it just happened naturally. Friends and relatives helped by clipping articles and saving magazines, photos, and reviews. We have stacks of newspapers and magazines that featured our overnight success band—just five average guys from the northwest side of Chicago one minute, and, the next, we're flying first class across the country playing to screaming audiences. Before our success, on Fridays we would all meet after school,

60

load up the van with all our gear, drive straight through to our Friday-night gig, unpack the van, set up the equipment, play, tear down the equipment, repack the van, hop in, and we were off again, doing the same thing all weekend long until we drove back to school on Monday. That all calmed down when we were able to hire a road crew. Then that allowed us time to relax a bit between shows. A lot of Chicago-based neighborhood newspapers mentioned the happenings of the Buckinghams, and when they couldn't quite get any new scoop on us, they looked to uncles, aunts, and distant relatives for any bit of news that they could write about.

When I think about it, the one collection I do have is T-shirts. Of course, that too began unintentionally. Most radio stations that we did air time for, most cities that we toured, and most other bands that we played with gave us T-shirts. I have hundreds of them. My T-shirt collection continues to grow even more today. It's nice to come across a shirt that represents a moment in our history. I also have three Buckinghams suits that I wore in the sixties. One is gray wool with faint chalk pin stripes, the second is brown with a black lapel, and the third is the ever popular Neru jacket in grayish-brown. Now there's a memory!

My father, who toured with Glen Miller for awhile, has a great record collection mostly from the thirties and forties. I have cartons of old albums, starting with the 1950s, but none of them are categorized or make any sense. I have a prize collection of Beatles studio mixes, and it's interesting to hear how Beatles songs first developed and to find out that they were written pretty much as they were recorded. You can hear John Lennon hacking it out on his acoustic guitar, take after take, during "Strawberry Fields." The Beatles did things just like everyone else.

During the sixties, there were numerous two-page programs from our concerts that were sold and/or distributed by the show's promoters. There was only one concert program that we designed ourselves, back in 1968, I believe. It was a 12-page program featuring each guy in the band. It included a bio on each of us and a series of original photos. We sold them at concerts for one year. Then, in 1985, we joined the Happy Together Tour with other bands such as Gary Lewis and The Playboys, The Grass Roots, and The Turtles. On occasion, Tommy James and the Mamas and Papas would join us. A program was put together and sold during that concert tour. Through the years, we've received keys to various cities. Our most recent addition to that collection is the key to the city of Boonesville, Mississippi, which we received in April 1990.

I never cease to be flattered by fans who share their Buckinghams collections with me. They are paying me the highest tribute that they can by collecting items that I was a part of. It makes me feel like I've left some kind of mark in the music business. That's something we all want to do—leave something behind so we can be remembered when we're gone. It makes me feel special that people collect Buckinghams items and keep them for sometimes as long as 25 years. That means it must be significant, that it must have touched their lives and made some kind of an impact. Very few people have that opportunity.

I'll never forget a fan who showed me an almost empty pack of Lucky

Strikes cigarettes sealed air-tight for a keepsake. She picked it up backstage during my smoking days in the sixties and she hung onto it ever since. And, once in awhile, I'll meet someone with a guitar pick with the Buckinghams stamped across it or a handwritten set list from the stage.

As many times as fans show me a Buckinghams item that I am familiar with, they show me two that I didn't even know existed.

THE BUCKINGHAMS FAN CLUB

A $15 yearly dues includes four quarterly newsletters, a 10% discount on most Buckinghams merchandise, an 8″ × 10″ personally autographed photo, past issues of the newsletter, a special invitation to two "Fan Club Members Only" events (one is normally held in February or March, the second is a picnic in the summer), a membership card, special seating at concerts and special discounts on ticket fees when possible, and special mailings such as a birthday greeting and holiday card. Write to: The Buckinghams, P.O. Box 32137, Chicago, IL 60632–2137; 24-Hour Hotline: (312) 254–6672.

CRAWDADDY

1966

#1 ....$40–80
#2–#6 ....$25–50

1967

Jan. #7 Raga & Raga Rock, The Supremes, The Remains, Jefferson Airplane, Rock History: The 50s, Simon & Garfunkel, The Animals $25–50
Mar. #8 The Kinks, Blues Project, The Four Tops, The Lovin' Spoonful, The Rolling Stones, Buffalo Springfield, The Aesthetics of Rock $25–50
May #9 The Rolling Stones, The Doors, Beatles, Youngbloods, Jefferson Airplane, Junior Wells $25–50
Aug. #10 Byrds, Doors, Moby Grape, The Who, Grateful Dead $25–50
Oct. #11 The Beatles: The Sgt. Pepper Report, Elton John, The Byrds..................$25–50

1968

Jan. #12 Van Dyke Parks, The Rolling Stones, Wilson Pickett, Jefferson Airplane, Buffalo Springfield, Country Joe & the Fish, Eric Clapton of the Cream...............................$20–40
Feb. #13 Rolling Stones, Jefferson Airplane, Wilson Pickett.......................................$25–50
Mar./Apr. #14 John Wesley Hardin, The Who, Paul Williams, The Hollies............$20–40
May #15 John Wesley Harding, The Bee Gees, Jimi Hendrix, Van Dyke Parks.....$20–40
June #16 Oh Caroline: The Doors in Concert, Smokey Robinson, The Beau Brummels, Randy Newman, The Kinks & The Who...$20–40
July #17 Traffic, Rolling Stones, Joni Mitchell, Blood, Sweat & Tears.................$20–40
Aug. #18 Grace Slick & Jefferson Airplane, Moby Grape, Joni Mitchell, Blood, Sweat & Tears, The Buckinghams, Jimi Hendrix $25–50
#19 The Doors: Banging Away at the Doors of Convention, Janis Joplin, Paul Williams, Mocha Blues, The Young Rascals..$35–70

1969

#20 An Afternoon With Roger McGuinn, The Beatles' Yellow Submarine..............$20–40
#21 Jim Morrison & the Doors...$20–40
#22 Kansas & Quicksilver Messenger Service, Joan Baez, Greg Allman, The Grateful Dead $20–40
#23 John Mayhall interview, Savoy Brown..$15–30

1970*

Vol. 4, #1 Mick Jagger & the Stones, Joe Cocker: The Brightest Face, The Beatles: The Bodhisattva-making Machine, Frank Zappa, Jimi Hendrix, James Cotton, Alvin Lee interview, Manfred Mann, The Grateful Dead: Snowflakes, The Kinks: A Few Looks, Captain Beefheart..$35–70
Vol. 4, #2 The Rolling Stones, James Taylor, Marc Bolan interview, T. Rex, Johnny Winter, Psychedelic Art & Music, Procol Harum, The Nice, The Byrds.............................$25–50
Vol. 4, #3 B.B. King, Frank Zappa, Zephyr, interviews with Steve Miller, Little Richard, Eric Mercury, David Crosby & Steven Stills, Leon Russell.....................................$15–30
Vol. 4, #4 Joe Cocker, Taj Mahal, Elvis Presley, Leon Russell interview, Felix Pappalardi & Lou Reed, Humphrey Osmond $15–30
Vol. 4, #6 Johnny Cash, A Special Country Music Section, The Incredible String Band, Paul McCartney's Misgivings, Stevie Wonder $15–30
Vol. 4, #7 George Harrison, The Mothers, Manfred Mann, Adventures of a Groupie....$10–20
Vol. 4, #8 Rock Roots: The Early Years, Creedence Clearwater Revival at the Plaza, Jethro Tull: Everyone Will Start to Pulsate, The Beatles, Elvis Presley..............................$15–30
Vol. 4, #14 Jimi Hendrix Dead in London, interview with Ray Davies, The Who ..$50–100

1971

May 16 Sea Train's Lee Michaels interview, Jake & the Family Jewels, Funkadelics, Jimi Hendrix $25–50

Crawdaddy's format changes from magazine to tabloid.

CRAWDADDY, 1970,
VOL. 4, #6

CRAWDADDY,
1971, 7–18

CRAWDADDY,
1971, 12–5

CRAWDADDY,
1972, 3–19

CRAWDADDY,
1972, 4–2

CRAWDADDY,
1972, 34–30

CRAWDADDY,
1972, Oct.

CRAWDADDY,
1974, Sept.

CRAWDADDY,
1979, Nov.

June 6 Ray Davies, Sly Stone, Viva, Tina Turner, The Doors: Half Notes, Carly Simon, Rita Coolidge, The Pentangle $20–40

June 20 The Beach Boys: 10 Years After, Procol Harum, Life in Woodstock, Cat Stevens, The Monkees: Half Notes, The Doors: L.A. Woman, The Jackson Five, Crosby, Stills, Nash & Young, John Lennon & Paul McCartney...$20–40

July 18 Ian Anderson interview, Terry Knight of Grand Funk Railroad, Buckminster Fuller, Paul Williams, Swamp Dog, Country Joe, Lenny Bruce..$20–40

Aug. 1 Emerson, Lake & Palmer Ascending, Poco, Shaun Phillips, Alice Cooper: Half Notes, Loretta Lynn, Dolly Parton, Canned Heat $15–30

Aug. 15 Dustin Hoffman, Ray Mungo, Rod Stewart, James Gang, John Lennon & Yoko Ono are Getting it On, Shaft...$15–30

Aug. 29 John Lennon & Yoko Ono, Pete Townshend, Taj Mahal, Brewer & Shipley, Keith Moon, Jim Morrison: Goodbyes, No More Fillmore Anymore, Joni Mitchell, Gordon Lightfoot $20–40

Nov. 7 Bobby Sherman: Tempest in a Teapot, The Allman Brothers, Tracy Nelson, The Rascals, Moby Grape, Elvis Presley: Love Letters, Hank Williams, The Byrds, War.......$15–30

Dec. 5 On the Road With the Who, John Lennon Reviews *"Imagine,"* Yoko Ono Reviews *"Fly,"* Peter Fonda, Howlin Wolf, Allman Brothers, Hot Tuna, Chuck Berry $15–30

Dec. 26 Rod Stewart, Frank Zappa & 200 Motels, Wings, Leon Russell, John Lennon, The Grateful Dead, Big Mama Thornton, Jefferson Airplane, The Beach Boys, Van Morrison, Cat Stevens, Randy Newman, Judy Collins, Poco...$15–30

1972

Jan. 16 Mountain, Randy Newman, Van Dyke Parks, Kim Foley, Isaac Hayes, Bob Dylan, The Mamas & the Papas, John Mayall, Little Richard, Chicago, J. Geils Band.....$15–30

Feb. 20 Blood, Sweat & Tears: Their History, The Kinks, Laura Nyro, Marc Bolan: "I'm Important," Melanie, David Bowie, Rick Nelson, Dion, *A Clockwork Orange* $15–30

Mar. 5 Traffic: Flowing Freely, Ravi Shankar, John Cassavettes, Bo Diddley, Todd Rundgren, Nelsson, Williams & Mungo in Japan, Wings, Keith Jarrett....................$15–30

Mar. 19 *A Clockwork Orange*, A Mad Morning With Commander Cody, Mahalia Jackson, Capt. Beefheart, Bangladesh, Elton John, John Mayall, Seals & Crofts....................$12–25

Apr. 2 Rock-&-Roll Women: A Special Issue—Joni Mitchell, Melanie, Linda Ronstadt, Mama Cass Elliot, Grace Slick, Enid, Fanny, Suzi Young, Susan Evans, Al Green, Eyewitness in Bangladesh, Harry Chapin, Jerry Garcia, Jackson Browne $15–30

Apr. 16 Chuck Berry Exclusive Interview, Yes, Jimi Hendrix & Voodoo, also Jimi Hendrix: To Die Too Easily...$30–60

Apr. 30 Grace Slick & Paul Kanter: The Mind Bogglers, Neil Young, Wilson Pickett at the Copa, Buffy St. Marie, Paul Williams, Little Feat, Stone the Crows $15–30

May 14 John Kay, Loggins & Messina, Link Wray, Black Oak Arkansas, Todd Rundgren, Bangladesh, Hot Tuna, Linda Ronstadt, B.B. King, Nitty Gritty Dirt Band.............$12–25

May 28 Delaney & Bonnie's Mad Dog Domino Theory, Exclusive Marty Balin Interview, Deep Purple, Nils Lofgren, Jimi Hendrix, ELO, Elvis Presley, The Beatles $20–40

June 11 Joe Cocker Exclusive, John Sebastian, Eric Clapton, Delaney & Bonnie, Humble Pie, The Mothers, The Everly Brothers, The Rascals, Savoy Brown, Lee Michaels....$12–25

July Mick Jagger interview: The Rolling Stones '72, Billie Holiday, Mahavishnu, Neil Diamond's Game Plan..$12–25

Aug. Inside the Music Business, The Rolling Stones, The Beach Boys, Jethro Tull, Randy Newman, Jeff Beck, John Mayall, Bonzos, David Bowie, Joan Baez, Burritos $12–25

Sept. Bob Weir Steps Out: The Grateful Dead's Diamond in the Rough, Joan Baez, Dr. John, Michael Jackson..$10–20

Sept. 11 The Truth About Led Zeppelin, The Fillmore Legacy, Donny Osmond, The Rolling Stones: A Real Kick in the Ass, with a special Rolling Stones game section, Rick Nelson, The Fillmore's Last Days...$12–25

1972*

Oct. Exclusive Joan Collins Interview, The Byrds: Byrds of a Feather, Tina Turner Turns 40 ....$10–20

Nov. Stevie Wonder, Rick Nelson & Rock 'n' Roll Revivals...................................$10–20

Crawdaddy returns to magazine format.

1973

Jan. Jefferson Airplane Flies Again, Bill Withers, Poco $5–10
Feb. Jack Nicholson, Chicago, The Grateful Dead, Poco...$5–10
Apr. The Beach Boys, Paul Williams, Carly Simon, Joe Cocker, Traffic, Elvis Presley, The Beatles..$6–12
May Exclusive Muhammed Ali Interview, Mike Bloomfield $5–10
June The Beatles: Fixing a Whole, Little Feat...$5–10
July Marvin Gayle, Gram Parson & Chris Hillman Together.......................................$5–10
Aug. Jeff Beck, Roy Wood, Barry Sadler, Clevinger's Trial $5–10
Sept. Bob Dylan: Pledging His Time, Swapping Stories With Willie Nelson.............$5–10
Oct. The Allman Brothers: Macon Whoopee at Watkins Glen, Roger McGuinn, New York Dolls..$5–10
Nov. Mahavishnu, The Pointer Sisters, Raspberries, Todd Rundgren, Buffy St. Marie ..$5–10
Dec. Woody Allen, Elvis Presley in Las Vegas, Labelle, Zappa & the Mothers, Mick Jagger
....$5–10

1974

Jan. Quadro Who?: The Whole Truth, Jackson Browne..$5–10
Feb. Who Killed Buddy Holly?, Elton John & Rod Stewart Battle the Age Barrier, Marty Balin Takes Off Again, Brian Ferry, Bette Midler, Ringo Starr....................................$5–10
Mar. John Lennon: "Our Year is 1974," Dave Mason Remembers, Yoko Ono, Rod Stewart, The Kinks, Average White Band, Wings, Beach Boys, Bruce Springsteen, Traffic ...$5–10
Apr. Kurt Vonnegut Jr., Bob Dylan on the Move, Paul McCartney on the Run, Graham Nash, Carly Simon, The Band, Joni Mitchell, Gram Parsons...$5–10
May The Evil Weed Goes Legit, Todd Rundgren, Keith Carradine, Smokey Robinson...$5–10
June Dr. John: How's Bayou?, Linda Ronstadt Cares, Herbie Hancock: Head Hunting, Boz Scaggs, Maggie Bell, Hot Tuna, Johnny Winter, Larry Coryell, The Pointer Sisters $5–10
July Souther, Hillman & Furay, The Eagles on the Border, Crosby, Stills, Nash & Young, Ringo, Argent, Poco $5–10
Aug. Gerald Ford, Bill Wyman, David Bowie, Al Stewart, Robert Fripp, Kris Kristofferson
....$5–10
Sept. Inside Miss U.S.A., The Beatles, War, Peter Frampton, Nektar, Edgar Winter, Sandy Denny, Sun Ra, Leon Russell, Lynyrd Skynyrd...$5–10
Oct. Crosby, Stills, Nash & Young: A Four-way Street at the Crossroads, Bad Company, Joe Cocker, Weather Report, The Grateful Dead, Eric Clapton $5–10
Nov. The Rolling Stones Connection, Little Feat, Alice Cooper, 10CC, Sly Stone ...$5–10
Dec. Uptight With Stevie Wonder, Jefferson Starship, The Return of Roy Orbison ..$5–10

1975

Jan. Who Killed Jimi Hendrix?, Labelle's Silver Strut, Lou Reed, The Last Days of Jimi Hendrix $10–20
Feb. Muhammed Ali, Steve Miller Speaks: An Exclusive, The Beatles on the Road, Jan & Dean, Centipede, Bachmann-Turner Overdrive..$5–10
Mar. J.D. Salinger, Jack Bruce, Mick Taylor, Leonard Cohen, Sandy Denny, Aretha Franklin $5–10
Apr. Gordon Lightfoot: Rises After "Sundown," Bob Dylan on the Tracks, Roger Daltry on *Tommy*, Disco: The Latest Twist, David Essex: The Stardust Kid $5–10
May Bill Walton, Keith Moon Talks Trashing, Emmylou Harris on the Verge, Roxy Music, Nico, Janis Ian, Velvet Underground, Melissa Manchester $5–10
June Led Zeppelin: Jimmy Page & Rock Music, John Lennon, Erica Jong, Chaka Khan, Country Joe, Annette Funicello Keeps Abreast..$5–10
July The Stones '75: The Spark Behind the Brave New World Tour, Ray Davies, Lynyrd Skynyrd Scorches the South, "Tommy": The Who, Alice Cooper: Nightmare or Sleepwalk?
....$6–12
Aug. The Whole Earth Conspiracy, The Beach Boys, Judy Collins, Carly Simon $5–10
Sept. Ted Kennedy, Lenny Bruce, Alice Cooper, Rick Wakeman, Tom Waits, Roger McQuinn, The Eagles..$5–10
Oct. Bruce Springsteen: Burning Up the Backstreets/A Star is Born to Run, Steve Stills Carries On, Bob Dylan, The Doobie Brothers, Ronnie Wood.....................................$7–15

CRAWDADDY,
1974, Dec.

CRAWDADDY,
1975, Jan.

CRAWDADDY,
1975, Nov.

CRAWDADDY,
1976, Jan.

CRAWDADDY,
1976, Apr.

CRAWDADDY,
1976, June

CRAWDADDY,
1976, Aug.

CRAWDADDY,
1977, Jan.

CRAWDADDY,
1977, Aug.

Nov. Eric Clapton: "Why I'm Returning to Rock 'n' Roll," At Home With Al Green, Melissa Manchester After "Midnight" $5–10
Dec. Marlon Brando, James Browne: Papa's Got Big Trouble, Bob Dylan on TV, Woody Guthrie on Film...$5–10

1976

Jan. Bob Marley: The Reggae Rebellion, Bob Dylan on Tour, The Who, Bonnie Raitt's Home Recipes, Diane Keaton..$5–10
Feb. Paul Simon Speaks: Conversations With a Crazy Man, James Dean Beyond the Grave, Janis Ian at 24, The Tubes Scrapbook, Buddy Holly, The Kinks, Robert Palmer......$5–10
Mar. Ray Davies Revealed: Kinks Konfessions, Robbie Robertson Interview: The Band's Man Steps Out of Bob Dylan's Shadow, The Jimi Hendrix Experience $6–12
Apr. Paul McCartney Unveils Wings Tour, Bryan Wilson, Robert Plant, Emmylou Harris Speaks Up, Bette Midler $5–10
May Henry Winkler: The Fonz, Peter Frampton Was Here, Roy Wood, Bruce Springsteen Loves the Asbury Jukes, Jim Morrison Flunked Out, David Bowie............................$5–10
June The Brian Wilson Interview: Back With the Beach Boys, Little Feat, Genesis, Smokey Robinson, Asleep at the Wheel $5–10
July Paul Newman, The Brian Wilson Interview: "It's Scary," Reggae Roundup, Santana on Tour $5–10
Aug. The Mick Jagger Interview: "We're Not as Good as People Think," Alice Cooper Tees Off, Labelle Cools Out, The Runaways, Todd Rundgren, Ian Hunter $6–12
Sept. Carly Simon Speaks Freely, Abbie Hoffman Exclusive, Rod Stewart Faces the Music, Peter Max Comes Back, Nash Blasts Stills & Young, Southside Johnny $5–10
Oct. The Runaways: Teen Lust, Linda Ronstadt $10–20
Nov. Fleetwood Mac Confidential, Elvis Presley Redux: Viva Las Vegas, Frank Zappa, Hall & Oates $10–20
Dec. William Shatner & *Star Trek*, The Band, Tommy Bolin, Patti Smith.................$5–10

1977

Jan. Marty Balin, Jefferson Starship, Elton John, Robert Palmer...................................$4–8
Feb. George Harrison Interview: The Beatle Finally Talks, Frankie Valli's Season in Hell, Brenda Lee, Frank Zappa, Foghat, Melanie, Joni Mitchell...$4–8
Mar. Dr. J., Abbie Hoffman & Tim Leary, The Eagles vs. the Cookie Monster, Graham Parker Howls, Queen, Blondie/Debbie Harry: Punk's Harlow With the Babys, Genesis $5–10
Apr. The Eagles: Life in the Fast Lane, Emmylou Harris, David Bowie, Fleetwood Mac: Fact or Rumour? $5–10
May Bette Midler: The Trash Trials of "Miss M," Brian Wilson, Willie Nelson, The Kinks Sell Out..$4–8
June John Belushi, Steve Winwood Speaks, Van Morrison Returns, Debbie Harry: Punk Harlow Dresses to Kill, Rita Coolidge, Bryan Ferry, Rick Derringer............................$4–8
July Steve Miller: His Rock of Dreams Comes True, Ronnie Spector Comes Home, Kenny Loggins, Abbie Hoffman, Alice Cooper: St. Alice Day Massacre $4–8
Aug. Marie Osmond: Cheesecake & Growing Pains, Special Beatles Hamburg Photos, Chicago, Greg Allman, The Dictators, Steve Miller, James Taylor $5–10
Sept. KC & Barry Manilow: The Song & Dance Men, Heart's Aches & Breaks, Eric Carmen, CSN, The Tubes, Peter Frampton: Safe as Milk, Yes......................................$4–8
Oct. Bjorn Borg, Steve Martin, Hall & Oates, Average White Band, Jerry Garcia, Pete Townshend, Firefall, The Bay City Rollers, Carloe King, Johnny Cash $4–8
Nov. Elvis Presley, Bob Seger's Nightmares, Linda Ronstadt: One Broken Heart for Sale, Ian Hunter, Talking Heads, The Rolling Stones Burnin' Love.....................................$4–8
Dec. CSN's Stephen Stills, Randy Newman...$4–8

1978

Jan. Ted Nugent, Dan Aykroyd, Graham Parker & Rod Stewart, David Bowie, Boz Scaggs $3–6
Feb. Claudine Longet, David Bowie's Breakdown, Dolly Parton, Lynyrd Skynyrd's Legacy, Joni Mitchell: Four Sides Now...$3–6
Mar. John Travolta & Gilda Radner: Looking for the Heart of Saturday Night, Sal Mineo:

End of a Hollywood Dream, The Elvis Costello Interview, Bette Midler, Genesis: The Things We Do on Stage...$4–8
Apr. Clint Eastwood, Stevie Wonder, Ry Cooder, Little Feat, Warren Zevon..............$3–6
May Susan Sarandon, Raquel Welch: Wild Dreams/Wicked Desires, Nick Lowe, Lou Reed, Patti Smith: Power of Babble, Brian Eno...$3–6
June Frank Langella/*Dracula*, Paul McCartney's "London Town," Frank Zappa: Plastic Man, Elvis Costello: Below the Belt, Chaka Khan..$3–6
July *Grease*'s Olivia Newton-John: The Sweetheart Next Door Gets Pinned, Nick Lowe: Power Pop's Mastermind, Carly Simon, Bob Seger, Olivia Newton-John's Story......$6–12
Aug. The Bee Gees: Behind Barry Gibb's Hot Streak, The Power of Rock 'n' Roll, The Kinks, Bruce Springsteen: Wounded in the Badlands, The Rolling Stones...................$4–8
Sept. Chevy Chase, Tom Petty, The Beach Boys, Laura Nyro: Safe at Home, Bob Dylan $3–6
Oct. Bruce Springsteen: Heart of Darkness, Dolly Parton, Firefall, Foreigner.............$4–8
Nov. Billy Joel: The Stranger in Paradise, Cheryl Ladd, Linda Ronstadt.....................$3–6
Dec. John Belushi & Dan Aykroyd: The Blues Brothers, The *Wiz* Kid: Michael Jackson's Gamble, Blondie/Debbie Harry: Be Her Little Baby, Yes, Al Stewart, Hall & Oates........$4–8

CRAWDADDY FEATURE
1979

Jan. #1 Sly Stallone, The Fearful Freedom of Elton John, Bryan Ferry: Lonely Days, Southside Johnny Makes a Movie, Chicago, Frank Zappa & the New Reich..............$4–8
Feb. #2 Lilly Tomlin, Al Stewart's Fantasy World, The Clash, The Grateful Dead....$3–6
Mar. #3 Gerry Garcia/The Grateful Dead: Rave-up on Shakedown Street, The Boomtown Rats, Nicolette Larson, Dire Straits, J. Geils, XTC, Joan Armatrading.....................$4–8
Apr. #4 Jane Fonda Speaks for Herself, Andy Kaufman, Little Feat's Lowell George, George Harrison, Charles Mingus...$3–6
May #5 Nicolette Larson...$3–6

CREEM
1969

Vol. 2, #6 The Paul McCartney Death Hoax & How it Grew, Johnny Winter, Tyrannosaurus Rex, Country Joe & the Fish, Ike & Tina Turner, Arlo Guthrie, Mitch Ryder, Joe Cocker $25–50
Vol. 2, #8 Adolf Hitler Live & Well at the Fillmore: Mention of Jefferson Airplane & The Youngbloods, The Family Dog, MC5: John Sinclair—A Letter from Prison, Mick Jagger/ The Stones: Detroit, The Stones & Alta Monte, John & Yoko, Rod Stewart...........$15–30
Vol. 2, #9 Ted Nugent of the Amboy Jukes, John Lennon & Yoko Ono's Erotic Drawings, Altamont Part II, Bob Dylan interview, Delaney & Bonnie, Jimi Hendrix & Miles Davis Dead at the Fillmore, Iggy Pop...$30–60
Vol. 2, #10 Scott Richardson of the SRC, Led Zeppelin, The Who, John Lennon & Yoko Ono, Stooges, The Michigan Bands: Commander Cody & MC5, The Bob Seger System, Grand Funk Railroad, James Taylor, Mitch Ryder...$20–40
Vol. 2, #10 This issue is actually Vol. 2, #11, The Rationals, Ray Davies, The New MC5, Country Joe, The Rod Stewart Plan, The Grateful Dead...$15–30

1971

May The Velvet Underground R.I.P.: Long Live Lou Reed, Judy Garland is Dead but the Memory of Brian Jones Lives on in All of Us, Wilderness Road, Jim Morrison in Europe, Beach Boys...$20–40
June The Grateful Dead, Grand Funk Railroad, Aretha Franklin, Bucky Fuller, Frank Zappa $20–40
Sept. The Jackson Five at Home, Commander Cody Meets Merle Haggard...........$15–30
Oct. Mick Jagger/The Rolling Stones, Howlin' Wolf, The Who, MC5, Jethro Tull, Mott the Hoople...$15–30
Nov. Grand Funk Railroad, The Johnny Otis Story...$12–25
Dec. Pete Townshend/The Who in Concert, Black Sabbath: Don't Scare Nobody, Edgar Winter: Not Just Johnny's Brother, Jimi Hendrix/Rainbow Bridge Review, The Godz.................$15–30

1972

Jan. Alice Cooper: All American, Rod Stewart on Jeff Beck, Van Morrison, The Band, James Taylor, Black Sabbath, Traffic, Elvis Presley..$15–30
Feb. Bob Dylan: A Slice of American Pie, Procol Harum: It's Only Realism, Behind the Blue Oyster Cult, Crabby Appleton Zaps the Zombies, Chicago at Carnegie Hall, Led Zeppelin, T. Rex, The Who, Cat Stevens, Frank Zappa's 200 Motels............................$15–30
Mar. John Lennon: Free John & Yoko, Elvis Presley & the A-bomb, *Jesus Christ Superstar*, *A Clockwork Orange*, Bob Dylan, Grand Funk, "Grapefruit" by Yoko Ono Reviewed, Nils Lofgren, Miles Davis...$17–35
Apr. Smokey Robinson Retires, The New Music of Sly Stone, Rod Stewart Joins Faces, Charlie Rich, Capt. Beefheart, Persuasions, The Jackson Five....................................$15–30
May T. Rex, Al Green, Aretha Franklin, Bob Seger $15–30
June Black Sabbath, Grand Funk Railroad, Chuck Berry, Creedence Clearwater Revival..$15–30
July The Beach Boys: A Fan Tells All, the Black Sabbath Extravaganza, Dr. John's Gumbo, Lou Reed vs. the Velvet Underground, England's Great T. Rex Dilemma, Ozzy Osbourne Speaks: Bring Your Mother to the Gas Chamber, Fillmore, Todd Rundgren, Deep Purple $15–30
Aug. Rod Stewart: The Daring Young Man & the Flying Chimpanzees, Todd Rundgren Meets Wolfman Jack, An Early Christmas With Phil Spector & John Lennon, The Beach Boys, Janis Joplin in Concert $15–30
Sept. The Sixties Starring the Rolling Stones, James Brown & Leslie Gore, J. Geils Band $15–30
Oct. Humble Pie Eat Out, Van Morrison, Rod Stewart, Alice Cooper $15–30
Nov. Allman Brothers: Deep in the Heart of Dixie, Is Rock Music a Commie Plot?, Miles Davis, Muddy Waters, Howlin' Wolf...$10–20
Dec. Leon Russell: Mad Greek in Oil City, Deep Purple Reveal Schizophrenia, Rod Stewart, T. Rex, Otis Redding, Ziggy at Top..$12–25

1973

Jan. Rolling Stones: "Can't Get No Satisfaction," Jefferson Airplane.......................$10–20
Feb. Chuck Berry: Back on Top, Leslie West, Elvis on Tour, Bette Midler $10–20
Mar. Edgar Winter After Dark, The Poop on Iggy Pop, Sam the Sham & The Pharoahs $10–20
Apr. The Amazing Spiderman, Alvin Lee: The Invulnerable Bullock, Gary Glitter: Android Superstar, Mick Jagger, Hank Williams, Diana Ross Review, Beach Boys, Marvin Gaye, Wilderness Road, Rundgren...$10–20
May Jethro Tull in Vietnam?, Asleep at the Wheel: Mugged in Nashville, Can the Groundhogs Save the World?, Beyond Glitter With Roxy Music, Alice Cooper's Billiondollar Baby, Van Morrison, Bruce Springsteen, Elvis Presley, Blue Oyster Cult, Kinks, Traffic $10–20
June Alice Cooper, Slade, The Rolling Stones, Allman Brothers, Rod Stewart, Led Zeppelin $10–20
July Johnny Winter's Back & Kicking Hard, Marc Bolan Says a Mouthful, Waylon Jennings, Kris Kristofferson, Bob Dylan, A Generation of Teen Dictatorship With the Beatles, Ron Wood to Join the Stones, Deep Purple Split?, The Guess Who, Sha Na Na Review, Temptations..$10–20
Aug. David Bowie: Best Dressed Mainman at the Twilight Zone Ball, Words of Wisdom from Jeff Beck, John Cale, J. Geils, Paul McCartney...$10–20
Sept. Led Zeppelin's Unnatural Acts, Allman Brothers Soar On, Paul Simon, Yes $10–20
Oct. First Annual Guitar Break Issue, Pink Floyd, Shoot the Moon, Van Morrison Talks Back Exclusive, The New York Dolls Have Come for Your Children, Diary of a Faces Roadie, Alice Cooper's School Daze $10–20
Nov. Jimi Hendrix: Experience from Beyond the Grave, Mott the Hoople: Surviving the Rock-&-Roll Circus, The Beatles in Your Living Room, Dick Clark, The Sweet, New York Dolls, Steve Stills, David Bowie's Secrets, Grand Funk Railroad, Jimmy Cliff, The Guess Who...$15–30
Dec. The Stones 1973 Nervous Breakdown: The Keith Richards Interview, Uriah Heep, Jimi Hendrix $15–30

1974

Jan. Pete Townshend Interview: Quadrophenia Strikes The Who, The Grateful Dead: Showing Off New Bodies, Savoy Brown, Leslie West, Alice Cooper Goes Aerosol, Bowie Takes a Dare, Seals & Crofts...$10–20

Feb. Elton John's Heavy Hundred, Dr. Hook, Martin Mull, Steely Dan, John Lennon, Talkin' Trash With Patti Smith...$10–20

Mar. Emerson, Lake & Palmer Charged Up, Carlos Santana & John McLaughlin, Pete Townshend Come Home, Jerry Lee Lewis: Loud & Proud, J. Geils.........................$10–20

Apr. Iggy Pop: The Saga of the Stooges, Mott the Hoople, Rock Couples: Mick & Bianca, David & Angela, Paul & Linda, Commander Cody, Foghat, Bob Dylan, Country Joe Behind Bars, Bruce Springsteen Review, Jimi Hendrix: A Biography Review......................$11–22

May Alice Cooper, David Bowie, Jimmy Page, Todd Rundgren, Elton John, Mott, Allmans, J. Geils, Emerson, New York Dolls, Bette Midler, The Stooges, Grace Slick interview, Led Zeppelin, Yardbirds, Kinks, Billy Preston, The Final Word on Bob Dylan, Three Dog Night, Kiss Party...$10–20

June The Only Naked Uncastrated David Bowie, Deep Purple, Kiss, Slade, Maria Mauldaur, Bob Dylan $10–20

July The Rolling Stone: The Golden Decade, Black Sabbath's Night of Terror, Rick Derringer, Steve Miller, Exclusive Mick Jagger Interview & Poster, Bad Co., Mott, Free, Suzi Quatro, King Crimson, Bette Midler, Ray Davies, Roxy Music $10–20

Aug. Alice Cooper's Tour of Tinseltown, Mick Jagger Exclusive Interview, David Bowie, Onstage Antics With the J. Geils Band, Maggie Bell: Last of the Red Hot Mamas, Fanny Show Their Feathers, Ringo & Nilsson, Mott, Aerosmith, Blue Oyster Cult, Lynyrd Skynyrd...$10–20

Sept. Rick Wakeman Says No About Yes, Frank Zappa's Secret Signals, Stills, Elton John's Dream Band, Blue Oyster Cult Rise from the Depths, Bryan Ferry's Blindfold Test, Flo & Eddie, Eric Clapton, Mick Jagger, Cheech & Chong, Leon Russell...........................$10–20

Oct. Rod Stewart Gets a Facelift, Eric Clapton: Re-amped & Re-vamped, The Who: Is Ten Years Too Much?, On a Drunk With Bob Dylan, Ron Wood & Keith Richards, Jimi Hendrix, John Cale, Kiss, Alice Cooper Retires, Johnny Winter's 108 Inches, Lenny Bruce, Neil Young, Frank Zappa Special...$10–20

Nov. The Allman Brothers: Strained at the Crossroads, Todd Rundgren in the Raw: Complete Story & Poster, Led Zeppelin's War Games Exclusive, Robert Plant interview, Suzi Quatro's Leather Lips, The Beatles, Lynyrd Skynyrd, David Bowie, Stevie Wonder, Pete Townshend, Rick Wakeman Breakdown, Steppenwolf & Jimi Hendrix Return..........$10–20

Dec. Frank Zappa: The Main Mother Mouths Off—An Exclusive Interview Plus a Complete Illustrated History, Keith Richards Reveals His Ravaged Past, Roger Trower, Alice Cooper Attacks the Silver Screen, Uriah Heep, Genesis: Bad Habits, George Harrison, Jimi Hendrix Rip-off, Rick Wakeman Dream Band, Rod Stewart, Stevie Wonder...........$10–20

1975

Jan. David Bowie Blacks Out, A Hollywood Farewell With the N.Y. Dolls, Iggy & the Strip Scene, Jethro Tull Exposé, Bachman-Turner Overdrive, Roger Daltry Exclusive Interview, Mott, Mick Ronson, Mahogany Rush, J. Geils, Alice Cooper's Breakup, Grace Slick Bared, Elton John...$10–20

Feb. Jimmy Page Tongues His Axe: The Interview, David Bowie Exclusive Interview, Rick Wakeman, The Guess Who, J. Geils, ZZ Top, Chicago, Leslie West, Traffic, The Naked Flo & Eddie, Elton John, Rod Stewart, Van Morrison, Stars' Cars Poster #1..........$10–20

Mar. Lou Reed: King of the Slag Heap, BTO, Mick Taylor Shatters, The Stones, Bad Co., The Who, Pete Townshend Exclusive Interview, Stars' Cars Poster #2—Genesis, Labelle, Bryan Ferry & James Bond, Carly Simon/Creemmate of the Month, Roxy & Eno, Stevie Wonder, Tina Turner...$10–20

Apr. Gregg Allman on the Good Old Days, Todd Rundgren's Secret Fantasies, John Entwistle, Mott, The Ultimate in Heavy Metal, Billy Preston, Kris Kristofferson, Dead Beatle, Kiss Komix, Rod Stewart, John Lennon, Dylan, Crosby & Nash, Suzi Quatro, Roxy Music, Bad Company...$10–20

May Elton John Exclusive Interview: "I Was a Groupie," Led Zeppelin's Holy Thunder, Rod Stewart & the Faces: A Day at the Races, Humble Pie, Bob Dylan: The War Drags On, Alice Cooper's New Play, Roxy Music, Gregg Allman poster, Olivia Newton-John Takes Off, Grace Slick, Cher Dresses Up, Dr. John's Voodoo...$10–20

June Play on Forever Issue/Gallery of Graves—Jimi Hendrix, Janis Joplin, Jim Morrison, James Dean, Hank Williams, Buddy Holly, Jim Croce, Duane Allman, Brian Jones, Otis Redding, Big Bopper, Cass Elliot & Others, Alice Cooper's Living Nightmare, Deep Purple: Ritchie Blackmore Expresses Himself, Roxy Music: The Elegant Paranoia of Bryan Ferry, Who Killed the Beatles?, Joe Walsh, Alvin Lee: Eleven Years After, Tommy, Average White Band, Labelle in the Flesh, Grand Funk poster, King Crimson, Rolling Stones: Road Map to the Mother Lode, Chaka Khan Creammate, John Lennon...........................$15–30
July Alice Cooper: The Hollywood Square Hits the Highway, Nilsson, Sparks: Expatriates in Ecstasy, Rick Wakeman Gets Slashed, Eno, Leo Sayer, Queen, Bob Seger: Nine-year Overnight Success, Bette Midler, Lesley Gore, Kiss, Elvis Presley, Chuck Berry, Little Richard, Dick Clark, Stones in the Streets, Robert Plant, Bad Co., Aerosmith Derriere, Grand Funk Farming With Farner...$10–20
Aug. Exclusive Mick Jagger Interview, Jeff Beck Turns Respectable, Kinks Then & Now/ "I Was a Kissette," Alice Cooper's Monster Stroke, Jerry Garcia Joins the Establishment, Suzi Quatro: Creammate of the Month, Hunter & Ronson, Lynyrd Skynyrd, Bad Co., Elton John Looks Back, Wishbone Ash, The Allman's Roadie Band....................................$10–20
Sept. Pete Townshend Zaps Jagger, Page, Beck & The Who, The Beach Boys, Aerosmith Takes Off, Pink Floyd, Kraftwerk, Jefferson Starship: Grace Slick Gives it Away, Cat Stevens, Paul & Linda McCartney, Gregg & Cher, Ron Wood, Queen, Little Feat, The Stones & Labelle Get Dressed, King Crimson, Neil Young...$7–15
Oct. Stones/Jaggernaut, Alice Cooper: Farewell, Willie Nelson, Pete Townshend interview, Bruce Springsteen: Dues of a Street Poet, Todd Rundgren, Dylan Tapes, Eric Clapton, Suzi Quatro, Jim Morrison Interview: "When I Go Down to be a Man," Rod Stewart, Ron Wood, Grand Funk Railroad $7–15
Nov. Rod Stewart Slaps Faces, Roger Daltry Responds to Townshend Interview, Deep Purple, Stephen Stills, Neil Young in the Danger Zone, Marshall Tucker, The Eagles: All-American Macho, Bruce Springsteen in the Jungle, Keith Richard in Bed, Bay City Rollers, Eric Clapton, Alice Cooper...$6–12
Dec. David Bowie on the Silver Screen: An Exclusive Interview & Movie Preview, The Allmans on Tour, Doobie Brothers, Frank Sinatra, Bob Dylan Goes Protest, The Outlaws, Tubes on the Beach, The Stones Stateside Shakedown, Faces, Bad Company, Kiss Kar, Elton John...$6–12

1976

Jan. John Denver is God, Bruce Springsteen is Not God, Jethro Tull, Frank Zappa/ Beefheart, Patti Smith: The Poet Priestess of Rock-&-Roll, Bay City Rollers, ZZ Top, Wakeman & Daltry, Tubes, Allmans, BTO, Tina Turner, Chicago, Mick Jagger, Cher, Bryan Ferry, Bob Dylan, Elton John...$6–12
Feb. Bob Dylan Exclusive Interview, The Who: Reaching Their Climax, Lou Reed, Roxy Music, Chicago, Crosby & Nash, Sparks Spin Out, 10CC, Patti Smith, Jim Dandy, Time Traveling With Jefferson Starship..$6–12
Mar. Tracking Kiss Special, Lynyrd Skynyrd, Black Sabbath, Goodbye Faces, Bruce Springsteen...$10–20
Apr. Beatles Confidential: The Things You Never Knew or Never Say—Pre-history, Their Women, Rare Pix, Jimi Hendrix Lives: First Interview in Five Years, Bob Dylan Dies, Elton John, Skin Tight With Patti Smith, BTO, Leslie West, David Bowie, Bay City Rollers, Eno, Bette Midler, Fleetwood Mac $7–15
May Led Zeppelin: The Robert Plant Interview, David Bowie Exclusive Interview, Stones/ Bill Wyman Talks, Queen: A Real-life Fairy Tale, Sweet, Chaka Khan, Bad Co., Lynyrd Skynyrd, Elton John, The Monkees, Peter Frampton, Bay City Rollers, Ted Nugent....$6–12
June The Unknown Stone: An Exclusive—Breaking the Lifetime Silence, Roxy Music's Last Stand, Ted Nugent, Bad Co., Bob Marley & the Search for Jamaica, Keith Moon, Paul McCartney, Grand Funk, Grateful Dead, Tangerine Dream, Baez, Scorpions, Dr. Feelgood $6–12
July Kiss Special, Paul McCartney, Aerosmith, Patti Smith, Peter Frampton, Rolling Stones, Led Zeppelin, Television, Tubes, Welsh...$7–15
Aug. Paul McCartney: He Did it All For You, Stones on Tour, Bob Seger Bites the Silver Bullet, Jeff Beck Gets Mellow, Aerosmith Profile, The Runaways Full-page Full-color Pin-up—At the Beach & in Bikinis, Steely Dan, Patti Smith, Rick Derringer, Bob Marley, Elton John, Frampton Poster, Todd Rundgren, Ramones, Foghat...$7–15

Sept. Rod Stewart: Faceless Lover Gets it Up Again, Kiss Blitz London, Yes, David Bowie Flick Flops, Bernie Taupin Tattles on Elton, Rick Derringer, Alice Cooper Lives His Own Nightmare, Zappa Meets Grand Funk, The Beach Boys, Led Zeppelin, Steve Miller, Stones...$5–10

Oct. The Rolling Stones/Keith Richard Exclusive Interview: The Pusher Behind the Stones, Ringo: The Beatles are Dead, Jimmy Page, ZZ Top, Elton Off the Road Forever, Brian Wilson: Beach Blanket Breakdown, Roxy Music, Aerosmith, Winter Brothers, Bob Seger, Bob Marley...$5–10

Nov. Sex & the Art of Rock 'n' Roll, The Who, Eric Clapton: Death of a Legend, The Runaways/Cherry Bombs NYC, Thin Lizzy, David Byron, Grand Funk, Linda Ronstadt, Kiss, "Saturday Night Live," Gallagher...$5–10

Dec. Steven Tyler/Aerosmith on Tour & Backstage, Linda Ronstadt: Heartbreak Kitten, Blue Oyster Cult, Elvin Bishop, The Ramones: White Punks Unglued, Lou Reed Mouths Off, Kiss Meet Flo & Eddie, Patti Smith, Lynyrd Skynyrd, Hall & Oates, The Beatles Unite, Sylan, Rollers $5–10

1977

Jan. Kiss Special, Peter Frampton, Ted Nugent, Hall & Oates, Queen, Led Zeppelin, Bob Seger, Eric Clapton, Starz, Boston, Patti Smith, Bruce Springsteen, Rick Springfield, Kim Carnes $7–15

Feb. Peter Frampton Talks, Kiss/The Gene Simmons Interview: "I'll Lick it for You Wholesale," Eric Clapton, Nils Lofgren, The Runaways: Loud-Mouthed Lolitas, Kiki Dee, Frank Zappa, Thin Lizzy, Hall & Oates, Black Sabbath, George Harrison, Led Zeppelin, Deep Purple, Jackson Browne, Elton John...$5–10

Mar. Jefferson Starship: The Strange Truth, Ron Wood: The Stone Tells Tales, Patti Smith: Punk Pansy, Earth, Wind & Fire, Abba, Dickey Betts, Kiss, Heart, Eagles, Angel, Queen, McCartney, Todd Rundgren, Blue Oyster Cult, Stones, Beatles, Rollers, Stevie Wonder, Linda Ronstadt $5–10

Apr. Jimmy Page/Led Zeppelin: Getting the Led Out, Bruce Springsteen: Blinded by the Hype, The Kinks Interview: Ray Davies in Disgrace, Parliament/Funkadelic, Leo Sayer, Kiss Dream Date—Whips, Chains & Twinkies, Sex Pistols Last Shot, David Bowie, ZZ Top, Beatles, Lynyrd Skynyrd, The Runaways, Mitch Ryder, Rollers, Marshall Tucker, Blondie, Abba..$5–10

May Queen: Dethroned/Deranged, Burton Cummings Talks About Guess Who, Television, Thin Lizzy, Kansas, Blondie: Sex Offender, Todd Rundgren, Ramones, Rick Derringer, Marshall Tucker, David Bowie, Iggy Pop, Kinks, Boc, Pink Floyd, Fleetwood Mac, Runaways, The Eagles, Aerosmith, Jethro Tull, Bruce Springsteen, Alice Cooper, Lou Reed, Flo & Eddie $5–10

June Exclusive Interview With Keith Richard: This Could be the Last Time, The Stones: Inside the Canadian Connection, Jethro Tull: Interview with Ian, Atlanta Rhythm Section, Todd Rundgren: Cosmic Conversations, Rush, The Reincarnation of Ian Hunter, Rick Derringer, Ted Nugent, Cheap Trick, Foghat, The Band, Bad Company, BTO, Iggy Pop ..$5–10

July Robert Plant: Naked Under Leather—An Intimate Interview, Led Zeppelin on the Road, Boston, Fleetwood Mac: Million-dollar Melodrama, Bob Seger, Angel Makes Up, Ian Anderson, Beach Boys, Dickey Betts, ELP, Iggy Pop & David Bowie, Garland Jeffreys.................$5–10

Aug. Kiss: The Phenomenon, Alice Cooper, Bad Co., Hall & Oates, Heart, The Allman Brothers, Sex Pistols $7–15

Sept. Ted Nugent: Recipe for Rock 'n' Roll Mania, Steve Miller, Frankie Miller, Fleetwood Mac, Small Faces, What Makes Heart Beat?, Iggy Pop: Godfather of Punk, Peter Frampton, Jeff Beck, ZZ Top, Abba, J. Geils, Cat Stevens, Neil Young, Moody Blues, Tubes, *Star Wars* $5–10

Oct. Peter Frampton: Past His Peak?, Pink Floyd: Past & Present, J. Geils, Marshall Tucker, Mink De Ville, Climax Blues Band, *Star Trek* to *Star Wars*, Kiki Dee, Kiss, Heart, Steve Miller, Roger Daltry, Yes, James Taylor, Crosby, Stills & Young $5–10

Nov. Rod Stewart: Telling All the Stones, Lynyrd Skynyrd, Boz Scaggs, Steve Winwood, Boston, Linda Ronstadt, Robin Trower, Nilsson, Cheap Trick, Firefall.........................$4–8

Dec. Grace Slick/Jefferson Starship—Up Against the Wall Again, Robin Trower, The Runaways, The Grateful Dead Never Die, Peter Frampton & the Bee Gees, Heart, Doobie Brothers, Ringo, Iggy Pop, Elvis Presley, Suzi Quatro, Rundgren, Babys, Hall & Oates, Kiss $4–8

CREEM, 1974, Jan.

CREEM, 1974, May

CREEM, 1976, Nov.

CREEM, 1976, Dec.

CREEM, 1977, June

CREEM, 1977, Nov.

CREEM, 1977, July

CREEM, 1977, Sept.

CREEM, 1977, Oct.

1978

Jan. Mick Jagger Talks: The Shape of the Stones to Come, Blue Oyster Cult: Leather & Laster, Elvin Bishop, Commodores, Lynyrd Skynyrd, Mark Farner, Dolly Parton, The Ramones, Steely Dan, Black Oak, REO, Linda Ronstadt, Rod Stewart, Queen, Iggy Pop, Elton John...$4–8

Feb. Jimmy Page/Led Zeppelin Flys Again: The Page Interview, David Bowie, Elvis Costello is Real, Sex Pistols, Kiss Special Report: Not for Fans Only, Aerosmith, ELO, Boz Scaggs, Eric Clapton, Bruce Springsteen, Punk Invades Canada, Joni Mitchell, Alice Cooper, Cher $4–8

Mar. Johnny & Edgar Winter, The Beatles, Foreigner, Fleetwood Mac, Jethro Tull, Lynyrd Skynyrd $3–6

Apr. Super Punk Johnny Rotten Spits Out the Truth, Queen: Back to Basics, Eric Clapton Exclusive Conversation, Elvis Presley, Punk Record Guide, Ted Nugent, Paul McCartney, Foghat, Abba, The Ramones, Angel, Tubes...$3–6

May Ted Nugent: The Animal Bites Back Exclusive, Beatles, Beyond Punk, ELP's Keith Emerson, Elvis Costello: Angry Alien Ex-Stone, Mick Taylor, Zappa, Patti Smith Babels, Bostons Back, Bob Weir, Sammy Hagar, Cheap Trick, ELO, Little Feat, Blondie $3–6

June Jethro Tull/Ian Anderson Exclusive Interview: Will Tull Go Punk?, Bee Gees: The Life & Times of the Brothers, Gibb, Marianne Faithful on Jagger, Junk & Jujubes, Ramones: America's Sex Pistols, Sea Level, Patti Smith, Beatles, Punk in Detroit, Warren Zevon, Godz, Van Halen..$3–6

July Mick Jagger & Ron Wood: The Stones Return from Exile, Foghat, Bob Marley, Frankie Miller, The Clash: New Princes of Punk, Lou Reed, Ted Nugent, Patti Smith, Aerosmith, Stevie Nicks, Heart, Steve Hacket, Ron Wood Talks Exclusive, Van Halen, Wings, Peter Frampton, Jethro Tull, Sweet, The Band, Andy Gibb, Carly Simon, Elvis Costello, REO Speedwagon...$4–8

Aug. Bob Seger: Can He Survive Success?, Broken Wings: The Paul McCartney Interview, Tom Petty & the Heartbreakers, David Johansen, Paul McCartney's Secret Life, Todd Rundgren, Foghat, Kinks, Cheap Trick, Ian Dury, Dickey Betts, Kraftwerk, Starz......$3–6

Sept. David Bowie: The Berlin Interview, Boston, The Second Coming of Patti Smith, Generation X, Tom Robinson, Punk Flicks: Sex Pistols, Devo, Blondie & Others, Bruce Springsteen, Moody Blues, Foreigner, Kiss, The Rolling Stones Onstage Rampage, Dead Boys, Alan Parsons, Beatles, Graham Parker, Rick Derringer, Bob Dylan, Gerry Rafferty $4–8

Oct. Bruce Springsteen Candid Conversation: His Strange Odyssey, Todd Rundgren Says Goodbye to Rock, Thin Lizzy, The Kinks, Bob Dylan, Sgt. Pepper, Foreigner, Bob Marley, Jefferson Starship Orbits Without Grace Slick, Stones, Joe Walsh, Kiss, Neil Young, Journey...$4–8

Nov. The Who's Last, On the Road With the Stones: Bill Moves/Charlie Talks, ENO, Robert Fripp, Stranglers, The Cars, Stones Tour, Meat Loaf, Bowie, Rick Wakeman, Boston, Alice Cooper, Buddy Holly..$4–8

Dec. Mick Jagger & Keith Richard interview, Cheap Trick, Kiss, Linda Ronstadt, Keith Moon, Heart $4–8

1979

Jan. Ted Nugent Reveals His Shocking Secret, The Keith Richard Interview: "Beast of Burden," Rod Stewart: Old Face, New Story, Steve Gibbons, Patti Smith, Memories of Jim Morrison, Sid Vicious, Van Morrison, David Bowie, Styx, Yes, Heart, Jimmy Page color poster & pullout calendar, Meat Loaf, Joe Cocker, Bryan Ferry, Black Sabbath, Elton John...$4–8

Feb. Led Zeppelin: A Psycho History, The Elton John Interview, Dave Edmunds With Nick Lowe & Rockpile, Dead Boys, P-Funk, David Cassidy, Stevie Nicks poster & calendar, Ted Nugent, Lou Reed, Rush, Billy Joel, Steve Martin, The Cars, Devo, Aerosmith, Kiss, Flick, Elvis Presley...$4–8

Mar. Winners Poll Issue—Debbie Harry, Stones, Led Zeppelin, Cheap Trick, Devo, Elvis Costello, Linda Ronstadt, The Cars, Who, Patti Smith, Kiss, Sid Vicious, "Saturday Night Live," Beatles, Rick Wakeman, Heart: Do They Still Have It?, Devo, Lou Reed, Gallagher, Talking Heads, Queen, The Clash, J. Geils, Tanya Tucker, Rod Stewart, Blues Brothers,

CREEM, 1978, Jan.

CREEM, 1978, Apr.

CREEM, 1978, May

CREEM, 1978, July

CREEM, 1978, Aug.

CREEM, 1978, Sept.

CREEM, 1981, Apr.

CREEM, 1981, June

CREEM, 1982, May

Southside Johnny, Eric Clapton, Peter Tosh, The Stiff, ELP, Ted Nugent, Bruce Springsteen poster & calendar..$4–8

Apr. The Blues Brothers: The Untold Story, J. Geils: Ten Years Hard Labor, Captain Beefheart, 25 Years of Outrageous Rock 'n' Roll, Kiss/Gene Simmons Talks Dirty, Blondie/ Debbie Harry Pin-up poster, Peter Wolf, Johnny Rotten's Public Image, Mitch Ryder, Kiss/ Zen Marketing, Elvis Costello, Cheap Trick, Tosh, Starship, Boomtown Rats, XTC, Eno, Good Rats, Werewolves..$4–8

May Elvis Costello Exclusive Interview: Confessions of an Angry Soul, The Clash: First U.S. Tour, Alice Cooper on Booze & Babes, Outlaws, The Ramones Hit Hollywood, Fabulous Poodles, Bob Seger Poster & Rock History Calendar, Bee Gees, Gallagher, Cheap Trick, Police, Gilda Radner, Who, Sid Vicious, Angel, Jam, Robert Gordon................$4–8

June Blondie/Debbie Harry: Blondie's Roots—An Intimate Interview With Debbie Harry, Bad Company, Dire Straits, The Police, A History of Punk: The Good, the Bad & the Ugly, Sex Pistols, Cheap Trick, Roxy Music, Zappa, Elvis Costello Poster & Rock History Calendar, Boomtown Rats, The Warriors, Graham Parker, Clash, Joe Jackson, Godz.......$4–8

July Cheap Trick: Budokan Beatles, Nick Lowe interview, Joe Jackson, Roxy Music: Bryan's Ferry Tale, Roots of Punk: From the Seeds to Seger, Stones/Richard Poster, Elvis Costello, Van Halen, Ramones, Suzi Quatro, Village People, Ron Wood, Jerry Lee Lewis $4–8

Aug. Stones/Behind the Scenes With Keith & Woody, Rod Stewart Calendar Poster, The Who, Tom Robinson, The Band, Patti Smith, The Damned, Thin Lizzy, Be-bop Deluxe, Meat Loaf, Elvis, Sweet, Rockets, Mods..$4–8

Sept. The Who: An Intimate Conversation With Pete, Roger, Kenny & John, The Cars: Life in the Fast Lane, The Babys, Patti Smith & Doc Rock, Graham Parker: Rumour & Rage, Wings, Dylan, Frampton, Bowie, Elvis Costello, Ted Nugent Poster & Rock History Calendar, Abba, Ian Dury, Marshall Tucker, Robert Fripp, ELO, Cheap Trick, Supertramp.....$4–8

Oct. Special Heavy Metal Issue—Aerosmith, Ted Nugent, Led Zeppelin, Kiss, Heart, Queen, Boston, Van Halen, Kinks, Cars, Cheap Trick, Devo, Blue Oyster Cult, The Knack $4–8

Nov. Jimmy Page Interview: The Return of the Zeppelin, David Edmunds: New Wave Rockabilly, The Clash, Dr. Iggy & Mr. Pop: Double Talk, Pere Ubu, Talking Heads, The Who poster & calendar, Blondie, Ian Hunter, Joni Mitchell, Devo, David Johansen, Southside Johnny, Ry Cooper, Cars..$4–8

Dec. Cheap Trick interview, Led Zeppelin: Coming of Age, Bob Dylan, The Records: Vinyl Virgins, Ray Davies' Kinks, B-52's: Buzz Bombs, Clash/Trash, Van Morrison, Sammy Hagar, Randy Numan, Tom Verlaine..$4–8

1980

Jan. Joe Jackson Shoots His Mouth Off, Bram Tchaikovsky, Rock in the 80s: Survival Report, Cheap Trick, Stevie Nicks/Fleetwood Mac are Back, Hunter & Ronson, The Knack Attack, Police, Bruce Springsteen, Debbie Harry/Blondie, Led Zeppelin Poster & Calendar..$4–8

Feb. Blondie Meets Meat Loaf/The Beauty & the Beast on the Set of Roadie, Police Beat Their Rap, Boomtown Rats, The History of Rockabilly, Elvis Presley, Gene Vincent, Annie Golden & the Shirts, Pat Benatar, Bruce Springsteen poster & calendar, The Mutants, Toto, Iggy Pop, B-52's, Eagles, Stevie Wonder, Tom Petty, Joe Jackson, The Rolling Stones.....$4–8

Mar. Winners Poll Issue—Debbie Harry, Jimmy Page, Cheap Trick, The Who, The Knack, Stones, Clash, Iggy Pop, "Saturday Night Live," The Cars, ZZ Top: Back in the Saddle, Graham Parker, The Romantics, The Police poster & calendar, Tom Petty, Pink Floyd, Starship, Bee Gees, John Cale, NRBQ..$4–8

Apr. The Knack, The Jam, Clash, Specials, Rick Derringer, Romantics, Police, The Pretenders, Tom Petty..$4–8

May Debbie Harry/Blondie: Special Report—Women in Revolt: The Future of Women in Rock—Pat Benatar, Ellen Foley, Rachel Sweet, Marianne Faithful, The Saga of Pink Floyd, The Inmates Break Out, Rock Artifacts, Can Iggy Pop Again?, Heart, Bob Seger wall poster, The Clash, Gary Numan, Ramones, The Knack, The Babys, Warren Zevon, Flying Lizards, Lene Lovich, Doug Sham..$4–8

June The Clash Conquer America, Pink Floyd Off the Wall, Ted Nugent wall poster, Pat Benatar, Bob Seger, Elvis Costello, Linda Ronstadt, Billy Joel, Iggy Pop Marches On,

CREEM, 1979, Sept.

CREEM, 1979, Oct.

CREEM, 1979, Nov.

CREEM, 1980, Jan.

CREEM, 1980, May

CREEM, 1980, Dec.

CREEM, 1981, Nov.

CREEM, 1981, Jan.

CREEM, 1981, Feb.

Ramones on the Run, Gary Numan, Public Image, Lene Lovich, Bette Midler, Rachel Sweet...$4–8

July David Lee Roth/Van Halen: The Band You Love to Hate, J. Geils: The Sweet Smell of Success, On the Road With Lene Lovich, The Motors, Heart wall poster, Cheap Trick, Grace Slick, Robert Fripp, Squeeze $4–8

Aug. The Pretenders on Tour: Talking About Top Ten Trauma, Joe Perry, Public Image of Johnny Lydon, Warren Zevon, The Cramps, Gang of Four, Graham Parker, Pete Townshend, Boz Scaggs, Def Leppard, Robin Lane, Blondie/Debbie Harry wall poster, Bob Seger, Lou Reed, Paul McCartney..$4–8

Sept. The Bob Seger Interview, The Kinks' Ray Davies Interview: A Career Retrospective, Hall & Oates Still Exist, Southside Johnny & the Asbury Jukes: Their Untold Story, Lou Reed's Secret Life, Paul McCartney, Alice Cooper, Ted Nugent, Chrissie Hynde wall poster...$4–8

Oct. Judas Priest, Heavy Metal Special: "Back from the Dead," The Rolling Stones Emotional Rescue, The Blues Bands: The Return of Paul Jones, Rockets, The Jags, Bebe Buell, The Clash vs. Led Zeppelin, Pretenders, B-52's, Nina Hagen, Kiss, Jeff Beck, Roxy Music, Queen, Dylan, X, Mitch Ryder, Jackson Browne, Phil Lynott, Blue Oyster Cult, Van Halen, AC/DC, Iron Maiden, Pat Benatar Special Calendar Poster Pin-up...................$4–8

Nov. Pete Townshend Exclusive Interview: The Why, How & Who, Punk Woodstock Heatwave Festival—Elvis Costello, Pretenders, Talking Heads, B-52's, Joe Jackson: The Man Talks Back, Secret Affair, Magazine, Records, Rachel Sweet, Bernie Taupin, Dave Edmunds, Carolyne Mas, The Heaters, Elvis, Mink Deville, Chicago, Grateful Dead, Cheap Trick wall poster...$4–8

Dec. Cheap Trick/Rick Nielsen interview, The B-52's: Beach Blanket Blow-out, John Cougar, The Motels, Tremnlers: Peter Noone Remembers, The Wimp Rock Hall of Fame, Cars, Elvis Costello, Yes, Pat Benatar, Psychedelic Furs, Van Morrison, Carlene Carter, Hall & Oates, Nina Hagen, Tull, Kingbees, Springsteen wall poster..................................$4–8

1981

Jan. Bruce Springsteen, Pat Benatar, Ronnie Spector, The Kinks, Queen, Talking Heads, David Bowie..$4–8

Feb. Rockpile, Dire Straits Exclusive Non-interview, Neil Young: Too Young to Rust, The Stranglers, Rubber City Rebels, Kiss Bonus: Without Their Makeup, Joan Jett: After the Runaways, John Waters, Joe Jackson, Cheap Trick, Bruce Springsteen, The Knack, Van Halen poster...$4–8

Mar. Winners Poll Issue—Bruce Springsteen, Pat Benatar, The Who, Led Zeppelin, Pretenders, AC/DC, Clash, Stones, Iggy Pop, Van Halen, Queen, Devo, Talking Heads/David Byrne interview, The Jam, Capt. Beefheart, Jim Carroll, Bus Boys, Iggy Pop Won't Stop, Nina Hagen: Fraulein Punkette, Police, Heart, Rod Stewart, Blondie, The Cars wall poster...................$4–8

Apr. The Police Interrogated, Stiff, Split Enz, Steve Winwood: No More Traffic Jams, Grace Slick: Starship Survivor, Alone Again, Arthur Lee/Love: 15 Years After, Van Halen, Eagles, REO, The Clash, AC/DC Poster $4–8

May Heavy Metal Guitar Heroes—Eddie Van Halen, Jimmy Page, Pete Townshend, Brian May & Keith Richards, Elvis Costello Still Not Talking, Boomtown Rats Beat the Press, Squeeze, Clash interview, Echo & the Bunnymen, The Teardrop Explodes, Styx, Todd Rundgren, Ian Dury, Divine, Dexy's Midnight Runners, B-52s wall poster, Marha Davis.$4–8

June Debbie Harry/The Man Behind Blondie—Chris Stein's Diary, Rush, Rick Nelson: The Travelin' Man is Back, Garland Geffreys, Adam & the Ants, Carlene Carter, Van Halen, Rainbow, Boomtown Rats, Jerry Lee Lewis, Smokey Robinson, Marvin Gaye, Rosanne Cash, Police poster...$4–8

July Angus Young's Wall of Noise, The ABCs of AC/DC, Todd Rundgren: Captain Video in Utopia, Dave Edmunds, Pearl Harbour, The Velvet Underground: The Untold Story, Joe Ely, XTC, REO Starship, Judas Priest, The Who, Lounge Lizards, Ozzy, Hall & Oates poster...$4–8

Aug. Judas Priest, Queen: Their Secret Life, John Cale: The War of Dogs, Bram Tchaikovsky, Spandau Ballet, Moody Blues, Tom Petty, Squeeze, Tina Turner, Gary U.S. Bonds, Molly Hatchet, Gang of Four, Public Image Ltd., Robert Fripp, Dead Kennedys, X, Keith Richards poster $3–6

Sept. Journey: The Prisoners of Rock Interviewed, Van Halen, Clash, Plasmatics: Wendy in Wonderland, Krokus, Ramones, Robert Gordon, Pat Benatar, AC/DC, Blackfoot, Adam Ant, Fridays, Hank Williams, George Harrison, Psychedelic Furs, Tom Petty wall poster..$3–6
Oct. Backstage With Van Halen, Billy Squire, Blue Oyster Cult: 61 Secrets, David Johansen, Steve Strange Dresses Funny, The History of L.A. Punk, Ramones, Yoko, Peter Tosh, Joe Jackson, ZZ Top, Joe Perry, Foreigner, The Plastics, Village People, Siouxsie & the Banshees, Cramps, Pat Benatar wall poster $3–6
Nov. Pat Benatar: Rock 'n' Roll Wonder Woman, Stones, ZZ Top, Ozzy Osbourne, Pretenders Interview: Chrissie Hynde Lets Loose, The Go-go's: L.A. Woman Unleashed, Debbie Harry, Rick Springfield, Bob Dylan, Kim Carnes, The Rockats, Robert Gordon, Ian Hunter, Bruce Springsteen poster $4–8
Dec. Ray Davies Exclusive Interview, Stones Tour '81, Pix, Rick James, Debbie Harry: Blondie Goes Koo-koo, John Enwistle Without the Who, Billy Squier, Go-go's, Hall & Oates, Grace Slick, Motorhead, Meat Loaf, Tim Curry, Nils Lofgren, Pat Benatar: 81's Pet, Bruce Springsteen: Still Boss, Van Halen: Top Dogs?, Mick Jagger wall poster $4–8

1982

Jan. Mick Jagger Exclusive Interview: Telling Torrid Tales, Ian Hunter, Devo: Can They Still Whip It?, Psychedelic Furs Talk, Genesis & Phil Collins, John Enwistle, Stray Cats, Mink Deville, J. Geils, James Brown, Jamie Lee Curtis, Bow Wow Wow, Ultravox, Lene Lovich, The Cure, Steve Hackett, Bill Burnette, The Police wall poster $4–8
Feb. Keith Richards Exclusive Interview: Secrets of a Slavedriving Man in a Black Limousine, The Knack, Marianne Faithful: Stone Survive Still Walks on the Wild Side, George Thorogood, Robert Fripp, Ozzy Osbourne, Elvis Presley, Jimi Hendrix, Grand Funk, J. Geils, Go-go's, Stray Cats, Quarterflash, Prince, Neil Young, U2, AC/DC poster...$4–8
Mar. Winners Poll Issue—Pat Benatar, Mick Jagger, Keith Richards, The Go-go's, Van Halen, Ray Davies, Angus Young, Bruce Springsteen, The Cars, Rod Stewart, Elvis Costello, Queen, Bob Dylan, Mink Deville, NRBQ, David Bowie, Joan Jett, Loverboy, Kinks, The Clash, AC/DC, J. Geils poster...$3–6
Apr. The Police: Every Little Thing is Magic, Black Sabbath: Life After Ozzy, Loverboy, Rock on Cable TV Exclusive, Soft Cell, U2, Blasters, Del Shannon, Elvis Costello, AC/DC, Black Flag, Rod Stewart poster...$3–6
May The Cars, Nick Lowe, Blasters, Fleshtones, Jerry Lee Lewis, AC/DC: Angus Speaks, Waitress, Lou Reed, B-52's, The Go-go's, Van Halen, Dylan, Altered Images, Au Pairs, Janis Joplin, Teardrop Explodes, Abba, Ozzy Osbourne $3–6
June Joan Jett Runaway Hit: beautiful Joan Jett cover photo, Hall & Oates, Quarterflash, Del Shannon, Huey Lewis, X, XTC, Utopia, Sammy Hagar, Van Morrison, Bonnie Raitt, Graham Parker, David Lee Roth, Muddy Waters...$4–8
July The B-52's: Wig Poppin' Time, J. Geils, Girlschool, Aldo Nova, Fear, Sammy Hagar, Asia, Talking Heads, Paul McCartney, The Jam, Sting, Rick Springfield, Haircut 100, Sparks, Greg Kihn Band $3–6
Aug. Blondie/Debbie Harry Captured—fantastic cover photo, Asia, Rosanne Cash, Dwight Twilley, Country Music, Rainbow, Marshall Crenshaw, Jerry Lee Lewis, Van Halen, Elton John, McCartney, John Cougar, Heart poster $4–8
Sept. David Lee Roth/Van Halen, John Cougar Fools America, Dave Edmunds, Marshall Crenshaw, Iron Maiden, The Clash, Roxy Music, David Bowie, Rick James, Haircut 100, Fun Boy Three, Squeeze, Heart, Abrian Belew, Ray Parker Jr., Ted Nugent poster....$4–8
Oct. Robert Plant is Back Exclusive Interview, Stones Roll Over Europe, Roxy Music: Bryan Ferry is Still Cool, Circle Jerks, X, Motorhead, Squeeze, Laurie Anderson, REO, Queen, Stevie Wonder, Pete Townshend, King Crimson, Rosanne Cash, Kid Creole, David Johansen...$3–6
Nov. John Cougar, Jimi Hendrix R.I.P., Keith Richards: No Comment, David Lee Roth, The Who Exclusive Pete Townshend Interview, Frank & Moon Zappa, Joe Cocker, Gang of Four, Van Halen, Robert Plant, Elvis Costello, The Go-go's, Stray Cats, Judas Priest, Lydia Lunch, Juice Newton $3–6
Dec. The Who Tour '82 Photo Album, The Go-go's Back from Vacation, Billy Squier, David Johansen, Kid Creole & the Coconuts, Thomas Dolby, Bad Company, Fleetwood Mac, Judas Priest, Pink Floyd, Ted Nugent, ABC, Vanity, Bananarama, Psychedelic Furs, John Cougar poster, The Blasters $3–6

1983

Jan. Mick Jagger Exclusive Interview, The Police, Stray Cats, Devo, Ian Hunter, Genesis $3–6

Feb. Keith Richards Exclusive Interview, Elvis Presley, The Knack, Jimi Hendrix, The Go-go's, The Stray Cats $3–6

Mar. Winners Poll Issue—Pat Benatar, The Who, David Lee Roth, Robert Plant, The Clash, Eddie Van Halen, Adam Ant, Peter Gabriel, Missing Persons, Ric Ocasek, English Beat, Lene Lovich, Rush, Devo, Plasmatics, The Beatles, Yoko Ono, Grace Jones, Culture Club, David Bowie poster $3–6

Apr. Tom Petty After Dark, Ozzy Osbourne: From Iron Man to Bat Man, Pat Benatar, Who Needs the Beatles? Grace Jones, Bob Seger, Michael Jackson, Mick Jagger, Black Uhuru, Lords of the New Church, Keith Richards, Neil Young, Rick Ocasek, Supertramp, John Cale, Chic, Yaz $3–6

May Prince: Sex God or Future King?, Bob Seger: Still the Same, Phil Collins, Capt. Beefheart, Toni Basil, Members, Fabulous Thunderbirds, Thompson Twins, Buddy Holly, John Cale, Randy Newman, Heaven 17, The Bangles, Ozzy Osbourne, Duran Duran, Black Sabbath, The Pretenders, Stray Cats poster $3–6

June Michael Jackson, Culture Club, The Pretenders, Bow Wow Wow, Dexy's Midnight Runners $3–6

July Joan Jett, Duran Duran, George Clinton, Thomas Dolby, Thompson Twins $3–6

Aug. Ray Davies of the Kinks, Molly Hatchet: Buried Alive, Thompson Twins, Wall of Voodoo, Lita Ford, Flesh Eaters, David Bowie Scandal, ZZ Top, Vanity 6, Marshall Crenshaw, Bryan Adams, Men at Work poster $3–6

Sept. David Lee Roth/Van Halen, U2: Bono's War Games, ZZ Top, Mitch Ryder, The Ramones Graduate, Talking Heads, David Bowie, Men at Work, Clash, Kinks, Joan Jett, Marshall Crenshaw, B-52's, Human League, Flock of Seagulls, Billy Idol, Dave Edmunds, R.E.M., The Blasters, Def Leppard poster $3–6

Oct. Robert Plant Exclusive Interview: Farewell to Led Zeppelin, Iron Maiden, Dave Edmunds, A Flock of Seagulls, Sparks, System: Post-Prince Funk, Fastway, Stevie Nicks, Joe Walsh, Bryan Adams, The Police, Tears for Fears, Violent Femmes, Richard Thompson, Fun Boy Three, Zebra $3–6

Nov. The Police Tell All: Exclusive Interview, *Creem's* Guide to Rock Magazines: Why They All Stink, Krokus: Swiss Metal Gods, The Hollies, Joan Armatrading, Asia, Robert Plant, Neil Young, Billy Joel, Elvis Costello, Graham Parker, Peter Tosh, Billy Idol, The Fleshtones, Standells $3–6

Dec. Brian Stezer/Stray Cats Exclusive Interview, Loverboy, Fastway vs. Motorhead, Ian Hunter, Robert Palmer, The Blasters, AC/DC, Big Country, Rick James, Robert Plant, NRBQ, Jackson Browne, Cheap Trick, The Bongos $3–6

1984

Jan. John Cougar Exclusive Interview: Down on the Farm, The Fixx, Carly Simon, Eddy Grant, The Animals, Altered Images, Y & T, INXS, Culture Club, The Doors, Talking Heads, Motley Crue, Aldo Nova, Herbie Hancock $3–6

Feb. Mick Jagger interview, Eurythmics: Strange Bedfellows, Motley Crue, Paul Rogers: Smell of the Buffalo, New Order, Alan Vega, John Cougar, Quiet Riot, Duran Duran, Paul McCartney, Bob Dylan, Black Sabbath, Rick James, Blue Oyster Cult, Paul Simon, Green on Red, Altered Images, Yes $3–6

Mar. Winners Poll Issue—Michael Jackson, Quiet Riot, Eddie Van Halen, The Police, Def Leppard, Mick Jagger, Gang of Four Can Count, Brian May: Queen for a Day, Soft Cell, Huey Lewis, Twisted Sister, Ozzy Osbourne, Billy Idol, Genesis, David Lee Roth, Was (Was Not), T-bone Burnett, Ray Parker Jr., Black Sabbath, Paul Rogers, Van Halen calendar poster ...$3–6

Apr. Duran Duran, Eric Clapton, Big Country, Jimmy Page & Jeff Beck, Billy Idol, Debbie Harry, Nick Heywood $3–6

May David Lee Roth/Van Halen '84: Going Down With David, Adam Ant Stripped Bare, Spandau Ballet Solid Gold, Girlschool, Jonathan Richman, Lords of the New Church, Michael Jackson, Boy George, XTC, Cyndi Lauper, Christine McVie, Huey Lewis, Eurythmics, John & Yoko, Judas Priest, Pretenders, The Sounds of the Sixties With—Jimi Hendrix, Beatles, Stones, The Who & Others, Billy Idol poster $3–6

June Boy George & Ozzy Osbourne Exclusive Interviews, Rick Derringer: Back & Proud, The Smiths: Handsome Devils, Re-flex, ABC, T-bone Burnett, Queen, Thompson Twins,

Cyndi Lauper, Motley Crue, Nena, The Alarm, Laurie Anderson, Jason & the Scorchers...$3–6

July Judas Priest: Screaming Hot Meatflakes, Eurythmics: Dangerous Strangers, Thomas Dolby, The Alarm, Was (Was Not), Rory Gallagher, Motley Crue, Scorpions, The Cars, Huey Lewis, R.E.M., Joe Jackson, Lou Reed, Madness, Black Flag, Joe Ely, Spinal Tap, Los Lobos, Style Council, The Pretenders pullout calendar poster.............................$3–6

Aug. Chrissie Hynde Off the Record, Scorpions: No Sour Krauts, The Go-go's: Vacation's Over, Missing Persons, Roger Waters, Rush, Dwight Twilley, Psychedelic Furs, Berlin, Annie Lennox, Everly Brothers, Bananarama, Weird Al Yankovic, Huey Lewis poster calendar...$ 3–6

Sept. Prince Returns Exclusive: Inside Purple Rain, Thompson Twins, Slade, Bruce Springsteen, Bowie, Elvis Costello, Scorpions, R.E.M., Tracey Ullman, Berlin, Duran Duran, Human League, Ultravox, Shannon..$3–6

Oct. Michael Jackson & David Lee Roth: Duets from Hell, The Clash Talk, Joan Jett: Her Misspent Youth, Ratt, Boy George, Jacksons, Prince, Billy Idol, R.E.M., Rod Stewart, Stray Cats, Little Steven, John Belushi, Accept, The The, Jason & the Scorchers, Bruce Springsteen poster..$3–6

Nov. Quiet Riot, The Cars, Lou Reed, Prince: Purple Passion, Cyndi Lauper: No Nude Photos, Pink Floyd, Little Steven, Bananarama: Fruit from Space, Greg Kihn, Yoko & John, Peter Wolf, Twisted Sister, Ratt, Elton John, Flock of Seagulls, Tina Turner, Scandal, Siouxsie & the Banshees, Eddy Grant, Rain Parade, INXS, Prince calendar poster...................$3–6

Dec. Billy Squier: Bad Boy Breakout, Huey Lewis: News at Ten, Human League, Twisted Sister, Lita Ford, David Bowie, Quiet Riot, Cyndi Lauper, Ratt poster calendar.........$3–6

1985

Jan. Bruce Springsteen Exclusive Interview: The Bruce on Fire, Van Halen, Patti Smith & Scandal, Yoko Ono Speaks, Little Richard, Lita Ford, Twisted Sister, John Waite, U2, Frankie Goes to Hollywood, The Church, Ramones, Everly Brothers, Styx, Billy Squier calendar poster..$3–6

Feb. Ratt vs. Motley Crue, Elvis Costello Exclusive Interview, Kiss: Super Studs from Heck, John Waite, The Fixx, Lindsay Buckingham Goes Insane, Frankie Goes to Hollywood, Tina Turner, Culture Club, Iron Maiden, Deep Purple, Hall & Oates, Rolling Stones, King Sunny Ade, Los Lobos, Lou Christie, Sheila E., DB's, David Lee Roth calendar poster...$3–6

Mar. Van Halen, Pat Benatar, Deep Purple, Madonna, The Bangles, The Kinks, Julian Lennon, Whitesnake, Talking Heads, Grim Reaper, The Church, Dokken, Krokus......$3–6

Apr. David Lee Roth: Too Cool to Live?, Big Country, Boy George, Hall & Oates, John Fogerty, Exclusive Jimmy Page Interview, Bryan Adams, David Bowie, Kinks, Foreigner, Moodists, Mr. T...$3–6

May Ratt, Motley Crue, Billy Idol, W.A.S.P., Missing Persons, Madonna: The Biggest Bozos of the 80s, Jimmy Page Exclusive Interview, The Firm, Tears for Fears, David Lee Roth, Hall & Oates, Duran Duran Reborn, Waterboys, The Commotions, John Haitt, Slade, U2...$3–6

June John Fogerty, Julian Lennon, W.A.S.P., Prince, The Bangles, Foreigner, Lita Ford, Motorhead..$3–6

July Prince: The Royal Scam, David Lee Roth, Iron Maiden, General Public, REO Speedwagon, U2: The Unforgettable Bobo, Tom Petty, Power Station, Motley Crue, Tears for Fears, Fiona, Husker Du, Eric Clapton, The Judds...$3–6

Aug. Inside Madonna, Eurythmics, Autograph: Best New Band Yet, Jason & the Scorchers, Bon Jovi: "Turn Me On," Tears for Fears calendar poster, Prince, Ratt, Howard Jones, Let's Active...$3–6

Sept. Robert Plant Exclusive Interview, Sade, R.E.M., Guiffria, Alison Moyet, Aztec Camera, Tenna Maria, Beach Boys, Suzanne Vega, Beastie Boys, Bongos, Eurythmics, New Order, Dire Straits, Lone Justice, Sting calendar poster...$3–6

Oct. Tom Petty: Song of the South, Paul Simon, Scorpions, Katrina & the Waves, Howard Jones, Talking Heads, Ratt, Bryan Ferry, Sting, Beach Boys, Mary Jane Girls, The Smith, "Till Tuesday," Live Aid poster...$3–6

Note: No issues were printed for November and December 1985 or for January 1986.

1986

Feb. John Cougar Mellencamp: Big Sound from a Small Town, Thompson Twins, Dire Straits, ABC, The Smiths, Heart: In the Right Place, Prefab Sprout............................$3–6
Mar. Van Halen: The Real Thing?, Del Fuegos, Psychedelica '86: Ghosts from the Coast, Arcadia, Robyn Hitchcock, ZZ Top Can't Stop, The Cure, Roger Daltry $3–6
Apr. Simple Minds: What's in a Name?, Clarence Clemons, Motley Crue, The Alarm, Waterboys, INXS, Pete Townshend Face to Face...$3–6
May U2: The Band of the Year, The Dream Academy & The Cult: Peace, Love & the Dollar, The Jesus & Mary Chain, The Starship, Sade: So Hot, She's Cool, Twisted Sister..$3–6
June The Hooters: How Long Will it Last?, David Lee Roth & Van Halen: What Really Happened, Husker Du, The Bangles, Aerosmith, OMD, Stryper, Brian Setzer Cuts Through $3–6
July Prince: The Parade Passes by Rating the Rock Magazines, Charlie Sexton, Ozzy Osbourne's Solution, Depeche Mode, Firm, Fine Young Cannibals, The Pogues.........$3–6
Aug. Billy Idol, Bill Wyman: The Only Stone That Matters, Julian Lennon, Katrina & the Waves, Fabulous T-birds, The Church, Pil, The Call $3–6
Sept. The Original Bob Seger: Accept No Imitations, Keith Richards: The Mickless Wonder, Judas Priest: Butchers from the Planet Hell, Pet Shop Boys, The Replacements, Feargal Sharkey, The Pogues...$3–6
Oct. David Lee Roth, Belinda Carlisle Fer Shure, Metallica, Joan Jett, Let's Active, Emerson, Lake & Powell, Siouxsie & the Banshees, A Night With R.E.M., Nady Wireless $3–6
Nov. R.E.M.: Giving it Away, Genesis: Scientifically Incorrect, Peter Gabriel Blows His Horn, Meat Puppets, George Clinton, Tangerine Dream, Gene Simmons, Eurythmics.....$3–6
Dec. The Cure, Run-DMC, 38 Special, Bananarama, The Monkees: The Next Beatles, The Moody Blues: Guys in the White Satin, Phil Collins $3–6

1987

Jan. John Fogerty Lets it Rock, Bon Jovi: The Wetter the Better, Darryl Hall, Jerry Lee Lewis Exclusive Interview, Robert Wyatt, Bodeans...$3–6
Feb. David Byrne the Talking Heads, Iggy Pop vs. Iggy Soda, Tina Turner, Big Country, Motorhead, Quicksilver: Best New Band...$3–6
Mar. Robyn Hitchcock, Billy Idol, Alice Cooper: Goodness Snakes, Human League, OMD, Jason & the Scorchers...$3–6
Apr. The Bangles, Van Halen, David Lee Roth, The Pretenders, Cyndi Lauper, Debbie Harry: Backer Than Ever, Chrissie Hynde: Without Cruelty......................................$3–6
May Beastie Boys: Boom Boxes from Hell, The Kinks, Timbuk 3, Gene Loves Jezebel, Heavy Metal Must Die, Ray Davies Face to Face..$3–6
June Richard Butler of the Psychedelic Furs: God & Country Second, Los Lobos, Husker Du, Billy Vera: Back to the Future, Shriekback $3–6
July The Smiths Exclusive Interview, Patti Smith: From Scandal to Hell, XTC, REO Speedwagon, Crowed House, Dave Edmunds, Simply Red: Red-haired Soul for the 80s $3–6
Aug. The Cult, Thompson Twins, Lou Gramm, Suzanne Vega, Julian Cope, Concrete Blondie..$3–6
Sept. Stevie Nicks/Fleetwood Mac: Back in Focus, The Replacements, Heart & Other Major Organs, Squeeze, Bryan Adams, Little Steven, Wire, Celibate Rifles, Hoodoo Gurus, The Beatles & Joe Orton $3–6
Oct. The Cure: Buy Them, Aerosmith: Sing da Blooze, Warren Zevon, John Hiatt, Genesis, Marshall Crenshaw, Chris Isaal, L.L. Cool J Raps...$3–6
Nov. Lou Reed & the Velvet Underground, The Monkees, Simple Minds $3–6
Dec. John Cougar Mellencamp, George Harrison: His Secret Beatle Past, Fabulous Thunderbirds, X: Lacking Nothing, DB's Duane Eddy, Angry Samoans, R.E.M. & The End of the World $3–6

1988

Jan. The Cars: This Year's Model, Tom Waits, Pet Shop Boys on the Gravy Train, The Ramones: Gabba in the Night, Bodeans, George Harrison: The Interview Continues, Metallica: Thrash Lords or Teddy Bears? $3–6

Feb. Pink Floyd: There's a New World Coming, Bruce Springsteen & Michael Jackson: Duets from Hell, INXS, Yes, Mick Jagger: Solo But Still Talking, Jethro Tull, The Neighborhoods, Alex Chilton...$3–6

Mar. David Lee Roth: Big Rock Mountain, Candy, George Michael: The 9th Beatle?, The Jesus & Mary Chain, Megadeth, Sting Looks at a Crumbling World, Pere Ubu, The Alarm, Ry Cooder...$3–6

Apr. U2: Band of the Year, The Replacements, Depeche Mode, Screaming Blue Messiahs, Bryan Ferry, Love & Rockets, The Pogues, Paul Simon: Life After Graceland, Opal, Dead Milkmen, The Reivers $3–6

Note: No issue was printed for May 1988.

June Madonna/Tiffany/Belinda Carlisle: The Truth is Not Sexist, The Church, Ted Nugent, Zen & the Art of Robert Plant...$3–6

July The Return of Steve Winwood: After the High Life, Anthrax, Firehose, The Smithereens, Robyn Hitchcock, T-bone Burnett, Icehouse, 1001 Uses for Frank Zappa, Clannad $3–6

Note: No issue was printed for August 1988.

Sept. Rod Stewart Gets His Wings, Georgia Satellites, Pontiac Brothers, Thomas Dolby, The Uncensored, Iggy Pop...$3–6

Oct. Jimmy Page: Turn, Turn, Turn, Brian Setzer, Prefab Sprout, The Moody Blues, The Byrds, Midnight Oil, Gamper Van Beethovan, Crowded House.......................................$3–6

Nov. Robert Cray: Blues for Allah, Was (Was Not), Pat Benatar: Married to the Mob, Blue Oyster Cult $3–6

1990*

Aug./Sept. #1 Billy Idol: Looking Both Ways at the Crossroads, Little Richard's Almanac: Richard Penniman Remembers His Former Guitarist Jimi Hendrix, Adam Ant Dons His Own Wardrobe, Door's Maven Danny Sugarman, Debbie Harry: Blondie on Blondie, Joey Ramone/The Ramones: White Punks on Hope, The Tom Tom Club: Funky But Sweet, Jerry Harrison...$3–7

Oct./Nov. #2 Chrissie Hynde: The True Blue Pretender, LL Cool J, Dave Stewart, The Sundays, Soul Asylum...$3–6

CREEM, BEST OF (THE)

1980

Fall Ten Years of Rock 'n' Roll—Special Collector's Edition, contains full-color Jimmy Page wall poster, Debbie Harry, Van Halen, Ann & Nancy Wilson/Heart, Lene Lovich, Chrissie Hynde, Bruce Springsteen, Alice Cooper, Joe Jackson, Mick Jagger, The Who, Cheap Trick, Sex Pistols, Led Zeppelin, Police, Clash, N.Y. Dolls, Beatles, Bowie..$5–10

1981

Summer Special Heavy Metal Edition—Van Halen, Led Zeppelin Interview With Jimmy Page, Rush, AC/DC, Queen, Heart: Metal a Go-Go $3–6

CREEM CLOSE UP

1982

Oct./Nov. Women in Rock Special—Pat Benatar: Rock's Reigning Queen?, The Go-go's Back from Vacation, Joan Jett Still Hot, Fleetwood's Stevie Nicks on Air 'n' Stuff, Girl Groups of the 60s, Chrissie Hynde, Heart, Blondie, Blondie/Debbie Harry, Quarter Flash, Missing Persons, Kim Carnes, Girlschool, Martha Davis, Patti Smith, Tina Weymouth, Grace Slick, contains full-color Go-go's poster...$5–10

1983

Apr./May Metal Music—Judas Priest, Van Halen, Ozzy Osbourne, AC/DC, Zeppelin, Rush, Queen, Ted Nugent, Deep Purple, Kiss, Bad Company, Scorpions, Jeff Beck, Aerosmith, Blue Oyster Cult, Grand Funk Railroad, Alice Cooper...$2–4

*New larger format/new publisher: Alternative Media Inc.

Aug./Sept. Heavy Metal—Def Leppard, Van Halen: U.S. Festival Hot Shots, Judas Priest, Iron Maiden, Krokus, Ozzy Osbourne, Billy Squier, AC/DC, The Scorpions, Motorhead, Kiss, Saxon, Lita Ford, Quiet Riot, Fastway..$2–4

Oct./Nov. The Heavy 100—Keith Richards, The Who, Robert Plant, Kinks, Van Halen, Adam Ant, Culture Club, Police, Stray Cats, Def Leppard, Men at Work, David Bowie, Prince, Journey, Duran Duran, Joan Jett, Loverboy, The Clash, Marshall Crenshaw, Billy Squier, The Go-go's, Pete Townshend $3–6

1984

Jan. Gold Soul—Michael Jackson, Prince, Rick James, Grandmaster Flash, Donna Summer, Vanity 6, Marvin Gaye, Stevie Wonder $3–6

Feb. Rock Chronicles—The Police, David Bowie, Stray Cats, Michael Jackson, Prince, Quiet Riot, ZZ Top, The Fixx, Def Leppard, Duran Duran, Spandau Ballet, Culture Club, Talking Heads, The Kinks, The Eurythmics..$3–6

May The New Wave—Van Halen, Motley Crue, Quiet Riot, Ozzy Osbourne, Def Leppard, Heavy Metal on Video $3–6

June The British Invasion—Duran Duran, Boy George, The Who, The Beatles Forever, The Clash $3–6

Aug. Van Halen Special Issue—The 1984 Report, David Lee Roth, Eddie Van Halen, Michael Anthony & Alex Van Halen interviews, Everything You Ever Wanted to Know, includes 1984 color wall poster $3–6

Sept. Michael Jackson & the Jacksons Special Issue—Their Complete Story, Revealing Interviews, Inside Michael's Wardrobe, At Home With the Jackson Five, Special Discography, Posters, Rare Photos $3–6

Oct. The Best of Metal—Van Halen, Quiet Riot, Motley Crue, Judas Priest, Def Leppard, Rush, Ozzy Osbourne, Black Sabbath, Iron Maiden...$3–6

Dec. Fifteenth Anniversary Issue—Mick Jagger, Boy George, Jimi Hendrix, Prince, Jimmy Page, David Lee Roth, Bruce Springsteen, Elvis Presley, The Velvet Underground, Journey, MC5, Kiss, Blondie, Queen, Jim Morrison & Others $3–6

1985

Jan. Metal Rock 'n' Roll Issue—Ratt: Rodent Rock, Motley Crue: Crue Confessions, Van Halen Still on Top, Twisted Sister Take It, Iron Maiden, Kiss, Scorpions, Dio, Bon Jovi............$3–6

Feb. Rock Chronicles—Prince: Purple Rain, Ratt: Out of the Sewer, Bruce Springsteen: A Cool Rockin' Daddy, Van Halen, Tina Turner, Madonna, David Bowie, Huey Lewis, Cyndi Lauper, Pat Benatar, Joan Jett, The Cars, R.E.M., Billy Idol, The Jacksons, Twisted Sister, Boy George...$3–6

Mar. Kiss & Tell, Van Halen, Twisted Sister Bent City, Ratt, Alice Cooper: Dead Baby Joke, Led Zeppelin: Classic Screech, Sex in Metal..$3–6

May Twisted Sister, Iron Maiden, Dokken, W.A.S.P., Kiss, Tongue Dynasty, Metal Church, British Metal Belfegore $3–6

June W.A.S.P., Ratt, Iron Maiden: Casket Case, The Firm, Metallica, Dio, Belfegore......$3–6

July Twisted Sister: All the Metal Facts, W.A.S.P.: Sting o' Death, Motley Crue, David Lee Roth, Deep Purple, Hanoi Rocks, Keel, Loudness $3–6

Aug. Jimmy Page Exclusive Marathon Interview, Krokus, Accept, Queensrche, Bon Jovi: "Never Again," Girlschool, Slayer, Alcatrazz, Belfegore $3–6

Sept. Giuffria, The Scorpions, Ratt, Yngwie Malmsteen, Alcatrazz, Bon Jovi, Mountain...$2–4

Oct. Motley Crue, Ratt, Accept, Venom, Uli Jon Roth, Phenomena, Belfegore...........$3–6

1986

Mar. Kiss: Feel the Heat, Motley Crue, AC/DC, Ozzy Osbourne, Dio, Venom, Anthrax, Ratt, Grim Reaper..$3–6

May Aerosmith: Mirror Reflection, Motley Crue Exclusive Interview, Y & T, Bon Jovi, Iron Maiden, Kiss, Possessed, Joe Lynn Turner...$3–6

July Judas Priest: Metal Lords Rule Again, Exclusive Van Halen Interview, Twisted Sister: Dee Talks, Dokken, Megadeth, W.A.S.P., Quiet Riot, Metal Church...........................$3–6

Sept. Black Sabbath: Who Needs Ozzy?, Rush: Better Than Ever, Accept, Yngwie Malmsteen, Ted Nugent, Autograph, Keel, Motley Crue, Saxon, Dio, King Kobra.....$3–6

Oct. Bon Jovi Exclusive Interview, Metallica, Venom, Honeymoon Suite, Wendy O, Alcatrazz, Krokus, Motley Crue, Triumph...$3–6

Nov. Quiet Riot: Just Like Starting Over, Kiss: On the Set With Gene Simmons, Motorhead: Death in Their Wake, Anthrax, Scandinavian Metal Scene, Nasty Savage, Ratt, Poison, Celtic Frost, Naked Raygun $3–6

1987

Jan. Iron Maiden: Shriek of the Savage Swordsman, Megadeth, Def Leppard: Return of the Renegades, Queensryche, Great White, Die Kreuzen, AC/DC, Scorpions, Alvin Lee, King Diamond...$3–6
Feb. Motley Crue & Bon Jovi: Metal Takes a Stand, Jimi Hendrix & Phil Lynott: The Real Black Metal, Cinderella, Poison, W.A.S.P., Scorpions, Discharge, Zodiac Mindwarp, Cub Koda...$3–6
Mar. Ratt, Bon Jovi's Kingdom of Love, Saxon, Blue Oyster Cult, Corrosion of Conformity, Slayer, Motorhead, Megadeth, CJSS, Poison $3–6
Apr. Megadeth, Stryper, Deep Purple, Blue Velvet, Yngwie Malmsteen, Metallica, Manowar, Loudness, Ratt, W.A.S.P., David Lee Roth, Paul Di Anno..........................$3–6
May David Lee Roth: Bigger Than Metal, Cinderella, Bon Jovi: On Top to Stay, Meat Loaf, Bad Brains, Metal Church, Bad Co., Slayer, Night Ranger, GBH.......................$3–6
June Motley Crue: Girl Happy, Alice Cooper: Follow That Dream, Iron Maiden, Halo of Flies, Crumbsuckers, Paul Stanley, W.A.S.P., Lita Ford...$3–6
July Scorpions: The Greatest Story Ever Told, Europe, Cinderella vs. Snow White, Keel, Motorhead, Alice Cooper Part II, Yngwie Malmsteen, Deep Purple, Iron Maiden, Suicidal Tendencies, Tesla, Queensryche, Meatmen $3–6
Aug. Ozzy Osbourne: His Tribute to Randy Rhoads, Poison, Anthrax, Vinnie Vincent: Better Than Kiss?, Lizzy Borden, Manowar, Dokken, C.O.C., Ratt.............................$3–6
Sept. David Coverdale/Whitesnake, Europe Blitz America, Ratt: Backstage Bombast, King Diamond, Quiet Riot, Led Zeppelin, CJSS, The Cult, Y & T, The Rods, EZO, TNT, DC3, John Butcher...$3–6
Oct. Motorhead: The Men, the Myth, the Madness, Judas Priest: Life After Leather, Motley Crue, Waysted, Ace Frehley: Kiss o' Death, Tesla, Slayer, Megadeth, Pretty Maids, Ramones...$3–6
Nov. Kiss: Their Legacy of Wit, Def Leppard: 10 Years After, Motley Crue, Aerosmith: The Vacation's Over, Poison, Boston, Bon Jovi centerfold, Great White, The Cult, Grim Reaper, Raven, Gary Moore, Helloween $3–6
Dec. Sammy Hagar: Solo Shriek, W.A.S.P.: Return from Hell, Dio, Kiss: Video Fun, Heart: Beat of the Beasts, Loudness, Sacred Child, Anthem, Redd Kross, Faster Pussycat, Marillion, Motley Crue, Stryper $3–6

1988

Jan. Metallica: World Conquerers from the Garage, Def Leppard: Their Metal Boots, Poison: A Bizarre Photofeature, Jon Bon Jovi: Man or Superman?, Slayer, Dokken, Twisted Sister, Tsol, Exodus, Keel $3–6
Feb. Kiss: Why They're Still Cool, Stryper, Poison, Slade, Dri, Metallica, Helix, White Lion, Alice Cooper centerfold, Motley Crue, Voi Vod, Jetboy, Whitesnake $3–6
Mar. Def Leppard, Alice Cooper Out for Blood, Cinderella, Vinnie Vincent, Motley Crue, Megadeth, Great White, Aerosmith, Bathory, Rush, Circle Jerks, Shok Paris, Bloodgood, Flipper..$3–6
Apr. Dokken, Anthrax, Def Leppard, Great White, Iron Maiden: Eddie's Revenge, Metallica, Stryper, W.A.S.P., Lizzy Borden, Kiss, Motley Crue, Triumph, Keel, Ratt, Poison, Motorhead, Vinnie Vincent..$3–6
May Stryper: Money Talks, Lita Ford Strips, Thrash Photo Spectacular, AC/DC, Poison, Guns 'n' Roses, White Lion, Helloween, David Chastain, Black 'n' Blue, Zodiac Mindwarp, Overkill..$3–6
June Motley Crue: Studio Shocker, Queensryche, Girlschool, Bon Jovi, L.A. Guns, Dokken, Poison, Verbal Assault, Zodiac Mindwarp, Sanctuary...................................$3–6
July Iron Maiden, Killer Van Halen & Metallica Posters, The New Ozzy, Joe Satriani, Scorpions, Dokken...$3–6
Nov. Judas Priest Ram On, Joan Jett: Runaway Child Running Wild, Ace Frehley: Give Him a Great Big Kiss, Deep Purple, Soul Asylum, Fifth Angel, Testament...............$3–6
Dec. Stryper, Scorpions, Anthrax, Europe Play Ball, Jimmy Page, Leslie West, Quiet Riot, Vinnie Moore...$3–6

1989

Sept. Guns 'n' Roses: Axl Answers Everything, Bon Jovi in Concert, Ratt, The Cult, Skid Row, Def Leppard, Metallica Lowers the Boom, Def Leppard & L.A. Guns Super Pullout Poster $3–6

Oct. Guns 'n' Roses, Winger Exclusive, Giant Cinderella/Metallica Poster, Great White, Slayer, Alice Cooper, Joan Jett, Tora Tora, Skid Row, White Lion, Poison: Rappin' With Rikki, Faster Pussycat, Motley Crue, Mr. Big $3–6

Nov. Motley Crue, Winger, Skid Row, L.A. Guns, Great White, Bon Jovi, The Cult, Faster Pussycat, Exodus, Tesla, Badlands, White Lion...$3–6

1990

Jan. Aerosmith Pump it Up, Motley Crue: Feelin' Alright, Atomic Playboys, Killer Whitesnake, Tora Tora poster, Mr. Big, White Lion, Def Leppard, Law & Order, King Diamond, Ozzy Osbourne, Faster Pussycat, Soundgarden, Poison $3–6

CREEM CLOSE-UP METAL SPECIAL EDITION

1988

Savage/Scorpions Poster, Van Halen, Metallica, Kingdom Come, Killer Dwarfs, Sonic Youth, Yngwie Malmsteen, Dag Nasty, Nuclear Assault, Ronnie Montrose, Krokus ...$3–6

CREEM CLOSE-UP PRESENTS THE BEST OF CREEM

1988

#2 Bruce Springsteen: Rock 'n' Roll Glory Days, Motley Crue, Muddy Waters, Iggy Pop Profile, Frank Zappa, The Cure, Los Lobos, Run DMC, The Beastie Boys, David Lee Roth, R.E.M., Pink Floyd...$4–8

CREEM CLOSE-UP PRESENTS THRASH METAL

1988

#3 Exodus, Death, Celtic Frost, Hirax, The Florida Scene, Megadeth, Slayer..............$3–6

CREEM CLOSE-UP THRASH METAL

1988

Nov. Anthrax: Euphotic Reaction, Holy Terror, M.O.D.: Surf Cats from Hell, Connecticut Scene Report $3–6

1989

Nov. White Zombie, Excel, Cro-Mags, Bad Brains, Testament Spreads the Word, Anthrax/Slayer/Dark Angel poster, Exodus, King Diamond: Tales from Beyond, Annihilator.......$3–6

CREEM CLOSE-UP TRASH METAL

1987

#1 Metallica, Megadeth, Motorhead, Slayer, Metal Church, Metallica centerfold poster, includes the Encyclopedia of Thrash Metal, Speedmetal & Hardcore Bands...................$4–8

1988

#11 Metallica, Voi Vod, Anthrax, Megadeth, Inside the New York Scene, Thrash in the U.K..$3–6

CREEM COLLECTOR'S EDITION/BRUCE SPRINGSTEEN

1986

#1 The Early Years, The "Dark" Years, The Glory Days, The Concerts, Clarence Clemons, Miami Steve, Max Weinberg, includes full-color pullout poster $6–13

The Doors

Collecting
THE DOORS

The Doors were one of America's biggest selling groups of the sixties. They topped the charts with unforgettable hits like "Light My Fire," "Touch Me," "Hello, I Love You," and "Riders on the Storm." Their lead singer, Jim Morrison, turned out to be one of the most controversial artists of their time. He was known to be the first one to add psychedelic poetry to rock music. After his death in Paris in 1971, the group disbanded. Today they sell more records than in the sixties and still gain new followers. Their lives and music are featured in Oliver Stone's film about the group. Jim Morrison's grave in Paris is the most visited plot in Paris—each day more than 200 fans visit the grave.

Following is a list of Doors' memorabilia sold at auction.

Fully autographed copies of the first Door's Albums (signed by all four members); from $800
A copy of "L.A. Woman" with Jim Morrison's signature (signed a few days before he died) $7,000

Gold awards dedicated to one of the Doors..$18,000

Platinum awards for "Greatest Hits," "Waiting for the Sun," and "The Doors"....$4,500

An original copy of a Doors' Acetate (five copies are known to have been made); each $25,000

Autographed photo signed by all four Doors...$900–1,800

Autographed photo signed by Jim Morrison..$750–1,500

Jim Morrison's handwritten lyrics to "L'America"...$3,000

Jim Morrison's jacket, worn on "Morrison Hotel" cover......................................$7,500

Jim Morrison's high school yearbook including sketches and poems...................$13,000

Jim Morrison's handwritten poetry from Pan's sold to Morrison's estate............$80,000

More than ever, Doors memorabilia is now desired by both collectors and investors, with record prices being attained at auction and through private sale. The best reference source from which to learn about the Doors and to be informed of upcoming auctions and sales of memorabilia is the *Doors Quarterly Magazine.* This magazine, printed in English, is published by the Official Doors Fan Club, based at AM Oelvebach 5, D. 4150 Krefeld-Stratum 12, West Germany. It has existed since 1983 when Ray Manzarek himself told Rainer Moddemann (founder and editor) to start a fan club.

Since its inception, the fan club (the only authorized Doors fan club in the world) has been going strong and features the only fan magazine devoted entirely to Jim Morrison and the Doors. The fan club has regular contact with all three remaining Doors—Robby Krieger, Ray Manzarek, and John Densmore. It also has contact with their managers and friends—Danny Sugarman, Frank and Kathy Lisciandro, Rich Linnell, Linda Kyriazi, Jerry Hopkins, and photographer Henry Diltz.

Each issue features never-before-published photos, news about the Doors, old and new articles on Jim Morrison and the Doors, and a list of rare collectors' items for sale and auction. Each issue is at least 44 pages in length, and also includes a bonus poster. It is published every three months and is a must for the serious Doors fan. Subscription rate is $20 per year (four issues). Sample copies are also available for $5.

Direct all subscriptions and inquiries to: Doors Quarterly Magazine, AM Oelvebach 5, D. 4150 Krefeld-Stratum 12, West Germany; Phone: 02151–571862.

CREEM COLLECTOR'S SERIES/KISS

1987

#6 A Complete Guide to America's Hottest Band, Kiss Klassic Pix: Then & Now, Historical Stories, Gene Simmons Remembers, Records: 21 Pieces of Gold, Peter Criss & Bruce Kulick poster, eight-page centerfold—Kiss Before and After.....................................$6–13

CREEM GUITAR HEROES

1986

#3 Yngwie Malmsteen, Eddie Van Halen, Jimi Hendrix: The Legend Lives On, Jimmy Page, Jeff Beck, Eric Clapton, Andy Summers...$3–6

CREEM PRESENTS

1987

#10 Dec. Issue The Best of Metal Issue—Poison, Bon Jovi, Motley Crue, Kiss, Def Leppard, Metallica, Aerosmith, Ozzy Osbourne, Iron Maiden, Ratt, Rush, Van Halen, Cinderella, AC/DC, W.A.S.P., Judas Priest, Kiss centerfold $4–8

CREEM PRESENTS HITMAKERS/WOMEN ROCKERS OF THE 80S

1987

#8 Aug. Issue Madonna, Whitney Houston, The Bangles: Their Climb to the Top, Heart, Tina Turner, Chrissie Hynde, Belinda Carlisle, Joan Jett, Cyndi Lauper, Janet Jackson, Stevie Nicks, Christine McVie, Rosanne Cash, Aretha Franklin, Patti Smith, Sheila E., Lisa Lisa, A History of Girl Groups $4–8

CREEM PRESENTS MASTERS OF METAL

1988

#12 Aerosmith: Cosmic Blooze, Jimi Hendrix: Heaviest of the Heavy, Whitesnake, Kiss: Party Everyday, AC/DC, Iron Maiden, Megadeth, giant wall poster of Aerosmith & The Cure...$3–6

CREEM PRESENTS METAL LETTERS

1986

#2 Motley Crue: Why They're Number One, Van Halen, Black Metal, Ozzy Osbourne, Ratt, Stryper, Dio, Bon Jovi, Kiss, Censorship $2–4

CREEM PRESENTS METAL POSTER CALENDAR 1990 MAGAZINE

1990

Skid Row, Def Leppard, Guns 'n' Roses, Kiss, L.A. Guns, Lita Ford, Whitesnake, Winger, Bon Jovi, Cinderella, White Lion, Aerosmith, Great White, issue includes giant color pull-out poster $2–4

CREEM PRESENTS METAL POSTER MAGAZINE

1988

Motley Crue, Def Leppard, Bon Jovi, Poison, Van Halen, Kiss, Metallica, Ozzy Osbourne, Ratt, Whitesnake, Dio, Jimmy Page, A Year's Worth of Facts & Photos.....................$4–8

CREEM PRESENTS THE MONKEES

1987

#5 April Issue The Monkees Remember—Exclusive Interviews With Micky, David, Peter & Mike, Complete History & Impact, The TV Years, The Records, The Movie, The Future $4–8

CREEM PRESENTS MOTLEY CRUE
1986
Nov. Their Complete History, The Records, The Tours, Backstage Exclusive Interviews ...$4–8

CREEM PRESENTS ROCK '86: THE PEOPLES' CHOICE
1986
#1 U2: Band of the Year, Bruce Springsteen, Madonna: Sex Object, John Cougar Mellencamp, Heart Back on Top, Motley Crue, Dire Straits, R.E.M., Hooters $5–10
#2 Motley Crue: Why They're #1, Van Halen, Bon Jovi, Kiss, ELO, Ozzy Osbourne, Ratt, Stryper, Black Metal: Inspired by Satan $3–6

1987
#7 Motley Crue: Is Their Reign Over?, Stryper, Metallica, Bon Jovi, Ozzy Osbourne, Ritchie Blackmore wall poster, Poison, Kirk Hammett posters $3–6

CREEM PRESENTS ROCK '87
1987
#4 R.E.M.: Return to Rockville, David Lee Roth, Tina Turner, The Monkees, Run DMC, Madonna, Van Halen, Prince, Whitney Houston, The Church, Motley Crue, ZZ Top, Cyndi Lauper, The Smiths, Metallica, Ozzy Osbourne, Janet Jackson, Gene Loves Jezebel, Screaming Blue Messiahs, Peter Case........................$3–6

CREEM SPECIAL EDITION/THE COMPLETE LED ZEPPELIN STORY
1980
Winter Issue. The Page Memoirs, Candid Conversations With Jimmy Page, Robert Plant: His Tragedy & the Long Road Back, 12 Years on Top, Behind the Scenes, Led Zeppelin poster........................$9–18

CREEM SPECIAL EDITION/GUITAR HEROES OF ROCK 'N' ROLL
1982
Jan./Feb. Jimi Hendrix, Keith Richards, Jimmy Page, Jeff Beck, Eric Clapton, Eddie Van Halen, Dave Edmunds, Pete Townshend, Leslie West, Bruce Springsteen, Rick Nielsen, Ted Nugent, Neil Young, Duane Allman, Angus Young & More, includes a full-color Keith Richards wall poster $8–16

CREEM SPECIAL EDITION/THE POLICE
1982
July/Aug. In-depth Interviews, Rare Photos, Police Interrogations, Photo History, Double Pullout Poster $5–10

CREEM SPECIAL EDITION/THE ROLLING STONES
1981
Oct./Nov. An Intimate Interview with Mick Jagger, Keith Richards: Rock's Greatest Guitarist, Bill Wyman & Charlie Watts Talk, Ron Wood, Complete Stones' Discography, The '81 Tour........................$5–10

CREEM SPECIAL EDITION/VAN HALEN
1982
May/June From the Beginning: A Complete History, Outrageous Interviews, Hot Photos & Double-size Pullout Poster $5–10

1989

Sept. Guns 'n' Roses, Bon Jovi in Concert, Metallica, White Lion, Ratt, The Cult, Def Leppard, Anthrax, Exodus, Helloween...$2–3

Nov. Predictions for the 90s, Motley Crue, Winger, Skid Row, L.A. Guns, Bon Jovi, Britny Fox, Testament, Great White, Poison, Badlands, The Cult, Faster Pussycat................$2–3

CREEM'S AMERICAN BAND

1984

Nov. Exclusive Interviews With Judas Priest, Glen Tipton, Yngwie Malmsteen, Motley Crue, Eddie Van Halen, Kiss, Accept, The Scorpions, Joan Jett....................................$3–6

1985

Jan. Special Exclusive Interview Issue—Interviews With Huey Lewis, John Entwistle, Gary Moore, Weinberg, Porcaro...$2–4

Mar. Stevie Wonder Exclusive Interview, Joey Ramone...$2–4

CREEM'S ROCK 'N' ROLL CALENDAR AND DATEBOOK

1981

Issue includes 12 full-color poster pin-ups of Led Zeppelin, Pat Benatar, Debbie Harry, The Who, The Rolling Stones & Elvis Costello, Rock History: All the Important Days of Rock
....$3–6

CREEM'S ROCK SHOTS

1981

Fall Debbie Harry, Bob Marley: 1945–1981, The Clash, David Lee Roth, Pat Benatar: Women Unchained, Grace Slick, The Police, Judas Priest, Van Halen, Keith Richards, Bruce Springsteen, Bob Seger, Elvis Costello, Pete Townshend, Queen, The B-52's $3–6

1982

Mar./Apr. The Rolling Stones: Rolling Across America, The Police Picture Postcards, Van Halen, Rolling Stones poster, Journey, Foreigner, The Pretenders, Pat Benatar, The Go-go's, Kim Carnes, Devo, REO Speedwagon...$3–6

Dec./Jan. Van Halen, The Go-go's, Joan Jett, Stevie Nicks, Debbie Harry, Martha Davis, The Who, Rolling Stones, The Clash, Elvis Costello, Ted Nugent, Robert Plant, John Cougar $3–6

1983

June The Who's Farewell Tour '82, The Clash, Van Halen, Stray Cats, Keith Richards, Joan Jett, Prince, Adam Ant, David Bowie, Men at Work, Missing Persons, Bruce Springsteen.........$3–6

Nov. U.S. Festival Photo Scrapbook: 12 Pages With David Bowie, Van Halen, The Clash, The Pretenders, Judas Priest & Others, Stray Cats, Quiet Riot, The Fixx, The Eurythmics......$3–6

1984

Mar. Jimmy Page, Quiet Riot, David Lee Roth, Angus Young, Keith Richards & Jerry Lee Lewis, ZZ Top, Mick Jagger, Van Halen, Andy Summers, Genesis, Kiss, David Bowie ...$3–6

July David Lee Roth, Motley Crue, The Romantics, John Cougar, The Eurythmics, ZZ Top, The Pretenders, Van Halen poster, Mick Jagger, Cyndi Lauper, Huey Lewis, Michael Jackson, Ozzy Osbourne...$3–6

Oct. Judas Priest, The Pretenders, Scorpions, Motley Crue, The Clash, Berlin, The Go-go's, The Cars, Loverboy, Nena, Billy Idol, ZZ Top & Prince double poster, The Jacksons, John Cougar..$3–6

1985

Feb. Prince: Up With Purple, David Lee Roth, Twisted Sister, Ratt, Paul McCartney, Bruce Springsteen, Boy George, Hall & Oates, The Bangles, Kiss, Patti Smith....................$3–6

Apr. David Lee Roth, Motley Crue, U2, Pat Benatar: The New Bob Dylan, Iron Maiden, Ratt, Prince, Quiet Riot, Bruce Springsteen, Lita Ford, Bion Jovi, ZZ Top, Bryan Adams, W.A.S.P. $3–6

Oct. The Exposed Madonna: Virgin Tour Photos, Wham, Ratt, Katrina & the Waves, Bruce Springsteen, Julian Lennon, Bon Jovi, REM, 'Til Tuesday, Bryan Adams $3–6

1986

Apr. Sting: From Music to Movies, Madonna: What's Next?, Billy Idol, Duran Duran, Adam Ant: Behind the Scenes, Simple Minds, Wham, A-Ha, Corey Hart, Michael J. Fox, Tears for Fears $2–4

1987

Jan. Duran Duran, Arcadia, A-Ha, David Lee Roth, Bananarama: Their Secrets, The Monkees, Dweezil Zappa, A-Ha poster, The New Edition, U2, Whitney Houston, Tears for Fears, Level 42...$2–4

July Dweezil Zappa, Cyndi Lauper, The Monkees, Cinderella, Bon Jovi double poster, The Bangles, Duran Duran, The Jets, Genesis, Janet Jackson, Kirk Cameron $2–4

1990

Jan. New Kids on the Block Special Containing Many Photos, Bon Jovi: The True Wedding Story, Paula Abdul, Bobby Brown, Milli Vanilli, Skid Row $2–3

CREEM'S SMASH ROCK HITMAKERS OF 1981 MAGAZINE

1981

Nov./Dec. REO Speedwagon, Foreigner, Journey, Jefferson Starship, The Moody Blues, Electric Light Orchestra, The Rolling Stones, AC/DC, Bruce Springsteen, Billy Squier, Bob Seger, Tom Petty, Pat Benatar, The Police, Kim Carnes, Debbie Harry, REO poster..$3–6

D

DAILY PLANET (Tabloid)

All issues $3–6

DAVE CLARK FIVE (Charlton Publications)

1965

#1 & #2 ....$5–10

DATEBOOK

1966

Spring All About the Beatles, America's Top DJs Interview the Beatles, Beatles Love Poems, Sally Field: Gidget, The Byrds, David McCallum, The Rolling Stones, Sonny & Cher, Herman's Hermits, The Beach Boys, Peter, Paul & Mary, The Yardbirds, DC5, James Brown, Donovan, Bob Dylan: Poet or Phony? $15–30

Sept. Paul McCartney: "It's a Lousy Country Where Anyone Black is a Dirty Nigger," John Lennon: Rock 'n' Roll & Christianity, Len Barry, Scott Walker, Bob Dylan: "Message Songs are a Drag" $12–25

Oct. Paul McCartney Exclusive: The Marriage of Paul & Jane Bird, Walker Brothers: Please Come Home, All About the Beatles, Secret Vacation for Ringo & John, Bob Dylan, Lovin' Spoonful, Lunch With Peter Noone, Troggs, Small Faces, Dennis Wilson...$12–25

Dec. Paul McCartney Talks About Jane, All About the Beatles, The Monkees, What the Beach Boys Hid from You, On the Road With the Beatles, Donovan's Pad, Yardbirds, Peter & Gordon, Beatle Poetry, Interviews With the Rolling Stones, Raiders, Hermits, Jay & the Americans & The Lovin' Spoonful...$12–25

1969

July The Beatles & the Big Group Break-ups, Will the Beatles be Next?, Paul McCartney's Wedding, Mick Jagger Talks About Stones' Capers, Lulu's Wedding, Janis Joplin: Her Personal Protest, The Doors: Jim Morrison's Philosophy, Canned Heat, Tom Jones, Interviews With Mary Wells, Country Joe & Boyce & Hart, Jefferson Airplane $20–40

Nov. Glen Campbell: A Past He Wants to Forget, Bee Gee Woes, John Kay Off Guard, 12-page Beatles section, Raiders Secrets, Buffy Sainte-Marie, The Union Gap, Mary Hopkin, Jim Morrison's Poem for Brian Jones, Janis Joplin, Everly Brothers: Then & Now, Lulu & Maurice Gibb, Jeannie C. Riley, Iron Butterfly, Stones $15–30

1970

Sept. Exclusive: Why Paul McCartney Quit the Beatles—The Inside Story, Mick Jagger on Sex & Love, Festivals 1970, The Doors: Interview with John Densmore, Joe Cocker, Twiggy: Her Life Today, The Association, The Byrds, Fifth Dimension, Three Dog Night, Ravi Shankar, Delaney & Bonnie, Bob Dylan & Johnny Cash $15–30

All other issues $15–50

DETAILS
1987
Aug. Debbie Harry cover & feature story: Unharried Debbie at Home, Michael Monroe: Up from Hanoi Rocks..$10–20

DIG
1961
Jan. Annette Funicello, Why Dion Left the Belmonts, The Secret Dreams of the American Bandstand Regulars, Connie Stevens Surprise Package, Portrait of Troy Donahue & Bobby Darin..$15–30
June Troy Donahue, Annette Funicello's Beauty Secrets, Bobby Vee's Embarrassing Moment..$12–25
Aug. The Incredible Jack Chapmam, Tuesday Weld, Brian Hyland..........................$10–20
Oct. Frani Giordano's Scrapbook, The Jack Chaplain Story....................................$10–20
Dec. Bobby Rydell..$10–20

1962
Mar. Flashback Star Calendar, Exclusive Report on Bandstand, Troy Donahue, Dick Chamberlain..$10–20
May Dick Chamberlain, Dig Defends Chubby Checker, Natalie Wood....................$10–20
Aug. James Dean: The Miracle of James Dean, Why Bandstand is Going Down the Tube, World's Largest Picture of Vince Edwards...$20–40
Oct. Vince Edwards, Dick Chamberlain, Connie Stevens, Teen Stars Report Cards, 74 Teen Stars Wallet Photos..$10–20

1963
Feb. Johnny Crawford Feature Scoop & Pinup, Ann-Margret, Connie Stevens, Dick Chamberlain, Paul Petersen's Puzzle Page..$10–20
Mar. 1963 Trajen Awards, Dick Chamberlain, Vince Edwards, Paul Petersen, Bobby Picket..$10–20
Apr. Vince Edwards, Dick Chamberlain's Twin, Elvis Presley Profile....................$10–20
May Dick Chamberlain, Seven Questions Hayley Mills Couldn't Answer, Shelley Fabare's Farewell..$10–20
July Ann-Margret, Connie Stevens, Dick Chamberlain Asks 47 Embarrassing Questions, Vince Edwards..$10–20

1964
Oct. The Beatles: Have the Beatles Had It?, Annette Funicello.................................$15–30

DISCOVERIES
1988
Jan./Feb. #1 Elvis Presley Interviewed, Buddy Holly: Separating Fact from Fiction......$2–5
Mar./Apr. #2 Donovan Story & Discography, Ketty Lester, Dwight Yokum, Beatles Memorabilia: A Collector's Guide, Early Elvis Presley Concert & Interview.....................$2–4
May/June #3 Janis Joplin, Hank Williams Jr., Buddy Holly & the Crickets, Beach Music, Beatlediscs..$2–4
July/Aug. #4 Peggy Lee: 30 Years of Fear, The Beatles on Compact Disc, Justin Tubb, Is Elvis Presley Alive?: A Most Incredible Story, Elvis Presley in Print..........................$2–4
Oct. #5 Elvis Presley, Rick Nelson, The Earliest Chuck Berry Recordings, The Archies, The Ron Dante Story..$2–4
Nov. Creedence Clearwater Revival/John Fogerty, The Doug Clifford Interview, Willie Nelson..$2–4
Dec. #6 Captain Beefheart & His Magic Band, Zoot Horn Rollo interview, Johnny Okeefe, Sid King & the Five Strings, The Latest Jailhouse Rock Discovery............................$2–4

1989
Jan. #7 Elvis Presley's First Recordings, Counting the Elvis Presley Cover Songs, A Year in the Life of James Browne..$2–4

Feb. Beatles' International Picture Discography, Beatles' Novelty Recordings, Did the Beatles Really Ruin the Music? $2–4

Mar. #8 Joan Jett & the Blackhearts, Joan Jett Propelled, Little Anthony Interviewed, Elvis Presley Meets the Jones Brothers, Buddy Holly & the Space Shuttle, The Beatles, Yesterday's Memories: The Crickets, The Sixties: Part One...$3–6

Apr. #9 Dick Clark: Bandstand to Golden Greats, Dick Clark: An American Legend, Roy Orbison: When the Legend Began, Roy Orbison: London, England 1966, Tony Orlando, The Sixties Part II $2–4

May #10 George Jones: The Lone Star Legend, The Return of Big Brother: An Interview With J.P. Richardson, Kenny Rogers & Dolly Parton in Concert, The History of Records, The Blenders, The Sixties Part III, Lacy J. Dalton $2–4

June #11 Judy Garland: "I Could Go on Singing," Ann-Margret: More Than Meets the Eye, Ann-Margret: Discography & Filmography, Skeeter Davis, Susan Anton $2–4

July #12 Frank Sinatra: The Capitol Years, Sinatra: 50 Years of Unusual Songs, Ted Nugent interview, Jeff Healey..$2–4

Aug. Elvis Presley on TV, Elvis Picture Discs, Dee Presley's Untold Story, Eastern Bloc Elvis, Dean Martin, Paul Horn..

Sept. Marty Robbins: A 20th-Century Drifter, The Buckinghams: An Interview with Carl Glamerse, Randy Travis, Elvis Presley on TV Part II, Frank Sinatra Part II, The Rocketones...$2–4

Oct. The Beach Boys: Music Myths & Memories, Annette (Funicello): America's Favorite Mouseketeer, The Honeys interview..$2–4

Nov. The Hollies: 25 Years in Harmony, The Yardbirds, Keeping the Faith in Eric Burdon, A Quick Visit With Yoko Ono, The British Invasion, Frank Sinatra Part III, Ronnie Lane Speaks $2–4

Dec. Tony Williams interview, B.B. King interview, Bobby "Blue" Bland, Frank Sinatra Part IV $2–4

1990

Jan. Melanie: Prematurely Blonde, Poco: Creating a New Legacy, NRBQ: What's in an Acronym?, The Madonna Picture Discs, Sandy Denny & Fairport Convention................$2–4

Feb. The Sensual World of Kate Bush, Johnny Otis: In His Own Words, Ritchie Valens: The Spirit Continues, Frank Sinatra Part V, The Busters...$2–5

Mar. Nat King Cole: Unforgettable, Connie Francis: Among Her Souvenirs, The Many Faces of David Bowie, Vanilla Fudge: An Interview with Carmine Appice & Mark Stein, Roland James..$2–4

Apr. Pop Hits of the Pacific Northwest, The Sonics, The Ventures interview, The Kingsmen $2–4

May Billy Vera: At This Moment, Del Shannon Interviewed, Archie Bell, Bubble Puppy, Johnny Vincent, Jerry La Croix...$2–4

June Teresa Brewer: Still Making Music, Music, Music, Renaissance of Progressive Rock, Interview With Jimmy Beaumont of the Skyliners, Whiting Girls, The Coachmen, The Vibranaires $2–4

July Led Zeppelin Discography, Robert Plant in Manic Nirvana, Jimmy Page: The Early Years, Rarest of the Rare: Led Zeppelin Memorabilia, How They Became the Beatles, Cliff Richard: Nearly Famous Now, The Del-Vikings interview $3–6

Aug. Elvis Presley, Joe Espositi interview, Collecting Elvis Presley Compact Discs, Led Zeppelin Discography Part II, 35 Shades of Black: The Johnny Cash Story, The Box Tops............$2–4

Sept. Jimi Hendrix: What is Hendrix Worth?, Frank Sinatra Part VII, Aerosmith: Back in the Saddle Again, Frank Valli & the Four Seasons...$2–4

Oct. Screamin' Jay Hawkins story & interview, The Kosmic Spark of Janis Joplin, Big Brother & the Holding Company, Nanci Griffith, An Interview With Ramblin' Jack Elliot, Still Crazy After All These Years—The Ramones Enter the Nineties.........................$2–4

Nov. Nancy Wilson Exclusive Interview, special feature on The Four Aces, Interviews with Donna Marie, Josefus & Mark Barkan $2–4

1991

Feb. British Beat Issue, The Dave Clark Five, Badfinger, Chapter One: "Music History for Earthlings (More or Less)," Crispian St. Peters..$2–4

D.I.Y. (Tabloid)

All issues $3–6

DOWN BEAT

All issues $2–5

DRUMMER (Tabloid)

1976

#423 Tales of Jethro Tull: Too Old to Rock-&-Roll, Cheap Trick: A Novel Approach to Rock 'n' Roll, BTO, Gentle Giant..$4–8
#426 Frank Zappa, The Allman Brothers' Last Lick: Got Love if You Want It, Rory Gallagher: Going Against the Grain..$3–6

1977

#435 The Strawbs: Ye Old Strawbs—A New Mood, Climax Blues Band, Chick Corea, Kris Kristofferson $3–6
#475 Tom Waits: For No Man, Leo Sayer, Kansas, The Beatles Forever $2–4
#478 Keith Jarrett Exclusive: New Music in the Wind, Phoebe Snow: Learning to Love Thy Self, Susan Dey..$2–4
#479 Burt Reynolds, Kris Kristofferson..$2–4
#480 Nona Hendryx: Out on Her Own $2–4
#481 Johnny Rotten: Bring Me the Head of Johnny Rotten, Ray Charles, Earth, Wind & Fire, Rod Stewart..$3–6

1978

#503 Slyvester Stallone, Jefferson Starship Grounded, Chuck Mangione......................$2–4
#525 Still Neal Young After All These Years, REO Speedwagon, The Who..............$2–4

1979

#551 Boomtown Rats: Life in the Rat Trap, Bubblegum Boogie With the Rubinoos, Sex Pistols: Nothing Rotten, Johnny..$2–4
#552 Issue is marked #551 by error.... No Sad Songs for Sad Cafe........................$1–2
#555 George Benson: Selling Records or Selling Out?, Suzi Quatro $2–4

DYNAMIC TEEN HEROES

1978

Oct. #7 Kiss: Will Cher Join Them?, Andy Gibb: Girl Watcher, Donny Osmond's Long Search is Over, Hardy Boys, John Travolta, Wings, Brooke Shields............................$5–10
Dec. #8 Spying on Kiss, Why Marie Osmond Left Home, John Travolta: Near Tragedy at His Wedding, Secrets of Shaun Cassidy, Andy Gibb, The Private Life of Robby Benson, The Real Kristy McNichol, Leif Garrett, Rod Stewart, Natalie Cole $5–10

E

EAST COAST ROCKER (Formerly *The Aquarian*)
1986

#1 Madonna: Making it in Her Own Way, On Her Own Terms, Pete Seeger interview, The Pogues, Chuck Berry, Ron Wood, Elvis Presley...$7–15

#2 Bob Dylan: What's Happening Here?, Jefferson Starship: Amazing Grace, Lou Reed, Jimmy Bufett, The Cure, 10,000 Maniacs..$5–10

#3 David Lee Roth: Diamond Dave Does it Alone, The Moody Blues: Does Anyone Know What Time it Is?, The New Church, PIL, Van Halen, Graham Nash interview, Van Morrison: In Philly $5–10

#4 The Ramones interview: Nobody's Perfect, Joe Jackson, The Eurythmics: Revenge, Elvin Bishop...$5–10

#5 Michael Been of the Call, The Monkees: The Summer Story in Philly, The Monkees: Deja Vu in Middle America, Neil Young: Still Strange After All These Years, The Feelies, Gary U.S. Bonds $5–10

#6 Katrina & the Waves interview, Queen: Still the Dragon Slayers, Joan Armatrading, X, The Smiths, Pharoah..$5–10

#7 Billy Joel: The Piano Man Heads for Home, Alice Cooper, Level 42, Paul Butterfield, The Psychedelic Furs, Fine Young Cannibals, David Steele interview: Off the Beat-en Path $5–10

#8 Big Country: Getting Taller, Tom Waits: Tom at Play, Talking With Richard Barone of the Bongos, Fleshtones, Paul McCartney...$4–8

#9 Steve Winwood: A Profile, Rick Nelson, Suicide: White Man's Civilization as it Really Is, MTV Awards Party $4–8

#10 R.E.M. interview, Emerson, Lake & Palmer, The Eurythmics: Enigmas are So Much Better, Paul Simon: A Mixed Bag, Bruce Springsteen, The Feelies, John Denver, David Bowie $4–8

#11 The Smithereens interview, John Lennon, Pet Shop Boys Pop Off, Annie Lennox: Sex Bomb, Journey, Steve Winwood, James Taylor: No More Fire, No More Rain, John Fogerty: Trying to Live Up to the Part, The Zombies...$5–10

#12 Elvis Costello: Blood & Chocolate, Joe Jackson, Bob Seger $4–8

#13 Cyndi Lauper Profile: The New Woman Taking Over, Sid & Nancy/Sex Pistols Film, Metallica, Pretenders, Elton John in Philly..$5–10

#14 Bananarama interview: Venus Envy, Doctor & the Medics, The Circle Jerks $5–10

#15 Iggy Pop interview: "I've Always Been a Regular Guy," Third World..............$5–10

#16 Talking Heads: More Than Middle Brow, Less Than a Cutting Edge, Billy Joel: Manipulation or Fine Art?, David Lee Roth: Arena Sex, Warren Zevon $4–8

#17 General Public interview, Huey Lewis & the News, Fairport Convention, Poison, John Prine, Arlo Guthrie...$4–8

#18 Orchestra Maneuvers in the Dark interview, The Pretenders: Pretending, Elvis Costello: Three Nights With Elvis, Lionel Richie..$4–8

#19 Doctor & the Medics, The Ramones: Old Soldiers of Punk Greet the Faithful, Johnny Paycheck, Boston, R.E.M. $4–8
#20 Joan Jett interview: "You Can't Back Off," Little Richard, Cyndi Lauper, Billy Idol: Only His Hairdresser Knows for Sure, Elliot Murphy interview, Johnny Winter, Gene Loves Jezebel, Iggy Pop: Rage Against the Dying of the Light $6–12
#21 Eric Clapton: A Strong Comeback From One of Rock's Forefathers, Robyn Hitchcock, Guadalcanal Diary interview, Love & Rockets, The Band $4–8
#22 Duran Duran, Jason & the Scorchers, James "Blood" Ulmer, Garland Jeffreys ...$4–8
#23 Bruce Springsteen: A Box of Bruce, Jackson Browne, Peter Gabriel: The Blend Wasn't Magic, Steve Ray Vaughn $4–8

1987

#24 Debbie Harry, Women in Rock, New Order, Jon Bon Jovi $5–10
#25 Metallica interview, Cyndi Lauper: No Colors Here—Just Shades of Glory.........$4–8
#26 Ray Davies of the Kinks: "I Am Determined Not to Forsake Music," David Lee Roth, Husker Du, Van Halen, Jason & the Scorchers, Georgia Satellites.................................$4–8
#27 The Beastie Boys interview, The Jim Morrison Legend, The Radiators, Bob Geldof, The Rainmakers interview $4–8
#28 The B-52's interview, Dave Edmunds, Johnny Thunder, The Beatles, Jerry Lee Lewis: Whole Lot of Achin' Goin' On...$4–8
#29 Bruce Willis, Crosby, Stills & Nash, Otis Rush, Spandau Ballet, Human League....$3–6
#30 Husker Du: Music is Our "Sanity Lever," Carl Perkins, The Roaches.................$3–6
#31 Joan Jett, Michael J. Fox, Bruce Hornsby, Billy Bragg, Husker Du, Gregg Allman, Dave Edmunds $4–8
#32 Special Music Directory Issue, The Smithereens..$3–6
#33 Dan Baird of the Georgia Satellites interview, The Kinks, The Return of the Hit Man, The Pretenders, Iggy Pop, Vanilla Fudge, Dickey Betts, Livingston Taylor, Dead Milkmen...$4–8
#34 Timbuk 3 interview: Keep it Small, Kate Bush short, Dave Clark, The Human League, David Bromberg, Sheila E. $4–8
#35 The The's Matt Johnson interview, Prince, Paul Young, Georgia Satellites...........$4–8
#36 Women in Music—Patty Smith, Linda Ronstadt, Dolly Parton, Emmylou Harris, Patti Labelle, Kinks, Richard Lloyd...$4–8
#37 U2, Colin Hay interview, Megadeth, B.B. King, Allman Brothers..........................$4–8
#38 Jerry Garcia/The Grateful Dead: Hey They Do Keep on Truckin', Three Cheers for the Doobie Brothers & U2, Joe Jackson/David Bowie/The Fall, Flesh for Lulu, Los Lobos, Julian Cope, Joan Jett: From the Hearts...$4–8
#39 Prince: His Purpleness Does it Again, Ratt/Poison $4–8
#40 Bryan Adams: The Reluctant Star, Paul Simon, Bon Jovi, Cinderella, A Private Moment With Ravi Shankar, C.C. Deville interview $4–8
#41 Fleetwood Mac: The Magic is Back—Hot Stuff for Early Summer Nights, Heart, Patti Smith, Elvis Presley, Nanci Griffith, The Roches Come Back for the Seventh Time....$6–12
#43 The Return of Tom Petty, Paul Butterfield, U2, Iron Maiden at Madison Square Garden, Kansas, Paul Simon at Radio City Music Hall, Pete Seger...$4–8
#44 Interview With Julian Cope, Exclusive U2 Concert Coverage, Buddy Holly, Crowded House interview, Lone Justice...$4–8
#45 Profile of Genesis: They Never Stop Moving, Rolling Stones, Whitney Houston, Patti Smith: Just Being Herself, Bo Diddley...$4–8
#46 Summer Concerts Issue, Patti Smith, Huey Lewis & the News, The Dead Boys, cover—Heart, Bangles, Madonna, Whitney Houston...$4–8
#47 Madonna—Women in Music: Carly Simon, Jennifer Rush, Ronnie Spector, Irene Cara, Whitney Houston, Jone Justine, John Mayall, Wang Chung (this issue is marked #48 in error) $4–8
#48 Women in Music—Cyndi Lauper, Carly Simon, Jennifer Rush, Irene Cara, Ronnie Spector, Whitney Houston, John Mayall...$4–8
#49 Bryan Adams Concert Exclusive, Michael Jackson, The Hooters: Staying Ahead of Sophoritis, Rodney Crowell interview, The Stranglers $3–6
#50 A Profile of Bob Dylan—Rainy Days, An Occasional Sun, The Cult, Anthrax, Cromags, Metal Church..$4–8

#52 Peter Gabriel Profile—Why It's Saint Peter Himself, Duran Duran, Ozzy Osbourne, Adriam Belew...$4–8

#56 Los Lobos interview, Billy Joel, Run DMC, Tom Waits, Todd Rundgren: Rundgrenmania...$3–6

#57 Roger Waters interview, David Bowie, XTC interview $3–6

#59 Simple Minds' Jim Kerr interview, Bruce Springsteen, David Bowie, Whitney Houston, Marshall Crenshaw: An Inspired Evening $3–6

#60 John Cougar Mellencamp Profile, Motley Crue, Whitesnake...............................$3–6

#61 Michael Jackson: He's Back & He's Bad, Tina Turner Concert Exclusive, Madonna, Michael Jackson: Alone at the Top, Billy Idol, The Cult, Neil Young.........................$4–8

#62 The Cars: An interview With Rick Ocasek & Greg Hawkes, The Beastie Boys, Motley Crue: That Old Primal Feeling...$4–8

#63 X: An interview with Exene Cervenka & John Doe, Georgia Satellites, Alice Cooper, Paul Stanley..$4–8

#64 R.E.M.: Interview with Mike Mills, Heart, Belinda Carlisle, Ace Frehley............$4–8

#65 Mick Jagger Profile: A Stone on His Own, Los Lobos, Taj Mahal, The Outfield, Glen Burtinick...$4–8

#67 Chuck Berry: The Man, the Myth & the Movie, Simply Red, Grim Reaper, Little Steven...$4–8

#68 An Interview With Marshall Crenshaw, Dan Fogelberg, Warren Zevon, Wendy Waldman $4–8

#69 Sting: A Profile of the Police, Def Leppard, Pink Floyd......................................$4–8

#70 Jethro Tull Returns, Stevie Nicks/Fleetwood Mac Concert Exclusive: Stumbling Through, Bon Jovi...$6–12

#72 The Doors—Then & Now: An interview With John Densmore & Ray Manzarek of the Doors, Guns 'n' Roses: Owning 1988...$6–12

#73 George Harrison: The Return of a Mystic, Meat Puppets, Husker Du, Alice Cooper..$4–8

#74 Ironweed: Local Kids Make Good, Stevie Wonder Profile $3–6

#75 The Celebration of Life: The Harry Chapin Tribute & an Interview With Bill Ayers of World Hunger Year, Aerosmith...$4–8

1988

#78 The Alarm Sounds Off: An interview With Mike Peters & Dave Sharp, The Debut from Terence Trent D'Arby...$4–8

#79 Issue is marked 1987 in error ... Joe Strummer interview: In and Out of the Clash, Bruce Springsteen & Michael Jackson, Madonna..$4–8

#80 Ry Cooper interview: A Roots Rock Originator, Hall of Fame Awards, Port Arthur Remembers Janis Joplin, Heart Break-up Rumors, Foreigner, Bruce Springsteen, Mick Jagger...$4–8

#81 A Look at David Lee Roth & "Skyscraper," Kiss Exclusive, Gladys Knight & the Pips, Sting, Frank Zappa...$4–8

#82 An Interview With the Pogues: A Longterm Accident, Bon Jovi $4–8

#83 Bene King interview, Sting: Live from Tampa, Talking With Keith Richards, The Del-Lords, Power Station interview...$4–8

#85 Talking With the Bo Deans, Whitesnake Exclusive, The Fall $3–6

#86 Exclusive Grammy Issue: Whitney Houston, Suzanne Vega, U2, They Might be Giants interview $3–6

#87 Talking With Nanci Griffith: "The Eyes of a Child," Exclusive: Bruce Springsteen Live from Philly, Underworld...$4–8

#88 Frank Zappa interview: Artist, Businessman, Politician, Sting, Robert Plant: A Tip of the Hat $4–8

#91 Robyn Hitchcock: Interview With the "Balloon Man" $3–6

#92 Poison interview, Club MTV, Cyndi Lauper, Can Madonna Survive? $4–8

#93 James Taylor & Joni Mitchell: The Return of the Singer/Songwriter, Jimmy Cliff interview...$4–8

#94 George Thorogood interview: "Born to be Bad," Sonic Youth $4–8

#95 Eric Clapton at the Crossroads: 25 Years at the Crossroads, Talking With Carl Perkins, 10,000 Maniacs, Arlo Guthrie...$4–8

#96 White Lion interview, Talking With Joe Satriani, John Cale, Madonna on Broadway: Critics in a Rage..$4–8

#97 The Latest from Bruce Hornsby & the Range, Christine Lavin interview, The Atlantic Records Party, Bruce Springsteen, The Smithereens...$4–8

#98 The Church interview, Swans Label, Paul McCartney................................$3–6

#99 Robert Plant: In and Out of Zeppelin, Steve Winwood, Moody Blues................$4–8

#101 Van Halen Exclusive: Thunder Rock & Much Lightning, Graham Parker: A Modest Success, Guns 'n' Roses, Pat Benatar, Iggy Pop...$4–8

#102 Bob Dylan: Another Chapter in the Legacy, Livingston Taylor, At Last: The Return of Patti Smith, Pink Floyd...$4–8

#103 Iggy Pop interview: He's Vacuuming His Way to Heaven, The Fall, The Pixies, Camper Van Bethoven, Squeeze..$5–10

#105 Judas Priest: Interview With Rob Halford, The Godfathers, Pharoah, Heavy Metal $4–8

#106 Richard Marx interview, Butthole Suffers, The Dreggs, Rodney Crowell, Gloria Estefan $4–8

#108 Talking With the Meat Puppets, Frank Zappa, Pete Seger Jailed, Bon Jovi Joins Drug Fight, Prince: Love, Sex, God, Heaven & Dancing, Timbuk 3, Tracy Chapman: Too Good to be a Star, Patti Smith & Brian Wilson: Two Strong Souls Return With Creativity Intact, Run DMC: A Report..$4–8

#109 Guns 'n' Roses interview: America Will Never be the Same, Prince Arouses Paris, Johnny Hates Jazz, Paul Winter $4–8

#110 Dweezil Zappa interview, Poison, Suzanne Vega, Bruce Springsteen, Testament, Destruction, Anthrax...$4–8

#115 Robert Cray interview, Jack Bruce, The Rascals: Fond Memories Rekindled.....$3–6

#116 Jackson Browne: Benefit for the Christic Institute, Andy Summers interview, Talking With Shawn Colvin, Erasure, The Escape Club, The Bangles, Everly Brothers, Pat Benatar $4–8

#117 Jimmy Page interview—On a Rock Foundation: New Approaches, Eric Keifer of Cinderella, Elton John, Iron Maiden, Ozzy Osbourne, Prince, Run DMC, Melanie $4–8

#118 Midnight Oil interview: The Fight Never Ends, Judas Priest, The Judds, The Beach Boys, John Lennon: Man or Monster?, The Grateful Dead: Doing it for Rainforests, Tom Rush $4–8

#119 The Feelies: Still the Next Big Thing, Prince: God & Sex at Madison Square Garden, Let's Active, Devo: Mark Mothersbaugh interview, They Might be Giants, Tom Waits, Sparks..$4–8

#120 Bon Jovi interview: Bring it All Back Home, The Roches, The Ramones, Michael Jackson: Too Much Candy Ain't so Dandy, Midnight Oil: Troubled Waters, Southside Johnny, Quiet Riot: No Pain, No Gain, Blue Oyster Cult's Buck Dharma interview..$4–8

#121 Ozzy Osbourne interview: What Am I Doing?—Vaudeville, Keith Richards, John Hiatt & the Goners, Hothouse Flowers interview, Skid Row, Slaughterhouse, Wet Wet Wet...$4–8

#122 UB40 Interview: England's Working Class Heroes, Paul McCartney Meets Husker Du, The Cavedogs, Tom Chapin...$3–6

#124 Metallica Breaks Through, Bon Jovi, Pink Floyd, B.B. King, Peter Beck of R.E.M. Special Feature...$3–6

#126 The Bangles: "We're Just Down-to-earth Gals"—interviews with Vicki & Debbie Peterson, Roy Orbison: 1936–1988—A True Original, John Denver, Youth in Judas Priest Case Dies, Michael Hedges interview. Rodney Crowell, Nanci Griffith $4–8

1989

#128 The Best of 1988—Roy Orbison, Van Halen, Brian Wilson, Vixen: These Girls Just Want to Rock Out, Warren Zevon, Southside Johnny....................................$4–8

#129 Michele Shocked: A Knee-jerk Anarchist, Dream Syndicate, The Waterboys, Kevin Meaney, Melissa Etheridge, Widespread Panic...$3–6

#130 Keith Richards & Ivan Neville: The Past & Future of Rock, Skid Row, Was (Was Not), Mike & the Mechanics, Transvision Vamp, Jeff Healey.....................................$4–8

#133 The Replacements: Interview With Paul Weterberg, Debbie Harry, Raging Slab, Black & White..$3–6

#134 The New Bohemians: An Interview With Edie Brickell, Lou Reed, Violent Femmes, Georgia Satellites, Tom Grant..$3–6

#135 Violent Femmes: An Interview With Gordon Gano, Roy Orbison, Ronnie Earl, Kitaro, Kirk Kelly, Bon Jovi to be Sued..$3–6

#139 Elvis Costello: Tales of a Sleeping Pit Bull, Poison, Telsa, Nick Cave, The Saints, Sting..$4–8

#140 Lyle Lovett, Fine Young Cannibals, Marc Almond, Bon Jovi, Guns 'n' Roses, Bruce Cockburn...$3–6

#141 Robyn Hitchcock interview: "Just an Ordinary Guy," David Crosby on Politics, Parenthood & Personal Triumphs, The Who..$3–6

#142 Ratt: Stephen Pearcy interview, Doro Pesch, Tesla, Suicidal Tendencies, Femme Fatale, Simply Red, Apollonia, Wendy & Lisa...$3–6

#143 Madonna & the Power of Prayer—Madonna & Music: No Other Woman Comes Close, Mick Fleetwood of Fleetwood Mac: Positive Stuff Feature Interview, The Reivers, Matt Dillon...$4–8

#144 XTC interview: "Gloriously Out of Time," Grace Pool......................................$3–6

#145 Richard Marx interview, Joe Jackson, Boy George, Indigo Girls, Nanci Griffith, Paquito D'Rivera, Tiny Tim...$3–6

#146 Great White interview: "A Fast-moving Freight Train," The Who Reunion Tour, Tom Petty, John Eddie, Warrent, King Diamond, Debbie Harry: Blondie Dips Once More into the Bleach..$4–8

#147 Joe Jackson interview: Carrying on With "Blaze of Glory," Lou Reed, Marley Marl, De Le Soul, Ice-T, Love & Rockets, Miracle Legion, Bon Jovi Croons, Meat Loaf, Tom Petty...$4–8

#148 Living Colour interview, R.E.M., Madonna, Pointer Sisters, The Bongos, Iggy Pop $3–6

#149 Cyndi Lauper interview: "Looking for the Center of the Song," Tom Tom Club, Phoebe Snow, Sting, Frank Zappa, Prince..$4–8

#150 John Cougar Mellencamp: The Little Bastard's Bitchin' Career, Radiators interview, Simple Minds, Matthew Sweet, The Neville Brothers, Alex Moore, Animotion, Ziggy Marley...$4–8

#151 Bon Jovi interview: "Maybe I'm Getting Older," Kingdom Come interview, Gary Moore, Extreme, Graham Parker, Swans...$4–8

#152 Bonnie Raitt interview, The Traveling Wilburys, Bon Jovi...............................$3–6

#154 10,000 Maniacs: Out of the Tribe, into the Zoo, Johnny Winter, Ringo Starr, Naughty Crissie Hynde Catches Hell, The Stern/Bon Jovi Fiasco, The Washington Squares.....$4–8

#155 Black Sabbath interview: Cozy Powell & Tony Tommi, Paul McCartney, Stray Cats, Fabulous Thunderbirds, Motley Crue...$4–8

#156 The Beastie Boys: Boys Will be Boys, Concrete Blonde, The Return of Edgar Winter, Prince: Holy Ambivalence...$4–8

#158 The Doobie Brothers interview: Rockin' Down That Same Highway Again, Pil, Cutting Crew, Loudon Wainwright...$3–6

#159 White Lion interview: "We're Trying to Give Something Back," Blue Murder, Mr. Big, Tin Machine, The Ramones, Adrian Belew...$3–6

#162 Film: *Wired*, The Pogues interview, Nitty Gritty Dirt Band, Soul II Soul, Neneh Cherry...$3–6

1990

#212 A Talk With Debbie Harry, Brian Wilson Loses First Round of Suit With Cousin, Chuck Berry & Child Abuse..$4–8

#217 Women in Music, Robert Plant, ZZ Top..$2–4

#218 to present...$2–3

EAST VILLAGE EYE

1982

#21 Soft Cell interview, Gang of Four...$3–6

Aug. Nina Hagen interview: "I Met Jesus on an Acid Trip," Richard Hell..................$3–6

1983

Apr. The Thompson Twins: High Tech Trio...$3–6

May Violent Femmes: Milwaukee's Non-violent Trio...$3–6

June The Blasters, Rank & File $3–6
Aug. Eurythmics: Annie Lennox interview $3–6

1984
Sept. Run DMC: Sucker MCs or Serious Rappers?, Billy Idol, John Sex $3–6

EBONY
1989
Oct. Tina Turner cover & feature story: "The Foreign Affairs of Tina Turner," issue includes beautiful color photos of Tina..$2–4

ELVIS (The Official Memorial Fan Club publication)
1978
Official Memorial Issue, A Message from Elvis Presley's Father, G.I. Blues, Elvis: Year by Year, includes full-page color pics $2–4

ELVIS: A PICTORIAL TRIBUTE (A poster magazine)
1977
The Last Tour, Exclusive Photographs & Story by Elvis' Brother $2–4

ELVIS: A TRIBUTE TO THE KING (Cousins Publications)
1977
#1 Issue includes color pullout poster, Elvis Presley as a G.I., Grief at Graceland, Love, Marriage & Divorce, In the Beginning..$3–6

ELVIS 1988 CALENDAR MAGAZINE (Harris Publications)
Issue includes daily events in the life of Elvis Presley..................................$3–6

ELVIS IN CONCERT (Bat Productions)
1987
#1 Issue contains 34 color pages of Elvis Presley in concert, Elvis' Life from Dirt Poor to Multimillionaire, Why Elvis Never Lost Touch With His Fans $2–4

ELVIS: ONE YEAR LATER (Dell)
1978
Fall Exclusive Never-before-published Photos of Elvis, The Mystery Girl in Elvis' Life, The Elvis Imitators, centerfold poster $3–6

ELVIS PRESLEY (Charlton)
All issues..$5–10

ELVIS PRESLEY MEMORIAL EDITION MAGAZINE
(Ideal Publishing)
1977
#3 Special Memorial Edition, Remembering His Life, Elvis in the Movies, His Mother: A Tribute, The Girls Who Taught Him About Life, His Life With Priscilla, Milestones of His Career..$3–6

ELVIS PRESLEY: THE LIFE & DEATH OF (A Manor magazine)
1977
Collectors' Issue—The Early Years, His Love Life, poster, The Final Years & His Tragic Funeral, The Hit Records & Movies..$3–6

*ELVIS PRESLEY
MEMORIAL EDITION,*
1977, #3

ELVIS, 1988 CALENDAR

*ELVIS: THE LEGEND
LIVES ON,* 1978, #1

*ELVIS: THE KING
LIVES ON,* 1987

ELVIS IN CONCERT,
1987

*ELVIS, A PICTORIAL
TRIBUTE,* 1977

*ELVIS: ONE YEAR
LATER,* 1978, FALL

*ELVIS, THE TRIALS &
TRIUMPHS,* 1978, May

*ELVIS: 10TH
ANNIVERSARY
(CELEBRITY SPOTLIGHT),*
1987, #1

ELVIS: THE KING LIVES ON, 1987

ELVIS . . . REMEMBERED, 1979, Aug.

THE ELVIS YEARS, 1956–1977, 1979, #1

THE ELVIS YEARS, 1979, #2

EXCLUSIVELY ELVIS, 1987, FALL, #3

ELVIS PRESLEY, THE LIFE AND DEATH OF, 1977

ELVIS, THE ONLY WOMAN ELVIS EVER LOVED, 1977–1978

ELVIS: A TRIBUTE TO THE KING, 1977, #1

ESQUIRE, 1980, Nov.

ELVIS REMEMBERED (Ideal's Celebrity Series magazine)
1979
#5 Elvis Photo Album: Loads of Intimate Family Pix, His Women, His Films, His Concerts, Elvis Auctions, includes 35 color pin-ups $2–4

ELVIS: THE KING LIVES ON (Tempo Publishing)
1987
#1 Issue includes two lifesize portrait wall posters, complete guide to all his movies & records, His Heart of Gold, His Rags to Riches Story, over 100 photographs..................$3–6

ELVIS: THE KING LIVES ON POSTER MAGAZINE
1987
Special Anniversary Issue, opens to become a two-sided 17″ × 22″ color wall poster, rare photos of Elvis in concert..$2–4

ELVIS: THE LEGEND LIVES ON (Manor Books)
1978
All New Memorial Edition—The Elvis Imitators, Inside Graceland, Elvis Presley Discography & Filmography, issue includes color wall poster, rare photos & movie stills, Elvis Memorabilia..$3–6

EIVIS: THE ONLY WOMAN ELVIS EVER LOVED
1977–1978
Priscilla Presley's Story, Why He Couldn't Forgive Her, Rare Pix $2–4

ELVIS: THE TRIALS AND TRIUMPHS
OF THE LEGENDARY KING OF ROCK-&-ROLL
1976
May A Tattler Special Issue—His Bizarre Private Life, His Personal Horoscope, His Luxurious Lifestyle, The Women in His Life..$2–4

ELVIS YEARS (A Sterling magazine)
1979
#1 1956–1977, Issue includes 42 loving stories from leading magazines from 1959–1977 with 36 Elvis magazine covers in color, Elvis' Last Words, Intimate Interviews, The Greatest Elvis Stories Ever $3–6
#2 A Loving Tribute to the King: 1957–1977, 1959: 1001 Facts About Elvis Presley, 1977: The Final Tour of the King, His Fabulous Life in 32 Color Portraits, Special Color Pin-up Section $3–6

ESQUIRE
1980
Nov. John Lennon's Private Life: A Madcap Mystery Tour...$2–4

EXCLUSIVELY ELVIS (Presley)
1987
Fall #3 Ten Years Later: A Decade of Devotion, Memories: The Stars Remember Elvis, The Concert Years, Rare Color Photos, The Selling of Elvis, issue includes rare photos from the private collection of Jim Curtin..$3–6

EYE, 1968, Mar. (#1)

EYE, 1968, Aug. (#6)

EYE, 1968, Sept. (#7)

EYE, 1968, Nov. (#9)

EYE, 1969, Mar. (#13)

EYE, 1969, May (#15)

EYE (Hearst Publications)

1968

Mar. #1 Donovan: Pop Visionary, Jimi Hendrix mention in *Eye*'s Guide to Rock, Creem major feature with double-page color photos, Ravi Duck cartoon featuring the Beatles, issue includes the big fat wall poster in psychedelic color $25–75
Apr. #2 The Internal Woody Allen, Beau Bridges $20–40
May #3 Ravi Shankar Raps, Mick Jagger portrait poster, The Rascals Review, Jimi Hendrix Review—Axis: Bold as Love, New York: Home to Rock's Greatest, Procol Harum Songbook, The Who: The Last of the Pop Groups, Aretha Franklin, issue includes full-page color poster ad for *Speedway* starring Elvis Presley & Nancy Sinatra..............................$25–50
June #4 Janis Joplin & Grace Slick: The Queen Bees of San Francisco, Arlo Guthrie feature story, Country Joe & the Fish, Jimi Hendrix wall poster $50–100
July #5 The Super Psychedelic Soul of Jumpin' Jimi Hendrix, The Persecution & Assassination of Rock-&-Roll, as Performed by the Jimi Hendrix Experience—Under the Direction of Jumping Jimi Himself, issue includes a two-page color photo spread of Jimi Hendrix, rock portfolio containing color photos of Jimi Hendrix, The Who, Jack Bruce, Roger Daltry, The Soft Machine, B.B. King & Pete Townshend, Hugh Hefner Raps......................$35–75
Aug. #6 The Bob Dylan Gang: Positively 4th Street, Brian Wilson: The Beethovan of Rock, The Beatles & The Blue Meanies poster & feature, Tiny Tim, Peter Noone: Mrs. Brown Review...$25–50
Sept. #7 John Lennon cover & feature: 101 Hours With John Lennon & Paul McCartney, Bob Dylan Returns poster page, Rock Jamming With Traffic, Arthur Brown..........$20–40
Oct. #8 The Doors' Jim Morrison Raps, Big Pink $30–60
Nov. #9 The Beach Boys: Riding the Crest, Mick Jagger Raps About Politics, Movies & Money, Aretha Franklin: The Lady of Soul, Grace Slick & Frank Zappa: What Turns Them On, The Byrds: Phoenixes Forever, B.B. King, Traffic: A Tight Little Band Getting Bigger all the Time, Newport Folk Festival '68, Janis Joplin, Joan Baez, Arlo Guthrie.....$20–40
Dec. #10 Candice Bergen: Making a Film in Rome, The Bee Gees: Are They as Sweet as They Sound?, God Bless Tiny Tim, Janis Joplin photo & review, At Home With Harry Nilsson, Peggy Lipton, Roger McQuinn, Eric Burdon, Van Dyke Parks, Canned Heat's Bob "The Bear" Hite, Joni Mitchell & John Phillips, Randy Newman: Bittersweet Romantic, *Eye*'s First Annual Rock 'n' Roll Poll featuring a Jimi Hendrix photo $17–35

1969

Jan. Beauties in Baby Sweaters, Private Wardrobes: Peek into the Closets of Jimi Hendrix, Peter Fonda, Buffy St. Marie & Liza Minelli, Abbie Hoffman, Smothers Brothers, Jimi Hendrix review: Electric Ladyland, Blood, Sweat & Tears: Still Looking for Their Finest Hour, Al Kooper Interviews Al Kooper...$25–50
Feb. Steve McQueen: Centerpunching, Beauty Secrets of the Super Girls—Olivia Hussey, Dionne Warwick, Janis Ian, Peggy Lipton, Tim Hardin.............................$12–25
Mar. The Rolling Stones: Drugs & Young Girls—Absolute Dirt, Arlo Guthrie Filming *Alice's Restaurant*, The Beatles, Bill Graham: The P.T. Barnum of Rock 'n' Roll, Joe Cocker: England's Newest Raving Rocker $20–40
Apr. Boys & the Pill, Everly Brothers, Jeff Beck: A Weekend Gig in San Francisco, At Home With New York's Pop Stars: Richie Havens, Steve Katz, Janis Ian, Jill O'Hara & Woody Allen, Dionne Warwick interview, The Rolling Stones Part II: The Easy Life of a Wicked Band $20–40
May Sexy Nice Girls in Summer Underwear, Laura Nyro: New York Princess, Dustin Hoffman Graduates, The Diet Plans of Jim Morrison, Mick Jagger, Sly Stone, Wilson Picket...$15–30

F

FACES ROCK (Captain Jack Publications)

1984

Mar. AC/DC's Angus Young, Black Sabbath interview, Rainbow, Hall & Oates, Paul Rogers, Joe Perry, Robin Gibb, Juice Newton, Rainbow, Joan Jett: A Hard Rockin' Centerfold, Michael Stanley Band..$3–6

Apr. David Lee Roth: Van Halen's Sexy Bad Boy, Adam Ant Strips Down, Billy Idol, Black Sabbath: A Marriage Made in Heaven, Van Halen giant poster, Rodney Dangerfield interview $3–6

May Ozzy Osbourne: Diary of a Mad Housewife, Michael Jackson: *Thriller*, Asia in Asia, Eurythmic Mania, Elton John, Duran Duran...$3–6

Aug. Scorpions, "My Lost Weekend With Van Halen," Making a Motley Crue Video, Queen's Brian May, The Pretenders interview, Nena $3–6

Sept. David Lee Roth, Cyndi Lauper, Nikki Sixx of Motley Crue, Night Ranger, Queen's Freddie Mercury interview, Bruce Springsteen..$3–6

Nov. Ratt: Back for More, Prince, Scorpions, Quiet Riot's Kevin Dubrow, Billy Squier & Helix, Jacksons: What Price Victory, Life Ford, INXS, Dan Aykroyd $3–6

Dec. Billy Squier, Joan Jett, Making a Twisted Sister Video, Dee Snider interview, Joan Jett, Ratt, Lita Ford, Night Ranger, Kiss, Aerosmith..$3–6

1985

Feb. Dio, John Waits, W.A.S.P., Zebra, Honeymoon Suite, Hanoi Rocks.....................$2–4

Apr. David Lee Roth, Pat Benatar, Billy Idol, Motorhead, Helix, Hanoi Rocks..........$2–4

May Iron Maiden, Ozzy Osbourne, Scorpions, Rock in Rio Festival, Triumph, Earl Slick, Dokken..$2–3

June Deep Purple, Bryan Adams, Ozzy Osbourne, Ratt, Whitesnake.........................$2–3

July Foreigner, Jimmy Page interview, Giuffria, Vince Neil, Loudness, Accept..........$2–3

Dec. Motley Crue Special, Richie Blackmore, Robert Plant, Helix, Heavy Pettin, Bryan Adams, Madonna, David Bowie..$2–3

1986

Jan. Kiss, AC/DC, Ratt, Spinal Tap, Heart, Motley Crue, Malmsteen...........................$2–3

Feb. The Scorpions, Kiss, Ratt, Dio, Power Station, Night Ranger $2–3

Mar. 2nd Annual Readers Poll Issue, Jeff Beck, Giuffria, Castle Donnington Rock Festival... $ 2–3

Apr. Dire Straits, Dio, Keel, Aerosmith, W.A.S.P., Bon Jovi......................................$2–3

May Twisted Sister, John Paul Jones, Deep Purple, Marillion, Motley Crue, Yngwie Malmsteen, Rocker & Slick, Phantom $2–3

July Dokken, Kiss, Ozzy Osbourne, Black 'n' Blue, Ted Nugent, Rush.....................$2–3

Aug. Special Summer Tour Issue: Rock on the Road, Ozzy Osbourne, Judas Priest, Metallica, Krokus, Dokken, Aerosmith, Twisted Sister, Raven, issue contains giant color pullouts..$2–3

Sept. David Lee Roth, Rob Halford of Judas Priest, Paul Stanley, Keith Richards, Black Sabbath, Bon Jovi, Quiet Riot, Rainbow, Saxon, King Kobra, Paul McCartney.........$2–3

Oct. Special: Ozzy Osbourne Backstage, Judas Priest in Hollywood, Mayhem, Van Halen, Metallica & Van Halen posters, Keith Richards, Kiss, Peter Frampton........................$2–3

Nov. Bon Jovi Takin' it to the Top, Gene Simmons, Paul Stanley, Ozzy Osbourne, David Lee Roth, Iron Maiden, The History of Heavy Metal Part III, Queensryche, .38 Special, Dio $2–3

Dec. David Lee Roth: Let the Good Times Roll, Stephen Pearcy: Leader of Ratt, Alice Cooper: Shock-rock King Returns, Iron Maiden, ZZ Top, Accept, Metallica, posters......$2–3

1987

Jan./Feb. The Year in Metal '86, Alice Cooper, David Lee Roth, Bon Jovi, Ozzy Osbourne, Paul Stanley, Cinderella, Van Halen, Ratt, Metallica, Queensryche, issue includes eight posters...$2–4

Mar. Cinderella: Rags to Rock Sensation, Ratt: A Special Tribute, Bon Jovi, Billy Squier, Iron Maiden, W.A.S.P., Journey, issue includes two giant wall posters of Ratt & Cinderella...$2–3

Apr. Motley Crue '87, Concert Violence, Iron Maiden, Cinderella, Kiss, Heart, Van Halen...$2–3

1988

Feb. Guns 'n' Roses: The No Bull Interview, Metallica: Justice Served at Last, Ozzy Osbourne, Slash & Joe Perry poster, Pat Benatar, Winger, Lita Ford $2–3

Mar. Issue includes pullout posters, Kiss: Celebrating 15 Years of Kisstory, Dokken, Danzig, Rock City Angels, Vixen, House of Lords $2–3

May Def Leppard, Metallica: Headbanger Heroes, Motley Crue '89, Poison, Gene Simmons, Quiet Riot, Bon Jovi, Ratt, Celtic Frost, Badlands, Britny Fox..........................$2–3

June Guns 'n' Roses: Ain't No Stopping, Dokken's Farewell, Metallica, Winger, Tesla, Jane's Addiction, Ratt, Def Leppard, Roughhouse...$2–3

July/Aug. Metallica: Metal's Mightiest, The All New Motley Crue, Def Leppard, Great White, The Replacements, Metal Church, Exodus, Skid Row.......................................$2–3

Sept. White Lion: The Cat's Meow, The Cult, Metallica, Motley Crue, Skid Row, Guns 'n' Roses, Great White, W.A.S.P., Kingdom Come, Dirty Looks, Winger, Bon Jovi.........$2–3

Oct. Sebastian Bach, Kip Winger, The Cult, Mr. Big, Heather Locklear: Love & Marriage Metal Style, White Lion, Sea Hags, Great White...$2–3

Nov. Skid Row, The Ghost of Hanoi Rocks, The Cult, Faith No More, Vain, Testament, Faster Pussycat, King's X, Badlands...$2–3

Dec. Motley Crue: Down 'n' Dirty, Kiss: Turning Up the Heat, Faith No More, King Diamond, A Night With Warrent, Aerosmith, Skid Row, Tangier, The Cult....................$2–3

1989

Jan. Metal Memories '88, a giant double issue featuring Bon Jovi, Guns 'n' Roses, Jimmy Page, Poison, Metallica, Deep Purple, Testament & many other heavy metal groups......$2–3

Feb. Guns 'n' Roses, Metallica, Exclusive Bon Jovi Map Pullout, Winger, Europe, Stryper, Anthrax, Britny Fox, Ozzy Osbourne..$2–3

Mar. Danzig, Kiss: Celebrating 15 Years of Kisstory, Def Leppard, Metallica, Dokken, Tom Keifer, Bon Jovi $2–3

Apr. Guns 'n' Roses, Axl Rose & Steven Tyler pullout poster, Bullet Boys, Circus of Power, Kix, Skid Row, Jake E. Lee, Poison, Ozzy Osbourne, Def Leppard $2–3

May Def Leppard: Bring on the Leppard, Britny Fox, Metallica, Rush, Manowar, Guns 'n' Roses, Rockers' Kitchen...$2–3

June Ain't No Stopping Guns 'n' Roses, Metal Maidens: Hard Rock's Leading Ladies, Winger, Def Leppard, Skid Row, Dokken, Guns 'n' Roses..$2–4

July/Aug. The All-new Motley Crue, Warrent, Metal Church, Exodus, Poison, Jale E. Lee, Bullet Boys, Skid Row..$2–3

Sept. White Lion, Whitehead's Lemmy Speaks Out on Concert Violence, Dirty Looks, Metallica, W.A.S.P., M.O.D., Winger, Skid Row $2–3

Oct. Sebastian Bach, The Cult, Heather Locklear on Life With Tommy Lee, Mr. Big, EZO, Great White, Skid Row, Queensryche, Sea Hags...$2–3

Nov. The Cult, Vain, Bad English, Faith No More, Badlands, King's X, Michael Monroe, Testament, Skid Row, Faster Pussycat $2–3
Dec. Motley Crue: Down & Dirty, Aerosmith, So F.I.N.E., King Diamond's Diabolical Demise, Kiss: Rock's Precious Stalwarts Turn up the Heat, Warrent, Faith or Fear?, Soundgarden, L.A. Guns, Mr. Big, Skid Row, Tangier, The Cult, Tora Tora, Aerosmith... $2–3

1990

Jan./Feb. Heavy Metal: The Year '89, The Most Memorable Moments: Motley Crue, Steven Tyler, Axl Rose, Kiss, Skid Row, Aerosmith, Dangerous Toys, Loudness, Poison, Billy Squier, Badlands $2–3
All other issues $2–3

FEELINGS (Issued by High Society)

1980

June Blondie's Debbie Harry: The Marilyn Monroe of Rock-&-Roll $5–10

FIFTEEN FEVER

1978

Sept. #1 Shaun Cassidy's Most Lovable Secrets, Andy Gibb, John Travolta's New Life, Kiss: From A to Z, Olivia Newton-John, A Fan Meets Donny Osmond, Bay City Rollers, Rosetta Stone $10–20
Nov. #2 Kiss: They Dare You, Rollers You Never Knew, Rosetta Stone interview, Abba: Superpop Sensation, Shaun Cassidy: More Than What Meets the Eye, Peter Frampton, Two Sides of Andy Gibb, David Cassidy, Donna Summer, Leif Garrett, Tom Petty: Rock-&-Roll in the Heat of the Night, Striker, Fleetwood Mac, Olivia Newton-John $10–20

FLIP

1965

Aug. Freddie & the Dreamers, The Beatles Backstage, Soupy Sales: Meet the Mouse Man, Herman's Hermits: Herman Sounds Off, The Moody Blues: "The Girls We Like," The Beach Boys Backstage, On the Set With the Dave Clark Five, The Kinks Konfess, Shindig: Made in England, The Men From U.N.C.L.E., The Righteous Bros., Peter & Gordon Answer Back, The Animals Exclusive: Alan Price Quits, Chad & Jeremy are Splitting?, The Zombies, The Searchers, Gary Lewis & the Playboys, Sonny & Cher, The Yardbirds $20–40

1966

Jan. Sonny & Cher Swap Secrets, Soupy Sales Flips Out, Catch the Dave Clark Five, The Boy Behind the Beach Boys, The Beatles Visit the Byrds, Paul Revere & the Raiders, Dino, Desi & Billy, A Cool Conversation With the Lovin' Spoonful, The Beau Brummels, Jay & the Americans Are Here to Stay, Here are the Turtles, The McCoys, Marianne Faithful's Future, Lesley Gore, Meet Billy Joe Royal, Donovan, The Yardbirds, All About Bill Wyman, John Lennon Talks, What Herman is Really Like, Herman in Hollywood, Eric Burdon, David Jones, The Men from U.N.C.L.E., Chad & Jeremy $20–40
July Herman's Hermits, Keith Allison's Story: "I'm Not Paul McCartney," Meet Lou Christie, Are the Mamas & the Papas True?, The Young Rascals, The McCoys, Paul Revere Says Goodbye, Lovin Spoonful: John Sebastian Tells All, The Knickerbockers, The Turtles' Loves & Hates, The Beatles' Greatest Interview Part II, Bob Lind, Lesley Gore's Private World, Herman, John Lennon Scrapbook, Bobby Vinton: "I'm Glad I'm Not a Teen," Sonny & Cher, Nancy Sinatra, Spencer Davis, The Kinks, The Rolling Stone No One Ever Sees, Batman, Peter & Gordon, The Animals.. $20–40
Dec. All About the Monkees, The Lovin' Spoonful, Paul Revere, Exclusive: The New John Lennon, Bruce Johnston: The Perfect Beach Boy, Dennis Wilson: The Most Exciting Beach Boy, Keith Allison, 6 Weeks With Herman, Man from U.N.C.L.E., Chad & Jeremy, The New Yardbirds, What the Rolling Stones Love & Hate, All About the Troggs, The Beatles' Column, Mark Lindsay.. $15–30

1967

Apr. Micky Dolenz, The Monkees, Davy Jones' Very Private Pix, Paul Revere & the Raiders, The Beatles, Mitch Ryder, Herman's Hermits, Fang, Peter Tork, The Hollies, Donovan, Rascals, The Lovin' Spoonful, Gary Lewis, The Association $15–30
May Peter Tork, How the Monkees Have Changed, Paul Revere & the Raiders, The Association, Rascals, Keith Allison, The Beach Boys, The Rolling Stones, Mitch Ryder, Peter & Gordon, The Beatles, Herman's Hermits, Donovan..$15–30
June Davy Jones, All About the Monkees, Micky Dolenz in London, 76 Facts About Mike Nesmith, Peter Tork, Paul Revere & the Raiders, Dino, Desi & Billy, The Beatles, Herman's Hermits..$15–30
July Mike Nesmith Talks About Everything, Davy Jones' Greatest Interview, 70 Secret & Personal Facts About Micky Dolenz, What the Raiders are Really Like, The Beatles, Mick Jagger Answers Your Questions, Dave Clark Flips Out, "My Life With the Monkees," Peter Tork Visits *Flip*, Herman, Mark Lindsay, The Standells, Mitch Ryder, Sonny Bono, The Buckinghams, *Harper's Bizarre*, The Vagrants, Guardsmen, Kurt Russell $15–30
Aug. Micky Dolenz, The Monkees, The Newest Raider: Fred Weller, Micky Dolenz' Girlfriend Samantha, Peter Noone/Herman's Hermits, Tommy Boyce & Bobby Hart, Peter Tork Answers Questions, Mark Lindsay, Nitty Gritty Dirt Band, My Life With the Monkees, The Doors, The Grateful Dead, The Seekers, Kurt Russell, "My Life With the Raiders" by Their Manager Roger Hart, Spencer Davis, The Beatles, Young Rascals, two pin-ups of Davy Jones, Davy Jones' Early Days..$15–30
Sept. Davy Jones & the Monkees Special Issue, Neil Diamond, Mark Lindsay......$15–30
Oct. Peter Tork's College Days Revealed, The Two Faces of Micky Dolenz, Davy Jones' Early Days, The Monkees on Tour, The Real Mike Nesmith, Raiders, Kurt Russell, Moby Grape..$15–30
Nov. Davy Jones, The Monkees Exclusive Tour Photos, Herman's Flick, Peter Tork's Secret Early Life, Mark Lindsay, The Beatles, The Mamas & the Papas $15–30
Dec. The Monkees, issue includes foot-long Monkees pin-up, Davy Jones' Diary, Herman's Hermits, The Rascals, Lewis & Clarke, Paul Revere & the Raiders, Mark Lindsay, The Beatles, Kurt Russell, Freddie & the Dreamers, Dino, Desi & Billy $15–30

1968

Jan. Young Rascals, The Monkees, One Dozen Color Pin-ups of Davy Jones, The Mamas & the Papas Take You Home, Go Fishing With the Monkees, Herman's Best Friend, Paul Revere & the Raiders Life Stories, Dave Clark Five, The Real Mike Nesmith, The Association, The Monkees' Secret Diary..$15–30
Feb. Paul Revere & the Raiders, Spend a Day With Davy Jones, The Mamas & the Papas at Home, Mark Lindsay, The Real Rascals, The Beatles Yesterday & Today, Herman's Best Friend, Monkee Fax, Lewis & Clarke, Herman's Life..$15–30
Mar. The Monkees' Madness, The Raiders Spook Out, Mark Lindsay, How Much Do You Know About Peter Tork?, Visit the Young Rascals, The Mamas & the Papas Talk About Their Future, Around the World With Herman, The Beatles, Sally Field, Lewis & Clarke, The Who Flip Out, Stone Poneys, The Sunshine Company, Meet the Doors, This is Jim Morrison..$15–30
Apr. Davy Jones, Why the Monkees Have Changed, Jay North, Micky Dolenz' New Car, The Doors, The Association, Rascals, Raiders...$15–30
May Jay North, Sajid Khan, Micky Dolenz Takes Off, Davy Jones Flips Out, The Bee Gees, The Rascals Invite You Home, The Beatles, The New Paul McCartney, The Monkees, Sally Field, The Buckinghams, Raiders..$15–30
June Sajid Khan: 67 Fax, Davy Jones, Monkee Scoops, Jay North, The Cowsills, Raiders, The Bee Gees, Mark Lindsay $15–30
July Mike Nesmith, The Monkees Movie Preview, Sajid Khan, The Bee Gees, Walter Koenig & *Star Trek*, Raiders, Mark Lindsay, The Cowsills, Jay North, Rascals..........$15–30
Aug. Davy Jones's New Dance, The Monkees Movie Preview, Walter Koenig at Home, Sajid's Secret, Raiders, Mark Lindsay, The Bee Gees, *Star Trek*................................$15–30
Sept. Sajid Khan, The Monkees, Davy Jones Gets a Haircut, Meet the Box Tops, Herman, The Rascals Speak Out, The Bee Gees Find a Friend, Paul Revere, How the Monkees Rocked England, Barry Gibb, The Cowsills, "My Adventures With the Bee Gees," The Association, Micky Dolenz at Home, The Union Gap, Leonard Nimoy........................$15–30

Oct. Davy Jones, The Monkees, Micky Dolenz Takes You Cherry Pickin', Union Gap interview, Glen Campbell, A Summer Day With Davy Jones, Herman/Peter Noone's Own Story, Sajid Khan, The Raiders, The Nazz at Work, Beatle Fashions, Mark Lindsay, A Visit With the Rascals, The Cowsills, The Bee Gees on Tour, Grace Slick $15–30

1969

Jan. Twiggy, The Monkees, "Mod Squad," The Beatles, Walter Koenig $15–30
Feb. Sajid Khan, "The Mod Squad," The Beatles, Mark Lindsay, Bobby Sherman .$15–30
Marc. Jonathan Frid/"Dark Shadows," Leonard Nimoy Speaks Out, Sajid Lets His Hair Down, The Beatles, The Bee Gees, The Monkees $15–30
Apr. Paul McCartney, "The Mod Squad," A Day With the Union Gap, Davy Jones, Jonathan Frid/"Dark Shadows," The Rascals, The Bee Gees, Jefferson Airplane, Mary Hopkins..$15–30
May Bobby Sherman, "The Mod Squad," Mark Lindsay, The Union Gap, The Bee Gees' Wedding, The Real Peggy Lipton, Steppenwolf, The Smothers Brothers, Sajid, The Cowsills $15–30
June Cast of "The Mod Squad," Jonathan Frid Backstage on "Dark Shadows," The Rascals Controversy, How the Cowsills Have Changed, Bobby Sherman, Sajid, The Beatles, The Raiders' New Life...$15–30
July Mike Cole's Life in Pix, "The Mod Squad," The Monkees & The Raiders Together, Bobby Sherman's Hideaway, Jonathan Frid/"Dark Shadows," The Doors, Elvis Presley, The Cowsills, Sajid, Rascals, Glen Campbell, Grass Roots, Shindig..................................$15–30
Aug. Bobby Sherman's Summer Love Wish, Michael Cole's Baby Pix, The Beatles, Sajid Khan, Davy Jones, Peggy Lipton, Mark Lindsay, Jonathan Frid, Tom Jones, Barry Cowsill, Glen Campbell, Donovan, Paul Revere Coming and Going, Jose Feliciano, Grass Roots, Why Diana Ross is Leaving the Supremes, What the Shondells Think of Tommy James, The Monkees, The Bee Gees Break Up..$15–30
Oct. Bobby Sherman, Michael Cole, Leonard Nimoys' Mission, The Monkees, The Beatles, "Dark Shadows" Family Tree...$15–30

1970

Jan. "Dark Shadows": Selby & Stroka, The Beatles, *Hair*, *Star Trek*, Bobby Sherman, The Cowsills, David Cassidy, Osmonds $15–30
Feb. David Cassidy: David's Love Test, Bobby Sherman, Donny Osmond, The Beatles, Neil Diamond, Mark Lindsay, Three Dog Night, Jack Wild, Jackson Five, Grass Roots $15–30
Apr. Bobby Sherman, Michael Cole, Paul Revere & the Raiders' New Life, Beatles, Tom Jones..$15–30
Aug. Bobby Sherman, "Dark Shadows," David Cassidy's Life Story, Three Dog Night $15–30
Sept. David Cassidy, The Osmonds, Beatles, "Dark Shadows," Three Dog Night ..$15–30

1971

Apr. David Cassidy: The Two Days That Changed His Life, Rick Ely, Bugaloos, Young Rebels, Grass Roots, Osmonds, Bobby Sherman, Mike Cole, Chris Knight, Barry Williams $15–30
May David Cassidy: His Day-to-Day Life, Three Dog Night, Jackson Five, Bobby Sherman, Partridge Family Secrets, The Osmonds, The Brady Bunch........................$15–30
June David Cassidy's Secret Escape, The Osmonds' New Love Pin-ups, Bobby Sherman, The Jackson Five's Life, The Bradys, Rick Ely's Strange Dream, Susan Dey, Donny Osmond, Partridge Family $15–30
July David Cassidy's Confession: The Hardest Decision of His Life, The Osmonds on Stage, Bobby Shermans' Big Movie, Jackson Five, Michael Cole, Farewell to "Dark Shadows," Ronnie Howard, Bradys...$15–30
Aug. David Cassidy: "How Well Do You Know Me?," "Dark Shadows," The Osmonds, Bobby Sherman, Three Dog Night, The Jackson Five...$15–30
Sept. David Cassidy: His 21st Birthday, A New Life for Bobby Sherman, Three Dog Night, Carpenters, Jackson Five, Pete Duel, Osmonds...$15–30
Oct. David Cassidy: His Personal Backstage Tour of the Partridge Family Set, Donny Osmond, Jackson Five, Susan Dey, Bobby Sherman $15–30

Nov. David Cassidy by Two Girls Who Know Him, David's Summer Illness, Bobby Sherman, Donny Osmond, Jackson Five, Chad Everett, Creedence Clearwater Revival, Partridge Family $15–30
Dec. David Cassidy in Concert, Bobby Sherman, Davy Jones: Where's He Been?, Jackson Five Exclusive, Three Dog Night, Partridge Family..$15–30

1972

Jan. An Intimate Weekend With David Cassidy, Bobby Sherman, Donny Osmond, David on Glen Campbell Show, Jackson, Five, Partridge Family Bus $10–20
Feb. David Cassidy's Life in Pictures, Bobby Sherman, The Beatles: What They're Like Today, Donny Osmond, Elvis Presley, Jackson Five, Partridges $10–20
Mar. David Cassidy Leaves Home, Bobby Sherman, Donny: Look at His Diary, Three Dog Night, Susan Dey, Jackson Five, Grass Roots, Chad Everett $10–20
Apr. David Cassidy: Saving Him from the Girls, Donny Osmond Concert Album & Poster, Jackson Five, Bobby Sherman, Peter Duel's Tragic Death $10–20
May David Cassidy's Step-by-step Lovers' Guide, Donny Osmond, Three Dog Night, Bobby Sherman, Andy & David Williams, Grass Roots, Michael Cole....................$10–20
June Donny Osmond Eight-page Special, David Cassidy, Bobby Sherman, Jackson Five $10–20
July Donny Osmond, David Cassidy, Bobby Sherman, Andy & Dave Williams, Jackson Five $10–20
Aug. David Cassidy, Donny Osmond, Susan Dey: She Gets Skyjacked, Three Dog Night, Jack Wild, Butch Patrick, Donovan, Karen Valentine..$10–20
Sept. David Cassidy Takes it Off, Donny Osmond, Bobby Sherman, Jackson Five....$10–20
Oct. David Cassidy Says He Quits, Donny Hides, Bobby Sherman $10–20
Nov. David Cassidy & Donny posters, Susan Dey: The Ugly Rumor That Made Her Cry, Bobby Sherman, Michael Jackson, Andy & Dave...$10–20
Dec. David Cassidy wall poster, Susan Dey's Love Hints, Donny Osmond, Bobby Sherman, Brady Bunch, Jermaine Jackson $10–20

1973

Jan. David Cassidy & His Future, Partridge Family poster, Andy & Dave, Sonny & Cher, Jackson Five, Raspberries, Susan Dey, Three Dog Night $10–20
Feb. David Cassidy: His London Photo Diary, Sonny & Cher: Medieval Madness, Donny Osmond, Rick Springfield, Brady Bunch, Bobby Sherman, Three Dog Night, Jackson Five, Jermaine Jackson...$10–20
Mar. David Cassidy: The Girl He Couldn't Love, Jackson Five: Twenty Red Hot Fax, Andy & Dave Williams, Three Dog Night, Donny Osmond, Raspberries, Sonny & Cher: Please Don't Break Up, Bobby Sherman...$10–20
Apr. David Cassidy & Susan Dey in the Bushes Together, David's Mystery Illness, The Day Donny Was Ready to Die, Andy & Dave Williams, Jackson Five, Three Dog Night, Rick Springfield $10–20
May David Cassidy Flees the Country, Rick Springfield, Donny Osmond, Bobby Sherman & His Marriage, Jackson Five, Michael Lloyd $10–20
June David Cassidy: The True Story, The Osmonds Split Up, Rick Springfield.....$10–20
July David Cassidy Leaves the Partridge Family, Donny's Sexy Thoughts, The Osmonds Robbed, Michael Jackson, Rick Springfield, Marie Osmond, Susan Dey, The New Seekers, Andy & Dave Williams..$10–20
Aug. David Cassidy: "Don't Leave Me Now," Donny Runs, Jermaine Jackson, Three Dog Night, Andy & Dave Williams, Heywoods, Marie Osmond......................................$10–20
Sept. David Cassidy's Family Feud, Donnie's Split Personality, Andy & Dave Williams, Rick Springfield, Sonny & Cher, Raspberries..$10–20
Oct. Donny Osmond: Why He May Never Date, David Cassidy: The Search for His Replacement, Rick Springfield, The New Seekers, Jan Michael Vincent......................$10–20
Dec. Donny Threatened, David Cassidy at the Olympics, Jackson Five, Rick Springfield, Marie Osmond, Brady Bunch $10–20

1974

Jan. Donny & the Osmonds Stage Accident, Jackson Five, Rick Springfield, David Cassidy's Dynamite Dream, Sonny & Cher $10–20

Feb. The Brady Bunch's Sneak Scrapbook, Donny's Wedding, The Jackson Five on the Move, Sonny & Cher, David's Last Partridge Family Day, Rick Springfield on Tour....$10–20
Mar. David Cassidy Takin' Off, The Brady's Foreign Adventures, Rick Springfield Locked Up, Alice Cooper: Freakiest of Them All, The Rookies, Donny Osmond, The Partridge Family, Sonny & Cher, The Stones, Bread, Heywoods, Elvis Presley, Jackson Five...$10–20
Apr. The Brady Bunch's Shocking News, Michael Jackson, Jermaine Jackson, Rick Springfield in Action, David Cassidy, Alice Cooper, The Carpenters, Peter Noone, The New Seekers, Defrancos, Andy & Dave Williams $10–20
May Donny Osmond Rebels, Sonny & Cher, The Rookies, Defrancos' Family Secrets, The Bradys' Wild 'n' Wacky Adventures, Rick Springfield's Slick Trick, Jackson Five, David Cassidy, Andy & Dave Tell on Each Other, Alice Cooper.......................................$10–20
June Donny Osmond Escapes: Why He Had To, Bradys' Sneak Peek, Andy & Dave, Jackson Five, Rick Springfield: Come to My Beach House, David Cassidy, Sonny & Cher, Rookies $10–20
July Donny Osmond & the Osmonds: Haunted, The Bradys' Cancelled, Defrancos Magic Act, Rick Springfield, Richard Thomas, David Cassidy, Rookies, Andy & Dave, Heywoods, Sonny & Cher $10–20
Sept. Donny Osmond, Defrancos, Waltons, Sonny & Cher, Heywoods......................$7–15

1975

Jan. Heywoods, Osmonds, *Planet of the Apes*, Marie Osmond, Waltons $6–12

FLIP SUPERSTARS POSTER ANNUAL
1972

Summer David Cassidy on the Set, Bobby Sherman, Osmond Brothers, The Partridge Family, Michael Jackson, Butch Patrick $15–30

FLIP'S SUPERSTARS PHOTO ANNUAL
1974

Summer Donny Does It & Talks About It, Michael Jackson: Hang Out With the Jackson Five, Rick Springfield, Complete Defrancos Lifelines, Alice Cooper, David Cassidy ..$10–20

FORUM
1980

Oct. Blondie Exclusive Interview: Debbie Harry Talks About Sex $3–6

FOURTEEN
1979

May Kiss: What Makes Them Kill, Kristy McNichol: Has Success Spoiled Her?, Debbie Boone, Shaun & David Cassidy: Love Them Tender, Peter Frampton A New Career, Andy Gibb: No Disco Duck, John Travolta: His Secret Fear, Olivia Newton-John, Barry Manilow, Frankie Valli, Leif Garrett...$5–10

FRAMPTON (Peter Frampton's life story magazine)
1977

Every Album Revealed, Contains the Largest Collection of Photos and Pin-ups Never Before Published...$2–4

FRESH
1985

May #1 Prince: Can He Keep His Secret?, Cosby Kids, The Jacksons, New Edition, Chaka Khan, Eddie Murphy $2–4
July #2 Prince Battles Love, Sex & God, Debarge, Kool & the Gang, Lionel Richie, New Edition...$2–4

1986

Jan. #3 Apollonia: Too Hot for TV, New Edition, New Edition's Drummer Tells All, Tina Turner, Whitney Houston, Eddie Murphy...$2–4

Feb. #4 Whitney Houston, Freddie Jackson, Stoney Jackson...$2–4

Mar. #5 Cosby Kids, Vanity's New Movie, Kurtis Blow, New Edition................................$2–3

Apr. #6 The New Edition, Apollonia vs. Phillip Michael Thomas, The Jets, Jacksons, Force MDs, Stephanie Mills...$2–3

May #7 Whitney Houston: "I'm Changing," American Music Awards, The New Edition Tour, El Debarge poster $2–4

June #8 Michael Jackson, Exclusive Interview With Janet Jackson, Whitney Houston, New Edition..$2–4

July #9 The New Edition Special: Latest Tour Facts & Photos, Janet Jackson: What She's Really Like, Prince: The Greatest Photos...$2–4

Aug. #10 The New Edition: Eight-page Color Special, Five Star, Prince: The New Movie, Whitney Houston: Thin Like Her..$2–4

Sept. #11 New Edition's Ralph: Things You Never Knew, Prince: His Girlfriends Tell All, Vanity, Force MDs, Michael Jackson..$2–4

Oct. Ronnie De Voe, Special 11-Page New Edition Section, Prince Panics in Hollywood, Janet Jackson, Lionel Richie, Vanity...$2–4

Nov. The New Edition: Seven-page Color Special, Why Run DMC Won't Change, Five Tells All Exclusive Interview, The Jets...$2–3

Dec. #14 New Edition Seven-page Color Special with color wall poster, At Janet Jackson's Party...$2–3

1987

Jan. #15 New Edition Seven-page Color Special with color wall poster, Michael Bivins Interviewed, The New Edition Tour Party...$2–3

Feb. #16 New Edition: As You've Never Seen Them With Personal Messages from Each, Janet Jackson's Future Plans, The Jets...$2–3

#17 New Edition pullout color poster, Run DMC, The Jets, Janet Jackson Tour: Full of Surprises...$2–3

#18 Huge New Edition Special With Dozens of Photos, The Jets, 5 Star, Billy Ocean $2–3

#19 New Edition's Night of Triumph With Photos, Chico Debarge, The Beastie Boys, 5 Stars' Likes & Dislikes $2–3

#20 New Edition As You've Never Seen Them, On Tour With Bobby Brown, Janet Jackson's New Life...:....$2–3

#21 New Edition: Their Long Kept Secrets, Bobby Brown on Tour $2–3

#22 New Edition, On the Road With Freddie Jackson, Bobby Brown's Past Secrets, Lisa Bonet, The Jets, Run DMC..$2–3

#23 Special Hollywood Hunk Issue, Ralph Tresvant, Eddie Murphy, Bobby Broen, The Beastie Boys, Janet Jackson, Lisa Lisa, New Edition $2–3

#24 Special Rumors Issue—Janet Jackson, New Edition, Five Star, Bobby Brown, The Fat Boys, Prince, Whitney Houston...$2–3

#25 A Visit With Five Star, New Edition's Secret Hideaway, On Tour With the Beastie Boys, Whitney Houston, Michael Jackson...$2–3

#26 New Edition: Then & Now, The Beastie Boys, Run DMC, Force MDs..............$2–3

#27 Michael & Janet Jackson: The Whole Truth About Their Secret Lives, The Jets, LL Cool J, Run DMC, The Beastie Boys...$2–3

#28 Michael Jackson Super Special Issue, Force MDs, The Jets, LL Cool J, The Beastie Boys $2–3

#29 Five Star Exclusive Interview & sexy color wall poster, special Rap Music section, New Edition Latest Fax, LL Cool J $2–3

#30 Unmasking Michael Jackson Exclusive, Prince's Pleasure Palace, Tempest Bledsoe, Madonna, New Edition, Janet Jackson...$2–3

#31 LL Cool J: Be His Forever, The Jets' Secret Desires, Lisa Bonet.........................$2–3

#32 Lisa Bonet, The Jets, Jody Watley, Force MDs, 1988 Predictions $2–3

1988

Jan. Prince: So, You Think You Know Him, LL Cool J: How Cool is He?, The Jets' Haini Goes Solo, Lisa Bonet's New Husband, Michael Jackson, Gloria Estefan Speaks Her Mind, Royalty, New Edition...$2–3

1989

Jan. Big Daddy Kane, Karyn White, Al B. Sure, Johnny Gill, The New Edition feature & poster, George Michael...$2–3
Oct. The Boys, Bobby Brown, Lisa Lisa, Prince, The Cult, The Jam, Donna Summer, Patti Labelle, Jackie Jackson...$2–3
Nov. Bobby Brown Exclusive Memory Pictures, The Boys Talk, Arsenio Hall, The Many Faces of Janet Jackson, Full Force...$2–3
Dec. Janet Jackson's Back: Come to Her Private Party, Why Girls Love Al B. Sure, Eric Gable, Lisa Lisa & Cult Jam, Diana Ross $2–3

FRESH MAGAZINE PRESENTS YO

1989

Nov. LL Cool J, On the Road With N.W.A., Kwane, Public Enemy............................$1–2
Dec. Salt 'n' Pepa, Redhead Kingpin, Kid 'n' Play, LL Cool J....................................$1–2

FRESH POSTERAMA (Each issue includes 10 giant color wall posters)

1988

#1 New Edition, Lisa Bonet, Force MDs, Five Star, Zoro...$2–5
#2 New Edition, The Jets, Chico Debarge, Janet Jackson, Bobby Brown, Run DMC $2–5
#3 New Edition, Run DMC, Five Star, Janet Jackson, Ralph Tresvant, The Beastie Boys, Jody Watley, Bobby Brown...$2–5
#4 Michael Jackson, Janet Jackson, Force MDs, LL Cool J, The Jets, Run DMC, Five Star, Beastie Boys, Salt 'n' Pepa, New Edition..$2–5

FUSHION

1969

Jan. 20 Bobby Darin, The Rolling Stones $10–20
July 12 Bob Dylan, The Who & *Tommy*, Jeff Beck..$10–20
Aug. 22 Elvis Presley, Bob Dylan's Children, John Lennon: Get Back....................$10–20
Sept. 5 The Boston Sound, Easy Rider, Frank Zappa interview................................$7–15
Oct. 3 Robert Kennedy, T. Rex...$5–10
Nov. 14 Mick Taylor interview, Abbey Road $7–15
Nov. 28 The Kinks: Better Than Never, Talks With: The Rolling Stones, Gene Vincent, Ray Davies, Crosby, Stills, Nash & Young...$10–20
Dec. 12 Mick Jagger: The Rolling Stones interview, Sam the Sham, Joe Cocker...$12–25

1970

Mar. 6 Arthur Lee, The Velvet Underground, The Nice $7–15
Apr. 3 Van Zandt, The Archies, Altamont on Film $7–15
Apr. 17 #31 Neil Young at Large, Paul Williams in the West $10–20
May 1 #32 The Woodstock Movie, Steve Miller, Lenny Bruce $10–20
May 15 #34 John Sebastian's Music, Johnny Otis interview.....................................$7–15
July 10 #37 The Punk Muse: The Lowdown on Grease...$5–10
Aug. 21 #39 Andy Warhol, Elvis Presley $5–10
Sept. 18 #40 The Folks That Gave Us Altamont, The Rolling Stones & Their Tour ..$7–15
Oct. 16 #42 Iggy Pop & the Stooges: The Pro & Con..$10–20
Nov. 27 #46 Jefferson Airplane, The Jackson Five $7–15
Dec. 25 #47 The Hollies, The Altamont Film $7–15

1971

Jan. 22 #49 A Christmas Poem by Lou Reed..$5–10
Feb. 19 #50 John Lennon & George Harrison: Two Who Made Good.....................$7–15

Mar. 19 #52 A Casualty Report on Rock: Brian Jones, Jimi Hendrix, Janis Joplin & Others, Capt. Beefheart, Michael Lydon $15–30
#54 Eric Burdon Special Report...$7–15
#55 Ike & Tina Turner...$6–12
#56 Mick Jagger & the Rolling Stones: No Dead Flowers $10–20
#59 Johnny Cash Goes West, The Youngbloods...$6–12
#60 John Mayall, Lenny Bruce $6–12
#61 Rod Stewart & the Faces, Ray Mungo, Frank Zappa: Another Look..................$7–15
#63 The Who Special, Country Comfort: Johnny Cash, Tammy Wynette $7–15
#64 Creedence Clearwater Revival, Bangladesh, George Harrison, Ray Charles........$7–15
#65 Kris Kristofferson $5–10
#66 John Lennon & Yoko Ono: The John & Yoko Show...$10–20
#67 Crosby, Stills, Nash & Young $7–15
#68 Chuck Berry: Chess Records, Traffic, Little Richard...$7–15
#69 Stalking Charles Manson, Fleetwood Mac, The Band, Todd Rundgren.............$7–15

1972

#70 Dustin Hoffman, Keith Emerson, Robert Palmer, Ray Charles, Dionne Warwick...$7–15
#71 Bob Dylan, The Beach Boys..$7–15
#72 Paul McCartney, Johnny Mathis, The Beatles $7–15
#73 Yoko Ono, Elvis Presley: The King as a Subject $7–15
#74 Bob Dylan: Way Back When & Now, Otis Redding, Ricky Nelson....................$7–15
#75 Frank Zappa Unfurled, Pat Boone Revived, Rock Fanzines & the Underground Press, Whatever Happened to Peter Tork?, Cilla Black, Mitch Mitchell & Others...............$7–15
#76 The Fifties: Grown Up Absurd, Murray the K, Simon & Garfunkel...................$7–15
#77 The Rolling Stone Magazine Story, Manfred Mann, Rock Radio $7–15
#78 Lou Reed: Revising the Legend, Randy Newman, James Brown, Phil Spector..$7–15
#79 Mick Jagger: The Rolling Stones American Exile, Eric Clapton........................$10–20
#80 Special Report on the Zombies & Moby Grape...$7–15
#83 Pete Townshend, The Band, Bread, Johnny Rivers..$7–15
#84 Mott the Hoople: All the Young Dudes, Raspberries, Joni Mitchell, Neil Diamond $6–12
#86 Little Feat, The Wailers $5–10

1973

#89 The Beatles: Capital Records, Black Oak Arkansas...$7–15
#90 Charlie Rich, Two Ex-Beatles, Martin Mull $5–10
#91 The Beau Brummels, New York Dolls..$5–10
#92 Free John Lennon, Deep Purple, Forgetting Dick Clark...$6–12

1974

#94 The Byrds..$4–8
#95 The Bob Dylan Tour, Led Zeppelin $6–12
#98 The Elton John Bon-bon Story, British Rock $4–8

Stevie Nicks

Collecting
FLEETWOOD MAC AND
STEVIE NICKS

Fleetwood Mac's first album (Peter Green's Fleetwood Mac) was released in 1968 and Stevie Nicks first appeared on the Buckingham Nicks album in 1973. Since then, there have been eager fans waiting to collect their albums and memorabilia.

Fleetwood Mac's earliest albums were released on the Blue Horizon label in England and the Epic label in the U.S. The Blue Horizon albums are nearly impossible to locate here (and in England); you are much more likely to find the Epic pressings or the CBS reissues of the pre-1975 recordings.

Aside from the Blue Horizon- and Epic-released albums, there are several European smaller label pressings of the early Fleetwood Mac recordings.

Most are live performances; others are recordings that were never included on their standard albums—songs like "Tutti Frutti" and "Great Balls of Fire."

Albums released since 1975 are still readily available, but since the CD now rules the record stores, you may have to find a store that will order them for you if they aren't in stock. Albums such as "Bare Trees," "Penguin," and "Mystery to Me" have been found in "cut-out" bins in the past few years. The albums "Kiln House" and "Heroes are Hard to Find" can still be occasionally found at used record shops. All of these albums can be found on CD, but it isn't quite the same. Stevie Nicks' standard release albums are still readily available, as are the 1975 and after Mac albums.

Special radio concerts and interview programs are very popular with collectors. They often come in two or three LP sets, sometimes boxed. All promotional discs like this are expensive, so be prepared to pay considerably for them.

In general, U.S. 7″ picture sleeve singles have been fairly easy to find, but they will soon vanish from the common record show as they now have from record stores. Since all of the recording companies in this country stopped producing vinyl as of 1990, current or recent singles on vinyl must now be found in record specialty shops, record shows or ordered through the mail from ads placed in special record collector magazines. Beginning with Fleetwood Mac's "Behind the Mask" and Stevie Nicks' "The Other Side of the Mirror" (in 1989 and 1990), fans were forced to look outside of the U.S. for new vinyl singles. Before 1989, the imported single was an extra addition to the standard U.S. single; now it has become the only commercial source of 7″ vinyl for Fleetwood Mac and Stevie Nicks collectors.

Imported 7″ picture sleeves have always been rare; the older the single, the rarer it is. Often import sleeves feature a completely different photo from the U.S. sleeve and it's not uncommon for the sleeves to vary from country to country. Japan usually includes the song lyrics, sometimes with laughable translations, so be sure to look for them. Germany often features photos of the individual band members and a brief history on the back of the sleeves. Sound quality varies from country to country, with Japan ranking number 1. But, sound quality is not the main reason import 7″s are sought after by collectors—it is for their variation on sleeve pictures that make them so valuable.

Mac collectors should be aware that the "Family Man" box set is a big disappointment. The graphics on and inside the box are less than satisfactory and certainly not worth the extra money.

Many fans complained about the "Behind the Mask" album cover, which is not a photo of the band but a photo of complete strangers. Each single released from this album features an ugly mark or equally unappealing artwork.

The only other Mac picture sleeve that may not appeal to fans is "Tusk," which features a dog baring its teeth. All the others have exceptionally nice photos or artwork that's pleasing to the eye.

The picture sleeves of Stevie Nicks' 7″ singles are uncommonly beautiful, and that fact alone makes them so desirable. Herbert Worthington III, who has a special talent for capturing the essence of Stevie through photography, created most of the photos for the sleeves. All are photographs of Stevie, except for one. "If Anyone Falls" features an enchanting drawing of Stevie holding a crystal ball. The "Talk to Me" sleeve is the album cover photo and the Buckingham Nicks singles feature the black and white version of the album cover photo. These exceptions aside, all the other sleeves are different from the album covers. All of Stevie's U.S. singles are on the Modern Records label, while those pressed outside of the U.S. are either on the EMI or WEA label. Promo singles from the "Bella Donna" album do not have the standard red ink on the label design; promos from "The Other Side of the Mirror" simply have "Promo" stamped on them in black ink. Stevie's imported singles cost considerably more than the Mac's, ranging from $20–$40.

It would be impossible to list and describe all of the different imported picture sleeves, so when buying or ordering an imported sleeve "sight unseen," have a clear understanding as to whether or not the sleeve in question is different from the U.S. version. Often when ordering through a record collector's magazine, you can call to get any additional information you may need.

Probably the three most valued things about the 12″ singles and EPs are that they often consist of extended/remixed/dubbed versions of songs, their picture jackets, and the fact that often they are promos.

The U.S. maxi singles from the "Tango" album have Warner Brothers' standard yellow and green jacket that says "12-inch Specially Priced Maxi Single." The U.K. released three 12″ picture disc singles from this same album.

The picture jackets for the "Bella Donna" promo 12″ singles are definitely the hardest to find and the most stunningly beautiful. Two U.K. single releases include two-sided posters in specially limited editions from "The Other Side of the Mirror" album.

Compact discs have only been on the market for a few years but, in that short amount of time, some truly unique ones have emerged. Radio programs and promos of Fleetwood Mac and Stevie Nicks are now on CDs, a couple with pictures printed on them.

There seem to be two groups of Fleetwood Mac fans—those who are interested in the early "Blues" Mac (the Peter Green era), and those who aren't interested in anything prior to Stevie Nicks and Lindsey Buckingham joining the band in 1975. For this reason, the listings under Fleetwood Mac with an asterisk (*) indicate recordings that include Stevie Nicks and/or Lindsey Buckingham.

There have been several books written about Fleetwood Mac and many magazine articles and interviews. Several books have been written prior to Bob Brunning's first book, but they are out of print and difficult to find. The same is true for the Stevie Nicks and Evangeline Walton books.

The best sources for Fleetwood Mac and Stevie Nicks collectibles of all kinds are record shows, specialty record stores, dealers who specialize in rock rarities, Rumours conventions, pen pals, used book stores, and record collector magazines.

TOUR PROGRAMS

"Behind the Mask World Tour 1990," 32 pages..$15
"Tango in Europe," 36 pages...$25–40
"Tango in the Night," 32 pages..$10–15

BOOKS

"A Book of Legends," 1989, compiled by Linda Iorio $25
"Blues—The British Connection," Blandford Press, by Bob Brunning $14.95

"Fleetwood Mac Behind the Masks," UK Hodder and Stoughton, by Bob Brunning, check for U.S. release.
"Fleetwood," William Morror, by Mick Fleetwood $19.95
"Rumours Magazine," editor Ann Morgan, per issue $4.50

MOST RARE AND SOUGHT-AFTER FLEETWOOD MAC AND STEVIE NICKS MEMORABILIA

Fleetwood Mac rarest 7" singles
Any Fleetwood Mac single on the Blue Horizon label or the Epic label, average per disc
....$10–20
DJUS-1007, first pressing in violet-colored vinyl...$25–50
DJUS-1008, second pressing in blue vinyl $25–75
*EP German Democratic Republic Amiga label, #5 56 088 ....$10–20
*"Go Your Own Way"/"Silver Springs" (non-LP), WBS 8304.............................$10+
"Hold Me"/"Eyes of the World"/"Oh Diane"/"Gypsy" graphic sleeve.................$25–50
"Man of the World" (mono)/**"Silver Springs"** (stereo), DJM Records.................$25–50
*"The Chain"/"Oh Diane"/"Rhiannon," UK WEA Fleet 1P disc............................$25–50

BUCKINGHAM/NICKS SINGLES

All Buckingham/Nicks singles are extremely rare. Stevie Nicks and Lindsey Buckingham's only album together was released in 1973, prior to joining Fleetwood Mac. The singles released on Polydor Records from Buckingham/Nicks are:
"A My Name is Alice," by Marie Osmond, mono, PD, 14333 on back, no picture sleeve, super rare..$50+
"Crying in the Night" promo mono/stereo, PD 14428...$25–50
"Crying in the Night"/"Stephanie," PD 14428...$25–50
"Don't Let Me Down Again"/"Crystal," UK 2066 700 ....$25–50
"Don't Let Me Down Again" promo mono/stereo, PD 14335 ....$25–50
"Don't Let Me Down Again" promo stereo, PD 14335 on front $25–50

STEVIE NICKS' RAREST 7" SINGLES

"Long Way to Go"/"Real Tears" (non-LP), UK EMI 97 ....$7–9
"Nightbird"/"Gate & Garden" (picture sleeve), Modern 7-99799 ....$20–45
Robbie Patton "Smiling Islands," ATL 7-89955...$4–5
The Rotters "Sit on My Face Stevie Nicks," Rotten Records, TR-002, no picture sleeve.
....$25+
Stevie doesn't sing on this listing; it is a crude and rude tribute to her and much sought-after by collectors.
Tom Petty "Refuge"/"Insider," UK PIC DISC MCAP 778B.................................$15–25
Walter Egan "Magnet & Steel"/"Tunnel O' Love," COL 3–10719 ....$3–6

FLEETWOOD MAC'S RAREST 12" SINGLES AND EPS

*"Can't Go Back"/"Rhiannon"/"Tusk"/"Over & Over," UK WEA W 9848T.....$20–25
*"Fireflies" promo, WBS PRO-A-932 ....$10–15
*Fleetwood Mac Special Radio Sampler from the "Tusk" album, WBS promo, PRO-A-866..$25–50
*"Go Your Own Way"/"Silver Springs" promo, WBS PRO 652......................$25–50
*WEA Promo-Eisco Internacional, No. 41, Brazil, WEA 6WP.0044-A, sampler includes "When I See You Again" from "Tango"...$15–20

STEVIE NICKS' 12" SINGLES—ALL ARE RARE

All of the following have picture jackets.
"Edge of Seventeen" promo, Modern DMD-315..$25–50

*Indicates item featuring Stevie Nicks.

"Has Anyone Ever Written Anything for You"/"No Spoken Word"/"I Can't Wait," UK EMI 5574..$15–25
"I Can't Wait"/"Rock a Little," UK Parlophone 12R 6110 ....$15–25
"I Can't Wait"/"The Nightmare" maxi single, Modern 0-96825 ....$15–30
"If Anyone Falls" promo, Modern PR-533...$25–30
"Long Way to Go"/"Real Tears," Gatefold UK EMI 12 EMG 97......................$10–20
"Long Way to Go"/"Real Tears," UK EMI 12EM 97 ....$8–12
"Rooms on Fire"/"Alice"/"Has Anyone Ever Written Anything for You," UK EMI 12EM 90..$8–12
"Rooms on Fire"/"Alice"/"Has Anyone Ever Written Anything for You," UK poster pack (includes poster), EMI 12EMP 90...$15–35
"Stand Back," promo, Modern PR-507..$25–50
"Stand Back"/"Garbo"/"Wild Heart," UK WEA U9870 (T)..............................$15–30
"Stop Draggin' My Heart Around" promo, Modern PR394 ....$25–50
"Talk to Me" promo, Modern PR-807..$15–25
"Talk to Me"/"One More Big Time Rock-&-Roll," Imperial UK Parlophone 12R 6124 ....$15–35
"Whole Lotta Trouble"/"Edge of Seventeen"/"Beauty & the Beast" (live), UK poster pack (includes poster), EMI 12EMP 114...$15–35

RAREST FLEETWOOD MAC ALBUMS

"Black Magic Woman," Germany, Platinum Records, three-album box set includes: "Oh Well," 24082, "Rattlesnake Shake," 24076, "Madison Blues," 24077 ....$25–35
"English Rose," Epic 26446..$25+
*"Fleetwood Mac," Czechoslovakia, Supraphon 1113 2569..................................$40–60
*"Fleetwood Mac," UK, white vinyl...$30–50
*"Fleetwood Mac Limited Edition Interview Picture Disc," UK Baktabak 2126...$50–150
"Fleetwood Mac Songbook," as performed by Danacers Image, Pickwick International SPC 3631-A..$1–3
*"Hot Rocks," 5/11/90...$50–75
"Japanese Fan Club Album," pressed in Japan only $150–200
"King Biscuit Flower Hour," 7/27/86..$50–100
"Live in Boston," Germany, Line Records LLP 5348, yellow vinyl......................$20–30
*"Masters of Rock Radio Show," aired 2/89 ....$25–50
"Mr. Wonderful," UK Blue Horizon 63205...$25+
"Peter Green's Fleetwood Mac," UK Blue Horizon 63200 ....$25+
    US Epic 26402...$20+
*"Rumours," Holland, white vinyl, WB 56344..$30–50
"Super-duper Blues," UK Blue Horizon SPR 31 ....$25–50
"Super Hits of Fleetwood Mac," promo sampler, Japan, Warner Pioneer PS-308 ....$50–75
*"Superstars in Concert," 7/8/88..$50–100
"The Marquee Collection, Volume 3," UK England Records, Mar 3.........................$10
"The Pious Bird of Good Omen," Blue Horizon 7-63215 ....$25+
*"Westwood One in Concert Fleetwood Mac Show," 85-1 ....$75–250

RAREST STEVIE NICKS ALBUMS

"BBC Rock Hour," UK radio show, BBC 241 ....$25–50
"Buckingham Nicks," Polydor PD 5058, 1973, Gatefold.....................................$20–50
"Earth News Radio," Special of the Month, 1982 ....$25–50
"Hot Rocks," two-LP interview, 5/26/86..$40–60
"Off the Record With Mary Turner," radio show 81-23 ....$75–125
"Reflections from the Other Side of the Mirror" promo, Modern Records PR 2881 ....$25–50
"Robert Klein," two-LP interview, 7/13/81..$35–75
"Startrak Profiles," two-LP interview, 6/2/86 ....$40–60
"The Other Side of the Mirror," UK EMI EMD 1008, includes oval-shaped hologram $25–40

*Indicates item featuring Stevie Nicks.

"The Source," radio concert, NBC 83-13...$75–250
"Westwood One," Rock-a-Little Tour Special...$75–125
"Westwood One," Superstars Concert Series, CO 89-32 ....$150–250

RAREST STEVIE NICKS APPEARANCES ON OTHER ALBUMS

Louise Goffin, "Louise Goffin," Asylum 6E-333 ....$2–5
Robbie Patton, "Orders from Headquarters," ATL 80006 ....$3–5
Sandy Stewart, "Cat Dancer," Modern 7 90133...$15–25
Walter Egan, "Fundamental Roll," COL PC 34679 ....$8–15
Walter Egan, "Not Shy," COL JC 35077 ....$8–15

RAREST STEVIE NICKS SOUNDTRACKS

"Against All Odds," Atlantic 7801521 E...$5–8
"American Anthem," Atlantic 81661 1 ....$5–8
"A Very Special Christmas," A & M 7502-13911-4 ....$18
"Fast Times at Ridgemont High," Full Moon/Asylum 66158 ....$5–10
"Heavy Metal," Full Moon/Asylum DP 90004...$8–20

RAREST FLEETWOOD MAC COMPACT DISCS

"'As Long as You Follow"/"Oh Well" (live), WBS 2-27644 ....$5–8
"The BBC Sessions," EEC SPA 02-CD 3316..$15–22

RARE ALBUMS STEVIE NICKS SINGS ON

"'Fleetwood Mac—The Interview," UK C.I.D. Productions CIDO16 ....$35–75
"'In the Studio," radio program, 8/7/89 ....$35–50
"Need Your Love So Bad"/"Albatross," Austria CBS 655491 1, the greeting card CD!
....$10–25
"'The HMV Classic Collection," Rumours, individually numbered 1-35,000.........$25–50

RAREST STEVIE NICKS COMPACT DISCS

"Long Way to Go"/"Real Tears," UK EMI CDEM97 ....$12–15
"Rooms on Fire" promo, Modern PR 2691-2...$10–15
"Rooms on Fire"/"Alice," UK EMI CDEM 90 ....$12–15
"Rooms on Fire"/"Alice," West Germany EMI/Electrola CDP 560-2033522, maxi CD featuring cover photo on the CD $15–25
"Two Kinds of Love" promo, Modern PR 2875-2..$10–15
"Up Close," two-CD interview for radio $75–125
Walter Egan, "Fundamental Roll," Columbia 34679 ....$8–12
"Whole Lotta Trouble," promo, Modern PR 2977-2...................................$10–15
"Whole Lotta Trouble"/"Beauty & Beast," UK EMI CDEM 114 ....$12–15

RAREST TOUR PROGRAMS

"Rock-a-Little World Tour," 28 pages $30–50
"Rumours," 28 pages $35–50
"The Other Side of the Mirror," 36 pages $25
"The Wild Heart Tour 1983," 20 pages $40–75
"Tusk," 32 pages...$35–75

RAREST BOOKS

Everything You Want to Know About Stevie Nicks, Ballantine Books, by Ethlie Ann Vare & Ed Ochs...$5–25
Fleetwood Mac, Proteus Books, by Steve Clarke...$25–50

'Indicates item featuring Stevie Nicks.

Stevie Nicks Tour Books

Fleetwood Mac Softcover Books

Fleetwood Mac: Rumours 'n' Fax, Harmony Books, by Roy Carr & Steve Clarke
....$25–50
Headliners, Tempo Star, by Charley Walters $25–50
Prince of Annwn, by Evangeline Walton, Ballantine Books, begins the story on
"Rhiannon" $5–20
Rock's Biggest Ten, Scholastic Books $3–5
Superwomen of Rock, by Susan Katz, Tempo Books........................$10–20
The Authorized History of Fleetwood Mac, Warner Brothers, by Samuel Graham
....$25–50
The Rock Video Book, Pocket Books $10–25
The Song of Rhiannon, Ballantine, by Evangeline Walton, tells the story of "Rhiannon"
....$5–50

RAREST POSTERS

Barnyard Shot, by Penguin Promo, 1977.......................................$50+
Behind the Mask, promo with band pictured $10–15
Behind the Mask, U.K. promo, different from U.S. $10–15
"Bella Donna," promo of album cover...$15–75
"Bella Donna," promo of "Stop Draggin'," pic sleeve....................$25–75
Door #6310, by Penguin Promo, 1977, group at door....................$25–50
Dreams Unwind . . . , black & white collage drawing ....$25+
Giant Poster by Penguin Promo, 1977 ....$30–50
Greatest Hits, promo with band photo $10–15
Greatest Hits, U.K. promo with more photos $10–15
HBO Presents Stevie Nicks in Concert, promo $50–75
Japan, promo from "Tusk" era with blue sky & clouds...................$50–75
Live, promo with individual member shots.....................................$20–30
"Long Way to Go," U.K. giant poster...$25–30
Manchester Evening News Pop Special, U.K. newspaper...............$25–30
Mick & Penguin, small, color illustration $10–25
Mirage, promo of album cover..$20–30
Oakland Stadium, Bill Graham Presents lithograph, 1977.............$75–125
"Rock a Little," promo, handtinted on heavy stock.......................$25–40
Rolling Stone Cover, Stevie Nicks promo.....................................$50–75
"Rumours" Convention II, gorgeous black & white drawing.............$6
"Rumours" promo picture from album insert $50–100
"Rumours" U.K. album cover $15–25
"Rumours" promo with older albums at bottom.............................$15–25
Schlitz Light, Mirage Tour promo concert poster............................$25–40
Small poster of band, Stevie with scarf wrapped on head $5–15
Stevie at Wembley Arena, U.K. promo, giant hot pink with pic......$20–30
Stevie in black-hooded top, U.K., by Anabas...............................$10–25
Stevie in pink/purple-sequined top, Holland #RO 059..................$15–25
Stevie in white outfit, seated, U.K. Masterpiece Ent. $10–20
"Tango," Europe album cover and group photo................................$10–20
"Tango," promo of album cover..$10–15
"Tango," promo with Lindsey which was discarded.........................$25–35
"Tango," U.K. giant Wembley concert poster with group pic $20–30
"Tango," U.K. promo, back of album group photo $10–20
"The Other Side of the Mirror," promo, handtinted portrait...........$12–15
"The Other Side of the Mirror," U.K. promo album cover $12–15
"Tusk," Germany concert poster...$25–50
"Tusk" promo, two-sided with black & white photos of band & dog....................$20–30
"Tusk" promo, two-sided with color picture of band $30–40
Wild Heart, promo, handtinted on heavy stock................................$25–40

RAREST FLEETWOOD MAC MISCELLANEOUS

Backstage Passes, prices vary...$5–10
Enamel Pin, penguin on top of Warner Brothers emblem...............$10–20

"Mirage" cardboard stand-up, promo of album cover...$25–50
"Mirage" coffee mug, promo $150
Polish postcard, is a 45 RPM, plays "Rhiannon" $15–25
Press Kits, usually includes photo & bio...$15–25
"Rumours" LP cover mirror, two or more versions..............................$20–30
"Rumours" postcard, promo, barnyard show, with autographs........$10–20
"Rumours" promo cardboard stand-up, two penguins with LP.............$30–75
"Rumours" silk-screened tapestry, back of LP picture $20–50
"Tango," two-sided puzzle, front & back of album..............................$15–25
"Tango" 3-D counter pop-up promo..$10–15
"Tusk" Scarf, promo, white, black, gold with penguins $150–175
Tour Jackets, promo, satin, large or extra large $200–300

RAREST STEVIE NICKS MISCELLANEOUS

Backstage Passes, prices vary...$5–15
"Bella Donna" cardboard cut-out, promo $25–50
"Bella Donna" licensed necklace, goldtone..$15–25
1985 Calendar, by Herbert Worthington III..$20–30
"I Can't Wait," 45 counter stand-up, U.K. promo...............................$15–25
"Mirror" Kaleidoscope promo...$20–30
"Mirror" make-up bag promo..$25–40
"Mirror" red banner, promo with album cover.....................................$10–20
"Mirror" silver banner, promo with words only....................................$10–15
Polish postcard, is 45 RPM, plays "Castaway"....................................$20–25
Postcards & prints by Herbert Worthington III, prices vary $5–20
"The Other Side of the Mirror," postcard, promo $5–10
"The Other Side of the Mirror" press kit deluxe................................$20–40
Tour jackets, promo satin in large or extra large...............................$200–350
Warner Brothers Publications 1990 calendar promo.............................$5–10
"Whole Lotta Music," U.K. promo sampler cassette...........................$15–25
"Wild Heart" pop-folio folder..$3–5
"Wild Heart" violet, promo served as press kit...................................$20–50

RUMOURS

Rumours is a magazine for fans with information on Stevie Nicks and Fleetwood Mac. The goal is to publish the best magazine possible, to be informative, to serve as a forum for Stevie and Mac fans, to bring fellow fans in contact with each other, and to print the best contributions from readers.

Rumours began in the fall of 1987 with the release of the "Tango in the Night" album. Some of the regular features are: Stevie and Mac News, interviews, Pen Pal Page, recording info, classified ads, reader's forum, media info, photos, articles, reviews, European news, and more. *Rumours* encourages fans to contribute original articles, reviews, and photos, and will credit each person whose contributions are used.

Beside the magazine, *Rumours* has held three conventions. Each convention had an art exhibit, video viewing, an auction of Stevie and Mac items to benefit the City of Hope, a trader's market, and social gathering.

Many of *Rumours* readers have greatly increased their collections through information that we have published in *The Back Issue* and through the pen pals that they have located on the pen pal page.

Rumours magazine is $4.50 per issue or $26 for six issues. For more information, send a self-addressed stamped envelope to: *Rumours*, P.O. Box 7210, Virginia Beach, VA 23458.

G

GIG (Premiere Publishing)

1990
Jan. White Lion's Early Days...$1–2
All other issues $1–2

GIG (Tabloid)

Kiss cover issues..$10–20
All other issues $5–10

GO MAGAZINE

1969
Oct. 3 #185 Review of Jimi Hendrix's Harlem, N.Y. Concert................................$20–40
Most all other issues...$5–20

GOLDMINE (Krause Publications)

1976
#12 Jack Scott, Bo Diddley, "For Elvis Fans Only"...$4–8

1977
#16 "Teenage Cruisers," Elvis Presley, X-rated Rockabilly $4–8
#17 Annette Funicello, Bobby Comstock, Nolan Strong......................................$4–8
#18 King Elvis Presley Rocks, What Ever Happened to Tommy James?.................$4–8
#19 Elvis Presley is Eternal: The King of Rock 'n' Roll......................................$4–8
#20 Joey Dee: The Other King of the Twist, Elvis Presley...................................$4–8
#21 Bing Crosby Memorial 1904–1977, Annette Funnicello................................$4–8

1978
#23 The Freniers: Special Brex-in Discography...$3–6
#24 The Flamingos, Elvis Presley $3–6
#25 Rockabilly Invades England $3–6
#26 Buddy Holly: The Day the Music Died..$4–8
#27 Pat Boone Exclusive Interview, James Browne Story...................................$3–6
#28 Annette Funicello & Frankie Avalon, The Crickets, Bobby Helms, Elvis Presley....$3–6
#29 Ivory Joe Hunter, Orville Jones, Percy Marshall...$3–6
#30 Screamin' Jay Hawkins, Dodie Stevens, The Beatles, Elvis Presley.................$3–6
#31 Jan & Dean, The Dore Story, Bill Watkins, Dale Davis.................................$3–6

1979

#32 Lenny Bruce, The Jordanaires, Gary U.S. Bonds..............................$3–6
#34 Lesley Gore: Changing With the Times, Ronnie Spector interview, The Delta Rhythm Boys $3–6
#35 John Stewart, The Fleetwoods, David Bowie, Van Morrison...................$3–6
#38 Petula Clark, Laura Lee, Deep River Boys, The Royal Teens, Charlie Feathers, The Roches, Boomtown Rats...$3–6
#39 Bobby Rydell interview, Bill Doggett, Renaissance, Elvis Presley.............$3–6
#40 The Smothers Brothers, The Four Knights, Buddy Holly $3–6
#41 Roy Orbison, Minnie Riperton, Asleep at the Wheel $3–6
#42 Chuck Berry interview, Johnny Sayles, The Zantees $3–6
#43 Waylon Jennings, The Gems, Gregg Kihn, Gary Puckett, The Kinks..................$3–6

1980

#44 Elvis Presley: The '68 Comeback, Herman's Hermits, The Tornadoes, Southside Johnny, Tom Rush, Gene Chandler..$3–6
#45 The Angels interview, Ray Charles, Procol Harum, Bo Diddley, Charles Bridges, The Hanson Brothers..$3–6
#47 Tiger Haynes, Herb Alpert, Bill Haley, Elvis Presley, Brenda Lee $3–6
#48 Collecting Bob Dylan, Spike Jones, Lenny Kaye, Cleftones......................$3–6
#49 A Talk With Carl Perkins, The Association, Nightcaps...............................$2–5
#50 The Beatles, The Troggs, The Shoes, Tommy James.................................$3–6
#52 The Shirelles, The Innocents, Michelle Phillips, Robert Fripp.......................$3–6
#53 Special Motown Issue, The Temptations, Hank Cosby, Mary Wells, Elvis Presley ..$3–6
#54 The Ruth Brown Story, The Beach Boys, The Rumblers.............................$3–6
#55 Phil Spector, The Crystals, Ronnie Spector, Elvis Presley, Payola.....................$2–5
#56 Special Elvis Presley Issue..$3–6

1981

#57 Fats Domino, John Lennon, Garland Jeffreys, Bruce Springsteen, Murray the K, Johnny & the Hurricanes...$3–6
#58 Bobby Darin, Bobby Vee, Johnny Horton, The Slits, Peter Noone, Marty Robbins, Eddie Fontaine..$3–6
#59 The Kinks: An Interview With Dave Davies, Bill Haley, Dr. Hook, Little Anthony, The Clash, Elvis Presley, Humble Pie $3–6
#60 Little Milton, The Vee-Jay Story, Dee Clark, The Standells...................$3–6
#61 The Dave Clarke Five, The Searchers, Cliff Richard, The Jam, The Idle Race, Martha Reeves Exclusive Interview..$3–6
#62 The Blues Project, The Vagrants on the Road With Jerry Lee Lewis, The Ventures, The Buckinghams, Stray Cats, Adam & the Ants, Steely Dan & Tom Petty......................$3–6
#63 The Four Seasons, Ben E. King, Leiber & Stoller, Gary U.S. Bonds, The Isley Brothers, The Four Tops, Sha Na Na..$3–6
#65 The Beach Boys: 20 Years on Badfinger, Asbury Park Music, The Tokens, Billy Joe Royal, Junior Walker, The Jacksons, Rachel Sweet, Tiny Tim, The Monkees, Bruce Springsteen...$3–6
#66 James Brown: Godfather of Soul, Hank Ballard, Bobby Lewis, Randy Newman, Vanilla Fudge, Elvis Presley, Grass Roots, Ramones $3–6
#67 John Entwistle, The Hollies, B.J. Thomas, Del Shannon, The Knack $3–6

1982

#69 Cher, Marianne Faithful, Dusty Springfield, Vicki Carr, Lulu, U2, Five Satins....$3–6
#70 The Beatles Special, Louis Armstrong, The Teenagers................................$3–6
#71 Jefferson Airplane, The Mamas & Papas, Jan & Dean, Otis Rush, Peter Tosh....$3–6
#73 New Orleans Sound, Nick Lowe, The Crewcuts, The Fleshtones $3–6
#75 Iggy Pop, The Champs, Beach Boys, New Jersey Doo-wop, The Leaves, The Impalas $3–6
#76 Special Country and Rockabilly Issue..$3–6
#77 The Beatles, A Talk With Pete Best, David Crosby, The Byrds, Billy Stewart....$3–6

1983

#80 Annual Elvis Special, Gene Pitney, Elvis Costello, Johnny Rivers, Rachel Sweet, Cousin Brucie, Lewis Lymon...$3–6
#82 Sandy Nelson, Conway Twitty, The Harptones, Brian Eno.................................$3–6
#85 B.B. King, Clyde McPhatter, The Impressions, King Sunny Ade.........................$3–6
#87 Frankie Valli Exclusive Interview, Marshall Crenshaw, King Floyd.................$3–6
#88 The Supremes: Exclusive Interview With Mary Wilson, Neil Diamond...............$3–6
#91 Elvis Costello Interview, The Beatles on TV, Little Feat, Bob Dylan, David Bowie, Gran Parsons, Herbie Smith...$3–6

1984

#92 Elvis Presley: His Unreleased Recordings, Julie London, The Beatles, The Shirelles....$3–6
#96 Mary Travers Talks About Folk Music & Peter, Paul & Mary...............................$2–5
#97 "Big Chief" Russell Monroe, Jim Capaldi, Chad & Jeremy.................................$2–5
#99 Don Pierce, The Righteous Brothers, Harry Nilsson, Casey Kasem.....................$2–5
#100 Bobby Fuller: His Music & Mysterious Death, Neil Sedaka, The Dells, Southside Johnny, Wynton Marsalls..$3–6
#102 Kingston Trio, Freddie King Revealing Interview, Boswell Sisters.....................$2–5
#103 Lillian McMurry's Story, The Manhattan Transfer: Then & Now.......................$2–5
#105 Elvis Presley: A Guide to Elvis Films, The Dells: 70s & 80s...........................$2–5
#106 Joey Dee, Elliot Horne interview, Tommy Maken & Liam Clancy.....................$2–5
#108 Stan Rogers, The Ink Spots, The Picks: Behind the Crickets Sound..................$2–5
#109 The Kendalls, Steeleye Span: The Return, Alvin Lee: 15 Years After................$2–5
#110 The Association, Timi Yuro, Bill Evans, Introspective Discography.....................$2–5
#111 Mott the Hoople, Leiber & Stoller, Hank Williams: Some New Light.................$2–5
#114 John Lennon: Recollections, Steve Goodman, Country Joe McDonald...............$3–6

1985

#116 Michael Bloomfield $2–5
#117 Elvis Presley, Solomon Burke, Mickey Gilley..$2–5
#118 Roy Orbison: Cadillac & Diamond Ring, Bobby Fuller, Alan Freed...................$2–5
#119 Roy Buchanan: Oldie but Goodie, Atlantic Collectibles Guide.........................$2–5
#121 Sam the Sham & the Pharoahs, Gordon Jenkins, Mel Carter, Harvey Fuqua.....$2–5
#122 Dave Clarke Five, The British Invasion 1964 Style..$2–5
#124 Tim Buckley, Lee Rogers: The D-town Story, Tania Maria..................................$2–5
#125 Bill Doggett, Tim Buckley: The Interview $2–5
#127 Eddie Rabbit, Orion, Baker Knight $2–5
#129 Audio Video: Then & Now...$2–4
#131 Poco: Rusty Young Looks Back, Gamble Rogers: Modern Day Troubadour.....$2–4
#132 The Beatles: In Person & On the Air: Their Solo Years....................................$2–5
#133 Elvis Presley, Southside Johnny Talks About Elvis, Leslie West.......................$2–5
#134 Ray Charles: The Genius, The Ventures: Surviving the 80s...............................$2–4
#135 Quicksilver Messenger Service: Happy Trails in Psychedelic Music.................$2–5
#136 Cream: As Told by Ginger Baker, Jack Bruce & Felix Pappalardi.....................$2–4
#137 P.F. Sloan, Tom Russell, Idle Race, Chas & Dave $2–4
#138 The Chi-lites: From Street Corners to Court Room, Lonnie Mack.....................$2–4
#139 60s' Albums: A Basic but Subjective Guide to Collecting, Chi-lites...................$2–4
#140 Big Jay McNeely, Dino, Desi & Billy: Silver Spoon Rebels $2–4
#141 The Buckinghams, Johnny Cash: The Sun Sound...$2–4

1986

#143 Eric Anderson, Joe Turner, The Microgroove Revolution $2–4
#144 Skeeter Davis: They Don't Make 'em Any Sweeter...$2–4
#146 Taj Mahal: The Blues & Beyond, Jerry Merritt..$2–4
#147 The Beau Brummels...$2–4
#148 Johnny Winter, Rolling Stones: To Box or Not to Box, Jorgen Ingmann...........$2–4
#149 Gary Lewis: Count Him In, Johnny Winter, Duane Allman, Kate Bush: Longing in Love & Other Excursions, Elvis Presley Session Background $2–5
#150 Peter Asher of Peter & Gordon, Tommy Sands, Victor Pearlin interview..........$2–4
#151 Spirit: The Most Neglected Rock Group of the 60s, James Brown, The Juniors...$2–4

#152 Bobby Day: His Mysterious Recording History, Spirit Part II, Blue Cheer $2–4
#154 Motown: A Look at Motown's Success & Failures...$2–4
#155 Keith Before & After '98, 6″, Genesis Part II, Peter Grendysa..........................$2–4
#156 Buddy Holly: Those Who Knew Him, Norman Petty: Setting Labels Straight...$2–5
#157 Eddie Bond: A Reluctant Rockabilly, Ike & Tina Turner, Frank Zappa, Ray Davies
....
#159 The Music Machine, Buddy Holly: Those Who Knew Him Part II, The Supremes,
Ricky Nelson, Elvis Presley, Sonic Youth, Jonathan Richman $2–5
#160 Canned Heat: Living the Blues, Peter Gabriel: The Solo Years, The Velvets: Motown's
Colorful Girl Group Sound, The Beatles, The Who, The Ramones, Chuck Berry.......$2–5
#161 Carl Perkins, John Lennon, Del Shannon, Dusty Springfield, Bob Dylan..........$2–4
#162 The Zombies, The Kinks, The British Invasion Special..$2–4
#163 Captain Beefheart, The Critters: Don Cicone interview...$2–4
#164 Bob Dylan: 25 Years of Chaos, Patti Page is Still a Rage.....................................$2–4
#165 Bobby Darin: Encouraging Signs, Johnny Ace, The Contours...............................$2–4
#166 Donovan, Gordon Lightfoot, Jesse Belvin, Buddy Holly, The Honeys, Little Richard
....$2–4
#167 Phil Ochs, The Jury, Elvis Presley, Bob Dylan, Tina Turner, The Beatles, James
Brown..$2–4

1987

#168 Sam Cooke, Ritchie Valens: The 17-year-old Recording Sensation, Joan Jett.....$2–5
#169 Commander Cody, Elvis Presley's Generosity Lives On, Robert Palmer.............$2–4
#170 Neil Young: A Rock Legend Talks About His Winnipeg Years, Bruce Springsteen: A
Collector's Look at Live/1975–1985, Graham Parker, Charlie Rich $2–4
#171 Buffalo Springfield, Van Halen, Neil Young: A 20-year Vinyl Retrospective, Isaac
Hayes, Eric Carmen, Kool & the Gang, The Chordettes $2–4
#172 Sex Pistols, Australian Rock, The Allman Brothers Band: Live at the Fillmore East,
Husker Du: Another Day Rising $2–4
#173 Ricky Erickson & the 13th-Floor Elevators, Big Bopper, Janis Joplin, ZZ Top, The
Fabulous Thunderbirds, Junior Parker, Freddie King..$2–4
#175 Little Richard Leaves a Message, Pointer Sisters, The Teddy Bears, Robert Parker,
Champaign, Psychedelic Furs, Sandie Shaw, Tim Hardin $2–4
#199 New York Dolls, Michael Jackson, Donna Summer $2–4

1989*

#233 The Guess Who, Cowboy Junkies, The Ugly Ducklings, Terry Jacks $1–2
#237 Bob Dylan Goes Digital: A Guide to Dylan on Disc, Dylan in Print, Dylan's Foreign
Albums, Dylan Discography & Price Guide, Dylan as a Student, Joan Baez, Cub Koda ..$2–5
#239 The 100 Most Valuable Albums, Rarest Elvis Presley Disc, Harry Chapin, The
Thrashmen vs. the Rivingtons...$1–2
#241 The Rolling Stones, Stones on Tour '89, The Stones' Price Guide & Discography, Cub
Koda..$1–3
#243 The Beatles: The Solo Years—Exclusive Interview With Beatle Historian Mark
Lewisohn, Guide to Beatle Books, Badfinger: Then & Now, A Special Beatles issue $2–4
#244 One-hits Wonder, Berlin, Debby Boone, Patty Duke, Aaron Neville...................$1–2

1990

#247 Bob Marley & the Wailers, Johnny Nash $1–2
#248 Dionne Warwick, Little Eva, Janis Ian, Dorothy Moore, Lorraine Ellison, Nancy Wilson, Kate & Ann McGarrigle, The GTOs $1–2
#249 Buck Owens, The Nitty Gritty Dirt Band, Steve Earle, Rodney Crowell, The Maddox
Brothers & Rose, Jerry Reed..$1–2
#250 Willie Dixon, John Mayall, John Hammond, Lowell Fulson, Mercy Dee Walton,
Charles Brown, Peppermint Harris, Frank Frost, Buddy Guy, Floyd Dixon $1–2
#252 Bruce Springsteen, The E Street Band, Clarence Clemons, Del Shannon $1–3
#253 The Laddins, The Cadillacs, The Five Chances, The Cardinals, The Staple Singers,
Gene Mumford, The Flamingos, Richard Lanham, The Hornets, Mickey Newbury $1–2

*1988—All issues $2–4.

#255 The Hollies, Petula clark $1–2
#256 Prince, NRBQ, Dave Brubeck, Flo & Eddie vs. De La Soul............................$1–2
#257 The Beach Boys, Jan & Dean, Wilson Phillips..$1–2
#258 Otis Redding, Carl Perkins, Steve Cropper, Ronnie Hawkins, Rufus Thomas, Howlin' Wolf, Bill Justis, Arthur Conley...$1–2
#259 Kiss, Billy Joe Royal, Frankie Lee..$2–5
#260 Miles Davis, Tom Petty, K.D. Lang, Shel Talmy.......................................$1–2

GOOD HOUSEKEEPING

1978

Apr. Marie Osmond: Why TV Fame Can't Spoil Her..$4–8

1979

Aug. Marie Osmond: A Mother's Dream Come True...$4–8

1980

Mar. Marie Osmond: What Grown-up Daughters Owe Their Mothers $4–8

1983

Sept. Marie Osmond: "For Me, Happiness is Having a Baby" $3–6

1985

May Marie Osmond: "How My Husband & I Saved Our Marriage" $3–6

GOOD TIMES (Tabloid)

All issues...$4–20

GRAFFITI

1988

Aug., Vol. 4, #8 Iggy Pop Exclusive Interview, Run DMC, Jane Wieldlin Remembers, Ohio Players, OMD..$3–6

GREASE POSTER MONTHLY

#1–#3...$2–4

GROOVES

1978

Mar. The Who: Who are You?, issue includes a giant color Who wall poster, The Triumphant Return of Alice Cooper, The Alice Cooper Diary & Personal Profile, The Alice Cooper Show, Cars $10–20

1979

May Paul Stanley: The Kiss Explosion, Electric Light Orchestra, Donna Summer: Heat Wave, Van Halen: Overnight Superstars, Exclusive Paul Stanley Interview, Joni Mitchell, Bob Welch: Ex-Fleetwood Mac...$12–25
June Bruce Springsteen: Frenzied Flight, Glorius Landing, Meat Loaf's Rock Opera Exclusive Interview, Angel: Coming in for the Kill, Parliament, Sha Na Na, Eddie Money, Ramones, Lou Reed, Nicolette Larson, Ray Charles, Steve Forbet, Alicia Bridges $6–12
Sept. Kiss Tours the World, Blondie: From Punk to Platinum, The Allman Brothers: Phase Three, Joe Simon, Nazareth, Black Sabbath, TKO...$12–25
Oct. David Bowie: "I am the New Wave," Blondie/Debbie Harry: An Up-close Look at the Early Days, Marshall Tucker Exclusive Interview, Jefferson Starship: Surrealistic Voyage, Styx: Doing it on the Road, The Police, Chuck Berry, Roxy Music, Triumph $10–20
Nov. Rod Stewart: Still Sexy After All These Years, The Cars: Out of the Garage & into the Spotlight, Moody Blues: Will They Play Forever?, Cheap Trick Exclusive: Backstage Concert Soundcheck, Rush interview, The Doors, Patti Smith, Graham Parker $7–15

Dec. Paul Stanley: Kiss Blasts New Dynasty, Ted Nugent color wall poster, Jethro Tull interview, Commodores: Motown Magic, Journey: Long Day's Voyage to the Top, Carmine Appice, The Romantics, Everly Brothers, Ian Hunter, Blackfoot, Ellen Foley, Melissa Manchester $12–25

GUITAR FOR THE PRACTICING MUSICIAN
1989
Nov. Metallica, Guns 'n' Roses, Stevie Ray Vaughan, The Traveling Wilburys $2–3
All other issues $2–3

GUITAR PLAYER
1967
June #1 Premier Issue...$25–50
Aug. #2 The Byrds..$20–40
Oct. #3 Laura Weber..$10–20
Dec. #4 Pete Seeger $10–20

1968
Feb. #5 Juan Serrano...$10–20
Apr. #6 Special: Guitar Construction...$10–20
June #7 Cream $15–30
Aug. #8 Special New Product Issue $10–20
Oct. #9 The Dobro..$10–20
Dec. #10 Jimi Hendrix $30–60

1969
Feb. #11 Buddy Guy..$10–20
Apr. #12 Glen Campbell..$10–20
June #13 Buffy Sainte-Marie $10–20
Aug. #14 Albert King $10–20
Oct. #15 Chet Atkins $10–20
Dec. #16 B.B. King..$10–20

1970
Feb. #17 Les Paul $10–20
Mar. #18 Special Artists Issue $10–20
Apr. #19 Howard Roberts, Crosby, Stills, Nash & Young $10–20
June #20 Chistopher Parkening, Eric Clapton $10–20
Aug. #21 Taj Mahal $10–20
Sept. #22 Special AMP Issue, Jose Feliciano..$10–20
Oct. #23 Barney Kessel..$5–10
Dec. #24 String Symposium Special..$5–10

1971
Feb. #25 Chuck Berry...$6–12
Mar. #26 Annual Artists Issue $6–12
Apr. #27 Jerry Garcia of the Grateful Dead $10–20
June #28 Segovia $5–10
Aug. #29 Terry Kath $5–10
Sept. #30 Special Guitar Issue..$6–12
Oct. #31 Alvin Lee $10–20
Dec. #32 Folk Guitar in Britain Special..$5–10

1972
Feb. #33 Chet Atkin's Own Story $5–10
Mar. #34 Annual Artists Issue $6–12
Apr. #35 Mountain $6–12
May/June #36 Pete Townshend $10–20
July/Aug. #37 Doc Watson...$5–10
Sept. #38 Guitar on Record..$5–10

Oct. #39 Dickey Betts..$4–8
Nov./Dec. #40 Rusty Young...$4–8

1973

Jan./Feb. #41 John Cipollina..$4–8
Mar. #42 Annual Artist Issue...$4–8
Apr. #43 Steve Howe..$4–8
May/June #44 Serranito, Duane Allman Tribute...$5–10
July/Aug. #45 Wes Montgomery $4–8
Sept. #46 Pete Drake $3–6
Oct. #47 Brownie McGhee...$3–6
Nov./Dec. #48 Jeff Beck $5–10

1974

Jan. #49 George Benson..$5–10
Feb. #50 J. Geils...$5–10
Mar. #51 Joe Pums & Chuck Wayne...$3–6
Apr. #52 Andres Segavie..$3–6
May #53 Tut Taylor, Robert Fripp...$4–8
June #54 Wishbone Ash..$4–8
July #55 Earl Scruggs...$3–6
Aug. #56 Johnny Winter...$5–10
Sept. #57 Greg Lake...$4–8
Oct. #58 Byrd-Kessel-Ellis...$3–6
Nov. #59 Carlos Santana..$3–6
Dec. #60 Larry Coryell..$3–6

1975

Jan. #61 Kim Simmonds $3–6
Feb. #62 John McLaughlin..$3–6
Mar. #63 B.B. King...$3–6
Apr. #64 Paul Simon..$4–8
May #65 Jan Akkerman...$3–6
June #66 Joe Walsh...$3–6
July #67 Stanley Clarke...$3–6
Aug. #68 Rick Derringer $3–6
Sept. #69 Jimi Hendrix Special (two different editions)..................$6–12 ea.
Oct. #70 Dave Mason..$3–6
Nov. #71 John Entwistle $3–6
Dec. #72 Ron Wood $4–8

1976

Jan. #73 Stephen Stills $3–6
Feb. #74 Elvin Bishop $3–6
Mar. #75 Richard Betts..$3–6
Apr. #76 Joe Pass..$3–6
May #77 Toy Caldwell...$3–6
June #78 Jorma Kaukonen $3–6
July #79 David Bromberg $3–6
Aug. #80 Eric Clapton...$4–8
Sept. #81 Marie Travis, Frank Marino $3–6
Oct. #82 Roy Buchanan...$2–4
Nov. #83 Django Reinhardt...$2–4
Dec. #84 Robertson & Danko..$2–4

1977

Jan. #85 GP's 10th Anniversary Issue, Frank Zappa....................................$3–6
Feb. #86 Jim Messina...$2–4
Mar. #87 Charlie Daniels $3–6
Apr. #88 J.J. Cale...$3–6
May #89 Bonnie Raitt $3–6

June #90 Pat Martino $2–4
July #91 Jimmy Page...$4–8
Aug. #92 Leo Kottke $2–4
Sept. #93 Albert King $2–4
Oct. #94 Todd Rundgren...$4–8
Nov. #95 Keith Richards $4–8
Dec. #96 Les Paul $2–4

1978

Jan. #97 Steve Miller..$2–4
Feb. #98 Al DiMeola $2–4
Mar. #99 Roy Gallagher $2–4
Apr. #100 Herb Ellis $2–4
May #101 Steve Howe $2–4
June #102 Carlos Santana $2–4
July #103 Jose Feliciano..$3–6
Aug. #104 John McLaughlin $3–6
Sept. #105 Ritchie Blackmore $3–6
Oct. #106 Jerry Garcia..$4–8
Nov. #107 Roy Clark $2–4
Dec. #108 Bill Wyman...$4–8

1979

Jan. #109 Ace Frehley..$10–20
Feb. #110 Lee Ritenour $2–4
Mar. #111 Joe Perry..$3–6
Apr. #112 Mike Bloomfield..$2–4
May #113 Larry Carlton $2–4
June #114 Howard Roberts $2–4
July #115 George Benson $2–4
Aug. #116 Ted Nugent $3–6
Sept. #117 Mick Ralphs $2–4
Oct. #118 Chet Atkins $2–4
Nov. #119 Rick Nielsen $3–6
Dec. #120 Nancy Wilson, Roger Fisher $2–4

1980

Jan. #121 Pat Travers $2–4
Feb. #122 Tommy Tedesco...$2–4
Mar. #123 Ry Cooder $2–4
Apr. #124 Eddie Van Halen $3–6
May #125 Stanley Clarke $2–4
June #126 Alex Lifeson $2–4
July #127 Robin Trower $2–4
Aug. #128 College Guitar, Leslie West $2–4
Sept. #129 B.B King..$2–4
Oct. #130 Jeff Beck $3–6
Nov. #131 John Williams $2–4
Dec. #132 Jeff Baxter..$2–4

1981

Jan. #133 Hank Garland...$2–4
Feb. #134 Billy Gibbons..$2–4
Mar. #135 DiMeola, DeLucia, McLaughlin $2–4
Apr. #136 Kenny Burrell $2–4
May #137 Albert Lee $2–4
June #138 Japan World Guitar Superpower..$2–4
July #139 Shaw, Young, Panozzo (Styx) $2–4
Aug. #140 George Van Eps..$2–4
Sept. #141 The Ventures..$2–4

Oct. #142 Special Issue: Duane Allman...$4–8
Nov. #143 Peter Frampton $3–6
Dec. #144 Pat Metheny..$2–4

1982

Jan. #145 Craig Chaquico $2–4
Feb. #146 Gary Richrath $2–4
Mar. #147 Charlie Christian...$2–4
Apr. #148 David Lindley..$2–4
May #149 Special Issue Equipment..$2–4
June #150 The Legend of Buddy Holly $3–6
July #151 Neal Schon..$2–4
Aug. #152 Steve Morse $2–4
Sept. #153 Andy Summers $3–6
Oct. #154 Special Equipment Issue $2–4
Nov. #155 Randy Rhoads...$3–6
Dec. #156 Allan Holdsworth $2–4

1983

Jan. #157 Brian May $3–6
Feb. #158 Frank Zappa..$3–6
Mar. #159 Women in Rock...$5–10
Apr. #160 Keith Richards...$5–10
May #161 Jim Hall $2–4
June #162 Special Equipment Issue $2–4
July #163 Judas Priest $3–6
Aug. #164 Muddy Waters With Johnny Winter..$3–6
Sept. #165 Rockabilly Revival, Frank Marino..$2–4
Oct. #166 Andres Segovia..$2–4
Nov. #167 Iron Maiden $3–6
Dec. #168 Roots of Rockabilly, Eddie Cochran...$3–6

1984

Jan. #169 Adrian Belew $2–4
Feb. #170 AC/DC's Angus Young...$3–6
Mar. #171 Talking Heads: Byrne & Weymouth..$3–6
Apr. #172 Steve Lukather $2–4
May. #173 James Taylor...$3–6
June #174 Rock Guitar Pioneers $3–6
July #175 Eddie Van Halen..$3–6
Aug. #176 Joe Pastorius..$2–4
Sept. #177 Mark Knopfler $2–4
Oct. #178 Stevie Ray Vaughan, Steve Vai...$2–4
Nov. #179 David Gilmour, Steve Morse...$3–6
Dec. #180 Night Ranger...$3–6

1985

Jan. #181 Rick Emmett, Chet Atkins..$2–4
Feb. #182 New Directions in Acoustic Steel-string, Allan Holdsworth $2–4
Mar. #183 Special Equipment Issue $2–4
Apr. #184 John Fogerty, Yngwie Malmsteen..$2–4
May #185 Yngwie Malmsteen, Arlen Roth $2–4
June #186 The Edge of U2, Benjamin Vandery..$3–6
July #187 Special Issue: The Eric Clapton Story, Billy Connors $3–6
Aug. #188 Earl Klugh, Roy Buchanan $2–4
Sept. #189 John McLaughlin, Bob Brozman $2–4
Oct. #190 Stanley Jordan...$2–4
Nov. #191 Jeff Beck, Raybeats & Paul Johnson...$3–6
Dec. #192 Personal Studios, John Scofield $2–4

1986

Jan. #193 Robert Fripp...$3–6
Feb. #194 Al DiMeola...$2–4
Mar. #195 Billy Gibbons, Billy Sheehan $2–4
Apr. #196 Geddy Lee, Kazumi Watanabe $2–4
May #197 Eric Johnson..$2–4
June #198 Guitar Synthesizers & Midi, Henry Kaiser & Bill Frisell $2–4
July #199 Jimmie Vaughan, D. Robillard $2–4
Aug. #200 Joe Pass...$2–4
Sept. #201 Steve Howe, Steve Hackett, David Tanenbaum.....................$2–4
Oct. #202 Steve Vai, Michael Hedges..$2–4
Nov. #203 John Abercrombie, Brad Gillis $2–4
Dec. #204 Billie Sheehan, Christmas Jazz: Ron Eschete $2–4

1987

Jan. #205 20th Anniversary: Frank Zappa, Dweezil Zappa $2–4
Feb. #206 Los Lobos, Hubert Sumlin $2–4
Mar. #207 Mike Stern, Adrian Belew $2–4
Apr. #208 Warren De Martini, Jimmy Bryant $2–4
May #209 Robert Cray, Eric Clapton..$2–4
June #210 John Scofield, Jorge Morel...$2–4
July # 211 Lifeson, Emmet, Boud, Rickert..$2–4
Aug. #212 Strat Mania, David Starobin $2–4
Sept. #213 Speed Tips...$2–4
Oct. #214 Van Halen & Hagar, Albert Lee $2–4
Nov. #215 George Harrison, David Torn...$2–4
Dec. #216 Sneak Previews Guitar Gear '88, Herb Ellis' Xmas Jazz $2–4

1988

Jan. #217 Lynyrd Skynyrd, Carlos Santana, C. Thompson $2–4
Feb. #218 Joe Satriani $2–4
Mar. #219 Chuck Berry, Cooder & Vai's Crossroads $2–4
Apr. #220 Joe Walsh, Tuck Andress..$2–4
May #221 Albert Collins, Jerry Donahue $2–4
June #222 Frank Gambale, John Patitucci $2–4
July #223 Jerry Garcia, B. Jones & J. Blackthorne..................................$2–4
Aug. #224 Eric Clapton, Derek & the Dominos $2–4
Sept. #225 Robert Ford...$2–4
Oct. #226 Vernon Reid $2–4
Nov. #227 AMPS Special Edition, U.S.S.R. Guitar: Nikita Koshkin......$2–4
Dec. #228 Guitar in the U.S.S.R., Foley $2–4

1989

Jan. #229 19th Annual Readers Poll Awards, Hans Reichel.....................$2–4
Feb. #230 The Art of Improvisation, Frank Gambale...............................$2–4
Mar. #231 Unknown Greats, Danny Gatton $2–4
Apr. #232 Metallica, Eliot Fisk..$2–4
May #233 Jimi Hendrix...$3–6
June #234 Digital Magic, Jimi Hendrix...$3–6
July #235 Jennifer Batten, Kalle Rademacker $2–4
Aug. #236 Jeff Healey, Allman Brothers $2–4
Sept. #237 Pete Townshend, Stu Hamm $2–4
Oct. #238 Steve Morse, Billy Sheehan & Paul Gilbert $2–4
Nov. #239 Joe Satriani $2–4
Dec. #240 Keith Richards, Christmas Medley...$2–4

1990

Jan. #241 Johnny Marr...$2–4
Feb. #242 Stevie Ray Vaughan & Jeff Beck, Joe Pass $2–4
Mar. #243 Allan Holdsworth..$2–4

Apr. #244 Buddy Guy, Dave Tronzo...$2–4
May #245 Steve Vai...$2–4
June #246 Julian Bream, Steve Morse & Jeff Watson.........................$2–4
July #247 Paul McCartney...$2–4

GUITAR SCHOOL (Harris Publications)
1989

Apr. #1 Steve Vai, Jimi Hendrix: Like a Rolling Stone, Edward Van Halen, Jimmy Page, Ry Cooder..$4–8
July #2 Def Leppard: Armageddon Ain't Foolin', Steve Ray Vaughan: Rude Mood, Eric Clapton, INXS, Rush, Winger...$3–6
Sept. #3 Yngwie Malmsteen: Rising Force, Vinnie Moore: Pieces of a Picture, Jeff Beck, Jimmy Page, Buddy Guy..$3–5
Nov. #4 Bon Jovi's Richie Sambora, Skid Row, The Who, Pete Townshend, Van Halen, Jimmy Hendrix, Killer Covers...$3–5

GUITAR STARS
1979

Apr. #6 Keith Richards Guilty in Toronto: Who Breaks a Butterfly Under a Rolling Stone?, Discographies of Jimi Hendrix & Neil Young, Histories of Fleetwood Mac & The Beatles, Tom Petty, Kiss Picker Pix: Paul Stanley & Ace Frehley, Tom Verlaine, Mick Jones, Pete Townshend, Warren Zevon, Bruce Cockburn, Jerry Garcia, Van Halen, Stevie Nicks, Talking Heads...$5–10
All other issues...$3–6

GUITAR WORLD
1980

July #1 Johnny Winter...$10–20
Sept. #2 Pat Metheny..$6–12
Nov. #3 Al DiMeola..$4–8

1981

Jan. #4 Eddie Van Halen..$5–10
Mar. #5 The Pretenders/Chrissie Hynde..$4–8
May #6 Andy Summers, Keith Richards, Frank Zappa.............................$4–8
July #7 John McLaughlin...$4–8
Sep. #8 Jeff Beck..$4–8
Nov. #9 Alex Lifeson...$3–6

1982

Jan. #10 Neal Schon..$3–6
Mar. #11 Frank Zappa...$3–6
May. #12 Adrian Belew...$3–6
July #13 Sting..$4–8
Sept. #14 Steve Howe...$3–6
Nov. #15 Eddie Van Halen...$4–8

1983

Jan. #16 Robbie Krieger..$3–6
Mar. #17 Les Paul...$3–6
May #18 Jaco Pastorius...$3–6
July #19 Steve Morse, King Sunny Ade, Mark Knopfler, Bow Wow Wow, Jeff Beck..$3–6
Sept. #20 Steve Lukather..$3–6
Nov. #21 Pete Townshend...$3–6

1984

Jan. #22 Eddie Van Halen...$3–6
Mar. #23 Angus Young..$3–6

May #24 Billy Gibbons $3–6
July #25 Judas Priest's K.K. Downing & G. Tipton $3–6
Sept. #26 The Car's Elliot Easton $3–6
Nov. #27 Quiet Riot's Carlos Cavazo.....................................$3–6

1985

Jan. #28 Jeff Beck $3–6
Mar. #29 Ron Wood $3–6
May #30 Brian Setzer $3–6
July #31 Eddie Van Halen...$3–6
Sept. #32 The Ultimate Tribute! Jimi Hendrix...........................$4–8
Nov. #33 Stevie Ray Vaughan $3–6

1986

Jan. #34 Yngwie Malmsteen $3–6
Mar. #35 Keith Richards $3–6
May #36 Steve Stevens $3–6
July #37 Special Jimmy Page Issue $3–6
Sept. #38 Eddie Van Halen $3–6
Nov. #39 Billy Gibbons $3–6

1987

Jan. #40 Yngwie Malmsteen $2–4
Mar. #41 Steve Vai & Billy Sheehan.......................................$2–4
Apr. #42 Andy Summers $2–4
June #43 Randy Rhoads $2–4
July #44 The Edge $2–4
Sept. #45 Chris Squire $2–4
Nov. #46 Mark Knopfler $2–4
Dec. #47 Joe Perry $2–4

1988

Jan. #48 Michael Schenker..$2–4
Mar. #49 Hendrix Lives!: A Tribute to a Genius $3–6
Apr. #50 Alex Lifeson & Geddy Lee (Edition 1)........................$2–4
Apr. #51 George Lynch (Edition 2)..$2–4
May #52 Steve Vai $2–4
June #53 Yngwie Malmsteen $2–4
July #54 Eddie Van Halen...$2–4
Sept. #55 Stevie Ray Vaughan $2–4
Oct. #56 Jimmy Page...$2–4
Nov. #57 Metallica...$2–4
Dec. #58 Keith Richards $2–4

1989

Jan. #59 Robert Cray...$2–4
Feb. #60 Night Ranger: Jeff Watson & Brad Gillis.....................$2–4
Mar. #61 Guns 'n' Roses: Izzy & Slash...................................$2–4
Apr. #62 State of the Bass: J. Bruce & B. Sheehan....................$2–4
May #63 Allan Holdsworth..$2–4
June #64 Zakk Wylde $2–4
July #65 Stevie Ray Vaughan $2–4
Sept. #66 White Lion's Vito Bratte $2–4
#67 Guitar Buyer's Guide $2–4
Oct. #68 Steve Stevens $2–4
Nov. #69 Joe Satriani $2–4
Dec. #70 Eric Clapton $2–4

1990

Jan. #71 Steve Vai $2–4
Feb. #72 Eddie Van Halen...$2–4

Mar. #73 Aerosmith $2–4
Apr. #74 Joe Satriani & Steve Vai $2–4
May #75 Special Issue: Metal Cutting Edge $2–4
June #76 Zakk Wilde & Ozzy Osbourne...$2–4
July #77 10th Anniversary Special Issue $2–4
Sept. #78 Special Issue: Blues Power $2–4
All other issues to present $2–4

H

HARD ROCK
1970
#1 The Grateful Dead's Jerry Garcia interview..$12–25

HARD ROCK
1978
Apr. #1 Kiss: War of the Worlds, Led Zeppelin: The Truth to the Rumors, Peter Frampton Welcomes Strangers in the Night, The Rolling Stones Banned by Parliament, Blondie: The Platinum Sex Queen of Rock, AC/DC: The Slobbering Drool Comes Alive, AC/DC, Aerosmith, Yes, Bad Company, Dead Boys, The Ramones..$7–15
June #2 Rod Stewart: Crying His Po' Little Heart Out, Eric Clapton Makes His Comeback, Ted Nugent: Mad Bad Ass of Rock-&-Roll, Peter Frampton: More Lustful Groupie Stories, Kiss: Don't Show This Story to Pops, Neil Young, Foghat, The Best Fleetwood Mac Photos in the Entire World, Bob Dylan, Alice Cooper, Jimmy Page......................................$5–10
Sept. #3 Peter Frampton's Lonely Hearts Club Band, Fleetwood Mac: The Model 1970s Band, Kiss' New Movie, Jefferson Starship interview, The Band's Last Stand, Aerosmith, Van Halen, Patti Smith, Ronnie Monrose, Tubes interview..$5–10

1979
Apr. #6 Kiss: Their New Movie, Kiss Comic Novel, Aerosmith's Steven Tyler, Led Zeppelin, The Moody Blues are Back, Linda Ronstadt: It's so Easy, The Grateful Dead in Egypt, Eric Clapton, Peter Frampton, Mick Jagger, A History of the Beatles, Pat Travers, The Steve Gibbons Band, Tom Petty: Guaranteed to Break Your Heart, Triumph, Cruising With the Cars, Joe English...$5–10

1989
#1 Issue includes eight giant full-color wall posters, Skid Row, Motley Crue, Britny Fox, Bon Jovi Rocks Russia, Badlands, Scorpions, Cinderella, Warrent...............................$2–4

HARPER'S BAZAAR
1990
June Madonna: Eye on Madonna Feature Story—The Sellout Tour, The Knockout Film, The Breakout Album: The Coolest Queen of White Heat Strikes Again and Again and Again, issue contains five full-page color photos of Madonna......................................$3–6

HEAD
1977
Jan. /Feb. Interview With Patti Smith...$5–10

HEAVY METAL

1980

Oct. Special Rock Issue, Elvis Presley, illustrated fiction: "Worlds Among Us" by Jimi Hendrix $7–15

1981

Dec. Deborah Harry Meets Alien Artist H.R. Giger, issue includes several pages of color photos of Deborah Harry...$10–20

HIGH TIMES

1977

June Debbie Harry: Blondie—The Marilyn Monroe of Punk Rock, issue includes full-page color Debbie Harry photo $10–20
Oct. Johnny Rotten & the Sex Pistols: "If They Mean to Destroy Us, We'd Bloody Well Better Destroy Them First"...$10–20

1980

June Mick Jagger: Jagger Bares His Breast—An Exclusive Interview $5–10
Nov. Johnny Rotten & Willie Nelson, Johnny Rotten & the DOA Film—Is There Life After Sex Pistols?, Waylon Jennings, Elvis Presley's Dope Doctor $5–10

1986

Feb. ZZ Top: Ridin' High With ZZ Top...$3–6

1990

Sept. Jimi Hendrix: Who Killed Jimi Hendrix?...$2–5

HIT PARADER

1959

Jan. Ricky Nelson, Johnny Mathis, Connie Francis...$10–20

1960

Sept. Dion & the Belmonts, Elvis Presley...$10–20

1964

Nov. The Beatles: Backstage on *A Hard Day's Night*, Dave Clark 5, Billy J. Kramer, A Talk With Peter & Gordon, Roger Miller, Gerry & the Pacemakers, Lesley Gore, Tracey Dey, The Rolling Stones: Bringing the Beat Scene to a Boil, Chubby Checker, Dionne Warwick, Bobby Bland...$15–30

1965

May John Lennon: A Beatle's Early Days, Jackie DeShannon: "I Toured With the Beatles," Gale Garnett, Under Siege With the Rolling Stones, The Fantastic World of Frank Sinatra, James Brown, Jan & Dean, The Beach Boys, The Supremes, Lesley Gore, Marvin Gaye, Backstage With Johnny Rivers, Peter & Gordon, Manfred Mann, The Detergents, Bobby Bland & the Animals..$15–30
July The Childhood of Paul McCartney, Gary Lewis, Herman's Hermits Come Out of Hiding, TV's Hullabaloo, Chad & Jeremy: Where Do We Go from Here?, The Ronettes Ride Again, Frankie Valli & Annette Funicello: Live It Up With the Party Gang, The Mersey Beats, Julie Rogers...$15–30

1966

Mar. Sonny & Cher: Behind the Scenes at a Recording Session, The Lovin' Spoonful, Beatle Secrets by the Girls That Knew Them, Bob Dylan's Early Days, The McCoys Hang, Bobby Vinton, Jay & the Americans, Johnny Rivers interview, Mick Jagger, Ringo, Marianne Faithful, Herb Alpert, Bill J. Royal, Dave Clark 5 ....$15–30
Apr. The Rolling Stones: The Big Bash—Keith Richards interview, The Beatles Abandoning Rock 'n' Roll, Elvis Presley: What is His Future?, Sonny & Cher, The Byrds, Lovin' Spoonful, The Yardbirds, Beau Brummels, Four Tops $15–30

May A Beatle Gets Married, John Lennon's Future, The Kinks, Elvis' Private Life, The Beach Boys: Secrets of Their Past, Tom Jones, Herman's Hermits, Bob Dylan, The Animals..$15–30
June The Beatles, Lou Christie, Dick Clark, The Animals in London, Herman's Hermits, Mamas & Papas, Yardbirds, Simon & Garfunkel $15–30
July Batman & Robin, The Byrds, Lovin' Spoonful, The Ex-Animal, Sonny & Cher, Dave Clark, Jay & the Americans, The Kinks...$10–20
Aug. Mick Jagger: Do the Rolling Stones Hate Their Fans?, Simon & Garfunkel, Jan & Dean, The Turtles, Lovin' Spoonful Baby Pix, Gary Lewis, Jay & the Americans.....$15–30
Sept. Meet the Beatles, special Lovin' Spoonful section, Dennis Wilson: The Private Life of a Beach Boy, Bob Lind, The Byrds, John Sebastian, The Beatles' Inner Circle, Bob Dylan..$15–30
Oct. The Beatles: 10 pages of Their Crazy World, The Big Beach Boys Bash, Bob Dylan in Nashville, The Mamas & the Papas, Lovin' Spoonful in London, Petula Clark, The Remains, The Four Seasons $15–30
Nov. Paul McCartney: A Talk With the Bachelor Beatle, Exploding The Bob Dylan Myth, The Mindbenders, Blue Magoos, Special Group Breakup Report—The Animals, The Yardbirds, The Mamas & the Papas & The Byrds, Roy Orbison, Blues Project, The Lovin' Spoonful..$15–30
Dec. The Beatles, Herman's Hermits: Another Side of Peter Noone, The Association, The Byrds Concert, The Yardbirds, Gene Pitney, The Hollies, The Outsiders, The Beach Boys...$15–30

1967

Jan. Paul Revere & the Raiders, Mamas & Papas, Understanding Bob Dylan, Beatle Dreams: John & Paul, Gary Lewis, Sonny & Cher on the London Scene, *Yellow Submarine*
....$15–30
Feb. Have the Rolling Stones Gone Too Far?, The Four Tops, Lothar, Otis Redding, The Beach Boys, Tommy Roe..$15–30
Mar. Confessions of a Raider—Phil Volk, Winchester Cathedral, The Rolling Stones Talk, Bob Dylan, The Supremes, Elvis Presley, James Brown, Beach Boys, Brenda Lee, Gene Pitney $15–30
Apr. The Young Rascals, Kinks, Youngbloods, Wilson Pickett, Paul Revere & the Raiders, "I Knew Peter Tork Before the Monkees," The Four Seasons, Moby Grape, Johnny Rivers, The Beatles...$15–30
May The Beatles' Sgt. Pepper, Jefferson Airplane, The Monkees, Royal Guardsman, The Beach Boys, Spencer Davis Group, The Who, Lovin' Spoonful, Herman, The Supremes
....$15–30
June Moby Grape, The Monkees, Mothers, Hollies, Rascals, Neil Diamond, The Animals, Tom Jones, The Beatles $15–30
July Monkee Mayhem, Jeff Beck, Lovin' Spoonful, The Animals, Frank Zappa, The Hollies, Tommy Roe, The Cream, The Temptations...$15–30
Aug. Jefferson Airplane, The Doors, Hollies, Rascals, The Who, The Association, Eric Burdon, Mick Jagger on "Buttons," The Turtles, Donovan, The Monkees, Paul Revere, Paul Simon $15–30
Sept. The Mamas & the Papas Split, Bee Gees, The Doors, Moby Grape, The Who, Cream, Peter Tork, The Yardbirds, The New Cream...$15–30
Oct. The Monkees, The Four Seasons, Beatles interview, Turtles, Kinks, The Who, Frank Zappa, Scott McKenzie, Stax Story. Jefferson Airplane...$15–30
Nov. The Beatles: Sgt. Pepper, Mark Lindsay, Jefferson Airplane, Recording With the Monkees, Herman's Hermits, The Supremes...$15–30
Dec. Roy Orbison's Rock History, Neil Diamond, Mark Lindsay, Paul Butterfield, Rolling Stones, Jefferson Airplane, The Bee Gees, Bobbie Gentry, Moby Grape...................$15–30

1968

Jan. The Monkees, The Rascals, The Rolling Stones, Jimi Hendrix, Jefferson Airplane, Spencer Davis Group, At Home With Paul McCartney, Traffic, Canned Heat, Moby Grape...$15–30
Feb. Jefferson Airplane, Eric Burdon, The Doors, The Rascals, The Hollies, The Association, The Who, Procol Harum, Roy Orbison, Herb Alpert, Moby Grape..................$15–30

Mar. The Monkees: How Their Album was Really Made, Country Joe & the Fish, Jefferson Airplane's Marty Balin Talks, Eric Burdon, The Who, Eric Clapton & the Cream.....$15–30
Apr. The Beatles: Their Last Big Movie Kick, The Monkees, The Rolling Stones, The Buckinghams' Personal Profiles, Procol Harum, Buffalo Springfield, The Kinks, Vanilla Fudge, Motown $15–30
May The Bee Gees, The Satanic Rolling Stones, The Supremes, At Home With the Monkees, Lonnie Mack, Peter Townshend, The Doors $15–30
June Groovin' With the Rascals History, Otis Redding, interview with Martha & the Vandellas, Beginning of Buffalo Springfield, Frank Zappa, The Bee Gees, Elvin Bishop, Phoney Monkee Facts, A Stone at Home: Charlie Watts $15–30
July Jimi Hendrix: Rough as Loves, The Cream on Top, Moby Grape, The Bee Gees' Lead Guitarist, The Rock Revolution, Rascals $20–40
Sept. The Problems of Being a Byrd or a Beatle, Steppenwolf, Manfred Mann, The Rolling Stones Back on the Rampage $15–30
Oct. The Beach Boys, The Beatles & George Martin, The Big Cream interview, Hollies, Donovan, The Impressions, Turtles, Laura Nyro..$15–30
Nov. Simon & Garfunkel: Their Despair & Hope, The Bee Gees, Cream, Incredible String Band, Elvis Meets Tom Jones, The Byrds in Nashville, Bill Hayley & the Comets Comeback, Janis Joplin, Eric Clapton, B.B. King $15–30
Dec. The Bee Gees are Back, The Association: The Real Hippies, The Very Real Tom Rush, Eric Burdon: Born Leader of the Pack, What Janis Joplin is Really Like, John Sebastian, Johnny Barbata..$15–30

1969

Jan. Judy Collins, Jimi Hendrix: Experiences of Bass Player Noel Redding, Donovan, Country Joe & the Fish, The Story of Spanky & Our Gang, Traffic, The Beatles Meet the Press $15–30
Feb. Cream: Playing With Fire, Jose Feliciano, Arthur Brown, Magical Mystery Trip With Paul McCartney, The Bee Gees, Gary Puckett, The Staple Singers, Bobby Gentry in England $15–30
Mar. Steppenwolf Explosion, John Sebastian, Blood, Sweat & Tears, Buffalo Springfield: Last Time Around, interviews with Carl Wilson & Alan Price, Deep Purple $15–30
Apr. The Beatles: *Yellow Submarine* Preview & Feature, interview with Keith Moon, Cream's Jack Bruce & George Harrison, The Doors in England, Barry Gibb on the Bee Gees Split, Sly & the Family Stone, Traffic, Steppenwolf $15–30
May George Harrison, The Moody Blues, Bee Gees, Donovan, Canned Heat, Rooting the Beatles, Harvey Mandel, Steppenwolf, Willie Dixon, Jackie Lomax $15–30
June Paul McCartney on the Beatles, interviews with Canned Heat, Martha Reeves, Aretha Franklin, Curtis Mayfield & Richie Havens, Jimi Hendrix............................$15–30
July Special Guitar Issue, George Harrison, The History of the Guitar, Great Soloists—Jimi Hendrix, Canned Heat, Cream, The Who, Steppenwolf, Ten Years After, Creedence Clearwater Revival, Jeff Beck...$15–30
Aug. Johnny Winter's Texas Blues, Chambers Brothers, Amboy Dukes, Left Banke, Eric Clapton, First Edition, Steve Winwood...$15–30
Sept. Creedence Clearwater Revival: Long Live Rock 'n' Roll, A Recording Session With Crosby, Stills & Nash, interviews with Johnny Winter, Nina Simone, Jack Bruce, Mary Hopkin, Judy Collins, Taj Mahal...$15–30
Oct. An interview with Ringo Starr, The Beach Boys, Jethro Tull, Rock's Surfing Days, The Nice, Pentangle, Jerry Lee Lewis..$15–30
Nov. Bob Dylan Loves Country Pie, John Lennon Seeds for Peace, John Mayall's History of British Blues, The Doors' Kingdom Has Crumbled, Three Dog Night................$15–30
Dec. John Lennon: The Renaissance Man, Paul Simon, Jack Bruce, The Kinks Today
....$15–30

1970

Jan. Jimi Hendrix: The Gypsy Sun, Taj Mahal, Joni Mitchell, John Lennon, The Phil Spector Interview, Creedence Clearwater Revival, The Rolling Stones, Blind Faith.....$25–50
Feb. Mick Jagger & Keith Richards: A New Day for the Rolling Stones, John & Yoko's New Adventure, Beach Boy Mike Love Still Meditates, Plastic Ono Band, Phil Spector, Deep Purple, Johnny Cash, Nitty Gritty Dirt Band, Bunky & Jake $10–20

HIT PARADER,
1968, Sept.

HIT PARADER,
1969, Aug.

HIT PARADER,
1969, Sept.

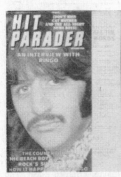

HIT PARADER,
1969, Oct.

HIT PARADER,
1970, May

HIT PARADER,
1970, Oct.

HIT PARADER,
1972, May

HIT PARADER,
1972, Dec.

HIT PARADER,
1973, May

Mar. Joe Cocker & Friends, Van Morrison, Bonzo Dog Band, Robin Gibb, Creedence Clearwater Revival, Blind Faith, Pentangle, Jeff Beck, Tom Paxton $10–20
Apr. Grace Slick: Jefferson Airplane: Can They Really Fly?, Bee Gees, Jack Bruce, Eric Clapton, Frank Zappa & the Mothers, Jimmy Page, The Youngbloods, Lonnie Mack ...$10–20
May The Beatles Conversations, Ian Anderson is the Pied Piper, The Rolling Stones Answering Back, King Crimson, Led Zeppelin, Mary Hopkin, Nitty Gritty Dirt Band, B.B. King $10–20
June Harry Nilsson's Talkin' Ten Years After, King Crimson, Ray Davies & the Kinks, John Sebastian, Spirit, Eric Mercury, John Mayall $10–20
July Alvin Lee: Ten Years Later, The Ike & Tina Turner Interview, Sha Na Na, Mick Jagger's Movies, David Ackles, Conversations With Al Cooper.......................................$10–20
Aug. John Lennon & Yoko Ono: Their London Interview, Joe Cocker, Al Cooper, Jerry Butler, Ian Anderson, The New Canned Heat, The Moody Blues, Rod Stewart, Joshua Light...$10–20
Sept. Janis Joplin: First Lady of Rock 'n' Roll, The New Iron Butterfly, Jack Bruce, Allman Brothers, Manfred Mann, Mason Williams, Simon & Garfunkel, Nitty Gritty Dirt Band $20–40
Oct. Paul McCartney Goes it Alone, Delaney & Bonnie, More of the Moody Blues...$10–20
Nov. The Who: Getting it Together, The Beatles Letting it Be, B.B. King, Archies Break-up, Canned Heat, John Mayall, Ginger Baker...$10–20
Dec. Blood, Sweat & Tears, The Rolling Stones Film Pics, The Band: Woodstock & California, Grand Funk Railroad, Jack Bruce, Brook Benton, Beatle Mania, Reggae Beat $10–20

1971

Jan. Mick Jagger: Notorious Ned, Creedence Clearwater Revival: The Eleven-piece Group, Kris Kristofferson, The Nice Split, Jefferson Airplane, Led Zeppelin $10–20
Feb. Neil Diamond: Where is He Going?, Linda Ronstadt, Free, Melanie: Writing & Audiences, Traffic, Christie, Laura Nyro, The Byrds: Nashville Acceptance....................$10–20
Mar. Eric Burdon & War, Stone Section: Mick Jagger/Keith Richards, John Phillips, Sly & the Family Stone, Chicago, Leon Russell, Eric Clapton, Ringo in America........$10–20
Apr. Melanie: Interview in Depth, Jimi Hendrix: A Few Last Words, James Brown, Eric Burdon, Moody Blues, Al Kooper, Tommy James, Three Dog Night, Rod Stewart, Richie Havens $10–20
May Jethro Tull, Johnny Winter's Changing Scene, Randy Numan, Graham Nash, The Who: Evolution of a Group, Grand Funk Railroad, Elton John.................................$10–20
June Ray Davies & the Kinks, Harry Nilsson's Talkin' Ten Years After, King Crimson, John Mayall, Spirit, John Sebastian $10–20
July Grand Funk Railroad, Black Sabbath, Blood, Sweat & Tears, Creedence Clearwater Revival, The Rolling Stones, James Taylor, Harvey Mandel, Deep Purple, The Byrds $10–20
Aug. John Lennon & Yoko Ono: Their London Interview, Jerry Butler, Joe Cocker, The Moody Blues, The New Canned Heat, Ian Anderson $10–20
Sept. James Taylor Makes a Flick, Jethro Tull, Neil Diamond, "My Father was a Hippie," The Rascals, Eric Burdon, Santana, Black Rock: Emerging Musical Form $10–20
Oct. Janis Joplin: Just Call Her Pearl, Mountain, Tina Turner, Johnny Winter, The Who, Joe Cocker, Badfinger, T. Rex, James Brown, Poco, Procol Harum $10–20
Nov. Paul McCartney: Working With Paul & Linda, Neil Diamond: Introspective, Melanie: The Good Book, The Who, Grand Funk Railroad & the Establishment, Jethro Tull, Steve Winwood..$10–20
Dec. Blood, Sweat & Clayton, Beatlemania is Still Here, Wayne Cockran: White-haired Rocker, The Band: Woodstock & California, The Rolling Stones Film Pics, Grand Funk Railroad, Jack Bruce...$10–20

1972

Jan. Mick Jagger: The Rolling Stones, Jim Morrison: Died July 4, 1971, Rod Stewart, ELP, Three Dog Night in Depth, Jefferson Airplane, Tom Fogerty....................................$10–20
Feb. John Lennon & Yoko Ono: "I Don't Like All This Dribblin' Popopera-Jazz," Sly & the Family Stone, Ginger Baker, Jack Bruce, John Kay, The Moody Blues $10–20

Mar. The Beach Boys: 25 Albums On, Jethro Tull: Sole Survivor, Cat Stevens, Rod Stewart: Working With Beck, The Drifters, Led Zeppelin: Page Talk In, Elton John, Dawn $10–20
Apr. Carole King: Nearly 400 Songs, John Lennon/Paul McCartney: Who Wrote What?, Grand Funk Railroad, B.B. King, Three Dog Night, Bread, Canned Heat, Creedence Clearwater Revival, Black Sabbath: The Critics $10–20
May Mick Jagger: The Rolling Stones Portrait Gallery, Judy Collins, Paul McCartney, Savoy Brown, J. Geils Band, Tommy James, Jeff Beck, Billy Withers $10–20
June Melanie: Not So Wide-eyed, *Jesus Christ Superstar*, Paul Simon, Paul Anka, Marc Bolan, Albert Collins, Neil Diamond: Reluctant Performer Retires, Procol Harem $10–20
July Faces & Rod Stewart, Muddy Waters, Anne Murray, Cat Stevens, Blood, Sweat & Tears, Rick Grech $10–20
Aug. Marc Bolan/T. Rex, The Doors, America, Guess Who, Don McLean, Badfinger, Young, Stills $10–20
Sept. The Bangladesh Movie, Elton John, Grateful Dead/Garcia Talks, George Harrison, America, Don McLean, Deep Purple, Hollies...$10–20
Oct. Elton John: Re-emergence, Carole King, Steven Stills, Capt. Beefheart Speaks, Savoy Brown, Laura Nyro With Labelle, Alice Cooper, Jimi Hendrix: A Manager Remembers, Chuck Berry in London..$10–20
Nov. 30-Year Anniversary Issue—David Cassidy: The Pop Star Business, Elvis Presley, Deep Purple, Johnny Mathis $7–15
Dec. Elvis Presley Meeting the Press, Emerson, Lake & Palmer, Bill Wyman: The Insecure Stone, Rod Stewart Recording Session, Mick Jagger: Solo Tangents, The Band, Blood, Sweat & Tears...$10–20

1973

Jan. Alice Cooper: Power to the Pupil, Led Zeppelin: Laying Down the Truth, Black Sabbath: Up From Downers, Blood, Sweat & Tears Moving On, The Who, The Taylor Family '72, Sha Na Na..$10–20
Feb. David Bowie, Gilbert O'Sullivan, Sly Stone, Jeff Beck, Marc Bolan, Alice Cooper, Paul McCartney & Wings, Rod Stewart...$7–15
Mar. Blood, Sweat & Tears, Led Zeppelin Unchanged, Roberta Flack, Neil Diamond, Van Morrison, Black Oak Arkansas, Kinks...$7–15
Apr. David Cassidy cover & interview, Grand Funk Railroad Speak Out, John Lennon, Johnny Cash, Rock History, Led Zeppelin, Neil Diamond, Bo Diddley $7–15
May Alice Cooper, Black Sabbath, Raspberies, O'Jays, Curtis Mayfield, Charlie Pride, Donovan, Simon Turner, The Osmonds: Nice Guys...$7–15

1974

May Mick Jagger: The Stones Do Europe, Pete Townshend: No More "Tommys," The Beatles, The Grateful Dead's First Seven, Black Oak Arkansas, Riders of the Purple Sage ....$ 7–15
Aug. Mott's Ian Hunter, Alice Cooper, ELP, Maggie Bell $5–10
Sept. Grand Funk Railroad, Edgar Winter, The Rolling Stones Movie, Jimmy Page, Paul Simon, Foghat...$5–10
Oct. Carly Simon, Led Zeppelin, Bill Wyman, Genesis, Ringo, Jeff Beck $5–10
Nov. The Return of Eric Clapton, Jimmy Page, Cat Stevens, Paul Rogers, Johnny Winter $5–10
Dec. Rick Wakeman—After Yes, David Bowie on Tour, Eric Clapton: On the Road, Pete Townshend, Robin Trower, Nash & Young...$5–10

1975

Jan. Jimmy Page Talks About Swan Song, ENO, Eagles, Todd Rundgren interview, Elton John...$5–10
Feb. Bad Company, John Lennon's New Music, Two Faces: Rod Stewart & Ron Wood, Crosby, Stills, Nash & Young: On the Road Again, Encore With Jimmy Page, Elton's Abandoned Dreams...$5–10
Mar. John Lennon Exclusive Interview, Led Zeppelin, Rolling Stones, Mick Jagger Backstage, Alice Cooper Exposed, Ronson Joins Mott, Pink Floyd: Dark Side of the Moon $5–10

HIT PARADER,
1974, May

HIT PARADER,
1974, Sept.

HIT PARADER,
1974, Nov.

HIT PARADER,
1974, Dec.

HIT PARADER,
1975, May

HIT PARADER,
1975, Aug.

HIT PARADER,
1978, June

HIT PARADER,
1979, Feb.

HIT PARADER,
1979, June

Apr. Exclusive Keith Richards Interview, Ray Davies Interview from London, Johnny Winter, George Harrison, Wayne County Remembers Dusty Springfield $5–10
May Paul & Linda McCartney Exclusive Interview, David Bowie: Trying to Sort Out His Confused Image, The Kinks & The Pretty Things, The Beach Boys, Led Zeppelin $5–10
July Ian Anderson Exclusive Interview, On Tour With Led Zeppelin: Backstage Flying, Concerts & More, Alice Cooper Invents the Human Shock Absorber, Rick Derringer, Roxy Musician Bryan Ferry Does it Here, Ron Wood Tells of Rod Stewart $5–10
Aug. Mick Jagger: Exclusive—The Stones on the Road Again: New Boy in the Band, Queen in the U.S.A., Average White Band, Jim Dandy interview, Blue Oyster Cult, Led Zeppelin Gets Physical, Alice Cooper..$5–10
Sept. Ian Anderson Reveals the Story Behind the Mott Break-up, Elton John Under Attack, Joe Walsh, Do the Who Hate "Tommy"?, Life at the Bowies: Weird Tales from Their London Home, Where Rock Stars Hang Out, Rock Stars' Teeth, Aerosmith color poster ..$5–10
Oct. Edgar Winter Talks About Rick Derringer, Mick Jagger interview, Has Success Spoiled Elton John?, Aerosmith's Steven Tyler, Robin Trower, Steve Harley, Kiss $5–10
Nov. Elton John Wants to Sing More Songs & be Less Bizarre, David Bowie: Memories of Friendship With a Superstar, Peter Frampton, Ray Davies: Is Flash Taking Over His Life?, Paul Rogers Talks About His Idols & Himself, John Cale, Hollies, Lynyrd Skynyrd ...$5–10
Dec. Freddie Mercury: His Electric Touch & Other Queen Stories, Aerosmith: Do Steven Tyler's Tight Pants Help the Music?, John Lennon Exclusive Interview, Bryan Ferry: All This & Roxy Too, issue includes a special Rolling Stones section, Leslie West, Alice Cooper Celebrates the Bicentennial...$7–15

1976

Jan. Eric Clapton, Ian Anderson, Richie Blackmore, The Doobie Bros., Mick Jagger & Keith Richards Exclusive Interviews, Patti Smith...$5–10
Feb. Roger Daltry: "Tommy" & Ten Years With The Who, Jim Dandy, David Bowie's First Film, Exclusive Interview With Bruce Springsteen: "It Ain't Easy" Says Rock Messiah, 10CC, Uriah Heep, Beyond Alice Cooper With the Tubes $5–10
Mar. A Special Who Issue, The Who: Ten Years Touch—Rock Without the Opera, David Essex, Ian Anderson Frustrated by Success, Roxy's Ritzy Rock, Jimi Hendrix Strikes With "Midnight Lightning"...$7–15
Apr. Bryan Ferry: Does He Rule Roxy?, Bruce Springsteen: Greased Lightning on the Thunder Road, Lou Reed, Patti Smith, ZZ Top, Crosby & Nash, Bob Dylan $5–10
May Aerosmith Rocks Out the U.S.A., Labelle, Patti Smith valentine centerfold, Ray Davies, Roger Daltry Speaks Out, The Sparks...$5–10
Aug. Bad Company: Paul Rogers' Soulful Side, David Bowie: The Illusions of the Thin White Duke, Lynyrd Skynyrd: How Rowdy is Ronnie?, Fleetwood Mac Draw a Pair of Aces, Tommy Bolin: New Punch in Purple, Foghat, Dr. Feelgood, David Johansen, Nazareth Charting the Road, issue includes Jimmy Page poster...................................$6–12
Sept. Mick Jagger Tells Tales, Wings, Aerosmith, David Bowie, Kiss, Bob Marley.....$5–10
Oct. Led Zeppelin Exclusive, Jimmy Page Talks, Paul McCartney, Kiss, Genesis, Ian Anderson: "I Wanted to be a Cop," Bad Company, The Rolling Stones, Elton John $5–10
Nov. Elton John: Superstar Sensation for the Seventies, Paul McCartney: America Goes Silly Over Wings, Yes: The Band That Went Solo, The Stones, David Bowie, Patti Smith & Bryan Ferry European Journal, Jeff Beck: Wired & Inspired, Thin Lizzy's Rock & Romance, Ian Hunter: Deeper Than Dylan?, David Bowie's Genius in *The Man Who Fell to Earth*, Iggy Pop Pops Up Again, issue includes Steven Tyler poster $5–10
Dec. Peter Frampton, Ringo, Kiss: Re-studding Their Bodies, Aerosmith, Jefferson Starship, Emmylou Harris: A Rare Interview, Bryan Ferry & Roxy Music, Led Zeppelin, Bad Company...$4–8

1977

Jan. Lynyrd Skynyrd: Ronnie Van Zant Saves the Fox, Kiss color centerfold poster, The Eagles: How They Hatched a California Legend, Ted Nugent, John Lennon: A Day in the Life of a Permanent Resident, Fleetwood Mac: Success in the (Stevie) Nick of Time, Aerosmith: Joe Perry Helps His Friends, Jethro Tull, Led Zeppelin Movie: Behind the Silver Screen...$6–12
Feb. Led Zeppelin: Heavy Metal's Celluloid Heroes, Aerosmith's Joe Perry Exclusive Interview, Kiss: Gene Simmon's Jewels Instant Photos, Roger Daltry: How the Who Survived,

Rebel Rock, Patti Smith: Lady on Lead Noise, Linda Ronstadt: Tears to the Top, Johnny & Edgar Winter: Winters' Summer Reunion, Queen poster..$6–12

Mar. Kiss: The Best or the Worst?, Jefferson Starship: Grace & Paul on a New Enterprise, Peter Frampton, Blue Oyster Cult: Road Agents Reap Riches, Linda Ronstadt Exclusive Interview, Thin Lizzy, Neil Young: Lonesome Guitar Singer, Lou Reed, Led Zeppelin special section...$10–20

Apr. Rod Stewart: Too Many Nights on the Town?, Elton John: The Way He Is, Paul Stanley: The Kiss You Can Count On, Lynyrd Skynyrd: The Wild Bunch, Led Zeppelin: Jimmy Page & Robert Plant Exclusive Interview, Grand Funk: Behind the Break-up, Bob Marley: Reggae Rebel With a Cause, Boston: More Than a Feeling, Aerosmith & Jeff Beck..$5–10

May Fleetwood Mac: The Truth Behind the Rumors, ELO, Ted Nugent, Blue Oyster Cult, George Harrison, Eric Clapton, The Eagles, The Ramones, Television, Jonathan Richman...$5–10

June Queen, David Bowie, Boston, Patti Smith, ZZ Top, Fleetwood Mac: The Years That Fame Forgot, Graham Parker, Alice Cooper: Still a Punk, The Sex Pistols...............$5–10

July Led Zeppelin: They're Back, Queen, Genesis, Ted Nugent, Pink Floyd: Fear on the Farm, ELO, Television, Kiss..$5–10

Aug. Boston: Behind the Scenes of the Success, Peter Gabriel, Angel, Led Zeppelin: The Tonsils That Stopped the Tour, Fleetwood Mac: "We Seem to be an Enigma" Says Christine McVie, Television, Bruce Springsteen Exclusive Interview, Bryan Ferry: He Wants to be Alone..$5–10

Sept. Peter Frampton: Still Mr. Nice Guy, Rolling Stones: A Surreal Rock Dream in Toronto, Kiki Dee, Led Zeppelin, Brian Wilson, The Ramones, Southside Johnny & the Asbury Dukes, Peter Gabriel, Journey, Lou Reed..$5–10

Oct. The Beatles Six-page Special, Kiss Color Bonus, ELP, Joe Walsh, Television, Sex Pistols, Bob Seger, Iggy Pop, The Beach Boys, Elton John $4–8

Nov. Led Zeppelin: Behind the Majesty an Annual Tour, ELP, Peter Frampton, Gregg Allman, Bad Company, Elton John, Dolly Parton: Rock's Newest Star, Phil Spector.....$5–10

Dec. Rolling Stones: "Love You Live" Exclusive Mick Jagger Interview, Bad Company: Too Good to be Bad, Lou Reed, Led Zeppelin: More Road Adventures, Carly Simon: Her Not So Secret Fears, Blondie: Debbie Harry—Day of the Commie, Bryan Ferry: In With the In-crowd, Hall & Oates, issue includes Joe Perry poster $7–15

1978

Jan. A Tribute to Elvis Presley, interviews with Aerosmith, Crosby, Stills & Nash Together, Eric Carmen, Elton John & Kiki Dee...$4–8

Feb. Yes: On the Same Wavelength Again, Heart is No Accident, interview with Blue Oyster Cult's Allen Lanier, KC Keeps it Comin', The Dictators: A Fantasy......................$4–8

Mar. Linda Ronstadt interview, Patti Smith: Guitar Maniac, Foreigner: Strangers Band Together, Aerosmith: Culture Shock, Punk Update...$4–8

Apr. Ram Jam, Steely Dan, Mark Farner interview, Lynyrd Skynyrd: Ronnie Van Zant Remembered, David Bowie...$4–8

May Gene Simmons: Kiss, Linda Ronstadt, Neil Young, ELO, Blue Oyster Cult, Hall & Oates: Alone Together, David Bowie, Queen, Patti Smith, The Babys $5–10

June Rod Stewart: Who Does He Think He Is?, David Bowie, Patti Smith, Sex Pistols, Eric Clapton, Kansas, Meat Loaf, Boz Scaggs, Bob Dylan, Boomtown Rats....................$5–10

July The Bee Gees: More Than Staying Alive, Ted Nugent, Patti Smith, Billy Joel, David Bowie interview, Bob Dylan, Sex Pistols: No Future, Jackson Browne, Alice Cooper.....$4–8

Aug. Fleetwood Mac: Platinum Payoff, Meat Loaf Fever, David Johansen interview, Aerosmith: LP Retrospective, Television: New Sounds from the Twilight Zone..........$4–8

Sept. Hall & Oates: Do it Live, Elton's Ego, Kiss, David Bowie: Hero to Go, Linda Ronstadt, Patti Smith, Jimmy Page: Zep Up Again, Television, David Johansen.........$4–8

Oct. The Rolling Stones Exclusive: Mick Jagger Talks, Eagles, Wings, Rolling Stones on Tour, Kansas, Tom Waits, Little Feat, David Bowie, Elton John, Kiss, Patti Smith, Kraftwerk..$4–8

Nov. Elvis Costello: Bog Top Fantasy, Bob Seger: No Secret for Success, Steven Tyler, Led Zeppelin, Rolling Stones on Tour, ENO & the Talking Heads, Foghat, Beach Boys Celebrate, Kiss Backstage, Bruce Springsteen: "My Songs are Like Italian Westerns" $4–8

Dec. Andy Gibb: Nice Guys Finish First, The Rolling Stones Backstage, Kraftwerk, Who's Bigger Than Kiss?, Ted Nugent, Todd Rundgren: Back from Utopia, Bruce Springsteen: Drive in Rock, Journey, The Moody Blues, Bob Dylan in Concert, Led Zeppelin Discography........$4–8

1979

Jan. Led Zeppelin Sing it Again, Journey, Foreigner, Buddy Holly Movie, Tom Petty: Rock Heartbreaker, Beach Boys Changes, Jimi Hendrix Retrospective, Meat Loaf, Kiss: Paul Stanley, ELO, Jefferson Starship, Patti Smith Backstage, Cheap Trick, ELO..............$4–8
Feb. Kiss/Gene Simmons: The Kiss Dream, Ted Nugent: Normal Wild Man, Tom Petty, UFO, Willie Nelson, Michael Jackson: Motown to Movies, Tom Scholz/Boston, The Black Sabbath Story, Exclusive Kiss Interviews, Bob Seger, Patti Smith, Tom Waits, Roxy Music, Linda Ronstadt, The Ramones, Jefferson Starship, Bee Gees.....................$5–10
Mar. Boston, The Cameras Roll for Kiss, Meat Loaf, Billy Joel Gets Tough, The Moody Blues, Yes Backstage, Kenny Loggins, The Who Discography, Queen, Foreigner.......$4–8
Apr. Aerosmith: Bootleg Gold, Paul Stanley, Elton John, Al Stewart, Queen, Bob Dylan, Ace Frehley, Steven Tyler color poster, The Stones Backstage, Neil Young, David Johansen, Keith Richards Jams, Devo: New Look, New Sound, Kiss pictures.............................$4–8
May Neil Young, Blondie Interview at Home, Queen, Billy Joel, Elton John, Rory Gallagher, Mick Jagger's Rock Reggae, Kiss, Aerosmith $4–8
June Paul Stanley: The Sexiest Kiss, Special Kiss Report, Aerosmith, Boston, Yes, Pink Floyd: Which One's Pink?, Fleetwood Mac, Chicago, Boomtown Rats, Jim Morrison Redux, The Ramones Movie, Jefferson Starship, Foreigner...........................$4–8
July Foreigner, Rod Stewart, Keith Richards: Last Rock Hero, The Blues Brothers, Peter Criss: Tossin' & Turnin', The Outlaws Across the Border, Robert Gordon, Steve Miller, Ace Frehley Sets the Controls to the Heart of the Sun, New Wave Records, Rory Gallagher, Peter Criss, Steven Tyler, Stevie Nicks, The Eagles.....................$5–10
Aug. Exclusive Cheap Trick Interview, Dire Straits, Elvis Costello: Armed Forces Accidents, Too, Bob Seger, The Clash Blast N.Y.C., Cher: She Won't Stop the Rock, Paul Stanley: Rock Heartbreaker, Elton John, Patti Smith, Kiss Disco, Aerosmith $4–8
Sept. Ted Nugent Exclusive Interview, Blondie/Debbie Harry Tells Her Story, Jefferson Starship: Kanter Refuels, Patti Smith, ENO, The Ramones' Movie, Bob Welch, Kiss' New Look, Stephen Stills, Cheap Trick, David Bowie in the Studio, Aerosmith Offstage, Elvis Costello's Mistake, Wings $4–8
Oct. Pete Townshend: The New Who—Behind the Scenes, The New Babys, Joe Jackson, Keith Richards: It's Only Rock 'n' Roll, Dire Straits, Ted Nugent, Kiss World Tour: Paul Stanley Says They're a Fresh Kiss, Bryan Ferry Explains Why Roxy Did It..............$4–8
Nov. Paul Stanley: Kiss—New Show, New Look, New Music, The Cars, David Bowie Dresses Up, Cheap Trick in Japan, Journey, Patti Smith, Van Halen, Bad Company..$4–8
Dec. Aerosmith's Joe Perry Exclusive Interview, Kansas: Building Their Own Monolith, The Kiss Super Show Exclusive, Wings, Peter Frampton, The Cheap Trick Story, Robert Fripp Tells the Secrets of Fripptronics, The Village People, Bad Company, Ted Nugent, Talking Heads Record at Home, Blue Oyster Cult...$4–8

1980

Jan. Robert Plant: Led Zeppelin Rock Back—Exclusive Behind-the-scenes Coverage, Ted Nugent: Nothing but the Facts, Kiss on Tour: Paul Stanley Talks, Cheap Trick Help the Who Rock, The Blue Oyster Cult: Rock Through the Looking Glass, Blondie, The Knack, The Doobie Brothers, Patti Smith, REO Speedwagon, Japan, Nick Lowe, The Rolling Stones...$5–10
Feb. Freddie Mercury/Queen Exclusive: Dressing Room Photos, The Cars Stand Up for Rock-and-Roll, Kiss on the Road, ELO, Robert Palmer, Suzi Quatro: Up All Night, The B-52's Explain Everything, Charlie Daniels, Southside Johnny Finally Gets the Image Across, Patti Smith, The Tim Curry Cult, Elton John, Ted nugent $5–10
Mar. Jimmy Page/Led Zeppelin Remain Unchallenged, The Who: Pete Townshend on Film, The Eagles: History Lesson, Paul Stanley: Backstage Talk, Blondie Stars in Meat Loaf Movie, Talking Heads, Fleetwood Mac Super Tour, Cheap Trick, Joe Perry Tells Why He Quit Aerosmith, The Knack, Edgar Winter, Patti Smith $4–8
Apr. Exclusive Cheap Trick Interview, Debbie Harry: The Blondie Sensation, Bob Marley, Iggy Pop, Journey, Fleetwood Mac: Tell N.Y. About "Tusk," Molly Hatchet, The Eagles, Boomtown Rats, Robert Plant, Rick Derringer, Rick Nielsen..................................$4–8

HIT PARADER,
1979, Sept.

HIT PARADER,
1979, Nov.

HIT PARADER,
1980, Jan.

HIT PARADER,
1980, Apr.

HIT PARADER,
1980, July

HIT PARADER,
1980, Oct.

HIT PARADER,
1980, Nov.

HIT PARADER,
1981, Apr.

HIT PARADER,
1981, Jan.

May Led Zeppelin, Fleetwood Mac: The Forgotten British Band, The Police, Boomtown Rats, The Clash, Aerosmith, B-52's in Japan, Tom Petty, Foreigner, The Specials $4–8

June Tom Petty: Rock Heartbreaker, Blondie: On the Set With Debbie Harry, Boomtown Rats, A Kiss Wedding, Jefferson Starship, Journey, Foreigner, Cheap Trick, Joe Perry's New Band, The Eagles, The Police, Cat Stevens $4–8

July Blondie/Debbie Harry Backstage in Europe, Tom Petty: Guitar Talk, The Police: Sting Exclusive, Gary Numan, Journey Tour, Queen, Foreigner Plans, Cheap Trick, Steven Tyler Talks, Kiss Strikes Back, The Knack, REO Speedwagon, The Romantics, Bob Seger, The Eagles, The Clash: Their Story...$4–8

Aug. Aerosmith, Linda Ronstadt Rocks, The Clash, ZZ Top, Pink Floyd, Blondie, J. Geils, Fleetwood Mac's Oriental Nights, Police, Journey, Cheap Trick, Foreigner $4–8

Oct. Mick Jagger & Keith Richards Exclusive Interviews, Journey's N.Y. Knockouts, Van Halen, The Clash Talk Back, Gene Simmons Explains the New Kiss, Rock Action With David Bowie in Japan, Boomtown Rats Photo Session, Genesis, The Led Zeppelin Tour, Elton John...$4–8

Nov. Exclusive Chat: Heart to Heart, The Police in Japan, Mick Jagger & Keith Richards, Kiss & the Creepy Reporter, Behind the Scenes With Blondie, Escape With Olivia Newton-John, Joe Perry, Southside Johnny, Genesis, Pete Townshend.......................................$4–8

1981

Jan. The Cars Exclusive Interview, Joe Jackson interview, AC/DC, The Rolling Stones centerfold poster, The New Yes, Ted Nugent, Judas Priest, The Doobie Brothers: Born Again Legends, Gene Simmons, Peter Criss, David Bowie, Alice Cooper, Utopia......$4–8

Feb. The New Cheap Trick, Kansas, Deep Purple, Molly Hatcher, REO Speedwagon, Journey centerfold, Teddy Pendergrass, Hall & Oates..$3–6

Mar. David Lee Roth: Van Halen: They Live by Night, Pat Benatar: Platinum is a Girl's Best Friend, Black Sabbath's Family Feud, The Kinks: One for the Road, Jethro Tull: When Will it End?, ELO, Gary Numan, Chicago, Al Stewart, John Cougar..........................$3–6

Apr. Fleetwood Mac: Fact & Friction, John Lennon Remembered, Billy Joel centerfold poster, Exclusive Interviews with Heart, Rush, Paul Simon, Dire Straits & Steve Forbert, the B-52's...$4–8

June Blondie/Debbie Harry: Domestic Bliss With Debbie & Chris, Mick Jagger: The Mouth That Roared, Styx, Bruce Springsteen: Caught in the Act, Led Zeppelin's Last Waltz, Journey, Bob Seger, Joan Jett, Steely Dan, Grace Slick, The Beach Boys, Elvis Costello, Supertramp, Thin Lizzy, Marshall Tucker Band...$3–6

Sept. Van Halen: The Wild Bunch, Linda Ronstadt: A Night at the Opera, Jefferson Starship: Doing What They Want, Tom Petty, Ted Nugent, Ringo Starr, Cheap Trick centerfold poster, Adam & the Ants, Styx, Kim Carnes, Johnny Ramone, Paul Stanley, Grace Jones, Ann Wilson, Southside Johnny, Blondie, Dave Edmunds $3–6

Oct. Queen: Fun in Space, The Ramones, Def Leppard, The Doors: Still Lighting Fires, Roger Daltry: Actor, Fighter & Family Man, Pat Benatar: The Real Thing, Scorpions centerfold poster, Joan Jett, Mick Fleetwood, Mahogany Rush, Van Halen, Iron Maiden, Tubes...$3–6

Dec. Blondie/Debbie Harry: Debbie's Darkest Roots, Rossington Collins Band, The Moody Blues, ZZ Top, Hall & Oates, Judas Priest centerfold poster, Alice Cooper, REO, Foreigner, Jefferson Starship, Nazareth, Iron Maiden, Psychedelic Furs, Triumph, Black Sabbath....$3–6

1982

Feb. AC/DC: Rock's First Family, Rod Stewart: Wine, Women & Song, Ozzy Osbourne, The Kinks, Scorpions, Sammy Hagar, Kiss Controversy, The Knack, .38 Special, Devo....$3–6

Mar. Sting/The Police, The Rolling Stones, The Kinks, AC/DC, The Doobie Brothers, Genesis, Ringo Starr centerfold, Van Halen, Billy Squier, Aerosmith, Def Leppard, Blackfoot, Meat Loaf, The Tubes, Elvis Costello, Marianne Faithful, Greg Lake..........................$3–6

May AC/DC: Rock's First Family, Ozzy Osbourne centerfold, Rod Stewart: Wine, Women & Song, The Kinks, Scorpions, Sammy Hagar, The Moody Blues, The Kiss Controversy, The Knack, Blackfoot, Devo, Saxon, .38 Special, Talking Heads, Jahn Waite, Joe Perry $3–6

June Judas Priest: Call of the Wild, Paul Stanley centerfold poster, REO Speedwagon, Ozzy Osbourne, Rainbow, Jim Morrison, Jimi Hendrix & Janis Joplin: Angels With Dirty Faces, The Outlaws, Queen, XTC, Rick Springfield, Neal Schon $3–6

July Led Zeppelin: The Second Coming, The Police, Pat Benatar: Torrid Zone, The Pretenders: Rhythm & Boose, Blue Oyster Cult: Great Balls of Fire, Judas Priest, Saxon, Roxy Music, J. Geils, Thin Lizzy $3–6

Aug. Heart: Picture of Health, AC/DC, J. Geils Band, The Beatles: Picture Perfect, The Police, The Cars, The Motels, The Outlaws, Iron Maiden.......................................$3–6

Oct. REO Speedwagon, Cheap Trick, Blondie: Guys & Dolls, Heart: Missing Persons, Queen, Van Halen, Jethro Tull, Black Sabbath, April Wine, Triumph, Journey...........$3–6

1983

Jan. Ozzy Osbourne: #1 Rock Act in America, The Who, Bad Company: Only the Strong Survive, Fleetwood Mac: Trouble in Paradise, The Go-go's: Return to Fantasy Island, Led Zeppelin, REO, The Police, Bow Wow Wow, The Beatles, Elton John, Jimmy Cliff.....$3–6

Feb. Pat Benatar: Ball of Fire, Ozzy Osbourne vs. Black Sabbath, Led Zeppelin in Their Own Words, Bruce Springsteen: King of the Boardwalk, Neil Young: Mind Expansion, Robert Plant centerfold, Blondie, Kansas, Triumph, Van Halen, Mick Jagger, Ted Nugent, Fleetwood Mac...$3–6

Mar. Robert Plant in His Own Words, Kiss: Lady Killers, Rush, Billy Squier, Alice Cooper: Joker's Wild, Pat Benatar centerfold, Van Halen, Judas Priest, Roger Daltry, John Cougar, Lene Lovich, Rachel Sweet, Jefferson Starship, Pat Travers $3–6

Apr. Tom Petty: Hot Spell, AC/DC: Thunder Down Under, Def Leppard, Linda Ronstadt: Built to Last, The Scorpions, Greatest Guitar Heroes—Jeff Beck, Richie Blackmore, Eric Clapton, Ace Frehley, Jimi Hendrix, Jimmy Page & Others, Devo, Toni Basil, Missing Persons, Blue Oyster Cult, Plasmatics, Van Halen, Adam Ant, Magnum, Aerosmith.......$3–6

May Eddie Van Halen: In Search of the Lost Chord, Kiss: Tales from the Road, Bob Seger: Going the Distance, Foreigner, J. Geils Band, Pat Benatar: Rock's Platinum Princess, Ozzy Osbourne centerfold, UFO, The Who, Cheap Trick, Black Sabbath, Quiet Riot, Girl School $3–6

Aug. David Lee Roth/Van Halen: Trouble in Paradise, Exclusive Interviews With—AC/DC, Loverboy, Robert Plant, The Rolling Stones, Rick Springfield & Def Leppard, Cheap Trick centerfold poster, ELO, Kiss, Aerosmith, Neil Young, Journey, Randy Rhoads, Sly Stone $3–6

Sept. Def Leppard vs. Iron Maiden, Journey, Aldo Nova, Pink Floyd, Kiss centerfold, Stevie Nicks: That Magic Touch, Scorpions, Styx, Cheap Trick, ZZ Top $2–4

Oct. Robert Plant: On the Road Again, Ozzy Osbourne, Jimi Hendrix: The Legend & the Man, Black Sabbath interview, Asia, Iron Maiden, Rod Stewart, Cheap Trick, Tom Petty, Kiss, Fastway $2–4

Nov. AC/DC: To Hell & Back, Def Leppard, Scorpions, Randy Rhoads, Van Halen, Loverboy, Joan Jett: Bad to the Bone, The Doors, U2, Marshall Crenshaw, Meat Loaf, Quarterflash, Scandal, Asia $2–4

Dec. Judas Priest: The Metal Conquers, Rainbow, Heart: Seductive Reasoning, Motley Crue, Rolling Stones: Mick Speaks Out, Iron Maiden: Exclusive Steve Harris Interview, Def Leppard, Ted Nugent, Free, Wendy O'Williams, Dave Edmunds, Ian Hunter.............$3–6

1984

Jan. Eddie Van Halen: #1 Rock Act in America, Pat Benatar: Life in the Spotlight, Kiss: Unmasked at Last, Robert Plant, Scorpions, Black Sabbath, Billy Joel, Krokus centerfold poster, Billy Idol, Carly Simon, Motorhead, ZZ Top, Iron Maiden, The Animals.......$2–4

Feb. Ozzy Osbourne, AC/DC, Cheap Trick, Judas Priest, Quiet Riot, Rush, Tom Petty, David Lee Roth, Creedence Clearwater Revival...$2–4

Mar. Def Leppard: A Year to Remember, Interviews With—Kiss, AC/DC, Rainbow, Jimmy Page, Girl School, Pat Benatar, Sammy Hagar/ Neal Schon, Randy Rhoads, Quiet Riot, ZZ Top, Black Sabbath, Yes, Keith Moon, Dokken, J. Geils $2–4

Apr. David Lee Roth: Van Halen: The High Life, Ozzy Osbourne, Triumph, Ted Nugent, Billy Squier, Aerosmith, Black Sabbath, Motley Crue, Night Ranger, Waysted...........$2–4

May Judas Priest: The Metal Machine, Kiss, Queen, Van Halen, Scorpions, Foreigner, Def Leppard, Randy Rhoads Remembers, AC/DC, Keith Moon, Black Sabbath................$2–4

June Motley Crue: The Sleeze Patrol, Ozzy Osbourne Night Ranger, Quiet Riot, Van Halen centerfold, Iron Maiden Journey, Lynyrd Skynyrd, AC/DC, Heart, Eddie Money, Scorpions, Duran Duarn, Golden Earring...$2–4

HIT PARADER,
1981, June

HIT PARADER,
1981, Dec.

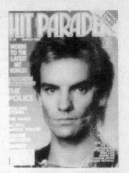

HIT PARADER,
1982, Mar.

HIT PARADER,
1983, Jan.

HIT PARADER,
1983, Feb.

HIT PARADER,
1983, Mar.

HIT PARADER,
1983, Apr.

HIT PARADER,
1983, May

HIT PARADER,
1986, Aug.

July Ozzy Osbourne: Inside the Asylum, Judas Priest, Van Halen, Kiss, The Who, Saxon, Def Leppard, Styx, AC/DC, Ace Frehley, Blue Oyster Cult, Iron Maiden..................$2–4
Aug. David Lee Roth: Van Halen: Too Hot to Handle, Scorpions, Accept, Judas Priest, Def Leppard, Motley Crue, Ozzy Osbourne, Rush, Iron Maiden, Yardbirds.......................$2–4
Sept. Motley Crue vs. Quiet Riot, Van Halen: The Rock Brigade, The Scorpions, Ozzy Osbourne, Def Leppard Speak Out, Iron Maiden: Metal Mad, Judas Priest, Krokus, Dio...$2–4
Oct. Scorpions: Animal Magnetism, Def Leppard, Motley Crue on the Set, Black Sabbath: Ashes to Ashes, Robert Plant the Legend, Deep Purple Together Again, Judas Priest, Quiet Riot, AC/DC, Rush, Kiss Go for Blood, Ozzy Osbourne, Slade, W.A.S.P., Iron Maiden...$2–4
Nov. Iron Maiden: Search & Destroy, Motley Crue, Quiet Riot, Krokus, Robert Plant: In His Own Words, Judas Priest, Ozzy Osbourne, Triumph, Scorpions, Van Halen, Ratt, Kiss...$2–4
Dec. Van Halen on the Edge, Exclusive Interviews With—Ozzy Osbourne, Iron Maiden, Def Leppard, Scorpions, Aerosmith, Quiet Riot, AC/DC, Rush, Kiss, Ratt..................$2–4

1985

Jan. Motley Crue: #1 in America, Van Halen: The Gripes of Roth, Iron Maiden: The Metal Noblemen, Def Leppard, Twisted Sister: The Night Stalkers, Billy Squier..................$2–4
Feb. Kiss: A Call to Glory, Iron Maiden: Show No Mercy, Dio, Motley Crue, Dokken, Joan Jett: Rock 'n' Roll Queen, Scorpions, Zebra, Triumph, Jimmy Page, Billy Squier.....$2–4
Mar. Motley Crue, Kiss: Call of the Wild, Queensryche, Krokus, Blackfoot, Helix, Iron Maiden: In for the Kill, Black 'n' Blue, Jimmy Page, Armored Saint, Ratt, AC/DC, Twisted Sister, Quiet Riot, On the Set With the Scorpions, Def Leppard................................$2–4
Apr. Van Halen's David Lee Roth: Just a Gigolo, Exclusive Interviews With—Iron Maiden, W.A.S.P., Kiss, Motley Crue, Ratt, The Firm, Ozzy Osbourne, Deep Purple, Twisted Sister...$2–4
May Judas Priest vs. Iron Maiden, Motley Crue: Life on the Edge, Def Leppard, Kiss: Out for Blood, Ratt Speak Out, AC/DC Shoot to Kill, Accept, Sammy Hagar, Firm $2–4
June Motley Crue: The Beginning or the End, Scorpions, Ratt: The New Breed, Accept, Judas Priest Delivering the Goods, Iron Maiden: Commitment to Excellence, Def Leppard: Answering Readers' Mail, Loudness, Aerosmith, Ozzy Osbourne, Deep Purple, Kiss, Armored Saint, Billy Idol, Jimmy Page, Keel, Journey, Black Sabbath.......................$2–4
July Ozzy Osbourne, Sin After Sin, Motley Crue: Trouble in Paradise, Iron Maiden: Metal Supermen, Scorpion: On the Road to Rock, Ratt: Of Mice and Men...........................$2–4
Aug. Motley Crue: A Time of Decision, Ozzy Osbourne, Twisted Sister, Judas Priest, Deep Purple, Scorpions, Van Halen, The Firm, AC/DC, Keel, Ratt, Black Sabbath, Madame X, King Kobra, Loverboy, Dio $2–4
Sept. Ratt: Leaders of the Pack, Exclusive Interviews With Judas Priest, Motley Crue, Iron Maiden, Bon Jovi, Raven, Loudness, Alice Cooper, Lita Ford, Ozzy Osbourne $2–4
Oct. Blackie Lawless of W.A.S.P., Dee Snider of Twisted Sister: The Kings of Shock Rock, Interviews With Motley Crue, Kiss, AC/DC, Ratt, Dio, Deep Purple $2–4
Nov. AC/DC: Return to Glory, The Heavy Metal Hall of Fame, Kiss: Under the Gun, W.A.S.P.: Blood & Guts, Ratt, Dio, Saxon, Bon Jovi, Aerosmith, Judas Priest, Planet...$2–4
Dec. Paul Stanley/Kiss: Inside the Asylum, W.A.S.P.: The Shock Brigade, Motley Crue, Scorpions, Dio, Grim Reaper, Judas Priest, Dokken, AC/DC: Sudden Impact, Ratt centerfold poster, Bon Jovi, Malice...$2–4

1986

Jan. Motley Crue #1 in America Again, Dokken, Interviews With—Ratt, Kiss, AC/DC, Van Halen, Judas Priest, Ozzy Osbourne & Black Sabbath, Night Ranger, Yngwie $2–4
Feb. Dio: The King of Rock 'n' Roll, Ratt, Ozzy Osbourne, ZZ Top, Quiet Riot, Aerosmith, W.A.S.P, Dokken, Kiss centerfold, Cheap Trick, Roger Daltry, Bon Jovi, Ted Nugent, Robert Plant...$2–4
Mar. Twisted Sister: Wild in the Streets, W.A.S.P., Triumph, Kiss, Iron Maiden, Stryper, Dokken, Quiet Riot, Van Halen, Def Leppard, Motley Crue, Armored Saint, Ted Nugent..$2–4
Apr. Judas Priest: Metal Avengers, Black Sabbath, Motley Crue, Iron Maiden, Def Leppard, Aerosmith, Van Halen, Dokken, Accept, Ratt, Keel, W.A.S.P. centerfold poster, Led Zeppelin, Heart, Autograph $2–4

June Ozzy Osbourne: The Madman Returns, Van Halen, Aerosmith centerfold, Kiss, Raven, Judas Priest, Dokken, Deep Purple, Def Leppard, Anthrax, Accept $2–4

July Motley Crue: The Kings of American Metal, Judas Priest, David Lee Roth, Ozzy Osbourne, Lita Ford: Love & Confusion, Dokken, AC/DC, ZZ Top, Loudness, Van Halen, Kiss $2–4

Aug. Robert Plant: Led Zeppelin Born Again, Van Halen: Meet the Press, Motley Crue: Entertainment of Death, Judas Priest, Dokken, Quiet Riot, Metallica, Krokus, Bon Jovi on the Road to Platinum, W.A.S.P., Ratt, Lita Ford foldout, Fiona, Kobra $2–4

Sept. Van Halen vs. David Lee Roth: The War Heats Up, Motley Crue, Accept, Keel, Kiss & Judas Priest foldouts, Iron Maiden Power & Passion, Ozzy Osbourne, AC/DC................$2–4

Oct. Metallica, W.A.S.P. & Motley Crue posters, Ozzy Osbourne, Judas Priest, Dokken, David Lee Roth, Jimmy Page, Dio, Van Halen, Billy Idol, Queensryche, Guffria, Triumph, Deep Purple..$2–4

Nov. Bon Jovi: Sexy, Wet & Wild, Motley Crue, Stryper, Ratt, AC/DC, Scorpions, Iron Maiden, Metallica, Cinderella, David Lee Roth & Judas Priest posters, Manowar, Led Zeppelin's John Paul $2–4

Dec. Ratt: Out for Blood, AC/DC, Bon Jovi, W.A.S.P., Motley Crue, Deep Purple, Dokken, Metallica, Scorpions, Malmsteen, Judas Priest, Loudness, Jimmy Page, Poison, Queensryche, Van Halen centerfold...$2–4

1987

Jan. Motley Crue: #1 Rock Act in America, David Lee Roth, Ratt, Iron Maiden, Bon Jovi: Living in the Limelight, Stryper: Angels With Dirty Faces, AC/DC, Metallica, Ozzy Osbourne, Cinderella..$2–4

Feb. Stryper vs. W.A.S.P., David Lee Roth, Motley Crue, Deep Purple, Iron Maiden, Billy Squier, Led Zeppelin, Alice Cooper..$2–4

Mar. Bon Jovi: Too Hot to Handle, Cinderella centerfold, Waysted, Kiss, Warlock, Rogue Male, Balls of Fire, Iron Maiden, Aerosmith, David Lee Roth, Malmsteen, Twisted Sister, Scorpions, AC/DC..$2–4

Apr. The New Metal Explosion—Stryper, Cinderella, Megadeth & Guns 'n' Roses, W.A.S.P., Def Leppard, Metallica, Ozzy Osbourne, Van Halen, Deep Purple, David Lee Roth, Bon Jovi, Scorpions, Ratt, Krokus..$2–4

May Motley Crue: Return of the Sleeze Patrol, Kiss: Turn it Loose Bruce, Whitesnake: Back on Target, Ratt, Scorpions, W.A.S.P., Iron Maiden, Stryper, Guns 'n' Roses, Cinderella, Aerosmith $2–4

June Ozzy Osbourne & Randy Rhoads: The Inside Story, Bon Jovi, Judas Priest, Deep Purple, Dokken, Dio, Megadeth, Motley Crue, Lita Ford, Cinderella, Ace Frehley, Tesla—Special Anniversary Issue...$2–4

July Motley Crue: A Dash of Flash, Poison centerfold poster, Kiss: Grass Under Pressure, Ozzy Osbourne Answers the Questions, Led Zeppelin: To Be or Not to Be?, Europe, Bon Jovi, Anthrax, David Lee Roth, Through the Looking Glass with Def Leppard, Black Sabbath: Born Again..$2–4

Aug. Bon Jovi: Glory Days, Metallica vs. Megadeth—Feud of the Year, Dokken, Def Leppard, Ace Frehley: Lost in Space, Bow Wow, Judas Priest, Poison Talkin' Dirty, Ozzy Osbourne, Through the Years With Kiss: A Photo Exclusive, Iron Maiden, Tesla........$2–4

Sept. Kings of Flash Metal Issue—Poison, Cinderella, Judas Priest, Metallica, Kiss: Legends at Work, Sammy Hagar: Return of the Road Rocker, Europe, Dio, Whitesnake: Overcoming Adversity $2–4

Oct. Judas Priest: Blood, Sweat & Cheers, Motley Crue centerfold, TNT: Set to Explode, AC/DC, Europe, Bon Jovi, Kiss: A Pace, Dokken, Autograph, Raven, Megadeth, Cinderella, Poison...$2–4

1988

June Poison: The Second Coming, Def Leppard, Sanctuary, David Lee Roth, Stryper, Ozzy Osbourne, Robert Plant, Lita Ford, Black Sabbath...$2–3

July Metal Tour Spectacular, Judas Priest, Megadeth, Guns 'n' Roses, Scorpions, Ace Frehley: Live & Dangerous, Def Leppard centerfold poster, Bon Jovi: The Heat is On, Van Halen, Dokken..$2–3

Aug. Iron Maiden: Master Mayham, Van Halen centerfold poster, Udo Dirkschneider, David Lee Roth, Cinderella, Megadeth, Poison, AC/DC on the Prowl, Europe, Aerosmith: Metal Pioneers...$2–3

Sept. Van Halen: The Monsters of Rock, Guns 'n' Roses poster, Billy Sheehan, Judas Priest, Poison Opening Up, Kingdom Come: The Song Remains the Same, Iron Maiden, Lita Ford, Def Leppard, Metallica, Megadeth, Cinderella, L.A. Guns, Jimmy Page....$2–3

Oct. Stryper: Heaven Can Wait, Poison poster, Overkill, Guns 'n' Roses, Van Halen, Kingdom Come, Anthrax, Bon Jovi: Idol Chatter, Zakk Wilde: Ozzy Osbourne's Speed King, King Diamond, Black 'n' Blue...$2–3

Nov. Guns 'n' Roses: The Kings of Sleeze Metal, Ozzy Osbourne & Zakk Wilde poster, King's X, Judas Priest, Bon Jovi, Stryper, Van Halen, Dio, Ratt, Europe, AC/DC, Hurricane, Scorpions, Whitesnake, W.A.S.P...$2–3

Dec. Metallica: No Guts, No Glory, Killer Dwarfs, Poison: The Greatest Show on Earth, Ozzy Osbourne, Guns 'n' Roses, Cinderella, Bonfire, Ace Frehley: Miracle Man, Ratt Back on Top, Van Halen...$2–3

1989

Jan. Bon Jovi: The Mania Returns, Europe, Whitesnake Poster, Jon Norum: Life After Europe, Motley Crue, Metallica, Britny Fox, Deep Purple: Twenty Years of Greatness, Anthrax, Dokken..$2–3

Feb. Ozzy Osbourne: Too Wild to Tame, Def Leppard, Whitesnake, Guns 'n' Roses, Van Halen, Bon Jovi, Metallica, Europe, Motley Crue...$2–3

Mar. Guns 'n' Roses: Band of the Year, D'Molls, Dokken, Metallica, Ozzy Osbourne, Bon Jovi, Cinderella, Kix, Kiss: Legends Never Die, House of Lords, W.A.S.P., Ratt, Queensryche..$2–3

Apr. Bon Jovi: Rockin' the Nation, Guns 'n' Roses centerfold, Quiet Riot: A New Beginning, Ozzy Osbourne, Motley Crue, Ratt: Reaching for Greatness, Poison, Megadeth, Badlands, Metallica, Vixen, Jet Boy, Blue Murder: Metal Killers, Dokken, Skid Row: Glory Bound $2–3

May Guns 'n' Roses: Lies, Lies, Lies, Motley Crue, Britny Fox poster, Bullet Boys, Ratt, Bon Jovi, Aerosmith: Kings of the Hill, Tesla, Aerosmith, Europe, Metallica, Ozzy Osbourne, House of Lords..$2–3

June Metal's Platinum Explosion Special Issue—Ozzy Osbourne, Kiss, Metallica, Aerosmith, Badlands, Anthrax, Stryper, W.A.S.P., Poison, Motley Crue centerfold, Circus of Power, Blue Murder, Vengence..$2–3

July Motley Crue: Return of the Titans, Richie Sambora centerfold, Wrathchild: Seeking an Identity, Metallica, Poison, Ratt, Dio, Whitesnake, Megadeth: Armed & Dangerous, Lita Ford, Kiss, Dio...$2–3

Aug. Skid Row: From Outhouse to Penthouse, Celtic Frost: Heavy Duty, Poison centerfold, Aerosmith: Rock Royalty, Kingdom Come, Bullet Boys, Whitesnake, Bon Jovi, Def Leppard, Tesla, Mr. Big: Out of the Shadows, Bango Tango, Great White, Vixen......$2–3

Sept. White Lion: Big Game Hunting, Lita Ford centerfold, Masters of Reality: Strangers in the Night, Poison, Whitesnake, Motley Crue, Bon Jovi: Road Fever, Tesla, Faster Pussycat: Against All Odds, L.A. Guns, Metallica, Aerosmith: Men at Work $2–3

Oct. Guns 'n' Roses: Slash Speaks Out, Tesla centerfold, Motley Crue, Bon Jovi, Warrent, Bullet Boys, Banshee, Badlands, The Cult, Extreme.......................................$2–3

Nov. Motley Crue: Clean & Mean, Skid Row centerfold, White Lion, Tesla, Warrent, Badlands, Mr. Big, Little Ceasar, Metallica..$2–3

Dec. Aerosmith: Pride & Passion, Winger centerfold, Skid Row, Great White, Bad English, Bon Jovi, Badlands, The Cult, L.A. Guns..$2–3

1990

Jan. Skid Row: Tales from the Road, Metallica centerfold, Accept, Great White, Lita Ford, Vain, Junkyard, Bon Jovi, Warrent...$2–3

Feb. David Coverdale/Whitesnake: The Heat is On, King's X: Mental Metal, Motley Crue: Kings of Crude, White Lion, Lita Ford: Set to Explode, Britny Fox, Def Leppard, Kiss Back for More, Guns 'n' Roses, Dangerous Toys, King Diamond: From the Dark Side, Metallica, D.A.D., Aerosmith: Rock Royalty, Alice Cooper: Roots, Skid Row, Bon Jovi...........$2–3

Mar. Nikki Sixx/Motley Crue: Hard Lessons, Princess Pang: Survival of the Fittest, Def Leppard: A Tough Act to Follow, Warrent, Bon Jovi, Skid Row, Aerosmith, Ozzy

Annette today, at home with two teen magazines that span more than thirty years of her being a covergirl

Collecting
ANNETTE FUNICELLO

Annette Funicello memorabilia is becoming increasingly harder to acquire. This is expecially true as she has been largely inactive in the recording and film industries. A possible explanation for this phenomenon could be that the "baby boomers" who grew up with her have been exercising their indulgence for nostalgia of times gone by and the things which bring about a reminiscence of "better times."

You can still find a good many of Annette's LPs in Goldmine and Discoveries. It is increasingly difficult to find some of the more obscure LPs and the 45s which came with picture sleeves. There are also many vintage record stores across the U.S. where you can occasionally find some of these rarities.

Her movie memorabilia is getting tougher to find as well. *Movie Collector's World* is an excellent publication for tracking down those rare posters, lobby cards, and press books. There are a few movie memorabilia stores located in the U.S., with the majority being in N.Y.C. or the L.A. area, mostly along Hollywood Blvd. and its side streets.

Paper collectibles of all kinds have gotten especially hard to find. Movie magazines featuring Annette, original photos from her films or for publicity purposes, and the many products that Disney licensed as merchandise are very difficult to locate. Paper dolls, coloring books, *Babes in Toyland* activity books, puzzles, and the like are usually found by accident at paper collectible shows and sometimes in the pages of *Toy Shop*.

Other related memorabilia such as jewelry, lunchboxes, dolls, and cosmetic sets are almost impossible to locate.

A good source for the more common memorabilia is through fan club publications. There is generally an auction of items to augment the club coffers for publication costs and almost always a photo shop offering both old and new photos.

In the following listings, all items are priced with ranges for near mint condition.

COLORING BOOKS

Watkins-Strathmore #1844 ....$25–40
Whitman #1131, 1961 ....$25–40
Whitman #1186, 1962 ....$25–40
Whitman #1145, 1964 ....$25–40

Annette Funicello Coloring Books

Annette Funicello Paperdolls

PAPER DOLLS

Whitman #1958, 1956 ....$25–50
Whitman #2083, 1958 ....$35–45
Whitman #1971, 1960 ....$35–45
Whitman #1969, 1961 ....$35–45
Whitman #1956, 1962 ....$35–45
Whitman #1953, 1964 ....$35–45
Boxed set #4621, 1962 ....$25–50

CUT-OUTS

Aldon, Annette & Zorro, three formed plastic cut-outs............................$50–75

FILM MEMORABILIA—MOST VALUABLE

This includes memorabilia other than records, posters, and lobby cards from
her films.
Annette vs. Haley $300
Beach Party one-sheet..$50
Teenage Wedding 45 with picture sleeve $100–150

BOOKS

Babes in Toyland Golden Picture Story Book (comic format)....................$12–15
Babes in Toyland Punch-outs
Forever Hold Your Banners High, 1976..$5–8

Giant Golden Punch-out, 1961...$25–40
Lady Lovely Locks & the Pixietails..$5–10
Little Golden Book (blue cover & green cover)..................................$5–10
Mickey Mouse Club Annuals
   1956 ....$15–25
   1957 ....$15–25
   1958 ....$15–25
Muscle Beach Party, paperback...$5–8
Of Mice & Mickey, 1975...$5–8
Rock 'n' Roll in the Movies, Alan Clark...$6–13
Shaggy Dog Picture Book (inside LP)..$6–12
Sticker Fun, Whitman #1693...$15–25
The Official Disney Trivia Book...$2–4
The Toymaker, Golden, 1961...$25–40
Tops in Pops—A Rock 'n' Roll Round-up, 1961..................................$6–12
Walt, Mickey & Me, Paul Petersen...$5–8
Whitman Great Big Punch-out, 1961...$25–40
Whitman series
   Desert Inn Mystery...$5–10
   Misadventures of Merlin Jones..$5–10
   Mystery at Medicine Wheel..$5–10
   Mystery at Moonstone Bay..$5–10
   Sierra Summer...$5–10

TOYS AND GAMES

Annette cosmetic set, rarest of memorabilia.....................................$200–400
Annette Dress Designer Kit, Colorforms..$25–50
Annette jewelry, rarest of memorabilia..$50
Annette Mousketeer doll, rarest of memorabilia..............................$150–300
Annette's Secret Passage Board Game...$40–75
Babes in Toyland puzzle, #4454...$15–25
Babes in Toyland puzzle, boxed, #4605..$15–25
Babes in Toyland puzzle, boxed, #8666–29...$15–25
Disney Trivia: A Family Game of Fun, Facts & Fantasy $2–5
View Master Reels, *Babes in Toyland*...$15–20
View Master Reels, MMC..$15–20

MISCELLANEOUS

Beach Party 1989 calendar (box C)...$10
Mickey Mouse Club Lunchbox, no thermos..$50
Script (autographed), "Fantasy Island," Mary Ann & Miss Sophisticate..............$35–50
Two-D Mickey Mouse Club Display for Mickey Mouse Club video...........$10
Walt Disney Super-8 Home Movies, highlights from the Mickey Mouse Club...........$25

FAN CLUB

The original Annette Funicello Fan Club is an active club with the full cooperation of Annette and features her input in each publication. Our newsletters
are informative and usually mix a blend of Annette's current activities along
with a look at past projects.

    Each member receives a black and white glossy photo of Annette, a color
candid, photo membership card, and four journals that range in size from
25–40 pages. They almost always include an auction of Annette memorabilia
for those members wishing to add to their collections, as well as a photo shop
where there is an offering of current candids and older, more obscure, shots.

Annette provides members with the current candids and they often have her family pictured as well.

Membership runs for one year and the dues are a low $12 per year. We keep the dues low so that everyone can participate. Many friendships are formed through the club and that may be the best of the many benefits. Dues should be sent to Sandi Kreml, Co-Pres., P.O. Box 26610–313, Sacramento, CA 95826.

Osbourne: Madder Than Hell, White Lion, Tora Tora: The Memphis Hit Men, L.A. Guns, Dio, Banshee, Ace Frehley, Lita Ford, Guns 'n' Roses centerfold $2–3

Apr. Aerosmith: Fast Lane Frolics, Kiss: Mind Over Matter, Icon, Def Leppard: Back to Work, L.A. Guns, Skid Row, Guns 'n' Roses: Call of the Wild, Tora Tora: Feeling the Power, Warrent, Michael Monroe, Faster Pussycat, Ozzy Osbourne, EZO, Motley Crue centerfold, Live on Stage: Metallica, Hangin' Out With Britny Fox, Alice Cooper $2–3

HIT PARADER ANNUAL

1975

Winter Led Zeppelin Special, Mick Jagger, Eric Clapton, Jimmy Page, Ron Wood, Elton John, Alice Cooper, Todd Rundgren, Keith Richards, Paul McCartney & Wings $5–10

1980

Debbie Harry: The Blondie Story, Special Kiss Report, Aerosmith, The Cars, Fleetwood Mac, Elvis Costello, Stephen Stills, Dire Straits, Patti Smith, Bryan Ferry, The Bee Gees, Ian Hunter, Cheap Trick, Linda Ronstadt, Led Zeppelin...$4–8

1981

Debbie Harry/Blondie: The Real Story, Ted Nugent, Cheap Trick, Boomtown Rats, Pete Townshend, The Little River Band, Linda Ronstadt, The Romantics, Gary Numan, J. Geils, The Clash, Heart, Journey, The Pretenders, The Rolling Stones, Judas Priest, Ace Frehley, Triumph, Southside Johnny $4–8

1984

Spring Judas Priest, Ozzy Osbourne, Journey, Pat Benatar, Heart, Steve Perry, Rainbow, Billy Idol, Y & T, Rush, Iron Maiden, Jimmy Page, The Rolling Stones, Black Sabbath...$3–6

1985

Spring Motley Crue, Van Halen, Def Leppard, Joan Jett: Rock 'n' Roll Queen, Kiss: The Call to Glory, Zebra, Lita Ford, Helix, Dokken...$3–6

1987

Spring Motley Crue, Twisted Sister, Cinderella, Bon Jovi, Judas Priest, Iron Maiden, Metallica, Ratt, Yngwie Malmsteen, Alice Cooper, Ace Frehley $2–4

1989

Fall Guns 'n' Roses, Whitesnake, Eddie Van Halen centerfold, Motley Crue, Iron Maiden, Badlands, Celtic Frost, Lita Ford, Vixen & Others $2–4

HIT PARADER'S GUITAR GODS MAGAZINE

1984

Winter Interviews With Eddie Van Halen, Jimi Hendrix, Jimmy Page, Ted Nugent, Ace Frehley, Pete Townshend, Eric Clapton, Jeff Beck & Others $3–6

HIT PARADER'S HEAVY METAL AWARDS '84 MAGAZINE

1985

Spring Motley Crue, Judas Priest, Scorpions, Ratt, Van Halen, Iron Maiden, Led Zeppelin, Black 'n' Blue, Kiss, Dio $2–4

HIT PARADER'S HEAVY METAL CALENDAR 1990 MAGAZINE

1989

Guns 'n' Roses, Aerosmith, Skid Row, Anthrax, Badlands, Motley Crue, Whitesnake, Great White, Winger, Blue Murder, Lita Ford, Bon Jovi, issue includes beautiful full-page glossy photos...$2–4

HIT PARADER'S HEAVY METAL HEROES (Each issue contains two 3′ × 2′ posters)

1984

Dec. Def Leppard vs. Judas Priest, Pin-ups & Outrageous Articles $2–4

1985

May AC/DC vs. Ozzy Osbourne...$2–4
June Robert Plant vs. David Lee Roth $2–4
July The Scorpions vs. Judas Priest $2–4
Aug. Kiss vs. Twisted Sister...$2–4
Sept. Motley Crue vs. Ozzy Osbourne $2–4
Oct. Jimi Hendrix vs. Randy Rhoads $3–6

1986

Jan. Ratt's Stephen Pearcy vs. W.A.S.P. $2–4
Mar. Def Leppard vs. Dio..$2–4

1988

Winter Exclusive Interviews With Jon Bon Jovi & Richie Sambora...........................$2–4

HIT PARADER'S HEAVY METAL HOT SHOTS

1984

Fall Judas Priest, Iron Maiden, Van Halen, Def Leppard, Ted Nugent, Rainbow, ZZ Top, Randy Rhoads, Kiss, Sammy Hagar, AC/DC, Dio $2–4

1985

Sept. Motley Crue, Kiss centerfold, Iron Maiden, Ratt, Ozzy Osbourne, Night Ranger, Aerosmith, Lita Ford, Accept, Van Halen, Dokken, W.A.S.P., ZZ Top.....................$2–4
Nov. Scorpions, Ratt, Ozzy Osbourne centerfold, Accept, Led Zeppelin, Kiss, Loudness, Bon Jovi, Lita Ford, Ted Nugent, Metallica, Dio, Dokken, Iron Maiden, W.A.S.P.....$2–4

1986

Jan. Def Leppard, Motley Crue & Ozzy Osbourne centerfold, Judas Priest, Ratt, Dokken, W.A.S.P., Dio, Kiss, Bon Jovi, AC/DC, The Firm, Robert Plant, Twisted Sister.........$2–4
Mar. W.A.S.P., AC/DC, Motley Crue, Bon Jovi centerfold, Aerosmith, Dio, Judas Priest, Ratt, Keel, Robert Plant, Adam Bomb, Slayer, Kiss, Lita Ford, Grim Reaper, Jimmy Page
....$2–4
May Ratt, Kiss, Motley Crue, AC/DC centerfold, Bon Jovi, Keel, Alice Cooper $2–4

1987

Feb. Stryper, Motley Crue, David Lee Roth, Kiss, W.A.S.P., & Poison centerfold $2–4

1989

Aug. Aerosmith, Guns 'n' Roses, Ratt, Ozzy Osbourne & The Bullet Boys posters, Kiss, Bon Jovi...$2–4
Oct. Motley Crue, Guns 'n' Roses, Skid Row, Bon Jovi, Femme Fatale, Warrent, W.A.S.P..$2–4
Nov. White Lion, Motley Crue, Badlands, Great White, Bon Jovi, Tesla, Winger, Kiss, Lita Ford, King Diamond, Iron Maiden, Cinderella................................$2–3

1990

Jan. Guns 'n' Roses, Aerosmith, Skid Row, Motley Crue, Metallica, Little Ceasar, Ratt, Jimi Hendrix, Bon Jovi, Whitesnake, Ozzy Osbourne, L.A. Guns, Faster Pussycat.....$2–3

HIT PARADER'S HEAVY METAL SEX STARS

1989

Fall Lita Ford, Vince Neil, Bret Michaels, Axl Rose, Nikki Sixx, Joe Elliot, Paul Stanley, Jon Bon Jovi, Tempest $2–4

HIT PARADER'S HOT METAL STARS MAGAZINE
1989
Winter Lita Ford, Steven Tyler, Tommy Lee, Mike Tramp, Jon Bon Jovi, Sammy Hagar, Slash, Vince Neil $2–3

HIT PARADER'S INTERVIEW
1977
Winter Mick Jagger & Keith Richards, Janis Joplin, Neil Diamond, Paul Simon, The Doors, Fleetwood Mac, Jimmy Page..$5–10

HIT PARADER'S LEGENDS OF HEAVY METAL MAGAZINE
1989
Winter Kiss, Motley Crue, Ozzy Osbourne, Aerosmith, Led Zeppelin, Bon Jovi, Black Sabbath, Jimi Hendrix $2–4

HIT PARADER'S METAL OF THE 80S MAGAZINE
1990
Spring Def Leppard, Motley Crue, Guns 'n' Roses, Metallica, Lita Ford, Bon Jovi, Ratt, Whitesnake, Iron Maiden, W.A.S.P..$2–3

HIT PARADER'S POWER METAL (The Nastiest Magazine on Earth)
1989
Dec. King Diamond, Metallica & Slayer super posters, Anthrax, Black Sabbath, Megadeth, Exodus, Whiplash, Celtic Frost, White Zombie, Lizzy Borden, Kreator, Hydra Vein..$2–4

HIT PARADER SONGS AND STORIES
1973
May Alice Cooper: Violence Bag, The Osmonds, Lou Reed, Black Sabbath, Raspberries, Sinatra, Charley Pride, Donovan, The O'Jays..$5–10
July Alice Cooper Exclusive Interview, Alice Cooper in Concert, Blood, Sweat & Tears, Remembering Hank Williams, The Real Billy Holiday: She's No Diana Ross, Lobo ...$7–15

1974
Mar. The Allman Brothers: The Price, Triumph, The Price & the Tragedy, Mick Jagger Selling Out, Cheech & Chong, The Eagles, John & Yoko, Three Dog Night, Wolfman Jack, Rod Stewart: The Angriest Dude in the Empire..$6–12
All other issues $5–15

HIT PARADER SPECIAL
1983
Fall Exclusive Interviews With AC/DC, Van Halen, Saxon, Rush, Iron Maiden, Led Zeppelin, Bad Company, Black Sabbath, Randy Rhoads, Quiet Riot, Y & T......................$2–4

HIT PARADER'S TOP 100 METAL ALBUMS MAGAZINE
1989
Spring Guns 'n' Roses centerfold, Led Zeppelin, Kiss, Bon Jovi, Metallica, AC/DC, Alice Cooper, Ratt, Dio, Jimi Hendrix, Megadeth, Van Halen, Def Leppard, Ozzy Osbourne, Deep Purple, Bad Company..$2–4

HIT PARADER'S TOP 100 METAL STARS MAGAZINE
1990
Fall Issue includes Motley Crue centerfold poster, Sebastian Bach, Axl Rose, Edward Van Halen, Joe Elliot, Steven Tyler, Ace Frehley, Paul Stanley, Bon Jovi, Jimmy Page, Tommy Lee, Etc..$2–4

HIT PARADER YEARBOOK

1967
The Beatles, The Monkees, The Mamas & the Papas, The Beach Boys, The Byrds, Simon & Garfunkel..$10–20

1968
The Young Rascals, The Bee Gees, Donovan, The Four Tops, The Byrds, Steppenwolf, The Temptations..$10–20

1969
The Beatles, Creedence Clearwater Revival, Judy Collins, The Who, Blood, Sweat & Tears, Jimi Hendrix, Bob Dylan, Eric Clapton, Steppenwolf, Donovan................................$20–40

1973
Spring Mick Jagger, Paul Anka, Tom Fogerty Hanging Out, Elton John, Noel Redding, Savoy Brown, Paul McCartney, Jimi Hendrix: Remembering, Link Wray Back Again, Santana, J. Geils Band, Brewer & Shipley, John Lennon, The Who, Three Dog Night, John Kay, The Doors: Friends & Other Voices, Cat Stevens, Paul Simon Alone, Stephen Stills...$10–20

1975
Summer/Fall The Elegant Mr. Ferry, Robin Trower, Elton John, Paul Simon, Bachman-Turner, Ray Davies, Johnny Winter's New Direction, Led Zeppelin Talks, On Tour With David Bowie, Eric Clapton, Jeff Beck, Jimmy Page, On the Road With Led Zeppelin, Keith Richards: The Rolling Stone...$7–15

1977
Summer/Fall Peter Frampton, Kiss, Led Zeppelin, Joe Perry, Alice Cooper, David Bowie, Jimmy Page, Mick Jagger, John Lennon, George Harrison, Fleetwood Mac, Queen, The Beach Boys, Rod Stewart, Linda Ronstadt, Patti Smith...$5–10

1978
Summer/Fall Queen, Aerosmith, Ramones, Foghat, Elton John, Patti Smith, Angel, Lou Reed, Hall & Oates, Mick Jagger, Ted Nugent, Carly Simon, Andy Pratt, The Babys, Led Zeppelin, Blue Oyster Cult, ELP, Television, David Johansen, Kiss, Linda Ronstadt..$5–10

1980
Blondie: Debbie Harry's Dreams, Aerosmith, The Police, Kiss Tour Talk, The Cars, The Cheap Trick Story, The Clash Tell Why They Rock, Fleetwood Mac, Tom Petty, Madness, The Eagles, The B-52's, Boomtown Rats...$5–10

HOLLYWOOD STUDIO MAGAZINE

1984
June/July Elvis Presley..$5–10

1986
Apr. Elvis Presley..$2–5
Sept. James Dean & Sal Mineo...$5–10

1988
Feb. Barbra Streisand...$2–5
May Cher: Her Battle to Win This Year's Oscar...$2–5

HOLLYWOOD TEEN PARTY

1990
#9 New Kids on the Block: Over 189 New Kids' Secrets Revealed, issue includes eight exclusive New Kids posters, A Special All-new Kids on the Block Issue......................$2–3

HOME VIDEO
1982
Feb. Mick Jagger Feature Story: Mick Struts into Video $2–4

HOT MAGAZINE (Issued by Smash Hits)
1989
Nov. New Kids on the Block Exclusive, includes two New Kids giant posters, Corey Haim, Kirk Cameron, Johnny Depp, River Phoenix, Bon Jovi, John Stamos, Debbie Gibson ...$2–3
Fall New Kids on the Block exclusive interview with 2 color pin-ups, Alyssa Milano: Will She Quit Who's the Boss?, Madonna, Debbie Gibson, John Stamos, Johnny Depp, Kirk Cameron, Bon Jovi $2–3

HULLABALOO (The Pre-*Circus* magazine)

1968
Aug. Jim Morrison, Jimi Hendrix, Janis Joplin $25–50
Nov. Jim Morrison: An Interview With Five Pages of Color Photos, Janis Joplin in Color Extra, Cream's Last Interview, The Who, Jefferson Airplane, Rascals, The Band ...$25–50

1969
Jan. Pete Townshend: The Who on Groupies & Getting Mobbed, Slamming the Doors, Dion in Color $20–40
Feb. John Lennon & Yoko Ono: The Beatles Now, The Rolling Stones Beggars Banquet in Color, Jimi Hendrix interview...$15–30
All other issues $15–50

I

ILLINOIS ENTERTAINER

1974
Feb. Marked Vol. 2 .... $3–5
All other issues $2–4

IN CONCERT PRESENTS

1990
July/Aug. #1 New Kids on the Block Special, Summer Tour Preview, The New Kids in Concert, Up Close & Personal, Backstage $2–3

INTERNATIONAL MUSICIAN

1976
Apr. The Other Side of Keith Moon, Thin Lizzy, The Strawbs $3–6

1978
Apr. The Leo Fender Story $2–3
Dec. B.B. King, Joe Pass, Percy Jones, Andy McKay, Eddie Spence $2–3

1979
Jan. Al Dimeola, The Stranglers, Crawlers.. $2–3
Mar. John McLaughlin, Al Dimeola, Frank Zappa, Peter Gabriel.................................... $2–3
Apr. Steve Howe, Pete Sears, Joe Pass, The Clash, David Sancious $2–3
May Billy Cobham, Pat Metheny, Dave Edmunds, Chuck Mangione, George Thorogood
.... $2–3
June Stephen Stills Exclusive, John Entwistle, Robert Fripp, Roger McGuinn, Clark, Hill-man.. $2–3
Aug. Herbie Hancock Talkin' Synthesizers, Kenny Jones, Chris Spedding $2–3
Oct. Carmine Appice: On the Rod Stewart Beat, Taj Mahal, Jeff Porcaro.................... $2–3
Dec. Stanley Clarke, ELO, Genesis, The Magic of Grover Washington $2–3

1980
Mar. The Kinks: Ray & Dave Cut a New Attitude, The Clash: Keeping Time With Head-on $2–4
May Sonny Rollins, Joe Perry: Looking Beyond Aerosmith, The Pretenders, Robin Trower
.... $2–4
July Pat Travers: Beyond Guitar Heroics, Carl Palmer, Michael Walden.................... $2–3
Aug. The Genesis Phenomenon, Phil Lynott, Steve Gadd, Bruce Cockburn, Phil Ramone
.... $2–4

Sept. Southside Johnny, Tom Verlaine, Brand X, Gary Burton $2–3
Oct. Hall & Oates, Joan Armatrading, Bill Nelson, Van Halen................................$2–3
Nov. Max Roach: Beyond Technique, J. Geils Band, Merle Haggard, Stewart Copeland....$2–3
Dec. Atlanta Rhythm Section: A History, Pink Floyd...$2–3

1981

Jan. Neal Schon of Journey, The Jam, Lee Perry, Gary Numan $2–3
Feb. Steve Hacket: Beyond Genesis, Elvin Jones, Asleep at the Wheel......................$2–4
Mar. Chic: The Art of Dance Music for the '80s, Steve Winwood, Reggae Understood...$2–3
May Eric Clapton: Dead or Alive, Lester Bowie, Marl Knopfer $2–3
June Andy Summers: The Face of the 80s $2–3
July Dizzy Gilespie's Brass Revolution, Nazareth, B.B. King, The Who....................$2–3
Aug. Jimi Hendrix $3–6
Sept. Debbie Harry, Carlos Santana, Judas Priest..$3–6
Nov. Brian May, Miles Davis, Brian Eno, Iggy Pop...$2–4

1982

Jan. The Kinks at Konk, The Dregs $2–4

1983

Aug. Naked Eyes: The Art & Science of Pop...$2–3

1984

Oct. Bruce Springsteen Exclusive Interview: Working Class Hero, Southside Johnny, Quiet Riot, Wang Chung, Ratt $2–4
Nov. David Bowie: More Ch-Ch Changes, The British Invasion Revisited, Iron Maiden, The Fixx, Johnny Rotten, Dio $2–4

1985

Mar. Night Ranger: We're an American Band, Queensryche, J. Geils Band, Phil Collins..$2–4
Apr. Jimmy Page, Jimi Hendrix, Jeff Beck, Richie Blackmore, The Edge, Alcatraz, Planet P..$2–4
Nov. Billy Idol & Steve Stevens: The Glamour Twins, John Cougar $2–4

1986

Apr. The Dave Letterman Band, Pete Townshend, Nile Rodgers $2–3
July Robert Palmer, Stan Ridgway: Life After Voodoo...$2–3
All other issues $2–3

INTERNATIONAL MUSICIAN AND RECORDING WORLD EQUIPMENT SPECIAL

1985

Fall Robert Plant: Leaving the Past Behind Little by Little, Foreigner, The Hooters......$2–3

INTERVIEW (Andy Warhol's)

1979

June Blondie's Debbie Harry Special Feature: Platinum Blondie—An Interview by Glen O'Brien, issue includes full-page photos...$7–15

1983

Nov. Olivia Newton-John $5–10

1984

July Dolly Parton $3–6

1986

Apr. Cyndi Lauper..$5–10
May Tom Cruise...$3–6
Dec. Aretha Franklin $3–6

INTERVIEW, 1983, Nov.

INTERVIEW, 1984, July

INTERVIEW, 1986, Apr.

INTERVIEW, 1986, May

INTERVIEW, 1986, Dec.

INTERVIEW, 1987, Mar.

1987

Mar. Ric Ocasek of the Cars $4–8

IN THE KNOW

1977

July Donny & Marie Osmond: The Sweetness & Light is for Real $3–6

J

JAZZ AND POP

1968

July Jimi Hendrix cover & interview $25–50

1969

Feb. Critics Poll Issue, Jimi Hendrix Again by Tom Phillips, The Real Tiny Tim, The Other Revolution—James Brown, Marvin Gaye, Diana Ross & the Supremes, Smokey Robinson & the Miracles, Martha Reeves & the Vandellas, The Four Tops & The Temptations, John Lennon's Whimsy $20–40

July B.B. King, Special Newport Jazz & Folk Festival Issue, The Bee Gees: The Land of Dreams, The Chambers Brothers interview, Sonny Rollins, Frank Zappa, Jimi Hendrix: Music or Theatre?, Jim Morrison & the Doors, Jefferson Airplane $20–40

Aug. Cat Mother & the All-night Newsboys, Chuck Berry, San Francisco: The First Golden Era Begins—Jerry Garcia & the Grateful Dead, Bill Graham, The Steve Miller Band $10–20

Oct. Interviews With T-bone Walker & B.B. King, Herbie Mann in Japan, Led Zeppelin Feature Story, Buffy Saint-Marie, Elvis Presley, Jefferson Airplane: Flying High ...$10–20

Dec. Steppenwolf interview, Johnny Winter, The Best of Acappella, Sha Na Na......$7–15

1970

Jan. Tony Williams interview, Iggy Pop/Iggy Stooge Feature Story, Randy Newman interview, The Band, Herbie Hancock, Roger Daltry...$10–20

Feb. Pete Townshend, Pharaoh Sanders, NRBQ interview, The Beatles, The Who, Janis Joplin, Bob Dylan, Rolling Stones, B.B. King...$10–20

Mar. Paul McCartney: The Paul Perplex, John Lennon & Yoko Ono interview, Elvin Jones, The Amboy Jukes's Recording Session, Ted Nugent, The Rolling Stones Tour, Jefferson Airplane, Cher $10–20

Apr. Jethro Tull/Ian Anderson interview, James Taylor, Frank Zappa, Quicksilver Messenger Service, The Byrds, Crosby, Stills, Nash & Young, Fleetwood Mac, The Allman Brothers, Pink Floyd...$10–20

May Grace Slick: Best Female Pop Vocalist, Alvin Lee interview, John Lennon, The Doors, Buddy Rich..$10–20

June Arthur Lee interview, John Mayall interview, Pink Floyd, Kinks, Judy Collins, Jim Morrison, James Taylor $10–20

July Paul McCartney: The Beatles are Finished—The Real Facts on the Break-up, Ticket to Ride, The Pentangle interview, Jefferson Airplane, Jim Morrison on the Festival Mentality, Argent $15–30

Aug. Frank Zappa interview, Argent interview, John Lennon, Melanie, Jethro Tull, Ringo Starr, Paul McCartney..$10–20

Oct. Herbie Hancock interview, The Beatles: Saddest True Story, The Guess Who interview, Bob Dylan, The Doors $10–20

1971

Feb. Pop Talk With Paul Kanter, Jerry Garcia of the Grateful Dead, Neil Young ..$10–20

Apr. Paul McCartney: Thirty Years After, Frank Zappa, Conference With Joan Baez, Ike & Tina Turner, Steppenwolf's John Kay, Jim Morrison, John Lennon & Yoko Ono, Burt Bacharach...$10–20

May The Bee Gees: A Definitive Analysis of the Bee Gees, The Byrds Still Aloft, James Brown, Zappa, ELP $10–20

July Weather Report, Country Joe: Society's Cheerleader, Jackie Lomax, Grand Funk Railroad, Emerson, Lake & Palmer, Kate Taylor $7–15

K

KEYBOARD

1975
Sept./Oct. #1 Chick Corea...$10–20
Nov./Dec. #2 Herbie Hancock $5–10

1976
Jan./Feb. #3 Vladimir Horowitz $4–8
Mar./Apr. #4 Rick Wakeman $4–8
May/June #5 Keith Jarrett..$4–8
July/Aug. #6 Greg Allman...$4–8
Sept./Oct. #7 McCoy Tyner..$3–6
Dec. #8 Edgar Winter..$4–8

1977
Jan. #9 Ramsey Lewis...$3–6
Feb. #10 Billy Preston..$3–6
Mar. #11 Bill Evans..$3–6
Apr. #12 Brian Auger...$3–6
May #13 Daryl Dragon...$3–6
June #14 Vladimir Ashkenasy $2–4
July #15 George Duke..$2–4
Aug. #16 Isao Tomita...$2–4
Sept. #17 Josef Zawinul...$2–4
Oct. #18 Keith Emerson..$3–6
Nov. #19 Herbie Hancock...$2–4
Dec. #20 Dave Brubeck..$2–4

1978
Jan. #21 Liberace...$2–4
Feb. #22 Chick Corea...$2–4
Mar. #23 Oscar Peterson..$2–4
Apr. #24 Van Cliburn..$2–4
May #25 Gary Wright..$2–4
June #26 Randy Newman..$3–6
July #27 Tony Banks...$2–4
Aug. #28 Jimmy Smith..$2–4
Sept. #29 Les McCann..$2–4
Oct. #30 Jan Hammer...$2–4

Nov. #31 Duke Ellington $2–4
Dec. #32 Richard Tandy..$2–4

1979

Jan. #33 Cecil Taylor...$2–4
Feb. #34 Rick Wakeman..$3–6
Mar. #35 Virgil Fox...$2–4
Apr. #36 Dave Grusin..$2–4
May #37 Dr. John...$3–6
June #38 Suzanne Ciani $2–4
July #39 Robert Lamm $2–4
Aug. #40 Mike McDonald $2–4
Sept. #41 Keith Jarrett $3–6
Oct. #42 George Duke $2–4
Nov. #43 Joe & Gino Vannelli $3–6
Dec. #44 Wendy Carlos..$2–4

1980

Jan. #45 Booker T., Hohner Keyboards $2–4
Feb. #46 Peter Nero..$2–4
Mar. #47 Jimmy Destri..$2–4
Apr. #48 Keyboards in the Movies..$2–4
May #49 Larry Fast $2–4
June #50 Bill Evans...$2–4
July #51 Roger Powell $2–4
Aug. #52 Glenn Gould...$2–4
Sept. #53 Keith Emerson $3–6
Oct. #54 Christine McVie $4–8
Nov. #55 Aaron Copland $2–4
Dec. #56 Oscar Peterson $2–4

1981

Jan. #57 Dennis de Young $2–4
Feb. #58 Elton John $3–6
Mar. #59 George Shearing..$2–4
Apr. #60 Tangerine Dream $3–6
May #61 Andre Watts..$2–4
June #62 Stevie Winwood...$3–6
July #63 Brian Eno $3–6
Aug. #64 McCoy Tyner $2–4
Sept. #65 Larry Dunn $2–4
Oct. #66 Aart Tatum $2–4
Nov. #67 Patrick Moraz $2–4
Dec. #68 Billy Joel..$3–6

1982

Jan. #69 Bob James...$2–4
Feb. #70 Early Rock Pianists $4–8
Mar. #71 Kraftwerk...$2–4
Apr. #72 Earl Hines...$2–4
May #73 Jonathan Cain $2–4
June #74 The New Synthesizer Rock $2–4
July #75 Thelonious Monk $2–4
Aug. #76 Vangelis $2–4
Sept. #77 John Cage $2–4
Oct. #78 Toto's Keyboards $2–4
Nov. #79 Wendy Carlos $2–4
Dec. #80 Eubie Blake...$2–4

1983

Jan. #81 Barry Manilow...$3–6
Feb. #82 Herbie Hancock...$2–4
Mar. #83 Jon Lord..$2–4
Apr. #84 Roger Williams (Sans Broche)...$2–4
May #85 Klaus Schulze..$2–4
June #86 Here Come the Portables..$2–4
July #87 Chick Corea...$2–4
Aug. #88 Thomas Dolby...$2–4
Sept. #89 Paul Shaffer..$2–4
Oct. #90 Oscar Peterson...$2–4
Nov. #91 Geoff Downes..$2–4
Dec. #92 The Great Synthesizer Debate...$2–4

1984

Jan. #93 George Winston..$2–4
Feb. #94 Lead Synthesizer..$2–4
Mar. #95 Josef Zawinul..$2–4
Apr. #96 Joe Sample...$2–4
May #97 Nick Rhode (Duran Duran)..$3–6
June #98 Computer Software for Musicians...$2–4
July #99 Tony Kayes...$2–4
Aug. #100 Tom Bailey..$2–4
Sept. #101 Geddy Lee of Rush...$3–6
Oct. #102 The Secrets of Improvisation, Denny Zeitlin............................$2–4
Nov. #103 Tony Banks, Bill Evans...$2–4
Dec. #104 Dave Stewart of Eurythmics, Wendy Carlos.............................$3–6

1985

Jan. #105 Cecil Taylor, James Newton Howard..$2–4
Feb. #106 Seth Justman of J. Geils Band, Hugh LeCaine...........................$2–4
Mar. #107 Special Issue: J.S. Bach, Duke, Williams, Dolby......................$2–4
Apr. #108 Darryl Hall, Suzanne Ciani..$3–6
May #109 Howard Jones, Vooders...$2–4
June #110 The Art of Programming Synthesizers, Michael Boddicker.........$2–4
July #111 Kate Bush, Patrick Moraz...$4–8
Aug .#112 Keyboards in Japan Special, Isao Tomita...................................$2–4
Sept. #113 Jan Hammer..$2–4
Oct. #114 Chick Corea..$2–4
Nov. #115 Jerry Harrison, Mark Isham...$2–4
Dec. #116 Endangered Species: Piano, D. Stewart & B. Gaskin................$2–4

1986

Jan. #117 Midi Mania, H. Hancock & A. Howarth.....................................$2–4
Feb. #118 Nick Rhodes, Reader Tape Winner...$3–6
Mar. #119 Jean-Michel Jarre..$2–4
Apr. #120 Michael MacNeil, Sorabji...$2–4
May #121 Ivo Pogorelich, Ralph Grierson...$2–4
June #122 The Art of Recording, Porcaro & Bhatia....................................$2–4
July #123 Lyle Mays...$2–4
Aug. #124 Alan Parsons Project, Larry Fast..$2–4
Sept. #125 Keith Jarrett, Igor Kipnis..$2–4
Oct. #126 Depeche Mode, Jim Cox...$2–4
Nov. #127 Jonathain Cain, Wendy Carlos...$3–6
Dec. #128 Roy Bittan, T. Lavitz..$3–6

1987

Jan. #129 Experimental Music Special Issue, Avant-Garde Sampler...........$3–6
Feb. #130 Frank Zappa..$3–6

Mar. #131 Paul Shaffer, Reader Tape Winner $3–6
Apr. #132 Philip Gless...$3–6
May #133 Jam & Lewis, T. Coster & S. Smith $3–6
June #134 Special Issue: Using Sequencers, Jan Hammer......................................$3–6
July #135 Bruce Hornsby, Jazz in Russia..$3–6
Aug. #136 Jeff Lorber, Ursula Oppens $3–6
Sept. #137 Michael Omartian, Banks & Marinelli $3–6
Oct. #138 Miles Davis, Freff, Jazz in Russia...$3–6
Nov. #139 Todd Rundgren, Roger Powell $3–6
Dec. #140 Accordion Power, Stanley Buckwheat Dural $2–4

1988

Jan. #141 Special Issue: On Stage, Mike Oldfield $2–4
Feb. #142 Stewart Copeland, Davis Frank..$2–4
Mar. #143 David Foster, Reader Tape Winner $2–4
Apr. #144 Keith Emerson, Bob James $2–4
May #145 Thomas Dolby, Jill Fraser $2–4
June #146 Back to Basics Special, Terry Fryer $2–4
July #147 Herbie Hancock & Chick Corea, Patrick Leonard $2–4
Aug. #148 The Ultimate in High Tech: The Piano, Ciani, McPartland...................$2–4
Sept. #149 Kenny Kirkland & Delmar Brown, Patrick O'Hearn............................$2–4
Oct. #150 Attack of the New-age Snyth Heroes, T. Lavitz $2–4
Nov. #151 Rap, Nicholas Slonimsky...$2–4
Dec. #152 David Bryan, John Tesh $2–4

1989

Jan. #153 Buying & Selling Sounds, C. Corea & A. Laverne................................$2–4
Feb. #154 Randy Newman, Raymond Scott's Electronium $2–4
Mar. #155 Samplers, Reader Tape Winner $2–4
Apr. #156 Music Notation Software $2–4
May #157 Cyber Punk $2–4
June #158 Brian Eno $2–4
July #159 Paul Carrack & Adrian Lee...$2–4
Aug. #160 Howard Jones & Keith Emerson...$2–4
Sept. #161 New Gear for Next Year $2–4
Oct. #162 Peter Gabriel $2–4
Nov. #163 Chuck Leavell & Matt Clifford $2–4
Dec. #164 Laurie Anderson $2–4

1990

Jan. #165 Billy Joel..$2–4
Feb. #166 Vince Clarke of Erasure, Reader Soundpage Winner.............................$2–4
Mar. #167 Film Scoring $2–4
Apr. #168 Tears for Fears...$2–4
May #169 Jam & Lewis $2–4
June #170 Jane Child $2–4
July #171 Jonathan Cain of Bad English...$2–4

KICKS

All issues..$1–3

KICKS
1989

Sept. Debbie Gibson: Pop's Teen Queen Turns on Electric Youth, New Kids on the Block,
Metallica $2–3

KISS SPECIAL

1978

Winter #4 Kiss Members All Dead, The Great Death Hoax, The World in Mourning, Gene's New Body, The Secret Doubles $10–20

1979

Spring A Behind-the-scenes Special, How They Put Their Shows Together, The Real Kiss Story, Interviews, Their Secret Dreams, The Wild Nights of Kiss $10–20
All other issues $10–20

KYA BEAT

1967

July 15 Jimi Hendrix With Mama Cass & the Monterey Pop Crowd—Special Monterey Pop Festival Issue. (*Note*: This issue is believed to be Jimi Hendrix's first American magazine cover appearance.) $50–100

L

LADIES HOME JOURNAL
1981
Feb. Marie Osmond on Her Own, Fending Off Drugs, Sex & Cynicism $4–8

1989
Nov. Cher, Dolly Parton, Madonna, Tom Cruise $2–3

LADY'S CIRCLE
1977
Dec. Marie Osmond is Changing Her TV Image but Not Her Religious Life Style ...$4–8

1978
Aug. Marie Osmond: Singing & Sewing Star, Now You Can Sew Marie's Super Quick Dresses $4–8

1979
May Marie Osmond as Her Mother Sees Her...$3–6

LIFE MAGAZINE
1958
Dec. 1 Ricky Nelson $10–20

1959
Feb. 2 Pat Boone...$2–4
Aug. 3 Kingston Trio $2–4

1960
June 13 Hayley Mills: A Pert & Perfect Pollyanna......................................$10–20

1964
May 22 Barbra Streisand $2–4
Aug. 28 The Beatles..$12–25

1968
June 28 Jefferson Airplane: The New Rock, Jimi Hendrix.....................................$10–20
Sept. 13 The Beatles: The Days in the Lives of the Beatles—They Call it Their Authentic Biography..$10–20

LIFE, 1960, 6–13

LIFE, 1968, 9–13

LIFE, 1969, 5–2

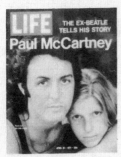

LIFE, 1971, 4–16

LIFE, 1972, 7–14

LIFE, 1971, 10–29

LOOK, 1966, 4–5

LOOK, 1968, 1–9

LOOK, 1969, 3–18

1969

May 2 Judy Collins: Gentle Voice Amid the Strife $3–6
Oct. 3 Issue contains an amazing fold-out front cover poster of Jimi Hendrix in a "Room Full of Mirrors," Jimi Hendrix interview with five full-color, psychedelic, full-page abstract special effects photo $35–70
Nov. 21 Johnny Cash: The Rough-cut King of Country Music $2–4

1970

Sept. 18 Top Pop Singers: Engelbert Humperdinck & Tom Jones $2–4
Oct. 16 Jimi Hendrix & Janis Joplin Obituary Issue...$20–40

1971

Apr. 16 Paul McCartney: The Ex-Beatle Tells His Story..$5–10
Oct. 29 David Cassidy: Teenland's Heartthrob..$10–20

1972

July 14 Mick Jagger: The Stones are Rolling Again...$10–20
Dec. 8 Diana Ross: The Star Shows Off Home, Husband & Babies.......................$10–20

1978

Dec. The Osmonds Show Biz Empire $3–6

1985

Jan. Special Issue—1984 in Pictures: Michael Jackson, Cyndi Lauper & Others........$3–6
Aug. Re-living the Fifties, An Exclusive At-home Interview With Tina Turner..........$2–4
Sept. Tina Turner & Mick Jagger, Live Aid, Paul McCartney, Madonna....................$2–4

1986

Dec. Madonna & the Camera: That Fabulous Couple...$2–4

LIFE SPECIAL EDITION

1969

Woodstock Music Festival Magazine, jammed with rare photos $10–20

LOOK

1958

Nov. 11 Ricky Nelson: "The Men in My Life" by Harriet Nelson............................$10–20

1966

Apr. 5 Barbra Streisand: The Not-so-funny Story of That Funny Girl $2–4
Dec. 27 The Monkees: TV's Latest, Craziest Sensation $10–20

1968

Jan. 9 Beatle John Lennon by Avedon, special pullout portfolio on the Beatles.....$12–25

1969

Jan. 7 Jimi Hendrix three-page special $10–20
Mar. 18 John Lennon & Yoko Ono: Lennon & Ono, Inc.: Beatle John & His Girlfriend Join Forces & Pow $12–25

1970

Aug. 25 The Music Business, The Jackson Five: Bubblegum Soul Takes Off, The Band: $25,000 a Night When They Feel Like It, Woodstock Feature...................................$10–20

1971

July 13 Kris Kristofferson: Country Music—Hillbilly No More, a 24-page special featuring Bobby Bare, Skeeter Davis, Tom T. Hall, Tammy Wynette, Hank Williams & others....$3–6

M

MADCITY MUSIC SHEET (Wisconsin's Original Music Magazine)
All issues...$2–4

MAGIC MAGAZINE
1977
Apr. Donny & Marie Osmond cover & feature story: The Great Osmondos $4–8

MARVEL SUPER SPECIAL
1977
#1 Kiss...$25–75
1978
#4 The Beatles Story, The Ultimate Unauthorized Beatles Magazine............................$3–6
#5 Kiss...$25–75

MASTERS OF ROCK
1990
#1 Jimi Hendrix Special Collector's Edition, The Definitive Hendrix Retrospective, Rare Hendrix Photos, Interviews & Remembrances, The Dark World of Jim Morrison by John Densmore, Janis Joplin: A Piece of Her Heart, full-page color Jimi Hendrix photos & poster..$3–7
#2 John Lennon: A Decade Later the Legacy Continues, issue includes many fine color photos & wall poster $3–6

McCALL'S
1985
Apr. Marie Osmond: Her Struggle to Save Her Troubled Marriage............................$2–5

MEMORIES
1989
June/July The Supremes: Where Did Their Love Go? $2–4

METAL
All issues...$2–4

METAL COLLECTORS EDITION
All issues...$2–4

METALLIX
All issues $2–4

METAL MADNESS
1989
June #1 Issue includes four gigantic color wall posters, Motley Crue, Led Zeppelin, Jon Bon Jovi, Kiss, Def Leppard, Poison, Guns 'n' Roses $2–5
#2 Bon Jovi, issue includes a 1990 Heavy Metal calendar, Lita Ford, White Lion, Danzig, Joan Jett, Kiss, Cinderella, Ozzy Osbourne..$2–4
Nov. #3 Special All-Kiss issue, Kiss stories & posters......................................$3–6
#4 Issue includes four gigantic color posters, lots of pin-ups, & picture-packed pages of Heavy Metal mischief..$2–4

1990
Feb. #6 Aerosmith, Britny Fox, Def Leppard, Slaughter, Jani Lane, Kip Winger, Kiss, Warrent, Ozzy Osbourne, Lita Ford, Skid Row, issue includes posters.........................$2–4
All other issues $2–4

METAL MADNESS FOTO FRENZY
1989
#1 The Fun & Funny Side of Heavy Metal, Packed With Candid Photos, issue includes four gigantic wall posters $2–4

METAL MADNESS MOTLEY CRUE TRIBUTE
1989
#2 Exclusive Candids, On & Off-stage Mischief, Video Clips, Trivia, Pullout Posters, Discography & History $2–4

METAL MADNESS 1990 HEADBANGER'S CALENDAR MAGAZINE
1989
Twelve Months of Metal, A Day-by-day Heavy Metal History Book, A Year Full of Classic Pin-ups $2–4

METAL MADNESS: THE MIGHT AND MAGIC OF KISS SPECIAL
1989
The Ultimate Kiss Kompendium, Loaded With Kiss Kaos..$2–4

METAL MADNESS WHITESNAKE YEARBOOK
1989
A Supergroup's Long Crawl to the Top, In Concert, History, Profiles & Interviews, Candids, eight pullout wall posters, with Great White & Motley Crue $2–4

METAL MUSCLE: '80S' METAL
1989
Metal Mega-stars of the Decade, Speed Metal, Glam-rock & Chartbusters, '70s' metal in the '80s $2–4

METAL MUSCLE: GUIDE TO HEAVY METAL
1989
The Grand Tour Through Heavy Metaldom, Video Directory, Underground Fanzines, The Ultimate Record Library..$2–4

METAL MUSCLE: GUNS 'N' LEPPARD SPECIAL
1989
What Makes Guns 'n' Roses & Def Leppard Unstoppable Bands So Successful? Exclusive
Interviews, Collectible Pullout Posters & Pin-ups...$2–4

METAL MUSCLE: HEAVY METAL IN THE RAGING '90S SPECIAL
1989
Today's Metal Gods Tomorrow, Metal Gurus, Heavy Metal Heavyweights Forecasting the
Future...$2–4

METAL MUSCLE: MEGASTARS OF METAL SPECIAL
1989
Today's Ruling Rockers, Four Decades of Metal Monsters, Skid Row, Def Leppard, Bon
Jovi, Metallica, Kiss $2–4

METAL MUSCLE: THE HEAVY METAL 100
1989
A Guide to the Most Influential & Best-loved Acts in Hard Rock History, The Legends, The
Leaders, The Latest, issue includes eight color pullout wall posters $2–4

METAL MUSCLE: TOP 10 GREATS OF HEAVY METAL
1989
The Best Bands, LPs, Guitarists, Songs, Vocalists, Drummers & Songwriters, issue includes
special collectors' pullout section...$2–4

METAL MUSCLE: WORLD SERIES OF HEAVY METAL SPECIAL
1989
Rock's Hardest Hitters, From the Rookies to the Hall of Famers, East vs. West, Heavy
Metal Speed Demons, Homeruns & MVPs, issue includes six pullout wall posters....$2–4

METAL RENDEZVOUS (America's Ultimate Heavy Rock Magazine)
All issues...$2–5

METAL RENDEZVOUS INTERNATIONAL
All issues...$3–6

METRONOME (Local Boston music tabloid)
1990
Sept. Jimi Hendrix: 20 Years Later—Hendrix Remembered $4–8
All other issues $1–3

M.I. (Musician's Industry Magazine)
All issues...$1–3

MODERN RECORDING AND MUSIC
1981
Feb. The Grateful Dead in Concert $2–4
Apr. A Session With the Dreggs, Steve Winwood Profile $1–2

June Rick Wakeman, Ian Stewart: The Sixth Rolling Stone............................$2–4
Aug. Mick Fleetwood on Location $2–4

MODERN SCREEN YEARBOOK
1986
#26 Special Ratt Color Spectacular, includes four posters & 12 centerfolds, Kiss, Bon Jovi, Billy Idol $2–4

MOJO-NAVIGATOR (Rock-and-Roll News)
1967
Apr. James Gurley, Blues Magoos, The Doors, Lovin' Spoonful............................$20–40
Aug. The Doors Return, Eric Clapton, Chuck Berry, Jimi Hendrix $20–40
All other issues $20–40

MOUTH OF THE RAT (Tabloid)
All issues..$3–6

MOVIE MIRROR
1989
Jan. Special 50 Metal Pix Issue—Includes 50 Unbelievable Color Pin-ups: Guns 'n' Roses, Warrent, Skid Row, Lita Ford, Metallica, Def Leppard, Ozzy Osbourne, Anthrax, Vixen, Bulletboys, Bon Jovi, Depeche Mode $2–4
Feb. Skid Row Color Spectacular: Up Close & Personal, issue includes two giant full-color wall posters, complete Skid Row history & discography................................$2–4

1990
Apr. Hot Metal Centerfolds Issue—includes 28 posters: Skid Row, Warrent, Motley Crue, Metallica, Tora Tora, Guns 'n' Roses, Ozzy Osbourne, Bon Jovi, Warrent, King Diamond, Anthrax, Alice Cooper, Bulletboys, Whitesnake, Steve Vai & others.........................$2–4
Aug. Hot Metal Centerfolds Issue—contains 17-page Skid Row section, Metallica, Axl Rose, Tora Tora, Motley Crue, Alice Cooper, Death Angel, Warrent, Def Leppard, Lita Ford, Aerosmith, Ozzy Osbourne, L.A. Guns, Shotgun Messia, Voivod, Joe Satriani, Slash $2–4
Sept. Metal Maniacs Issue—Slayer Exclusive, Voivod, Overkill, Bruce Dickinson, Coroner, Celtic Frost, C.O.C., King Diamond $2–4

MUSIC CONNECTION
1990
May14–27 Wilson Phillips...$2–4

MUSIC EXPRESS
All issues...$2–4

MUSICIAN: PLAYER AND LISTENER
1977
#8 Interviews with Herbie Hancock, Freddie Hubbard & others $5–10

1978
#14 George Benson's Midas Touch, Newport Festival '78....................................$4–8
#15 Chick Corea's Changes, The New Freedom Swing.......................................$4–8

1979
#17 Art & Funk, Charles Mingus Farewell...$4–8
#18 The Pat Metheny Method, ENO, Dire Straits...$4–8

1980

#22 Stevie Wonder, Robert Fripp: The New Realism $4–8
#23 Sonny Rollins Retrospective, Pete Townshend, Steely Dan $4–8
#24 Reggae: Bob Marley's Rasta Roots, Robert Fripp, Lester Bangs $4–8
#28 Dire Straits, Brian Ferry & Roxy Music, Robert Fripp, Japan $4–8
#29 Captain Beefheart, Michael McDonald, Surf Music $4–8

1981

#30 Bruce Springsteen interview, Miles Davis $3–6
#31 Steely Dan interview, John Lennon interview $3–6
#32 David Byrne & Talking Heads, Brian Eno, Muscle Shoals $3–6
#33 The Clash, Robert Fripp interview, Lindsay Buckingham $3–6
#34 Tom Petty interview, Carlos Santana, Dave Edmunds, John Cale $3–6
#35 Jim Morrison & the Doors Special Issue, Carla Bley, David Lindsay $3–6
#36 The Grateful Dead, Kid Creole, David Johansen, Journey, REO, Zappa, Miles Davis
....
#37 Bill Wyman: The Inside Story of the Rolling Stones, Rickie Lee Jones, Reggae, Robert
Fripp on King Crimson, Copeland, Ornette Coleman $3–6
#38 The Police, Robert Fripp, Africa, The Pretenders, The Go-go's $3–6

1982

#39 The Cars, Marianne Faithful, Lene Lovich, King Crimson by Robert Fripp $3–6
#40 Ringo, Devo, Rossington-Collins, Special Drummers' Issue $3–6
#41 Miles Davis, Genesis, Joan Jett's Bad Reputation, Lowell George $3–6
#42 Hall & Oates, Frank Zappa, Joan Armatrading, David Byrne in the Studio $3–6
#43 Eric Clapton, Robbie Robertson & the Band, Albert King, Rock Guitar Pioneers $3–6
#44 Nick Lowe: Pure Pop Prankster, Graham Parker, Dr. John, X, L.A. Punk $3–6
#45 Willie Nelson, The Motels, Marshall Crenshaw, Joe Cocker, Lou-ann Barton $3–6
#46 Pete Townshend & the Who, Squeeze, Warren Zevon, John Hiatt, Miles Davis ..$3–6
#47 Eddie Van Halen, The Clash, Quincy Jones, The Jam, Pete Townshend $3–6
#48 Steve Winwood Comes in from the Cold, Brian Eno, Steve Miller, Rosanne Cash ...$3–6
#49 Neil Young, Foreigner, The Go-go's $3–6
#50 Billy Joel: A Native Son Revealed, Pink Floyd: Inside 15 Years of Pink Floyd, Elvis
Presley, The Failure of Corporate Rock $3–6

1983

#51 Joni Mitchell interview, Peter Gabriel, Andy Summers $3–6
#52 Joe Jackson: Chameleon Cool, Men at Work, John Cougar: Rock's Complicated Brat,
Iron Curtain Rock, Emmylou Harris: The Alabama Angel $3–6
#53 Tom Petty: He's Sorta Like God, The Roaches: Fresh Folk Faces, Ric Ocasek/The Cars
.... $4–8
#54 Bob Seger: Nobody's Fool, Randy Newman, Missing Persons, Todd Rundgren, Dexy's
Midnight Runners $4–8
#55 David Bowie interview, Psychedelic Furs, Kenny Loggins, Sunnyade $3–6
#56 The Police, Home Recording Special $3–6
#57 Bob Marley Exclusive, The Ramones, Ultravox, Don Henley $3–6
#58 Ray Davies: The Kinks, Marvin Gaye interview, Roxy Music, R.E.M. $3–6
#59 Prince Talks: Stranger Than Fiction, Joan Jett: The Genius of Gum, The Beach Boys:
The Life of Brian, Billy Gibbons $3–6
#60 Elvis Costello Lets Down His Guard, Joe Walsh, Culture Club, Aztec Camera,
Motown $3–6
#61 Jackson Browne: A Precocious Pretender Cuts it Away, Eurythmics: Anything Goes,
Keith Jarrett $3–6
#62 Keith Richards & Mick Jagger: Glimmer & Gore, Big Country $3–6

1984

#63 Australian Rock, Midnight Oil, Jimmy Page, UB40, Ronnie Lane $3–6
#64 Stevie Wonder, Reggae 1984, X, Was (Was Not), Ornette Coleman $3–6

#65 Chrissie Hynde: The Pretenders—One Tough Mother, Linda Ronstadt, Paul Simon.....$3–6
#66 Laurie Anderson, AC/DC, Paul Weller Ambushed, Charlie Harden.......................$3–6
#67 Thomas Dolby, Steely Dan, The Alarm, Thompson Twins, Marcus Miller..........$3–6
#68 Van Halen: The Oddest Couple—Can it Last? The Cars, XTC, Joe Jackson, Black Flagg, Huey Lewis, The Smiths, Russian Jazz $3–6
#69 Michael Jackson, R.E.M., Charlie Watts $3–6
#70 Peter Wolf, King Crimson, Bass Drum Special...$3–6
#71 Judas Priest & The Scorpions: The Truth About Headbangers, Defending Dirt Bags Like Twisted Sister, Slade, Blue Cheer, Tina Turner, Heavy Metal Special................$3–6
#72 Prince: The Prince Who Would be King, Lou Reed, Rod Stewart, Glenn Frey, Cyndi Lauper, Bruce Springsteen, The Assembly $3–6
#73 Bruce Springsteen: A Pure Patriot Keeps His Promise, also Bruce Springsteen interview, The E Street Band, Phil Ramone, Miles Davis, John Lydon, Lindsay Buckingham Recovers His Sanity..$4–8
#74 David Bowie Under Pressure, Andy Summers, Yoko Ono: The Artist in Her Own Write, Sheila E., The Fixx, Steve Morse...$3–6
#75 U2: The Passion Players Catch Fire, Van Morrison, Culture Club, J. Geils Band $3–6
#76 Paul McCartney: After the Broad Street Fiasco—A Search for What Went Wrong, Rickie Lee Jones Exclusive Interview, Toto, Big Country..$3–6

1985

#77 John Fogerty: Alias—Creedence Clearwater Revival: Last Heard From in 1975, Los Lobos, Marsalis Hancock $3–6
#78 Mick Jagger, Felix Cavaliere, The Firm, Jimmy Page & Paul Rogers interview..$3–6
#79 Jeff Beck Gets Back Interview, Jimmy Page Talks Shop.......................................$3–6
#80 Phil Collins: A Musician Becomes a Star, Tom Petty, David Byrne, Husker Du $3–6
#81 Sting Solo: The Inside Story, Graham Parker, The Billy Idol Maker, Dave Edmunds $3–6
#82 Brian Wilson, Sting Part II, Jerry Garcia & the Grateful Dead $3–6
#83 Dire Straits, R.E.M., John Cage, Brian Eno $3–6
#84 John Cougar Grows Up, Bryan Ferry Opens Up, T-bone Burnett...........................$3–6
#85 Talking Heads: To Be or Not to Be?, Neil Young, CSNY $3–6
#86 Joni Mitchell: Having the Last Laugh, Simple Minds: Glorious Noise, Hall & Oates ..$3–6

1986

#87 ZZ Top: How Three Bad Boys Became the Kingpins of Cactus Crunch, Kate Bush Gets Her Head Shrunk, Marshall Crenshaw, Yngwie Malmsteen $3–6
#88 The New Van Halen: Will it Fly?, Pete Townshend Comes in from the Wasteland ...$3–6
#89 Elvis Costello, Al Green, Mick Jones $3–6
#90 James Brown: Behind His Long Strange Trip Back, Tom Petty Bares His Southern Soul, Brian Setzer: The Ex-Cat Shifts Gear...$3–6
#91 The Rolling Stones on the Rocks, Violent Femmes, INXS, The Bangles $3–6
#92 Joe Jackson, Bob Seger, John Lydon...$3–6
#93 Peter Gabriel, Steve Winwood, Lou Reed...$3–6
#94 Jimi Hendrix World Exclusive—Inside the Experience: Noel Reddings Startling Memoir of Music, Money & Drugs, The Cure, 38 Special, The Origin of Prince $4–8
#95 Pete Townshend: Host of the Big Guitar Issue, Jimi Hendrix: The Final Days, U2's Edge, Eric Johnson, Ron Wood..$3–6
#96 Tina Turner: Her Tag Team—Mark Knopfler, Terry Britten & Bryan Adams, Paul McCartney Mouths Off, Genesis, Frank Zappa...$3–6
#97 Eric Clapton in a Revealing Interview, Rick Ocasek's Pop Artbeat, Paul Simon's Amazing Graceland, Can Queen Conquer America?...$3–6
#98 The New Pretenders: Chrissie Hynde Goes Looking for Mr. Goodband, The Clash Reunion Producer Orgy, Richard Thompson...$3–6

1987

#99 Boston: The Untold Story, Georgia Satellites, Sun Ra, The Kinks $3–6
#100 Special Anniversary Issue—Bruce Springsteen, Sting, Van Halen, Prince, John Lennon, Joni Mitchell, Elvis Costello, The Beatles, David Bowie, Rolling Stones, Robert Fripp...$3–6

#101 Psychedelic Furs: Will They Sell Their Souls for Success?, Miles Davis, John McLaughlin, Elton John Undisguised..$3–6
#102 Robert Cray, Los Lobos, Simply Red $3–6
#103 U2, Steve & Jimmie Vaughn, Rick Rubin, Beastie Boys, Run DMC..............$3–6
#104 Bruce Springsteen Talks About His Journey From Introspection to Superstardom, Ginger Baker, Billy Cobham..$3–6
#105 John Coltrane: The Legacy Lives, Bruce Springsteen: The Boss on the Record, The Real Replacements, George Martin on the Beatles..$3–6
#106 David Bowie, Peter Wolf, Husker Du $3–6
#107 The Debut of Robbie Robertson: The Band's Leader Comes Back Strong, Mark Knopfler, Tom Petty Stands Up Against Selling Out, Andy Summers Walks the Solo Beat...$3–6
#108 U2 Hits the Top, Tom Waits Without the Jive, The Seven Trials of Squeeze....$3–6
#109 George Harrison: The Quiet Beatle Finally Talks About Everything, Who is Neil Young's Crazy Horse?, The Mick Jagger Philosophy: Music, God & Country............$3–6
#110 Slapping Sting Around: Can He Handle the Tough Questions?, The Life & Death of Jaco Pastorius, The Last Peter Tosh Interview, Def Leppard $3–6

1988

#111 R.E.M.'s Double Visionaries, The Year in Rock, George Michael Gets No Respect, Meat Puppets, 10,000 Maniacs..$3–6
#112 Paul McCartney Gets Hungry Again, Elvis Costello: Paul's Partner, The Two Faces of Buster Poindexter..$3–6
#113 Robert Plant interview: Zen & the Art of Led Zeppelin, Joe Strummer, Miles Copeland, INXS $3–6
#114 The Hidden John Lennon: Private Memories, Musical Diaries & New Beatles Tracks Come to Light, James Taylor's Darkest Past, Robyn Hitchcock's Bright Future..........$3–6
#115 Living Legends Issue—Stevie Wonder, Sonny Rollins, Joni Mitchell & Johnny Cash: Four Corners of American Music..$3–6
#116 Sinead O'Connor, Nothing Stops Neil Young, Why the Best New Artists of 1988 are Women, Toni Childs, Tracy Chapman, Michelle Shocked, Rush's Neal Peart..............$3–6
#117 Has Jimmy Page Still Got It?, Leonard Cohen, Dixie Dregs............................$3–6
#118 Pink Floyd: Happy at Last, New Order, Smithereens, The Sons of Aerosmith, Camper Van Beethoven..$3–6
#119 ZZ Top, Monsters of Guitar, Eddie Van Halen: Backstage on the Metal Express, Carlos Santana, Frank Zappa, Georgia Satellites, Vernon Reid's Living Color............$3–6
#120 Keith Richard's revenge, Crowded House, Steve Forbert's Nightmare, The Beatles '66...$3–6
#121 Prince vs. Prince: An Artist at War With Himself, Randy Newman's Big Problem, Brian Eno, Steve Winwood's American Connection..$3–6
#122 Guns 'n' Roses: Up from the Gutter, Going Down the Drain?, Midnight Oil Catches Fire, Who's Edie Brickell?, Glyn Johns $3–6

1989

#123 The Year in Music 1988—U2, R.E.M., INXS, Def Leppard, Joe Satriani, Metallica, George Harrison, Guns 'n' Roses, Robert Plant, Keith Richards, Randy Newman, Jack Bruce..$3–6
#124 The Replacements: The Last Best Band of the 80s, How Fleetwood Mac Fired Lindsay Buckingham..$3–6
#125 Elvis Costello in Love & War: A Major Interview, Bobby Brown....................$3–6
#126 Lou Reed & John Cale: A Historic Reunion, Joe Satriani..............................$3–6
#127 Miles Davis: Still Miles Ahead, XTC's Cottage Industry, Thomas Dolby Goes Hollywood, Fine Young Cannibals Success Recipe $3–6
#128 The Passion of Peter Gabriel, The Lost Memoirs of Charles Mingus, Bob Mould After Husker Du, Tone-loc, Drummers' Special Section...$3–6
#129 The Who: Never Say Never Again, Inside the Cure's Closed World $3–6
#130 10,000 Maniacs, John Cougar Mellencamp, Bonnie Raitt & Jackson Browne....$3–6
#132 Don Henley's Dirty Laundry: The Ex-Eagles Take on Joe Walsh & Others, The Rolling Stones on Steel Wheels, Love & Rockets: On the Road, Steve Stevens on His Own, Vengence and Bob Marley: The Wailers' Violent Legacy $3–6

#133 The Eighties Special: Year by Year, Blow by Blow, Everything That Mattered in the Decade of Excess—Prince, The Police, Madonna, Bruce Springsteen, U2, Paul Simon & Many, Many Others $3–5

#134 Night of the Grateful Dead: Jerry Garcia & Bob Weir Expose Their Demons, Stevie Ray Vaughan interview, Laurie Anderson $2–4

1990

#135 The Death & Rebirth of Aerosmith, NRBQ, Ricky Skaggs $2–4
#136 February Issue. . . . 62 Reasons it's Great to be Eric Clapton, The Private World of Kate Bush: Theatre of the Senses $2–4
#137 George Harrison: It Beat Being a Beatle $2–4
#138 Tom Petty & the Heartbreakers $2–4
#139 On Tour With Paul McCartney $2–4
#141 Jimi Hendrix: Playing With Jimi $2–4

MUSIC MAKERS (Published by Personics Corporation)

All issues $1–3

MUSIC PAPER (New York-based music magazine)

All issues $2–4

MUSIC REPORTER

All issues $1–2

MUSIC SOUND OUTPUT

1981

Aug. #5 Jefferson Starship: How America's Hippies Survived the Sixties, Joe Ely, John Cale, George Clinton $2–4
Oct. Robert Fripp, Black Uhuru, Tom Verlaine $2–3
Dec. Stevie Nicks: Bella Donna Stevie, Tom Petty & Stevie Nicks, Ian Hunter: The Perennial Rocker Rocks On, Duran Duran: Music Beyond Fashion, Deborah Harry's Solo Rock Excursion, Brian Eno, Western Swing $5–10

1982

Feb. The Cars: Their Unabashed Commercial Success, Foreigner, King Crimson, Marianne Faithful, Jerry Lee Lewis, Genesis, Frank Zappa, Rod Stewart, The Ventures $2–4
Apr. Rod Stewart, Human League, Genesis, Big Joe Turner $2–4
June J. Geils Band: The Past 15 Years, Sonny Rollins, Bobby Bare, Lizard Kings, Clarence Clemons $2–4
Aug. Squeeze, Graham Parker, The Dreggs, Chet Atkins..$2–4

1983

Dec. Robert Plant Exclusive: All Part of the Plan, Adrian Belew, Spandau Ballet, R.E.M., Shalamar, Ray Manzarek $2–4

1984

July The Eurythmics: Contrasting Images, The Alarm: Politics at the Front, Johnny Cash: The Early Classics of a Country Legend, Echo & the Bunnymen, John Cale, The Dice, Icicle Works...$2–4
Sept. Difford & Tilbrook: Emotional Squeeze, Bananarama: The Hard Road to Respect, Nashville British, Scritti Pollitti...$2–3
Nov. Hall & Oates: Responding to the Call of the Street, Yoko Ono: Fulfilling a Legacy, The Bangles: Good Old-fashioned Pop Harmony, Reggae: British Style, The Gun Club, Bluebells $2–4

1985

Jan. Big Country: Music Back to the People, Malcom McLaren: Restructuring the Classics, The Church...$1–2

Feb. Talking Head's David Byrne Talking Music, Human League: Don't You Want Them?, Los Lobos: Ethnic Music Crosses the Border...$2–4

Mar. The Washington Squares, Violent Femmes, XTC: Studio Impressionists.............$1–2

1987
Apr. Whitney Houston, Aretha Franklin, George Benson, Husker Du $2–3

MUSIC TECHNOLOGY
1990
Mar. The Thompson Twins: Rock 'n' Roll Royalty $2–4

MUSIC VENDOR
All issues $1–2

N

NATURAL BODY FITNESS MAGAZINE
1989
Nov. Sheena Easton cover & story: Sexy, Talented & Superfit, Billy Idol, George Michael, Bruce Springsteen $2–4

NEWSWEEK
1975
Oct. 27 Bruce Springsteen: Making of a Rock Star $6–12
1985
Aug. 5 Bruce Springsteen: Glory Days—Going Wild About Bruce $3–5

NEW WAVE ROCK
1978
Sept. #1 Kiss: What do They Mean?, Why Are They Here?, Debbie Harry/Blondie: Return From the Baricades—Tour Trials & Tribulations, The Jam: Tour Misunderstandings, The Dictators, The Clash, John Cale, Television, The Ramones: Four Boys from Queens, The B-52's..$15–30
Nov. #2 Bruce Springsteen With Patti Smith, Special Interview Issue, Patti Smith: The Resurrection & the Life, Billy Joel, Bruce Springsteen, XTC, Elvis Costello: Alienated Artist, Nico in Paris, Robert Gordon, The Roots of Punk, Debbie Harry $12–25
1979
Feb. #3 Tom Petty interview, Joan Jett & the Runaways: No More Favors for Fowley interview, Talking Heads: David Byrne Blabs, The Roots of Punk Part II, Dead Boys, Mink Deville, Sham 69, Eddie Jobson, Sid Vicious: An Anglo-American Tragedy, Iggy Pop, issue includes Runaways color poster..$12–25

NEW YORK ROCKER
All issues...$5–20

NEW YORK ROCKER PIX
1979
May #1 Donna Destri, Sister of Jimmy "Blondie" Destri, Joan Jett, Joey Ramone, Talking Heads, Lydia Lunch, Richard Hell & others $7–15

NIGHTLIFE MAGAZINE (Long Island, New York, music magazine)
1981
Apr. Kid Creole, Melba Moore...$1–2

1984

Feb. The Four Tops..$1–2
Mar. Ashford & Simpson $1–2
Apr. Kiss $4–8
May Scandal $1–2
June Patti Labelle, Duran Duran...$2–4
July Debarge $1–2
Aug. Style Council, Toni Tenille..$1–2
Sept. Madonna, Frankie Valli $2–4
Dec. Graham Nash...$1–2

1985

Apr. Mick Jagger, Connie Francis...$2–4
June Power Station..$1–2
July Tom Chapin $1–2
Aug. David Lee Roth $2–4
Sept. Tears for Fears $1–2
Oct. Rubin Blades $1–2
Nov. Rosemary Clooney...$1–2

1986

Jan. Dolly Parton, Sheila E. $2–4
Feb. China Crisis $1–2
May Alisha...$1–2
June Ziggy Marley, Chuck Mangione $1–2
July Robert Palmer...$1–2
Aug. Belinda Carlisle $4–8
Oct. Nia Peeples..$1–2
Dec. James Ingram...$1–2

1987

Jan. Joan Jett, Gloria Loring, Neil Sedaka, Bo Diddley.....................................$4–8
Feb. Debbie Harry, Roberta Flack, The Moody Blues...$4–8
June Liza Minelli, Buster Poindexter $1–2
Aug. The System, Joe Jackson...$1–2
Sept. XTC, Ace Frehley $2–4
Oct. Donna Summer..$2–4
Nov. Thompson Twins, Chris Hillman...$1–2
Dec. Gloria Estefan, Judy Collins, Debbie Gibson...$2–4

1988

Jan. Bobby Short, The Fabulous T-birds..$1–2
Feb. Mary Wilson, Dan Fogelberg, Gordon Lightfoot $2–4
July Expose, Natalie Merchant...$1–2
Sept. Taylor Dane $1–2
Oct. Nia Peeples..$1–2
Nov. Robert Cray, Smithereens..$1–2
Dec. Rod Stewart $2–4

1989

Jan. David Sanborn, Sheena Easton, Toni Childs, U2..$2–4
Feb. The Bangles, Eddie Money, Mike Rutherford..$2–4
Mar. Anita Baker, Duran Duran..$2–4
Apr. Samantha Fox..$2–4
May Dion, Harry Connick, Elvis Costello $2–4
June Richard Marx, David Crosby $2–4
July Cyndi Lauper, Rosanne Cash, Swing Out Sister...$2–4
Sept. Expose, Mel Torme, Paul McCartney..$2–4
Oct. Ron Wood, Melissa Etheridge, Lyle Lovettt, Don Henley $2–4

Nov. Gloria Estefan, Natalie Cole...$2–4
Dec. Roger Daltrey, Bob Dylan..$2–4

1990

Jan. Jellybean Benitez, Swing Out Sister, Kate Bush, Laurie Anderson.....................$2–4
Feb. Taylor Dane...$2–4
Mar. Roxette, Patti Labelle, Quincy Jones..$1–2
Apr. Desert Rose Band...$1–2
May Julia Fordham...$1–2
June Heart...$2–4
July Aerosmith, Joe Walsh...$1–2
Aug. Suzanne Vega...$1–2
Sept. Shawn Colvin..$1–2

NIGHT TIMES (Tabloid)

1971

#5 Commander Cody & His Lost Planet Airmen...$5–10

1972

#28 Boz Scaggs: His Berkeley Concert & the Start of His U.S. Tour.........................$5–10

NON LP B SIDE

All issues..$1–2

NORTHERN CALIFORNIA FOLK-ROCK FESTIVAL NEWSPAPER

All issues..$10–20

NOT FADE AWAY (The Texas Music Magazine)

All issues..$2–4

O

ON MUSIC AND MEDIA MAGAZINE
1982
July Blondie: Debbie Harry & Chris Stein interviews, The Motels, Haircut 100, Bow Wow Wow, Van Halen, Jim Carroll, Chic, Miles Davis, Paul McCartney, Laurie Anderson, Mamas & the Papas $5–10

OPEN CITY (Los Angeles tabloid)
1968
#84 The Moody Blues, Dillard & Clark..$5–10

ORGAN (Tabloid)
All issues..$15–30

OVERTHROW (Rock Against Racism)
1979
Apr. #1 Tom Robinson: Rebel on the Road, Todd Rundgren: Palladium Rocks for Refugees, The Clash are a Smash $6–12

Dylan and the Dead

Collecting

THE GRATEFUL DEAD

The Grateful Dead have already marked their 25th anniversary as a musical unit. With so many years behind them, it could be well imagined that they have amassed an incredible array of items worth collecting.

Perhaps the earliest accessible mementos are the original concert posters announcing the shows in the Bay Area put on at various venues like the Avalon Ballroom and the Fillmore. In their original printing, these posters are worth varying amounts of money (some have gone into second printings and others were bootlegged in the early '80s when the market values of the originals skyrocketed). Prices range from $30 to $500, with some very rare posters almost priceless.

Many pieces of Grateful Dead art have been made available by the veteran artists who did the original psychedelic concert posters, including Stanley Mouse, Alton Kelley, Rick Griffin, and Phillip Garris. They have produced some wonderful limited edition signed prints that range into the thousands of dollars, but the true collectibles they have to offer are the dwindling original pieces of art used in the production of posters, album covers, T-shirts, etc.

Since the Dead's 20th anniversary, more attention has been paid to their merchandising line. The band has sold licenses for everything from hacky sacks, frisbees, and wallets to belt buckles, mugs, trivets, pins, buttons, patches, decals, car license plate holders, car window sunscreens, and just about anything else that will hold a logo. There is, however, a huge selection of collectibles from the pre-licensing days that are worthy of collecting. Pre-'80s posters, buttons, patches, T-shirts, and other novelty items are all out there, worth looking for, and gaining in value.

The Grateful Dead boast the world's largest traveling circus, and those followers were the originators of many unique concepts. Due to a number of problems both personal and professional in the late '80s, following the release of their most successful album, "In the Dark," outdoor vending at the concerts was stopped. There are less unusual items easily accessible from the merchants that provide handmade collectibles. Many of these people have resorted to advertising in *Relix* magazine as a way to sell their wares. However, licensing is strictly enforced, and it can be a tedious task to get approval from the Dead to manufacture an item. Many companies have gotten the rights and include in their deals that a portion of the proceeds go to an environmental or charitable organization. For example, Ben & Jerry's Ice Cream uses proceeds from its "Cherry Garcia" flavor to help support the rain forest preservation.

The year 1989 marked a major change in the Grateful Dead's marketing strategy. After having been under license to Winterland for most of their career, the band started their own competing merchandiser (Winterland was formed by Bill Graham who helped launch the Dead's musical career). Their T-shirt designs are so different from the Winterland concepts that many fans displayed their dismay by not buying the new artwork, which steps away from the more colorful, hippielike designs of yesterday. This does, however, create a whole new line of shirts in the collectible market. No matter how you look at it, the most original and interesting shirts are those created in small quantities by the fans.

Grateful Dead records also represent some vintage material. Early 45s range from $15 and up. Promotional packages for recent releases will garner a good sum when the market is right. Many vinyl selections range around $50, such as the labels Seastones, Ace, and Vintage Dead, but this material is quickly becoming available on CD. It is a known fact that Deadheads prefer good sound and many of these original selections were not of the highest standards. Many of the CD versions have been remixed, adding additional value to the original vinyl.

The first pressings were old vinyl, green- or gold-label Warner Brothers products. Any of these are worth holding onto, in either album or 45-RPM form.

The Grateful Dead, as well as their earlier record companies, made a selection of promotional items, including stand-up displays, which are quite rare. Promo posters and album slicks from the record companies have been bootlegged over the years and should only be bought from a reputable source.

Grateful Dead-oriented magazines are probably the most easily accessible of collectibles, and once you get started you can get hooked! There have been about eight different magazines published on the Grateful Dead scene since the beginning that are now impossible to find. *Relix* magazine, with a publishing history of 18 years at about six issues a year, is the oldest Bay rock publication still in existence. *The Golden Road* was published for about seven years. *Relix* magazine never reprinted any of the early issues, and, as a result, some of the early issues are now valued in the hundred of dollars. *The Golden Road* may have reprinted issues, so their value as collectibles has yet to be established.

There are also many books that have been published over the years. The list is quite extensive and many are still available. The three most successful books are *The Official Book of Deadheads* by Paul Grushkin, *The History of the Grateful Dead* by William Ruhlmann, and *The Grateful Dead Guitar Anthology* by Warner Brothers Books, but these too are very difficult to find.

On the merchandising front, recent licenses include dancing bear plush dolls ($30), a line of tie-dyed shirts, mugs, trivets, decals, patches, posters, jackets, and towels, as well as a huge selection of buttons and other small items. None of the recent items have yet to exhibit any collecting opportunities.

For information on *Relix* magazine, please drop them a note and they will be happy to send you their brochure—*Relix*, P.O. Box 94, Brooklyn, NY 11229. A subscription to *Relix* magazine is $23 per year/$27 Canada and foreign.

P

PENTHOUSE

1980
Feb. Debbie Harry cover & feature story: Blondie, Sex Symbol of the 80s..........$ 10–20

1985
Sept. Madonna cover & nude photos $20–40

1987
Sept. Madonna cover & nude photos $15–30

PEOPLE WEEKLY

1974
May 6 The Beatles: Ten Years Later—And Ringo is the Big Surprise $3–6

1975
Jan. 15 Elvis Presley at Forty...$3–6
Apr. 21 Paul McCartney: "My Family is my Life, Then My Music" $3–6
June 9 Mick Jagger: His Stones Hit the U.S. While Bianca Conquers the Continent
....$5–10
Aug. 18 Elton John: His New Look—Everything is Slimmer but His Wallet.............$3–6
Sept. 8 Cher & Gregg Allman: She Helps Him Stay off Heroin & His Band is Hot Again
....$3–6
Oct. 20 Grace Slick: Love on a Rock Starship..$3–6
Nov. 10 Bob Dylan: "I Don't Consider Myself Reclusive, Exclusive Maybe," The Os-
mond's Mom & Pop..$4–8

1976
Mar. 29 Glen Campbell: It's a Sparkling New Life for the Rhinestone Cowboy.......$1–2
Apr. 5 The Beatles: Will They Sing Again for Fifty Million Dollars?, Olivia Newton-John,
John Lennon $3–6
June 7 Paul McCartney: "What Will Daddy Do When He Grows Up?".....................$2–4
July 12 Sonny Bono, Jerry Garcia's Grateful Dead Pass the True Acid Test & Still Play-
ing $2–4
Aug. 23 The Beach Boys: Still Riding the Crest 15 Hairy Years Later.....................$2–4
Sept. 6 David Bowie: With A Spacey Film & a Son Named Zowie, He's Rock's Weirdest
Act...$4–8
Oct. 25 Stevie Wonder: Life Offstage With the Musical Genius of His Generation ...$2–4
Nov. 29 John Travolta...$2–4
Dec. 20 Led Zeppelin: Robert Plant—His Songs Spin Heavy Metal Rock into Plati-
num $4–8

PEOPLE WEEKLY,
1975, 6–9

PEOPLE WEEKLY,
1975, 8–18

PEOPLE WEEKLY,
1975, 9–8

PEOPLE WEEKLY,
1976, 4–5

PEOPLE WEEKLY,
1976, 6–7

PEOPLE WEEKLY,
1976, 8–23

PEOPLE WEEKLY,
1976, 10–25

PEOPLE WEEKLY,
1976, 11–29

PEOPLE WEEKLY,
1977, 1–17

1977

Jan. 17 Ringo Starr: His Tax Exile, His New Fiancee, His Rap on a Beatle Reunion, Barbra Streisand..$2–4
Feb. 21 Rod Stewart & Britt Ekland: A Sexy Swede Tames the Rascal Rocker $2–4
Apr. 4 Hello Dolly Parton: It's Not Goodbye Nashville but Hello Hollywood, Frankie Valli $2–4
May 23 Dickey Bets on Cher & Greg Allman $2–4
June 6 Fleetwood Mac: Their Saga of Busting Charts While Breaking Hearts—Each Other's, Stevie Nicks...$7–15
June 27 Peter Frampton: He's More Alive Than Ever $2–4
Oct. 3 Tony Orlando's Breakdown, Mick Jagger, Annette Funicello $2–4
Oct. 10 Remembering Elvis Presley: The Imitators, The Fans & the Rip-offs, Carly Simon, Paul McCartney...$2–4
Oct. 31 Donny & Marie Osmond: Marie—at 18 She's Sexy..$3–6
Nov. 21 The Rolling Stones Keith Richards & Mick Jagger: Jagger's Genius Partner Keith Tells All...$3–6
Dec. 12 Crosby, Stills & Nash: Brawling & Bad Vibes..$2–4

1978

Jan. 16 The New Elton John: He's Given Up Touring & Nutty Glasses but Not Lasses, Greg Allman...$2–4
Mar. 13 Chick Corea & Herbie Hancock Making Jazz..$1–2
May 15 Shaun Cassidy: The Hottest Act in Rock..$2–4
Apr. 10 Cher & Her New Flame: Gene Simmons of Kiss $3–6
June 5 Loretta Lynn & Crystal Gayle, Elvis Presley $2–4
July 17 Carly Simon: She's Conquered Her Stage Fright but Not Motherhood $2–4
Aug. 21 The Elvis Presley Legend: One Year Later, Sgt. Pepper $2–4
Sept. 4 Sha Na Na: Still Greasy After All These Years, Alice Cooper in Wagonland, The Bee Bees, Allman Brothers, Donny Osmond...$3–6
Oct. 6 Chicago: America's Classiest Rock Group, Moving in With Olivia Newton-John $2–4
Nov. 20 Kristy & Jimmy McNichol, Donna Fargo...$1–3
Dec. 4 Priscilla Presley & Her Life With Elvis, Elton John $2–4
Dec. 26 Shaun Cassidy: Preadolescent America is Swooning Over Him.....................$2–4

1979

Jan. 1 John Travolta, Donna Summer Cleans Up, Grace Slick $2–4
Jan. 15 Diana Ross: Her Life isn't Just a Whiz..$2–4
Feb. 5 Rod Stewart Prefers Blondes, Tanya Tucker..$2–4
Feb. 19 Barbra Streisand, Donna Summer, Linda Ronstadt $2–4
Feb. 26 John Denver: The Unsung Story, Gene Simmons $2–4
Mar. 5 Special Fifth Anniversary Issue, Kiss, Elvis Costello $2–4
Mar. 19 Billy Joel Rocks Cuba: The Havana, Woodstock, Paul McCartney & Wings, Johnny Mathis...$2–4
Apr. 9 John Travolta & Donna Pescow, Kenny Rogers $2–4
Apr. 30 Linda Ronstadt & the Governor, Melba Moore...$2–4
May 7 Keith Richards' Drug Rap Concert in Toronto $2–5
July 16 Grease & Stockard Channing, Fleetwood Mac $2–4
Aug. 6 Hanging Out With the Bee Gees: A Backstage Look at the Summer's Hottest Tour...$2–4
Sept. 3 Conway Twitty, Roger Daltry Goes to Jail, Debbie Harry Meets the Real Blondie...$2–4
Sept. 10 The Music Business Blues, Debbie Harry, Paul McCartney, Kenny Rogers, Donna Summer, Peter Frampton, The Village People...$2–4
Oct. 1 Kiss: Peter Criss Divorces, Elton John's New Image.......................................$4–8
Oct. 22 Cher & Kiss' Gene Simmons Bare Their Life Together & Marriage Thoughts for the First time, Hank Williams Jr., Bee Gees..$3–6
Nov. 19 Mick & Bianca Jagger, Roger Daltry in New York $2–4
Nov. 26 Fleetwood Mac: They're Off Their Love-go-round & onto "Tusk," Elton John $5–10

PEOPLE WEEKLY,
1977, 2–21

PEOPLE WEEKLY,
1977, 10–3

PEOPLE WEEKLY,
1977, 11–21

PEOPLE WEEKLY,
1977, 12–12

PEOPLE WEEKLY,
1978, 1–16

PEOPLE WEEKLY,
1978, 5–15

PEOPLE WEEKLY,
1978, 7–17

PEOPLE WEEKLY,
1979, 2–5

PEOPLE WEEKLY,
1980, 5–12

Dec. 10 Kenny Rogers, Daryl Hall & John Oates $1–3
Dec. 24 Debbie Harry, Joan Baez, Olivia Newton-John, Bob Seger Dives into the New Wave, Ellen Foley...$3–6

1980

Jan. 28 Elvis Presley: How Did He Die?..$2–4
Mar. 31 Kristy McNichol, The Beach Boys...$2–4
Apr. 21 Andy Gibb & Olivia Newton-John, Chaka Khan: Rock's Queen of Sass......$3–6
May 12 The Who: Pete Townshend Talks About the Cincinnati Concert Tragedy, Keith Moon...$2–4
Mar. 10 Rod Stewart & Britt Ekland, John Lennon & Yoko Ono..............................$2–4
May 26 Mac Davis, Rock Star Recipes, The Bee Gees..$2–4
June 23 John Travolta: Urban Cowboy, Elton John's Partner, Bernie Taupin..............$2–4
June 30 Tanya Tucker & Glen Campbell, Willie Nelson..$2–4
Aug. 18 Kiss: Behind That Makeup, They're Rich, Raunchy & Not So Repulsive, Carly Simon is Slightly Off Form, John Travolta...$10–20
Sept. 1 Willie Nelson, John Lennon & Yoko Ono, Debbie Harry 4 Sale $2–4
Sept. 8 Jefferson Airplane, Rachel Sweet: Rock is Sweet on Rachel, Linda Rondstadt...$2–4
Sept. 29 Debbie Harry, Cher, Elton John Rocks Central Park....................................$3–6
Oct. 6 Carly Simon & James Taylor, Carrie Fisher, Paul Simon $2–4
Dec. 1 Kenny Rogers, The Fight Over Elvis Presley's Estate, Donny Osmond..........$2–4
Dec. 22 John Lennon & Yoko Ono: John Lennon Tribute 1940–1980 ....$2–4

1981

Jan. 12 Yoko Ono: How She is Holding Up...$2–4
Jan. 19 Dolly Parton, Petula Clark...$1–3
Feb. 23 Ringo Starr & Barbara Bach: Ringo Talks About John Lennon $2–4
Mar. 2 John Phillips & Mackenzie Phillips, Pat Benatar..$1–3
Mar. 16 Debbie Harry: Pop's Sassy Lady Cleans Up Her Act & Aims for Hollywood, Rosanne Cash, Andy Summers, Billy Joel $3–6
May 4 Tanya Tucker vs. Glen Campbell $2–4
May 18 Barbra Streisand, Kenny Rogers, Sting...$1–3
Aug. 17 John Travolta & Nancy Allen, Rick Springfield, Carly Simon.....................$1–3
Sept. 7 Kris Kristofferson, Black Sabbath & Ozzy Osborne....................................$2–4
Sept. 21 The Story of John Lennon's First Wife: Cynthia Lennon $2–4
Sept. 28 Pat Benatar's Sassy Talk About Music & Men..$3–6
Oct. 12 Mick Jagger on Tour: The U.S. Rocks as the Stones Roll Again.................$2–4

1982

Jan. 4 Mick Jagger, Barbara Mandrell, Linda Ronstadt..$2–4
Jan. 25 Cher: Moving to the Big Apple, Steve Miller..$2–4
Mar. 29 Kenny Rogers: A Neglectful Father Reforms, Bianca Jagger $1–3
Apr. 19 Mick Jagger $2–4
Aug. 2 Dolly Parton & Her X-rated Movie...$1–3
Oct. 11 Scott Baio, The Price of Being Pat Boone's Daughter, John Cougar, Robby Benson $1–3
Nov. 22 Mick Jagger & Jerry Hall: The Split & Scandal, Diana Ross, Billy Joel.....$2–4
Dec. 13 Yoko Ono & Sean: Two Years Later, In Ricky Nelson's Image $2–4

1983

May 2 Randy Newman Zings L.A., The One & Only Twiggy $1–3
May 16 Flashdance, Sonny & Cher & Daughter, David Cassidy...............................$2–4
July 25 John Travolta: Staying Alive, Olivia Newton-John, Wendy O.......................$2–4
Aug. 8 Diana Ross: The Concert, Controversy & Her Michael Jackson $3–6
Oct. 17 Michael Jackson: He's a Thriller, Elton John, Nina Hagen...........................$2–4
Nov. 14 Paul McCartney: Richest Man in Showbiz, Sassy Talk from Bette Midler, Barbra Streisand..$1–3
Nov. 21 The Karen Carpenter Story by Her Brother, Bonnie Tyler $2–4
Dec. 12 Barbra Streisand, Rob Lowe, Melissa Gilbert $1–3
Dec. 19 Olivia Newton-John & John Travolta, Annie Lennox Makes the Eurythmics Throb, Yoko Ono & Sean Lennon...$3–6

1984

Jan. 2 Michael Jackson & "Thriller," Dolly Parton...$2–4
Jan. 16 Death of a Beach Boy: The Drowning of Dennis Wilson at 39, Bette Midler & Mick Jagger..$3–6
Feb. 13 Michael Jackson: His Brush With Disaster...$2–4
Feb. 20 John Lennon & Yoko Ono: John's Last last Song, Van Halen.......................$2–4
Mar. 5 John Lennon, John Travolta, Grace Jones...$2–4
Apr. 23 Boy George: Joke, Freak or Pop Genius?, Rex Smith $2–4
May 7 Michael Jackson Tour: Behind the Scenes...$2–4
May 14 Rock's Hot Trio: The Thompson Twins...$2–4
May 28 Bruce Springsteen, Michael Jackson $2–4
July 9 Dolly Parton, Irene Cara of "Fame"..$1–3
July 16 Boy George, Bob Dylan in His Glory, Paul Simon Parties With Carrie Fisher, The Jacksons $2–4
Aug. 13 Loretta Lynn, Rod Stewart, Duran Duran...$1–3
Sept. 24 Michael Jackson: Being Sleek, Cher, John Travolta $2–4
Dec. 24 Bruce Springsteen, Tina Turner..$2–4

1985

Jan. 7 Olivia Newton-John's Wedding, Bette Midler, Julian Lennon, Carly Simon Cross-Dresses...$3–6
Feb. 25 The Night Rock Cried: Diana Ross, Michael Jackson, Bruce Springsteen, Bob Dylan, Willie Nelson, Lionel Richie, David Bowie & Others...............................$2–4
Mar. 11 Madonna: A New Star, Eddie Van Halen...$2–4
Mar. 18 Cher & the Movie *Mask*, Tanya Tucker...$1–3
Mar. 25 Prince, Dolly Parton, Tina Turner, David Bowie, Mick Jagger, Jackson Browne $2–4
Apr. 8 Billy Joel & Christie Brinkley: A Rare Interview & Personal Photos Reveal Their Chemistry...$2–4
May 13 Madonna: Man-smasher on Tour, Karen Carpenter & Death........................$2–4
May 27 Bruce Springsteen: The Midnight Marriage & the Starlet, The Pointer Sisters...$2–4
July 1 Cyndi Lauper, Elton John, Tears for Fears $2–4
July 15 Tina Turner, Meat Loaf...$1–3
July 29 Live Aid Exclusive: Backstage With the Rolling Stones, Tina Turner, Bob Dylan & Madonna, Heart: A New Beat, Whitney Houston, Billy Bragg...........................$2–4
Aug. 5 Bob Geldof's Story, Rita Coolidge $1–3
Aug. 26 Simon Lebon of Duran Duran: His Brush With Death at Sea.....................$1–3
Sept. 2 Madonna Weds Sean Penn...$2–4
Sept. 16 Has Rock Gone Too Far?, Prince, David Lee Roth & others $2–4
Sept. 30 Olivia Newton-John & Her Baby, Cher, Tina Turner................................$3–6

1986

Jan. 20 The Life & Death of the Boy Next Door: Ricky Nelson................................$2–4
Feb. 3 Bette Midler at Forty, Sade, Yoko Ono's Lost Daughter $2–4
Feb. 17 Diana Ross' Supreme Day: Her Wedding...$2–4
Mar. 10 Barbra Streisand, Phil Collins, The Grateful Dead, Sade $1–3
Mar. 24 Madonna's Beatle Boss: George Harrison $2–4
May 5 Dolly Parton: Peppery Talk, The Osmonds $1–3
May 19 Whitney Houston: America's Top New Star $2–4
July 21 On a Blind Date With Prince, Boy George $2–4
Sept. 23 David Lee Roth: Rock's Sexy Road Warrior, Ashford & Simpson................$2–4
Oct. 27 Ricky Nelson's Kids: Holding Fast as a Family, Whitney Houston $2–4
Dec. 1 Cher, Iggy Pop, Chrissie Hynde/The Pretenders..$2–4
Dec. 8 Bruce Springsteen's Best: The Boys in the Band, Boss History $2–4
Dec. 22 Whitney Houston, Bette Midler, Run DMC..$2–4

1987

Feb. 9 Janet Jackson, The Beastie Boys $2–4
Apr. 27 David Crosby: The Confessions of a Coke Addict.......................................$2–4

PEOPLE WEEKLY,
1980, 12–22

PEOPLE WEEKLY,
1981, 1–12

PEOPLE WEEKLY,
1982, 11–22

PEOPLE WEEKLY,
1984, 2–20

PEOPLE WEEKLY,
1985, 5–13

PEOPLE WEEKLY,
1985, 9–16

PEOPLE WEEKLY,
1986, 7–21

PEOPLE WEEKLY,
1987, 4–27

PEOPLE WEEKLY,
1988, 3–28

June 22 Summer Love Issue: Celebrating the 60s—A Be-in With the Beatles, Janis Joplin, Jimi Hendrix, Peter Max, Killing Joke, Elton John & Elvis Presley.............................$2–4
July 20 Patty Duke: A Troubled Coming of Age...$2–4
July 27 Whitney Houston, Run DMC...$2–4
Aug. 17 Elvis Presley: Ten Years Later—Private Scenes from the Life of Rock's Most Enduring Legend, Carly Simon's Victory Over Paralyzing Stage Fright.........................$2–4
Oct. 14 Michael Jackson Exclusive: A Message from Michael/Backstage With Michael Jackson..$2–4

1988

Jan. 25 Cher: The Ultimate Liberated Woman...$2–3
Mar. 28 Andy Gibb: The Short, Turbulent Life of a Fallen Teen Idol.........................$2–4

PEOPLE WEEKLY EXTRA
1984

Nov./Dec. All About Michael Jackson: A Souvenir Issue...$2–4

PHILLIP MORRIS MAGAZINE
1988

Winter Elvis Presley at Graceland...$2–4

PHONOGRAPH RECORD MAGAZINE (Tabloid)
1972

Jan. What's Wrong With the Byrds Recordings, An Interview With the Faces, Is David Bowie the Darling of the Avant Garde?, The Slowing Down of Traffic, Helen Reddy
....$10–20
Apr. The Doors' Aftermath: What We're Gonna Do Now, Alice Cooper, Bob Dylan: An Intimate Biography, Tom Fogerty, Cheech & Chong, The Stark Soul of Bobby Womack, Jackson Browne: Lonely Day Music—His Pals Present & Future, T. Rex: The Mania Never Stops, Black Oak Arkansas..$12–25
May Badfinger at the Crossroads, Seatrain: Everyday Drama of the New Rock, The Dillards, German Rock Expression...$10–20
July The Rolling Stones: Exile on Main Street—PRM Consumer Affairs Report, The Everly Brothers: Sliding Down Easy, The Roots of Ike Turner, Loggins & Messina, History of Eric Clapton, ZZ Top $15–30
Aug. Fanny: Cryptic Tales of America's Fanny, David Bowie, Slade, Rick Nelson, The Hollies Revisited, Jo Jo Gunne, Who Will Save the Groundhogs?, Uriah Heep, John & Yoko, Lou Reed $12–25
Sept. Flash: All About Them, Joe Cocker's Lost Audience, Jim Croce, Family, David Bowie's Mott the Hoople, Sandy Denny...$10–20
Oct. David Bowie's Glamorous Career, Making it With the Raspberries, Slade......$10–20
Nov. Slade: A Rock Chronicle, Rick Springfield: Survival of an Image $10–20
Dec. Ricky Nelson Grows Up, The Incredible String Band, Detroits' Rock Culture—Iggy Pop & the Stooges, MC5, Mitch Ryder, Mott the Hoople, Pete Townshend............$15–30

1973

Feb. Mott the Hoople's Complete History, The Move: Divide & Conquer, David Bowie's Love Letters, The Rolling Stones in Los Angeles, The Return of the Troggs, Slade, Neil Diamond...$10–20
Mar. Todd Rundgren's Inauguration, Pink Floyd, Hawkwind, The Raiders & Dusty Springfield Unearthed, Space Rock, The Monkees...$10–20
Apr. Alice Cooper & Heavy Metal Today, The Ian Whitcomb Story, Steve Winwood
....$10–20
May The Beach Boys: The Surf Music Revival, Kinks, The Left Banke: The Michael Brown Story, photo of the car that killed Eddie Cockran $10–20
June Paul McCartney & the Beatles—A Special Beatles Issue, Linda Rondstadt, The Zombies Rock Retrospective, Brownsville Station $12–25

July The Dr. John Story, Led Zeppelin, Jonathan King, Steeley Span & Dion, Anne Murray, Carole King $10–20
Sept. Special John Fogerty Issue—Creedence Clearwater Revival's Survival, Flo & Eddie Remembered, The Turtles & 1965, Zombies in the Hot 100, Jackson Browne, Jethro Tull $10–20
Oct. New York Dolls: New York's Brutal Music, Blue Oyster Cult, Charlie Rich in Retrospect, Bob Dylan's Last Showdown, Iggy $10–20
Nov. Elton John's New Career, The Sutherlands Arrive, Growing Up With Sonny & Cher, The Rolling Stones: You Can't Say They Never Tried, 10CC $10–20
Dec. The Jackson Browne Story, The Who's Mod Generation, Yoko Ono, Lou Reed & The Velvet Underground, New York Dolls, Iggy Pop on David Bowie $10–20

1974

Jan. Ray Davies & the Kinks: The Preservation of a Myth, Pop Music in 1974, Flo & Eddie as Rock Critics, Anne Murray, 10CC, Del Shannon, Alice Cooper, Rick Nelson, John Lennon $10–20
Mar. The Texas Rock-&-Roll Spectacular, Eric Burdon Discovers America, Todd Rundgren Explains Himself, Olivia Newton-John $7–15
Apr. Music on Television, The British Invasion: 1964–1974—A Decade of Anglo-Pop, The Grand Funk Revival, Aerosmith & the Boston Curse, TV: The David Bowie Special, Dick Clark, Flo & Eddie, Trashy Flashes from the New York Dolls, Bobby Womack $10–20
July David Bowie: Bowieart—Vampo, Mondo-Deco, Is David Doomed to be the First Martyr of the Rock-&-Roll Seventies?, Pete Townshend, Marvin Gaye, Roy Wood, Kiki Dee, 10CC, The Kinks $10–20
Aug. Suzi Quatro: Queen of Pop—Suzi in England & Elsewhere, Maria Mauldaur, Flo & Eddie's Media Mania, Joe Cocker Gets Down, Chaka Khan, Sly Stone's Guide for the Married Man, Elton John, Brenda Lee, Sweet...$12–25
Sept. The Rebirth of Paul Anka, Surfin' Music, The Beach Boys, Jan & Dean, Barry White, Nancy Wilson, Lou Reed's Popcicle Love $10–20
Nov. The Linda Ronstadt Coverup, ENO Music: The Roxy Rebellion, The Beatles, Todd Rundgren: An Advance Fanalysis of the New Utopia, Jackson Browne, Herbie Handcock $10–20
Dec. 1974 World Record Orgy, Keith Moon Goes Solo, Neil Sedaka: The Tra-La Days are Back, Wings, John Denver, B.B. King, Brenda Lee...$10–20

1975

Jan. Alex Harvey's Ultimate Rock Dream, The Hudson Brothers $5–10
Feb. Donovan in the Seventies, Genesis: The Future of the Rock Theatre, American Music Awards, Bob Dylan, Booker T., Kiss, Sweet, Nektar...$10–20
Mar. Led Zeppelin Ravages America, Monsters from the Crypt: Interest in the Legendary & Supernatural Jimi Hendrix, Jimi Hendrix: Raves from the Grave, Bruce Springsteen, Mingus, The Temptations Today, Michael Jackson..$15–30
Apr. The Pink Floyd Void, Del Shannon Returns, Faces on Tour, *Tommy* on the Silver Screen, Suzi Quatro, Minnie Riperton, Labelle...$12–25
May Carly Simon: Attitude Dancing, American Pop Scenes: Pop from Boston to Berkeley, Marty Balin Returns to the Fold: Starship Takes Off, Leon Russell's Tulsa Turnaround, Suzi Quatro in Cleveland, Billy Joel, Ben E. King, Smokey Robinson............................$10–20
June The Eagles: Defining the '70s, Hunter-Ronson, The Rolling Stones' New Face, Beau Brummels Regroup, Kinks, Jefferson Starship, The Hollies, Elton John, Donald Byrd & the Blackbyrds, Bobby Womack $10–20
July The Beach is Back—Featuring Jan & Dean, The Beach Boys & Johnny Rivers, Bobby Mann: Rock-&-Roll Survivor, Alice Cooper for President, The Tubes $10–20
Sept. The Nitty Gritty Dirt Band: The Original Rhinestone Cowboys, ZZ Top: Who's Buying All Those Records?, The Dudes, Dwight Twilley, Eric Clapton, Fleetwood Mac, Quincy...$10–20
Oct. Bob Marley: The King of Reggae, The Sweet: Glitter Relics Come to Life, Jackie De Shannon: "I Never Got an Even Break," KC & the Sunshine Band: Motown in Florida, Pink Floyd, Linda Ronstadt $10–20

Nov. Simon & Garfunkel: The Sounds Unsilenced, Paul McCartney & Wings: The Band on the Run, The Grateful Dead & Jefferson Starship: Reunion in the Park, Don McLean, Eric Carmen Beyond Raspberryism, Bruce Springsteen in Los Angeles $10–20
Dec. Little Feat Take Off, The Who in America, Janis Ian: Top Thirty Therapy, Patti Smith: Poetry in Motion, Abba: Doin' the Bomp With Rump, The Ozark Mountain Daredevils $10–20

1976

Sept. Hall & Oates: Deco-Disco Spreads Across America, The Future of ELO, New York Street Bands, Cliff Richards Rockets to Stardom, Blondie, Heartbreakers, Wayne Country, Mink Deville, Ramones, Talking Heads, Mumps, Television, War: In the U.S.A. $7–15

1977

Apr. Nils Lofgren Shakes Rock '77, David Bowie's Iggy Pop: From Russia With Love, Queen Deborah Harry/Blondie, Bad Company in 1977, Ronnie Spector Breaks Cleveland, The Sex Pistols: No Future but What a Past, Stevie Nicks: Fleetwood Mac's "Rumours," The Beach Boys, Muddy Waters at 62 ....$10–20

PHOTOSTAR
1990

June #1 Madonna: 1983–1990, Breathless Mahoney, Cher, Taylor Dayne, Gloria Estefan, New Kids on the Block, Milli Vanilli: Two for the Road, Johnny Depp, Janet Jackson..$2–4

PIZZAZZ
1978

July #10 Sgt. Pepper Special, The Bee Gees, Peter Frampton, Leif Garrett, Meat Loaf.$2–4
Sept. #12 Olivia Newton-John & John Travolta: *Grease*..$2–4

PLAYBOY
1985

Sept. Madonna Nude: Unlike a Virgin—For the Very First Time $15–30

1989

Mar. The Nude La Toya Jackson Special: A Thriller Pictorial...................................$5–10

PLAYING KEYBOARD

All issues...$2–4

POLYPHONY

All issues...$1–3

POPPIN
1969

#9 John Lennon & Yoko Ono, Jim Morrison, The Rolling Stones Ego Trip $12–25

POPSHOTS PRESENTS NEW KIDS ON THE BLOCK WITH MADONNA AND TOMMY PAGE
1990

Fall Issue includes double-sized wall posters..$2–4

POWERLINE
1989

May Poison Exclusive, Queensryche, Kiss, Metallica, Iron Maiden, TNT, Motley Crue, Stryper, Skid Row, Bon Jovi...$2–3

July Bon Jovi & Skid Row: The Year's Biggest Tour, Paul Stanley, King Diamond, Def Leppard, Britny Fox, Tesla, Defiance $2–3

Nov. Motley Crue: They're Back, Alice Cooper, Ozzy Osbourne, Skid Row, Poison, Slayer $2–3

1990

Jan. Aerosmith Pump it Up, Motley Crue, Onslaught, Warrent, Kiss, Bulletboys, Slayer, Poison...$2–3

All other issues $2–3

POWER METAL

1990

June Metallica: Blood & Guts, Slayer, Vengeance, Nuclear Assault, Sodom, Flotsam & Jetsam, Testament, Paradox, Evildead, Voivod, Death Angel, Overkill, Deadon, Kreator, Coroner, King Diamond, Dark Angel, Onslaught $2–3

PREMIERE

1988

Nov. U2: A Special Issue—Music in the Movies...$2–4

PRIVATE LIVES

1956

Dec. Elvis Presley: Music to Sin By—Is Rock 'n' Roll Making Savage Sex Sinners of Simple Teenagers?, Is Young Elvis Presley the Answer?...$15–30

PULSE (Tower Records)

All issues..$2–4

PUNK (Published by G.E. Dunn Jr.)

1976

#1 Lou Reed interview, The Ramones, The Original Punk 60s, Sluggo Interview ..$12–25

#2 Patti Smith: The Sophie Tucker of Rock-&-Roll, Talking Heads: Less is More, Lenny Kaye, The Leeches, The Marbles, Television: Intelligent Remarks, Punks Through History.....$12–25

#3 The Ramones' Story, David Johansen interview, Richard Hell interview, Tony Pigg, Legs in Leather, Patti Smith, The Star Trek Satire...$10–20

#4 July The Incredible Iggy Pop: The Only True Genius, Blondie: Incredible Photos of Debbie Harry from Childhood to 1976, Most Photos by Chris Stein, issue includes Debbie Harry poster & nude photo of Debbie with guitar, An Afternoon With Iggy Pop, Lester Bangs vs. Dick Manitoba, Theresa Stern interview, Harvey Kurtzman $15–30

#5 Aug. The Monkees: Four Has-beens Try to Act Clever & Cute, Ted Nugent: Motor City Man Eater, Alice Cooper, Humphrey Ocean, Patti Smith, David Bowie Falls to Earth, An Exclusive Interview With God...$10–20

#6 Nick Detroit, Richard Hell, David Johansen, Lenny Kaye, Blondie, Talking Heads $10–20

1977

#7 Patti Smith, Eddie & the Hot Rods, Dead Boys, Lou Reed, Blue Oyster Cult, Blondie .$10–20

#8 The Sex Pistols: Johnny Rotten to the Core interview, The Ramones, Hitler Interview, Frank Zappa..$7–15

1979

#16 Sid Vicious, Nancy Spungen Exclusive Interview, The Boomtown Rats $6–12

PUNK ROCK

1977

Dec. #1 Patti Smith interview, Debbie Harry: We Love Blondie, issue includes full-page Debbie Harry pin-up, Iggy Pop is Really Crazy, Sex Pistols Exclusive: The Pix That Got

Them Banned, DMZ, Television, Deaf School, Devo, A Fireside Chat With Iggy Pop, Dead
Boys $15–30

1978

Feb. #2 Debbie Harry: The Bombshell With Style, issue includes full-page color pin-ups,
The Jam, The Dictators, Sex Pistols: The Spirit of the Pistols, Mink Deville, The Criminals,
The Motor City Bad Boys, Iggy Pop's Lust for Life, Devo, Voidoid $10–20
Apr. #3 Johnny Rotten: Sex Pistols Super Special, David Bowie Exclusive: "I Was a UFO
Prisoner," Iggy Pop: Man or Worm?, Debbie Harry/Blondie: The Revealing Pix She Tried
to Hide, Punk Fashion, Patti Smith's a Survivor, Lookin' for Cheap Trick, Eddie & the Hot
Rods $15–30

PUNK ROCK SPECIAL

1978

Spring #1 Johnny Rotten & the Sex Pistols Exclusive, Meet if You Dare: Steve Jones, Sid
Vicious, Paul Cook & the One & Only Johnny Rotten, The Nothing-held-back Issue ...$15–30
Summer Kiss Special: Oh No, Is Gene Simmons Dead?, Everything You Ever Wanted to
Know About Kiss, The Black Magic, Voodoo Curse on Kiss, an all-Kiss issue with pin-ups
& posters $15–30

1979

Fall Rod Stewart: Will He Really Reform?, Dire Straits: Nothing Like the Name, Exclusive
Kiss' Wildest Night of Terror, Meat Loaf's Spashy Summer of Fun—The Inside Story, Led
Zeppelin: Are They Really at Their Peak?, The Doobie Brothers, Roxy Music Reforms, Jefferson Starship interview, George Harrison, Chicago, Paul McCartney, The Allman Broth-
ers, Elvin Bishop, Bob Welch..$7–15

PUNK ROCK STARS

1978

July #8 Debbie Harry/Blondie: Sex Fantasies of a Hot Punk Mama, Kiss: Did They Start
it All?, Johnny Rotten Tells All: The Real Reason the Sex Pistols Broke Up, Pattie Smith:
The Plot to Get the Punk Princess, The Latest on the Clash, The Runaways: The Sassiest
Punk Sisters in Town, The Ramones, Talking Heads, Voidoids, Boomtown Rats, DMZ,
Mick Jagger Muses About Punk, David Bowie: Where Does He Fit In?, Iggy Pop....$15–30
All other issues $15–30

R

RAP MASTERS
1989
Dec. Big Daddy Kane, D.O.C., Salt 'n' Pepa, Slick Rick, Public Enemy, issue contains four giant wall posters $2–3
All other issues $2–3

RAPPIN
1990
Jan. Ice T, Fab 5 Freddie, MC Lyte, issue includes pin-ups & giant color wall poster ..$2–3
All other issues $2–3

RECORD (Published by *Rolling Stone* magazine)
1981
Nov. #1 Exclusive: Bob Seger Returns, Elvis Presley: Sex & Sin, ZZ Top: Naturally Weird & Getting Weirder, Mick Jagger Centerfold Poster, Bruce Springsteen, the Go-go's Surprising Debut $20–40

1982
Jan. #3 Rod Stewart: A Candid Interview, Foreigner's Stormy Year, The Rolling Stones' Tour: The Essential Documents, Tina Turner in Action, Molly Hatchet, Debbie Harry: Videodrome, David Bowie, Queen, The Outlaws $5–10
Apr. #6 J. Geils' Main Men, Murray the K: An Appreciation, Todd Rundgren's Woes, Lindsay Buckingham, Rick James, Roger McGuinn Nikes Byrds Reunion, Journey, Van Halen, Jerry Garcia, Ginger Baker, Abba..$4–8
Sept. #11 Fleetwood Mac: The Trouble With Stevie, X, The Rolling Stones in London, Steve Miller interview, Marshall Crenshaw, Toto, Psychedelic Furs, Ted Nugent $10–20
Dec. The Who's Last Stand, Jimmy Page, The Pretenders, Joan Jett, ABC, The Blasters, Taking Stock of Jefferson Starship, Men at Work...$4–8

1983
Jan. Tom Petty: The War is Over, Ry Cooder Exclusive Interview, Jeff Beck, Eric Clapton, Joni Mitchell, Linda Ronstadt, Yaz, Miami Steve, Peter Gabriel Steals the Beat $4–8
Mar. Pat Benatar: Business as Usual, The Genesis of Phil Collins, Bob Seger, Neil Young, Rounding Up Missing Persons, Asia, English Beat, X Saga, Bow Wow Wow, Culture Club...$4–8
May David Bowie interview, Musical Youth Meets the Enemy, The Pete Townshend Tapes, A Solid Wall of Voodoo, Randy Newman, Lene Lovich, Bow Wow Wow, The Call, Jon Butcher Axis..$4–8
July Men at Work & the Spirit of Australian Rock, R.E.M.'s Enigma, A Muddy Waters Tribute, Maurice White Exclusive Interview, Lindsay Buckingham, Roxy Music, Robert Palmer, Rod Stewart, Marvin Gaye...$3–6

Oct. Keith Richards Exclusive: Reflections of a Rolling Stone, Eddy Grant, Contemporary Neil Young, Eurythmics: Sweet Dreams, Constant Friction, Elvis Costello, The Fixx, The Tubes...$3–6
Nov. Boy George Interview, Tom Waits, The Story Behind the Who, Yoko Ono, Keith Richrads, Musical Youth...$3–6
Dec. John Cougar: The Kid's Alright, Big Country, All Green $2–4

1984

Jan. David Byrne: A Head of His Times, Huey Lewis, Spandau Ballet, Debarge: Motown's First Family $2–4
June ZZ Top: Strange Tales of Sharp-dressed Men, The Clash: Take the Money & Run, R.E.M.: An Open Party, Michael Jackson: Dear Michael..$3–6
Sept. Paul McCartney Exclusive Interview, Prince Hits His Stride, Little Steven, Steve Ray Vaughan: Strings Attached, Missing Persons & Berlin: Bimbo Rock...........................$3–6

RECORD EXCHANGER (Vintage Records)

All issues...$2–4

RECORD REVIEW
1972

Sept. #1 Four-page trial issue, Dr. John, Jimmy Spheeris $10–20

1976

Jan. #2 Vol. 1, Issue A, Jeff Beck Interview, Elton John, Bill Withers, Emmylou Harris, Waylon Jennings, Dan Fogelberg...$6–12

1977

Feb #3 First regular issue, Thin Lizzy, Led Zeppelin, The Byrds...............................$4–8
Apr. #4 Jeff Beck, Queen, Paul McCartney, Santana, Cream Tribute $4–8
June #5 Emerson, Lake & Palmer, Bad Company, Pink Floyd, ZZ Top, Johnny Winter ..$4–8
Aug. #6 The Beatles, Allman Brothers, The Outlaws, John McLaughlin, Jack Bruce, Peter Frampton, Supertramp, Steve Miller, Traffic $4–8
Oct. #7 Coloseum With Gary Moore, UFO, Ted Nugent, Richie Blackmore, Rick Derringer, Kiss, Yes..$4–8
Dec. #8 The Rolling Stones Complete History, Robin Trower, Be-Bop Deluxe, Cheap Trick $5–10

1978

Apr. #9 Lynyrd Skynyrd Classic Tribute, Eric Clapton, Alice Cooper, Genesis, ELP, Queen, Santana, Aerosmith $3–6
June Frank Zappa, The Doors' Eric Dolphy: A Retrospective, Ted Nugent, Duke Ellington, Little Feat, Blondie, The Outlaws, Rufus $3–6
Oct. Mick Jagger, The Rolling Stones: Some Girls, Interviews With Led Zeppelin, Herbie Hancock, Freddie Hubbard & Cheap Trick, Bruce Springsteen, Mink DeVille, The Commodores, Sgt. Pepper, Thin Lizzy, Bob Dylan, Foreigner...$3–6

1980

June Van Halen, Heart, Rush, Bob James, XTC, Specials, Lene Lovich, The Band & Coleman Hawkins Retrospectives...$3–6

1981

Feb. Heavy Metal Magic: Thru the Past, Present & Future, Bruce Botnick: The Former Door's Producer Speaks, Larry Carlton, Sidney Bechet: Creedence Clearwater Revival Retrospective, Bruce Springsteen, Heart, Blondie, Neil Young, Eagles, David Bowie, Cheap Trick, The Police, John Lennon & Yoko Ono $3–6

1982

Oct. The Who: How it All Began, Motorhead: Madness Excess, Sonny Rollins, Bryan Ferry: The Continental Man, Haircut 100, Judas Priest, April Wine, The Rolling Stones, Robert Plant, Squeeze, Eddie Money, King Crimson, Rory Gallagher $3–6

RECORD REVIEW,
1978, June

RECORD REVIEW,
1978, Oct.

RECORD REVIEW,
1979, Oct.

RECORD REVIEW,
1980, June

RECORD REVIEW,
1980, Aug.

RECORD REVIEW,
1982, Oct.

RECORD REVIEW,
1982, Dec.

RECORD REVIEW,
1983, Apr.

RECORD REVIEW,
1984, Apr.

Dec. Billy Squier: A Man in Motion, John Cougar, The Who: Governors of Rock 'n' Roll, George Thorogood, Scorpions, Django Reinhardt, Rush, X, Elvis Costello, The Go-go's, Santana, Warren Zevon, Uriah Heep $3–6

1983

Apr. Journey: Looking for New Frontiers, The Cars' Rick Ocasek: He Hates Ozzy Osbourne, Def Leppart & British Metal, Deep Purple, Ozzy Osbourne, Led Zeppelin, Kiss, Sammy Hagar, All You Need to Know About Bluegrass $3–6
Dec. Def Leppard: Catching Fire With Pyromania, Eddie Jobson, Y & T, Supertramp, Tim Farris & INXS, Graham Parker, Robert Plant, Great White, Frank Zappa, Jackson Browne $3–6

1984

Apr. Motley Crue, Billy Sheehan of Talas, Van Halen, Judas Priest, Y & T, Alcatraz, Yes, Blue Oyster Cult's Eric Bloom, Heaven $2–4
Aug. Black Sabbath's Tommy Lommi, Michael Schenkar, Scorpions, Accept, Stray Cats' Brian Setzer Struts His Stuff, Fletcher Henderson, April Wine, David Gilmour..........$2–4
All other issues $2–6

RECORD WORLD

All issues..$1–5

RECORD WORLD PRESENTS A SALUTE TO FLEETWOOD MAC

1977

Sept. 17 Issue consists of 45 oversized pages dedicated to Fleetwood Mac, A Personal Voyage for Stevie Nicks, Christine McVie: Low Profile, Tremendous Contribution, The Fleetwood Mac Success Story, Lindsay Buckingham: Holding Things Together, Mick Fleetwood: Musician & Businessman, The Early Years $20–40

RELIX

1980

Vol. 6, #2 The Blues Brothers, The Grateful Dead on Tour $2–5
Vol. 6, #3 Debbie Harry, Women in Rock: Blondie, Janis Joplin, Linda Ronstadt & Others, The Byrds, Dire Straits, Peter Tosh..$3–6

1981

Vol. 7, #1 Music of the 70s $2–4
Vol. 7, #3 Pink Floyd..$2–4
Vol. 7, #4 Jerry Garcia Interview Part I, Ian Hunter, Greg Kihn, Tommy Tutone, Chick Corea, The Blues Brothers $2–4
Vol. 7, #6 1980 Photo Special: Exclusive Photos of Bruce Springsteen, Led Zeppelin, The Grateful Dead, Tom Petty, David Bowie, Pat Benatar, The Rolling Stones..................$2–5

1982

Vol. 8, #1 John Lennon Interview With Bill Graham, The Police, Bruce Springsteen, The Grateful Dead, Rolling Stones, Song Titles..$2–4
Vol. 8, #2 Memorial Special..$2–4

1984

Vol. 11, #1 The Police, Mickey Hart, Jorma, Arms Benefit..$2–4

1986

Vol.13, #2 Hot Tuna Reunion Tour..$2–4
Vol. 13, #3 Bob Weir With Kingfish, Grateful Dead, John Cipollina Interview, Trips Festival '86..$2–4
Vol. 13, #5 Frank Zappa $2–4
Vol. 13, #6 Year-end Special $2–4

By Arnold Skolnik. 8/15–17/69
Woodstock, White Lake, New York
Final Version (24″ × 36″)
Poster...$500–700

By David Byrd. 8/15–17/69
Woodstock, Wallkill, New York
First Version (13.5″ × 22.25″)
Poster...$50–60

By Mark Behrens and Burke.
5/15–16/70 **Iggy & The Stooges at**
The New Old Fillmore *First Edition*
(14″ × 20″) Poster...$300–600
Second Edition 1990 (17″ × 24″)
Poster...$10

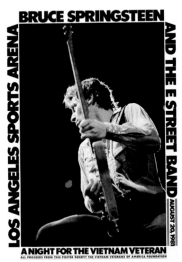

Artist and Photographer Unknown.
8/20/81 **Bruce Springsteen &**
The E Street Band
(22″ × 30″) Poster...$70–80

Artist Unknown. 1969
Newport 69 At Devonshire Downs
(24″ × 36″) Poster...$45–55

JS6 8/5/67 Poster...$15–25
The Doors, Lavender Hill Mob,
Joint Effort, Captain Speed

JS7 8/19/67 Poster...$15–25
Jimi Hendrix Experience, Moby
Grape, Captain Speed, Tim Buckley

JS9 9/16/67 Poster...$15–25
The Seeds, Thee Midnighters,
Chocolate Watch Band, West Coast
Pop Art Experimental Band

JS23 8/1/69 Poster...$15–25
Handbill...$15–20
Led Zeppelin, Jethro Tull,
Fraternity of Man

PHOTOS COURTESY OF JIM SALZER PRESENTS

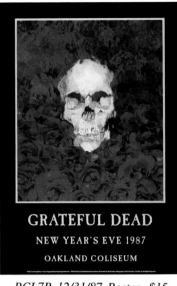

PCL7B 12/31/87 Poster...$15
Grateful Dead

PCL15 1989 Poster...$10
Led Zeppelin

PCL16 1989 Poster...$10
R.E.M.

PCL20 1989 Poster...$10
The Who Silver Anniversary

PCL23 1989 Poster...$10
The Who North American Tour

PCL28 1990 Poster...$10
Madonna Blond Ambition Tour

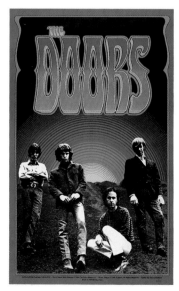

PCL29 1990 Poster...$10
The Doors

PCL30 1990 Poster...$10
The Beatles North American Tours

PHOTOS COURTESY OF PHILIP CUSHWAY LITHOS

Kiss *memorabilia:* *Halloween costume, dolls, garbage can, make-up kit, lunch box, radio, game, and colorforms*

Kiss *movie poster, puzzles, videos, and a double 8-track*

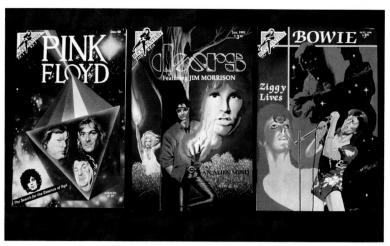

Rock Fantasy Comics #1, Pink Floyd
Rock Fantasy Comics #14, The Doors
Rock Fantasy Comics #13, David Bowie

Sh-Boom #1 (1–90)
Rock Scene (9–73)
Ideals' Celebrity Series #3, Led Zeppelin (4–79), $10–20

From top left: **Rock**, *6–79*, **Official Kiss Poster Book**, *1979 ($15–30)*,
Punk Rock *(Summer '78)*, **Teen Machine Presents Kiss**, *5–79*,
Circus *#171*, **TV Superstar**, *8–80*, **Grooves**, *5–79*,
Grooves, *12–79 (#18)*, **Super Rock**, *4–79*

1987

Vol. 14, #3 Special 20th-Anniversary Summer Love Issue...............................$2–4
Vol. 14, #6 Year-end Special $2–4

1988

Vol. 15, #2..$2–4
Vol. 15, #3 Grateful Dead, Dinosaurs...$2–4
Vol. 15, #4 Grateful Dead, Jerry Garcia...$2–4
Vol. 15, #5 Johnny Winter, The Grateful Dead, Ian Hunter...............................$2–4
Vol. 15, #6 Year-end Special $2–4

1989

Vol. 16, #1 Bob Dylan & the Grateful Dead...$2–4
Vol. 16, #2 Little Feat...$2–4
Vol. 16, #3 Summer Special $2–4
Vol. 16, #4 Woodstock..$2–4
Vol. 16, #5 The Rolling Stones, The Grateful Dead..$2–4
Vol. 16, #6 Year-end Special $2–4

1990

Vol. 17, #2 Jerry Garcia & Saunders, Neil Young, The Grateful Dead Photo Spread $2–4
Vol. 17, #3 The Grateful Dead's Silver Anniversary Issue, The Grateful Dead in Hartford, San Francisco: An Early History of the Grateful Dead, Jerry Garcia interview...........$2–4
Vol. 17, #5 Jimi Hendrix: His Life & Legacy, There & Back With Jeff Beck, The Grateful Dead Jam in the Northeast, Moby Grape: Escape, Where the Grateful Dead Goes When There Ain't No Tour..$2–5
All other issues $2–8

RIGHT ON

1981

Nov. Stephanie Mills, Michael Jackson Learns to Pop Rock, Dee Williams, In the Studio With the Emotions, Dana Plato, Prince: A Visit to His Bedroom $2–4

1984

Feb. Janet Jackson & Latoya Jackson: What It's Really Like Being Michael Jackson's Sisters, Shalamar: Splitsville, Lillo, D.D. Cabs..$2–4
Sept. Michael Jackson & Prince: Who Rules?, Jermaine Jackson: The Agony & Ecstacy, Stacy & Johnny, Jackson Five Mania..$2–4
Nov. Janet Jackson: "Fame" is the Name of the Game—An Exclusive Interview, The Pressure of Being a Jackson, O'Bryan, The Jacksons in Concert, Morris Day: Stealing the Scenes in Purple Rain $2–4
Dec. The New Edition, Prince, Jackie Jackson's Torture, Janet Jackson Becomes Legal: Her Scrapbook Through the Years, Guy Davis $2–4

1985

Jan. Prince & Purple Rain Tour Exclusive, Michael Jackson, Phillip Thomas, Stephanie Mills, Janet Jackson & James DeBarge, Sheila E. $2–4
Feb. Vanity, Apollonia 6, Andre Cymore, Morris Day, Sheila E., Prince's Erotic Subjects, The Cosby Kids, Randy Jackson, New Edition $2–4
Mar. The World's Most Eligible Bachelors: Michael Jackson, Prince, Eddie Murphy & Shabba-doo, Prince's Purple Rain, Lionel Richie...$2–4
Apr. The Cosby Kids, Eddie Murphy Exclusive, Madonna Sheds Her Virgin Image, Michael Jackson's Lucky Star, Janet Jackson $2–4
May Rebbie Jackson: An Intriguing Interview, Vanity Makes a Movie, Behind the Scenes With Lionel Richie & Michael Jackson, Fat Boys $2–4
June Prince: Is He Getting Too Big for His Lace Britches?, Todd Bridges interview, Debarge, Tina Turner, New Edition, Sheryl Lee Ralph...$2–4
Oct. What's Going on With the Fat Boys?, Sheila E., Run DMC & Kurtis Blow, Prince's Royal Dresser, Debarge, Billy Dee Williams, Sade..$2–4

1986

Apr. Sade: Smooth & Sleek, Prince: Purple Power, Five Starr, Blair Underwood, Malcolm-Jamal Warner, Bobby Brown, Stoney Jackson $2–4

May Janet Jackson: She's So Different from Anyone Else, The Truth About Shalamar, Michael Jackson, New Edition, LL Cool J, Prince $2–4

July Bobby Brown: A Visit to His Hotel Room, Prince: The Lies That Hurt Him, Michael Jackson, New Edition, Solid Gold Dancers, On the Cosby Show, Talking to Alfonso Ribiero, LL Cool J $2–4

Sept. Prince: His Intimate Friends Talk, Johnny Gill, Patti Labelle Tells All, El DeBarge, Michael Jackson & Pepsi, Cosby Kids $2–4

Nov. Janet Jackson's Pleasure Principle, Robin Givens, Esai Morales, In Concert With Jermaine Jackson, Whitney Houston, Rockwell $2–4

1987

Mar. Michael Jackson: "I'm Bad," Cameo's World, Is Prince's Kingdom Crumbling?, Chico DeBarge, Kool & the Gang, Chaka Khan $2–4

Sept. Rap Rules, Run DMC, Lisa Bonet, Beastie Boys, Robert Townshend, New Edition, Misha Mick, Cameo, Deniece Williams, Expose, Dana Dane $2–3

1988

Jan. The Favorite Movie Men: Michael Jackson, Prince & Eddie Murphy, Daniel Spencer interview, Lisa Lisa, Holly Robinson, Cult Jam, Whitney Houston...........................$2–3

Feb. The Fly Girls: Shanice Wilson, Kim Fields, Tempest Bledsoe, Jody Watley, Michael Jackson: His Bad Concert Tour, Salt 'n' Pepa, The Jets, Labelle..............................$2–3

Mar. Whitney Houston, Sheila E. on Prince, The Jets, MC Shan, 4 by Four $2–3

Apr. The Dating Game: How the Stars Play It—Michael Jackson, Eddie Murphy, Stephanie Mills, Whitney Houston, Lisa Lisa, LL Cool J, Curtis Baldwin: The Earth, Wind & Fire Reunion $2–3

1989

Feb. The Secret Meeting Between Michael Jackson & LL Cool J, Prince's "Lovesexy" Tour, MC Hammer, J.J. Fad, Bobby Brown, Cameo, D'Arby...$2–3

Sept. The Boys, New Edition, De La Soul, Slick Rick, Lisa Lisa, MC Hammer $2–3

Nov. Heavy D, The Confessions of LL Cool J, The Boys, Michael Jackson, Mica Paris, Public Enemy, New Kids on the Block, Party Rose, Jodi Watley $2–3

Dec. Big Daddy Kane, Kool Moe Dee, EPMD, Guy, The D.O.C., LL Cool J............$2–3

All other issues $2–4

RIGHT ON ANNUAL

1980

Spring Ashford & Simpson: Why They Almost Did Not Marry, Ray Parker, Lawrence Hilton Jacobs, David Hubbard, Natalie Cole..$2–4

RIGHT ON ANNUAL POSTER BOOK

1984

Fall #46 Issue includes 10 16″ × 22″ color glossy wall posters, Michael Jackson, Irene Cara, Rick James, Janet Jackson, Shari Belafonte, Prince, Latoya Jackson, Cameo, DeBarge, Shalamar $3–6

1985

Summer Issue includes 10 16″ × 22″ color glossy wall posters of the New Edition, Michael Jackson, Prince, Curtis Blow, Eddie Murphy, Kim Fields, Vanity, Ala Ray, Phillip Michael Thomas, Robert "Kool" Bell & James Taylor $3–5

1986

Spring Issue includes 10 16″ × 22″ color glossy wall posters of Prince, Michael Jackson, Michael Bivins, Ronnie Devoe, Ralph Tresvant, Ricky Bell, Stoney Jackson, El DeBarge, Ready for the World & Malcolm-Jamal Warner $3–5

AR   363

RIGHT ON, 1984, Nov.   *RIGHT ON*, 1985, Jan.   *RIGHT ON*, 1985, Feb.

RIGHT ON, 1986, May   *RIGHT ON*, 1987, Mar.   *RIGHT ON*, 1987, Sept.

RIGHT ON, 1988, Jan.   *RIGHT ON*, 1988, Mar.   *RIGHT ON SUPER
                                                        SPECIAL*, 1984,
                                                        SUMMER

RIGHT ON, BEST OF
1984

#3 The Jacksons, Prince's Bedroom, DeBarge, Todd Bridges, Teddy Pendergrass, Michael Jackson's Hair-raising Experience, Latoya Jackson, Ola Ray's Naughty Nighties, Rick James, Stevie Wonder...$2–4

RIGHT ON CLASS
1984

Oct. Eddie Murphy, Stephanie Mills, Lou Rawls, Charo, New Edition.......................$1–2

1985

Jan. Tina Turner: Love Has a Lot to Do With It, Michael Jackson Exclusive, Deniece, Miles Davis: The Return of the Prince of Darkness, Darcel Wynne's a Homebody, Shannon Green...$1–2
Feb. Tonya Pinkins, Michael Jackson, Rick James, Stevie Wonder, Billy Ocean........$1–2
Mar. Billy Dee Williams Exclusive, Chaka Khan: "My Life is Madness," The Four Tops Celebrate Three Decades of Harmony...$1–2
Apr. Little Richard: The Outrageous Original Rocker, Prince, Michael Jackson, James Brown, Diana Ross Gets a Leg Up $2–4
Dec. Smokey Robinson Lights the Motown Fire, Kim Fields, Sheila E., Bobby Womack
....$1–2

RIGHT ON FOCUS
1983

Fall Mr. T, Ted Lange, Eddie Murphy, Belinda Tolbert, Janet Jackson $1–3

1984

Fall Michael Jackson: Behind the Video Scene, Sexy Evelyn King, Rick James & Ebony, Eyes, Herbie Hancock, Lionel Richie $1–3
Fall This is the Winter issue, but is marked Fall (Vol. 4, #8). . . . Janet Jackson: The Fame Game, Latoya Jackson: Her TV Career...$1–3

1985

Winter Janet Jackson, Everybody "Gloves" Michael Jackson, Why Boy George Dresses "Girl," Eurythmics, Prince, Rick James, Latoya Jackson, Adam Ant, Break Dancing $1–3
Spring Janet Jackson: Can She Keep Up With Her Growing Fame?, Sheila E.: Did Prince Really Discover Her?, New Edition, Shannon, Billy Ocean..$1–3
June Run DMC, UFO, Kurtis Blow, Force MDs, Whodini, Fat Boys..........................$1–2

1986

Feb. Stephanie Mills, Sister Sledge: Surviving With Siblings, Nona Hendryx, Petronia Paley, Little Jamie, Annette Taylor $1–2
Sept. Darnell Williams, Stoney Jackson, Laura Carrington, Tracey Ross, Kim Fields, Kristoff St. John, Denzel Washington, Lisa Bonet...$1–2
Nov. Michael Jackson Unmasked, El Debarge, Billy Ocean, Princes Kisses & Tells, Lionel Richie, Smokey Robinson, Rick James, Rockwell...$1–2

1987

Jan. Ralph Tresvant of the New Edition, The Jets, Five Star, Janet Jackson: She's in Control, Cherie Johnson, Apollonia $1–2

1989

Feb. Bobby Brown, Public Enemy, EPMD, Grandmaster Flash, Vanessa Williams, New Edition, J.J. Fad $1–2
Nov. LL Cool J: Is He Too Sexy?, The Beastie Boys are Back, Kool Moe, The Fat Boys, Kid 'n' Play, Al B. Sure, Fab 5 Freddy, Eric B...$1–2

RIGHT ON MUSIC SPECIAL
1983
Winter Ashford & Simpson, Kool & the Gang, Luther Vandergross, Stacy Lattisaw, Morris Day, Brenda Richie...$1–2

1986
Summer Rap-&-Rock All-stars Special, A Look Back at Michael Jackson's Past, LL Cool J, Prince Reigns, Janet Jackson, Lisa Lisa...$2–4

RIGHT ON 1985 POSTER CALENDAR MAGAZINE
1985
Lionel Richie, Kool & the Gang, Eddie Murphy, Emmanuel Lewis, Kim Fields, Jayne Kennedy, Michael Jackson, Darnell Williams, The Jacksons, New Edition, Diahann Carroll, Mr. T...$2–3

RIGHT ON 1984 CALENDAR AND PIN-UP SPECIAL
1984 Billy Dee Williams, Diana Ross, Eddie Murphy, Donna Summer, Richard Pryor, Michael Jackson, Jackie Jackson, Kim Fields, Jayne Kennedy, Lionel Richie, Ron Glass, Michael Warren...$2–4

RIGHT ON POSTER SPECIAL
1987
Fall Issue includes 10 giant wall posters of Lisa Bonet, New Edition, Malcolm-Jamal Warner, Bobby Brown, Tresvant, Bivins, Bell, Devoe, Run DMC, Janet Jackson.......$3–5

1988
Spring Issue includes 10 giant wall posters of 4 by Four, Michael Jackson, Run DMC, Prince, Shanice Wilson, Tempest Bledsoe, Holly Robinson, Levert, Whitney Houston, Lisa Lisa..$3–5

RIGHT ON SPECIAL BEAUTY SPECIAL
1987
Winter Janet Jackson: She's Got the Look, Tempest Bledsoe's Ultimate Workout, Shanice Wilson..$2–4

RIGHT ON SUPER SPECIAL PRESENTS
THE BEST OF MICHAEL JACKSON MAGAZINE
1984
Fall Never-before-seen Photos of Michael, Behind the Scenes, His Rockin' Rock Concert & Other Stories...$2–4

RIGHT ON SUPER SPECIAL PRESENTS
THE BEST OF PRINCE MAGAZINE
1985
Fall Prince Special With Vanity, Sheila E., Jesse Bohnson, Alexander O'Neal, Apollonia
....$2–4

RIGHT ON SUPER SPECIAL PRESENTS PRINCE
1984
Everything You Ever Wanted to Know About Prince, Behind the Scenes, Prince Who's Who, His Mysterious Life, centerfold poster $3–6

RIP

1986

Dec. #1 Speed Metal, The Shagheads Meet the Mohawks, Ozzy Osbourne, interviews with The Ramones, Motorhead, Black Flag & Metallica..$3–6

1987

Jan. #2 ZZ Top: Drivin' While Blind, Special Rods-&-Rockers Issue, Ted Nugent, Mark Paline, David Lee Roth, David Johansen $3–6

Feb. #3 Alice Cooper interview, At Home With the Rock Stars, interviews with Charlie Sexton, Billy Idol, Ratt & DOA..$3–6

Mar. #4 Megadeth, Debbie Harry: It Was Crazy interview, Gene Simmons: Who is That Masked Man Anyway interview, B-52's, Love & Rockets...$3–6

Apr. #5 Iron Maiden's Bruce Dickinson interview, interview with The Dead Kennedys, Queenscryche, Stryper, Motorcross...$2–4

May #6 The Rising Force of Yngwie Malmsteen, interviews with Ron Wood, Guns 'n' Roses, Husker Du, AC/DC & Wendy O'Williams..$2–4

June #7 Slayer Gets Tough on Rock Censorship, Suicidal Tendencies: Under the Gun, interviews with Twisted Sister, Black Sabbath & Frank Zappa.................................$2–4

July #8 Vince Neil, Lita Ford Confesses, The Wild Women of Rock: Wendy O, Siouxsie Sioux, The Pandoras & Others, Frightwig, Motley Crue $2–4

Aug. #9..$2–4

Sept. #10 Judas Priest Escapes the System, Metal Church, Redd Kross, The Cult, Exodus, Poison, DRI, Ace Frehley $2–4

Oct. #11 Kiss: Midnight Masquerade, King Diamond, Lizzy Borden, Led Zeppelin, Grim Reaper, The Cramps, Misfits, Butthole Surphers $2–4

Nov. #12 Aerosmith's Steven Tyler: Still Rockin' New Ground, Poison, Whitesnake '87, Motley Crue on the Ropes of the Road, Venom, Celtic Frost $2–4

Dec. Dokken, Sammy Hagar, Ace Frehley, Dio: A Legend Raps, Tesla, Metallica.....$2–4

1988

Jan. Metallica: Christmas Dudes, Kiss, Marillion, Y & T, White Lion, The Death & Rebirth of Quiet Riot, Blackie Lawless, Scorpions...$2–4

Feb. Whitesnake's David Coverdale Exclusive Story, Anthrax on the Warpath, Dee Snider, Armored Saint, Great White, Motorhead..$2–4

Mar. Def Leppard Special Exclusive Story With Photos of the Year's Wildest Concert Tour, Warlock, Dokken's George Lynch, EZO, The Triumphant Return of Alice Cooper, Backstage Hysteria With Def Leppard...$2–4

Apr. David Lee Roth: The Serious Partying Begins, Aerosmith, Joe Satriani, Megadeth, Loverboy, Triumph, Exodus, Whitesnake...$2–4

May AC/DC, Ozzy Osbourne, Mick Jagger Exclusive: 25 Years of Rock Madness, Anthrax, Lita Ford, Black 'n' Blue, Dweezil Zappa, Vinnie Vincent...$2–4

June Guns 'n' Roses: Metal's New Supergroup, The Iron Maiden Onslaught, Agnostic Front, Ted Nugent, Kiss, Dio, Great White, Motley Crue, Zodiac Mindwarp..............$2–4

July $2–4

Aug. Megadeth's Anarchy in Los Angeles, Van Halen: Monsters of Rock, Metallica, Kingdom Come, Scorpions, Dokken, Steve Vai...$2–4

Sept. DRI, The Odyssey of Yngwie Malmsteen, Hurricane, Iron Maiden's Bruce Dickinson, Voivod, Krokus, Cinderella, Queenscryche, AC/DC...$2–4

Oct. Lita Ford Exclusive: Lita Grows Up, Judas Priest Count Their Millions, The Definitive Led Zeppelin Retrospective in Words & Photos, King Diamond, White Lion, Ace Frehley, Death Angel...$2–4

Nov. Metallica Exclusive Story With Photos of the Band That Slayed the Monsters, Sodom, Stryper, Flotsam & Jetsam, Slayer, Ratt $2–4

Dec. Ozzy Osbourne: 20 Years Later—From Black Sabbath On, Nuclear Assault, Danzig, Europe, Cinderella, Dokken, Scropions, Def Leppard $2–4

1989

Jan. Anthrax, Keith Richards Rolls His Own, Nikki Sixx Speaks Again, House of Lords, Judas Priest, Van Halen, Overkill, Winger...$2–4

RIP, 1987, Apr. (#5)

RIP, 1987, May (#6)

RIP, 1987, Sept. (#10)

RIP, 1987, Oct. (#11)

RIP, 1987, Dec.

RIP, 1988, Feb.

RIP, 1988, May

RIP, 1988, Aug.

RIP, 1988, Sept.

Feb....$2–4

Mar. Def Leppard Exclusive, Guns 'n' Roses, Helloween, Quiot Riot, Magnum, D'Molls, Ratt, Metallica pin-ups, Circus of Power..$2–4

Apr. Exclusive Axl: The First Truly Honest Interview, Motorhead, Slayer, Rock City Angels, Winger, Metallica, Jetboy, Europe...$2–4

May Ratt is Back, Dokken: Why Did it End?—An Insider's Report, Living Colour, Gary Moore, Manowar, Joan Jett's Rock Chronicle, Some Cheap Talk With Keith Richards, Anthrax, DRI, Badlands $2–4

June Doro Pesch & Lita Ford Exclusive Stories & Photos, White Lion, Metallica, Warrent, W.A.S.P., Ozzy Osbourne, Rush, Kix...$2–4

July Winger: Metal's New Stud, The Cult Returns, Vixen, Bon Jovi Does Dallas, Bulletboys, The Resurrection of Metal Church, Danzig, Annihilator............................$2–4

Aug. Motley Crue's Sober Return, Never-seen Guns 'n' Roses Pin-ups, Anthrax, Great White, Investigating Blue Murder, M.O.D., House of Lords, Black Sabbath: Out of the Darkness, Dog D'Amour, Kingdom Come $2–4

Sept. Cinderella Exclusive, Great White, Paul Stanley, Leatherwolf, TNT Explodes, Steve Jones: A Sex Pistol Fires Again, The Sea Hags, The Cro-Mags, Tesla, Extreme Rock 'n' Roll...$2–4

Oct. Alice Cooper Live: The Trashman Cometh, Skid Row: Youth Gone Wild on the Road, Fishbone, Poison, Faith No More, Def Leppard's Rick Savage, Junkyard, God Save Queen, UFO, Testament, Metallica...$2–4

Nov. Skid Row, Exclusive Led Zeppelin Rare Photo Scrapbook, Mr. Big, The Cult: Greeting from Asbury Park, The Far Side of Ozzy Osbourne, The Queensryche Conspiracy, Richie Sambora...$2–4

Dec. Metallica: Justice is Done, Aerosmith Pumps Again, The Dark World of King Diamond, White Lion: Stormy Weather, L.A. Guns, Plane Talk With Bon Jovi, The Surprise Attack of Tora Tora, Warrent, Axl Rose...$2–4

1990

Jan. Aerosmith: New Decade/New Decadence, Kiss: For the Love of Kiss, Faster Pussycat in Heat, Nuclear Assault, Princess Pang, Motley Crue, Living Colour, Getting Ugly With Junkyard, Great White, Billy Squire...$2–4

Mar. Skid Row Exclusive, Guns 'n' Roses, Def Leppard, Joe Satriani, Tesla, DRI Enuff Z'Nuff, Steve Stevens...$2–4

June Kiss: Paul Stanley & Gene Simmons—A Kiss Exclusive, Bon Jovi: Off the Road Finally, Aerosmith, Slaughter, Europe, Skid Row, L.A. Guns, Coroner, The Front, Jethro Tull, Sebastian Bach $2–4

July Metallica Exclusive: Is There Life on Lars?, XYZ, Celtic Frost, Poison Gets Serious, Danzig, Black Crowes, Faster Pussycat, Salty Dog, Sebastian Bach Part II, Aerosmith $2–4

Sept. Uncensored Opinions from Ozzy Osbourne, Guns 'n' Roses, Alice Cooper, Frank Zappa, Metallica, Anthrax & Others, Van Halen Does Mexico, Stryper, Y & T, Thunder, Hurricane, Warrior Soul, London Quireboys $2–4

Oct. The New Poison, Joe Perry Exclusive, Slaughter Flirts With Stardom, The Cult, Bonham Marries, Led Zepellin Reunites, Ratt...$2–4

Nov. Metallica: Behold the Mighty Hetfield Speaks, Megadeth: Back from the Dead, Queenscryche's Empire, Anthrax Returns, Faith No More $2–4

Dec. Party With the Cure, The Persecution of Judas Priest, Inside Queenscryche's Empire, Savatage, Jani Lane & Sebastian Bach...$2–4

1991

Feb. Queensryche's Mental Metal Gymnastics, AC/DC Exclusive, Killer Megadeth Centerfold, Iron Maiden, Little Ceasar, Electric Boys, Annihilator, Riverdogs, Scorpions, Poison, Winger $2–4

Mar. The Making of Metallica Part III: Tracking With James, Motley Crue, Bulletboys, Cheap Trick, Warrent, Lynch Mob, Anthrax, King's X, Nelson, Tesla, Slaughter, Testament, Megadeth, Suicidal Tendencies $2–4

Apr. The Latest Temptations of Great White, Led Zeppelin Lives: An Exclusive Interview With Jimmy Page, Danzig, Extreme, Cinderella, Testament, Lita Ford, Judas Priest, David

Lee Roth, Dirty White Boy, The Making of Metallica Part IV, Black Crowes centerfold $2–4
All other issues $2–4

RIP PHOTO SPECIAL

All issues $3–6

RIP PRESENTS

All issues $3–6

ROCK (Tabloid)

1969

Oct. 13 Crosby, Stills, Nash & Young, B.B. King, Sly Stone, Albert King: King of the Blues, Mountain $15–30
Nov. 10 Paul McCartney in Memoriam 1942–1968, Moondog, Sympathy for the Mothers..$15–30

1970

Oct. 11 Mick Jagger Feature Story, The Rolling Stones, Jimmy Page, Elvis Presley, Jimi Hendrix $15–30
Nov. 17 A Farewell to Janis Joplin, Jimi Hendrix Funeral, Poco, Get Ready for Elton John, Pink Floyd, Humble Pie, Eric Burdon $40–80
Nov. 30 Inside Sly Stone, Paul McCartney & Family, The Rolling Stones for Thanksgiving, Iggy Pop, The Beach Boys, The Cadillacs...$15–30
Dec. 14 Joe Cocker & His New Film, The Beatles in New York, Humble Pie, Black Widow, Bob Dylan $15–30
Dec. 28 Paul McCartney, The Beach Boys, Eric Burdon, Marianne Faithful, Grand Funk Railroad, Van Morrison Interview, The Grateful Dead, Elton John, Rod Stewart $15–30

1971

Jan. 11 Mick Jagger interview, The Year in Review: Jimi Hendrix, Janis Joplin....$20–40
Jan. 25 The Frankest Zappa Interview Ever, John Lennon's Film & Album, The Fillmore: Toys for Tots, Creedence Clearwater Revival, Motown, The Beatles Alone Together, Johnny Winter & Rick Derringer, Free, The Harptones Today..............................$15–30
Feb. 15 The Grateful Dead, Savoy Brown, Tom Rush, Bob Weir, Elton John, Elvis Presley, Paul McCartney, Frankie Lymon: The First Superstar, Big Brother..........................$15–30
Mar. 1 Chicago, Elvis Presley, Little Richard, Zappa, Taj Mahal: The Walking Anachronism, The Incredible String Band Minstrels, Janis Joplin, Poco, Neil Young..........$12–25
Mar. 15 The Yardbirds Revisited, Eric Clapton, Jimmy Page, Jeff Beck, Rod Stewart, Captain Beefheart, Grace Slick, The Who, Joan Baez, Mark Bolan, Sugarloaf, The Youngbloods $12–25
Mar. 29 Elton John, Bob Dylan Dribbles On, Howdy Doody, Rascals, Guess Who, Emerson, Lake & Palmer: On Their Way, Christine McVie: She's Not Perfect Anymore, Rod Stewart, Fanny, The Bee Gees $12–25
Apr. 12 Mountain: The Odd Couple, Ronnie Spector, Poco, Aretha Franklin, The Beach Boys in New York, Yoko Ono & Linda McCartney, The Jackson Five: One Bad Rumble, Keith Moon, Eric Burdon, Spencer Davis, Jimi Hendrix & Lonnie Youngblood—The Cry of Love Review, James Taylor $15–30
Apr. 26 The Allman Brothers, Simon & Garfunkel, The Rolling Stones, Paul McCartney: One Bad Apple, The Carpenters, The Chambers Brothers...$10–20
May 10 Ray Davis: King of the Kinks, Mary Travers: Mommy Goes it Alone, "Jesus Christ Superstar" interview, Tracy Nelson, Elton John..$10–20
May 24 Paul McCartney, Mick Jagger, John Lennon, Donovan, James Taylor, Paul Simon, Jimi Hendrix: Should the Hendrix Archives be Opened?, The Motown Saga From the Beginning, Blood, Sweat & Tears, Howdy Doody, Cat Stevens: Easy Does It, The Doors: L.A. Woman, Joan Baez, Bob Dylan...$20–40
June 7 James Brown: Soul Survivor, The Fillmore East 1968–71: Rest in Peace, Kate Taylor, Weather Report, B.B. King, The Doors, The Delfonics $10–20

June 21 Procol Harum, Mick Jagger Loves Bianca, John Lennon, Guess Who, Pete Seeger, The Temptations: Short Staffed, Buddy Miles, Blood, Sweat & Tears '71, Elvis Presley, Mick Jagger: Sticky Fingers, Edgar Winter, James Taylor...$10–20

July 5 Grand Funk: Love It or Leave It, Bob Dylan, Mitch Ryder, Carole King: A Natural Woman, Jeff Beck is Back interview, Todd Rundgren $10–20

July 29 Byrds is the Words, Jim & Roger McQuinn, John Lennon & Yoko Ono Come Out, Jackie Lomax, Quoth the Fillmore Nevermore, Seatrain, Rita Coolidge: Paying Dues, Paul McCartney, Flying Burritos Brothers...$10–20

Aug. 17 Moby Grape Preserved, John Mahall, B.J. Thomas, Lenny Bruce: The Agony & The Legacy, Taj Mahal: The Real Thing..$10–20

Aug. 30 Steve Stills, Keith Emerson, John Cale, Sonny & Cher: The Beat Goes Blech, Elvis Presley, Tina Turner, John Lennon & Yoko Ono..$10–20

Sept. 27 The Who, John Lennon, The Chapins, The Doobie Brothers, John Sebastian, Bob Dylan, Ringo, Pete Townshend Talks, George Harrison, Robert Plant $10–20

Oct. 11 The Extra Heavy Interview Issue, interviews with John Lennon, Elvis Presley, The Supremes, Rapping With Van Dyke Parks, John Lennon & Yoko Ono: The Wizard of Oz, Grace Slick, Moody Blues, The Beach Boys, James Taylor..$10–20

Oct. 25 Ringo: An Interview With a Forgotten Beatle, Sly Stone, Rod Stewart & His Merry Pranksters, Late Night Dialogue With the Lennons, The Fillmore & Filling the Void, Ten Years After: The Story of Alvin Lee, Flying Burritos Brothers, Jimi Hendrix at Berkeley, Carly Simon, Tina Turner $12–25

Nov. 8 Moody Blues, Three Dog Night, Ricky Nelson, Bangladesh..........................$10–20

Nov. 22 Jethro Tull, Peter Frampton, Gene Vincent Dead at 36, Iggy Pop, Yoko Ono, Savoy Brown, Jim Morrison, Alice Cooper, Mick Jagger, Johnny Maestro Crosses Over the Bridge, The Band, Bee Gees $12–25

Dec. 6 Duanne Allman Killed in Motorcycle Crash, Aretha Franklin, Janis Joplin: A Look Back, John Lennon, John Peel...$12–25

Dec. 25 Pink Floyd interview, Jose Feliciano, The New Doors, Elvis Presley $10–20

1972

Jan. 17 3rd Annual Year in Review Issue—Paul McCartney interview, Three Days With Rod Stewart, Grace Slick, The Doors, Janis Joplin, Mick Jagger, Diana Ross, Alice Cooper, Rod Stewart on Tour With Small Faces, Carly Simon..$10–20

Feb. 14 Paul Simon Talks About the Past & Future, Isaac Hayes, Alice Cooper: Killer Off the Cuff, John McLaughlin interview, Elvis Presley..$10–20

Feb. 28 Jefferson Airplane: In the Wake of the Airplane, John Lennon & Yoko Ono, The Night Before With J. Geils Band, Harry Nilsson interview, "Jesus Christ Superstar," Bob Dylan, Brian Jones, Janis Joplin: Bullfeathers Mythology—A Pantheon of Rock Gods & Goddesses, Grateful Dead, Elvis Presley, Isaac Hayes Raps $10–20

Mar. 13 Ms. Rockstar: The Time is Now—Carly Simon, Carole King, Melanie, Laura Nyro, Lulu, Cass Elliot, Janis Joplin, Joan Baez, Grace Slick, Linda Ronstadt, Carly Simon interview: Outspoken & Outgoing, John Lennon & Yoko Ono, The Return of Joe Cocker, Captain Beefheart, The Carpenters, Elvis Presley, Led Zeppelin, Grass Roots, Yes, Paul Simon..$10–20

Mar. 27 Kris Kristofferson: "I Get a Little Weary," Dave Mason, Jim Capaldi, Joe Cocker: "Mad Dogs," Elvis Presley, Oldies as Today's Hits, Paul McCartney, Top 40 Radio, Pete Seeger, Grace Slick...$10–20

Apr. 10 America Comes to America, Kiddy Rock: An Interview With David Cassidy, Bo Diddley: The Father of Us All, David Bowie is Hunky Dory, Steppenwolf, Fillmore East Reopening, Joe Cocker, Cheech & Chong, Donny Osmond, Marc Bolan Arrives, Neil Young, Linda Ronstadt $10–20

Apr. 24 Cream, Mountain: West, Bruce & Laing, B.B. King interview, Yes, Seatrain, Keith Moon: What's Next for the Who?, Joe Cocker, Jimi Hendrix: Hendrix in the West, Little Feat, Hot Tuna, Savoy Brown...$12–25

June 19 The Allman Brothers: Playing All Night, Stone the Crows, Carlos Santana, Chuck Berry Talks, Johnny Maestro, Bill Graham, Mothers $10–20

Aug. 28 Alice Cooper in London, Stones Roll into the Big Apple, Will Success Spoil Randy Newman?, John & Yoko $12–25

Sept. 25 The Complete Rod Stewart Interview, Free in Japan, Roberta Flack, Johnny Cash: Down to Business, Grand Funk Railroad, James Gang, Elvis Presley $10–20

Nov. 6 Elton John: A Peek Behind the Mask, Stevie Wonder: Blind Musicians, A Special Kind of Sight, Ron Wood: The Face in the Backround Comes Forward, Ronnie Hawkins, Seatrain, Yes, Little Richard $10–20

Dec. 4 The Moody Blues: In Search of the Lost Orgy, Don Kirshner, Argent, The Moody Blues: On the Road With the Salvation Army, James Taylor $1–20

Dec. 18 Procol Harum: Beyond the Pale & Shinning on Brightly, The Making of Tommy, The Incredible String Band, Alice Cooper, Jeff Beck $10–20

1973

Jan. 15th 4th Annual Year in Review Issue, interviews with Keith Moon, Paul McCartney, John Entwistle, Ronnie Spector, The Old Hollies, Rita Coolidge, Kris Kristofferson, Herman's Hermits, Jimi Hendrix: War Heroes $15–30

Jan. 29 Cat Stevens on the Run, Loggins & Messina on the Floor, Paul Butterfield, Trapeze, Poco, *Tommy* Live in London, Mott the Hoople: The Punks Rock On, Tom Rush Remembering, Roy Orbison...$10–20

Feb. 26 Mick Jagger: The Rolling Stones in Los Angeles, John Lennon & Yoko Ono: Imagine, Who Do the Deep Purple Think They Are?, The Rascals $10–20

Mar. 12 David Bowie, George Harrison, British Rock 1964–1973, Dick Clark, Shawn Phillips, The Doobie Brothers, Keith Moon, The Grateful Dead: Ghost Stories, Conversations With Bob Weir, Alvin Lee: Ten Years After...$10–20

Mar. 26 Traffic: Shanghaied at the Fantasy Factory, Peter Frampton: His Guitar & Camel, Fanny, Harry Chapin, Yoko Ono, Bob Dylan $10–20

Apr. 9 The Who: In Love With Pete Townshend, The Out-coming of David Bowie, The Rainbow Race: Bruce Springsteen & Carol Hall, Steeleye Span: The Up-side of Down, Chick Corea, Iggy Pop, Elvin Jones $10–20

Apr. 23 Bob Dylan at West Point, Al Green, Don McLean, So This is What Happened to Robin Trower, Dion & the Belmonts, Alice Cooper, Grateful Dead $10–20

May 7 At Home With Carly Simon, T. Rex, Tom Rapp, John Martyn, Pink Floyd Hangs a Moon, Byrds, The Temptations, Alice Cooper...$10–20

May 21 Rod Stewart & Faces, The Robert Klein Story, The Astounding Rock Hall of Fame, John McLaughlin, Bonnie Raitt, Procol Harum, Harry Nilssen, Michael Nesmith: No More Monkee Business, Todd Rundgren $10–20

June 18 Led Zeppelin's Jimmy Page Cornered, The Wailers, Ian Whitcomb, Rick Wakeman Profile, Yes: Getting Closer Than Ever, The Bee Gees in 1973; Gibb Fibs & Other Fables, Brewer & Shipley $10–20

July 23 Special 4th Anniversary Double Issue, Special Memorial Section: Legends of the Lost, A Time to Remember—Jimi Hendrix: There Will Never be Another Like Him, Jimi Hendrix & His Curtis Knight Days, In Search of Janis Joplin, Brian Jones was a Rolling Stone, Jim Morrison: James Douglas Morrison Remembered, Rock 'n' Roll Heaven, Seals & Crofts, Elton John, Chuck Berry, Jeff Beck, Slade, J. Geils........................$25–50

Aug. 27 The Return of Johnny Winter, The Electric Light Orchestra, Jimmy Cliff, Clarence White Dead, Sgt. Pepper Auditions, The Spinners, O'Jays, Stylistics, Pretty Things, Manfred Mann, Status Quo, Ray Davis Waterloo, Black Oak Arkansas...................$10–20

Sept. 10 An interview with the Garbage of Watkins Glen, Elton John's Rocket Launched in L.A., Climax Blues Band, Todd Rundgren $10–20

Dec. 3 Rod Stewart:The Amazing British Singing Sensation, Blue Oyster Cult, Iggy Pop, Mott the Hoople, Bobby Womack, The Raspberries...$10–20

Dec. 31 Roger Daltry: Bye Bye *Tommy*: Howdy Quadrophenia, Zappa Does it Again, Rolling Stones in Berlin: Waiting for the Walls to Fall, ZZ Top, Bob Dylan, History of the Juke Box, The Eagles, War, David Bowie, Roger McGuinn....................................$10–20

1974

Jan. 14 Pete Townshend: Happy Who Year, Elton John, Loggins & Messina, TV Rock, Jackson Browne, Marty Bolin, Black Oak Arkansas...$10–20

Mar. 25 10th Anniversary of the Beatles: John, Paul & Ringo, George, Chris Jagger, The Beach Boys, The Exploitation of Elvis Presley, Wendy Waldman...........................$10–20

Apr. Grace Slick at 34, Slade, Morgana King, ELO, Climax Blues Band, Linda Ronstadt, Jesse Colin Young, Richie Furay, The Beatles Tour, Phil Ochs.................................$10–20

July 5th Anniversary Issue, Jimi Hendrix: There Will Never be Another Like Him, James Brown is Superbad, an interview with John Lennon & Yoko Ono, The Rolling Stones

Interview Circa 1969, Paul McCartney Playing in the Band, Marty Balin, 15 years of Elvis Presley, Bob Dylan & the Sheik of New York, On Tour With Rod Stewart & Faces, Paul Simon, The Beatles, Brian Jones, Taj Mahal, Jim Morrison on Trial, Janis Joplin Still Rocking, Duanne Allman, Mick Jagger: Hard Working Playboy..$25–50

1975

Jan. Special Year in Review Holiday Issue, Elton John: 1975's Superman of the Year, Dick Clarke, John Sebastian, The Eagles, Neil Young, Uriah Heep, Linda McCartney, George Carlin, Mick Jagger, Sonny & Cher...$10–20

ROCK (Modern Day Periodicals Inc.), magazine format

1977

Jan. Lou Reed, Bob Dylan, Roger McGuinn: Rolling Thunder Redux, The Bay City Rollers Frenzy, Brian May of Queen interview, The Beach Boys, David Bowie Cries Wolf, Keith Richards' Hair, Kiki Dee, Elvin Bishop, Asleep at the Wheel, Southside Johnny, The Outlaws...$4–8

Mar. Steven Tyler: Aerosmith's Eros Myth Exclusive, Led Zeppelin: Wide-screen Celebration, Kiss Roll Over, ZZ at the Top, Stevie Wonder is Finished, Flo & Eddie, Marilyn Chambers Exclusive, Hall & Oates, Tommy Bolin, Be-bop Deluxe, Debbie Harry: Blondie's the Band, Not the Blonde, Rick Springfield, Graham Parker, issue includes full- page glossy color Kiss pin-ups..$6–12

May Dennis Wilson Flies Solo, Peter Frampton on Fire, Stevie Wonder, Bob Seger: Why Rock 'n' Roll Almost Forgot, Rod Stewart Exclusive, Linda Ronstadt: Through Her Image Darkly, Foghat, The Bee Gees, Rory Gallagher, Dave Mason, Kiss, Leo Sayer, Todd Rundgren, War, George Benson...$4–8

July Paul Stanley & Kiss, Alice Cooper: Freaky as Ever, Kiss on Tour of the U.S.A, Queen, Thin Lizzy, Rod Stewart, Aerosmith: Keeping a Tight Rudder, Led Zeppelin: Running Naked in the Sun, Grace Slick, The Eagles, Blue Oyster Cult: Rock's Vampires, Al Stewart, Neil Young, Fleetwood Mac & Stevie Nicks, ELO, Pink Floyd.................................$5–10

Sept. Led Zeppelin: Is There a Curse on Led Zeppelin?, Blondie, Kiss, The Who, Groupies: The Lovely Ladies of Rock, Cheap Trick, Bad Company, Boston, The Babys, Tom Petty, Rush, The Runaways, Andy Gibb, Tubes, Angel, Mink DeVille, Nils Lofgren $4–8

Nov. Led Zeppelin on Tour, Kiss: One Hot Night, Heart, Mick Jagger, Rod Stewart, Freddie Mercury, The Who, ZZ Top, Bee Gees, Taj Mahal, Climax Blues Band, Pez Band, David Bowie, Brian Ferry $4–8

1978

Jan. Steven Tyler & Aerosmith Forever, Pink Floyd Insanity, Rod Stewart: No More Britt, Led Zeppelin, Dead Boys, Peter Frampton, Kiss, Heart, Fleetwood Mac, Angel, UFO, Bebe Buel, Alice Cooper $2–8

Mar. Foghat Special: Why They're Shooting to the Top, Starz, Bay City Rollers, Kiss Exclusive: Gene Simmons—The Tongue That Tells All, Peter Frampton, Ted Nugent, Elton John, Crawler, The Babys, Thin Lizzy, Black Oak Arkansas, Tubes, Blue Oyster Cult $4–8

July Ted Nugent: The Madman Talks, Kiss Konfessions: Paul Stanly Speaks, Led Zeppelin's Flight Plan, Aerosmith: Soaring Skywards, Rod Stewart: Burning Hot, Peter Frampton, Fleetwood Mac: Number One With a Bullet, Meat Loaf, Bob Dylan, Judas Priest, Van Halen...$5–10

Sept. Peter Frampton, Paul Stanley Exclusive Interview, Queen: The Kings of Rock, Led Zeppelin posters, Buddy Holly, Mink DeVille, Mahogany Rush, Gene Simmons Gossip, Robert Palmer, Jimi Hendrix, Tangerine Dream, Heart: The World's Greatest Sister Act, Genesis, Strawbs $4–8

Nov. Peter Frampton, Led Zeppelin Exclusive: The Photo Files, Wings, The Bee Gees' History Part I, Bruce Springsteen: The Boss is Back, Bob Seger, Kiss: Kissteria Rocks the Nation, Uriah Heep, Van Halen, Eddie Money, John Hall on His Own, Nektar, Lou Reed, Olivia Newton-John: Not Average...$4–8

1979

Jan. Kiss Exclusive: Gene Simmons interview, Linda Ronstadt, The Sizzling Carly Simon, Todd Rundgren: History of a Runt, Partying With Aerosmith, Boston, Led Zeppelin, Foreigner, Southside Johnny, The Cars, Billy Joel, Savoy Brown...$4–8

Apr. Kiss Exclusive, Heart: Straight from the Heart—An Intimate Conversation With the Wilson Sisters, What's Next for the Who?, Cheap Trick Has Arrived, Lookin' Back With the Stones, The Future of the Stones, Van Morrison, On Tour With Aerosmith, Elton John Speaks, Devo, Boston, John Oates, Queen, Olivia Newton-John, Jethro Tull, Yes, The Blend, Peter Frampton, Ozzy Osbourne..$6–12
June Kiss Special: The Secret Messages of the Kiss Albums, The Unhappy World of Billy Joel, Meat Loaf Talks, The Kiss Hoax, Ted Nugent, Elvis Costello & Armed Forces Hits Town, The Definitive Kiss Discography, Al Stewart, Peter Frampton, Wings, Bruce Springsteen: What if the Boss Decides to Quit?, Blondie Builds...................................$4–8

ROCK (D.S. Magazines Inc.)

1989

Sept./Oct. Skid Row: Everyone's Going Wild, The Who: 25 Years & Still Rocking, It's the Rude, Lewd & All New Motley Crue, L.A. Guns...$2–4
All other issues...$2–4

ROCK ALIVE

All issues..$2–3

ROCK-AND-ROLL SONGS

1967

Sept. The Who, Peter & Gordon, The 5 Americans, Mitch Ryder, The Grateful Dead, Sam the Sham, Eric Burdon, Eddie Floyd, The Monkees..$10–20

1968

Sept. Pink Floyd, The Incredible Story of Buffalo Springfield, Meet Moby Grape, The Four Tops, The Troggs, Blood, Sweat & Tears, The Tremeloes, Classics Four................$10–20
All other issues...$10–20

ROCK-AND-ROLL SONGS

All issues..$2–4

ROCK AWARDS

1978

#1 Kiss Extravaganza: Special Section for Kiss-ophiles, issue includes 16 giant color posters, Blondie, Bob Seger, Led Zeppelin on Tour, Jethro Tull, Leo Sayer, Foghat, Jefferson Starship, Peter Frampton, David Bowie, Rex, Stevie Nicks.......................................$15–30

1979

Summer Kiss: A Contract Out on Their Lives, Cheap Trick, Meat Loaf, Boston, Southside Johnny & the Asbury Jukes, Jefferson Starship, The Doobie Brothers, ELP, Billy Joel, Todd Rundgren, Jethro Tull, Elton John, Jim Morrison Epilogue: An American Prayer, Master of the Macabre...$5–10

ROCK BEAT

1986

July Duran Duran Return, A-ha, Motley Crue, Wham Splits, Kiss Returns, Bon Jovi in Concert, Heart in Concert, Arcadia, Ratt, U2 ....$2–4
Sept. Motley Crue, Van Halen, Arcadia, Duran Duran: Then & Now, Bon Jovi, Kiss, Prince Marillion, Bruce Springsteen, Thompson Twins, A-ha, Ozzy Osbourne, Dokken........$2–4
Nov. Motley Crue, David Lee Roth, Ozzy Osbourne, Jon Bon Jovi, Stephen Pearcy interview, A-ha, Kiss, Iron Maiden, Blow Monkeys, The Pet Shop Boys, Julian Lennon, W.A.S.P., Judas Priest, Women in Music, Duran Duran, Ratt.......................................$2–4

1987

Winter Van Halen: Life After David—A Special Van Halen/David Lee Roth Collector's Issue, stories, pin-ups, posters..$2–4

Jimi Hendrix

Collecting

JIMI HENDRIX

Jimi Hendrix—what can be said about him that hasn't already been said many times before? The greatest guitarist and most revolutionary instrumentalist in rock-and-roll history!—that seems to be the general consensus. He was the most startling original and influential electric guitarist since Charlie Christian. He is the man who single-handedly changed the course and approach to electric guitar playing and forever increased its range and scope. He made electric guitar playing a world unto itself, permanently severing its identity from its acoustic brother. Even more amazing, however, is the fact that all of this was accomplished during a career that spanned only four short years from October 1966 to September 1970.

Jimi Hendrix was born on November 27, 1942, and died prematurely on September 18, 1970, at the age of 27. He was approximately 5′ 10″ tall and weighed 126 pounds. This, however, is irrelevant compared to his gigantic stature in rock-and-roll and, more specifically, his contribution to the history of his chosen instrument, the electric guitar. This, plus his amazing showmanship, exotic multiracial heritage, and gentle off-stage demeanor have made him an enduring legend, whose mystique increases rather than decreases with time.

Jimi Hendrix is considered to be the first acknowledged virtuoso genius in rock-and-roll. His influence extends beyond the boundaries of rock to affect pop, jazz, and even classical music. No other rock guitarist, past or present, can stake that claim. Twenty years after his death, his vision of a "new music" still speaks to those who can hear.

Needless to say, Jimi Hendrix memorabilia and recordings have risen in value astronomically in the past decade. The most dramatic example of this is the sale of Jimi's cream-colored "Woodstock" Fender Stratocaster guitar, which sold at auction for an astounding $330,000. Although prices are constantly rising, Jimi Hendrix memorabilia is quite plentiful, and, aside from the more exotic (and expensive) items such as guitars, stage clothing, and handwritten items, is still affordable.

RECORDS, 45 RPM (U.S. RELEASES)

Guitar player flexi-disc, 7375X5, "Beginnings" $10–20
Reprise, 0572, "Hey Joe"/51st anniversary, with picture sleeve..........................$100–500
  0572, "Hey Joe"/51st anniversary without sleeve $12–25
  0597, "Purple Haze"/"Wind Cries Mary" $10–20
  0641, "Foxy Lady"/"Hey Joe"...$10–20
  0665, "One Rainy Wish"/"Up from the Skies" $10–20
  0767, "All Along the Watch Tower"/"Burning of the Midnight Lamp" $10–20
  0792, "Crosstown Traffic"/"Gypsy Eyes"..$10–20
  0853, "Stonefree"/"If Six was Nine"...$10–20
  0905, "Stepping Stone"/"Izabella"...$15–35
  1000, "Freedom"/"Freedom" $12–25
  1000, "Freedom"/"Angel" $10–20
  1044, "Dolly Dagger"/"Dolly Dagger"...$20–40
  1044, "Dolly Dagger"/"Star Spangled Banner"...$12–25
  1118, "The Wind Cries Mary"/"Little Wing"..$7–15
  1118, "The Wind Cries Mary"/"The Wind Cries Mary"..$10–20
  K14286, "Hear My Train"/"Rock My Baby"..$7–15
  PRO-A-840, "Auld Lang Syne"/"Little Drummer Boy"/"Silent Night," radio promo
  ....$50–100
  29845, "Fire"/"Little Wing"..$3–6
  GRE 0728, "Foxy Lady"/"Purple Haze" $3–6
  1082, "Johnny B. Goode"/"Johnny B. Goode" $10–20
  1082, "Johnny B. Goode"/"Loverman"...$3–6

ALBUMS, 33⅓ RPM (U.S. RELEASES)
WHITE LABELS PROMOS

Reprise, R-6261, "Are You Experienced," mono.....................................$75–150
  R-6281, "Axis: Bold as Love," mono...$150–300
  2RS-6307, "Electric Ladyland," stereo..$100–200
  MSK2276, "Smash Hits," stereo $30–60
  MS-2029, "Monterey International Pop Festival," stereo $20–40
  MS-2034, "Cry of Love," stereo $20–40
  MS-2049, "Rainbow Bridge"..$15–35
  MS-2049, "In the West"...$15–35
  MS-2103, "War Heroes"..$15–35
  2RS-6481, Soundtrack to the film *Jimi Hendrix*...$20–45
  MS-2204, "Crash Landing"...$12–25
  MS-2229, "Midnight Lightning"..$12–25

2RS-2245, "The Essential Jimi Hendrix" $20–40
HS-2293, "The Essential Jimi Hendrix," Vol. II $10–20
HS-2299, "Nine to the Universe" $10–20
22306-1, "The Jimi Hendrix Concerts" $12–25
25119-1, "Kiss the Sky" $10–20
25358-1, "Jimi Plays Monterey" $10–20

BOOTLEGS (ORIGINAL RELEASE LABELS)

Sagittarius, "Live at Philharmonic Hall," 1969 ....$125–250
Munia, "Live at the Los Angeles Forum," 1970 ....$30–65
CSD, 1564, "Home at Woodstock," 1970 ....$65–125
Hen, 37, "Hendrix Live in Hawaii," 1971 ....$25–50
TMOQ, 71028, "Smashing Amps," 1971 ....$20–40
TMOQ, "Incident at Rainbow Bridge," 1971...................................$25–50
TMOQ, 7502, "Broadcasts/Maui," 1971 ....$25–50
TMOQ, 7509
   "Alive," 1971 ....$25–50
   "Big Broadcasts," 1971 ....$20–40
Kustom, 005, "Live Experience 67–68," 1971 ....$30–65
Kustom, 005, "Goodbye Jimi," 1971 ....$15–30
TMOQ, 71060, "Good Karma," 1971 ....$20–40
TMOQ, 71079
   "Good Karma," Vol. II, 1971 ....$30–60
   "Isle of Wight," Vol. I, 1971 ....$35–75
   "Isle of Wight," Vol. II, 1971..$35–75
   "Jimi Hendrix in Hawaii," 1971 ....$15–30
Shalom
   "Rainbow Bridge," 1971 ....$20–35
   "Wow—Woodstock & Monterey," 1971 ....$50–100
Red Lightning, 0015
   "Woke Up This Morning & Found Myself Dead," 1972.................$7–15
   "Rainbow Bridge," the unreleased out-takes from the movie, 1972 ......$20–40
Mushroom, 1850, "Good Vibes," 1972 ....$30–60
Rubber Dubber, 70001, "Enjoy," 1972 ....$40–75
Rubber Dubber, 9022–233470, "Scuse Me While I Kiss the Sky," 1972...............$35–65
TMOQ, 7509, "Hendrix Alive," 1972...$20–40
TMOQ, 7502, "Hendrix in Europe," 1972 ....$25–50
Out to Lunch, 1, "He Was a Friend of Yours," 1972 ....$25–50
Fruitend, 10168, "Live in Stockholm," 1972.....................................$35–75
Ken, 712/3, "Star Portrait," 1972...$7–15
Raven, JH6146, "Unknown Wellknown," 1972 ....$15–35
Berkeley, 2228, "Royal Albert Hall," 1973 ....$20–45
Figa, "Stereo Experience," 1973 ....$20–45
Phoenix, 44775, "Never Fade," 1974 ....$20–40
Sure Nice Shoes, 714, "Electric Lady Jams," 1974..........................$25–50
TMOQ, 71019
   "Broadcasts," 1974 ....$20–40
   "Jimi Hendrix Live, Isle of Wight," Vol. I, 1974.......................$35–65
   "Jimi Hendrix Live, Isle of Wight," Vol. II, 1974 ....$35–65
Napolean, NPL 11018, "Jimi Hendrix Vol. II, A Man of Our Time," 1974..........$15–25
QCS, 1447, "Music for Fans," Vol. I, 1975 ....$25–45
Impossible, 102, "Primal Keys," 1976..$35–75
K & S, 011, "Guitar Hero" 1978 ....$15–30
Horweite, "Foxy Hendrix," 1979 ....$25–50
Ruthless Rhymes, "Can You Please Crawl Out Your Window?," 1979 ....$30–60
Loma, 79–109/109, "Wink of an Eye," 1979.....................................$15–30
Towne, RG-2001, "Magic Fingers," 1980 ....$15–30
Alston, 45-4570, "Live in Ottawa, Canada," 1980.............................$20–45
White Knight, WK22, "The Good Die Young," 1981 ....$50–100

Rock Folders, Q9020-PRO
   "You Can't Use My Name," 1985 .... $12–25
   "Turn 'er On," 1985 .... $7–15
Spicy Essence, "Apartment Jam 1970," 1986 .... $75–150
Veteran Music Inc., MF243, "This One's for You," 1987 .... $10–20
Side Walk, JHX8868, "Gypsy Suns, Moons & Rainbows," 1988 .... $25–50
Toasted, TRW 1953, "Hoochie Coochie Man," 1988 .... $20–40
Pyramid, 023, "Electronic Church Music," 1989 .... $12–25
Joguardondi, 001/2, "Electric Jimi," 1989 .... $20–40
Swingin' Pig, 016, "Live in Paris '68," 1989 .... $10–20
Swingin' Pig, 018, "Fire," 1989 .... $10–20
Manic Depression, 01, "Winterland Days," 1989 .... $25–50
Wild Bird, 890 901,
   "Woodstock Nation," 1990 .... $25–50
   "Standing Next to a Mountain," 1990 .... $100–200
Tam, "Driving South With the Jimi Hendrix Experience," 1990 .... $50–100
Humphrey, "Lord I Can See the Blues," 1990 .... $100–200
Cops & Robbers, JTYM 01, "Happy New Year, Jimi," 1990 .... $125–250
Guitar Hero, 71056, "Electric Church Music, Part One," 1990 .... $50–100

RARE HENDRIX (SOLD AT AUCTION)

Abstract 19″ × 24″, multicolored felt-tip drawing by Jimi $5,500
"Are You Experienced" album cover signed by Jimi, Noel & Mitch $2,200
Gold album award for "Cry of Love" $3,000
Handwritten letter signed by Jimi $3,000–4,700
Jimi Hendrix autographed programs & posters (set sale) $800–2,000
Jimi Hendrix floral shirt $2,970
Jimi Hendrix handwritten lyrics to "Bold as Love" $5,000
Jimi Hendrix handwritten lyrics to "Purple Haze" $17,000
Jimi Hendrix signature only on paper $350–800
Jimi's "eye" jacket, featured on "Are You Experienced" album cover $13,000
Jimi's "Woodstock" Fender Stratocaster guitar $330,000
Other previously auctioned albums .... Up to $2,500
Other previously auctioned Hendrix guitars $20,000–50,000
Other previously auctioned, multicolored felt-tip drawings $4,600
Other previously sold handwritten lyrics $3,000–7,500
Platinum album award for "Axis: Bold as Love" .... Over $3,500
Silk crepe shirt $3,800
Watercolor painting by Jimi $3,300

THE JIMI HENDRIX INFORMATION MANAGEMENT INSTITUTE

J.I.M.I. was founded in 1985 and is one of the oldest and most active Jimi Hendrix fan clubs in America. It is extremely reliable with information as well as with its "collectors' corner" sales.

For more information about Jimi Hendrix collectibles such as CDs, bootlegs, photos, and memorabilia contact: J.I.M.I., c/o Ken Voss (Curator), P.O. Box 374, Des Plaines, IL 60016, or Lou Schwartz, 24 Hillside, Ansonia, CT 06401.

Spring Special All-metal Issue—Bon Jovi, Stryper, Slayer, Alice Cooper, Ozzy Osbourne, Warlock, Van Halen, Megadeth, Anthrax, The Firm..$2–4

1988

Feb. Def Leppard's Joe Elliot, Ozzy Osbourne, Alice Cooper, Motley Crue, Bon Jovi, White Lion, E-Z-O, Dokken, Guns 'n' Roses, Metallica...$2–3

Apr. Don Dokken, David Lee Roth, MSG, Def Leppard, Tesla, Dio, Alice Cooper, Poison, Sammy Hagar, Kiss, Aerosmith, Bon Jovi, Warlock $2–3

May David Lee Roth, Ozzy Osbourne, Bon Jovi, Savatage, Van Halen, AC/DC, Metallica, Aerosmith, Megadeth, L.A. Guns, Motley Crue, White Lion....................................$2–3

Oct. Cinderella's Tom Keifer, Scorpions, Metallica Delivering Justice, Europe, Poison, Stryper, Def Leppard, Judas Priest, Vince Neil...$2–3

Dec. Joey Tempest: Europe Mania, The Dreaded Van Halen Family Trait, Jimmy Page Tells All, Exporing the Mind of Tom Keifer, Flotsam & Jetsam, Guns 'n' Roses, Ozzy Osbourne, Def Leppard, Kingdom Come..$2–3

1989

Jan. Ozzy Osbourne & Zakk: Living History, Jet Boys, Def Leppard's Bizarre Backstage Bash, Bon Jovi's Latest, Tempest, C.C. Deville $2–3

May Guns 'n' Roses: Identity Crisis, Kiss Waiting for the Big One, Tesla, Cinderella, Winger, Europe, Whitesnake, Bon Jovi: Staying Sane $2–3

Aug. Warrent Exclusive, Kiss, INXS, Cinderella, Metalheads & Their Women, House of Lords, Blue Murder, Alice Cooper, Charlie Sexton $2–3

Nov. White Lion, L.A. Guns, Rock Star Recipes, Torrid Tales of Poison's Past, Faster Pussycat, Queensryche, Dangerous Toys, Bad English...$2–3

Dec. Motley Crue Exclusive: The Tatooed Lover Boys Return, Aerosmith color centerfold, Scandal & Bon Jovi, Faith No More, Alice Cooper $2–3

1990

Jan. Def Leppard 1990: Intimate stories, pin-ups, etc., Alice Cooper, Bret Michaels, Axl Rose centerfold, Law & Order, Sebastian Bach..$2–3

All other issues $2–3

ROCK BEAT'S METAL PIN-UPS MAGAZINE

1989

Fall Guns 'n' Roses, Skid Row, Great White, L.A. Guns, Bullet Boys, Motley Crue, Bon Jovi, Warrent, Cinderella...$2–3

ROCK CALENDAR POSTER MAGAZINE

1985

Van Halen, Michael Jackson, Cyndi Lauper, Boy George, David Bowie, Billy Joel, Quiet Riot, Huey Lewis, Sting, Motley Crue, Prince, Duran Duran $2–4

ROCKET (Stanhope Communications, Inc.)

1978

Mar. #1 Paul Stanley: Kiss Pounds the Pork, Blondie's Debbie Harry Nude, Stevie Nicks: 10 Years of Hills & Valleys Only Make Fleetwood Mac Stronger, Heart on Tour, Robert Plant, Interviews with Rick Wakeman, Andy Gibb, Foghat, City Boy, Andy Pratt & Eddie Money, Mick Jagger, David Bowie, Patti Smith, Kraftwerk, Rod Stewart, Elton John, Bob Dylan, Johnny Rotten $10–20

May #2 Rod Stewart, Peter Frampton: The Whole Story, Kiss, Linda Ronstadt, Carly Simon, Chicago, Boston, Sammy Hagar, Wings, Sex Pistols, Alice Cooper, Kansas: The Point of No Return, Queen: Up Close in Concert, Sea Level, The Temptations, Charlie Daniels $5–10

July #3 Peter Frampton: The Peter Piper of Pepperland, Rod Stewart: A Touchy Minute With Mr. "Hot Legs," Andy Gibb, Thin Lizzy, Led Zeppelin, Abba, Dr. Hook, Warren Zevon, Bob Dylan, Kiss Army, Billy Joel, Hall & Oates: Back Street Boys on the High Road $5–10

ROCK '79, 1979,
SUMMER

ROCKET, 1978, Mar. (#1)

ROCKET, 1978, May (#2)

ROCKET, 1978, July (#3)

ROCKET, 1978, Nov. (#5)

ROCKET, 1986, Dec. (#1)

ROCK FEVER AWARDS,
1979, SPRING (#2)

ROCK FEVER AWARDS,
1979, SUMMER (#3)

ROCK GOSSIP, 1979,
SPRING (#1)

Nov. #5 Foghat, Kiss: Ace Spills It—The Kiss Flick, The Solo Album, His Fans, His Private Life & His Solo Career as a Comedian, Amanda Lear & Andy Gibb, Rod Stewart Gives the Finger, Backstage With Bob Dylan, The Rolling Stones photo feature, Roger Daltry, Bruce Springsteen, Todd Rundgren, Joe Walsh, Pattie Smith $5–10

1986

Dec. #1 Billy Joel: Trials & Tribulations $2–4

ROCK EXPRESS (Canadian rock music magazine)

All issues $2–4

ROCK FANTASY COMICS (First editions, which are limited to a run of 10,000 copies)

1989

#1 Pink Floyd $7–15

1990

#2 Rolling Stones $3–5
#3 Led Zeppelin $6–12
#4 Stevie Nicks (never issued)
#5 Guns 'n' Roses $3–7
#6 Monsters of Rock—Ozzy Osbourne, Lita Ford, Def Leppard $3–5
#7 Sex Pistols $5–10
#8 Alice Cooper (never issued)
#9 Van Halen $3–5
#10 Kiss $5–10
#11 Jimi Hendrix $3–6
#12 Def Leppard $3–5
#13 David Bowie $3–5
#14 The Doors $3–5
#15 Pink Floyd #2 .... $3–6
#16 Great Gig in the Sky (double issue) $5–8
#17 Rock Vixens—Madonna, Debbie Gibson, Paula Abdul, Samantha Fox $3–6
#18 Metallica $3–5
#19 Ozzy Osbourne $3–5

ROCK FESTIVAL MAGAZINE

All issues $2–4

ROCK FEVER

1984

Oct. #4 Van Halen, Motley Crue, Duran Duran, Def Leppard Open File, Quiet Riot, Berlin, The Clash, Cyndi Lauper, Tracy Ullman, Ozzy Osbourne, Boy George, On Stage With Billy Idol, Huey Lewis, Heart $2–4
Dec. #5 Eddie Van Halen, Judas Priest, The Scorpions, Motley Crue, Ratt, The Eurythmics, Duran Duran, Quiot Riot, Accept, Boy George $2–4

1985

Feb. #6 Ratt Attack, Twisted Sister, Bruce Springsteen: The Stories They Tell, Mathias Jabs/Scorpions, Michael Jackson: The Making of an American Idol, Iron Maiden, Motley Crue, Quiet Riot, Krokus, Van Halen $2–4
Aug. David Lee Roth & Van Halen's Future, Madonna, Ratt, Iron Maiden, Deep Purple, Bruce Springsteen: The Bruce Nobody Knows, Bryan Adams, Queensryche, Tina Turner, Quiet Riot, Kiss, Bon Jovi $2–4

1987

Aug. Jon Bon Jovi, Simply Red, Andy Taylor, Michael Jackson, Ray Davies, Howard Jones, Huey Lewis, The Bangles, Cyndi Lauper, David Bowie $2–4
Sept. The Beastie Boys, David Bowie, Ten Years With U2, Duran Duran: Wild Boys on Film, Bruce Springsteen: The Boss' Glory Days, Heart, The Cult $2–4
Oct. Poison Laughs Last, Crowded House, Janet Jackson, Madonna: A Fantastic Photo Feature, Psychedelic Furs, Tom Petty, The Cure, Tina Turner $2–4
Nov. Run DMC, Heart: Animals Gone Bad, Jefferson Starship's History of Flight, The Cure, Billy Idol, The Nylons, Cutting Crew, The Hooters, George Michael, Wire Train, Beastie Boys, Fuzz Box, Pseudo Echo $2–4

1988

Jan. Duran Duran: "We're Not Dead Yet," Motley Crue, The Tale of Echo & the Bunnymen, Rappin' With Def Leppard, Sting, John Cougar Mellencamp, Michael Jackson: The New Look, Beastie Boys, Madonna, The Turtles, issue includes posters $2–4

ROCK FEVER AWARDS

1979

Spring #2 Kiss Confessions, Looking Back On, Kiss Make-up Off, The Rolling Stones, Led Zeppelin in Concert, Peter Frampton, On the Set With Sgt. Pepper $5–10
Summer Kiss, Blondie, Patti Smith: Rock's Prodigal Daughter, Heart: Girls are Better, Olivia Newton-John is Hot to Trot, Buddy Holly: The Roots of Rock, Meat Loaf's Favorite Recipes...$7–15

ROCK FEVER GIANT POSTER MAGAZINE

1984

Fall Issue contains eight giant color wall posters of Van Halen, Scorpions, Duran Duran, Boy George, Billy Idol, Quiet Riot, Michael Jackson & Cyndi Lauper.........................$3–6

1985

Winter Issue includes eight giant color wall posters of Van Halen, Scorpions, Michael Jackson, Vince Neil, John Taylor, Bruce Springsteen, & Def Leppard..................................$3–6

ROCK FEVER 1985 ROCK POSTER CALENDAR MAGAZINE

1985

Eddie Van Halen, Boy George, Scorpions, Michael Jackson, David Lee Roth, Van Halen, The Eurythmics, Quiet Riot, Ozzy Osbourne, Cyndi Lauper, Adam Ant, Simon Le Bon, Billy Idol, Joe Elliot, Police $2–4

ROCK FEVER POSTER MAGAZINE (Each issue contains 10 giant full-color wall posters, 16″ × 22″)

1986

Vol. 5 Judas Priest, Helix, Saxon, Fiona, The Ramones, Accept, Dokken, John Lydon/ Johnny Rotten, Van Halen...$4–8
Vol. 6 Heart, David Lee Roth, Giuffria, Poison, Quiet Riot, Europe, Jon Bon Jovi, Heaven, Cinderella, Black 'n' Blue $4–8

1987

Vol. 1 Heart, Madonna, David Bowie, Suzanne Vega, Crowded House, ABC, The Cure, Kim Wilde, John Waite, Michael Jackson $4–8
Vol. 2 Lizzy Borden, Dokken, Europe, Billy Idol, Poison, Platinum Blonde, Anthrax, Aerosmith, Fields of Nephilim, Def Leppard..$3–6

ROCK FEVER SPECIAL
1984
The One & Only Michael Jackson—His Tours, His Future, His Life...........................$3–6
1984 Duran Duran/Culture Club & Boy George—includes four wall posters $3–6

ROCK-FOLK-POP-BLUES SONG FOLIO (Charlton)
1966
Spring #1 How Did the Animals Get Their Names?, Bon Dylan: The Best Folk Musician Around Today, Joan Baez: Leading the Folk Music Revival, Phil Sloan..................$10–20
Summer #2 The Mamas & the Papas Switched to Rock, The Rolling Stones are Not an R & B Group, Phil Ochs, Simon & Garfunkel: Poet & A One-man Band...............$6–12
Fall #3 Muddy Waters & the Chicago Beat, Jimmy Reed: The Big Boss Man, The Byrds: A New Wave of Awareness, Judy Collins: A Logical Evolution................................$5–10

1967
Spring #5 Mike Bloomfield, Joe Butler, Phil Volk, John Sebastian..............................$3–6

ROCK GOSSIP
1979
Spring #1 Kiss Exclusive: They Take Off Their Make-up, Steve Tyler: Intimate Stories You Wouldn't Believe, Van Halen: Will Success Ruin Them?, The Beatles are Back, Led Zeppelin, Beneath the Scanty Clothing: The Real Linda Ronstadt, Meat Loaf

ROCK LEGENDS
1989
#1 Elvis Presley: The Original Idol, Ricky Nelson: The Rock 'n' Roll TV Star, Ricky Nelson's Complete Discography, Fabian, Bobby Rydell, Jimmy Clanton, The Beach Boys, Tribute to Roy Orbison, Jon Bon Jovi: Rock's New Idol, Bruce Springsteen, Elvis Presley Discography, The Beatles 25th Anniversary, Little Richard, Buddy Holly, Tribute to Richie Valens, Frankie Avalon...$3–5

ROCK LOVE
1979
Oct. #3 Bruce Springsteen: A False Legend?, Debbie Harry: The Hard Way, Andy Gibb, The Greatest Rock Movies, Aerosmith: Their Secret Life Style, Guitar Wars: Name the King $5–10

ROCK MAGAZINE
1983
Dec. David Bowie, Joan Jett: Life After Jailbait, The Eurythmics, Asia, Flock of Seagulls, Talking Heads, Men Without Hats, AC/DC, Bonnie Tyler, Mick Fleetwood, Def Leppard, Kiss, Oingo Boingo, Billy Joel...$2–4

1984
June Billy Idol: This Year's Elvis, Duran Duran Comes of Age, Quiet Riot, The Pretenders: What Chrissie Hynde Wants From You, Berlin, Grace Slick, Echo & the Bunnymen, Van Halen, Bette Midler, Menudo...$2–4
Aug. The Thompson Twins: Their Strange Past & Bright Future, Rush: Breaking Up, Kenny Loggins, Scorpions, Adam Ant, Pink Floyd, Bruce Springsteen, Missing Persons, REM..$2–4
Oct. Rod Stewart: Return of the Tartan Terror, Prince & Purple Rain, Cyndi Lauper on Love, Jermaine Jackson, Wang Chung, The Motel's Martha Davis: Her Secret Life, Ratt, Bruce Springsteen, Bangles, Linda Ronstadt, Michael Jackson in Concert, The Pointer Sisters..$2–4
Nov. Pat Benatar: A Rare Interview, Lindsay Buckingham, Bill Murray, The Fixx, Lou Reed, Ratt, Elton Johm, REM $2–4

1985

Feb. Prince, Hall & Oates, Frankie Goes to Hollywood, Vanity, Little Richard, Iron Maiden, David Byrne, Paul McCartney...$2–4
Oct. Mick Jagger, Tears for Fears, Paul Young, Supertramp, Tina Turner, John Fogerty, Randy Newman, Joan Jett: Burning Her Reputation, REM, Devo, Almost Nude Madonna, Run DMC, Loudness, Triumph...$2–4

ROCK MANIA (Stories, Layouts, and Press, Inc.)

1979

Spring Kiss Special, Gene Simmons: Why He Must Leave Kiss, Does Paul Stanley Really Have Ten Girlfriends?, Paul Stanley Interview Part I & Part II, Touring With Ted Nugent, Do it With Heart: Is Heart Just a Silly Bunch of Girls?, Peter Frampton: Can He Survive?, Wings, Queen, Aerosmith, Steve Martin, Led Zeppelin in Concert, Looking Back With the Rolling Stones, Rod Stewart, Talking With Olivia Newton-John, Kraftwerk, Meat Loaf, Stevie Nicks, David Bowie, Linda Ronstadt...$6–12
Summer Kosmic Kiss, Ted Nugent's Weekend Rampage, Meat Loaf, Cheap Trick: The Past They Want to Hide, The Clash Invade America, Talking Heads '79, Sid Vicious: "They Made a Moron of You"...$6–12

ROCK MANIA (Liberty Communications, Inc.)

1985

Spring #1 Giant Billy Idol poster magazine, opens to become a 22″ × 32″ color wall poster, all about his music, his life story..$3–6

ROCK MARKETPLACE

All issues...$2–4

ROCK 'N' ROLL CD SPECTACULAR (Digital Audio Special)

1988

#1 The Bangles are Back: Back With a Brand New Beat, Supertramp: The Transition of a Super Group, Alice Cooper: Still Outrageous After All These Years, Squeeze: Better the Second Time Around, John Mayall: The Master Bluesman Takes Center Stage, Ian Mathews...$2–4

ROCK 'N' ROLL SPECIAL

1978

Winter #1 Rock Party Issue, Keith Moon is Dead: A Special Farewell Issue With Mick Jagger, Kiss Gives the Eulogy, Peter Frampton Laughs, Led Zeppelin $5–10

1979

Spring #2 Kiss Takes Off Their Make-up, Gene Simmons interview, Meat Loaf in Motion, Don't Show This Kiss Story to Pops, Billy Joel: The Piano Man, Bruce Springsteen: The Boss is Back, Carly Simon: Devoted to You, Peter Frampton Joins Kiss, Rock Couples...$5–10
Fall #4 Kiss Facelifts, Blondie Has Swagger, Meat Loaf, Elton John.......................$6–12

ROCK 'N' ROLL SPECIAL KISS COLLECTION SERIES

Fall Gene Simmons, Gene's Tongue Tells All, Gene Needs Your Help, The Who: Still Going Strong & Standing Proud $10–20

ROCK 'N' ROLL SPECTACULAR

1988

#1 The Bangles are Back..$2–4

ROCK LOVE, 1979,
Oct. #3

ROCK MANIA,
1979, SPRING

ROCK MANIA,
1979, SUMMER

ROCK MANIA, 1985,
SPRING, #1

*ROCK'N'ROLL CD
SPECTACULAR*, 1988, #1

*ROCK'N'ROLL SPECIAL/
KISS COLLECTION
SERIES*, 1979, FALL

ROCK'N'ROLL SPECIAL,
1979, SPRING

ROCK'N'ROLL SPECIAL,
1979, SUMMER

ROCK ON SPECIAL,
1979, SPRING

ROCK 'N' SOUL ANNUAL
1980
Michael Jackson & Sister Sledge, Peaches & Herb, Earth, Wind & Fire, Village People, Teddy Pendergrass, The Isley Brothers, Donna Summer..$2–4

1986
Summer Prince, New Edition, Vanity, Tina Turner, Morris Day, Rick James, Michael Jackson, Stevie Wonder, Apollonia, Whitney Houston, Cameo, Atlantic Starr, Run DMC, Stephanie Mills, Kool & the Gang..$2–4

ROCK 'N' SOUL AWARDS
1987
Summer Prince, New Edition, Janet Jackson, Michael Jackson, Run DMC, Sheila E., Patti Labelle, Whitney Houston, Diana Ross $2–4

ROCK 'N' SOUL SONGS
1969
Mar. Sly Stone, A Marriage in the 5th Dimension, The Impressions..$3–6

1972
Jan. The Honey Cone, Tina Turner, Labelle, Howlin' Wolf, Isley Brothers, Roberta Flack, Percy Sledge, Donny Hathaway..$3–6

1976
Jan. Labelle, The Spinners, Al Green & Stevie Wonder: Their History, KC & the Sunshine Band, Van McCoy, Jimmy Walker..$2-4

1978
Oct. Brothers Johnson, Party With Stevie Wonder, The Jacksons, The Spinners, Bob Marley's Peace Concert, The O'Jays, Maurice White, Donna Summer..$2–4

1979
Nov. The Commodores Exclusive, Peaches & Herb, Rick James, The Hot Donna Summer, The Village People, Tavares Tour, Labelle, Isley Brothers, Chaka Khan, Earth, Wind & Fire, Michael Jackson, Teddy Pendergrass..$2–4

1981
Mar. Teddy Pendergrass Exclusive Interview, The Jacksons Rule the World, Millie Jackson, The O'Jays, Earth, Wind & Fire, Kid Creole $2–3
Apr. On the Road With the Commodores, Chaka Khan, The Doobie Brothers, Bob Marley, La Toya Jackson, Kool & the Gang, Pointer Sisters..$2–3
July Earth, Wind & Fire, Natalie Cole, Marvin Gaye: Alive & Well, Donna Summer, Sister Sledge, Barry White, Dione Warwick, Shalamar $2–3

1984
May Earth, Wind & Fire: The Impossible Dream, The Jacksons: A Special Conference, Lionel Richie, Cameo, Rick James, Musical Youth, My Private Thoughts by DeBarge, Pointer sisters, Melba Moore $2–3
June Lionel Richie: All the Right Moves, Prince on the Set, Jeffrey Osbourne, Zapp vs. Rick James, The Time, Eyewitness Exclusive: Michael Jackson's Tragic Accident, George Clinton, Diana Ross, The New Edition, Kool & the Gang, Stevie Wonder, Labelle ...$2–3
Aug. The Michael Jackson Death Threats, DeBarge, The Jackson's Tour Preparations, Prince Photo Gallery, Jermaine Jackson..$2–3
Dec. Michael Jackson & the Jacksons' Greatest Tour, The Who's Who in Purple Rain, Prince, Lionel Ritchie, Jermaine Jackson, Stevie Wonder, DeBarge Photo Gallery, Janet Jackson, Eddy Grant, Run DMC, Nona Hendryx $2–3

1985
Oct. Prince Vs. Michael Jackson: The Clash of the Titans, Stevie Wonder, New Edition, Mary Jane Girls, Tribute to the Apollo Theatre, Whitney Houston, Grace Jones, Atlantic Starr, Freddie Jackson..$2–3

1986

Apr. Prince: Space Cadet or Real Man?, Ray Parker Jr., Lionel Richie, Gregory Hines, On Location With El Debarge, Sade, The Jets...$2–4
Aug. Prince: Everything You Ever Wanted to Know, Vanity, Sheila E., Morris Day, Andre Cymore, Jesse Johnson, Apollonia, Cherrelle...$2–4
Oct. El DeBarge: A New Life, Prince: Inside the Mystery Man, Richard Pryor, New Edition, Michael Jackson: Adventure in New York, Pattie Labelle Photo Gallery, Whitney Houston, Grandmaster Flash, Anita Baker...$2–3

1987

Feb. Tina Turner, Chaka Khan, Sheila E.: Sexy Sensation, Whodini, Janet Jackson, Prince, El DeBarge, Jermaine Jackson, Kool & the Gang...$2–3
Oct. Run DMC & The Beastie Boys, Whitney Houston Photo Gallery, Prince, Jody Whatley, The Fat Boys, The Jets, Lisa Bonet, Jesse Johnson $2–3

ROCK 'N' SOUL YEARBOOK

1979

Fall Issue includes exclusive pin-ups of Donna Summer, Michael Jackson, Peaches & Herb, The Sylvers, Ashford & Simpson, Sister Sledge, Rick James.......................................$2–4

1984

Winter The Jacksons on the Road, Stevie Wonder, Michael Jackson: A Weekend Encounter, Prince: Mystery in Minneapolis, Lionel Richie, Diana Ross, DeBarge, Kool & the Gang, Irene Cara, Janet Jackson...$2–4

ROCK ON

All issues...$2–4

ROCK ON SPECIAL

1979

Spring Kiss, Paul Stanley Exposed, Bruce Springsteen, Can Kiss Lick Back?, Who is Kiss?: The Inside Story...$10–20

ROCK ON SPECIAL PRESENTS FRAMPTON (PETER) DEAD: THE GREAT HOAX MAGAZINE

1978

Fall The Secrets of His Long Hospital Stay, Why He is Alive.................................$2–4

ROCK POSTER MAGAZINE (Each issue contains 12 giant color wall posters)

1984

Vol. 5 The Cars, The Thompson Twins, Boy George, Judas Priest, Nena, Wham, Madness, Footloose's Kevin Bacon, Missing Persons, Huey Lewis, Parc & Lane, Thomas Dolby ...$4–8
Vol. 6 Bruce Springsteen, Prince, Bon Jovi, Quiet Riot, The Jacksons, INXS, Twisted Sister, Bananarama, Depeche Mode, Corey Hart...$4–8

1987

Vol. 8 Issue contains 10 giant wall posters of Bruce Springsteen, Billy Idol, Europe, Psychedelic Furs, The Pretenders, The Bangles, The Beastie Boys, Til' Tuesday, Joan Jett, Huey Lewis $3–6
Vol. 10 Issue contains 10 giant wall posters of Dokken, Joey Tempest, Motley Crue, Helloween, Cinderella, David Coverdale, Redd Kross, Poison, Jon Bon Jovi & Metal Church...$3–6

1988

Vol. 11 Issue contains 10 giant wall posters of Whitesnake, AC/DC, MSG, Metallica, Megadeth, Motley Crue, Kiss, Great White, Bon Jovi & Lita Ford.................................$3–6

ROCK POSTER MAGAZINE PRESENTS MENUDO POSTER MAGAZINE

1984

Issue contains 10 super color pull-out wall posters, stories, photos & the complete Menudo history $2–4

ROCK SCENE (Four Seasons Publishing)

1973

Mar. #1 A Visit With David Bowie, Alice Cooper: Never Ordinary, Rod Stewart: Three Years On, Van Morrison, Mark Bolin, Slade, The Dolls, Sha Na Na, Lindisfarne, Blues Magoos, The Remains $15–30
May #2 Ray Davis in America, Roxy Music & the New Rock, Alice Cooper in Paris, Todd Rundgren, Bette Midler, Uriah Heep, Arthur Lee, Rick Nelson, James Taylor, Wolfman Jack, Bob Dylan...$10–20
July #4 Slade: One by One, David Bowie: His First Movie, Alice Cooper: Object d'Art, Iggy Pop's Raw Power, John Lennon's Last Stand, Jimmy Page: Golden Zeppelin, Beach Boys, Sidewinders, Focus, Argent, Al Green, Flo & Eddie, Genesis Chronicles, Dolls $10–20

1974

Aug. #8 David Bowie: His Many Faces, Led Zeppelin, Rick Derringer at Home, Suzi Quatro: The Third Rock Rises, Silverhead, Sweet vs. Mud, Alex Harvey Band, Alice Cooper Making a Movie, Maggie Bell, Eno, David Essex...$7–15
Oct. #9 Mick Jagger, The Rolling Stones: Ladies & Gents, Blue Oyster Cult: Evil Rock, Television, Dolls, Bad Co., Led Zeppelin...$7–15

1975

Jan. #10 Roxy Music Run Down, Elton John & Kiki Dee, Grand Funk, Brownsville Station, Suzi Quatro Speaks, Eric Clapton is Back, David Bowie on Tour, Street Rock in New York, David & Cyrinda...$7–15
Mar. #11 Lou Reed: Pretty in New York, Todd Rundgren & Utopia, Marc Bolan: Past, Present & Future, Bad Co., Eno, Led Zeppelin, Mick Jagger & John Lennon, Kiss, Mick Ronson interview...$7–15
May #12 Peter Gabriel: What's He Doing?, Elton John, Kiki Dee & the Music, Queen, Sailor David Bowie in New York, Alice Cooper: Memory Lane, Ringo, Pretty Things Back to Stay...$7–15
July Elton John in *Tommy*, Queen: Inside Scoop, Rick Derringer in the Studio, Roxy Music American Tour, Led Zeppelin Special Section, Blondie Debbie Harry: Our New Sweetheart, Alice Cooper is Back, Patti Smith $5–10
Sept. Kiss: Good or Bad, Elton John: High Stepping With Labelle, Queen, Aerosmith, Robert Plant, Angela Bowie at Eton, Alice Cooper on Tour, Suzi Quatro at Home, The Jackson Five, Bay City Rollers, Wayne County, Ray Davies, Joe Walsh, John Cale.............$7–15
Nov. Aerosmith: Wonder Boys of Rock, Stones' American Tour Diary With 30 Pictures, Boogie With Elton John, David Bowie's Movie, Pattie Smith's Pics, Kiss, Backstage, Todd Rundgren, The Bee Gees, Alice Cooper: What a Party, John Cale, The Tubes........$7–15

1976

Jan. Mick Jagger's Secret Desires, Roger Daltry Deals With Fame, Patti Smith Rehearsal Pics, Stones' Private Tour Scrapbook Exclusive, Eric Clapton, Alice Cooper Cleaning Up New York, Kiss: Their First Big Year, Television, David Bowie on the Set Photo Exclusive, Paul & Linda McCartney, Dolls, issue includes Kiss rock sketch super centerfold poster $10–20
Mar. David Bowie: Bowie Mania, Kiss: Rock-&-Roll Firemen, Labelle on the Town, Elton John: Celluloid Hero, Roxy Music, Patti Smith on 48th St., Television, Debbie Harry: Blondie Rockin', Aerosmith, David Essex $9–18

May Patti Smith: Lioness of Rock, Aerosmith: Dream On, Patti Smith at the Bottom Line Exclusive, Kiss: 10 Super Photos, Led Zeppelin on Film, Bob Marley: Trenchtown Rockers, Bryan Ferry, Keith Moon, Tubes, New York Dolls...$6–12

July Kiss Goes Hollywood, The Private David Bowie Party, Queen in New York, Peter Gabriel, Robert Plant, Patti Smith Group, Lou Reed at Home, Pretty Things, The Spinners, Blondie, Ramones, Ted Nugent $7–15

Sept. Keith Richards, The Kiss Years, Bad Co., Patti Smith on "Saturday Night Live," David Bowie, The Dolls in New Orleans, Queen Party With Lynyrd Skynyrd, Alice Cooper, The Who, Peter Frampton, Rick Derringer, Feelgoods...$5–10

Nov. The Rolling Stones Tour Europe, Kiss' New Show, Peter Frampton, Aerosmith, Wings, David Bowie, Patti Smith in Paris, Jimmy Page & Bad Co., The Jam, MC5, The Dolls, Elton John, Pete Townshend Throws a Party...$5–10

1977

Jan. Robert Plant, The Led Zeppelin Movie, Elton John Backstage, Patti Smith's Diary, Aerosmith Special, Los Angeles Party With Kiss, The Ramones on the Coast, John Cale & Lou Reed, Fleetwood Mac, The Bay City Rollers...$4–8

Mar. The Ramones, Led Zeppelin Super Premiere, Aerosmith in London, Patti Smith in Amsterdam, David Bowie, Kiss: One at a Time, Starz, Lynyrd Skynyrd, Mick Jagger, Sex Pistols, Dwight Twilley..$3–6

May Ted Nugent, Gene Simmons, Lou Reed, Television, The Ramones, The Fast, Bee Gees, Aerosmith, George Harrison, Lynyrd Skynyrd, Angel $3–6

June Bryan Ferry, Aerosmith in New York, Kiss Backstage, Patti Smith, John Cale, Blondie, Cramps, The Sonics, Bay City Rollers, John Lennon...............................$3–6

July Iggy Pop, Kiss Scrapbook, Angel in Japan, Queen in New York, Aerosmith, Bryan Ferry, Genesis, Blondie, The Cramps, The Ramones, Bruce Springsteen, Patti Smith........$4–8

Sept. Television, Kiss in Japan, Led Zeppelin Tour, Angel in New York, Joe Perry, Sex Pistols, Boston, Brats, Patti Smith, The Damned, Sammy Hagar $4–8

Oct. Joe Perry, The Bay City Rollers Tour, Kiss Comic, The Ramones, Dolly Parton, Talking Heads, Angel, Deadboys, Brats, Bee Gees $3–6

Dec. Johnny Rotten, Dictators, Led Zeppelin, Kiss, Lou Reed, Television, Foreigner, Fleetwood Mac, Bob Marley, Bryan Ferry, Patti Smith $4–8

1978

Feb. Keith Richards, Elton John, Elvis Presley Tribute, Peter Frampton, Bob Marley, Aerosmith, The Rolling Stones, The Beach Boys, Steve Miller, Bryan Ferry, British Punk, Patti Smith, David Johansen $3–6

Mar. The Ramones, Elton John, Rod Stewart, Paul McCartney, Lynyrd Skynyrd Tribute, Rolling Stones, Pattie Smith, Aerosmith, Roger Daltry, Blondie....................................$3–6

May Queen: Claiming Rock's Crown, Patti Smith Poetry, Blondie in Europe, Kiss at the Garden, Dead Boys, Dictators, Doc Rock, David Bowie, Sex Pistols, The Stranglers, Steve Miller, Robert Gordon, Mick Fleetwood..$4–8

June Patti Smith Group, The Ramones, Kiss Imitation, John Travolta, Elvis Costello, David Johansen, The Jam, Paul Simon, Sex Pistols, Debbie Harry/Blondie $3–6

July David Johansen, Kiss, Angel on the Road, Abba, Leo Sayer, Lou Reed, Jefferson Starship, David Bowie, Sgt. Pepper Film, Meet Van Halen..$3–6

Sept. Kiss in Japan, Fleetwood Mac, Wings at Work, Suicide, Ron Wood, The Ramones Rock, Bobby Marley's Island, David Johansen, Patti Smith in Europe, The Band, David Bowie in New York, Blondie in London..$10–20

Oct. Bruce Springsteen, The Rolling Stones, Elvis Costello, Ted Nugent, David Bowie, Linda Ronstadt, Kraftwerk, ELO, Blondie, The Ramones, Leif Garrett, David Johansen, $30,000,000 Kiss...$7–15

Dec. The Four Faces of Kiss, Bob Seger, The Stones Blast Back, Steely Dan, Alice Cooper, Foreigner, Starship, Jimi Hendrix, Peter Frampton, Elton John...................................$7–15

1979

Feb. Queen, Todd Rundgren, Meat Loaf, Bruce Springsteen, Ace Frehley Speaks, Rolling Stones, Bee Gees, Ramones, Keith Moon, Joe Cocker, Genesis...............................$4–8

Mar. Meat Loaf, Linda Ronstadt, Abba, Bruce Springsteen, Phoebe Snow, Blondie Session, Hall & Oates interview, Gene Simmons, Suicide, Billy Joel, Boston, Peter Frampton, Patti Smith, David Bowie $4–8
May Aerosmith, Stonebolt interview, Ace Frehley Stays, The Bee Gees: Then & Now, Kiss History, The New Starz, Queen, Bruce Springsteen, Donna Summer, Elvis Costello, J. Geils, The Eagles $7–15
July Steven Tyler/Aerosmith, The Rolling Stones, Ace Frehley Looks Back, Peter Criss: Beatle Lover, Kiss World Tour, Aerosmith: Year by Year, Clash: The Complete Story, Foreigner, Rod Stewart, The Doobie Brothers $7–15
Sept. Debbie Harry/Blondie, Aerosmith: Their Story Part II, Boston, The Ramones: Rock 'n' Roll High School, The Clash, David Bowie, Mick Jagger.
Nov. The Clash U.S. Tour, Alice Cooper's New Success, The Pretenders, Public Image, Squeeze, Cheap Trick in Action, Boomtown Rats, Peter Criss Leaves Kiss.................$4–8

1980
Jan. Kiss: Super Nova, Aerosmith: The Joe Perry Story Part I, David Bowie: Check-out Time, Peter Frampton, Pete Townshend: Sort of Solo, Alice Cooper: Comics Hero, Debbie Harry: One Way or Another, Doobie Brothers, Southside Johnny, James Taylor, B-52's, Ramones, Clash, Cheap Trick, Devo $6–12
Mar. Queen, Fleetwood Mac, Cheap Trick, Meat Loaf Backstage, Johansen Tour, The Cars, Abba, Talking Heads, The Clash, Blondie Dreams, The Doobie Brothers, The Bee Gees in Depth, Foreigner, The Who Making Movies $4–8
May Led Zeppelin, Fleetwood Mac's Party, Doobie Brothers, Aerosmith: Rut Rockers, Carly Simon, Suzi Quatro Backstage, James Taylor, Foreigner, Bobby Marley, The Police, Iggy Pops Out $4–8
July Meet Dr. Hook, Blondie: Erotour, Damned, Clash, Rick Derringer, Joe Perry, Patti Smith, Tom Petty, Kraftwerk, Ramones, Abba..$4–8
Sept. Chrissie Hynde of the Pretenders, Clash in Concert, Ted Nugent: Is He Sexy?, On Tour With the Boomtown Rats, Kiss: The Boys in Black are Back, The Police, Billy Joel, Slits, Iggy Pop...$4–8

1981
Jan. The Rolling Stones: Going for a Walk, Paul Stanley Talks About Kiss' Peter Criss, Blue Oyster Cult: Ten Years Later, The Ramones World Tour, Public Image, The Clash, The New Kiss, David Bowie, Queen, Ted Nugent/Peter Gabriel, Cheap Trick, Dave Davies, X, Boomtown Rats, Pat Benatar...$4–8
Mar. Talking Heads, John Lennon's Last Photos, Ted Nugent interview, Peter Criss Without Kiss, The Cars' Rick Ocasek, Broadway Bowie, The Pretenders, Bo Diddley, Patti Smith in Detroit, B-52's, Cheap Trick Replacement, Pat Benatar Loves $3–6
May The Rolling Stones Photo Session, John Lennon Memories, Kiss Down Under, Led Zeppelin, The Police, Fleetwood Mac: Their Way, David Bowie, The Blondie Movie, Jan & Dean Still Goin', Iggy Pop, The Doobie Brothers, Peter Criss $3–6

1982
Jan. Debbie Harry, The Eagles: A Rock History, Remembering a Decade of Rock Heroes, Clash Mania, REO Speedwagon, Genesis of Phil Collins, Yoko Ono in New York, The B-52's, Iggy Pop, The Police..$3–6

ROCK SCENE (Tempo Publishing)
1985
Jan. Vince Neil/Motley Crue, Prince's Purple Rain, Quiet Riot, Duran Duran, Ratt interview, Van Halen, Boy George, The Pretenders, The Scorpions, Accept, Bon Jovi, Great White, Alice Cooper, with three color posters $6–12
Mar. Twisted Sister Exclusive Interview, Kiss, Women in Rock: Cyndi Lauper, Girl School, Madonna, The Go-go's, Siouxsie, Annie Lennox, Lita Ford, Joan Jett, Terri Nunn, Bruce Springsteen, AC/DC, David Bowie, Remembering Grace Slick & Jefferson Starship, Duran Duran, posters $4–8

1986
Apr. Nikki Sixx, The Sacred Heart of Dio Exclusive Interview, Gene Simmons interview, The Scorpions, Aerosmith, Marillion, Ratt, posters $3–6

Sept. Vince Neil, Gene Simmons interview, Bruce Kulick of Kiss, Lita Ford, Eddie Van Halen, Autograph, Dio, WASP, Dokken, King Kobra $2–4
Oct. Aerosmith: A Mirror on the Past, Black Sabbath & Deep Purple Reunite, Ratt, Kulick on His Own Kiss-history, Ozzy Osbourne, three wall posters...................................$3–6
Nov. Turbo, Ted Nugent Speaks, Raven, Aerosmith, Fiona, The Firm, Metallica, Queensryche, Judas Priest, posters $2–4
Dec. In the Studio With Bon Jovi, Peter Criss After Kiss, Robert Palmer, Marillion, Van Halen Takes the Heat, Gene Simmons & Ozzy Osbourne..$3–6

1987

Jan. David Lee Roth's Hired Guns interview: Vai & Sheehan, Dio, Alice Cooper is Back With a Vengeance, Yngwie, UFO, Alvin Lee, In the Studio With Gene Simmons, Husker Du, The Steady Rise of Dokken $2–4
Feb. In the Studio with Ratt, Billy Squier, Bruce Dickinson/Iron Maiden, Metallica's James Hetfield, Nikki Sixx, Stryper, Hanoi Rocks, Poison..$2–4
Mar. The Scorpions, Blackie Lawless, Kiss, Megadeth, Saxon, Motorhead, The Ramones, Queenscryche, Spitz, Black Sabbath, Metallica...$2–4
Apr. Dio, Paul Stanley Checks the Charts, Raven, King Kobra, Zebra, Q5, Precious Metal, Triumph, Slayer, Blue Oyster Cult: Inventors of Metal $2–4
May Metallica's Final Burton Interview, Alice Cooper Demands Criminal Justice, Krokus, Iron Maiden, Yngwie, Great White, Joan Jett, Cinderella...$2–4
Aug. The Pet Shop Boys, Ray Davies: King of Kinks, Beastie Boys, Bruce Dickinson: The Man Behind Iron Maiden, REO Speedwagon, Ozzy Osbourne, Dio, Bon Jovi, Eddie Van Halen, Gene Simmons $2–4
Oct. Ratt: Stephen Pearcy on Wine, Women & Rock, Motley Crue, Huey Lewis, Dokken, Glass Tiger, The Cinderella Story, Stryper, Foreigner $2–4
Nov. Motley Crue, Europe Invades America, The Woman Behind Poison, Kim Wilde, Night Ranger, Thompson Twins, The New King Kobra $2–4
Dec. Kiss: Bigger, Badder & Better, The New Improved Quiet Riot, The Cult, Dokken, Deep Purple Rocks On, Run DMC, Bangles, Duran, Europe, Bitch $2–4

1988

Feb. Partying With Poison, Remembering the Great Randy Rhoads, Alice Cooper: The Shock Master Returns, Def Leppard, Peter Criss Blows the Lid Off Kiss, ABC $2–4
Apr. Def Leppard: The Greatest Rock Band Ever, Bon Jovi, Motley Crue, Kiss, L.A. Guns, Twisted Sister, TNT, Guns 'n' Roses, Rush, Ratt, Faster Pussycat.................................$2–4
May Cinderella, Motley Crue's Tommy Lee, Whitesnake, Faster Pussycat, Kiss, Jetboy, Bon Jovi, Def Leppard, Ace Frehley, Savatage, Dokken $2–4

1989

Apr. Guns 'n' Roses, Bon Jovi Exclusive, Motley Crue, Stryper, Cinderella, Accept, Kiss, Kirk Hammett/Metallica, Iron Maiden, Dokken, Def Leppard.......................................$2–4
June Cinderella Exclusive, Winger, Skid Row, A Visit to Kiss World, Ratt, Guns 'n' Roses, Poison, Warrent, Def Leppard, Life & Loves of Bon Jovi...$2–4
Dec. White Lion Exclusive, Warrent, Danger Danger, Guns 'n' Roses Exclusive, Motley Crue, Bon Jovi's Richie Sambora, Britny Fox, Joe Elliot...$2–4

1990

Jan. Vain, Def Leppard, Mr. Big, Princess Pang, Steve Stevens, Bullet Boys, Skid Row, Tora Tora, Great White, Guns 'n' Roses, Heavy Metal Hunks.................................$2–4
All other issues $2–3

ROCK SCENE: BEST OF (Four Season Publishing)
1978

#1 Kiss: Rock-&-Roll All Night & Party Everyday, Aerosmith: Hard Rocks, Queen, Rolling Stones, Led Zeppelin, issue contains Kiss posters of Gene Simmons/Dragon & Kiss: The Boys Now & the Boys Then, Mick Jagger, Patti Smith, Joe Perry, Ramones, Blue Oyster Cult, Dolls, Blondie, Iggy Pop, David Bowie...$7–15

ROCK SCENE: BEST OF (Tempo)

1987

#1 Jon Bon Jovi Before Making It, The Evolution of Ratt & Roll, Tommy Lee on the Good Old Days, Gene Simmons on Fans, Ozzy Osbourne, Black 'n' Blue, King Kobra, Fiona, Eric Carr Comes Out, Heart: Anne Wilson Explains $4–8
#2 The Many Faces of Gene Simmons, Metallica & the Future of Rock, W.A.S.P., Queensryche, Judas Priest, Aerosmith, Ted Nugent, Dio, Ozzy Osbourne, Keel..........$3–5

1988

#3 Van Halen: Surviving the Gripes of Roth, Glass Tiger, Dio, Alice Cooper, Iron Maiden, Anthrax, Bon Jovi, Poison, Robert Palmer...$2–4
#4 Kiss: Second Generation Tells All, Cinderella, Scorpions, Motley Crue, Metallica's Last Days in the Garage, Triumph, Raven, Poison, Iron Maiden, Metal Church, Alice Cooper's Kane Roberts, Slayer $2–4

1989

#6 Bret Michaels, Guns 'n' Roses interview, Kip Winger Lets His Hair Down, Metallica, White Lion, Gene Simmon's 1001 Facts, Bon Jovi, Jetboy, Stryper, Kix, Ratt, L.A. Guns, Def Leppard, Cinderella $2–4

ROCK SCENE PRESENTS BRUCE SPRINGSTEEN

1984

Special Collector's Edition—The Life & Times of an American Dreamer, Tours, full-color poster portrait $3–6

ROCK SCENE PRESENTS CONCERT SHOTS

1985

#3 Backstage With Paul Stanley, Conversations With Ratt, Van Halen, Ronnie James, Dio, Krokus, The World According to Motley Crue, Inside Bruce Dickinson, The Firm, issue includes four color wall posters of Kiss, Ratt, Motley Crue & Van Halen, Judas Priest, Iron Maiden, W.A.S.P., AC/DC...$3–6

1986

#5 Backstage With Twisted Sister, Van Halen & Kiss, Exclusive AC/DC Interview, The Old & the New Days of Van Halen, Triumph, ZZ Top..$2–4
#6 Exclusive Interviews With Twisted Sister, Bon Jovi & Night Ranger, Kiss, Dokken, Scorpions, Black 'n' Blue, W.A.S.P., King Kobra, Cheap Trick, Battalion, Giuffria, issue includes four color wall posters...$3–6
#7 Vince Neil, Paul Stanley, Aerosmith, Van Halen, AC/DC, Bon Jovi, Ozzy Osbourne, Night Ranger, Jimmy Page, Twisted Sister, Dokken, Iron Maiden $2–4
#8 Ozzy Osbourne, Van Halen Exclusive, The Personal Side of Eric Carr, Stryper, ZZ Top, Motley Crue, Accept, Metallica, Ted Nugent, Kiss, W.A.S.P., Judas Priest, Tuff Luck, Black Sabbath, Iron Maiden, Ratt, issue includes three color wall posters............................$3–6

1987

#9 Issue includes 2′ × 3′ posters of Kiss & Motley Crue, Van Halen, Stryper, Judas Priest, Krokus, Quiet Riot, Bon Jovi, Keel, Helix, Ozzy Osbourne, King Kobra....................$3–6
#10 Issue includes two giant posters of Ratt & Ozzy Osbourne, Paul Stanley, Dokken, Keel, Pat Benatar, The Moody Blues, Glass Tiger, Raven, Julian Lennon, GTR.................$2–4
#11 Issue includes two life-size posters of Bon Jovi & Nikki Sixx, Poison, Ratt, The Fixx, Queensryche, Triumph, Quiet Riot, ZZ Top, Guns 'n' Roses, Eddie Van Halen $2–4
Sept. Issue includes two posters of Dee Snider & Lita Ford, Vinnie Vincent, On the Road With Poison, Queensryche: Behind the Heavy Metal Image, A Day in the Life of Megadeth, Kiss, London, Accept, Hurricane, Sammy Hagar..$2–4
Nov. Issue includes two posters of Steven Tyler & ZZ Top, Alice Cooper: The Nightmare Returns, Megadeth, On the Road With Stryper, Behind the Scenes With the Beastie Boys, Tesla, On Stage With Bruce Hornsby, Run DMC, Ratt, W.A.S.P., Triumph.................$2–4

1988

Jan. Issue includes two posters of Europe & Bret Michaels, Aerosmith Rocks On, On the Road With Boston, Santana: Behind the Iron Curtain, Billy Idol's Whiplash Tour, Motley Crue on Tour, Heart, Loudness..............$2–4
Mar. Issue includes two posters of Loudness & David Coverdale, On the Road With Ace Frehley's Comet, Whitesnake, Mark Slaughter, Bon Jovi, Dio, Madonna's Troubled Tour, Hurricane, Mick Jagger, A-ha, REO, Europe, Overkill, Prince $2–4

1989

Jan. Issue includes two posters of Metallica & Megadeth, White Lion's Mike Tramp, Poison, Guns 'n' Roses, Ratt, Europe, Def Leppard's Wicked Dreams, Georgia Satellites, Monsters of Rock Exclusive Pull-out Section, Kiss, L.A. Guns, Helix $2–5
Nov. Issue includes two posters of Bon Jovi & Winger, The Truth Behind Bon Jovi, Roxx Gang, Great White, Banshee, Cinderella's Tom Keifer, The Cult, Vixen, Kiss, Bad Company, Ratt, Def Leppard Mouths Off, Tesla, Guns 'n' Roses, Sea Hags..............$2–4

1990

Jan. Issue includes two posters of Poison & White Lion, Skid Row, Aerosmith's Steven Tyler, Bon Jovi, Rachel Bolan, Tommy Lee, King's X, Kiss, Bullet Boys, Tesla, Alice Cooper, Def Leppard, Cinderella, Queensryche..............$2–3

ROCK SCENE PRESENTS CONCERT SHOTS: BEST OF

1987

#1 Motley Crue, AC/DC, Ratt, Judas Priest, Van Halen, Kiss, Lita Ford, Dio, ZZ Top, Metallica, Guiffria, David Lee Roth, Bon Jovi, Iron Maiden..............$3–5

1988

#2 Eddie Van Halen, Exclusive: The Van Halens & the MC Roths, Ratt on Tour: The Naked Truth, Bon Jovi, Dokken, Ozzy Osbourne on Stage, Styper, Krokus $2–4
#3 On the Road With Poison, Touring With Guns 'n' Roses, Whitesnake, Vinnie Vincent Invades, Faster Pussycat, Megadeth, Sammy Hagar..............$2–4

ROCK SCENE PRESENTS PRINCE

1984

Special Collector's Edition—issue includes rare photos, The Complete Prince, Purple Rain, The Capri to Hollywood, Vanity, Apollonia & Sheila E., posters & pin-ups $3–6

ROCK SCENE'S METAL MANIA

1987

Apr. #9 Paul Stanley, Metallica: Before the Fall, Slayer, Great White, Celtic Frost, Exodus, Keel: Speeding With Farrari, Megadeth, Iron Maiden..............$2–4
May #10 Metallica: From Tragedy to Triumph, Metal Church, Lizzy Borden, Motorhead, Kreator, Fastway, GBH, Fates Warning $2–4
June #11 Paul Stanley: Kiss Exposed, Black Sabbath, The Other Megadeth, Manowar, Warlock, Malice, Armored Saint, Van Halen, Iron Maiden, Judas Priest..............$2–4
Aug. #12 Billy Sheehan: Covering the Bases for David Lee Roth, Saga of the Saxons, Yngwie Malmsteen, The Bizarre World of King Diamond, The Return of the Rods, Uncensored quotes of the Year, Slayer, At War, Judas Priest..............$2–4
Oct. #13 Possessed: The Eyes of Horror are Upon You, Saxon, Helix: Back to Basics, Voivod, Whitesnakes Returns, Malice, Waysted, Slayer..............$2–4
Dec. #14 Slayer: Headed for Hell, Motorhead, Wendy O'Williams, Helix, Maggots & the Plasmatics, Anthrax, Nuclear Assault, Abattoir, Mentor, Loudness..............$2–4

1988

Feb. Metal Church, King Diamond, W.A.S.P. Fights Back, Grim Reaper, Judas Priest, D.R.I., Blackie Lawless, The Florida Metal Scene..............$2–4
Apr. David Wayne Rips the Doors Off Metal Church, The Scorpions Bite Back, Anthrax, Metallica, Megadeth, Motorhead, Chastain, Frehley $2–4

July Metallica & Megadeth: The Feud is Over, Doro Pesch: Sex Kitten or Serious Musician?, Accept Exclusive Interview, Exodus, Anthrax, Savatage, Whiplash, Shok Paris, DOA, Heathen, Helloween's Ways $2–4

1989

Mar. Helloween in Hamburg, Accept: Worldwide Exclusive, Anthrax, Kiss, Slayer, Testament, Iron Maiden, David Lee Roth, Destruction..$2–4
May Ozzy Osbourne, Metallica, Megadeth, Exodus in California, Anthrax, The Crumbsuckers, Danzig, Slayer, Violence, Testament, Motorhead...$2–3
Sept. Guns 'n' Roses, Metallica Meets Middle America, Powermad, Anthrax, Kreator, Annihilator, Onslaught, Mod, King Diamond, Overkill...$2–3
Nov. Doro Pesch, James Hetfield, Tom Araya, Testament, Warlock, Slayer, Metallica, Waysted Youth, Crimson Glory, Black Sabbath, Anthrax $2–4

1990

Jan. Testament, King Diamond Exodus, Skid Row poster, Metallica, Death Angel, Cromags, Metal Church, White Zombie, Trust, Shok Paris..$2–4

ROCK SCENE'S METAL MANIA: BEST OF
1987

#2 The Best Kiss Yet, Motorhead, New Life for Megadeth, Metallica: Antirock Heroes, Yngwie Malmsteen, Accept, Saxon, Ozzy Osbourne, Motley Crue $2–4

1988

#3 Accept: Heavy German Artillery, Motorhead, Lizzy Borden, Iron Maiden, Queensryche, Aerosmith, Keel, Loudness, Slayer, Death Angel, Metallica, Voivod, Great White, Metal Church, Kreator, Celtic Frost...$2–4

1990

#5 Exclusive Interviews With Megadeth, Metallica, Ozzy Osbourne, Judas Priest, Scorpions, Snowhite, Guns 'n' Roses, Testament, Ace Frehley's Comet, Doro Pesch, Helloween, Kingdom Come, Seduce $2–4

ROCK SCENE SPOTLIGHTS
1987

#2 Kiss Exposed: Special All-Kiss Issue, The Official Kiss Magazine, Paul Stanley Talks, Exclusive Interview With Gene Simmons, Kiss Through the Years, Kisstory, A Conversation With Gene Simmons, issue includes two life-size color wall posters $5–10

1988

#3 Rock of the 80s, issue includes two life-size full-color wall posters of Jon Bon Jovi & Bret Michaels, Behind the Scenes With Bon Jovi, Megadeth, Stryper, Poison, Special Intimate Interview Issue...$3–6
#4 Special Rock Hunks, Including Two Juicy Life-size Posters, Poison, Motley Crue, Hurricane, Ratt, Jon Bon Jovi: Steamy Centerfold, Roxanne, Jetboy, Europe, Tuff...........$3–6

ROCK '79
1979

Apr. Kiss Exclusive, Heart: Straight from the Heart—An Intimate Conversation With the Wilson Sisters, What's Next for the Who, Cheap Trick Have Arrived, Lookin' Back With the Rolling Stones, The Future of the Stones, Van Morrison, On the Road With Aerosmith, Elton John Speaks, Devo, Boston, John Oates, Queen, Jethro Tull, Olivia Newton-John, Yes, The Blend, Peter Frampton, Osbourne...$5–10
Summer Meat Loaf Challenges Muhammed Ali, Chicago: Can They Survive Without Terry Kath?, Running on Empty With Jackson Browne, 10CC Splits Up, Billy Joel Grows a Beard, Willie Nelson, Sea Level, Bob Dylan: The Last Angry Man Returns, Peter Frampton & the Angel of Death, Dr. Hook, Aerosmith, The Bee Gees, Abba, Parliament, Peter Criss is Free $5–10

ROCK'S NOVA/BOWIE

1976

Issue includes 101 startling pics & a special 16-page pin-up section on David Bowie, The Man Who Fell to Earth & Other Bowie Stories..$10–20

ROCK SPECTACULAR (Bright Eye Publications)

1970

Summer David Cassidy, Three Dog Night, Poco, Creedence Clearwater Revival, Tiny Tim, Elton John...$10–20

ROCK SPECTACULAR (National Newstand Publishing)

1978

#1 Jimmy Page: A Curse on Led Zeppelin, Linda Ronstadt, Starz, Peter Frampton, Kiss: Destroys All Imitators, Aerosmith: Walks This Way, Rod Stewart, Robert Plant.....$10–20

1979

#6 Spring Billy Joel vs. Kiss, 1979 Kiss Interview, Kiss vs. Peter Frampton, 25 Reasons to Love Kiss...$7–15
#7 Summer Meat Loaf's Out to Flatten Kiss, Queen, Bob Seger, The Eagles, Rod Stewart's Untold Story as Told by His Enemies, BIlly Joel & His Own Town, David Bowie: All That Glitters is Fool's Gold, Dave Edmunds, Kansas: Live & Well $7–15
#8 Fall Gene Simmons Says Kiss is Better, Cheap Trick Rock it to the Top, A Collection of Rock Star Weirdness, Aerosmith: Alive & Kicking, Supertramp's Brilliant Brand of Rock, Rod Stewart: His Latest Stunt, Doobie Brothers Minus Two, Led Zeppelin, Kansas, The Who Survive, Van Halen, Meat Loaf, Suzi Quatro: The Secret Rocker, Boston, Billy Joel $7–15

ROCK STAR PAGEANT

1986

Sept. #9 The All-new Prince, Whitney Houston: Rock's Newest Star, The Madonna Nobody Knows, Wham: Go it Alone $2–4
Nov. #10 Madonna: Has She Lost the Only Man She Ever Loved?, The All-new Prince, Madonna's Latest Look, Her New Movie $2–4

ROCK STAR PARADE

1986

July #8 Wham: Their Music & Their Sex Lives, Prince: What Makes Him So Great, Bryan Adams Swings Big, Madonna & Sean, Rock Fashions...$3–6
Sept. #9 The All-new Madonna: Her New Movie, Her New Boyfriend, Prince: His New Look With Exclusive Photos, Sheila E. & Her Prince Charming, Phil Collins interview: His Personal Life $3–6

ROCK STARS PHOTO MAGAZINE

All issues..$2–4

ROCK SUPERSTARS POSTER MAGAZINE (Each opens to become a 36″ × 22½″ poster)

1975

#1 Elton John: How Reg Dwight Became Elton John Superstar, Elton's Tour, The Sparks are Flying, The Rolling Stones are Back..$3–6
#2 David Bowie: Space Oddity, Musical Rarity & the Man Who Fell to Earth, The Many Faces of David Bowie..$2–4
#3 The Who Story: Talkin' 'Bout Our Generation, The Who Tour 1975, Rod Stewart Sails Away, Peter Frampton: The Three-time Winner...$2–4

ROCK SPECTACULAR,
SUMMER, 1970

ROCK SPECTACULAR,
1978, #1

ROCK SPECTACULAR,
1979, SPRING

ROCK SPECTACULAR,
1979, SUMMER

ROCK SPECTACULAR,
1979, FALL

ROCK STAR PAGEANT,
1986, Sept., #9

ROCK STAR PAGEANT,
1986, Nov., #10

ROCK STAR PARADE,
1986, July, #8

ROCK STAR PARADE,
1986, Sept., #9

ROCK SUPERSTARS,
1975, #1

ROCK SUPERSTARS,
1974, #2

ROCK SUPERSTARS,
1975, #3

ROCK SUPERSTARS,
1975, #4

ROCK SUPERSTARS,
1975, #5

ROCK SUPERSTARS,
1975, #6

ROCK SUPERSTARS,
1975, #7

ROCK SUPERSTARS,
1975, #8

ROCK SUPERSTARS,
1975, #10

#4 Led Zeppelin: The Complete Story, How Led Zeppelin Got Off the Ground, David Essex, Simon & Garfunkel Reunion $3–6
#5 Bruce Springsteen: Is He the Future of Rock?, How the Great American Dream Came True in New Jersey, The Man Behind the Hype, Chuck Berry, Bob Dylan Comes Back With a Bang..$2–4
#6 Bob Dylan: From Minnesota Kid to the Eye of the Hurricane, The Story Behind Desire $2–4
#7 Paul McCartney & Wings, Wings' American Tour 1976, Yesterday & Today: Paul as a Beatle, Wing & Himself, Aerosmith, David Bowie..$2–4
#8 Rod Stewart: His Musical Journey from Street Singing to Atlantic Crossing & A Night on the Town, Kiss, Queen...$2–5
#9 Peter Frampton: The Complete Story, Peter Frampton Talks, Special Rolling Stones Edition, The Rolling Stones: Through the Past Starkly, Stones' American Tour 1975, The Stones Today $3–6
#10 The Rolling Stones Special, American Tour 1975 Style..$3–6

1984

Special Michael Jackson Edition, issue opens to become 2′ × 3′ poster of Michael, also 18 of the best color pictures of Michael..$2–4

ROCK VIDEO
1984

Apr. #1 John Taylor of Duran Duran Feature Story & Giant Wall Poster, Ozzy Osbourne, Boy George Exclusive Interview, David Bowie Nudity, Ramones Violence, Loverboy, Billy Joel, Men at Work, Zebra $3–6
Sept. #5 Boy George & Thomas Dolby color wall posters & scenes from their videos, On the Set With .38 Special, The Alarm, The Beatles' Video Guide, Lisa Robinson, Duran Duran, Scorpions, The Go-go's, Billy Idol, INXS $2–4
Oct. #6 Billy Idol Talks Intimately, interviews with Steve Perry & David Gilmour, wall posters of The Thompson Twins & The Scorpions, The Beatles, The Clash, Spandau Ballet, The Cars, Annie Lennox $2–4
Nov. #7 Duran Duran's Nick Rhodes, Is Michael Jackson the Real Miss America?, Duran Duran Tell-all Book, Satanism & Rock, The Go-go's & Judas Priest giant color wall posters, Quiet Riot, Phil Collins Exclusive, Wendy O'Williams, Twisted Sister, Bananarama $2–5
Dec. #8 Huey Lewis & the News & The Cars giant color wall posters & stories, Ratt & the Cure: Behind the Scenes Exclusive, Paul McCartney Movie Preview, The Eurythmics' Intimate Interview, Billy Squire, Madonna $2–4

ROCK VIDEO PRESENTS DURAN DURAN AND FIVE OTHER GROUPS POSTER MAGAZINE
1984

Issue contains 10 giant color wall posters of Duran Duran, Billy Idol, Queen, Spandau Ballet, The Eurythmics & The Police, complete with feature stories & photos.................$3–6

ROCK VIDEO PRESENTS THE BOY GEORGE POSTER MAGAZINE
1984

Issue contains 10 full-color wall posters (16″ × 22″), stories, pin-ups, facts & photos......$3–6

ROCK VIDEO PRESENTS TM POSTER MAG
1984

Issue includes 12 giant full-color wall posters of Boy George, Michael Jackson, John Stamos, Sting, John Taylor, Ricky Martin, Rob Lowe, Carlo Imerato, Tom Howell, Lance Quest, Zach Galligan $2–4

ROCK VIDEO SUPERSTARS/PRINCE

1984

Dec. The Inside Story With Fantastic Photos...$3–6

ROCK WORLD (Myron Fass Publishers)

1978

Fall Special All Rolling Stones Issue—The Stones' '78 Tour, Mick Jagger's Women, Stones' Discography, their movies, etc. $7–15

1979

Summer Kiss Goes to Hollywood: The Latest on Their Film, Meat Loaf, Billy Joel, Santana, Free Alice Cooper From Himself, Queen: Those Royal Rock Snobs, Fabulous Poodles, Elvis Costello, Steve Miller, The Police Move In, Stones Still Rolling Along, Peter Tosh...$7–15

1984

May #1 Police Exclusive, Andy Summers, Sting, Def Leppard, Stray Cats, Journey, Elvis Costello: Confessions of an Imposter, The Blasters, Zebra, John Cougar Mellencamp, INXS, Loverboy, AC/DC, David Bowie, Robert Plant, Iron Maiden Turns Up the Volume, Joe Perry, Duran Duran..$5–10
Nov. The Year of Van Halen, Ratt: Race to the Top, Wendy O'Williams, The Bruce Springsteen Tour File, Def Leppart, Duran Duran, Joan Jett & Her Misspent Youth, ZZ Top, Billy Idol, Styx, Zappa, The Call, Motley Crue $2–3

1985

Jan. Twisted Sister, Van Halen, Kick Axe, Cyndi Lauper: The Clown Queen of Rock, Quiet Riot, Bruce Springsteen, Scorpions, The Bizarre Legend Called Prince, Ozzy Osbourne, Lita Ford, Kiss $2–3
May Twisted Sister: Hardcore Outcasts, The Kinks, Frankie Goes to Hollywood, Stevie Wonder Exclusive, Hall & Oates: How the Duo Does It, Helping the Ramones, The Second Coming of Tina Turner, Kiss's Gene Simmons & Heavy Metal, Joan Jett...................$2–3

ROCK WORLD HEAVY METAL SPECIAL

1985

#1 Motley Crue, Judas Priest, Van Halen, Scorpions, issue includes four Headbanger color wall posters...$3–6
#2 Ozzy Osbourne, Twisted Sister, Iron maiden, Ratt, issue includes four giant Metal Monster color wall posters $3–6

ROLLING STONE MAGAZINE

1967

#1 John Lennon: "How I Won the War," The Grateful Dead: A Photographic Look, Donovan interview $150–300
#1 Reprint issue $5–15
#2 Tina Turner cover & feature story, Bob Dylan, Alive in Nashville, Jefferson Airplane, Marty Bolin Talks, Donovan...$100–200
#3 The Beatles: A New Thing for the Magical Mystery Tour, The Byrds: Clark Leaves, Bob Dylan Press Conference, The Youngbloods, Ravi Shankar, The Grateful Dead in London
....$100–200
#4 Jimi Hendrix, Donovan, Otis Redding...$100–200

1968

#5 The Beatles, The Doors' Movie, Al Kooper...$50–100
#6 Janis Joplin, Bob Dylan, The Rolling Stones, The Animals, The Beatles.........$75–150
#7 Jimi Hendrix cover & feature story, "It's Jimi," Jefferson Airplane $90–180
#8 Lou Adler & John Phillips, The New Bob Dylan, Steve Miller, Jimi Hendrix, The

Beatles Magical Mystery Tour, Rolling Stones Take on Traffic, Paul Revere, Mike Bloomfield, Frank Zappa & the Mothers of Invention...$50–100

#9 The Beatles Battle for the Blue Meanies, Eric Clapton Busted, Keith Moon, Zappa, Traffic, Blood, Sweat & Tears, Moby Grape..$50–100

#10 Eric Clapton interview, The New Byrds, Janis Joplin, Cream, Mike Bloomfield....$40–80

#11 Baron Wolfman, The Beatles, Ringo Snubs the Queen, Dylan, Johnny Cash, Simon & Garfunkel $40–80

#12 The Missing Bob Dylan Album: A Special Report, The Mararishi, The Mick Jagger Tour, Peter Tork of the Monkees...$40–80

#13 Tiny Tim, Jerry Lee Lewis, Aretha Franklin, John Lennon..............................$40–80

#14 The Frank Zappa Interview, Cream's Bomb, The Rolling Stone's Studio Fire, The Beatles & Apple Records, Little Richard, Dionne Warwick, Eric Clapton $40–80

#15 Mick Jagger: The Return of the Rolling Stones—A Stones Super Special, Creem $50–100

#16 The Band, Janis Joplin at the Newport Folk Festival, The Byrds, Yoko Ono, Booker T & The MGs...$50–100

#17 Pete Townshend Special Interview, John Lennon: "The Egg Man Wears White," The Doors' Long Island Concert, Eric Burdon, Jerry Garcia at the Newport Folk Festival, Jefferson Airplane..$45–90

#18 Pete Townshend interview Part II, Janis Joplin Leaves Big Brother & Co., The Stones, Country Joe, Smokey Robinson, Byrds, Buffalo Springfield $45–90

#19 Mick Jagger interview, Stones, Steve Miller, Tiny Tim, Sky River Festival, Van Dyke Parks, Booker T & MGs...$45–90

#20 The Beatles Today, Cass Elliot interview, The Doors, Jefferson Airplane in Middle Earth, Sly Stone, Brian Jones Fined in Dope Case, Ray Charles in London, Albert King $45–80

#21 The Beatles, Muddy Waters, Little Richard, Traffic...$45–80

#22 John Lennon & Yoko Ono Nude, Last Days of Cream $75–150

#23 The Beatles U.S.A. Tour, The New Joan Baez, Jimi Hendrix, Felix Paparelli, Dylan $30–60

#24 The Beatles: John Macrobiotics, Yoko Ono on Her Films................................$35–70

1969

#25 MC5, Traffic, Taj Mahal, Janis Joplin & Big Brother.......................................$40–80

#26 Jimi Hendrix: Performer of the Year, Memphis Debut of Janis Joplin............$50–100

#27 The Groupies & Other Girls: Anna, Trixie Merkin, The GTOs, The Plaster Casters, Beatles, Zappa $25–50

#28 Japanese Rock, Zabriskie Point interview, Johnny Winter, Joe Cocker, Two Virgins $25–50

#29 Janis Joplin cover & story: The Judy Garland of Rock, Bob Dylan, Johnny Cash, Trixie Merkin Topless, Melanie, Two Virgins $45–90

#30 American Revolution 1969, Jim Morrison Wanted in Dade County for Simulating Masturbation, Creedence Clearwater Revival, Small Faces, The Mamas & the Papas ...$40–80

#31 Sun Ra, Jim Morrison's Penis is Indecent, Jethro Tull, Cream $40–80

#32 A Last Look at Traffic, Jim Morrison Surrenders to Police, The Fillmore to Close, Early Julian Lennon Photo, Johnny Winter, The Beach Boys $35–70

#33 Joni Mitchell, The Band, Judy Collins, Larry Coryell.......................................$25–50

#34 Jimi Hendrix Busted in Toronto: cover & story, Bob Dylan's Nashville Trip, Johnny Cash in San Quentin, Janis Joplin in London, Delaney & Bonnie, John Lennon & Yoko Ono...$50–100

#35 Chuck Berry, Jean-luc Godard interview, Jefferson Airplane Busted in the South $20–40

#36 Boosting Peace: John & Yoko in Canada, Moby Grape, Mexican President Inks for the Doors, Hank Williams Perspective, Buddy Holly $30–60

#37 Elvis Presley in Hollywood, Pete Townshend on *Tommy*, The Beatles, Blind Faith, Jefferson Airplane Today, Reunion at Winterland $20–40

#38 Jim Morrison interview, Jimi Hendrix..$60–120

#39 Brian Jones: Sympathy for the Devil, Dylan, The Wild Things.......................$60–120

#40 Jerry Garcia: Good Old Grateful Dead, James Taylor, Aretha Franklin $25–50

#41 Joe Cocker at Atlantic City, Jane Fonda, Peter Fonda, B Boys, Kinks.............$20–40

ROLLING STONE, #16

ROLLING STONE, #20

ROLLING STONE, #33

ROLLING STONE, #35

ROLLING STONE, #37

ROLLING STONE, #39

ROLLING STONE, #45

ROLLING STONE, #44

ROLLING STONE, #40

#42 Woodstock, Dylan, Zappa, Jefferson Airplane, The Nazz.............................$20–40
#43 Bob Dylan on the Isle of Wight, Stones U.S.A. Tour, Sky River Festival $20–40
#44 David Crosby Cover, CSN & Young, John & Yoko: Rock-&-Roll Revival, George Harrison on Abbey Road, Zappa & Mothers, Tiny Tim & Miss Vicki, Joni Mithcell ..$20–40
#45 Tina Turner, Johnny Cash, Phil Spector interview $20–40
#46 The Beatles: Inside Apple, The Stones in Los Angeles, Keith Richards...........$20–40
#47 Bob Dylan interview, John Lennon: "Let it Be," Stones, Baez, Byrds.............$20–40
#48 Miles Davis, Robbie Robertson, Mick Jagger & the Stones, Janis Joplin Gets Busted, Joni Mitchell Hangs it Up, The Zombies, Brian Jones $25–50
#49 Mick Jagger cover & story: The Stones' Grand Finale, The Truth About Teen Movies, Neil Young, Curtis Mayfield, The Kinks.............................$20–40
#50 The Rolling Stones cover & story: The Rolling Stones Disaster at Altamont: "Let it Bleed," Jimi Hendrix, The Beatles, Yoko Ono, Leon Russell, James Brown, Laura Nyro $30–60

1970

#51 A Private Talk With John Lennon, Stones, The Who & *Tommy*, Jimi Hendrix $25–50
#52 John Fogarty interview, John Lennon & Yoko, Tiny Tim, Elvis Presley, Rod Stewart $20–40
#53 The Grateful Dead, John Lennon, The Crickets, Ringo.............................$20–40
#54 The Sly Stone Family, The Rolling Stones Circus, Peter Fonda, Little Richard.....$20–40
#55 Abbie Hoffman, Jefferson Airplane, Ringo, Iggy Pop $20–40
#56 The Varnished Truth About John Lennon, Peter Max, Woodstock, Johnny Winter $20–40
#57 Paul McCartney Returns, Neil Young, Stones, Janis Joplin, Lennon $20–40
#58 Capt. Beefheart, Peter Townshend Spills the Beans, Beatles Mystery $20–40
#59 Little Richard, Janis Joplin Back from the Jungle, Bob Dylan, Paul Simon, George Harrison, The Zombies, The Beatles, Elvis Presley.............................$25–50
#60 George Harrison in New York, Otis Spann, Joe Cocker, "Let it Be" $20–40
#61 Charles Manson, Eric Clapton, "Let it Be," Lennon, Little Richard...............$20–40
#62 "Let it Be" Revisited, Van Morrison, Roger Daltry, *Tommy*, Zappa, The Who $20–40
#63 David Crosby interview, The New Bob Dylan, John Phillips.............................$15–30
#64 Janis Joplin, The Return of Traffic, Ringo, Donovan, The Byrds $40–80
#65 Mick Jagger & His Film, Dr. John, Capt. Beefheart, Rod Stewart $20–40
#66 The Grateful Dead, The Beatles Album No One Will Ever Hear, Elvis Presley, Steven Stills $20–40
#67 The Rascals, The Rolling Stones on Tour in Europe.............................$20–40
#68 Jimi Hendrix Memorial Issue 1945–1970, Jackie Deshannon $50–100
#69 Janis Joplin Memorial Issue 1943–1970—Special Tribute Issue.....................$50–100
#70 Grace Slick, Dylan, Elvis, Tiny Tim, Janis Joplin, Beach Boys, Phillips..........$20–40
#71 The Beatles, Pete Townshend, Pink Floyd, The Jackson Five & Michael Jackson, George Harrison.............................$20–40
#72 The State of Rock: Leon Russell, Aretha Franklin, Ian Anderson $15–30
#73 Rod Stewart, Poco, Elvin Bishoop, Livingston Taylor, John Lennon.................$15–30

1971

#74 John Lennon Interview: Life With the Lions, Paul Simon, Creedence Clearwater Revival, Jefferson Airplane.............................$20–40
#75 John Lennon Interview Part II, McCartney Sues Beatles, Grand Funk Railroad.....$15–30
#76 James Taylor & Family: Carly, The Beatles, Mama Cass, Lennon.....................$15–30
#77 Bob Dylan, Stills, Led Zeppelin at the Garaden, Tom Fogerty, Jim Morrison..$15–30
#78 Muhammed Ali, An Evening With Linda Ronstadt, Yoko Ono & Her Sixteen-track Voice $15–30
#79 Capt. Beefheart, James Taylor, Ray Charles, David Bowie, Cat Stevens, Melanie $15–30
#80 Joe Dellesandro, Allman Brothers, Alice Cooper.............................$15–30
#81 Michael Jackson & the Jackson Five, Creedence Clearwater Revival, Jack Nicholson $20–40
#82 Peter Fonda, Dennis Hooper, Black Sabbath, The Motown Story: The Supremes—A Special Feature $15–30

ROLLING STONE,
1969, #47

ROLLING STONE,
1969, #49

ROLLING STONE,
1969, #50

ROLLING STONE,
1970, #52

ROLLING STONE,
1970, #57

ROLLING STONE,
1970, #64

ROLLING STONE,
1970, #65

ROLLING STONE,
1970, #68

ROLLING STONE,
1970, #69

#83 Country Joe McDonald, Crosby, Stills, Nash & Young.......................................$15–30
#84 Elton John, John Lennon, Mick Jagger, The Mamas & the Papas.....................$15–30
#85 The White House Romance, Lenny Bruce, Barbra Streisand, Jeff Beck, Jim Morrison
....$15–30
#86 John Lennon & Yoko Ono, Whole Earth, Tull, Nils Lofgren, Early Mick Jagger
....$20–40
#87 Jethro Tull, Fillmore East, The Stones on Their U.S.A. Tour $15–30
#88 Jim Morrison 1943–1971—A Special Memorial Issue $50–100
#89 Keith Richards interview, Grand Funk, Graham Nash, Alice Cooper $25–50
#90 George Harrison & Bob Dylan Concert, Paul McCartney, Todd Rundgren, The Grateful
Dead, Three Dog Night...$15–30
#91 The Incredible Hulk, Spiderman's Secret Life, Billy Preston, The Moody Blues, Marc
Bolan...$15–30
#92 Abbie Hoffman, Jefferson Airplane, Woody Allen, Elvis Presley, Dr. John, Stevie Won-
der...$15–30
#93 Sly & the Family Stone, The Rolling Stones, Steve Winwood $15–30
#94 The Beach Boys, Bangladesh, Mick Jagger & the Rolling Stones.....................$15–30
#95 The Beach Boys, Crosby, Stills, Nash & Young, The Fillmore London............$15–30
#96 Duane Allman's Final Days on the Road, The Doors, Edgar Winter Got His Trash
Together/Contains Nude Photo, Rod Steward...$15–30
#97 The Pete Townshend Essays, Cat Stevens, Johnny Mathis................................$15–30
#98 Elvis Presley in Concert, Carole King, Rock-&-Roll on Broadway, Manfred
Mann...$15–30

1972

#99 Cat Stevens, Maggie Bell, Cheech & Chong, Zappa, Bob Dylan $10–20
#100 Jerry Garcia of the Grateful Dead, Marlon Brando, Carly Simon, *A Clockwork Or-
ange*...$10–20
#101 The Grateful Dead, Bob Dylan, The Fillmore...$10–20
#102 Janis Joplin: A Reminiscence, The People's Beatle, Isaac Hayes.....................$25–50
#103 Bob Dylan Part I: An Intimate Biography, The Death of Mahalia Jackson $10–20
#104 Bob Dylan Part II, T. Rex, Jonathan Edwards, Quincy Jones, B. Winters......$10–20
#105 Alice Cooper & His Boys, Nils Lofgren, Mahavishnu.....................................$10–20
#106 Pete Seeger, The Bizarre Ballad of Todd Rundgren, Aretha Franklin in Watts $10–20
#107 Marvin Gaye, Mick Jagger, Fear & Led Zeppelin in New Zealand..................$10–20
#108 David Cassidy naked cover & feature story...$25–50
#109 Jane Fonda: The Woman & the War, The Desperate Comeback of Joe Cocker
....$10–20
#110 Rod Stewart's Drunken Dixie Days, Marty Balin, *A Clockwork Orange*, Beatniks
....$10–20
#111 Van Morrison, April in Paris With the Grateful Dead, Jackson Browne..........$10–20
#112 Mick Jagger cover & story: The Stones in America/The Heaviest Rock 'n' Roll Tour
Ever, Johnny Winter: "Just Act Like I'm a Person"...$10–20
#113 Paul Simon interview, A Tribute to Clyde McPhatter, Rolling Stones Tour Part II
....$10–20
#114 Huey Newton, The Further Adventures of the Rolling Stones/with six pages of special
photographs...$10–20
#115 The Eagles Take it Easy, The Rolling Stones Take a Fall $10–20
#116 Randy Newman the Amazing Human, Procol Harum, Paul McCartney & Wings, Mick
Jagger's Birthday, Bob Dylan $10–20
#117 Three Dog Night: See How They Run, James Brown.......................................$10–20
#118 The Grateful Dead, Benny Goodman, Dalliance With Alice Cooper $10–20
#119 Sally Struthers, The Grand Funk Papers, Herb Alpert, Arlo Guthrie...............$10–20
#120 The Naked Truth: Jeff Beck's Back, Lenny Bruce Remembered, Hayden.......$10–20
#121 Are You Enough for David Bowie?: cover & story, Bob Dylan, Hayden.......$10–20
#122 Chuck Berry, Curtis Mayfield, Joe Cocker Busted, Youngbloods Split, Boz Scaggs
....$10–20
#123 The Resurrection of Carlos Santana $5–10
#124 Keith Moon, In Search of the Moody Blues, Lee Marvin, Hell's Angels.......$15–30

1973

#125 James Taylor & Carly Simon on Their Honeymoon, revealing outfit on Carly, Alice Cooper...$10–20

#126 Genesis, The Rolling Stones Record in Jamaica..$10–20

#127 The Diana Ross Story, Joan Baez in Hanoi, "Jesus Christ Superstar" $15–30

#128 Bette Midler, The Rolling Stones Coast Concert $5–10

#129 The Rolling Stones in Hawaii, Johnny Cash...$10–20

#130 Robert Mitchum, Woodstock, Bob Dylan, Ms. Helen Reddy, Bob Vee............$5–10

#131 Dr. Hook, George Burns Meets Alice Cooper, The Four Tops, Ronettes.........$5–10

#132 Truman Capote, Willie Nelson, Claudia Lennear, Marianne Faithful................$5–10

#133 Mark Spitz, Stevie Wonder, Roger Daltry: Who's Lead Singer Solo...............$5–10

#134 Inside Alice Cooper, Liza Minnelli's Private Lives, The Beatles, John Lennon & Yoko Ono..$10–20

#135 Sonny & Cher, Neil Young: Movie Maker, Slade, John Prine $5–10

#136 Yes, Soul Train & Dick Clark, Country Joe, Wayne Cockran...........................$5–10

#137 Rod Stewart: From Gasoline Alley to Park Ave., Paul & Linda McCartney, War & Eric Burdon, Sandy Denny, Tom T. Hall $5–10

#138 Paul Newman: Portrait of an Artist, Carole King, The Pointer Sisters, John Fogerty...$5–10

#139 Tatum O'Neil, Chicago, B.B. King Homecoming $5–10

#140 Leon Russell, Little Feat, Alan Price: Ex-Animal, J. Geils $5–10

#141 Elton John interview, Dick Clark, David Bowie: Stardust Rock, Grank Funk & Todd Rundgren, Everly Bros., Black Oak Arkansas..$5–10

#142 Dan Hicks, Beatlemania, Ike & Tina Turner, Van Morrison, Sly Stone $5–10

#143 Stevie Wonder, John Phillips, Martin Mull, Anita Bryant, Disco.......................$5–10

#144 Stephen Stills, Paul Williams, Lou Reed, Monty Python, Dr. John $5–10

#145 Art Garfunkel, Santana, The Rolling Stones on Tour $5–10

#146 Gene Autry, Bizarre Death of Ex-Byrd Gram Parson, Jim Croce.....................$5–10

#147 Liza Minnelli & Ronnie Spector & Alice Cooper, Jethro Tull is Off the Road & Ian's Plans for a Movie, Goodbye David Bowie, Marley...$5–10

#148 A New Life for the Grateful Dead, Deadheads...$5–10

#149 The Allman Brothers Story, Bob Dylan Returns to the Arena, Bowie, Earth, Wind & Fire...$5–10

#150 Hugh Hefner, Ringo Reconvenes the Beatles $5–10

1974

#151 The Who's Plagued Tour, Bob Dylan, Funky Chic, Coal Town Massacre........$5–10

#152 Ringo: Regrouping the Beatles, Hank Williams Jr., Rick Wakeman $5–10

#153 Paul McCartney interview, How the Dylan Tour Began, Bobby Darin: Dead at 37, Maria Mauldaur, Bruce Springsteen Goes Gritty $5–10

#154 Knockin' on Dylan's Door $5–10

#155 David Bowie interview, The Band With Dylan, Fleetwood Mack Flak, Stevie Wonder..$5–10

#156 Bob Dylan: The Poet's Poet, The Smothers Brothers, Dave Mason $5–10

#157 World's Sexiest Calendar, Bob Dylan's 1974 Tour $5–10

#158 Marvin Gaye, Teen Fantasies, The Beatles Talk, Stones as Honkey-Tonk Women $5–10

#159 Kris Kristofferson, Beatle Tour, John Lennon's Hard Day's Night, ELP, Fleetwood Mac $5–10

#160 Paul Getty interview, The Stones' Movie "Jumpin' Jack" Flick, Tina Turner..$5–10

#161 Jackson Browne, Aretha Franklin, Gary Glitter, Stones Film Preview..............$5–10

#162 Gladys Knight & the Pips, Bill Wyman, Capt. Beefheart, ZZ Top: Hombres Riding North, Jim Morrison's Pam: A Final Curtain on Her Affair With Life....................$10–20

#163 James Dean: A New Biography, The Pointer Sisters, Abba, The Kinks, Pete Townshend's Busty Days, Led Zeppelin, Mott, Billy Joel, Jerry Garcia & the Grateful Dead, Buffy Saint-Marie...$5–10

#164 The Carpenters, Jane Fonda's Vietnam Journal, B.J. Tomas, David Cassidy: Death on Exit, War, Zappa: Continuity is the Mother, Bette Midler, Sha Na Na, Elvin Bishop.....$5–10

#165 Eric Clapton interview, Sly Stone's Wedding, The Hollies, Explaining Who-mania, For Pete's (Townshend) Sake, Allman Bros..$5–10

#166 Maria Mauldaur, Eric Clapton, Golden Earring, The O'Jays, Peter Frampton: Over the Hump $5–10

#167 Steely Dan Comes Up Swinging, CSN & Young, Diana Ross.........................$5–10

#168 CSN & Young: Anatomy of a Reunion, John Lennon, The Private Life of Raquel Welch, Mama Cass Dead: 1941–1974...$5–10

#169 The Tragic History of Jan & Dean, Eno, The Spinners, Rod Stewart, Steeleye Span $5–10

#170 Tanya Tucker at Fifteen, Todd Rundgren: The $50,000 Producer, Judy Collins, Strawbs, Jimi Hendrix, Grover Washington..$5–10

#171 Lily Tomlin & Richard Pryor, David Bowie Returns, The Moody Blues Trial Separation, John Lennon Back in the U.S.A...$5–10

#172 Lily Tomlin, The Beatles: Strange Rumblings in Pepperland, Paul Anka, Lynyrd Skynyrd in Sweet Home Atlanta, Yes, Ron Wood, Traffic..$5–10

#173 Evel Knievel, The Real Fleetwood Mac Rolls On, Randy Newman in Georgia, Tammy Wynette, Uriah Heep, Kiki Dee..$5–10

#174 Elton John: The Four-eyed Bitch is Back, George Harrison's Mystery Tour, Bob Dylan, Don McLean $5–10

#175 Dustin Hoffman as Lenny Bruce, Night of the Grateful Dead, Keith Richard, The Plot to Prosecute John Lennon, John Entwistle, Zappa..$5–10

#176 George Harrison, The Rolling Stones: It's Only Rock 'n' Roll, ELO, Donovan, Fripp $5–10

1975

#177 Suzi Quatro Flexes Her Leather, Elton in the Big Apple, Hall & Oates: Eating Up Times Square, Genes: To Them it's Only Rock 'n' Roll, Tom Rush.........................$5–10

#178 Greg Allman: Born a Travelin' Man, Bachman-Turner Overdrive, J. Geils, Bonnie Bramlett's Rebirth, Al Green, Harry Chapin $5–10

#179 Freddie Prinze, Rick Wakeman, Mick Jagger Explains the Rolling Stones Split $5–10

#180 Les Paul interview, Alvin Lee & Co., The Electric Muse $4–8

#181 Loggins & Messina, Bryan Ferry, Joe Walsh, Billy Preston, Mac Davis, Roxy Music ....$ 4–8

#182 Led Zeppelin: Jimmy Page & Robert Plant Talk, Dylan, Alice Cooper, Kool's Gang, Donna Fargo, Dan Fogelberg...$10–20

#183 Linda Ronstadt: Heartbreak on Wheels, Paul McCartney at the Mardi Gras, Jim Stafford..$5–10

#184 Roger Daltry: *Tommy*, Little Feat, The Grammys, Led Zeppelin, Richie Blackmore $5–10

#185 Peter Falk, Bryan Ferry, Robin Trower, Rod Stewart's Last Laugh....................$4–8

#186 John Denver: His Rocky Mountain Highness, Marilyn Chambers, Dylan, Joan Baez, Jerry Garcia, Neil Young, Queen, Pretty Things, Dr. Demento....................................$4–8

#187 Carly Simon: There Goes Sensuous Simon, Running With Led Zeppelin, Jamming With Jimi Hendrix, Deep Purple, Elton John, Bette Midler on Broadway, *The Wiz*: Michael Jackson..$10–20

#188 Phoebe Snow: The Suburbs of the Soul, A Conversation With John Lennon, Smokey Robinson, Freddy Fender, The Doobie Brothers, John Denver................................$5–10

#189 Stevie Wonder, The Kinks, Stones Ticket Frenzy, Average White Band, Fame Catches Up With Emmylou Harris, Nils Lofgren $5–10

#190 Labelle: Sex, Billy Jack, Bad Company, Jefferson Starship, Zappa $4–8

#191 The Rolling Stones 1975 Tour: Mick Jagger & Keith Richards cover, Eric Clapton, Paul McCartney, Janis Ian, Jimmy Buffett...

#192 Richard Dreyfus, Alice Cooper: The Band's Reformed but Has He/She, The Rolling Stones Fumble in New York, Elton Rallies at Wembley, John Lennon in Court $4–8

#193 Neil Young interview, The Stones Dazzle Memphis, Cher, Peter Frampton: Power of Love $4–8

#194 Doonesbury, The Isley Brothers, Bob Dylan, Yes, Tangerine Dream, Pure Prairie League...$4–8

#195 Mick Jagger cover: Rolling Stones Jumping, Booming, Bumping & Grinding to a Halt, Reggae's Hairy Explosion, Bob Marley, Stevie Wonder, Robert Plant, The Bee Gees, Roger Daltry...$5–10
#196 The Eagles: Chips Off the Old Buffalo, The Tubes, Fleetwood Mac, Aerosmith...$5–10
#197 Ali, Mick Jagger Calls on Me, Bruce Springsteen, Elton John, Black Sabbath..$4–8
#198 Bob Dylan, Crosby & Nash, George Harrison, Slade, Jefferson Starship, 10CC.....$4–8
#199 Rod Stewart & His New Pal Britt Ekland, Jerry Garcia: Afternoon With the Living Dead, Wings, John Lennon, Johnny & Edgar Winter: Two Hazy Shades of Winter, Deep Purple...$4–8
#200 The Who, Tony Orlando, Eric Clapton, Woody Guthrie $4–8
#201 Jack Nicholson, Bob Dylan, Elton's Finest Hour, Neil Sedaka, The Who: Quadromania...$4–8
#202 Bonnie Raitt, Simon & Garfunkel, Dylan Tour, Roxy Music, Linda Ronstadt, Commander Cody $4–8
#203 Jefferson Starship, Patti Smith, Crosby & Nash, The Who Split $4–8

1976

#204 Bob Dylan & Joan Baez, Bowie on Tour, Neil Young, Journey, O'Jays, ELO ..$4–8
#205 Pat Boone, Alice Cooper: Breaks the House at Tahoe, Earth, Wind & Fire, Faces, Herbie Hancock..$4–8
#206 David Bowie: Rolling on to Rule the World, Dave Mason, Mick Jager.............$4–8
#207 Howlin' Wolf 1910–1976, Tommy Bolin & Deep Purple, The Runaways, Joan Jett..$4–8
#208 The Later-day Osmonds: Donny Osmond & Text, Ronnie Montrose, Black Oak Arkansas, Allman Brothers, Grace Slick, Roxy Music...$4–8
#209 Mary Hartman, Kiss, Bill Wyman, Robert Plant & the Runaways, Joan Jett, Donna Summer...$4–8
#210 Robert Redford & Dustin Hoffman, Lou Reed, Fleetwood Mac: Look Who's Back, Early Stevie Nicks, John Lennon in Court Again, Laura Nyro, Seals & Crofts, Ted Nugent...$4–8
#211 Peter Frampton: The Pretty Power Rocker, Lynyrd Skynyrd Turns the Tables, Rod Stewart, Janis Ian, Genesis: A New Beginning..$4–8
#212 Santana Comes Home, Mick Jagger, Creedence Clearwater Survivor, Grateful Dead....$4–8
#213 Marlon Brando, The Outlaws, Loretta Lynn, The Animals are Back, Dr. Feelgood $4–8
#214 Freddy Fender, Mahavishnu..$3–6
#215 Yesterday, Today & Paul (Wings), Stevie Miller, Thunder, Steely Dan, The Yardbirds, The Grateful Dead $4–8
#216 Paul Simon, Woody Allen, Diana Ross, Bruce Springsteen's E-street Softballers $3–6
#217 The Beatles & You Know That Can't be Bad, Stones, Patti Smith, The David Bowie Film..$4–8
#218 Loggins & Messina Break-up, Randy Newman, Leon Russell, Bob Seger $4–8
#219 Bob Marley: Rastaman With a Bullet, The Beach Boys, Jimmy Page Beats the Devil, The Ramones are Punk, Todd Rundgren, George Benson $4–8
#220 Aerosmith: Platinum Punk, ZZ Top, Zappa, Alice Cooper's New Role, Hall & Oates...$4–8
#221 Stills & Young: Off the Road, Eagles, Linda Ronstadt, Jackson Browne, Allman Brothers...$4–8
#222 Neil Diamond: I Need, I Want—Linda Ronstadt Redeemed, Elton John, Tommy James...$4–8
#223 Elton John's Frank Talk, The Rolling Stones at the Fair, Charlie Daniels, Buddy Holly $4–8
#224 ELO, An Early Byrd: Hillman, Bob Dylan $3–6
#225 Brian Wilson & the Beach Boys, Greg Allman's Unhappy Confessions.............$3–6
#226 Janis Joplin Special Issue, The Who & the Grateful Dead Battle, Joe Cocker, Renaissance...$5–10
#227 Linda Ronstadt: The Million-dollar Woman, Jimi Hendrix Scandal, Led Zeppelin, Blue Oyster Cult, Starz, Heart, Kiss, Random Notes...$5–10
#228 Jackson Browne: Say a Prayer for the Pretender, Phoebe Snow, The Band, Paul McCartney..$4–8

#229 The Band's All-star Adieu, George Harrison, Robin Thrower, Ruth Copeland...$3–6
#230 Rod Stewart Abroad, Dan Akroyd & John Belushi, Leo Sayer, Tommy Bolin, Bob Marley..$4–8

1977

#231 Jeff Bridges, Jackson Browne, Tom Waits, Johnny Rotten..............................$3–6
#232 Peter Frampton: Rock Star of the Year, Backstage With Bob Dylan..................$3–6
#233 Boz Scaggs: The Slow Dancer, Bob Dylan, Melissa Manchester After Midnight....$3–6
#234 Princess Caroline, Arlo Guthrie, Jethro Tull's Ian Anderson is Back, Bob Seger......$3–6
#235 Fleetwood Mac, Women in Erotic Literature..$5–102
#236 Lily Tomlin, Kiss: Pagan Beasties of Teenage Rock, Keith Richard $4–8
#237 Hall & Oates: Chic to Chic, Stones, Manfred Mann, Genesis.........................$3–6
#238 Keith Richard: A Rolling Stone Meets the Mounties, Loretta Lynn, Freddie Mercury, The King of Queen, Rick Derringer, Peter Gabriel..$3–6
#239 Van Morrison interview, Iggy Pop, Shields & Yarnell, Muddy Waters, Crystal Gayle
....$3–6
#240 Crosby, Stills & Nash Reunion, Jesse Winchester, Roger Daltry, Asleep at the Wheel
....$3–6
#241 Deniro, The Grateful Dead on Their Feet Again, Steve Winwood, Rita Coolidge...$3–6
#242 Diane Keaton, The Beatles Live at the Hollywood Bowl, Elton John..................$3–6
#243 The Bee Gees: The Saga of the Not-so-average White Band, ELP, Led Zeppelin, Joan Baez: Relaxed at Last, Bruce Springsteen...$3–6
#244 Heart: Natural Fantasies/Natural Acts, Peter Frampton Gets Inside You, Stevie Wonder, Marshall Tucker, The Dictators, Tavares...$5–10
#245 Diana Ross: Reflections/A Question of Style, CSN & Young, Bruce Springsteen Reclaims the Future, Johnny Rotten in England, Carole Bayer, Bryan Ferry $4–8
#246 The Wizard of *Star Wars*, cast cover & Lucas interview, Ted Nugent, Dolly Parton, Fleetwood Mac Rock Madison Square Garden $5–10
#247 OJ Simpson, Led Zeppelin Disaster, Sex Symbols, The Emotions, Alice Cooper....$3–6
#248 Elvis Presley Dead Issue: 1935–1977, Jimmy Buffet, Carole King, J. Geils....$5–10
#249 Paul McCartney & Wings, Rick Wakeman, The Selling of Elvis Presley, Yes, Herbie Hancock $3–6
#250 Sex Pistols: Rock is Sick, Linda Ronstadt: Simple Dreams, The Beach Boys No More
....$3–6
#251 The Rolling Stones: Mick & Keith Mouth Off, Ron Wood Lives it Up, Elvis Costello $4–8
#252 Inside the Who: Reveries & Regrets by Pete Townshend, Randy Newman Snubs God, Leo Sayer: The Happy Hoofer, Talking Heads: Beyond Safety $4–8
#253 Steve Martin, Lynyrd Skynyrd: Victims & Survivors, Dead Boys $3–6
#254 Special 10th Anniversary Issue, Rock Photo Gallery, Diana Ross, John Lennon, Linda Ronstadt $3–6
#255 James Taylor, Linda Ronstadt, Steely Dan...$3–6
#256 Fleetwood Mac cover & story, Rod Stewart, Dan Akroyd, David Bowie........$6–12

1978

#257 Bob Dylan interview, Earth, Wind & Fire, Meat Loaf, Johnny Paycheck...........$3–6
#258 Jimmy Thudpucker interview, Ray Charles, Eddie & the Hot Rods...................$3–6
#259 Rita Coolidge & Kris Kristofferson, Emmylou Harris, The Sex Pistols in Texas, The Jam's Image Game, Michelle Phillips, Rod Stewart...$3–6
#260 Jane Fonda: A Hard Act to Follow, Jackson Browne: This Wheel's on Fire, Jane Oliver, Jimmy Webb, Warren Zevon..$3–6
#261 Donna Summer: Is There Life After Disco?, Warren Zevon, Richard Perry, Fleetwood Mac Headed for Moscow, Corea & Hancock, Elvis Presley $4–8
#262 Brooke Shields: Pretty Baby's Pretty Baby, Rod Stewart Under Siege, Lou Reed....$3–6
#263 The Bee Gees, Rock 'n' Roll Movies, Bob Weir, Patti Smith $3–6
#264 Ali, Foreigner, Jefferson Starship..$3–6
#265 Jefferson Starship: Starship Wars, Maria Mauldaur, Beatlemania, Van Halen.....$3–6
#266 Carly Simon: Land of Milk & Honey, Art Garfunkel, Hank Williams Jr., Hall & Oates
....$3–6
#267 John Travolta, Bob Seger, Eagles vs. The Rolling Stones, Lynyrd Skynyrd.......$3–6

#268 Mick Jagger interview, George Benson, Mick Jagger: "Jumpin' Jack Flash," Peter, Paul & Mary Reunite, Dylan, Neil Young, Nick Lowe $3–6
#269 Willie Nelson, Bruce Springsteen: Back on the Road With Bruce.....................$3–6
#270 Pattie Smith Catches Fire, Neil Young's World Tour, Olivia Newton-John, The Rolling Stones...$3–6
#271 John Belushi, Boston: The Band from the Platinum Basement, The Stones Back from Exile, Isley Brothers, Todd Rundgren's Fragile Utopia....................................$3–6
#272 Bruce Springsteen Raises Cain, ELO, Gerry Raferty, Stevie Nicks $3–6
#273 The Rolling Stones on the Road, Jill Clayburgh, Sgt. Pepper..........................$3–6
#274 Buddy Holly, Dylan & the Stones in the Seventies, Thin Lizzy, Elton John, The O'Jays $3–6
#275 Steve Martin's Secret Life, Sid Vicious: The Punk Murder Case, Van Morrison interview, Keith Richards Guilty but Free $3–6
#276 Linda Ronstadt interview, Black Sabbath, Tom Petty & The Heartbreakers, Keith Moon 1947–1978, Grace Slick Quits..$3–6
#277 Gilda Radner, The Kinks, The Grateful Dead in Egypt, The Blues Brothers, Aerosmith..$3–6
#278 Bob Dylan Interview II, Groupies Revisited 1978, The Selling of Meat Loaf, Yes, AC/DC, Anne Murray, Neil Young on Tour, Heroes of Rock 'n' Roll...................$3–6
#279 The Who: Why Don't They Do it on the Road?, Muddy Waters: The Real Rolling Stone, Bee Gees, Touring With Neil Young, 10CC, The Grateful Dead, Bob Dylan, The Village People, REO Speedwagon, Cars...$3–6
#280 Cheech & Chong, Billy Joel: The Miracle of 52nd St., Sid Vicious, Chicago, Joe Cocker, Blondie/Debbie Harry: The Toast of Europe, Nicolette Larson........................$3–6

1979

#281/#282 Special Double Issue, Richard Dreyfuss, Kenny Loggins, Diane Keaton, The Who's New Drummer, Bob Marley...$3–6
#283 The Cars: Best New Band, Paul Simon Sues CBS, Sid Vicious Jailed, Keith Richard, Al Stewart, The Clash, Jim Morrison, Blues Bros $3–6
#284 Neil Young: The Last American Hero, The Ramones, Rod Stewart, Wilson Pickett $3–6
#285 Dan Akroyd: The Blues Brothers, Aerosmith Bares Its Battle Scars, The Eagles $3–6
#286 Ted Nugent: Motor City Madman, Sid Vicious Dead at 21, Toto, Clash............$3–6
#287 Johnny Carson, Lou Reed, George Thorogood, Dr. Hook, Hall & Oates, Elvis Costello $3–6
#288 Michael Douglas, Dire Straits Fairy Tale, *Rocky Horror Picture Show*, Chaka Khan, The Pointer Sisters, Clapton, Bee Gees, Hell's Angels..$3–6
#289 The Village People, George Harrison: A Candid Conversation, "Hair," Willie Nelson..$3–6
#290 Richard Pryor, Allman Brothers: Rebirth of the Band, The Bee Gees, Keith Richard & Ron Wood, Judy Collins, Beach Boys, Police, Bad Co....................................$3–6
#291 The Bee Gees: Stayin' Alive, Elvis Costello on the Run, Elton John, Gloria Gaynor, Bob Welch, Who, Joe Jackson, Woodstock II, Graham Parker..........................$3–6
#292 Jon Voight, Ron Wood and the New Barbarians, Keith Richards, Concert for the Blind, Rickie Lee Jones, Peter Frampton, BB King, Roches...$3–6
#293 Cheap Trick: Japan Surrenders, Roches, Van Halen, Cars, Ian Hunter, Badfinger, Lou Reed $3–6
#294 Platinum Blondie/Debbie Harry Riding the Crest of the New Wave, Graham Parker, Jefferson Starship, Mick Taylor, Who, Patti Smith......................................$5–10
#295 Paul McCartney, Supertramp, The Bee Gees, Sister Sledge, Mudd Club, Donna Summer $3–6
#296 Joni Mitchell: Her First Interview in 10 Years, "Saturday Night's" Mr. Mike, Peter Frampton: A Private Struggle, Dylan, Who, Dixie Dreggs, Robert Fripp.................$3–6
#297 Rickie Lee Jones: The Story of a Runaway Success, The Who, 15 Years After/On Film, Tom Petty, Chicago, Southside Johnny, Lene Lovich, David Bowie...........$3–6
#298 Robin Williams, The Cars, Kansas, Aerosmith, Fleetwood Mac, Rachel Sweet, Hank Williams Jr., Roy Orbison, Gerry Raferty, The Crusaders $3–6
#299 James Taylor Interview, Bruce Springsteen: The Singer & His Record Company, Nicolette Larson, Ian Dury, Arlo Guthrie, Tammy Wynette, John Denver Protest.......$3–6

#300 The Doobie Bros: Jazzing it Up, Dylan, Rockpile, Raitt, Cooper.......................$3–6
#301 Jimmy Buffet, David Bowie: Bad Boy in Berlin, Led Zeppelin Live, Jackson Browne, Bruce Springsteen, The B-52's, Randy Newman $3–6
#302 Sissy Spacek: A Knockout, The Knack: New Fab Four are #1, Pete Seeger, The Beatles, Led Zeppelin $3–6
#303 Martin Sheen, Randy Newman, Charlie Daniels, The Eagles, Who, Little Feat, Cars, Fleetwood Mac: "Tusk," Beatles Reunion...$3–6
#304 Bruce Springsteen, Carly Simon, The Eagles, Dylan, Dionne Warwick, Fleetwood Mac, "Tusk" Sneak Preview, Abba, America, Elton John $3–6
#305 The Eagles: A Good Year in Hell, Talking Heads, Aerosmith, Blondie.............$3–6
#306 Bette Midler: The Rose, Jerry Lee Lewis, Fleetwood Mac at "Tusk," Zappa, Bob Dylan...$3–6

1980

#307/308 Special Double Issue/The Year in Music, "Saturday Night Live," Special Photo Gallery
#309 Pink Floyd, Rick James, "1941," Belushi, Neil Young $3–6
#310 Fleetwood Mac: Stevie Nicks, The Police $6–12
#311 Tom Petty: Damn the Torpedoes, McCartney Busted in Japan, Kool & the Gang, Bonnie Raitt, Santana Buzzcocks, BB King, Meat Loaf $3–6
#312 Richard Gere, McCartney Bust, Warren Zevon, Elvis Presley, Cliff Richard, Bob Dylan...$3–6
#313 Bob Hope, The Beach Boys, Rachel Sweet, Chevy Chase, John Belushi, The Ramones $3–6
#314 The Styles of Linda Ronstadt, J. Geils, Ron Wood, Bob Seger, Bill Wyman, The Clash $3–6
#315 The Clash: Rebels With a Cause, Jefferson Starship, Grateful Dead, Van Halen, Boz Scaggs, Marianne Faithful, Elvis Costello $3–6
#316 Bob Seger, Billy Joel's Glass House, Johnny Rotten's Public Image, Sex Pistols Film, Pat Benatar: A Classy Soprano...$3–6
#317 Heart/Ann & Nancy Wilson—"Heart Attack": Rock's Hot Sister Act, "Saturday Night Live," Patti Labelle: The Original "Lady Marmalade," Jam, The Searchers, Flying Lizards, Bob Seger $4–8
#318 The Pretenders: Thrilling America With Leather & Love, Jim Morrison: The Kinky Last Days of the Lizard King, Darryl Hall, Frank Zappa, Boz Scaggs $3–6
#319 Hard Rock Hits With a Hard Sell, *Star Wars II*, Smokey Robinson $3–6
#320 Pete Townshend interview, Paul McCartney, Selector..$3–6
#321 John Travolta, Lou Reed $3–6
#322 Cast of *The Empire Strikes Back*, Richard Pryor, Pat Benatar $6–12
#323 Jackson Browne interview, The Grateful Dead Celebrate, The Blues Brothers, Bobby Bare, Gladys Knight, Gang of Four...$3–6
#324 The Rolling Stones: The Band That Refuses to Die, Tom Wolfe $3–6
#325 Billy Joel is Angry, Heavy Metal Lust, Van Halen, Elvis Presley, Richard Pryor, Jackson Browne..$3–6
#326 The Commodores, Joe Jackson, Judas Priest, Peter Gabriel, The Undertones.....$3–6
#327 Robert Redford, Elvis Presley: The Final Years, Tom Rush, Irene Cara, Def Leppard $3–6
#328 Pat Benatar: This Year's Model/Slick & Sexy, James Dean Remembered, Jeff Beck, The Police, Talking Heads, Ronnie Spector, Paul Simon...$3–6
#329 The Cars: Fighting Their Critics, Art Garfunkel, Paul Simon, Van Morrison, Mink Deville, AC/DC...$3–6
#330 Mary Tyler Moore, David Bowie: Elephant Man, Jonie Mitchell, The Bee Gees, Dave Davies, John Otway, Chic...$3–6
#331 Jill Clayburgh, Bruce Springsteen: On the Road Again, Bus Boys, The Doors $3–6
#332 The Unsinkable Dolly Parton, The B-52s, The Shaggs $3–6
#333/334 Double Issue/The Beatles: How They Began, Photo Gallery, The Year in Music & Film $3–6
#335 John Lennon & Yoko Ono: A Special Memorial Issue.......................................$5–10
#336 Bruce Springsteen & the Secret of the World, Steely Dan...................................$4–8

#337 The Police: Bottle Blondes Go to the Bank, Marilyn Monroe, Saturday Night Dead/ Live $3–6
#338 Goldie Hawn: Her Secret Life, Bruce Springsteen, Talking Heads in Trouble, John Lennon $3–6

1981

#339 The Resurrection of Warren Zevon, REO Speedwagon, Frank Sinatra $3–6
#340 Roman Polanski, Elvis Costello, Mike Bloomfield $3–6
#341 Jack Nicholson, Chevy Chase, Smokey Robinson..$3–6
#342 Gary U.S. Bonds, Ringo Starr...$3–6
#343 Inside the Gun: John Lennon Murder Special, James Caan.................................$3–6
#344 Susan Sarandon, Elvis Presley: His Life & Movies..$3–6
#345 James Taylor, Queen on Tour in South America $3–6
#346 Harrison Ford of *Raiders of the Lost Arc*, Bob Marley Dead $3–6
#347 Margot Kidder, Kim Carnes, Yoko Ono's Search of Glass.................................$3–6
#348 Tom Petty, America, Paul McCartney $3–6
#349 Rickie Lee Jones $3–6
#350 Bill Murray, The Rolling Stones on Tour, Bruce Springsteen.............................$3–6
#351 Stevie Nicks cover & story, Harry Chapin Dead 1942–1981, The Moody Blues, Lee Marvin...$10–20
#352 Jim Morrison, Elvis Presley $3–6
#353 Yoko Ono, Santana, Stones Tour, Liberace, The Pretenders $3–6
#354 Meryl Streep, Foreigner, Stones Get Great, Simon & Garfunkel Get Back........$3–6
#355 Elvis Presley: The Party Years, Simon & Garfunkel Special Photo Report........$3–6
#356 Keith Richards, The Stones Tour: A Sloppy Start, Pointer Sisters.....................$3–6
#357 Bill Hurt, Backstage With the Rolling Stones: Special Report.............................$3–6
#358 Carly Simon: Life Without James, Stones on Tour, Jamie Lee Curtis.................$3–6
#359/360 Double Issue/1981 Yearbook—A Photographic History of the Year in Music & Film, Rolling Stones on Cover..$3–6

1982

#361 John Belushi, Mick Jagger: Will Success Spoil Him?...$3–6
#362 Timothy Hutton, Muhammed Ali...$3–6
#363 Steve Martin, Van Morrison, Rolling Stones interview, James Cagney at Home $3–6
#364 Peter Wolf, The Police's Sting Considers a New Career, Earth, Wind & Fire ...$3–6
#365 Simon & Garfunkel, Rod Stewart, Rolling Stones interview, Genesis $3–6
#366 Warren Beatty, Mister James Brown, The Cars, Mamas & Papas Reunite..........$3–6
#367 Mariel Hemingway, Crosby, Stills & Nash: Together Again, Blasters $3–6
#368 John Belushi, Joan Jett, Jimmy Webb, Tragedy Strikes Ozzy Osbourne Tour $3–6
#369 Sissy Spacek, John Belushi, Keith Richards, The Go-go's...................................$3–6
#370 Natassai Kinski, Bonnie Raitt, Paul McCartney, Rickie Lee Jones $3–6
#371 David Letterman, Arnold Schwarzenegger as Conan..$3–6
#372 Pete Townshend interview, Rick James, Huey Lewis, Asia..................................$3–6
#373 Sylvester Stallone, Human League, Jefferson Starship, The Dead........................$3–6
#374 *ET*: The Movie, The Rolling Stones in Europe..$3–6
#375 The Go-go's, Shark $5–10
#376 Tron, Jeff Bridges, The Clash, Fleetwood Mac..$3–6
#377 Elvis Costello interview, Creedence Clearwater Revival......................................$3–6
#378 Behind Pink Floyd's Wall, Donovan's Grief, Bruce Springsteen.........................$3–6
#379 Richard Gere Loosens Up, Roger Daltry Talks About the Who, X, Bette Midler ...$3–6
#380 John Lennon & Yoko Ono: The Private Years, Michael Jackson Teams Up With Paul McCartney, Bruce Springsteen, The Who's Sell-out, Joe Jackson, Billy Joel $3–6
#381 Billy Joel Takes Chances, Bruce Springsteen's Nebraska Connection, Fleetwood Mac, The Who...$3–6
#382 The Who, Linda Ronstadt, Stray Cats, Steve Winwood, Joni Mitchell.................$3–6
#383 Matt Dillon, Joni Mitchell: Woodstock's First Lady, The Who Sell-out...............$3–6
#384 Bette Midler: The Divine Ms. Midler, John Cougar, Jefferson Starship, A Flock of Sea Gulls..$3–6
#385/386 Double Issue/The Year in Music & Film...$3–6

#387 Paul Newman, Dire Straits, Yoko Ono's 48 Hours, Michael Jackson, Jamaican World Music Festival With Rick James $3–6
#388 Dustin Hoffman, Bob Seger, Phil Collins, The Who in Toronto $3–6
#389 Michael Jackson: Life as a Man, Culture Club...$3–6
#390 Stray Cats in Heat, Robert Mitchum, The Rolling Stones New Movie, Lionel Richie $3–6
#391 Jessica Lange, Videodrome Starring Debbie Harry/photos $3–6
#392 Dudley Moore, Randy Newman, Dylan Returns to Greenwich Village, U2........$3–6
#393 Joan Baez interview, Pink Floyd, Missing Persons...$3–6
#394 Prince & Vanity, Mick Jagger & Hells Angels, Men at Work $3–6

1983

#395 David Bowie, Duran Duran, Prince Rocks Bruce Springsteen..............................$3–6
#396 Sean Penn, Rap Music, David Bowie, *Flashdance* $3–6
#397 Health Clubs, U2, Talking Heads', Rosanna Arquette...$3–6
#398 Men at Work, Yoko's Mystery Man Speaks, The Police, Earl Hines $3–6
#399 Eddie Murphy Goes for the Gold, Stevie Nicks, Def Leppard, Bruce Springsteen, Christopher Cross, *Twilight Zone*: The Movie..$3–6
#400/401 Special Summer Double Issue—*Star Wars* Goes on Vacation, George Lucas interview..$3–6
#402 John Travolta, Linda Ronstadt: Snow White Goes to South Africa.....................$3–6
#403 The Police Brutality Sting Interview, Simon & Garfunkel's Uneasy Reunion $3–6
#404 Jackson Browne Rocks, Pete Townshend on Mick Jagger, Yoko Ono Readies New John Lennon LP..$3–6
#405 Eurythmics: Sweet Dreams of Success/Annie Lennox cover, Jackson Browne, Police at Shea Stadium $3–6
#406 Chevy Chase, Pete Seeger, Human League, Stray Cats, Mick Jones Fired from the Clash $3–6
#407 Sean Connery: The Real James Bond, The Animals $3–6
#408 Culture Club's Boy George, Simon Dumps Garfunkel $3–6
#409 Mick Jagger: Satisfaction, J. Geils Band, Dylan, Brooke Adams........................$3–6
#410 Michael Jackson & Paul McCartney Team Up for TV, Inside MTV, Big Country Untamed, The JFK Assassination $3–6
#411/412 Double Issue—Great Faces of '83 Special $3–6

1984

#413 The Concert of the Year Issue—Eric Clapton, Jeff Beck, Jimmy Page, Joe Cocker, Tom Waits, Bill Wyman, Jones, Rodgers & Lane: all on cover, Quiet Riot, Lionel Richie $3–6
#414 Duran, Duran: The Fab Five, Dennis Wilson Dead, Al Pacino, The New Yes, Pete Townshend Speaks to the Who: "Drop Dead," Eurythmics...$3–6
#415 Special Beatles Anniversary Issue..$3–6
#416 The Police Interview, The Gap Band, John & Yoko, The Mysterious Death of Mrs. Jerry Lee Lewis: An Exclusive, Bob Seger, The Return of the Clash.........................$3–6
#417 Michael Jackson: An Exclusive Look Inside a Musical Empire, Huey Lewis & the News $3–6
#418 Jack Nicholson interview, Billy Idol Struts Again, Joan Collins Talks Trash, Cher $3–6
#419 Eddie Murphy, ZZ Top, Quincy Jones, The Go-go's/Belinda Carlisle $3–6
#420 Darryl Hannah Speaks, The Cars, The Pretenders: Drugs, Death & Devotion, UB40, Debarge $3–6
#421 The Death of Marvin Gaye, Simple Minds, The Jacksons Update.......................$3–6
#422 Cyndi Lauper Laughs Last, Marvin Gaye Sr. Talks, Rockwell...............................$3–6
#423 Culture Club's Boy George interview, The Last Days of Dennis Wilson, Jackson's Tour in Chaos, Count Basie 1904–1984, Springsteen...$3–6
#424 Bob Dylan interview, Jackson's Jinx: The Inside Story, Van Halen, The Go-go's....$3–6
#425 The Go-go's cover & story—Women on Top, Bruce Springsteen, The Cars, Billy Joel, Bill Murray, Spend the Night With Rod Stewart...$3–6
#426/427 Super Summer Double Issue—The Thompson Twins, The Cars, Little Richard, Bruce Springsteen $3–6

#428 Bill Murray interview, On the Road With Michael Jackson, Bruce Springsteen $3–6
#429 Prince Scores a Hit Album & a Hot New Movie, Tina Turner, Piscopo $3–6
#430 Huey Lewis & the Good News, The Rolling Stones at Altamont: A Look Back, Morris Day, The Bangles, The History of Records $3–6
#431 John Belushi's Troubled Sleep, Ray Parker Jr., Patty Smith, U2, Aerosmith $3–6
#432 Tina Turner: She's Got Legs, Frankie Goes to Hollywood, David Bowie, Eddie & the Cruisers, U2...$3–6
#433 David Bowie, Herbie Hancock, Jamie Lee Curtis, Lindsay Buckingham $3–6
#434 Steve Martin, Prince's New Tour, Yoko Ono, Ed Begley Jr., Bananarama, Frank Sinatra $3–6
#435 Madonna Goes All the Way, Van Morrison, Culture Club, Twisted Sister, The Fixx, Rod Stewart $3–6
#436 Bruce Springsteen interview, Julian Lennon, Paul McCartney's New Movie, Bonnie Raitt...$3–6

1985

#437/438 Special Double Issue—Great Faces of '84 Photo Spectacular $3–6
#439 The Secret Life of Hall & Oates, Schwarzenegger Talks, Prince $3–6
#440 Billy Idol: Sneer of the Year, Vanessa Williams, Honeydrippers, John Fogerty, U2 in Concert, The Eurythmics...$3–6
#441 Mick Jagger Steps Out, Chaka Khan, Laurie Anderson, Ozzy Osbourne $3–6
#442 Bruce Springsteen, Prince, Cyndi Lauper, The Cars $3–6
#443 U2 cover & story, Fogerty, U.S.A. for Africa, 46 Stars but Not Prince...........$3–6
#444 Inside "Miami Vice," Wham, Mick Jagger, Tom Hutton, U.S.A. for Africa.......$3–6
#445 Van Halen's David Lee Roth, Richard Brautigan, Sting's Solo Show $3–6
#446 Richard Gere, Sade, U.S.A. for Africa...$3–6
#447 Madonna & Rosanna Arquette: Their New Movie, Martin Short.......................$3–6
#448 Phil Collins Beats the Odds, Tom Petty, Tina Turner & David Bowie, Sade, Madonna $3–6
#449 Julian Lennon: Here Comes the Son, Prince Goes Psychedelic, Beatles $3–6
#450 David Letterman, Eric Clapton interview, The Go-go's Craze, Petty..................$3–6
#451 Clint Eastwood interview, Led Zeppelin Exclusive: The Untold Story, The Return of Psychedelica, Bob Dylan Rocks again $3–6
#452/453 Double Issue—John Travolta & Jamie Lee Curtis, Bruce Springsteen Rocks Europe $3–6
#454 The Live Aid Concerts for Ethiopia: A Special Issue: The Day the World Rocked $3–6
#455 Mel Gibson & Tina Turner: Making Mad Max, Live Aid: What it Meant, Michael J. Fox, Aretha Franklin...$3–6
#456 Prince Talks: The Silence is Broken, Special: Music Greats of the Sixties & Seventies $3–6
#457 Sting: Losing His Cool, Bruce Springsteen in Concert, John Cougar.................$3–6
#458 Bruce Springsteen, Billy Crystal, Weird Al, Joe Piscopo.....................................$3–6
#459 Steven Spielberg, The Amazing Love Life of the Eurythmics, Stevie Wonder, Billy Crystal...$3–6
#460 Don Johnson interview, Rock Censors: Big Brother Meets Twisted Sister, Backstage With Farm Aid, The Thompson Twins $3–6
#461 Dire Straits: A Conversation With Mark Knopfler, How Drugs Destroyed David Crosby $3–6
#462 Bob Geldorf interview, Bob Dylan, The Stones, John & Yoko, ZZ Top............$3–6

1986

#463/464 Special Double Issue—1985 Rock Yearbook...$3–6
#465 Michael Douglas, Bob Dylan's Masterpiece, The Clash, Tom Petty $3–6
#466 John Cougar Mellencamp interview, Stevie Nicks, Sade, Tom Waits $3–6
#467 Ricky Nelson Special Memorial Issue: 1940–1985, The Rock 'n' Roll Hall of Fame $4–8
#468 Bruce Springsteen Does it Again, U2, Dire Straits, Tina Turner, Tears for Fears, Talking Heads, Witney Houston $3–6
#469 Jim McMahon, The Bangles, Hall of Fame, Rock's Night to Remember $3–6

#470 Bruce Willis, Bangles, Al Green, Elvis Costello, Joe Jackson..............................$3–6
#471 Stevie Wonder, Elvis Costello, Jackson Browne, Spring Fashion With Julian Lennon, Whitney Houston, Brian Setzer $3–6
#472 Wendy & Lisa: Prince's Women, Heart, Yoko Ono Tours Europe.......................$3–6
#473 Making Whoopi, The Everly Brothers interview, Yoko Ono Tour Behind the Iron Curtain, Julian Lennon, ZZ Top $3–6
#474 Michael J. Fox, Special Issue: The Hottest in Music, Movies, TV....................$3–6
#475 The New Madonna, Van Halen, Robert Palmer, Joe Jackson, Feargal Sharkey, Fleetwood Mac...$3–6
#476 Top Gun's Tom Cruise, Simple Minds, U2, Sting, Bryan Adams, The Amnesty Concerts...$3–6
#477 Van Halen: Hot & Happy Without David Lee Roth, Peter Frampton.................$3–6
#478/479 Double Issue—Bob Dylan & Tom Petty: Talking About the Road, Madonna, David Bowie, Heart...$3–6
#480 Jack Nicholson Gets Mad: The Interview, Boy George.......................................$3–6
#481 Boy George's Tragic Fall, Van Morrison, *Aliens*, Max Headroom $3–6
#482 Paul McCartney interview, Run DMC, Billy Joel, Special Issue: Where are They Now?—The Byrds, Big Brother, Gerry & the Pacemakers, The Crystals & Many Others...$3–6
#483 Don Johnson: Rock 'n' Roll Star, The Monkees, Tom Hanks, Cyndi Lauper, Lou Reed..$3–6
#484 Cybil Shepard, Rock Stars & Their Kids, Steve Winwood, John Fogerty, Bob Seger, Huey Lewis $3–6
#485 Tina Turner interview, Talking Heads, Pet Shop Boys, Eurythmics, Paul Simon's Daring Comeback..$3–6
#486 Billy Joel: The Good Life With Christie Brinkley, Tina Turner, Frank Zappa, Timbuk 3...$3–6
#487 Huey Lewis: Stuck With Success, George Michael Tells Why Wham Broke Up, John Fogerty, Iggy Pop, Anita Baker, Meet "Saturday Night Live's" New Cast $3–6
#488 Run DMC, Chuck Berry, Billy Idol, Elvis Costello, UB40 in the U.S.S.R.........$3–6
#489/490 Special Double Issue—1986 Yearbook..$3–6

1987

#491 Talking Heads, Bruce Springsteen, Eric Clapton, Cameo, Michael J. Fox Makes a Rock Movie, Joan Jett..$3–6
#492 Peter Gabriel, Jackson Browne, *Platoon* Director Oliver Stone, Justine Bateman..$3–6
#493 Pee-Wee Herman: Saturday Morning Fever, Cyndi Lauper, Beastie Boys, New Members in the Rock 'n' Roll Hall of Fame, Bruce Hornsby $3–6
#494 Bruce Springsteen, Peter Gabriel, Madonna, Run DMC, Genesis, Cyndi Lauper, Bruce Hornsby, David Lee Roth, Charlie Watts, Los Lobos, Billy Vera, Bob Dylan, Bruce Willis..$3–6
#495 The Private Life of Michael J. Fox, The Rock 'n' Roll Hall of Fame: A Night to Remember $3–6
#496 The Bangles Know What They Want, Los Lobos, Paul Simon, The Pretenders, Husker Du, The State of Rock in Russia, Kevin Costner...$3–6
#497 Woody Allen interview, U2, Beatles, Genesis, Andy Warhol 1928–1987...........$3–6
#498 David Bowie, 20th Anniversary Issue, Beastie Boys, Prince, 20 Years of Rock 'n' Roll Style: Lots of Rare Photos..$3–6
#499 U2 Burns Up the Charts, Fleetwood Mac, Club Nouveau, Kronos.....................$3–6
#500 Bon Jovi, U2 in the U.S.A., Bryan Adams, Special Issue: The Hottest in Music ...$3–6
#501 Jimi Hendrix 20th Anniversary Issue, Bruce Springsteen & Bon Jovi, The Cure, Suzanne Vega, Billy Idol, David Bowie, The Twenty Greatest Concepts of All Time—Elvis, Cream, Beatles, Led Zep, Stones, John Lennon, Jimi Hendrix, Who, Springsteen, Jacksons...$4–8
#502 Robert Cray, Jody Watley, A Special Tribute to Sgt. Pepper, Paul Butterfield 1942–1987, Sting & Jimi Hendrix, Suzanne Vega...$3–6
#503 Paul Simon: The Graceland Tour Hits the Road, Eddie Murphy, Prince, The Judds, The Neville Brothers, The Beastie Boys $3–6

#504/505 Special Double Issue—The New Dawn of the Grateful Dead, A Rock 'n' Roll Tour of America, Tina Turner, Joe Jackson, Tom Petty, Beatles......................................$3–6

#506 Heavy Metal: On the Road With Motley Crue, Rare Elvis Presley Photos, Whitney Houston, Brian Wilson: The Reclusive Genius, Boston, George Harrison, The Chicago Blues Festival...$3–6

#507 The 100 Best Albums of the Last Twenty Years—Jimi Hendrix, Jefferson Airplane, Springsteen, Marvin Gaye, Dylan, Prince, Etc., Michael Jackson Gets the Girl, Rockers of Russia, Madonna Live, Tracy Ullman...$3–6

#508 Madonna: On Being a Star, Where are They now?: A Special Issue—Delaney & Bonnie, Dr. Hook, Sopwith Camel, The Turtles, Etc., Bryan Adams, Def Leppard, Dylan, The Grateful Dead, Sting, Keith Richards, Elvis Presley...$3–6

#509 Michael Jackson in Fantasyland, The Far Side of Gary Larson, Bruce Springsteen, Billy Joel in Russia, David Bowie, The Cars, Bon Jovi, Def Leppard.........................$3–6

#510 Bono: U2's Passionate Voice, LL Cool J., John Mellencamp, Tina Turner, Boy George, Michael Jackson, Aretha Franklin...$3–6

#511 The Return of George Harrison, How Good is Michael Jackson's "Bad?," Bob Dylan in Israel, R.E.M., Pink Floyd, Prince, Peter Tosh...$3–6

#512 20th Anniversary Special—Interviews with Bob Dylan, Bruce Springsteen, Paul McCartney, Mick Jagger, George Harrison, Keith Richards, Stevie Wonder, Pete Townshend, Bono, Sting, Tom Wolfe, Etc., Yoko Ono, Jackson Browne, Baez, Brian Wilson: Pet Sounds, John Fogerty, Tina Turner...$3–6

#513 Pink Floyd: The Inside Story, The Return of Robbie Robertson, U2 Live, Terence D'Arby, Mick Jagger, Roy Orbison, Stevie Wonder...$3–6

#514 R.E.M./America's Best Rock 'n' Roll Band, Chuck Berry, Prince's Movie, Fleetwood Mac, Bruce Springsteen & Sting, U2, Echo & the Bunnymen, Tom Waits, Squeeze
....$3–6

#515/516 Special Double Issue—1987 Yearbook: Joan Jett, Bangles, Stones, Lauper, Jimi Hendrix, Madonna, Grateful Dead, David Bowie, Bon Jovi, U2, Springsteen..............$4–8

1988

#517 Michael Douglas, George Michaels, Sting Hits the Road, INXS in Prague, Tom Waits, Neil Young..$3–6

#518 George Michael: Life After Wham, John Cougar Mellencamp, Paul Simon, The Alarm, Aretha Franklin...$3–6

#519 Sting interview, The Rock 'n' Roll Hall of Fame, The U2 Movie: On Location, Michael Jackson, Def Leppard, Debbie Gibson & Tiffany: Bombos With Big Hits.........$3–6

#520 Robin Williams interview, Bono, U2, Rosanne Cash, Pink Floyd, Boston, Kiefer Sutherland..$3–6

#521

#522 Robert Plant interview, Led Zeppelin: Tribute to a Rock Legend, Ziggy Marley, Robbie Robertson, Frank Zappa, T-bone Burnett, Neil Diamond...................................$3–6

#523 Martin Luther King, INXS, Bruce Springsteen: The Boss & the "Bad Man," Eric Carmen, Talking Heads $3–6

#524 David Byrne interview, Can Tiffany Survive Her Success?, Eric Clapton's Greatest Work, Mrs. Bruce Springsteen...$3–6

#525 Bruce Springsteen on the Road, Neil Young's Comeback, Mick Jagger in Japan, Portrait of a Generation Part II, Van Halen, Stevie Wonder $3–6

#526 The Hot Issue Starring Lisa Bonet, Neil Young, Tiffany, Robyn Hitchcock, Michael Jackson, Graham Parker $3–6

#527 Neil Young interview, Ultimate Dead Head, Paul McCartney, John Lennon, Billy Bragg, Toni Childs, Tracy Chapman, *Beetlejuice*...$3–6

#528 Terrence D'Arby: A Legend in His Own Mind, INXS: Rock's New Sensation, Prince
....$3–6

#529 Tom Hanks, Van Halen, Tracy Chapman, Graham Parker: Flirting With Success, Backstage With Led Zeppelin & CSSN, David Byrne, Winwood.................................$3–6

#530/531 Special Double Issue—Van Halen: Monsters on Tour, Huey Lewis & the News, Brian Wilson: Surf's Up Again $3–6

#532 Tom Cruise, Brian Wilson: His Long Journey Back from Madness, Steve Winwood, Run DMC $3–6

#533 Eric Clapton interview, Robert DeNiro, Prince in Paris, Patti Smith, Where are They now?—Cat Stevens, Box Tops, Billy Kramer, Bay City Rollers, E Street Band Alumni, Yvonne Craig/Bat Girl $3–6

#534 Special Issue—The 100 Best Singles of the Last 25 Years $3–6

#535 Tracy Chapman, George Michael, Randy Newman, Stevie Nicks, Madonna $3–6

#536 Keith Richards Comes Clean interview, Jim Morrison, Bruce Springsteen, Sting, Bon Jovi, Tom Waitts $3–6

#537 John Lennon Remembered: A Special Photo Album, Character Assassination: The Goldman Attack on John Lennon, 5th Annual MTV Awards, Eric Clapton, The Lives of John Lennon $3–6

#538 Johnny Carson & David Letterman/Special Comedy Issue, Keith Richard..........$3–6

#539 Guns 'n' Roses: Hard Rock Heroes, U2s Rattle & Hum, Mick Jagger, James Brown..$3–6

#540 Steve Winwood, Elton John, Judas Priest, Tom Petty, Roy Orbison...................$3–6

#541/542 1988 Yearbook Special—Springsteen, Beatles, Jagger, U2............................$3–6

1989

#543 Mel Gibson, Metallica, R.E.M., Keith Richards, John Hiatt, Billy Bragg, CSNY, Robert Plant, John Fogerty $3–6

#544 Roy Orbison: 1936–1988—The Last Interview, Tributes from Bon Jovi, Bruce Springsteen, George Harrison, Dylan, Mick Jagger, Etc., Lou Reed, James Brown, Toni Childs...$3–6

#545 Bon Jovi: Rock's Young Gun, The Beatles: In the Studio With the Fab Four, Rock 'n' Roll Hall of Fame: Stones, Stevie Wonder, Dion, Temptations, Otis Redding, Tom Petty, Susan Sarandon $3–6

#546 Sam Kinison: Comedy's Wild Thing, Jim Morrison: The Lizard King Comes to Dinner, Lou Reed..$3–6

#547 Bono/U2: Voice & Band of the Year, Rock 'n' Roll Hall of Fame, Elvis Costello, Ornette Coleman $3–6

#548 Madonna: A Candid Talk About Music, Movies & Marriage, John Cougar Mellencamp, The Beach Boys, XTC...$3–6

#549 James Brown: Behind the Bars With the Godfather of Soul, Madonna, The Grammys, Linda Ronstadt, Debbie Gibson...$3–6

#550 R.E.M.: Down Home With America's Hippest Band, Fine Young Cannibals, XTC, Madonna: Pop's High Priestess...$3–6

#551 Lou Reed interview, Detroit Pistons, Edie Brickell, David Bowie, The Rolling Stones, Tom Petty $3–6

#552 Uma Thurman, Roger Daltry, Sonic Youth, Bob Mould/Husker Du, Dylan, Madonna, Phoebe Snow, Randy Newman...$3–6

#553 *Ghostbusters II*—Cast & Story, Elvis Costello interview, The Replacements, Paul McCartney, Retro-Rock: Graham Parker, Ringo, John Cougar Mellencamp, Abbie Hoffman Tribute 1936–1989 ....$3–6

#554 Paul McCartney: Setting the Record Straight About Yesterday & Today, 10,000 Maniacs, David Bowie's Tin Machine, Pete Townshend, Beastie Boys, Indiana Jones.....$3–6

#555 *Batman*: Can Michael Keaton Fill the Cape?, John Mellencamp's Broken Heartland, The Stones Search for Harmony: Mick & Keith Search, Grateful Dead, Billy Idol, Whitesnake, XTC, Beastie Boys, Clapton...$3–6

#556/557 Special Double Issue—The Who, The Beatles, Gilda Radner, The Cult, Jerry Lee Lewis & Dennis Quaid, The Allman Bros., REM...$3–6

#558 Axl Rose interview, The Rolling Stones in the Studio, Nenah Cherry, The Who: Tommy's Triumphant Return, Beastie Boys, Prince, Donny Osmond, Where are They Now?—Ginger Baker, David Essex $3–6

#559 Eddie Murphy interview, Rob Lowe, Ringo Starr, Woodstock Remembered, Prince & Batman, Aerosmith, The Rolling Stones...$3–6

#560 The Rolling Stones: Mick & Keith's Uneasy Peace, The Cure, Bobby Browan, Rickie Lee Jones, Cher...$3–6

#561 Madonna, Special Rock 'n' Roll Photo Album, Elvis Costello, Love & Rockets, Tracy Chapman...$3–6

#562 Roland Gift & Fine Young Cannibals, Tom Petty's Tour Diary, Tracy Chapman, Paul McCartney $3–6

#563 Andie MacDowell, On the Road With the Rolling Stones, Behind the Lines With Public Enemy, Janet Jackson, Grateful Dead, Bonnie Raitt $3–6

#564 Jay Leno & Arsenio Hall, Close Encounters With New Kids on the Block, Sting, Neil Young...$3–6

#565 Special Issue—The 100 Gratest Albums of the 80s, Tears for Fears, The Pogues, Joe Strummer, Paul McCartney $3–6

#566 Jerry Garcia interview, Paula Abdul, Trent D'Arby, Milli Vanilli, Jeff Beck, Stevie Ray, Billy Idol...$3–6

#567/568 Yearbook Double Issue—Stones, Madonna, Dead...$3–6

1990

#569 Tom Cruise: Nobody's Fool, Bruce Springsteen: Life After the E Street Band, David Byrne: The New Mambo King, Tina Turner, NRBQ $3–6

#570 Billy Joel interview, Jeff Beck, Stevie Ray Vaughn, Beatles $3–6

#572 Janet Jackson: Michael's Little Sister Grows Up, Midnight Oil.....................................$3–6

#574 The B-52's: The Return of America's Favorite Party Band, Sinead O'Connor Gets What She Wants $3–6

#575 Aerosmith: They're the Band That Won't Die, Death of a Deadhead.................................$3–6

#576 50s: A Celebration of Four Decades of Rock, Little Richard, Jerry Lee Lewis, Eddie Cochran, Elvis Presley, Chuck Berry, Everly Brothers, Pat Boone, Ricky Nelson, The Coasters, Buddy Holly, Fats Domino & Others $3–6

#577 Bonnie Raitt interview, Rickie Lee Jones, Prince...$3–6

#578 Look Who's Hot Issue, Claudia Schiffer, Wilson Phillips...$3–6

#579 Being Warren Beatty, Madonna: The Material Girl Reveals Her Blond Ambition Tour $3–6

#581 At Home With Bart Simpson, Midnight Oil Turns to Gold, Soul II Soul $3–6

#585 John Lennon, A Special Issue: The Sixties, Billy Joel on the Beatles, James Brown's Nuclear Assault, Motown Archives, Steven Tyler on the Rolling Stones, A San Francisco Oral History, Spector's Wall of Sound, Roger McGuin on Bob Dylan.......................................$3–6

#586 It's Mc Hammer Time: Nailing Down Number One, Faith No More.................$2–4

#588 The Women of "Twin Peaks," Sinead O'Connor, George Michael, Neil Young, Stevie Ray Vaughan: 1954–1990...$2–4

#590 Living Colour: Good Day for Black Rock $2–4

ROLLING STONE BOUND EDITIONS (Bound issues do not have the same value as the more highly desired subscription and newsstand issues)

Vol. I, Issues #1–#15...$450–900
Vol. II, Issues #16–#30 ....$200–400
Vol. III, Issues #31–#45...$200–400
Vol. IV, Issues #46–#60 ....$150–300
Vol. V, Issues #61–#75...$150–300
Vol. VI, Issues #76–#90..$125–250
Vol. VII, Issues #91–#105 ....$75–150
Vol. VIII, Issues #106–#120..$50–100
Vol. IX, Issues #121–#135..$50–100
Vol. X, Issues #136–#141 ....$35–70
Vol. XI, Issues #142–#150..$35–70
Vol. XII, Issues #151–#160...$35–70
Vol. XIII, Issues #161–#170..$35–70
Vol. XIV, Issues #171–#180..$35–70
Vol. XV, Issues #181–#190...$35–70
Vol. XVI, Issues #191–#200...$35–70
Vol. XVII, Issues #201–#210..$25–50
Vol. XVIII, Issues #211–#220...$25–50
Vol. XIX, Issues #221–#230...$25–50

ROLLING STONE: LIKE A (TSM Publishing Corp.)

1985

Summer Collector's bootleg parody of the original *Rolling Stone Magazine*—Bob Dylan: How Does it Feel?, Boy George, Madonna With Child, Duran Duran, Lennon & Yoko .$3–5

ROLLING STONES 1989 TOUR MAGAZINE

1989

The Official Collector's Edition, Exclusive 1989 Tour, full-page pics $3–6

ROLLING STONE SUPPLEMENT/THE NEW YORK FLYER

(Tabloid)

All issues...$5–15

ROLLING STONE SUPPLEMENT/SAN FRANCISCO FLYER

(Tabloid)

All issues...$5–15

R.P.M. (Record Profile Magazine)

All issues...$2–4

ROYAL'S WORLD COUNTDOWN

All issues...$25–50

Buddy Holly

Collecting

BUDDY HOLLY

Charles Hardin Holley, known to the world as Buddy Holly, was born on September 7, 1936, and perished in a plane crash on February 3, 1959, ending what was to be a super-successful career. As it has been more than 30 years since Buddy Holly has been on the music scene, some of his collectibles, especially personal items, are extremely rare.

The value of his early records, those released during his lifetime, have steadily risen in value, the greatest price coming after the release of the movie *The Buddy Holly Story* in 1978. Of the obtainable items, one of the most desirable is an authentic autograph.

Personal items belonging to Buddy Holly were always very hard to attain, until June 23, 1990, when the bulk of his items, including his famous Gibson and Stratocaster guitars, which had been held by his family, were sold at auction at Sotheby's in New York City.

As Buddy Holly's group, The Crickets, is still performing around the world, items by these persons are still relatively easy to collect, including autographs.

45S, NEAR MINT CONDITION

Brunswick 55009, "That'll be the Day"/"I'm Looking for Someone to Love".......$12–15
Coral 61885, "Peggy Sue"/"Everyday"..$10–12
Coral 62448, "Slippin' & Slidin' "/"What to Do"...$75–100
Coral 20526 (Chile), "Look at Me"/"Now We're One"..$60–75
Coral 72392 (England), "Heartbeat"/"Everyday" $20–30
Coral 93356 (Germany), "Bo Diddley"/"It's Not My Fault".................................$25–40
Coral DC 1059 (Japan), "It's so Easy"/"Lonesome Tears"..................................$50–60
Decca 29854, "Blue Days Black Nights"/"Love Me," DJ copy $80–100
Decca 29854, "Blue Days Black Nights"/"Love Me"..$100–125
Decca 30434, "That'll be the Day"/"Rock Around With Ollie Vee," DJ copy....$125–150
Decca 30434, "That'll be the Day"/"Rock Around With Ollie Vee" $175–200

EPS, 7" FOUR-TRACK 45S WITH CARDBOARD COVERS

Brunswick 71038, "The Sound of the Crickets"..$125–150
Coral 10400 (New Zealand), "Maybe Baby" $50–60
Coral 62007 (France), "Rip it Up" $60–75
Coral 81193, "Brown-Eyed Handsome Man"..$350–450
Decca 2575, "That'll be the Day" $500–550
Festival 10397 (Australia), "Blue Days Black Nights"......................................$75–100

LPS 12" WITH CARDBOARD COVERS

Ace of Hearts (England), "That'll be the Day"..$50–60
Bell 1021 (Korea), "The Buddy Holly Story"...$150–200
Brunswick 54038, "The Chirping Crickets"...$125–150
Caravan 33001 (Belgium), "Buddy Holly"..$30–40
Coral 57450, "Showcase"...$60–75
Coral 96101 (Holland), "Buddy Holly Countrywise" (This is a 10" LP with extremely limited known copies. *Note*: Beware of bootleg copies.) $1,000–2,000
Coral 97034 (Germany), "Buddy Holly Forever"..$50–60
Decca 8707, "That'll be the Day," DJ copy...$400–450
MCA 3275 (South Africa), "The World of Buddy Holly"....................................$50–60
Sir Val 7008 (Italy), "It Doesn't Matter Anymore"..$75–100
Vocalion 73923, "Good Rockin' " $100–125

78S, 10" RECORDS WHICH BREAK VERY EASILY

Brunswick 55035, "Oh Boy"/"Not Fade Away"..$150–175
Coral 61985, "Rave On"/"Take Your Time"...$125–150
Coral 62074 (Canada), "It Doesn't Matter Anymore"/"Raining in My Heart"....$125–150
Decca 29854, "Blue Days Black Nights"/"Love Me"..$300–500

OTHER COLLECTIBLE ITEMS

PICTURES

Any candid photos of Buddy Holly, with or without his group, which have been previously published can bring prices ranging from $25–30 to $300 or more, depending on the purchaser and the use of the picture.

AUTOGRAPH

The price depends on what was actually signed. Just his signature on a piece of paper sells for $400–700. A signed picture sells in the range of $700–1,500. A picture signed by all four Crickets from 1957 can sell for $1,500 or more. Signed contracts, personal letters, and such can sell for thousands of dollars.

PERSONAL CLOTHING

Although seldom obtained outside his family, a recent auction (6/90) of some of Holly's personal belongings brought the following prices:

Lot 362, orange V-neck sweater..$1,320
Lot 392, gray stage jacket seen on album cover...$5,500
Lot 394, a pair of brown trousers...$770
Lot 400, a pair of brown suede stage shoes...$1,870
Lot 406, light blue sweater seen in many photos $4,675
Lot 421, nine silk handkerchiefs...$880
Lot 457, black motorcycle boots..$7,425

INSTRUMENTS

Buddy Holly's famed 1958 Stratocaster guitar, his Gibson acoustic with a homemade handtooled leather cover, his banjo, and other accessories were sold recently at auction (6/90) and brought the following prices:

Lot 378, two guitar picks & a signed card...$1,980
Lot 381, banjo & case, ca. 1935 ....$6,500
Lot 395, guitar capo & signed card..$1,320
Lot 408, Gibson guitar with homemade cover, ca. 1945...............................$242,000
Lot 431, handmade guitar strap for Gibson...$7,975
Lot 433, Ampex tape recorder & microphone..$14,300
Lot 440, harmonica, ca. 1955...$3,025
Lot 458, Fender Stratocaster guitar #028228 ....$110,000

OTHER MISCELLANEOUS ITEMS SOLD AT AUCTION 6/90

Lot 389, Buddy Holly's first-grade report card and high school commencement announcement $3,850
Lot 393, homemade leather cowboy chaps $11,000
Lot 402, 26 pages of handwritten homework for school................................$4,400
Lot 404, Buddy Holly's social security card, damaged $4,675
Lot 405, bank check written & signed by Holly $3,300
Lot 423, seven-page handwritten autobiography, ca. 1953 ....$8,800
Lot 443, 1956 life insurance policy, receipt signed by Buddy Holly................$4,950
Lot 444, Buddy Holly lyric book, most pages handwritten by Buddy Holly..........$14,300
Lot 455, black horn-rimmed glasses..$45,100

BUDDY HOLLY MEMORIAL SOCIETY

The International Buddy Holly Memorial Society was founded by Bill Griggs in 1975 and is licensed by the Holly estate. It boasts of more than 5,400 members in all 50 states and 34 foreign countries. It is basically a research organization. They try to locate previously unseen photos and music, and they report on all news pertaining to Buddy Holly and the Crickets. In order to spread this information, Bill Griggs publishes the magazine *Rockin' 50s* (previously called *Reminiscing*) every other month. Content is limited to the true rock 'n' roll era with emphasis on west Texas music.

A one-time membership fee to become a member of the BHMS is $15 in the States and Canada (more overseas), and you receive a special packet of material.

To subscribe to *Rockin' 50s* magazine, the fee for 1990–1991 is $21 in the States and Canada (first class mail), $30 to Europe (airmail), $33 to Asia and Australia (airmail), and $21 anywhere overseas (by surface mail). You may send a self-addressed, stamped envelope and request the free information sheet, or simply send payment for the one-time membership fee and the annual subscription fee to: Bill Griggs, 3022 56th Street, Lubbock, TX 79413.

S

SHA-BOOM

1990

Jan. #1 Annette Funicello Goes All the Way: An Exclusive Interview, Dick Clark Talks About the Payola Scandal That Almost Ruined Him, Ben Weisman: The Man Who Wrote 57 Songs for Elvis Presley, Special Investigative Report That Reveals New Information About Buddy Holly's Fatal Airplane Crash, Complete With Rare Photos. *Note*: Only a few thousand copies of this issue ever made it to newsstands.)...$5–10

Feb. #2 Elvis Presley: Exclusive Photos of Graceland, Connie Francis: "My Father Committed Me to a Mental Institution," Herman (Peter Noone) Trumps the Hermits, Ed "Kookie" Byrnes, Motown..$3–6

Mar. #3 Pat Boone: Pat Tries to Set the Record Straight About His Goody-goody Image, Little Richard's Drummer Reveals the Wildman's Backstage Antics, A Tour of Memphis' Famous Sun Studios $3–6

Apr. #4 Diana Ross, Motown, Backstage With Chuck Berry, Bo Diddley & Ronnie Spector, The Supremes, Spencer Davis Group...$3–6

May #5 The Beatles: Special Feature Interview With Ringo Starr & Three Other Beatle Drummers Who Kept the Beat for John, Paul & George, A Tour of the Elvis Presley Automobile Museum..$3–6

June #6 James Dean: The Stars Talk About Their Relationship With James Dean, Eddie Cochran: Sharon Sheeley Recalls the Night She Almost Died With Eddie $3–6

July #7 A Visit With Sonny Bono, Johnnie Ray, Elvis Presley's Private Jet, Marilyn Monroe $3–6

Aug. #8 ....$3–6

Oct./Nov. #9 Buddy Holly: Inside the Myth, Ronnie Spector. (*Note*: Only three Xerox copies exist in booklet form of this issue.) ....Value Unknown

16 MAGAZINE

1959

May #8 Inside Elvis Presley by the Girl Who Knows Him Best, Fabian Revealed, Frankie Avalon Answers 40 Intimate Questions, Rick Nelson, Phil Everly, Connie Francis, Sandra Dee, Bobby Darrin, Backstage With Dick Clark, Pat Boone...................................$30–60

1960

All issues $20–40

1961

Jan. Troy Donahue Answers 40 Intimate Questions, Connie Stevens & Dating, Barbara Levick & Bill Cook, Bobby Rydell: "My Life in Pix," Why Do They Lie About Annette Funicello & Fabian?, Jimmy Clayton, Elvis Presley $25–50

Mar. Annette Funicello, Dion, Troy Donahue, Brenda Lee, Jimmy Clayton, Elvis Presley..$20–40

July Johnny Tillotson Answers 40 Intimate Questions, Paul Anka Says "I Confess," Dion Describes His Lonely Life, Yvette Mimieux, Elvis Presley: 10 Brand-new Pix & Giant Color Pin-up, Paul Petersen's Secrets, Chubby Checker, Neil Sedaka, Frankie Avalon, Annette Funicello $25–50

Aug. Share Your Secrets With Paul Anka, Dion Confesses, Bobby Vee Answers 40 Intimate Questions, Bobby Rydell, Annette Funicello Reveals Her Secrets, Deborah Walley, Johnny Burnette, Fabian: "Don't Go High Hat on Me," A Visit to "American Bandstand," Rick Nelson: Stop Those Terrible Lies, Johnny Tillotson poster...$25–50

Sept. "American Bandstand" Regulars' Private Lives, Buzz Clifford's Loves & Hates, Tuesday Weld Exclusive, Paul Anka, Fabian, Bobby Vee, George Chakiris, Tony Orlando, The Night Frankie Avalon is Trying to Forget $25–50

Oct. Connie Francis Answers 40 Intimate Questions, Bobby Rydell Blows His Top, Elvis Presley Tells Things He's Never Told Before, Annette Funicello Describes Her Hates & Loves, Jimmy Clanton, Don Grady, Brenda Lee, Shelley Fabares...........................$25–50

Nov. Arlene Askes Mike 40 Intimate Questions, Fabian Confesses, Bobby Vee Describes His Favorite Girl, Paul Anka: "I Ran Away From Home," Troy Donahue, Rick Nelson, Connie Francis, Johnny Tillotson, Debby Walley, A Visit to Frankie Avalon's New Home, Duane Eddy, What the Teen Idols Really Think of Each Other $25–50

1962

Jan. Bobby Rydell Runs Wild, Brenda Lee Answers 40 Intimate Questions, Frankie Avalon Describes His Loves & Hates, Rick Nelson's Private World, Shelley Fabares' Secret Hairdos, Troy Donahue, Connie Francis bigger than life-size pin-up, Paul Petersen & Rick Nelson giant color pin-ups, "American Bandstand," Secrets Kept From Annette Funicello: Her Mother's Moving Story $25–50

Feb. Bobby Rydell & Jimmy Clanton giant color pin-ups, Hayley Mills Answers 40 Intimate Questions, Debby Walley's Life Story, Troy Donahue's Loves & Hates, Secrets from Connie Francis' Diary, Annette Funicello's Dream Wedding, Frankie Avalon, Fabian, How to Act When you Meet Dion, Ann-Margret...$20–40

Mar. Ricky Nelson Giant Bonus Feature, Connie Francis: "Fast Girls are Losers," Connie Stevens, The Kookie Private Life of Bobby Vee, Elvis Presley Revealed: The True Facts, Hayley Mills' Life in Words & Pix, Frankie Avalon, The Inside Scoop on Chubby Checker, Johnny Tillotson, Annette Funicello's Amazing Change $20–40

May Sandra Dee Answers 40 Intimate Questions, Troy Donahue Answers His Critics, Rick Nelson's New Home, Linda Scott, Dion, Fabian, Frankie Avalon, Annette Funicello, Connie Francis, Connie Stevens, Dick Chamberlain, Brenda Lee $20–40

Aug. Connie Stevens life-size pin-up, Dick Chamberlain Confesses, Johnny Crawford Answers 40 Questions, Troy Donahue, Elvis Presley in Hawaii, Connie Stevens' Life in Pix, Bobby Rydell, Behind the Scenes on "American Bandstand," Annette Funicello: "When I Get Married," Fabian & Sandra Dee, Joey Dee, Chubby Checker, Shelley Fabares, Annette Funicello, Hayley Mills...$20–40

Sept. Paul Petersen Tells All, Bobby Vee Reveals His Life Story, Troy Donahue's Secret Photo Album, Dick Chamberlain, Shelley Fabare/Mystery Girl, Connie Francis: "I Was a Lonely Teenager," Bob Logan, Annette Funicello, Connie Stevens, Bobby Rydell, Rick Nelson, Chakiris..$20–40

Oct. Dick Chamberlain Answers 40 Questions, Connie Stevens Shows Her Secret Photos, Troy Donahue's Loves & Hates, Annette Funicello's Most Romantic Night, Bobby Vee Asks: "Will You be My Girl?," "American Bandstand" Birthday Party, Shelley Fabares & Paul Petersen color pin-ups, Bobby Rydell: Has Hollywood Changed Him?, Dion, Anita Bryant, Johnny Crawford...$20–40

Nov. Elvis Presley: What is He Afraid Of?, Connie Stevens, Has Troy Donahue Fallen in Love?, Rick Nelson, Dick Chamberlain, Shelley Fabare, Hayley Mills: Is She Trying to Grow Up Too Fast? Bobby Vee, Paul Petersen, Johnny Crawford, Mike Landon, Paul Anka...$20–40

Dec. Highlights of Vince Edwards Life, Connie Stevens, Two Years With Elvis Presley, Dick Chamberlain, Bobby Rydell, Paul Petersen, Chakiris, "Bonanza," Brenda Lee......$20–40

1963

Jan. Shelley Fabares: "When I Get Married," Vince Edwards & The Girls, Paul Petersen's Life Story, Eddie Hodges Squeals on Hayley Mills, Frankie Avalon's Love Letter to You, Bobby Vinton, Tommy Roe, Mark Rydell, Johnny Crawford, Mike Clifford, Dick Chamberlain, Maharis, Chakiris..$20–40

Feb. 101 Pix of Dick Chamberlain, Elvis Presley: "I Spent a Day With Him," Johnny Crawford Revealed, George Maharis, Shelley Fabares' Life Story in Pix, Connie Stevens, Brenda Lee, Frank Sinatra Jr., Vince Edwards...$20–40

Mar. Paul Petersen's Life Story in Pix, Vince Edwards, Johnny Crawford's Complete Life Story, Elvis Presley, Troy Donahue, Fabian, Hayley Mills, Rick Nelson, Bobby Vee, Dion, Frankie Avalon, Mike Landon, Bobby Rydell, Dick Chamberlain $20–40

Apr. Troy Donahue's Thrilling Life Story, Connie Francis, Michael Landon, Neil Sedaka, Ricky Nelson, Dion, Shelley Fabares, Timi Yuro, Vince Edwards, Elvis Presley: 101 Pix of Elvis, Johnny Crawford, Paul Petersen: His Life in Photos, Connie Stevens $20–40

May Paul Petersen & Shelley Fabares: 200 Pix, Troy Donahue, Dickey Lee, Brenda Lee
....$20–40

June Rick Nelson: 101 Pix, "American Bandstand" Bonus Issue $20–40

Sept. Shelley Fabares Squeals on Paul Petersen, Talking About Troy Donahue—Is He Married?, Elvis Presley, Hayley Mills, Don Grady, Dick Chamberlain, Ann-Margret: Why Don't You Dig Her?, Johnny Crawford..$20–40

Oct. 101 Private Pix of Michael Landon & the "Bonanza" Gang, The Boys of *West Side Story*, Jimmy Darin, Russ Tamblyn, Shelley Fabares, Annette Funicello, Troy Donahue, Connie Francis, Johnny Crawford & Paul Petersen Talk About Girls, Dick Chamberlain
....$20–40

Nov. Dick Chamberlain & Paul Petersen: Look What's Happened to Them, Elvis Presley & the "Bonanza" Gang full-length color feature, Shelley Fabares, Goodbye to "American Bandstand," Hayley Mills: Her Intimate Confessions, Sandra Dee, Johnny Crawford's Loves & Hates, Chakiris & Beymar, Anderson..$20–40

Dec. Elvis Presley & Ann-Margret, Bobby Rydell's Crazy Mixed-up Pix, Paul Petersen, Johnny Crawford, Luke Halpin, Davy Jones, Cliff Richard, Dick Chamberlain.......$20–40

1964

Jan. Hayley Mills' Very Private Pix, Paul Petersen: "My Wildest Night," Cliff Richard Exclusive, Bobby Rydell: Teasing the Girls, Annette Funicello, Tamblyn, Chakiris.....$20–40

Feb. The Beatles & Elvis Presley: What Really Happened at Their Secret Meeting?, David McCallum, Sonny & Cher: The Heartbreak Behind Their Laughter, Herman's Hermits, The Rolling Stones, Gene Pitney, Chris Jones, Keith Allison's Life in Pix, The Turtles, Yardbirds, Ian Whitcomb, Beau Brummels, Dino, Desi & Billy Meet the McCoys........$20–40

Mar. Patty Duke's Untold Secrets, James Franciscus' Life Story in 100 Pix, Paul Petersen, Chakiris, Ann-Margret & Hayley Mills' Loves, Are There Two Elvis Presleys?, Johnny & Bobby Crawford, Annette Funicello...$20–40

Apr. Paul Petersen's Book of Love, Janet Landgard, Troy Donahue, Hayley Mills, Lesley Gore: "How to Make the Most of Yourself," Patty Duke's Life Story in Words & Pix, Cliff Richards' Loves & Hates, "Mr. Novak," The Beach Boys, The Beatles $20–40

May The Beatles: 40 Pix & Fact Sheets, Bobby Rydell Answers 40 Forbidden Questions, James Franciscus, Paul Petersen: "The Night I Cried," Lesley Gore & Connie Francis, Elvis Presley: What He Does to Girls, Dick Chamberlain, Kurt Russell, Patty Duke, Hayley Mills: 101 Intimate Questions..$20–40

June The Beatles: 160 Intimate Questions, The Beach Boys in Color, Elvis Presley's 101 Untold Secrets, Bobby Rydell: "The Night I Almost Died," Sandra Dee & Hayley Mills: Their Red Hot "Freeze," Patty Duke: 80 Pix & Her Life Story, Paul Petersen's Party, Shelley Fabares, Mike Landon's Thrilling Romance, Yvette Mimieux, Cliff Richard, Lesley Gore, Annette Funicello & Frankie Avalon/Muscle Beach Party $20–40

July The Beatles Life Stories & All New Pix, Darryl Richard/Janet Langaurd, The Four Seasons, The Searchers, Swinging Blue Jeans, Dave Clark Five, Bobby Vinton: 40 Personal Questions, Yvette Mimieux, Patty Duke, Dick Chamberlain, Paul Petersen: 101 Top Secrets, Troy Donahue, Why Did Elvis Presley Kiss Ann-Margret Goodbye? Mike Landon, Connie Francis..$20–40

Aug. The Big Beatle Bonanza Issue, Paul Petersen, Patty Duke, Dick Chamberlain, Hayley

16 MAGAZINE,
1962, Mar.

16 MAGAZINE,
1963, Apr.

16 MAGAZINE,
1964, Oct.

16 MAGAZINE,
1965, Mar.

16 MAGAZINE,
1966, June

16 MAGAZINE,
1966, Oct.

16 MAGAZINE,
1971, Nov.

16 MAGAZINE,
1972, May

16 MAGAZINE,
1972, Dec.

Mills, The Rolling Stones: Has England Gone Too Far? Shelley Fabres Getting Married?, The Dave Clark 5: What They Did to American Girls...$20–40

Sept. The Beatles: All Four Married?, The Rolling Stones: They Get Away With Murder, The Dave Clark 5: 50 Intimate Questions, The Beach Boys "Feud," Elvis Presley, Paul Petersen, Michael Landon vs. Pernell Roberts, Beatles' Special Feature—A Girl's Three Days With the Beatles, Davy Jones, James Brown...$20–40

Oct. The Beatles Biggest Blast, Beatles Scrapbook, Peter & Gordon: An Intimate Talk With Them, Bobby Rydell's Secret Search, Jane Asher, Maureen Cox, Patti Boyd, The Dave Clark 5: Which Two Are Wed?, Patty Duke Super Signed Portrait Pin-up, The Rolling Stones, Beach Boys: 50 Questions, Hayley Mills: A Falling Star?, Jerry Kramer's Hates & Loves...$20–40

Nov. The Beatles' Wildest Years, The Rolling Stones 100 Explosive Pix & 200 Intimate Questions, Dick Chamberlain, The Beatles Personal Letter to You, Peter & Gordon: Our Hates & Loves, Should Patty Duke Leave Home?, Dusty Springfield, Jane Asher, Paul McCartney, The Animals, Lesley Gore Tells, Peter McEnry, Billy J. Kramer, Annette Funicello $20–40

Dec. The Beatles Red Hot Discovery: Never Before Printed—Their Baby Pictures & What Their Parents Say About Them, Peter McEnry: 50 Questions, Dave Clark 5 vs. the Rolling Stones, Beware of the Animals, Hayley Mills Learns About Love, Luke Halpin's Loves & Hates, The Three Wild Lives of Elvis Presley, Paul Petersen, Connie Francis $20–40

1965

Jan. The Beatles' Secret Wild Pix, Dave Clark 5 & the Animals in Raving Color, Jane Asher, Luke Halpin, How it Feels to be Kissed by Elvis Presley, The Rolling Stones Fight Back, "I Grew Up With Patty Duke," Dusty Springfield, Lesley Gore, Manfred Mann, Honeycombs, Kinks, The Zombies, Pretty Things, Chad & Jeremy, Peter & Gordon, Dave Berry, Meet Marvin Gaye $20–40

Mar. Alone With the Stones, The Beatles' Wild Wild Bash, George & John on a Desert Island, Paul's Most Secret Confession, Ringo Turns Cowboy, The Beatles Take Over Scotland, Luke Halpin, Hayley Mills, The Girl Who Tickles Elvis Presley, Peter & Gordon Tell on Each Other, Jane Asher: Her Life in Pix, Pattie Boyd, Peter McEnry, Maureen Cox, Paul Petersen, Shangri-las, Kinks, Dick Chamberlain, The Beach Boys, Four Seasons, Animals, Patty Duke, Mersey Beats...$20–40

Apr. The Beatles: A Visit to Their New Homes, Dino, Desi & Billy: 30 Pix & Facts, Peter & Gordon in Luv-lu Color, The Stones Top Secret Love Life, Gene Pitney: 40 Very Intimate Questions, Ringo's Loves & Hates, The Dave Clark Five: The Day They Almost Died, The Supremes & the Shangri-las Tell All, The Honeycombs, Halpin, The Legend of Buddy Holly, Lesley Gore's Life in Pix, Herman & the Hermits, The Boys in Patty Duke's Life, Fact Sheets on Chad & Jeremy, Paul Petersen...$20–40

May The Beatles & Me: Their Closest Friend Tells All—From Schooldays to Night Now, Dave Clark Five, Bobby Sherman & "Shindig," David McCallum & Robert Vaughn, The Stones Double-page Color Pin-up, Chad & Jeremy Tell Everything, The Beach Boys, Sheila James, Halpin, Gerry's New Bride, The Zombies, Marianne Faithful, Twinkle, Gary Lewis, Georgie Fame, Gene Pitney, The Animals...$20–40

June The Beatles, George & Ringo Confess, Paul McCartney Giant Signed Pin-up, The Stones Answer Questions You Don't Dare Ask, Gary Lewis Complete Fax & Pix, The Beatles & Me: a special feature with four pin-ups, Peter & Gordon Flip Out With Chad & Jeremy, Halpin, David McCallum, What It's Like to be Married to Ringo, Dave Clark Five, "Hullabaloo," Liz Montgomery, Georgie Fame, Roger Mobley, Jan & Dean, The Kinks, Freddie & the Dreamers...$20–40

July 100 Pix of David McCallum, Herman & the Hermits Answer 100 Questions, The Beatles Movie Pix & Color Pin-ups, Dave Clark Five, Dino, Desi & Billy, Freddie & the Dreamers, Chad & Jeremy, Bob Dylan, Petula Clark, Luke Halpin, Elvis Presley..$20–40

Aug. Herman's (Peter Noone) Life Story in 100 Pix, The Secret Life of David McCallum, 101 Untold Secrets of Peter & Gordon, The Rolling Stones' Picture Book, Gary Lewis & the Playboys Answer 100 Questions, Luke Halpin, Robert Vaughn, Dave Clark Five, The Beatles, What is John Lennon Hiding?, Ringo: Why is He Different?, Why is George Harrison Angry?, Paul in Color...$20–40

Sept. Herman's Hermits: Peter Noone's Life in Pix, The Beatles: Devils or Darlings?, David McCallum, The Beach Boys: "Our Hates & Loves," Mike Smith, Dennis Payton, Robert

Vaughn, In Liverpool With Gerry & the Pacemakers, The Stones: We Break the Rules, Chad & Jeremy: Life Story in Pix, Freddie & the Dreamers, Jan & Dean, Patti Boyd $20–40

Oct. The Beatles: The Truth About Their Girls, David McCallum Opens His Heart, Dino, Desi & Billy Confess, Herman: "My Hates & Luvs," Never-before-seen Pix of Peter Noone, Beatle Color Portrait Pin-ups, Sean "007" Connery, The Stones: 101 Sizzling Secrets, Chad & Jeremy Answer 80 Questions, Peter & Gordon, The Byrds, Kinks, Robert Vaughn Party, Patty Duke, Elvis Presley, Paul Revere & the Raiders......................$20–40
Nov. Herman's Whole Life Story, Patty Duke: How You Can be Her Best Friend, Dino, Desi & Billy: 120 Revealing Questions, David McCallum, Robert Vaughn, Flyin' With the Byrds, Ian Whitcomb, Sonny & Cher, Lovin' Spoonful, Patrick McGoohan, Chris Jagger Tells What it's Like Living With the Rolling Stones, What is Elvis Presley Hiding? ...$20–40
Dec. The Beatles & Me: Neil Reveals Red Hot New Secrets, Dino, Desi & Billy, Herman's Hermits Tell All on Each Other: 50 Flipped-out Pix & "Herman's Little Sister Suzanne," Paul Revere & the Raiders Pin-ups, Fax Sheets & Autographs, Sonny & Cher Answer 100 Questions, The Byrds, The Beach Boys, Ian Whitcomb, Chris Jagger Squeals on the Stones, Bruce Scott, Bob Dylan, Donovan, Marianne Faithful, Jane Asher, Kinks, Dave Clark Five, Meet the Lovin' Spoonful, Meet John Leyton & Pattie Boyds' Sister Jenny Boyd.......$20–40

1966

Jan. Herman: 100 Intimate Pix, Special Feature: "I Live With the Beatles," Bob Dylan, Dino, Desi & Billy: Their Personal Friends, Donovan, Ian Whitcomb's Complete Life Story in Pix, David McCallum, Thrills & Chills With the Dave Clark Five, Sonny & Cher Tell the Truth About Each Other, Patty Duke, Debbie Watson, Leslie Gore, Billy Joe Royal, Tony & the Tigers, Luke Halpin $20–40
Feb. Herman's Hermits, The Stones, Robert Vaughn, Gene Pitney, Dino, Desi & Billy: Life Stories from Birth With 100 Never-before Pix, David McCallum, Chris Jones, The Turtles, Yardbirds, Ian Whitcomb, Beau Brummells, Meet the McCoys, Keith Allison, Sonny & Cher: The Heartbreak Behind Their Laughter, Hayley Mills, Patty Duke, Sally Field, Cynthia Lennon, Peter & Gordon, Paul Revere & the Raiders, Lovin' Spoonful, Tony & the Tigers $20–40
Mar. The Beatles: 50 Wild Pix & Secrets, Dino, Desi & Billy, Lee Majors, Sonny & Cher, Chris Jones, Elvis Presley, Herman: The Truth About Those Terrible Rumors, Allison/ McCartney, Illya/Napoleon, Sally Field: The Secret Fear She Hides, Fang, Paul Revere, Mark Lindsay, Dave Clark Five: 55 Intimate Questions, Lovin' Spoonful, The Secret Life of Bob Dylan, The Stones: Their Very Private Lives, The McCoys $20–40
Apr. The Beatles Hair-Raiser: You've Never Seen Them Like This Before, Paul Revere & the Raiders: Intimate Pix & Daring Questions, The McCoys, Mark Lindsay, David McCallum, Chris Jones: The Truth About His Double Life, Peter & Gordon, Ian Whitcomb, Dave Clark Five: Their Secret Life by Their Closest Friend, The Gentrys, Gidget/Sally Field, Sonny & Cher: The Lies That Almost Destroyed Them, Billy Joe Royal, Mick Jagger, Keith Allison...$20–40
May The Beatles: New Hot Wild Pix With a Private Visit to Their Homes, Beatle Baby Pix & Secrets, Herman's Hermits: 101 Supersecret Secrets, Dino, Desi & Billy: Their Personal Letters, Paul McCartney, Tony & the Tigers, Fang, Alfy, Keith Allison, Mark Lindsay, Sonny & Cher Wear Clothes, The Mamas & the Papas, David Jones, Randy Boone, David McCallum, The Stones Blow Their Minds, Sally Field Fact Sheet, Knickerbockers......$20–40
June Paul McCartney: His Hidden Life With Top Secret Pix, Paul Revere & the Raiders: "Come Fly With Us," Dino, Desi & Billy Answer Your Letters, The Beatles, Keith Allison, Burt Ward/Batman, David McCallum, Chris Jones Confesses, Sally Field: "How to Get the Gidget Look," The Stones, The Byrds, Hayley Mills: Her Wild New Life, Lou Christie, Chad & Jeremy, Lovin' Spoonful, Lee Majors, Bruce Scott, Robin, Ringo & John......$20–40
July The Beatles: 66 Wow-ee Pix—"U Won't Believe Your Eyes," Raiders Fab Pix Plus Their Loves & Hates, Robin & Batman Unmask Each Other, Illya/Solo on the Loose, Keith Allison: New Look & New Sound, Dave Clark Five in Danger, Herman, Gary & the Playboys: Secret Fax & Uptight Pix, Bobby Fuller, Peter & Gordon, The Beach Boys, The Lovin' Spoonful, The Byrds, Young Ringo...$20–40
Aug. The Beatles Weird Wishes, The Mamas & the Papas Spin Out, Dino, Desi & Billy: Spend a Day With Them, Batman & Robin Answer 80 Questions, Dave Clark Five, Herman's Hermits Caught in the Act, The Raiders' 100 Wildest & Intimate Pix, Mark

Slade, Beach Boys, Cher's Brush With Death, Chris Jones, Michele Phillips: All-American Beauty, Tony & the Tigers, Ian Whitcomb..$20–40

Sept. The Beatles: 60 Hidden Pix, Shocking Rumors About John Lennon, Dini, Desi & Billy: What They Really Think of Each Other, Raiders' True Life Stories, In Hawaii With the Hermits, Lovin' Spoonful, Burt Ward, David McCallum, Paul McCartney, Keith Allison, Dave Clark Five, Fang, Keith Richards, Dear Cher...$20–40

Oct. The Beatles Explode: 50 Freakie New Pix & Their Secret Lives, Fang at Home, Mark Lindsay, Smitty, Herman & the Hermits, Dave Clark Five, Raiders, Paul McCartney, Keith Allison, David McCallum/Robert Vaughn, Stones, Beach Boys, Thomas Group......$20–40

Nov. At Home With the Rolling Stones, The Dave Clark Five, Herman's Hermits, Dino, Desi & Billy, Mark Lindsay, Sally Field's Sad Farewell, Jay North, The McCoys, Mindbenders, Beach Boys, The Monkees, John Law...$20–40

1967

Jan. The Monkees: 40 True Fax & Fab Pix, Raiders, The Beatles' Secret Plans, Herman Blows His Mind, Halpin, Raiders: 250 Hot Pix, Dave Clark Five: Fantastic Adventures, Lovin' Spoonful, Beach Boys' Wives, Beatles, Dino, Desi & Billy, Stones.............$20–40

Feb. Monkees Scoop: 100 Wow-ee Pix & Intimate Questions & Kolossal Kolar Pin-ups, David McCallum Makes It, Raiders, Mark Lindsay, The Beatles Freak Out, Hermits: Extra Secret Lives, Dino, Desi & Billy Super Surprise, Dave Clark Five, Squealing on the Stones, Peter McEnery, Lovin' Spoonful, Byrds, Leyton, Keith Anderson............................$20–40

Mar. The Monkees: 300 New Pix, The Monkees Secret Loves & Secret Lives, Includes nine color Monkee pin-ups, Mark Lindsay's Hidden Life Revealed, Fang, Beatle Shocker, Dino, Desi & Billy, Herman's Marriage Plans, Kurt Russell, Sonny & Cher, Hollies ...$20–40

Apr. Exclusive & Very Private Pix of the Monkees, Paul Revere & the Raiders Reveal Things They Tried to Hide, The Beatles Battle, Dino, Desi & Billy, Herman Needs Help, "The Monkees & Me" by Their Closest Friend, The Real Leonard Nimoy.............$20–40

June The Monkees Run Wild, Paul Revere & the Raiders, The Beatles & The Monkees Meet, The Rascals Revealed, Jim Morrison's Mystery Girl, Herman's Hermits, Dino, Desi & Billy..$20–40

July The Monkees: 100 Secret Pix, Davy's Lonely Nights, Micky's Hidden Life, Peter's Wild Flings, Mike's Mod Madness, The Monkees: A Visit to Their Homes, The Monkees True Life Stories, Beatles, Leonard Nimoy..$20–40

Aug. The Monkees, Herman's Hermits, Mark Lindsay & His New Farrari, We Remember Elvis, Micky Dolenz: His Life in Pix, Beatles, Kurt Russell, Dino, Desi & Billy, Phil Volk...$20–40

Sept. The Monkees, Mark Lindsay: The Bad Things He Does, Dino Martin, Freddy Weller Answers 40 Intimate Questions, Ex-Raiders Phil, Drake & Smitty, Herman's Hermits, Micky Dolenz Life in Pix Part IV, Who's Who in the Sgt. Pepper Band.................$20–40

Nov. The Monkees, Mike Nesmith, Beatles, Mark Lindsay, Sally Field Answers 20 Snoopy Questions, Raider Centerfold, "American Bandstand," Jon Provost, Jim Morrison & the Doors, Sajid Khan, Jay North, Dino Danelli...$20–40

1968

Jan. The Monkees' Private Conversations, The Rascals, Dear Cher, Jim Morrison & His Mystery Girl, Peter Tork, Slade, Peter Noone, Sajid Khan...$20–40

Feb. Davy Jones, Sajid Khan, Jay North, Jon Provost, Mark Lindsay: The Tears They Try to Hide, The Cowsills, Jim Morrison's Lost Love, Dino, The Monkees, Herman's Future
....$20–40

July The Monkees, Davy Jones, The Cowsills, Raiders, Slade, Sajid, The Beatles, Nazz, Herman, Dino, Desi & Billy, "Star Trek," Jim Morrison, The Bee Gees, Mark Lindsay..$20–40

Oct. The Monkees/Sajid Fight: The Whole Terrible True Story, Raiders: What They Do After Dark, Chris Jones Answers 40 Questions, Boone & Gorillas, The Cowsills: Barry Takes You to Bill's Wedding, Mike Vincent, Len Whiting, "Star Trek," "Dark Shadows," Dino, Desi & Billy, Billy Mummy, Slade..$20–40

Nov. Davy Jones: "Help Me—I'm Lonely," Jonathan Frid & "Dark Shadows," Boone, The Cowsills, Sajid, The Monkees Tragedy Strikes, Bobby Sherman, "Star Trek," Chris Jones, Dino, Desi & Billy, Slade, Schultz Kids, Sarrazin $15–30

Dec. Jonathan Frid is Missing: The Whole Weird Story, Sajid, Desi, Lucie, Dino & Billy,

Davy Jones & The Monkees: Their Loves & Hates, Michael Cole, Raiders Break Up, Nazz, The Doors, Union Gap, Darrow, Boone $15–30

1969

Jan. Davy Jones, Jonathan Frid, Sajid, Bobby Sherman, "Mod Squad," "Dark Shadows," The Beatles Like You've Never Seen Them Before, The Monkees, The Doors, The Union Gap, Herman's Hermits, The Cowsills in the Tunnel of Love, "Star Trek"............$15–30
Mar. Davy Jones' Shocking Decision, Sajid Khan, Elvis Presley, Bobby Sherman, The Beatles, "Mod Squad," "Dark Shadows": The Whole True Story, The Monkees' New Life, Bobby Sherman centerfold $15–30
Apr. Bobby Sherman: The Girl That Tried to Destroy Him, The Cowsills Throw a Family Party, Mark Lindsay & Davy Jones: Lonely & Love Starved, The Monkees Back on TV, Sajid Khan, Elvis Presley, "Dark Shadows," Cowsills centerfold poster, Jim Morrison $15–30
June Bobby Sherman & Mike Cole: Secret Diaries & 202 Red Hot Pix, Sajid Khan's Hidden Life, Barry & John Cowsill Talk About Girls, issue includes 16 huge color pin-ups, Davy Jones Married?, Jonathan Frid/"Dark Shadows"...$15–30
Aug. Bobby Sherman Takes a Bride, Michael Cole, The Cowsills, Davy Jones' Darkest Hour, Desi, Raiders, Jack Wild, "Dark Shadows," Tommy James.............................$15–30
Nov. Bobby Sherman, Mike Cole's Wedding, Selby's Life in Pix, Barry Cowsill Heart-to-Heart, Billy Mummy, Sajid Khan, Raiders, The Monkees...$15–30

1970

Jan. Bobby Sherman in the Flesh: Share His Secrets, Loves & Life, Mike Cole: Behind Closed Doors, The Cowsills: Their Secret Hiding Places, The Monkees, The Raiders..$15–30
Feb. Bobby Sherman's Secret Life, Mike Cole's Lonely Nights, The Cowsill's Love-In, Jack Wild, Barry Williams, Zooey Hall, Mike Parks, David Henesy, Peggy Lipton, The Monkees...$15–30
Mar. Bobby Sherman Elopes, Mike Cole, The Cowsills, Raiders, The Monkees, Sajid Khan $15–30
May Bobby Sherman Faces Death—Six Months to Live, The Cowsills: Most Wanted Lover-Boys, The Monkees, The Beatles, Raiders, The Osmond Brothers, Mike Cole, David Cassidy, Grass Roots, 3 Dog Night, Steppenwolf, Mountain, Kurt Russell, The Hagers $10–20
Aug. Bobby Sherman's Hidden Desires, Mike Cole, David Cassidy, Davy Jones & Grass Roots, The Osmonds, The Brady Bunch, Cowsills, The Jackson Five, Tom Jones..$15–30
Oct. Bobby Sherman: His Secret Love List, A Day With Donny & the Osmonds, Bob Cowsill's Wedding, David Cassidy, Partridge Family, The Jackson Five $15–30

1971

Apr. Bobby Sherman: The Tears He Tries to Hide, The Jackson Five, The Brady Bunch: Their Secret Hiding Places, David Cassidy Vanishes, The Cowsills, The Osmonds as You've Never Seen Them Before, Peter Duel, Ronny Howard, Chris Stone, Partridge Family, Danny Bonaduce $15–30
May David Cassidy: "Be My Summer Love," The Osmonds: Meet Them in Disneyland, Bobby Sherman, The Jackson Five, Susan Dey, The Bradys, The Cowsills, Mike Cole, Chris Stone, Danny, Rick Ely, Jack Wild..$15–30
Aug. David Cassidy Death Threat: His Life in Danger, Donny Osmond, Bobby Sherman's Love Schedule, The Osmonds, The Jackson 5, Bradys, Cowsills, David Cassidy's Life Story, Susan Dey, Peter Duel, Chad Everett...$15–30
Oct. David Cassidy: What They Whisper Behind His Back, Bobby Sherman, Donny & the Osmonds: Round the Clock, Susan Dey: Summer Love, Chris & the Bradys: New Fax & Pix, Mike Cole, Michael Jackson & the Jackson Five..$15–30
Nov. David Cassidy, The Brady Bunch Funtime: Rare Photos With Full-page Color Cast Photo, The Osmonds, Pete & Ben, Bobby Sherman, The Jackson Five, Night of Dark Shadows, David Cassidy's Life Story $15–30
Dec. The Osmonds, David Cassidy, The Partridge Family, Night of Dark Shadows, Bobby Sherman, Jack Wild, Susan Dey, The Jackson Five, Maureen McCormick, Kurt Russell, David Cassidy's Life Story Chapter 11 ....$15–30

1972

Jan. David Cassidy: His Weird Wicked Nights, Donny Osmond: "Be My Girl," Chris: His Life in Pix, The Jackson Five: 50 Funky Questions, Susan Dey, Butch Patrick, Mike Cole, Michael Jackson, Peter Duel, Bobby Sherman, Jack Wild, David Cassidy's Life Story Chapter 12...$12–25

Apr. David Cassidy: "Watch Out, I'm No Angel," The Osmond Wedding, Donny Osmond, Bobby Sherman's Wild New Life, The Jackson Five: What are They Hiding?, Peter Duel: His Tragic Story, The Carpenters, Butch Patrick $12–25

May Michael Jackson & Jermaine Jackson: Listen to Their Secret Phone Calls, David Cassidy Locked Up, Bobby Sherman, The Partridge Family Sing-along, The Bradys, Donny Osmond's First Date, Butch Patrick, Marie Osmond, Chris Knight.........................$12–25

June Donny Osmond, David Cassidy Invites You into His Bedroom, Marc Bolan & T. Rex, Michael Jackson & the Jackson Five: Funky Family Pix, The Brady Bunch, Bobby Sherman, Ben Murphy, Michael Tilson Thomas...$12–25

Aug. David Cassidy's Shocking Sin-secrets, includes two giant color posters of David Cassidy & Donny Osmond, The Bradys Bounce on Their Beach Blankets, Marc Bolan, Boone Girls, Mantooth, Butch Patrick, Bobby Sherman, Michael Jackson & the Jackson Five $12–25

Sept. David Cassidy: The Vicious Plot—His Life Wrecked?, includes two giant posters of David Cassidy & Donny Osmond, The Jackson Five Pass the Love Test, Bobby Sherman Fights Back, The Bradys, Marc Bolan, Mantooth, Maureen McCormick's Summer Beauty Secrets, Boone Girls $12–25

Oct. Donny Osmond Breaks Down, David Cassidy Alone in the Dark, includes two posters of Michael Jackson & the Jackson Five & Donny Osmond, The Jackson Five Wedding, Bobby Sherman, Bradys, Marc Bolan, 3 Dog Night...$12–25

Nov. David Cassidy Elopes, Donny Osmond, The Jackson Five: Sis Tells All, Is Donny a Father?, Michael Jackson Visits "American Bandstand" $12–25

Dec. David Cassidy Teaches You How to Kiss, Bobby Sherman: Is He Married?, Andy & David, Donny's Secret Steady, Spy on Michael Jackson, Bradys, includes two giant posters of The Osmonds & The Partridge Family...$15–30

1973

Jan. Donny Osmond: Fed-up & Quits the Osmonds, David Cassidy Arrested, Marc Bolan: Born to Boogie, The Jackson Five: Hanging Out With Them, Andy & Dave Tell on Each Other, Bobby Sherman, The Bradys, Rick Springfield, Two Posters of Donny & David Cassidy...$15–30

Feb. Michael Jackson & the Jackson Five in England, The Brady Bunch in Trouble: Cancelled, David Cassidy, Rick Springfield, Alice Cooper: Devil or Angel?, Donny Osmond, Maureen McCormick, The Heywoods, Andy & Dave, includes giant double poster of The Jackson Five & The Osmonds...$12–25

Mar. David Cassidy: Is He a Phoney?, Andy & Dave: At Their House, Rick Springfield's Loves & Hates, Donny Osmond & Michael Jackson Jailed, Alice Cooper: Devil or Angel? Part II, Heywoods, Partridge Family, Maureen McCormick, David Cassidy & Donny Osmond poster..$12–25

Apr. Donny Osmond Kicked Out, Rick Springfield, The Jackson Five, Jan Michael Vincent, Michael Jackson, Latoya Jackson, Giant Poster of Andy & Dave & TV's "Emergency"..$12–25

May Donny Osmond's Hush Illness, "Emergency," David Cassidy: Two-Faced, Two-Timer?, Rick Springfield, Michael Jackson: Feel His Muscles, Andy & Dave, The Osmonds on TV, Latoya Jackson, The Sylvers, The Heywoods, The Bradys, double poster of Donny Osmond & Mark Spitz $12–25

June The Osmond Bomb Threat, Andy & Dave: Hide in Their Closet, David Cassidy: The Girl He Got in Trouble, The Jackson Five: Where They Find Their Girls, Rick Springfield: Taste His Lips, Maureen McCormick & Eve Plumb, The Bradys: 60 Sexy Secrets, The Waltons, The Rookies, Mark Spitz, UFO, Alice Cooper, Double Poster of the Jackson Five & Donny Osmond $12–25

July The Jackson Five in Hollywood & at Home, David Cassidy, Donny Osmond.....$12–25

Aug. Spying on Donny Osmond: Sneak Pix & Secret New Home, Jackson Five: Jump on Their Soul Jet, Andy & Dave, Rick Springfield: Raw Power, David Cassidy: "Please Leave

Me Alone," Bradys, Elvis Presley, UFO, King Fu, includes giant double poster of The Osmonds & TV's "The Waltons" $12–25

Sept. Donny & Randy Shirtless Photos, Alice Cooper, David Cassidy Cracks, The Rookies, Rick Springfield, The Jackson Five Make Love in Japan, Double Poster of The Jacksons in Japan & The Osmonds $12–25

Oct. Donny Osmond, Linda Blair, Rick Springfield, Marie Osmond, The Hudsons, Alice Cooper: Between the Sheets, The Jackson Five, John Denver $10–20

Nov. Donny Osmond, Rick Springfield, David Carradine, David Cassidy $5–10

1974
All issues $5–10

1975
Mar. Tony Orlando, Donny Osmond, Mac Davis, Billy Jack, Alice Cooper, Robby Benson $5–10

1976
Oct. Bay City Rollers' Scrapbook—includes 119 Roller Pix, "Starsky & Hutch," John Travolta's Body Secrets, Donny Osmond: His Beautiful Dream, Mark Shera, KC: Hunk of the Month, Elton John's Love Test $3–6

Nov. The Bay City Rollers: More Rumors, Barry Manilow: What a Hunk, On Tour With Elton John, Meet Kiss, Leif Garrett, Donny Osmond: Learn His Hot Secrets, John Travolta's Love Test, Roller Diary $4–8

Dec. Bay City Rollers: 'Round the Clock Special, Donny & Marie: Enter Their World, Starsky: Secret Love Interview, John Travolta: The Teen Who Made His Dream Come True, Monkees, Fonzie, Aerosmith, Elton John Takes a Ride, Leif Garrett, Robby Benson, Davy Jones $4–8

1977
Feb. Bay City Rollers' Holiday Special, Ian Quits the Rollers, Their Real Life Stories, "Starsky & Hutch" Break-up, Donny & Marie: How They Rate Each Other's Dates, John Travolta: Tasting Heartbreak, Peter Frampton, Davy Jones Plays Badminton, Kiss $3–6

1978
Feb. The Bay City Rollers: Personal 'n' Private, Shaun Cassidy, Kiss Shocker: Gene Simmons Hurt, John Travolta's Got the Fever, Andy Gibb: An Intimate Interview, Donny & Marie, Leif Garrett, wall poster of Shaun Cassidy, Bay City Rollers & The Mouseketeers $5–10

Apr. The Bay City Rollers at Home—Peek into Their Private World, Shaun Cassidy: Behind the Scenes, Kiss: Pix Galore—As You've Never Seen Them Before, Leif Garrett, Kristy McNichols, The Babys, Scott Baio, Parker Stevenson, Rollers poster $5–10

May The Bay City Rollers in Hollywood: Their Secret Holiday Hideaway, Shaun Cassidy: Love Will Have to Wait, Kiss: Zany Interviews—Get to Know the Guys Behind the Masks, Leif Garrett, John Travolta, *Grease*, Scott Baio, Rosetta Stone, Andy Gibb, Kristy McNichol, The Mystery of the Missing Roller, Roller's Les & Eric color poster $6–12

July Kiss' Gene Simmons: "Meet the Real Me," Bay City Rollers, Shaun Cassidy, Leif Garrett, Parker Stevenson, Sgt. Pepper, Rosetta Stone, Andy Gibb on the Spot, Scott Baio, Mark Hamill $5–10

Sept. Bay City Rollers in Switzerland, issue includes giant color centerfold of the Rollers, Shaun Cassidy: What His Best Friends Won't Tell Him, Kiss: Their "Ace" in the Hole, Leif Garrett, Andy Gibb: Love is. . . ., The Bee Gees, Scott Baio, Rosetta Stone, Peter Frampton, Kristy McNichol $5–10

Oct. Paul Stanley of Kiss, Peter Criss: What Makes Him Purr, Leif Garrett, Rosetta Stone Juicy Centerfold, Scott Baio, *Grease*, Andrew Stevens, Andy Gibb, Shaun Cassidy & Parker Stevenson, The Bee Gees, Kristy McNichol $5–10

1979
Jan. Kiss 'n' Tell: What They Really Think of Each Other, Kiss in Concert, Andy Gibb—Long, Lean & Luscious Color poster, Leif Garrett, Shaun Cassidy's New Image, Exclusive Bay City Roller Fun Photos, Scott Baio, Bee Gees, Dirk Benedick, Rosetta Stone, Angel, Peter Frampton, Sgt. Pepper $5–10

Aug. Leif Garrett, Kiss' Peter Criss: How Well Do We Really Know Him?, T. Rex, Andy Gibb, Shaun Cassidy: A Personal Message, Bay City Rollers, Scott Baio, The Village People, Styx, The Bad News Bears, Rosetta Stone $5–10

Sept. Kiss' Gene Simmons, Andy Gibb & the Bee Gees: Their Mom & Dad Tell All in an Exclusive Interview, Shaun Cassidy, Bay City Rollers: A New Beginning, Scott Baio, Erik Estrada, Leif Garrett, Kristy McNichol, "Charlies Angels," Styx, T. Rex $6–12

Dec. Kiss Close-up: Get to Know Them, Village People, Sha Na Na, John Schneider, Kristy McNichol, "Little House on the Prairie," Scott Baio, T. Rex $6–12

1980

Apr. The Komplete Kiss: Know Them Inch by Inch, issue includes "Superific" color centerfold poster of Kiss, Styx, Leif Garrett, Jimmy McNichol, Erik Estrada, Cheap Trick: A Rap With Robin, Scott Baio, Andy Gibb, John Schneider, Willie's Wedding, T. Rex, Shaun Cassidy, The Village People $6–12

May Kiss' Ace Frehley, issue includes Kiss poster, John Schneider, Andy Gibb, Leif Garrett, The Village People, Kristy & Jimmy McNichol, Styx: What Turns Them On & Off, T. Rex, Bay City Rollers, Cheap Trick, Scott Baio.....................................$10–20

June Kiss, John Schneider: His Lonely Nights, Andy Gibb After Dark, Kristy & Jimmy McNichol, Scott Baio, Greg Bradford, Styx, Cheap Trick, T. Rex & The Village People, Paul Stanley, Sha Na Na, Rob Lowe, Queen, Leif Garrett............................$5–10

July Kiss' Paul Stanley's Life Story, Gene Simmons pull-out poster, John Schneider, Kristy & Jimmy McNichol, Scott Baio, Leif Garrett in Concert, Styx' Tommy, Cheap Trick's Robin poster, Tom Wopat, KC & the Sunshine Band, Andy Gibb, Village People, T. Rex, Tatum O'Neil & Kristy McNichol: "Little Darlings"................................$6–12

Aug. Kiss' Peter Criss Talks About That Horrible Rumor, Issue includes Kiss Poster, John Schneider, Sha Na Na, Matt Dillon, Barry Manilow, Mark Hamill, Robin Zandor & Cheap Trick, Andy Gibb, Kristy McNichol, Styx, T. Rex.......................................$6–12

Sept. Kiss Krack-up: Are They Really Breaking Up?, Gene Simmons' Life Story, Paul Stanley Centerfold Poster, Styx: A Friend Tells All, Leif Garrett: A Very Special Love, Matt Dillon, Andy Gibb, Scott Baio, Village People, "Little House on the Prairie," Billy Joel, Cheap Trick: In Concert With Robin centerfold poster, Kristy & Jimmy McNichol, Olivia Newton-John: *Xanadu*..$7–15

Oct. Kiss' Ace Frehley's Life Story, John Schneider, Scott Baio, The Village People, Tommy Shaw & Kiss poster, Styx: 30 Things You Never Knew, Leif Garrett, Cheap Trick, Matt Dillon, T. Rex, Brooke Shields, Def Leppard, Kristy McNichol, Sha Na Na, "Little House's" Melissa & Dean...$5–10

Nov. Kiss: Meet Their New Drummer, Gene Gives the Scoop on Eric Carr, John Schneider, Tom Wopat, Scott Baio, Leif Garrett: The Person Who Knows Him Best, Rex Smith, Matt Dillon, Rob Lowe, The Village People, Styx, Andy Gibb, Kristy & Jimmy McNichol, Cheap Trick, Lorenzo Lamas, Journey, Greg Harrison.....................................$5–10

Dec. Kiss: Behind the Scenes, Tom Wopat, Matt Dillon, Cheap Trick, Village People, Chris Atkins, Kristy McNichol, *Star Wars/The Empire Strikes Back*....................................$5–10

1981

Jan. Kiss & Peter Criss: Marching to the Tune of a Different Drummer, John Schneider, Tom Wopat, Cathy Bach, Robin Zandor & Cheap Trick, Ace Fehley & David Lee Roth double poster centerfold, Scott Baio, Matt Dillon, The Village People, Brooke Shields...$5–10

Feb. John Schneider, Van Halen: Love Notes from David & Alex, Kiss: Personal Handwritten Messages & Love, Peter Criss Exclusive In-depth Interview, Scott Baio, Cheap Trick story & color centerfold, Kristy & Jimmy McNichol, Matt Dillon $5–10

Mar. Kiss' Eric Carr Up Close, Matt Dillon & Kristy McNichol, Eddie Van Halen, Journey, Scott Baio, Barry Manilow, John Schneider, Greg Harrison, David Lee Roth $5–10

Apr. John Schneider: Secrets Revealed, The New Kiss in Concert, Paul Stanley Calendar, Van Halen's David Lee Roth, Scott Baio, Matt Dillon, Journey, Cheap Trick, Styx, Peter Criss at Home, Rex Smith, Tony Danza, Queen's Roger Taylor, Ralph Macchio, Chris Atkins, Tom Wopat..$5–10

May John Schneider, Kiss' Gene Simmons: His Lonely Search, Scott Baio: Come Home With Him, Eddie Van Halen Exclusive Intimate Interview, Matt Dillon, Cheap Trick, Tom

Wopat, Leif Garrett: Meet His Kid Sis, Olivia Newton-John, Ralph Macchio, Rex Smith, The Police, Journey $5–10
June John Schneider, Kiss: Unmasked, Van Halen, Scott Baio, Styx, Journey, Rex Smith, Greg Harrison, Ralph Macchio, Matt Dillon...$4–8
July John Schneider: The Night He Cried, Ralph Macchio, Tommy Shaw, Scott Baio, Kiss: The Fearsome Foursome Answer the Questions, David Lee Roth, Matt Dillon, Cheap Trick, Cathy Bach, Queen, April Wine, The Knack...$5–10
Aug. John Schneider: Daredevil Car Race, Ralph Macchio, Kiss: Down Memory Lane, Scott Baio, Matt Dillon, Cheap Trick, REO, Leif Garrett, Styx, The Doobie Brothers, Journey...$5–10
Sept. Styx, Ralph Macchio, John Schneider & "The Dukes of Hazzard," Tom Selleck, Cathy Bach, Meet Van Halen, REO Speedwagon, Kiss' Paul Stanley, Adam & the Ants, Scott Baio, Matt Dillon, Cheap Trick, Journey, Leif Garrett, Cliff Richard, Hall & Oates $4–8
Oct. "Dukes of Hazzard," Kiss & Scott Baio, Van Halen's David Lee Roth, Rick Springfield, Journey, Tom Selleck, Tommy Shaw, Brooke Shields, Ralph Macchio...............$4–8
Dec. The Kiss Look: 1982, REO Speedwagon, Rick Springfield, Ralph Macchio, Adam Gunn, Styx, Scott Baio, Journey, "Dukes of Hazzard" $4–8

1982

Jan. Kiss Exclusive: An Intimate Interview With Drummer Eric Carr, Styx, Van Halen: Their Most Private Facts, Scott Baio, Matt Dillon, Ralph Macchio, Hall & Oates, Rick Springfield in Concert, John Schneider, REO Speedwagon, Journey, AC/DC, Brooke Shields, Andy Gibb, The Police, The Doobie Brothers, TV's "Facts of Life".............$4–8
Feb. Kiss, Scott Baio, Journey, Rick Springfield, Billy Squier, Tom Wopat, Hall & Oates, Olivia Newton-John, David Lee Roth, John Schneider, Andrew Stevens......................$4–8
Mar. Kiss' Ace Frehley, Hall & Oates, Journey, Gregory Harrison, Pat Benatar, Rick Springfield, Matt Dillon, Ralph Macchio, Timothy Hutton, Scott Baio, Air Supply, Styx, John Schneider $4–8
Apr. Scott Baio Moves On, Rick Springfield, Styx: Where They Have Been, John Schneider, Kiss, Journey, Billy Squier, AC/DC, Ralph Macchio, Barry Manilow, "Little House on the Prairie," Matt Dillon, Hall & Oates, Nancy McKeon...$4–8
May Rick Springfield: Private Pix, Scott Baio, John Schneider, Styx, Journey's Steve Perry, Ralph Macchio, Kiss: Meet Gene & Paul's Special Friend, Hall & Oates, Gregory Harrison, The Police, Matt Dillon, Rod Stewart, Billy Squier...$4–8
June Scott Baio: Happy Days Gone Forever, Tim Hutton, Steve Perry, Loverboy, Rick Springfield, Eddie Van Halen, Mike Reno, Styx, The Police, Olivia Newton-John, "The Dukes of Hazzard," Ralph Macchio, The Solid Gold Dancers, Valerie Bertinelli........$4–8
July Rick Springfield, Will Olivia Newton-John Marry?, The Police, AC/DC, Scott Baio, Maxwell Caulfield, Billy Squier, Matt Dillon, Tim Hutton, Journey's Steve Perry......$4–8
Aug. Matt Dillon, 16's Silver Jubilee Issue, Queen's Freddie Mercury, John Stamos, Journey, The Cars, Van Halen's David Lee Roth, Scott Baio, Doug McKeon, The Outsiders...$4–8
Sept. Rick Springfield Feature & Poster, David Lee Roth & Van Halen, Journey, Loverboy, Queen, Harrison Ford, Cheap Trick, AC/DC, The Police, Hall & Oates.....................$3–6
Oct. Rick Springfield, Sting, Cheap Trick, "Dukes of Hazzard," Scott Baio, John Stamos, Rush, Van Halen, Journey, Sylvester Stallone, The First Ladies of Rock, The Outsiders ..$3–6
Nov. Rick Springfield: The Tears You'll Never See, David Lee Roth, Scott Baio, Ralph Macchio, Journey, Haircut 100, Chris Atkins...$3–6

1983

Jan. Matt Dillon, Scott Baio, Rick Springfield, Duran Duran's Roger & John Taylor, Def Leppard, John Stamos, Tom Howell $3–6
Feb. Rick Springfield, Scott Baio, Loverboy, Matt Dillon, Journey, Ralph Macchio, Kiss, Hall & Oates $3–6
Mar. Rich Springfield, Journey: Video Games, Def Leppard's Phil Collen, Tom Howell, Tom Cruise, Van Halen, The Police, Glen Scarpelli..$3–6
May John Schneider, Rick Springfield, Tom Wopat, Journey, Styx, David Hasselhoff, Tommy Howell, John Stamos $3–6

June Rick Springfield: Around the Clock, Hall & Oates, John Stamos, Matt Dillon, Ricky Schroder, Stray Cats, Loverboy, The Police $3–6

1984

Jan. Duran Duran: Exclusive Interview With Roger Taylor, A Chat With Andy Taylor, John Stamos, Rick Springfield, Def Leppard, Ricky Schroder, Matt Dillon $3–6
Feb. Duran Duran Exclusive, Def Leppard, Tom Cruise, Rick Springfield, Adam Ant, Journey..$3–6
Mar. Duran Duran, Simon Le Bon's Private Life, Menudo Exclusive Interview, Def Leppard, Rick Springfield's New Movie, Culture Club, Adam Ant, Kiss, *Footloose*: The Movie $3–6
May Duran Duran, Rick Springfield, Matt Dillon, Ricky Schroder, John Stamos, Tom Howell, Adam Ant, Ralph Macchio...$3–6
June Duran Duran Spill the Beans, Rick Springfield, Van Halen, Chris Atkins, Pat Benatar $3–6
July Duran Duran: More Secrets Revealed, Van Halen: David Lee Roth, Michael Jackson at the Grammys, Tommy Howell, John Stamos, Ralph Macchio, *Indiana Jones & the Temple of Doom*, Menudo, Boy George..$3–6
Aug. Duran Duran Conquers America, Michael Jackson, Ralph Macchio, Tommy Howell, Kevin Bacon, Ricky Schroder, Menudo, Van Halen, Rick Springfield, Matt Dillon, Def Leppard, Styx, John Stamos, Culture Club...$3–6
Sept. Duran's John & Nick, Ralph Macchio, Michael Jackson, Culture Club, Cyndi Lauper $3–6
Oct. Duran Duran, Rick Springfield on the Road Again, Ralph Macchio Interviewed, Tommy Howell, Menudo, Michael Jackson: Every Little Thing You Need to Know Plus Michael Jackson Centerfold, Night Ranger, Def Leppard..$3–6
Nov. John Stamos: A Very Special Interview, Duran Duran, Michael Jackson: The Boy vs. the Man, Menudo, Ralph Macchio, Hall & Oates, Culture Club, Quiet Riot, Rick Springfield, Lorenzo Lamas, Rob Lowe..$3–6
Dec. Duran Duran: Where Have They Been? (with centerfold), Scott Baio, Tommy Howell, Ralph Macchio, Michael Jackson: Live Magic, Ricky Schroder, Rick Springfield: Secrets You Never Knew, Menudo, Fame, John Stamos, Hall & Oates, Styx, Rob Lowe, Cyndi Lauper calendar, Night Ranger, Rex $3–6

1985

Jan. Duran Duran: The Weddings, Menudo centerfold, Ralph Macchio, Ricky Schroder, Prince on File, Scott Baio, Tom Howell, Culture Club, Bruce Springsteen, Michael Jackson, Matt Dillon, Rob Lowe, Hall & Oates $3–6
Feb. John Stamos, Scott Baio, Duran Duran: The Wild Boys Strike Again, Ralph Macchio, Menudo, Culture Club, Ratt, Quiet Riot, Rick Springfield, Prince, Thompson Twins, Chad Lowe, Hall & Oates, Jason Bateman...$3–6
Mar. Duran Duran: Their New Image, Ralph Macchio: The Moment of Truth, Ricky Schroder, Matt Dillon, Culture Club, Rick Springfield, Prince, Chad Lowe, Menudo, John Stamos, David Lee Roth, Scott Baio, Michael Jackson, Hall & Oates, Tim Hutton, Fame, Tom Howell..$3–6
May Andrew McCartney, Menudo, Simon Le Bon, Michael J. Fox, A-ha, Ralph Macchio, Julian Lennon, Wham, Tears for Fears, Kiss, Don Johnson, Platinum Blonde, Rob Lowe, Sean Astin, Madonna, Kevin Bacon, Corey Hart $3–6
June Duran Duran, John Taylor centerfold, Menudo, Madonna, Cyndi Lauper, Ricky Schroder, Julian Lennon, Matt Dillon, The Breakfast Club, Marc Singer.....................$3–6
July Duran Duran, Ricky Schroder, Ralph Macchio, Julian Lennon, Wham, Menudo, Rick Springfield, Sting, The Police, Madonna, Culture Club, Corey Hart $3–6
Aug. Duran Duran, Ricky Schroder, Chad Lowe, "Miami Vice," Julian Lennon on the Road, Rick Springfield, Menudo, Prince, Ralph Macchio, John Stamos, Madonna, Tom Cruise $3–6
Oct. Duran Duran: A Photo Souvenir, Wham, The Goonies, Tom Howell, Rob Lowe, Menudo, Michael J. Fox, Cyndi Lauper, Prince, Madonna, Ralph Macchio, Rick Springfield, Jack Wagner, Chad Lowe, Matt Dillon..$3–6

1986

May Andrew McCartney feature story & color centerfold, Menudo, Simon Le Bon, Michael J. Fox, Kirk Cameron, Ralph Macchio, Ricky Schroder, Julian Lennon, A-ha, Wham, Tears for Fears, Madonna, Kiss, Platinum Blonde, Don Johnson, Shean Astin.................$3–6

July Michael J. Fox, Menudo: A Talk With Sergio, Kirk Cameron: The Flip Side of Fame, A-ha at the Grammys, Rob Lowe, Duran Duran, Charlie Sexton, Julian Lennon, Loverboy, Pretty in Pink, John Cougar Mellancamp, Ralph Macchio, John Stamos, Ricky Schroder, Don Johnson, "Miami Vice"...$3–6

Aug. Menudo's Sergio's Personal Secrets, Michael J. Fox, Julian Lennon, A-ha: Everything You Ever Wanted to Know, Kirk Cameron, Duran Duran, The Monkees, Van Halen, Tom Cruise, Ralph Macchio, Pretty in Pink, Madonna, Culture Club, Don Johnson, Wham, Bruce Willis, Jason Bateman...$3–6

Sept. Ralph Macchio feature story & color centerfold, Mitch Gaylord, A-ha, Menudo, Alfonso Rebeiro, Kirk Cameron, Julian Lennon, Duran Duran, Michael J. Fox, Ricky Schroder, Madonna, Prince, George Michael, The Monkees, Rob Lowe...............$3–6

Oct. Ralph Macchio: Everything You Ever Wanted to Know, A-ha: Catch the Fever, Tom Cruise, Corey Hart, Madonna, The New Monkees, Rob Lowe..........................$3–6

Nov. Ralph Macchio: Straight from the Heart—A Very Private Interview, Menudo, A-ha, Michael J. Fox, The Monkees vs. MTV, Duran Duran, Madonna, Kirk Cameron, Mitch Gaylord, Tom Cruise, The Lost Boys, Wham, Ricky Schroder.............................$3–6

Dec. A-ha: Stories, Special Pin-ups & Posters, The Monkees, Ralph Macchio, Kirk Cameron, Sean Astin, Madonna, Michael J. Fox, Janet Jackson, Cyndi Lauper, Corey Feldman, Tom Howell...$3–6

1987

Jan. The Monkees, Davy Jones, A-ha: Hotel Capers—A Behind-the-scenes Exclusive, Sean & Mack Astin, Menudo, Kirk Cameron, Don Johnson, Ralph Macchio, MTV Awards, Michael Jackson, Journey, George Michael, Cyndi Lauper, David Lee Roth, Madonna, Michael J. Fox, Stars of *Stand by Me*..$3–6

Feb. The Monkees: New & Old, Brian Bloom, Cyndi Lauper, Ralph Macchio, Rob Lowe.$2–4

Mar. Micky Dolenz & the Monkees, Kirk Cameron, Madonna, Duran Duran, The Goonies $2–4

Apr. Davy Jones & the Monkees' Diary, Michael Fox, Kirk Cameron, River Phoenix, Menudo, The Outsiders, Duran Duran, Sean Astin, Madonna, Bon Jovi $2–4

Sept. Bon Jovi: What's Jon Really Like? Madonna: Movie Magic, Duran Duran, REO Speedwagon..$2–4

Nov. Kirk Cameron Talks, River Phoenix, Johnny Depp, The Monkees, Chad Allen, Jon Bon Jovi, Menudo, Madonna's Love Story, Michael Fox, Duran Duran, Def Leppard, The Beastie Boys, Richie Sambora, Ralph Macchio, Wil Wheaton..........................$2–4

Dec. The Real River Phoenix, Kirk Cameron, The Monkees' Personal Letters, Sean Astin, Chad Allen, Michael Jackson: He's So Good, Johnny Depp, Madonna: It's a Wonderful Life, Menudo, Duran Duran, Whitesnake, Alyssa Milano, John Stamos, Whitney Houston, Def Leppard...$2–4

1988

Jan. Kirk Cameron: He's So Shy, Chad Allen, Sean Astin, The Monkees, Def Leppard, Menudo, Madonna, Michael Jackson, George Michael, Kiss, Bon Jovi, The Lost Boys, Johnny Depp, John Stamos..$2–4

Feb. Kirk Cameron: Girl Questions, Corey Feldman, River Phoenix Grows Up, Sean Astin, The Monkees Exclusive Interview, Bon Jovi Diary, John Cougar, Johnny Depp, Micky Dolenz, Trey Ames, two posters $2–4

Mar. Kirk Cameron: Making Your Dreams Come True, River Phoenix: Is He Romantic?, Davy Jones & the Monkees: Secret Stuff, Corey Haim, Wil Wheaton, Sean Astin, Johnny Depp Answers the Questions, Madonna Leaves Sean, Bon Jovi, Def Leppard, George Michael, Chad Allen $2–4

Apr. Kirk Cameron: Getting Close to Him, River Phoenix, Sean Astin, The Monkees: They're Squealin' on Each Other, Bon Jovi, Patrick Swayzee, Johnny Depp, Menudo, Madonna, Shane Conrad, Corey Haim...$2–4

May Kirk Cameron: His Secret Battle, The Monkees, Shane Conrad Exclusive Interview,

Chad Allen, River Phoenix, Menudo, Tiffany, Michael Fox, Hall & Oates, Kiefer Sutherland, Rick Springfield..$2–4

July River Phoenix: King of Hearts, Kirk Cameron: Backstage at the People's Choice, Corey Feldman, Corey Haim, Shane Conrad, A-ha, Menudo, Patrick Swayzee, Rick Springfield, George Michael, Alyssa Milano, Chad Allen, Wil Wheaton, The Monkees $2–4

Aug. Wil Wheaton, Corey Haim, Kirk Cameron: His Secrets, Tiffany, A-ha, Alyssa Milano, Debbie Gibson Goes Hollywood, George Michael, The Jets $2–4

Sept. Kirk Cameron, Corey Haim: The Truth Behind the Rumors, River Phoenix, Patrick Swayzee, Chad Allen, Menudo, Johnny Depp: The Secret of His Success Part I, Cyndi Lauper, The Jets, Madonna, Rick Springfield, George Michael $2–4

Oct. Debbie Gibson: Her Secret Love, Wil Wheaton, River Phoenix, Kirk Cameron, Johnny Depp, Angelo of Menudo, The Monkees, A-ha, Patrick Swayzee, Trey Ames, Keiffer Sutherland $2–4

Dec. The New Kids on the Block: The Way They Were, The Debbie Gibson Fashion Look, Corey Haim, Kirk Cameron, George Michael Grows Up, The Monkees, Johnny Depp, Chad Allen..$2–4

1989

Jan. River Phoenix, Corey Haim, Debbie Gibson: A Star is Never Done, Bon Jovi, Kirk Cameron, Menudo, Tiffany, New Kids on the Block, The Escape Club........................$2–4

Feb. Kirk Cameron: Is He Still Number One?, Debbie Gibson: The Girl & the Woman, Menudo & Alyssa Milano centerfold, Corey Haim, Shane Conrad, New Kids on the Block, Tiffany, Ami Dolenz, Duran Duran, River Phoenix, Madonna, Bon Jovi $2–4

Mar. Kirk Cameron's Special Valentine: A Sneak Peak at His New Movie, Corey Haim, Debbie Gibson: Why Love Will Have to Wait, Alyssa Milano: Wallet Pix & Fax, Bon Jovi on Stage & Behind the Scenes, Johnny Depp, Shane Conrad, New Kids on the Block, Menudo, The Bangles, The Monkees, Keiffer Sutherland..$2–4

Apr. Alyssa Milano: Staying Fit, Jason Gedrick, Kirk Cameron, Johnny Depp, Corey Haim, Bros, Debbie Gibson Answers the Questions, The Monkees Speak: Their Private Thoughts, New Kids on the Block: Meet Donnie, Madonna, Bobby Brown..................................$2–4

May New Kids on the Block: Meet Danny, Corey Haim Interview, Backstage With Debbie Gibson, Chad Allen, The Monkee Life, Kirk Cameron, Alyssa Milano, Johnny Depp......$2–4

July New Kids on the Block, Debbie Gibson: In the Studio With Her, Johnny Depp, Young Riders, The Outsiders, Fred Savage $2–4

Aug. Debbie Gibson: The Making of Electric Youth, Tiffany: Her Heartfelt & Personal Message, The Monkees Part II of Talia & Davy's Family Pix, Shane Conrad, New Kids on the Block, Corey Haim, Kirk Cameron, Alyssa Milano, Bon Jovi, Bros......................$2–4

Sept. Kirk Cameron Confesses, Debbie Gibson Exclusive, Corey Haim, Jordon Knight, Bros, Shane Conrad, Ralph Macchio, Fred Savage, The Monkees: They're Being Sued, River Phoenix, Johnny Depp, Bon Jovi, Menudo, Tiffany, Alyssa Milano, Jeremy Licht, New Kids..$2–4

Oct. New Kids on the Block, Corey Haim, Monkees: Davy Jones & Talia Take You on Tour, Tiffany & Her Cartoon Movie, Debbie Gibson: Her Hometown Triumph, Michael Jackson, Johnny Depp, Bon Jovi, Ralph Macchio, Alyssa Milano, Ricky Schroder....$2–4

Nov. New Kids on the Block: Joe's Biggest Secret, Corey Haim, The Monkees: Behind the Scenes, Debbie Gibson: You Won't Believe What You Hear, Kirk Cameron, Alyssa Milano, Johnny Depp, Bros, Fred Savage, Grieco, Menudo, Eddie & the Cruisers...................$2–4

Dec. New Kids on the Block, The Monkees: Their Secret Tinseltown Rehearsal, The New Outsiders, Chad Allen, Debbie Gibson: Behind the Scenes at Her Video Shoot, Johnny Depp, Bros, Grieco, River Phoenix, Kirk Cameron, Alyssa Milano $2–4

1990

Jan. New Kids on the Block: Behind the Scenes, Debbie Gibson: Party at the Palladium, Grieco, Fred Savage, The Monkees: Talking About Their Hollywood Star, Corey Haim, Alyssa Milano, Kirk Cameron, Young Riders, Menudo...$2–4

Feb. New Kids on the Block, Tiffany, The Monkees: A Personal Message, Fred Savage, Corey Haim, Bros, Paula Abdul, Debbie Gibson on the Road: Hot Pix........................$2–4

Mar. New Kids on the Block: Time Out, Debbie Gibson: Success Isn't Easy, Corey Haim, Neil Patrick Harrison, Monkees: The Lo-down on Their Cenvention, Young Riders, Janet Jackson, Tears for Fears, Mr. Big $2–4

Apr. New Kids on the Block, Jordan Backstage, Corey Haim, Chad Allen, The Monkees, Debbie Gibson, Menudo, Bros, Martika, Paula Abdul, Janet Jackson, The Outsiders $2–4
May New Kids on the Block: Tour Diary, Ty Miller, Neil Patrick Harris, Corey Haim, Johnny Depp, The Monkees: Peter Tork's Lady Squeals, Mr. Big, Martika, Paula Abdul $2–4
June New Kids on the Block Weekend, Fred Savage, Janet Jackson & Madonna: Rock Queens Take Over, Young Riders, Chad Allen..$2–4
July The New Kids on the Block Go to the Grammys, Meet the New Kids' Friends, Debbie Gibson: Into Her Studio With Her, Young Riders, Johnny Depp: Hollywood's Cry-baby, Neil Patrick, Fred Savage, Chad Allen, Michael St. Gerard, Paula Abdul $2–4
Aug. New Kids on the Block: Backstage Pass, The Outsiders on Location, Young Riders, Madonna, Debbie Gibson, Paula Abdul, Corey Haim..$2–4
Sept. New Kids on the Block Fireworks Special, Outsiders, Janet Jackson, Johnny Depp $2–4

16 MAGAZINE PRESENTS JOHN LENNON AND THE BEATLES/A LOVING TRIBUTE

1981

Exclusive Candid Photos from *16*'s Private Collection, The Life of John Lennon, issue contains 11 glossy color pin-ups of John through the years & a full-color poster of John & the Beatles, The Story of His Tragic Death $5–10

16 MAGAZINE PRESENTS ROCKLINE

1979

Fall/Winter The Village People, Ralph Macchio: Trouble in Macholand, Andy Gibb in the Hot Seat, Rod Stewart: Can His Marriage Make It?, Billy Joel, Barry Manilow, Donna Summer, Kiss, Eddie Money, The Bee Gees, Doobie Brothers, Cheap Trick, The Babys, Van Halen, Kiss Special—Gene Simmons: Too Hot to Handle, Paul Stanley: Too Much Privacy, Ace Frehley: Not Enough Respect, Peter Criss: Not Enough Love..............................$6–12

1980

Summer Paul Stanley/Kiss: The Shocking Things They Say, Village People, Barry Manilow: The Reluctant Superstar, Van Halen: Macho Rockers, Blondie's Deborah Harry: Devil or Angel?, Cheap Trick on Camera, Styx: 150 Facts, Leif Garrett: His Tragic Accident, The Bee Gees: Down Memory Lane, Fleetwood Mac, The Knack, Abba, Diana Ross, Rod Stewart, Styx poster, Bay City Rollers, Commodores, Andy Gibb.....................$8–16
Fall/Winter Gene Simmons/Kiss: The Women Behind Them, Cheap Trick Exposed, Styx, Andy Gibb & the Girls, Village People, Leif Garrett, Michael Jackson, Kenny Loggins, David Lee Roth, Olivia Newton-John, Blondie, Queen, Donna Summer, Tom Petty, Barry Manilow, Rex in Concert $6–12

1980–81

Winter David Lee Roth/Spotlight on Van Halen, Styx Close-up, Bob Seger, Peter Criss: He Takes it Off, Kiss Profile, Journey Exclusive Interview, Cheap Trick, Michael Jackson: Trapped by Fame, The Village People, Olivia Newton-John, Rex, Barry Manilow, Sha Na Na, The Doobie Brothers, Queen, The Blues Brothers, Hall & Oates, Manhattan Transfer, Gene Simmons & Journey wall posters..$8–16

1981

Spring Styx on Styx: Their Personal Thoughts, Pat Benetar: Her Secret Life, Queen, Eric Carr Profile, Journey Exclusive Interview, John Lennon: A Pictorial Portrait, Van Halen, The Two Sides of the Doobie Brothers, Donna Summer, Barry Manilow, Eddie Rabbitt, Cher, Cheap Trick, Sha Na Na, Air Supply, Michael Jackson, Peter Criss.................$6–12
Fall REO Speedwagon, Styx, Van Halen: Who are the Women in Their Lives?, Hall & Oates Exclusive Interviews, Barbara Mandrell, Kiss: What They Do When They're Not Making Music, Adam & the Ants, Journey: 99 Things You Never Knew About Them, Doobie Brothers, The Clash, Cheap Trick, Elvis Costello, Frankie & the Knockouts, Rush,

16's ROCKLINE,
1981, SUMMER

16's ROCKLINE,
1984, Nov.

16's ROCKLINE,
1985, Feb.

16's ROCKLINE,
1986, Apr.

16's ROCKLINE,
1986, Aug.

16's ROCKLINE,
1986, Sept.

16's ROCKLINE,
1986, Oct.

16's ROCKLINE,
1986, Dec.

16's ROCKLINE,
1987, Feb.

The Who, Bruce Springsteen, Talking Heads, Deborah Harry, Rod Stewart, Neil Diamond, Benatar...$6–12

1981–82

Winter Journey: Going Back in Time, REO Speedwagon Exclusive Interview, Van Halen: They're Picture Perfect, Kiss 1982, Styx, Rick Springfield, Hall & Oates, AC/DC, Heart: An Intimate Talk With Ann Wilson, Bruce Springsteen, Andy Gibb, Squeeze, Billy Squire, Paul McCartney, Cheap Trick, Spider, Tom Petty, Split ENZ, Kim Carnes, Pat Benatar, Freddie Mercury, Nazareth, The Elecktrics..$6–12

1982

Summer Rick Springfield, Olivia Newton-John, Journey, Hall & Oates, Billy Squier, AC/DC, The Cars, The Police, David Lee Roth...$5–10
Fall David Lee Roth, Kiss, Rick Springfield, Blondie, Hall & Oates, Journey, The Go-go's, Mike Reno, Elton John, REO Speedwagon, Queen, Rush, AC/DC, Billy Squier, Loverboy, Barry Manilow $5–10

1982–83

Winter Hall & Oates, Bruce Springsteen, Loverboy, Tom Petty, REO, Loverboy, Rick Springfield, The Who, Billy Squier, AC/DC, Olivia Newton-John, Stevie Nicks, Rock Drummers $5–10

1984

Jan./Feb. Boy George/Culture Club, The Stray Cats, David Bowie, Def Leppard, Quiet Riot, Motley Crue, Loverboy's Matt Frenette, Men at Work, Hall & Oates, Duran Duran, The Police...$5–10
May/June Eddie Van Halen, Culture Club/Boy George, Duran Duran, Def Leppard, AC/DC, Adam Ant, Eurythmics, Rick Springfield, Quiet Riot $5–10
July/Aug. Duran Duran, Quiet Riot, Michael Jackson, Judas Priest, The Go-go's, Culture Club, Van Halen, AC/DC, Journey..$5–10
Sept. Special Jackson Issue, Duran Duran Exclusive, Thompson Twins, Bruce Springsteen, The Cars, Quiet Riot $4–8
Oct. Michael Jackson & the Jacksons Part II: Meet Them One-by-one, Quiet Riot, Rick Springfield, Rod Stewart, Billy Squier, Night Ranger, Krokus, Ratt, Devo, Eurythmics, Van Halen, Duran Duran, Weird Al, Flock of Seagulls, Prince, Air Supply, Joan Jett, Missing Persons, Saxon $5–10
Nov. Hall & Oates Exclusive, Quiet Riot's Kevin Dubrow Talks, Michael Jackson & the Jacksons on the Road, Rick Springfield: Rock's Man for All Seasons, Duran Duran, Prince, Bruce Springsteen, Ratt, Elton John, Scorpions, Huey Lewis, Cyndi Lauper, Lionel Richie, Madonna, Night Ranger, Van Halen, Culture Club, Sammy Hagar $5–10
Dec. Hall & Oates: Close Personal Ties, Quiet Riot Interview Part II, Duran Duran, Michael Jackson: The Family Takes it on the Chin, Culture Club, Bruce Springsteen, Ratt, The Go-go's, Billy Idol, Zebra, U2, Iron Maiden, Psychedelic Furs, Thompson Twins, Berlin, Night Ranger, Nena Hagen, Twisted Sister, Motley Crue, Van Halen, Dennis DeYoung.......$4–8

1985

Jan. Culture Club: The Clone War Begins, Hall & Oates: Penetrate Their Wall of Sound, Kiss, Duran Duran, Quiet Riot, The Pretenders, John Cougar Mellencamp..................$4–8
Feb. Ratt's Robin Crosby Talks, Billy Squier, Culture Club, Quiet Riot, Billy Idol, Kiss, Prince, Honeymoon Suite, Night Ranger, Lita Ford, Rick Springfield, Bryan Adams, Duran Duran, The Ramones, The Fixx $4–8
Mar. Duran Duran Breaking Up, Boy George, Van Halen's David Lee Roth, Hall & Oates, Tommy Shaw, Dio $4–8
Apr. Motley Crue & Hanoi Rocks Tragedy: The Accident That Changed Their Lives, Def Leppard, Frankie Goes to Hollywood, David Lee Roth, Kiss: Ripping Up the Road, Duran Duran, Twisted Sister, Culture Club, Accept, Madonna, Hall & Oates, Big Country, Dio, Blackie Lawless...$4–8
May Duran Duran, Wham, Bon Jovi: Meet Rock's Hottest New Star, Ratt: An Exclusive Interview, Hall & Oates, Def Leppard, Morris Day/Purple Rain, Thompson Twins, Kiss, Chaka Chan, Guiffria, U2, W.A.S.P., John Parr..$4–8

June Rick Springfield: The Greatest Man is Nobody, Wham on the Road, Duran Duran, Corey Hart, Twisted Sister, Foreigner, Kiss, Sting, Hall & Oates, Madonna, Iron Maiden, Dio, Bryan Adams $4–8
July Sting, Wham's George Michael, Rick Springfield, Duran Duran, REO, Vanity Interview, Guiffria, Debarge, Prince: A Royal Backlash, Madonna, Julian Lennon, Mick Jagger, Tom Petty, Thompson Twins, Ozzy Osbourne, Triumph $4–8
Aug. Ratt, Desperately Seeking Madonna, Julian Lennon, Corey Hart, Power Station, John Waite, Rick Springfield, Bon Jovi, Sting, Madonna, David Lee Roth, Deep Purple, Krokus, Night Ranger $4–8
Sept. Madonna, Power Station, Wham, Bon Jovi, Julian Lennon, Tina Turner, U2, Rick Springfield $4–8
Oct. Power Station, Rick Springfield on the Road Again, Huey Lewis, AC/DC, Tom Petty, Madonna, Corey Hart, Julian Lennon, Accept, Frankie Goes to Hollywood, Wham, Bryan Adams, Phil Collins...$4–8
Nov. Power Station, Andy Taylor, Corey Hart, Madonna, Tears for Fears, Bruce Springsteen, Howard Jones, Wham, Paul Young, Survivor...$4–8
Dec. Corey Hart, Duran Duran, Power Station, Arcadia, Adam Ant, Cheap Trick, Stevie Nicks, Heart, Twisted Sister, Billy Idol, Motley Crue, Loverboy, Wham $4–8

1986

Jan. Twisted Sister: Just a Little Off Beat, Power Station, Kiss, Adam Ant, Loverboy, Corey Hart, Gilly Idol: The Idol Truth, Arcadia, Ratt Exclusive, Motley Crue, Dead or Alive, Rick Springfield, A-ha, Y & T...$4–8
Feb. Arcadia/Power Station: Adventures in the Pleasure Zone, Julian Lennon, Twisted Sister Exclusive Interview, Kiss' Gene Simmons: As You Never Have Seen Him, Eurythmics, Howard Jones, Farm Aid, The Hooters, Heart, Billy Idol, The Motels, Loverboy, Dio.....$4–8
Apr. Twisted Sister, Arcadia, A-ha, Julian Lennon, Exclusive Interviews With—The Hooters, Adam Ant, Kiss, Eddie Van Halen, Pat Benatar, Olivia Newton-John, Billy Idol & Bryan Adams..$4–8
July Julian Lennon, Prince, Wham, Madonna, Duran Duran, The Nelsons, Tommy Shaw, A-ha, Charlie Sexton, Robert Palmer, Culture Club, Peter Frampton, Sade..................$4–8
Aug. Prince: "Under the Cherry Moon," Madonna: The Truth About All Those Racy Rumors, David Lee Roth, Julian Lennon, A-ha, Darryl Hall, Duran Duran, Billy Squier, Sting, Wham, Culture Club, Van Halen, The Bangles, Dennis DeYoung..............................$4–8
Sept. David Lee Roth on Van Halen, Duran Duran: Time Out for Roger, A-Ha, Billy Idol, Julian Lennon, Madonna, Journey, Prince, The Hooters, Janet & Jermaine Jackson, Tom Petty, Brian Setzer, Bon Jovi, Billy Squier $4–8
Oct. Madonna: Trouble in Paradise, Wham: Their Last Hurrah, Corey Hart, Cyndi Lauper, A-ha, Exclusive Interviews With—David Lee Roth, The Monkees, Duran Duran, Prince, Quiet Riot, Billy Joel, Air Supply, Joan Jett, Eurythmics, Julian Lennon, Ace Frehley, Rod Stewart, Peter Criss..$4–8
Dec. A-ha: What are They Hiding?, Madonna: Is She Showing Her True Colors?, Corey Hart, The Monkees: Doing it Live, Cyndi Lauper, Duran Duran, Howard Jones, Julian Lennon, The Jets, Quiet Riot, George Michael, Darryl Hall, Van Halen & David Lee Roth $4–8

1987

Feb. The Monkees Then & Now, Bruce Springsteen, George Michael, Bon Jovi, Madonna, Duran Duran, Lionel Richie, Huey Lewis, Ratt, Don Johnson, David Lee Roth, Elton John, Darryl Hall, A-ha, Cyndi Lauper, Quiet Riot, Corey Hart................................$3–6
Apr. The Monkees: The Truth Behind Them, Don Johnson, Cyndi Lauper: Her Sizzlin' Secrets Revealed, Menudo, The New Monkees, Joan Jett, Ratt, Kirk Cameron, Duran Duran, New Kids on the Block, Darryl Hall, Ricky Schroder...$3–6
June Bon Jovi, The Monkees: What's Davy Really Like?, Bruce Willis, Janet Jackson, Bryan Adams, Michael J. Fox, Joan Jett, Europe, Kirk Cameron, Cinderella, Rob Lowe, Cyndi Lauper, Duran Duran, A-ha, Don Johnson, Michael Jackson, Billy Idol, issue includes Bon Jovi giant wall poster bonus $3–6
Aug. Jon Bon Jovi, Kirk Cameron Comes Clean, Madonna & Friends on the Road, River Phoenix, The Monkees: What's Micky Dolenz Really Like?, Janet Jackson, Bruce Willis,

Corey Hart, Duran Duran, The Lost Boys, Michael Fox, David Bowie, U2, Whitney Houston, Bon Jovi poster $3–6

16 MAGAZINE PRESENTS SUMMER SUPERSTARS

1990

Summer New Kids on the Block: Personal Reports, issue includes 17 color pin-ups & a wall poster $2–4

16 MAGAZINE PRESENTS TV TATTLE-TALES

1976

Vol. 3, #4 Starsky & Hutch, Fonzie: His Secret Love Life, Donny Osmond: TV Sure Changed His Life, John Travolta: Behind Closed Doors, Marie Osmond: Does She or Doesn't She?, Tony Orlando, Freddie Prinze $5–10

1979

Vol. 5, #1 Shaun Cassidy: His Most Embarrassing Moment, With Shaun Cassidy's Steady, Kiss: What Really Goes on Behind the Scenes, Andy Gibb, Leif Garrett: His Girls, Richard Hatch, Bay City Rollers: Their Troubled Lives, posters of Shaun Cassidy, Andy Gibb & Parker Stevenson $5–10

1981

Spring Scott Baio, Matt Dillon, John Schneider, Tom Wopat, Cathy Bach, Greg Harrison, Chris Atkins, Brooke Shields, Kristy & Jimmy McNichol, Valerie Bertinelli, Rex Smith $4–8
Summer Ralph Macchio: Watch Him Working Out, Scott Baio: Will He Marry?, John Schneider, Matt Dillon, Tom Selleck, Rex Smith, Valerie Bertinelli, Kristy McNichol $4–8
Fall John Schneider, Christopher Reeves, Scott Baio, Kristy McNichol: Her Private Photo Album, Ralph Macchio, Tom Selleck, Matt Dillon, Brooke Shields, Gregory Harrison, Nancy McKeon, Catherine Bach $4–8

1981–82

Winter Scott Baio, John Schneider, Rick Springfield, Matt Dillon, Tom Selleck, Gregory Harrison...$3–6

1983

Summer *Return of the Jedi*, David Hasselhoff, Matt Dillon, Rick Springfield, Richard Gere $3–6
Fall David Hasselhoff, John Stamos, Matt Dillon, Rob Lowe, Tom Selleck, Bruce Penhill $3–6

1983–84

Winter John Stamos, Matt Dillon, Tom Cruise, David Hasselhoff, Tom Cruise, Chris Atkins, Ricky Schroder, John James $3–6

1984

Spring John Stamos Tells All, Rick Springfield, Scott Baio & Erin Moran, Ricky Schroder, Ralph Macchio, Michael Fox, Kate Jackson, "Fame," Rob Lowe $3–6
Summer Tom Howell, Kevin Bacon, Harrison Ford, Rob Lowe, Ralph Macchio, Ricky Schroder, David Hasselhoff...$3–8

16 MAGAZINE'S ANNUAL SPECTACULAR

1963

#1 Issue includes six huge color pin-ups, Private Photo Albums of Dion & Shelley Fabares, First Annual Gee Gee Awards, The Secret World of Connie Stevens, Paul Petersen, Chakiris, Annette Funicello, Troy Donahue, Dick Chamberlain, Bobby Rydell, Vince Edward's Secret, Hayley Mills' Life, Elvis Presley, Rick Nelson.............................$30–60

1964

#2 Issue includes 500 Pix of the Top 'Teen Stars, Color Pin-ups & Signed Portraits, "Things a Guy & a Girl Never Tell" by Annette Funicello & Frankie Avalon, Paul Petersen, Shelley

Fabares, Johnny Crawford, Dick Chamberlain, Hayley Mills, Troy Donahue, Connie Stevens, Elvis Presley, Maharis, Chakiris, Mike Landon, Connie Francis, Bobby Vee, Vince Edwards, Lennon Sisters $25–50

1965

#3 No longer is issued annually. ... Elvis Presley & Ann Margret in *Viva Las Vegas*, Bobby Rydell's Loves & Hates, Mike Landon, Troy Donahue Secret Pix, Johnny Crawford, Patty Duke, Kurt Russell, The Beatles, Shelley Fabares, Hayley Mills, *West Side Story* Boys' Exclusive, Paul Petersen, Dick Chamberlain...$20–40

#4 The Beatles Whole Story in 50 Pix, issue includes 40 wallet photos of The Beatles, Elvis Presley & The Beatles, Patty Duke, Paul Petersen Married?, Is Ringo Dying?, Is George Harrison Leaving the Beatles?, John Lennon Divorcing, Dave Clark Five, Hayley Mills Personal Photo Album, Bobby Vee, Brenda Lee, Bobby Rydell, Del Shannon, The Ronettes, England's Crazy Groups...$20–40

16 MAGAZINE'S BEATLES WHOLE TRUE STORY

1966

Issue includes seven Exclusive Color Pin-ups, Over 100 Never-before-seen Pix, Complete Story of the Beatles "On Stage," How They Make a Record, Lyrics, Complete Discography, Interviews, Their Women, The History of the Beatles Around the World $25–50

16 MAGAZINE'S BEATLES MOVIE MAGAZINE

1965

The only magazine of the entire story of *A Hard Day's Night*, issue includes 100 action photographs with color pin-ups..$25–50

16 MAGAZINE'S FUN TIME

1972

Oct. #1 Donny Osmond: Be His Bride & See What Happens on Your Wedding Day, David Cassidy: A Date With David, Donny & the House of Horrors, Brady Bunch Crunch, pin-ups of David Cassidy, Donny Osmond & Bobby Sherman $25–50

Dec. #2 David Cassidy & the Cat-witches, A Love Letter from Donny Osmond, Maureen McCormick's Crazy Clothes Caper, pin-ups of Donny, David & the Osmonds $20–40

16 MAGAZINE'S HOLIDAY SPECIAL

1973

Summer #1 Donny Osmond, The Osmonds Special With 250 Very Personal Pix, 36 in Wild Color, Be With the Osmonds on Stage in Vegas, in Their Hotel, on Their Ranch in Utah, at Their Home in Hollywood & in Provo, Meet & Talk With Fans, Go to Their Concerts & Make Records With Them, Michael Jackson & the Jackson Five: On Dates, at Plays, at Home, on Stage, on Vacation, Cutting Records, Backstage in Japan & in England, Andy & Dave...$25–50

16 MAGAZINE'S LOVING FASHIONS

1970

Oct. #1 Secret Boy Signals $20–40
Dec. #2 Crazy Fashion Fads..$20–40

1971

Nov. #7 David Cassidy: Dress David, Bobby Sherman, David's Eyes.....................$20–40

1972

Sept. David Cassidy: Your Trial Marriage With Him—Will it Last?, Don Raye, Donny Osmond Trial Marriage..$15–30

16 MAGAZINE SPEC (Formerly 16 *Magazine's Spectacular*)

1965

#5 The Beatles: 100 Red Hot New Pix, Herman's Hermits, Elvis Presley: 101 Untold Secrets, Dave Clark Five: Their Secret Love Life, David McCallum, Robert Vaughn, Peter & Gordon, The Beach Boys, The Rolling Stones, Chad & Jeremy, Patty Duke...........$30–60

1966

Winter Sonny & Cher's Life Story in Pix, Chris Jones Heartbreaking Story, Paul McCartney, Paul Revere & the Raiders: 50 Great Pix, Peter & Gordon's Life Story in Pix, Ian Whitcomb, A Sneak Preview With Herman's Hermits, A Salute to Elvis Presley, Keith Allison, The Dave Clark Five, The Beatles Personal Calendar, Hermits' Life Story in Pix, Paul Petersen, The McCoys, Lee Majors, The Rolling Stones.................................$20–40

Summer The Beatles Return to Liverpool, Raider Smitty's Life in Pix, At Home With Dino, Desi & Billy, Adam West's Favorite Girl, Herman & the Hermits: Full Fact Sheets, The Rolling Stones, Raiders, David McCallum, A Date With Paul McCartney, Peter & Gordon: 30 Intimate Questions, A Day With Tony & the Tigers, Mark Lindsay's Life in Pix, Keith Allison, Sonny & Cher Movie, The Beach Boys Go Wild, Dave Clark Five Life in Pix, At Home With Hayley Mills $20–40

1968

Spring Davy Jones, Raiders, Dark Shadows, The Doors, The Monkees, The Dark Past of the Beatles, Sajid Khan, Mark Lindsay, Barry Cowsill, Dino, Desi & Billy, Mark Slade, Peter Noone, Walter Koenig, The Bee Gees $20–40

Summer The Monkees, Sajid Khan, 100 Monkee Pix, Monkee Cars, Jay North, Slade, Peter Noone, The Bee Gees, Billy Mummy, "Star Trek"..$20–40

Fall The Monkees, Davy Jones Vanishes, Chris Jones, Sajid Khan, The Cowsills, Raiders, "Star Trek," Sing Along With Jim Morrison & the Doors, Jonathan Frid, Billy Mummy, The Many Faces of Peter Noone, Boone & the Gorillas, Mark Lindsay.......................$20–40

Winter The Monkees, Davy Jones in *Oliver*, Lyrics to the Monkees' "Pisces & Aquarius," Sajid Khan, Jay North Answers 50 Intimate Questions, Mark Lindsay, The Beatles Through the Looking Glass, Mark Lindsay, The Cowsills, Chris Jones, Mark Slade, The New Rascals, Walter Koenig, Dave Clark Five, Grass Roots, Jim Morrison & the Doors $20–40

1969

Winter The Monkees Break-up: The When, How & Why, Sajid Khan, Jay North, Mark Lindsay's Secret Love Letters, The Beatles, Slade, Chris Jones, The Cowsills, Walter Koenig...$20–40

Spring Bobby Sherman, The History of the Beatles, Mike Cole, Donovan, Sajid Khan, Davy Jones, Nazz, Dark Shadows, Elvis Presley, The Cowsills, Simon & Garfunkel, Dave Clark Five, Peter Noone's Wedding Special..$20–40

1971

May David Cassidy & the Partridge Family: 100 Rare Pix, Color Posters, 200 Intimate Questions & Their Love-life Secrets, Bobby Sherman, Donny & the Osmonds, Susan Dey, Mike Cole, Michael Jackson Squeals on the Jackson Five, Jim Brolin, Chad Everett, The Music Career of David Cassidy...$15–30

July David Cassidy's Tragic Illness: His Deep Dark Secret Revealed at Last, The Bugaloos, The Jackson Five on TV, Raiders, Ronny Howard, Mike Cole, The Osmonds, Bobby Sherman, The Carpenters, Peter Duel $15–30

Aug. David Cassidy: His Tragic Illness Part II, Susan Dey Tells on David, Mike Cole, The Jacksons Sock it to You, Bobby Sherman, The Osmonds, The Cowsills, Kurt Russell, Desi Arnez...$15–30

Sept. David Cassidy: How He Keeps in Shape, Susan Dey, The Bradys, Danny Bonaduce, Bobby Sherman, The Monkees, Jimmy Osmond's Life Story, The Jackson Five: Their Secrets Revealed, Michael Jackson, Peter Duel $15–30

Oct. David Cassidy, Donny Osmond, Bobby Sherman, Susan Dey, Peter Duel, The Jackson Five: "What Love Means to Us," Maureen McCormick, The Bradys......................$15–30

Nov. Donny Osmond: Meet the Girls He Loves, David Cassidy, Bobby Sherman, The Brady

Bunch: "We are Growing Up Too Fast," The Jackson Five, Susan Dey, David Cassidy Hospitalized, Maureen McCormick $15–30

1972

Jan. David Cassidy & the Partridge Family: Their Most Intimate Pix, David Cassidy: Singin' in the Shower, Peter Duel, Night of Dark Shadows, The Jackson Five, Bobby Sherman: Talking About Wes Stern, The Cowsills, Donny Osmond, Rick Ely, Jack Wild...$15–30
Feb. David Cassidy, Bobby Sherman, Donny & the Osmonds, Butch Patrick, The Jackson Five, Peter Duel, Michael Jackson, The Boone Girls, Barry Williams, The Four Leaves, Maureen $12–25
Mar. Donny Osmond, David Cassidy: What He Expects from Girls, Susan Dey & Danny Bonaduce, The Carpenters, Jim Morrison & the Doors, The Temptations, Chicago, Maureen McCormick, The Bradys, Peter Duel, The Jackson Five, Bobby Sherman, Butch Patrick, Osmonds $12–25
Apr. Michael Jackson & the Jackson Five, David Cassidy: In Action & at Ease, The Brady Bunch: "Come to Our Party," Donny & the Osmonds, Bobby Sherman: His Future Plans, Peter Duel: His Tragic Story, Butch Patrick...$12–25
May The Osmonds House Party, David Cassidy & the Partridge Family, Jan Michael Vincent, Butch Patrick, Chris Knight, The Bradys, Marc Bolan & T. Rex, Davy Jones, Three Dog Night, Spending the Night With Donny Osmond, The Jackson Five, Maureen McCormick, Desi Arnez, Michael Jackson...$12–25
June Donny Osmond & the Osmonds: The Family Wedding, David Cassidy: How Can You Ring His Bell, Chris Knight & the Bradys, Marie Osmond, Bobby Sherman, T. Rex, America, Bob Dylan, The Grass Roots, Raspberries, The Jackson Five $12–25
July Michael Jackson & the Jacksons, Meet Marie Osmond, Chris Knight, Butch Patrick, Maureen McCormick, Marc Bolan, T. Rex, David Cassidy, Bobby Sherman, The Bradys, The Heywoods, Billy Mummy, The Moody Blues, The Hudsons, The Cowsills $12–25
Aug. Donny Osmond, Marie Osmond, Bobby Sherman, Butch Patrick, Mitch Vogel, Billy Mummy, The Bradys, The Jackson Five, Marc Bolin, Vince Van Patten..................$12–25
Sept. David Cassidy: "Please Show Me You Love Me," The Jackson Five, The Osmonds: Special Pictures, Bobby Sherman, Donny Osmond, Kurt Russell, The Bradys, Marie Osmond, Billy Mummy, Marc Bolin, Vince Van Patten...$12–25
Nov. David Cassidy Goes All the Way, Donny Osmond: He's in Love, Marc Bolin, Michael Jackson, Rick Springfield, The Jackson Five, Marie Osmond $12–25
Dec. Donny Osmond: His Secret Love Message, David Cassidy: A Jealous Lover?, Michael Jackson & the Jackson Five: The Secret Girls in Their Lives, Marie Osmond: Secret Sister, Bobby Sherman, Butch Patrick, Rick Springfield, Randy Mantooth, Marc Bolan, The Brady Bunch..$12–25

1973

Jan. Donny Osmond: 10 Things You Can Do to Drive Him Wild, David Cassidy Quits: Partridge Family Shocker, Jermaine Jackson to Wed, Marc Bolin, Bobby Sherman: Married?, Chris Knight & Eve Plumb: Are They Having a Secret Romance?, Butch Patrick, Marie Osmond, David Bowie, The Jackson Five: They Visit Sonny & Cher, Andy & Dave, Rick Springfield $12–25
Feb. Donny Osmond Attacked, David Cassidy: "I'll Never Marry," Michael Jackson, Rick Springfield's Love, Andy & Dave, Marc Bolan, The Bradys, Chris Knight, Bread, Slade, The Osmonds, The Heywoods, Alice Cooper, Bobby Sherman a Father?, Cher $12–25
Mar. Michael Jackson, Donny Osmond Collapses, David Cassidy Takes You to England, The New Seekers, Rick Springfield, Sonny & Cher's Greatest Guests, The Heywoods, Davy Jones & Micky Dolenz, Marie Osmond, Bobby Sherman, David Cassidy's Love ...$12–25
May The Osmond's Fight: The Girl That Came Between Them, Rick Springfield, "The Waltons," The Bradys, David Cassidy, The Jackson Five Super TV Special, Randy, Andy & Dave, Marie Osmond, Vince Van Patten, Bobby Sherman $12–25
June David Cassidy on Trial, Donny Osmond & the Osmonds: Their Sneak Dates, Rick Springfield Deported, Randy, Andy & Dave, Marie Osmond, The Jackson Five, Sonny & Cher, Butch Patrick, Susan Dey, Special Jackson Five Poster....................................$12–25
July Michael Jackson & the Jackson Five: Bare-chested & Ready for Action, Are the Osmonds Leaving the U.S.A?, Donny Osmond: His Body Secrets Revealed, Rick Springfield:

16 MAGAZINE,
1979, Jan.

16 MAGAZINE,
1979, Aug.

16 MAGAZINE,
1982, Jan.

16 MAGAZINE SPEC,
1971, May

16 MAGAZINE SPEC,
1971, July

16 MAGAZINE SPEC,
1971, Nov.

16 MAGAZINE SPEC,
1972, Feb.

16 MAGAZINE SPEC,
1972, Mar.

16 MAGAZINE SPEC,
1972, Apr.

His Love Test, Randy, Jan Michael Vincent, Alice Cooper, The Heywoods, The Bradys, David Cassidy, Andy & Dave, Edgar Winter, J. Geils, Spinners, The Doobies, War...$12–25
Aug. Donny Osmond: His Bitter Love Affair Part I, Andy & Dave: 100 Hot Fax & Pix, The Jackson Five: To Their House & Meet the Whole Clan, Rick Springfield, David Cassidy: Gone Forever, Marie Osmond, The Bradys...$12–25
Sept. Donny Osmond's Secret Hideout—Never-before-seen Pix, The Jackson Five: Their Funky Japanese Bash, Jan Michael Vincent: Behind the Closed Door, Andy & Dave, My Bitter Love Affair With Donny Osmond Part II, Rick Springfield, Simon Turner, "The Waltons," Maureen McCormick, David Cassidy...$12–25

1974

Jan. Donny Osmond's Awful Secret, The Osmond Hotel Fire, David Cassidy Sounds Off, Michael Jackson: Ruff Tuff Cream Puff, Randy, Andy & Dave, Alice Cooper & His Freaky *Rocky Horror* Friends, The Bradys, Robby Benson, Rick Springfield.......................$12–25

16 MAGAZINE SPECIAL EDITION
1987

Davy Jones feature story & color centerfold, The Monkees Forever, The Real Michael J. Fox, Kirk Cameron, Menudo, A-ha, Rob Lowe, Andrew McCarthy, Hall & Oates, River Phoenix, Julian Lennon, Madonna, Ralph Macchio...$2–5

16 MAGAZINE'S SCOOP: BEATLES COMPLETE STORY FROM BIRTH TO NOW MAGAZINE
1965

The Beatles' Pictures from Childhood, Over 100 Exclusive Photos, issue includes seven huge color pin-ups, Hamburg Days & Early Liverpool Days, The Strange Story of the Beatle Who Vanished, Fact Sheets on all four Beatles..$25–50

16 MAGAZINE'S '62 SECRET BANDSTAND ALBUM
1962

Includes All Your Favorite "Bandstand" Regulars...$25–50

16 MAGAZINE'S THE TWIST
1962

Learn the Twist Step by Step, Completely Illustrated, How Joey Dee Twisted to Stardom, Chubby Checker: King of the Twist, Shirley MacLaine $20–40

16 MAGAZINE'S 3-IN-1 SPECTACULAR
1959

Edd Byrns, Fabian & Frankie Avalon, includes 101 rare photos $15–30

16'S ALL-STAR FAMILY SPECIAL '88 MAGAZINE
1987–88

Winter Kirk Cameron & His Family, The Monkees: Behind Closed Doors, River Phoenix, George Michael: Before & After, Corey Haim, Def Leppard, Twisted Sister, Michael J. Fox, Patrick Swayzee, John Stamos, Johnny Depp $3–6

16'S PRESENTATION OF THE BEATLES MOVIE "HELP"
1965

The Un-cut, Full-length Story of *Help*, Pin-ups & Pix...$25–50

16'S SUPER STARS MAGAZINE
1989

Spring Alyssa Milano Exclusive Interview & Color Pin-ups, Jon Bon Jovi: At Home With His Favorite Things, Corey Haim, Debbie Gibson: At Her Party & Talking About Electric

Kiss

Collecting
KISS

From its inception in 1973, Kiss has been a highly unusual band—but no one can argue with their amazing success. They brought wild makeup, glamorous costumes, and bombastic stage theatrics to the otherwise dull 1970s. They've sold over 70 million albums, baffled critics, and delighted fans for almost 20 years. They continue to make hit records and play live for their millions of fans worldwide.

Although they weren't the first band to be mass-merchandised, Kiss, with the help of Casablanca Records, brought rock memorabilia to a level never seen before. During Kiss's peak merchandising years of 1976–1980, hundreds of items were released with Kiss's logo and trademarked facial makeup emblazoned on them. In addition to dolls, T-shirts, and posters, there were Kiss pens, shoelaces, beach towels, and even a pinball machine.

Only Elvis and the Beatles equal Kiss in merchandise and collectibility, and the popularity of Kiss music and Kiss collecting has increased dramatically in the last few years. There are over 50 Kiss fan clubs in the United

States and many more overseas. Kiss conventions have been held in various parts of the United States and Canada in the last several years. Record-collecting magazines such as *Discoveries* often contain large numbers of advertisements for Kiss records and merchandise.

MISCELLANEOUS KISS COLLECTIBLES

Backpack, in package $25–50
Backpack, without package $20–40
Ball-point pens, Paul, Gene, Ace, Peter
  Sealed on original illustrated blister pack; each.........................$7–15
  Sealed set of four..$25–50
  Without blister pack; each..$4–8
  Set of four without packaging $12–25
Bedspread, sealed in package $50–100
Bedspread, without package $45–90
Belt buckle, lettered brass, 1976..$15–30
Belt buckles, Pacifica
  "Love Gun," 1977 ....$20–40
  Paul Stanley, 1977 ....$20–40
  Rock-and-Roll Over, 1977...$20–40
  Kiss logo, 1977, several color combinations available $20–40
Books
  Kiss: The Real Story, by Peggy Tomarkin................................$17–35
  Kiss, by Robert Duncan $7–15
  Headliners: Kiss, by John Swenson $7–15
Chu-bops, record-shaped bubble gum in "album cover"
  Dynasty $6–12
  Unmasked $4–8
Colorforms..$15–30
Dolls, Mego, 12"–13", Gene, Ace, Paul, Peter
  With original box; each..$75–125
  Set of four in original boxes $200–400
  Without box; each..$40–80
  Set of four without boxes $120–300
Eric Carr drumsticks, 1980–present $22–45
Garbage can/wastebasket $30–60
Gold chain, Australian import...$10–20
Halloween costumes, Paul, Gene, Ace, Peter
  Complete with box; each..$20–40
  Costume & mask without box; each $10–20
  Masks only; each $5–10
Jewelry
  Gold logo necklace, 1977...$7–15
  Silver logo necklace, 1978..$7–15
  Solo-album rings, 1978, Paul, Gene, Ace, Peter; each....................$12–25
  "Signature" necklaces, 1978, Paul, Gene, Ace, Peter; each.............$12–25
  "I Was There" 3" button, 1978 ....$7–15
  Logo sticker pin, 1980, gold or silver $7–15
"Kiss Your Face" makeup kit, first edition, sealed $30–65
"Kiss Your Face" makeup kit, second edition, sealed $30–65
Logo/faces beach towel..$20–40
Logo/faces shoelaces...$7–15
Logos only shoelaces...$6–12
"Love Gun" beach towel...$20–40
Lunchbox, with thermos...$25–50
Lunchbox, without thermos...$20–40
Mardi Gras coins, 1979 & 1983, red or silver; each...........................$5–10
Microphone..$20–40

Model van, sealed $15–30
Model van, open but unassembled $12–25
"On Tour" game...$20–40
Paul Stanley "Firehouse" hat, several styles available $150–300
Pencils, sealed set of four..$7–15
Pencils, without package; each..$2–4
Peter Criss drumsticks, 1973–1979...$25–50
Pinball machine, operating condition..$500–1,500
Pinball machine, not operating..$200–400
Plastic tumblers, 1978, Majik Markets
   First series, Ace, Paul, Gene, Peter; each..$20–40
   Second series; each..$25–50
Poster art, sealed, with pens..$17–35
Puffy stickers/"Rockstics," Paul, Gene, Ace, Peter
   Sealed in package; each $7–10
   Set of four $20–40
Puzzles
   Paul Stanley $12–25
   Gene Simmons $12–25
   Ace Frehley $12–25
   Peter Criss $12–25
   Destroyer..$15–30
   Love Gun $15–30
Radio, with box...$30–60
Radio, without box..$25–50
Record player...$80–160
Remote control van, with box..$20–45
Remote control van, without box $15–30
"Rub & Play" set..$15–30
Sleeping bag, sealed in package $65–125
Sleeping bag, without package...$55–110
Solo-album plastic shopping bag, 1978..$5–15
Songbooks
   Destroyer..$12–25
   The Originals..$25–50
   Rock-and-Roll Over $12–25
   Love Gun $12–25
   Alive II $17–35
   Double Platinum...$12–25
   Paul Stanley...$10–20
   Gene Simmons $10–20
   Ace Frehely $10–20
   Peter Criss $10–20
   Dynasty...$12–25
   Unmasked...$12–25
   Crazy Nights...$7–15
Spiral notebooks
   Paul Stanley $7–15
   Gene Simmons $7–15
   Ace Frehley $7–15
   Peter Criss $7–15
   Solo-album art $7–15
   Posed shots, 1978..$10–20
   Posed shots, 1979..$10–20
Thermos alone..$10–15
Tour books (U.S.A.)
   "Kiss on Tour, 1976" $35–70
   "Kiss on Tour" ("Destroyer"), two different available $25–50
   "Kiss World Tour '77 & '78" $20–40
   Dynasty Tour book, three different available $17–35

"Kiss 10th Anniversary Tour" $40–80
"Kiss World Tour 1984" $15–30
"Kiss World Tour 1984–85," with Mark $10–20
"Kiss World Tour 1984–85," with Bruce $10–20
"Kiss Asylum Tour" $10–20
"Kiss Crazy Nights World Tour 1987–88" $12–25
"Kiss Hot in the Shade World Tour 1990–91" $12–25

Tour books (Foreign)
Japan 1977 ....$40–85
Japan 1978 ....$40–85
Australia 1980 ....$30–60
Europe 1980 ....$30–60
Japan 1988 ....$30–60
Monsters of Rock (Kiss With Iron Maiden & others) '88 ....$10–20

Toy guitar, sealed in package $45–90
Toy guitar, without packaging $25–50

Trading cards
First series (#1–66), per card ....$.50–1
First series (#1–66), full set of 66 cards $15–30
First series, seven cards in unopened wrapper $2–4
First series, wrapper only $1–2
First series, illustrated box, empty $5–10
Second series (#67–132), per card ....$.50–1
Second series (#67–132), full set of 66 cards $15–30
Second series, seven cards in wrapper $2–4
Second series, wrapper only $1–2
Second series, illustrated box, empty $5–10
First series, revised with Eric Carr, Australia $10–20
Per card, without Eric $1–2
Per card, with Eric $3–5
Full set of 66 cards $17–35
Seven cards in wrapper $6–12
Wrapper $1–2
Empty box $5–10

Viewmaster reel, sealed in package $7–15
Viewmaster reel, in opened package $5–10
Viewmaster reels, set of three in package $10–20

NEW ENGLAND KISS COLLECTORS' NETWORK

The New England Kiss Collectors' Network, run by John and Karen
Lesniewski, is a Kiss fan club that promotes Kiss conventions. They held the
first-ever U.S. Kiss convention on March 1, 1987, and have run at least seven
Kiss conventions so far. Their February 1990 convention featured Eric Carr
as a special guest.

The New England Kiss Collectors' Network newsletter is issued four to six
times a year. The newsletter features Kiss news, information about Kiss collecting, and exclusive Kiss photos and interviews. Subscription to the newsletter is $6 for the United States and Canada, and $10 (surface mail) to all
other countries. For a sample copy of the newsletter, send a self-addressed
stamped envelope (United States and Canada only) to: The New England
Kiss Collectors' Network, 168 Oakland Avenue, Providence, RI 02908.

Youth, Tiffany, New Kids on the Block, Madonna, Bros, Wil Wheaton, Tiffany wall poster...$3–6
Fall New Kids on the Block, Corey Haim, Debbie Gibson, Bros, The Monkees: Davy Jones Has Been Hurt, Kirk Cameron, Johnny Depp, John Stamos, Menudo, Ralph Macchio, Tiffany, Red Savage, Alyssa Milano, River Phoenix, Sara Gilbert.....................................$2–6

1989–90

Winter Exclusive New Kids on the Block—16-page section with wall poster & pin-ups, Debbie Gibson, Bros, Chad Allen, Corey Haim, Fred Savage, Johnny Depp, Grieco, Young Riders, Paula Abdul, Michael Damian..$2–4

1990

Spring New Kids on the Block, Tiffany, Young Riders, Fred Savage, Debbie Gibson: What Success Has Cost Her, Paula Abdul, Janet Jackson, Martika, Alyssa Milano, Kirk Cameron, Johnny Depp...$2–4

SLASH (Tabloid)

All issues...$4–10

SMASH HITS

1981

May #1..$3–6
July #2 .38 Special, The Whispers, Emmylou Harris..$3–6
Sept. #3 Ted Nugent, Ray Parker Jr. & Raydio, Mel Tillis.......................................$2–4
Nov. #4..$2–4

1982

Jan. #5...$2–4
Mar. Triumph, Kool & the Gang, Mac Davis...$2–4
May Rod Stewart, George Harrison, Willie Nelson...$2–4

1983

June Men at Work, Michael Jackson, Alabama...$2–4
Oct. Thomas Dolby Exclusive Interview, Prince, The Oak Ridge Boys.......................$2–4

1984

May Sting, Stewart, Copeland of the Police Exclusive Interview, the Jones Girls, John Denver..$2–4
July Kiss/Paul Stanley, An Exclusive Interview With Gene Simmons of Kiss, Lionel Richie, Emmylou Harris..$3–6
Oct. Eurythmics, Luther Vandergross, The Statler Brothers..$2–4

1988

Oct. INXS: On Tour, Bros, Debbie Gibson at Home, Prince: Secrets from His Past, Tiffany on the Road, Terence Trent D'Arby, INXS poster, Corey Hart, Michael Jackson, Thomas Dolby, OMD, Poison, Richard Marx, Wet Wet Wet..$2–3
Nov. Guns 'n' Roses, Terence Trent D'Arby, Billy Idol's Motorcycle Madness, Fat Boys, Huey Lewis, Tracy Chapman, Def Leppard, Cyndi Lauper, 10,000 Maniacs...............$2–3

1989

Feb. The Return of Duran, Duran, Bon Jovi for a Day, Pet Shop Boys: Are Washed Up, U2, George Michael, UB40, Guns 'n' Roses...$2–3
Apr. Pet Shop Boys, Def Leppard, 25 Amazing Facts on Duran Duran, Phil Collins, Poison, Breathe, Psychedelic Furs, The Bangles..$2–3
Aug. Madonna: Expressin' Herself, The Cure: Bob is Back, Brother Beyond, Milli Vanilli, Fine Young Cannibals, Love & Rockets, Bon Jovi, Depeche Mode, Debbie Gibson, Escape Club...$2–3
Dec. New Kids on the Block: Their Wildest Secrets, Being Kookie with Madonna, The

Cure, Paula Abdul, Fine Young Cannibals, Bon Jovi Goes Bonkers, Debbie Gibson: She's Delirious, Martika, Neneh Cherry..$2–3

SMASH HITS PRESENTS METALLIX

1989

Oct. Issue includes posters & interviews—Bon Jovi, White Lion, Beastie Boys, Lita Ford, EZO, Kingdom Come, Ozzy Osbourne, Blue Murder..$2–4
Dec. Metallica, Warrent, White Lion, Backstage With Skid Row, The Cult, Guns 'n' Roses & Aerosmith special feature & poster, Motley Crue's Nasty Past, Metallica..............$2–4

1990

Jan. Nikki Sixx, Skid Row, L.A. Guns, Bang Tango, Nuclear Assault, The Cult, Whitesnake, Guns 'n' Roses, Warrent, Aerosmith, Metallica, Tora Tora, Danger Danger..$2–3

SMASH HITS PRESENTS THE SMASH HITS SUMMER SPECIAL MAGAZINE

1989

Madonna, Def Leppard, Bros, Belinda Carlisle, Michael Jackson: A Shocking Story, Boy George, Debbie Gibson, The Pet Shop Boys Story, Breathe, Yazz, Roachford............$2–4

SMASH HITS SPECIAL

1987

#5 Metallix—Guns 'n' Roses: Road Warriors Exclusive, Poison Talking Trash, Metallica's Killer Justice, Judas Priest: True Rockets Forever, Killer Backstage Interviews & Centerfolds With Def Leppard, Cinderella, Lita Ford, Ace Frehley & Bon Jovi........$2–4

SOHO NEWS

Issues that feature pop music performers on cover $4–10

SONG HITS

1966

Mar. Herman's Hermits, Mick Jagger & James Brown are Too Sexy, The Lovin' Spoonful, Jackie De Shannon, The Toys, The Walker Brothers $15–30
Apr. Frank Sinatra: The Whole Life Story, Johnny Mathis: New Lease on Life, Gene Pitney: Simon & Garfunkel, The Kinks, Paul Revere & The Raiders......................$15–30
June On the Road With the Lovin' Spoonful, The Animals & The Four Seasons Get New Members, The Temptations, Bob Dylan, Bobby Vinton..$15–30
July The Beach Boys: Having a Midas Touch, Simon & Garfunkel, The Who, Paul Revere, The Kinks, Bobby Fuller Four, Moody Blues..$15–30
Aug. Dusty Springfield Returns, Walker Brothers, The Outsiders, Young Rascals, Mitch Ryder, The Knickerbockers, Lesley Gore, Percy Sledge..$15–30
Nov. The Mamas & the Papas, Tommy Roe Makes a Comeback, Tommy James & The Shondells, The Happenings, Sunrays, The Leaves, Eric Burdon, Los Bravos, Sandy Posey, Andrew Oldham $15–30

1967

Jan. Elvis Presley: Dying at the Box Office, Tracking Down the Lovin' Spoonful, Count 5, The 5 Stairsteps, The Wild Ones..$15–30
Feb. An Exciting Visit With the Byrds, The Four Seasons, Herman/Peter Noone Grows Up, Lou Rawls, Peter & Gordon, The Happenings, The McCoys......................................$15–30
Apr. The Young Rascals in London, Roy Orbison in Hollywood, Herman in Holland, Sonny & Cher, The Sunrays, The Left Banke, Otis Redding, Wilson Pickett, Tim Rose $15–30
May The Whole Truth About the Monkees, Problems for the Spencer Davis Group, Gene Pitney, Bobby Goldsboro, Spyder Turner, The Woolies, Electric Prunes, Peaches & Herb $15–30

June The Monkees: Can They Last?, The Blue Magoos, The Association, The Hollies $15–30
July Paul Revere & the Raiders: The Bare Facts, The Left Banke, The Monkees Meet the Beatles, The Hollies, Dave Clark Five, Jefferson Airplane $15–30
Aug. Mick Jagger on "Buttons," The Monkees, The Turtles, The Who, Donovan, Paul Simon, Paul Revere, Otis Redding $15–30
Sept. Micky Dolenz Speaks Out, Moby Grape, The Bee Gees, Mothers, The New Raiders $15–30
Oct. Davy Jones: Does He Want Out?, The Doors: Musicians & Poets, Janice Ian, Procol Harum, Grass Roots, The Association $15–30
Nov. The Monkees: Are They Different?, Bobbie Gentry, Mark Lindsay, The Hollies, Bobby Vinton, Van Morrison, Lewis & Clarke $15–30
Dec. Davy Jones, Mick Jagger Turn On, The Association, The Everly Brothers, Jimi Hendrix $15–30

1968

Jan. Micky Dolenz: His Girls Tell All, Bobby Vee's Comeback, To Lulu With Love, Neil Diamond, The Tokens $15–30
Feb. Strawberry Alarm Clock, Jefferson Airplane, Every Mother's Son, Chad & Jeremy, The Beach Boys, Nilsson, Blue Magoos, The 5th Dimension $15–30
Mar. Jim Morrison: The Key to the Doors Success, The Bee Gees, The Animals $20–40
Apr. Davy Jones: Will He Leave America?, Neil Diamond, Donovan, On Tour With the Cowsills, Spanky's Gang $15–30
May Meet Davy Jones, Neil Young of Buffalo Springfield, "My Beautiful Experiences With Jim Morrison" by a Teen Fan, The Soul Survivors, Donovan $15–30
June Peter Tork: The Mystifying Monkees, Neil Diamond Confessions, Lulu $15–30
July Davy Jones, Lesley Gore, Waylon Jennings, Neil Diamond, Jefferson Airplane....$15–30
Sept. The Union Gap, Every Mother's Son, Spanky & Our Gang $15–30
Oct. Boyce & Hart, Jim Morrison: Behind the Bad Reputation, Pete Townshend & the Who, The Troggs, Strawberry Alarm Clock $15–30
Nov. Digging John Kay of Steppenwolf, Eric Clapton, Traffic, The Box Tops, Strawberry Alarm Clock $12–25
Dec. The Bee Gees are Back, The Real Hippies: The Association, The Very Real Tom Rush, Eric Burdon, Janis Joplin, Jim Webb $15–30

1969

May The Doors, The Impressions, Sheb Wooley $15–30
June Merle Haggard, Tommy James, The Temptation $10–20
Sept. The Who, Jerry Butler, Jim Ed Brown, Peter Townshend $10–20
Dec. Classics IV, Joe Simon, Jeannie C. Riley $10–20

1970

Jan. Oliver, Gladys Knight & the Pips, Johnny Cash...$8–15
Mar. Creedence Clearwater Revival, Jim Reeves...$10–20
Aug. Simon & Garfunkel, The Delfonics, Jeannie C. Riley......................................$10–20

1971

Jan. Ray Charles, Buck Owens...$4–8
Feb. Canned Heat, Eddie Floyd, Jim Ed Brown $3–6
Apr. Tommy Roe, Funkadelic, Skeeter Davis...$4–8
June The Who, Clarence Carter, Buddy Alan $4–8
July The Partridge Family, The 5th Dimension, Dolly Parton...................................$15–30
Sept. Canned Heat, Floyd Cramer, Tyrone Davis...$4–8

1972

Nov. Aretha Franklin, Elvis Presley, Hanson Cargil $4–8

1973

Jan. Chicago, Frederick Knight, Porter Wagoner $4–8
Feb. The Who, Bobby Bare, Charles Wright...$4–8

Mar. Beverly Bremers, The Persuasions, The Hagers.................................$4–8
Apr. Lobo, Isaac Hayes, George Jones...$4–8
June Gary Glitter, The Intruders, Don Gibson $4–8
July Carly Simon, The Four Tops, Charlie Rich................................$5–10
Aug. Bread, Kris Kristofferson, Timmy Thomas $3–6
Oct. Vicki Lawrence, Bobby Womack, Del Reeves $4–8
Dec. The Carpenters, Marvin Gaye, Donna Fargo............................$5–10

1974

Jan. Charlie Daniels, Ray Charles, Diana Trask...............................$4–8
Feb. Billy Preston, O.B. McClinton..$3–6
Mar. The Doobie Brothers, Bloodstone, Anne Murray $4–8
Apr. Seals & Crofts, Al Green, Roger Miller.....................................$3–6
May Todd Rundgren, Gladys Knight & the Pips...............................$5–10
July Elton John, Billy "Crash" Craddock $4–8
Aug. Three Dog Night, The Spinners, Mel Tillis...............................$4–8
Oct. Jim Stafford, Stevie Wonder, Joe Stampley.............................$3–6
Nov. Paul McCartney, War, Bobby Bare $4–8
Dec. John Denver, Charley Pride, Bobby Womack $3–6

1975

Jan. The Righteous Brothers, Tower of Power, Merle Haggard $3–6
Mar. Gordon Lightfoot, Curtis Mayfield, Larry Gatlin......................$3–6
Apr. Kiki Dee, Rufus, Moe Bandy...$3–6
July Olivia Newton-John, America, The Miracles..............................$5–10
Aug. Charlie Rich, The Eagles, Blue Magic.......................................$3–6
Sept. Karen Carpenter, Mel Tillis, The Ohio Players.........................$3–6
Nov. The Bee Gees, Roberta Flack, Freddy Fender $4–8

1976

Jan. The Captain & Tennille, Minnie Riperton $3–6
Mar. Billy Swan, Tanya Tucker, Van McCoy....................................$3–6
May Seals & Crofts, Asleep at the Wheel, Emmylou Harris..............$3–6
June Neil Sedaka, Natalie Cole, Conway Twitty $3–6
July Electric Light Orchestra, KC & the Sunshine Band...................$3–6
Aug. Gary Wright, Diana Ross, Billie Jo Spears...............................$3–6
Oct. Elvin Bishop, The Sylvers, Marty Robbins $3–6
Nov. America, Aretha Franklin, Freddie Hart $3–6
Dec. Jefferson Starship, Eddie Rabbitt, Al Wilson $3–6

1977

Jan. Helen Reddy, Joe Stampley, The Brothers Johnson..................$3–6
Feb. Boz Scaggs, Jessi Colter, The O'Jays......................................$3–6
Mar. England Dan & John Corey, Marilyn McCoo...........................$3–6
Apr. Rod Stewart, The Staple Singers, Emmylou Harris....................$3–6
Aug. The Bee Gees, Rufus, Glen Campbell $3–6
Sept. Fleetwood Mac, The Commodores, Tom T. Hall......................$10–20
Oct. Leo Sayer, Tavares, Hank Williams Jr. $3–6
Nov. The Steve Miller Band, Marvin Gaye, Charlie Pride.................$3–6
Dec. Kiss, The Isley Brothers, Crystal Gayle $10–20

1978

Jan. Foreigner, KC & the Sunshine Band, Freddy Fender.................$3–6
Feb. Andy Gibb, Rose Royce, Merle Haggard...................................$3–6
Apr. Kansas, Barry White, Kenny Rogers...$3–6
July Jackson Browne, Eric Clapton, George Benson $3–6
Sept. Wings, Carly Simon, Heatwave, Barbara Fairchild....................$3–6
Oct. Warren Zevon, Patti Smith Group, Dolly Parton.......................$3–6

Nov. Joe Walsh, Gerry Rafferty, The Oak Ridge Boys..$3–6
Dec. Rita Coolidge, Foreigner, Taste of Honey $3–6

1979

Jan. Pablo Cruise, Eddie Money, Ronnie Milsap $2–4
Feb. Exile, Barbara Mandrell, Sylvester...$2–4
Mar. Linda Ronstadt, Ambrosia, Chaka Khan, Bobby Bare......................................$3–6
Apr. Jethro Tull, Chicago, Diana Ross, Waylon Jennings $3–6
May Queen, Eric Clapton, Gladys Knight, Bill Anderson..$3–6
July The Bee Gees, Poco, Rick James, Willie Nelson $3–6
Aug. George Harrison, Nicolette Larson, The Pointer Sisters $3–6
Nov. Electric Light Orchestra, Rex Allen Jr..$2–4

1980

Jan. Kiss, The Kinks, Diana Ross, Earl Scruggs $5–10
Feb. The Eagles, Foreigner, Ashford & Simpson...$3–6
Apr. Jefferson Starship, The Police, Stevie Wonder, Carlene Carter $3–6
May ZZ Top, Dan Fogelberg, The Spinners, Donna Fargo..$3–6
July Billy Joel, Bob Seger & the Silver Bullet Band, Michael Jackson, Loretta Lynn....$3–6
Aug. Van Halen, Linda Ronstadt, Whispers, Charlie Pride...$3–6
Sept. Ambrosia, Boz Scaggs, Isley Brothers, Mac Davis..$2–4
Oct. Pete Townshend, Stephanie Mills, Hank Williams Jr...$3–6
Nov. Ted Nugent, Alice Cooper, Natalie Cole, Larry Gatlin..$3–6
Dec. Christopher Cross, Queen, Chic, Alabama...$3–6

1981

Jan. Paul Simon, The Allman Brothers, Diana Ross, Don Williams............................$3–6
Feb. The Doobie Brothers, Carly Simon, L.T.D., Mickey Gilley $3–6
Mar. Kansas, David Bowie, John Lennon: In Memoriam, The Jacksons, Crystal Gayle....$3–6
Apr. Dire Straits, Rod Stewart, Kool & the Gang, Charlie Rich...................................$3–6
May REO Speedwagon, AC/DC, Heatwave, Johnny Lee..$3–6
June Steve Winwood, Nicolette Larson, The Gap Band, Dolly Parton.........................$3–6
July Loverboy, April Wine, The Bellamy Brothers...$2–4
Sept. Santana, Gary U.S. Bonds, Ozzy Osbourne $2–4
Oct. Kim Carnes, Rosanne Cash, Lee Ritenour..$3–6

1982

Jan. The Allman Brothers Band, ZZ Top, Al Jarreau $3–6
Mar. Journey, Luther Vandergross, John Lennon, Terri Gibb......................................$3–6
Apr. Kiss, The Cars, Earth, Wind & Fire, Reba McEntire...$5–10
May Quarterflash, Lindsay Buckingham, John Anderson...$3–6
June Sammy Hagar, Sheena Easton, Emmylou Harris..$3–6
Aug. Rick Springfield, Asia, Third World, Joe Sun..$3–6
Nov. The Alan Parsons Project, Fleetwood Mac, Bobby Bare......................................$3–6
Dec. Patrick Simmons, Robert Plant, Donna Summer...$3–6

1983

Apr. Jefferson Starship Exclusive Interview, Supertramp, Marvin Gaye, Merle Haggard
....$3–6
July Hall & Oates Exclusive Interview, Janet Jackson, Styx, Shelley West................$3–6
Sept. Men at Work, Supertramp, Joan Armatrading, Mel Tillis....................................$2–4
Oct. Loverboy, Journey, Al Jarreau, T.G. Sheppard..$2–4
Dec. Joe Walsh Exclusive Interview, Billy Joel..$2–4

1984

Mar. John Cougar Mellencamp Exclusive Interview, Peter Schilling, Dionne Warwick, Gary
Morris..$2–4
Apr. Quiet Riot's Kevin Dubrow, .38 Special, The Commodores, Deborah Allen.......$2–4
Aug. Christine McVie Exclusive Interview, April Wine, The Deele, Dolly Parton......$4–8
Sept. David Lee Roth, Night Ranger, Culture Club, Michael Jackson, Earl Thomas Con-
ley...$2–4

Nov. Rush, Bruce Springsteen, King Crimson, Del Shannon $2–4
Dec. REO Speedwagon, Wang Chung, Ratt, Peabo Bryson $2–4

1985

Jan. Triumph, Bon Jovi, Tammy Wynette, Chris Deburgh..............................$2–4
Feb. Billy Squier, Elton John, Lionel Richie, The Scorpions, Rick Springfield, Ronnie Milsap $2–4
Mar. Billy Idol Exclusive Interview, Chicago, Corey Hart, Johnny Lee, Stacy Lattisaw...$2–4
Apr. Darryl Hall Exclusive Interview, Tommy Shaw, Exile, Dennis DeYoung, Patrice Rushen $2–4
May Patti Smyth Exclusive Interview, Iron Maiden, Lindsay Buckingham, Nitty Gritty Dirt Band $2–4
Sept. Kenny Loggins, The Power Station, Emmylou Harris, Survivor, Diana Ross $2–4
Oct. Madonna, Bon Jovi, Eric Clapton, Crystal Gayle $2–4
Nov. John Waite, Phil Collins, Motown Returns to the Apollo, Michael Martin Murphy ...$2–4
Dec. Night Ranger, Heart, Tears for Fears, Mary Jane Girls, Alabama $2–4

1986

Feb. REO Speedwagon, Roger Daltry, Rosanne Cash $2–4
Apr. Special Report: Mick Jagger & Tina Turner, John Cougar, John Cafferty, The Judds ..$2–4
June Pat Benetar, Triumph, Mr. Mister, Bobby Womack $2–4
July Phil Collins, John Parr, Kiss, Whitney Houston, Marie Osmond $2–4
Sept. Culture Club, Jefferson Starship, Ronnie Milsap, Loverboy, James Brown $2–4
Oct. Journey, Mike & the Mechanics, Ozzy Osbourne, Prince, Waylon Jennings $2–4
Nov. Genesis, Miami Sound Machine, Run DMC...$2–4
Dec. Robert Palmer, The Bangles, El DeBarge, Honeymoon Suite, Dan Seals............$2–4

1987

Jan. David Lee Roth, David Bowie, The Jets..$2–4
Feb. Darryl Hall, Triumph, Julian Lennon $2–4
Mar. Bon Jovi, Elton John, Randy Travis, Sister Sledge $2–4
Apr. Cyndi Lauper, Kansas, Bruce Springsteen, Tina Turner, Restless Heart............$2–4
Aug. Lou Graham, U2, Sheila E., Anne Murray...$2–4
Oct. Night Ranger, Poison, Stach Q., Prince $2–4
Dec. Bon Jovi, Cinderella, Motley Crue, Ferry Aid..$2–4

1988

Feb. Fleetwood Mac: An Exclusive Interview With Christine McVie & Mick Fleetwood, Boston Interview, Whitney Houston, Rosanne Cash, U2, Richard Marx, Night Ranger, David Bowie, Motley Crue, John Cougar Mellencamp, Def Leppard...............................$2–4

SONG HITS OF THE SUPER '70S
1975

Fall The Doobie Brothers, John Denver, Maggie Bell, Jethro Tull, Bad Company $2–3
Nov. America, Loggins & Messina, Cher, Charlie Rich, The Spinners........................$2–4

1976

Mar. 10CC, Jefferson Starship, Three Dog Night, Helen Reddy, Orleans $2–4

1977

Spring Hall & Oates, The Bay City Rollers, Barry Manilow, Kiss, Dr. Hook $2–4

1979

Spring The Who, Hall & Oates, The Kinks, The Cars, Little River Band $2–4

SONG HITS SPECIAL
1986

Fall Heart feature story, ZZ Top, Ozzy Osbourne, The Rolling Stones, Slade & Others $3–6

SONG HITS' SUPERSTARS
1990
Fall New Kids on the Block Special, issue includes two giant color 2' × 3' New Kids posters, Janet Jackson, Madonna, Paula Abdul $2–3

SONG HITS YEARBOOK
1976
Summer The Captain & Tennille, Willie Nelson, Staple Singers $2–4

1977
Summer/Fall Rod Stewart, Waylon Jennings, Marilyn McCoo & Billy Davis............$3–6

1978
Summer/Fall Kiss, Loretta Lynn, Leo Sayer, Styx, Paul & Linda McCartney............$3–6

SPIN
1985
May #1 Madonna Cover and special feature story..$7–15
June #2 Sounds Like Talking Heads: A Talk, Billy Joel Talks Back, UB40: Stength in Numbers, Sting, Mick Jones, The Fat Boys...$5–10
July #3 Sting, A Private Conversation With General Public, The Beastie Boys are the Bigfoot of Rap, David Bowie, Men at Work, The Pogues, Katrina & the Waves, Lone Justice, Nick Cave $4–8
Aug. #4 Annie Lennox: Who's That Girl?, Midnight Oil, Dee Snider, Weird Al Yankovic, Sonic Youth, Ike Turner Exclusive: The Flip Side of Tina's Story $4–8
Sept. #5 Pat Benetar: An Extraordinary Interview, New Order, ENO, George Thorogood, Screamin' Sirens, Aerosmith, Bob Geldof, Chuck Norris, The Underground $4–8
Oct. #6 Keith Richard: A Stone Unturned, The Blasters, D.O.A., George Clinton, Buddy Rich, A Special Report: The Tragic Story of David Crosby's Living Death.................$4–8
Nov. #7 Bruce Springsteen: Fanfare for the Common Man, X, Jesus & Mary Chain Gang, Miles Davis, Henry Rollins, Yngwie Malmsteen, Tom Waits $4–8
Dec. #8 Bob Dylan: Not Like a Rolling Stone Interview, Sly Stone's Heart of Darkness, Squeeze, Husker Du, Miles Davis Part II, Rock 10,000 Maniacs................................$4–8

1986
Jan. #9 Debbie Harry Exclusive Interview, Motley Crue: Asleep at the Wheel, 'Til Tuesday, Ginger Baker, 10th Anniversary of Punk, The History of Punk: A Cartoon.............$5–10
Feb. #10 ZZ Top: America's Road Scholars, Nina Hagen: Lost in Space, The Dead Kennedys, Blow Monkeys, Invasion of the Elvis Zombies, The Pet Shop Boys.................$3–6
Mar. #11 Mick Jones Makes Good, the Pete Townshend Interview, Fear, The Cult, Robyn Hitchcock, Redd Kross, Madonna $3–6
Apr. #12 David Lee Roth Alone, Special First Anniversary Collectors' Edition, On the Road With Black Flag, Rick Nelson Remembered by Stephen King, Patti Labelle, Fine Young Cannibals, The Swans, The Residents, Rock Memories, John Lee Hooker $3–6
May Charlie Sexton: The Second Coming or What?, The Rolling Stones: What a Drag it is Getting Old, U2, Hunter Thomson: Still Crazy After All These Years $3–6
June Billy Idol, The Pogues, The Fall, INXS, Jackie Gleason, Siouxsie & the Banshees
....$3–6
July Prince: Black Narcissus, Lou Reed, Aerosmith & Run DMC Walk This Way, Simply Red, The Fabulous Thunderbirds..$3–6
Aug. Mick Jagger/The Rolling Stones: It's Almost Over Now—The Stones Run Out of Reasons for Staying Together, Run DMC, The Ramones & the Ties That Bind, The Philosophy of James Brown, Metallica, Joey Ramone interview, Pia Zadora........................$3–6
Sept. Ozzy Osbourne, Peter Gabriel, Jello Biafra, Bodeans $3–5

SPIN, 1985, June (#2)

SPIN, 1985, Aug. (#4)

SPIN, 1985, Oct. (#6)

SPIN, 1985, Dec. (#8)

SPIN, 1986, Jan. (#9)

SPIN, 1986, Feb. (#10)

SPIN, 1986, Apr.

SPIN, 1986, July

SPIN, 1986, Nov.

Oct. R.E.M.: Are We There Yet?, Boy George Exclusive Interview: The Full Story, Kool & the Gang, Jailhouse Rock...$3–5

Nov. Iggy Pop: His First interview in Four Years, Elvis Costello: Rare Photos, Cro-mags, Richard Hell, House Music in Chicago...$3–6

Dec. Chrissie Hynde: The Great Pretender, Timbuk 3, The B-52's, Fountainhead, Violence at L.A. Concerts..$3–6

1987

Jan. Janet Jackson: Damn it Janet—The Battle for Control Over Janet, Paul Simon, Ozzy Osbourne on Trial, Belinda Carlisle, Ike & Tina Turner, ZZ Top, issue includes special *Spin* 1987 color glossy poster calendar featuring—Madonna, David Bowie, Jimi Hendrix, Woodstock, Bruce Springsteen & others...$3–6

Feb. Duran Duran: Making Up is Hard to Do—A Pop Group Grows Up, Sheila E.: The Glamorous Lie, Chris Lowe of the Pet Shop Boys...$3–6

Mar. The Beastie Boys: Fighting for the Right to Party in Hell, David Bowie: What's Next?—Put-together Man, The Scorpions in Nuremberg & Behind the Iron Curtain, Megadeth, Simply Red...$3–6

Apr. Madonna: Sex as a Weapon—What Did She Start?, Bon Jovi, The The, Luther Vandergross, Joe Ely, Sonny Bono, Elvis Presley interview.....................................$3–6

May Joan Jett Finds the Promised Land, Julian Cope, The Cult.................................$5–10

June Michael Jackson: Running Scared, U2: Out of the Blue, Al Green, Crowed House, Rock Censorship..$3–6

July Susanna Hoffs of the Bangles, Sting, Motorhead, Bob Dylan, Tom Verlaine, Lisa Lisa, Susanne Vega, Anthrax, Boy George, The Return of the Grateful Dead: The Jerry Garcia Interview, The Cure...$3–6

Aug. Simple Minds: Live & Kicking, Fuzzbox, Little Steven, Disco: What Was It?, Marianne Faithful on the Set, Joe Strummer...$3–6

Sept. John Cougar Mellencamp Exclusive Interview, LL Cool J, Tom Waits, The Petrol Emotion..$3–6

Oct. & Nov. No issue printed

Dec. Sting: Oedipus Rising, Motorhead, George Michael..$3–5

1988

Jan. Aerosmith's Steven Tyler Mouths Off, Guns 'n' Roses, Public Enemy, Waylon Jennings, Lisa Lisa, Captain Beefheart..$3–5

Feb. INXS: Michael Hutchence Kicks Butt, Madonna Exclusive Interview, Def Leppard, Tony Bennett, Cabaret Voltaire, Bryan Ferry...$3–5

Mar. The Cure: Robert Fripp Stays Cool, Debbie Gibson: Baby It's You, Annie Lennox/ The Eurythmics, David Lee Roth, Pere Ubu, Megadeth, The Clash.........................$3–5

Apr. Sa-fire, The Unpublished Patti Smith Interview, Megadeth, Echo & the Bunnymen, L.A. Guns, Sisters of Mercy...$3–5

May Run DMC: In Your Face, Guns 'n' Roses, Joni Mitchell, New Order, Robyn Hitchcock, Talking Heads...$3–5

June Ex-Smith/Morrissey: The Importance of Being Earnest, James Brown on Neil Young, Salt 'n' Pepa, Terence Trent D'Arby, Frank Zappa, The Byrds....................................$3–5

July Belinda Carlisle—*Spin's* Special Swimsuit Issue, Johnny Cash, Jon Bon Jovi, The Weather Girls, LL Cool J, Meat Puppets, Hall & Oates, Megadeth, Poison, Leslie West..$3–5

Aug. Comics, Depeche Mode, Kingdom Come, Timbuk 3, Dirty Dancing, Boogie Down Productions: A Rapper's Success Story..$2–4

Sept. Tracy Chapman, Peter Gabriel, Little Steven, Billy Bragg, Public Enemy: There's a Riot Going On, Merle Haggard, The Smithereens, Is Elvis Presley Alive?...............$2–4

Oct. Jazzy Jeff & the Fresh Prince, John Lennon Exclusive Unpublished Interview, Slayer, Devo Try Again, Tom Wolfe...$2–4

Nov. Bon Jovi: Some Guys Have All the Luck, Midnight Oil, Crowded House, Cuba: The Real Birthplace of Rock 'n' Roll...$2–4

Dec. The Bangles: L.A. Women, Bobby Brown, Buck Owens, James Brown, Sham 69, Billy Idol, Bananarama, The Year in Music, Patti Smith...$3–6

SPIN, 1987, Mar.

SPIN, 1987, Apr.

SPIN, 1987, May

SPIN, 1987, Sept.

SPIN, 1987, Nov./Dec.

SPIN, 1988, Jan.

SPIN, 1988, Mar.

SPIN, 1988, Dec.

SPIN, 1989, May

1989

Jan. U2, Belfast, Gary Oldman, Sonic Youth, Michelle Shocked, Russ Meyer, Shinehead, The Feelies $2–4

Feb. Nick Cave, Roy Orbison, Erasure, Husker Du, R.E.M. $2–4

Mar. Edie Brickell & the New Bohemians, Julian Cope, Big Daddy Kane, Kiss, Charles Burns, Nicolas Cage, John Hiatt.................$2–4

Apr. Special 4th Anniversary Issue—Madonna, The Replacements, The Greatest Albums, Singles, Movies & Books of All Time, First Annual Reader's Poll, XTC, Sun Ra, Pussy Galore, Ann Rice.................$2–4

May Elvis Costello, Karyn White, Slayer, De La Soul, Brian Eno, Living Colour, Rap Music.................$2–4

June John Cougar Mellencamp, Tone 10CC, Jerry Lee Lewis, Raggae, R.E.M., Fine Young Cannibals, Boy George, Apollonia.................$2–4

July Elvis Presley, 3rd Annual Swimsuit Issue, Neneh Cherry, Tin Machine, The Cure, The Women of Heavy Metal, David Byrne, Billy Bragg, The Knights of Malta $3–5

Aug. Tom Petty, Love & Rockets, Indigo Girls, Simple Minds $2–4

Sept. 10,000 Maniacs, Expose, The Who, Sonic Youth Meet LL Cool J, Matt Dillon, The Cult, Public Enemy.................$2–4

Oct. Terence Trent D'Arby, The Beastie Boys, Timothy Grimes, Ziggy Marley, Sandra Bernhard, Jefferson Airplane.................$2–4

Nov. Michael Hutchence, Alice Cooper, Taylor Dane, Rickie Lee Jones, Malcolm McLaren, The Moscow Music Peace Festival $2–4

Dec. The Rolling Stones, Skid Row, Michele Shocked, Steve Tyler.................$2–4

1990

Jan. Motley Crue, Young MC, Belinda Carlisle, Tina Turner, David Byrne, Teens for Life.................$2–4

Feb. The Red hot Chili Peppers, 2 Live Crew, The Nineties $2–4

Mar. The B-52's, Eric Clapton, Spring Break $2–4

Apr. Sinead O'Connor, 5th Anniversary Issue, Midnight Oil, The Ten Most Interesting Musicians of the Past 5 Years, A Day in the Life of Rock-and-Roll, Dee Dee Ramone, Screamin' Jay Hawkins $2–4

May Jazzie B: Soul II Soul, Stones Roses, Lou Reed & John Cale.................$2–4

June Lisa Stansfield, The New Kids on the Block, Hip Hop.................$2–3

July Depeche Mode, 4th Annual Swimsuit Issue, Farm Aid, Butthole Surfers, Lenny Kravitz $2–3

Aug. Depeche Mode, Peter Hook, Delicious Vinyl, Butthole Surfers, Lenny Kravits, Aids $2–3

Sept. Billy Idol, 2 Live Crew, Sonic Youth, Jane's Addiction, Concrete Blonde.........$2–4

Oct. Spike Lee, Eddie Murphy, Living Colour, Joie De Lee $2–3

Nov. Bon Jovi: Back in the Saddle Again, AXL Rose Comes Clean to Danny Sugarman, Judas Priest Beats the Rap, Rick Rubin & the Geto Boys, Special College Music Report.................$2–3

Dec. Faith No More: Artists of the Year, Sinead O'Connor, Aerosmith, Depeche Mode, Digital Underground, The Cure, Neil Young, INXS.................$2–3

SOUL MAGAZINE

1970

Nov. 2 "What Killed Jimi Hendrix" $20–40

SOUL TEEN

1974

July Diana Ross, Billy Dee Williams, Roberta Flack.................$2–4

Sept. Aretha Franklin, Al Green on Screen, Michael Jackson $1–3

1982

Oct./Nov. Donna Summer: There's a Lot Going On Here $1–3

Dec. Cheryl Lynn Rocks the Roxy, Michael Jackson & Paul McCartney.................$1–3

SPLICE
1989
Oct. #17 Richard Grieco Exclusive Interview, Kirk Cameron, New Kids on the Block, Jason Donovan, Debbie Gibson, Expose $2–3

STAR FLASH
1987
July #8 The Beastie Boys: How Bad are They?, Bon Jovi Tells All, Alyssa Milano, Kirk Cameron, Michael J. Fox, Madonna, John Stamos, Poison, River Phoenix, Don Johnson, Charlie Sheen $2–3
Nov. #9 Kirk Cameron: Shedding His Image, Charlie Sheen, Meet the Monkees, Madonna Off Guard, Michael J. Fox, Alyssa Milano, Bon Jovi: Has Fame Hurt Him?, issue includes four posters $2–3

STAR FLASH POSTER MAGAZINE
1987
July #2 Includes ten wall posters of Kirk Cameron, Alyssa Milano, Bon Jovi, Michael J. Fox, The Beastie Boys, Poison, Cinderella, Europe's Joey & Ian $3–5

STAR HITS
1984
Feb. #1 Duran Duran: Big as the Beatles, Debbie Harry: Rush Rush, The Doors: Still Open for Business, ZZ Top, Billy Joel, Romantics, David Bowie: Ziggy Stardust, Culture Club, The Alarm, Pat Benatar: Lipstick Lies, Big Country, Rolling Stones, Eurythmics, Madonna $4–7

1986
Mar. Madonna: Love Her/Hate Her, Tina Turner, The Alarm, A-ha, OMD, Arcadia, Depeche Mode, INXS, Wham, John Cougar Mellencamp, Paul Young, Sheila E.: A Love Bizarre, Paul McCartney, Pat Benatar..$2–3
July Charlie Sexton: Meet the Mouth from the South, INXS: Live from London, Sigue Sigue Sputnik, The Bangles: Our Magic Monday, A-ha, Madonna, Whitney Houston, Culture Club, Simple Minds, Miami Sound Machine, Julian Lennon, Depeche Mode, The Alarm, Janet Jackson, Jefferson Starship, The Rolling Stones: Harlum Shuffle, Sade, Dream Academy, Level 42, The Bangles, Pet Shop Boys, Platinum Blonde, Howard Jones, Simon Le Bon, Ozzy Osbourne, Blow Monkeys..$2–4
Aug. Billy Idol: The Rebel Returns, Culture Club: By George, Depeche Mode: Lust, Pet Shop Boys, Blow Monkeys, The Bangles: If She Knew What She Wants, Tears for Fears, Psychedelic Furs, Simply Red, Depeche Mode, Arcadia, ABC, Falco, The Monkees, Mr. Mister, Diana Ross: Chain Reaction, Robert Palmer, George Michael, Julian Lennon, OMD, Feargal Sharkey..$2–3
Sept. Madonna: The Whole Truth, Belinda Carlisle: Mad About Her, George Michael, The Cure, Big Country, OMD, Erasure, Nu Shooz, Genesis: Invisible Touch, Culture Club, The Fixx, Howard Jones, Bryan Ferry, David Bowie: Underground, Simply Red, Falco....$2–3
Oct. Boy George: Is This the End?, Eurythmics: Sweet Revenge, Billy Idol, The Madonna Story Part II, Bananarama, Wham, Sigue Sigue Sputnik, Berlin, Robert Palmer, A-ha, Peter Gabriel, Depeche Mode poster, Dressed to Kill, The Outfield, Liar Liar $2–3
Nov. A-ha: What's Morten Got Up His Sleeve?, Belinda Carlisle: From Biloxi or What?, INXS, Blow Monkeys, UB40, The Smiths, The Cure, Bananarama, Fine Young Cannibals, Huey Lewis, Prince, The Jets, Simply Red, Glass Tiger, Arcadia, Dr. & the Medics, The Bangles..$2–4
Dec. Bananarama, Tina Turner, Pet Shop Boys, Janet Jackson, Blow Monkeys, The B-52's, Cyndi Lauper, Talking Heads, The Smiths, The Beatles, Sigue Sigue Sputnik, Big Country, Don Johnson $2–3

1987
Jan. In the Studio With Duran Duran Exclusive, Andy Taylor, Billy Idol, Human League, OMD, Sigue Sigue Sputnik, Madonna, Cory Harey Hart, Lisa Lisa & Cult Jam, Aretha Franklin, Ric Ocasek, Doctor & the Medics, Cyndi Lauper, A-ha $2–3

Feb. Billy Idol: Insane in Spain, Cyndi Lauper Goes Hawaiian, Rob Lowe, Tom Cruise, Howard Jones, Pet Shop Boys, Glass Tiger, Banarama, Wang Chung, The Pretenders, Berlin, A-ha, The Monkees, Duran Duran, U2, Huey Lewis, Depeche Mode....................$2–3

Mar. Howard Jones, Duran Duran Gets Notorious, The Monkees, Madonna Meets an Idol (Billy), Paul Young, 'Til Tuesday, Dead or Alive, Cyndi Lauper, Corey Hart, The Eurythmics, Tina Turner, General Public, Fine Young Cannibals, The Police, Gene Loves Jezebel $2–3

Apr. Glass Tiger: Best New Band, Duran Duran: Back on Top Again, The Bangles, A-ha, Bon Jovi, The Beastie Boys, U2, Grace Jones, The B-52s, Huey Lewis & the News, Timbuk 3, Frankie Goes to Hollywood, Bon Jovi, Human League, Sigue Sigue Sputnik.........$2–3

June Jon Bon Jovi, The Pretenders, The Bangles, Beastie Boys, Talking Heads, Human League, The The, Wang Chung, Dead or Alive, Charlie Sheen, Psychedelic Furs...$2–3

Aug. U2: The Whole Story, Poison: Warning, The Cure, Crowed House, Duran Duran & The Smiths Centerfold Poster, Dr. Robert, Curiosity Killed the Cat, Oingo Boingo, B.A.D., Breakfast Club, Fuzzbox $2–3

Sept. Billy Idol: The Rudest Man in Rock, Beastie Boys: Censored Song Words, Robert Smith, Pseudo Echo, Depeche Mode, The Cult, Stranglers, Duran Duran, Cutting Crew, Allison, Erasure, Swing Out Sister, Thompson Twins, Janet Jackson, Howard Jones $2–3

Oct. Madonna: "I Know Exactly What I Want," George Michael, Pet Shop Boys, Curiosity Killed the Cat, Beastie Boys, Boy George, Fuzzbox, David Bowie, Suzanne Vega, Simon Le Bon, Simple Minds, ABC, The Smiths, Echo & the Bunnymen, Nick Kamen......$2–3

Nov. Pee Wee Herman Rocks, Madonna: Live for Life, Simple Minds, U2: Bono Speaks, Depeche Mode/Strange Love Centerfold, Elvis Presley, Pepsi & Shirley, A-ha, Boy George, Chatterbox..$2–3

Dec. Billy Idol: Vital Billy/This Dude is Rude, Pet Shop Boys, The Smiths Split Scoop, Duran Duran, Curiosity Killed the Cat, Swing Out Sister, INXS, LL Cool J., REM, Pseudo Echo, New Order, Pil, Siouxsie, Kim Wilde, David Bowie: Never Let Me Down......$2–3

1988

Jan. Sting Comes Clean, Depeche Mode: The History of Leather, Echo & the Bunnymen, Pil: Rotten to the Core, Gene Loves Jezebel, Madonna, Robert Smiths, Billy Idol, The Silencers, Bananarama, The Cure, New Order, Terence Trent D'Arby............................$2–3

Feb. INXS: A Bunch of Good-looking Guys from Australia, Belinda Carlisle: A Girl Who Used to be in the Go-go's, U2's Larry Alone at Last, Depeche Mode, ABC, George Michael, Pet Shop Boys, Swing Out Sister, Love & Rockets, Debbie Gibson: A Teenage Girl by Day, A Pop Star by Night, The Cure, Jesus & Mary Chain...................................$2–3

Mar. George Michael: "I'm Bored," U2: Godlike Geniuses, Billy Idol: The Rude Dude Rides Again, INXS poster, Depeche Mode, Def Leppard, Bananarama, Boy George, Robert Smith, The Dream Academy, Bryan Ferry, The Cure, The Alarm.................................$2–3

Apr. U2, Billy Idol: Best Undressed, Duran Duran, Robert Smith, Curiosity Killed the Cat, Madonna in the Spotlight, INXS, A-ha, Depeche Mode, Tiffany, Eurythmics, Prince, Swing Out Sister, Whitesnake, Rick Astley $2–3

July/Aug. Summer Special—Pet Shop Boys: What are They Up to in New York?, INXS: Michael Hutuence Exclusive, OMD, Debbie Gibson: Making a Video, issue includes three posters—U2, George Michael & Richard Marx, Michael Jackson, Kingdom Come, Glass Tiger, Poison, Bananarama, Bryan Ferry, Scarlett & Black $2–3

STAR HITS PRESENTS THE BEST OF SMASH HITS

1987

#1 Madonna, Nick Kamen, Curiosity Killed the Cat, Go West, Pet Shop Boys, Prince, Cutting Crew, The Cure, Dr. Robert, Depeche Mode, Pepsi & Shirlie, Boy George: Travels Through His Life, Thompson Twins, The Mission UK, Spandau Ballet, The Beastie Boys $2–3

STAR HITS PRESENTS STAR HITS SPECIAL

1985

#4 The *Star Hits* Collection—Madonna: A Fashion Report, Simon Le Bon, Eurythmics, Paul Young, Foreigner, Rick Springfield, John Taylor, Adam Ant, Tears for Fears, Howard Jones, David Lee Roth, Thompson Twins, Strawberry Switchblade $2–4

#8 The Best of *Star Hits* 1986—issue is loaded with color pin-ups, Madonna, Wham: In Their Own Words, Duran Duran, Billy Idol, OMD, Simple Minds, Depeche Mode, Eurythmics, Dream Academy, Style Council, The Cult, Spandau Ballet, Go West, the Damned, Howard Jones, A-ha, Sade, Adam Ant, The Cure, Robert Palmer $2–4

1986

#12 *Star Hits* Summer Special—John Taylor: Angry Young Man, Billy Idol, Randy Rhodes, Sigue Sigue Sputnik, Blow Monkeys, Feargal Sharkey, The Rolling Stones Get Some Satisfaction, The Damned, Simon Le Bon, Level 42, The Cure, Stevie Wonder, Mr. Mister, U2, Madonna, David Bowie, Whitney Houston $2–4

#13 *Star Hits* Seriously Cool Scrapbook 1986—Billy Idol: Around the World, Madonna, Culture Club: Mucho Gusto, Nick Rhodes: Genius or Madman?, Depeche Mode, Pet Shop Boys, The Blow Monkeys, OMD in 3D, Sade, Roger Taylor, Sputniks, Judas Priest Unleashed, Robert Smith, Blue in Heaven $2–4

#14 *Star Hits* A to Z, The Who's Who in Rock—over 300 stars & 30 color pin-ups, Madonna centerfold poster, Prince, Sting, David Lee Roth, Arcadia, Blow Monkeys, The Cure, Duran Duran, Eurythmics, Falco, Peter Gabriel, Stevie Nicks, Queen, ZZ Top, Violent Femmes, U2, Soft Cell & Hundreds of Others $3–6

#15 *Star Hits* Confidential—Belinda Carlisle: California Screamin', Madonna: "I Used to Torture People," Wham Apart, Eurythmics Behind Bars, John Taylor, A-ha, Dr. & the Medics, Fuzzbox, The Bangles, Bananarama, The Jets, Genesis, Berlin $2–5

#17 *Star Hits* 1987 Yearbook—In Their Own Words: Simon Le Bon, A-ha, Billy Idol, George Michael, Andrew Ridgeley, Corey Hart & Depeche Mode, Berlin: Our Favorite Things, OMD, Pet Shop Boys Exclusive, Annie Lennox: "My Story," Kate Bush, The Monkees, Sting, David Bowie, Talking Heads, Madonna $2–5

1987

#2 *Star Hits* Present Metallix—Ozzy Osbourne Strikes Back, Bon Jovi, Motley Crue: Nikki Sixx Speaks, Def Leppard, Kiss, Anthrax, Whitesnake: Here They Go Again, Poison: Talking Dirty, Stryper, Great White Megadeth, Aerosmith, Motorhead, Dio, Metallica, Iron Maiden, Twisted Sister, Faster Pussycat $2–4

1988

#3 The *Star Hits* 1988 Yearbook—A Day in the Life of Billy Idol, The Secret Life of U2, Curiosity Killed the Cat Personal File, Pet Shop Boys: 20 Questions, A Trip to Sting's House, Madonna, The Life of Morrissey, ABC, Simon Le Bon, Robert Smith, The Beastie Boys Photo Album, Bon Jovi, Swing Out Sister, ABC, Duran Duran, Bananarama ...$2–4

STARLINE PRESENTS

1990

#17 New Kids on the Block Pullouts, Pin-Ups & Special 1990 Calendar, Alyssa Milano's Many Loves, Debbie Gibson Questions & Answers, Fred Savage, Martiks, Paula Abdul Talks, Kirk Cameron...............................$2–4

#18 New Kids Holiday Issue With Posters, Damian, Paula Abdul, Fred Savage, New Kids Personal Facts & Interviews, Def Leppard...............................$2–4

#20 New Kids on the Block, Paula Abdul & the Royal Ladies of Rock, Tiffany, Debbie Gibson, Martika, Fred Savage, issue includes 25 color pin-ups...............................$2–3

#23 New Kids on the Block Special Mini Mag Feature, Paula Abdul $2–3

#24 New Kids on the Block Special Photo Gallery Scrapbook Issue, Janet Jackson, Paula Abdul: Beauty & the Beat $2–3

STARZ
1990
#1 Madonna: Has She Gone Too Far?, New Kids on the Block, Paula Abdul............$2–3

STARZ POSTER MAGAZINE
All issues..$2–4

STREET, THE (Elroy Enterprises)
All issues..$1–3

STROBE (Picture Magazine, Inc.)
1969
July #1 Janis Joplin Up Front, Slaughter House Five $25–50
Sept. #2 Buffy St. Marie: Public & Private, The Apotheosis of Johnny Winter, Sly & the Family Stone, Fillmore East: Silence & Sound..$15–30
Nov. #3 Grace Slick cover & feature story, The Frank Zappa Column?, B.B. King, Creedence Clearwater Revival's True Philosophy of Life..$15–30

SUPER ROCK (National Newsstand Publications)
1977
June #1 Mick Jagger & Keith Richards, Mick Jagger: "Fame Can be a Lonely Place," Paul McCartney interview: Tragedy & Triumph of an Ex-Beatle, Peter Frampton, Rick Derringer, Allman Brothers Reunion, Ted Nugent Meets the Who: A Super Rock Comic, Black Sabbath's Ozzy Oxbourne: The Satanic Whirlwind, The Roots of Rock: From Bobby Darin to Jimi Hendrix, Donny & Marie: Happy Talk, Barbra Streisand & Kris Kristofferson, Elton John: "My Unreal Jet-set Life Must Stop," Charlie Daniels & Marshall Tucker, The Todd Rundgren Story, Patti Smith on Tour in Florida, Boston: The Long Trip to the Top, Cher, Kiss color centerfold: Growing Up With Kiss $15–30
Aug. #2 Special Punk Rock Issue: Iggy Pop—The Original Sixties Punk, Dead Boys, Nite City, Mink Deville, Natalie Cole, Abba, Ramones: Fear of Basements, Fleetwood Mac: Spreading Rumours, Lynyrd Skynyrd: A Bloodbath Every Night, Bay City Rollers......$10–20
Oct. #3 Peter Frampton: "I'm in You," The Who Part II, Queen, The Grateful Dead, Thin Lizzy, The Bee Gees, John Miles, Bad Company, Patti Smith, Kiss color pin-ups, Debbie Harry/Blondie, Led Zeppelin Hits New York, The Monkees, Sex Pistols, Yes, Peter Tosh, Supertramp, Lou Reed at the Bottom Line, the Dictators, Procol Harum: A Whiter Shade of Pale & Beyond, Tom Waits & Patti Smith, Southside Johnny & the Asbury Jukes, Uriah Heep, John Cale, Sammy Haggar..$7–15
Dec. #4 Robert Plant: Led Zeppelin's Heartbeat Tour, Peter Frampton: "I Can't Believe This is Happening to Me," Alice Cooper interview, Bad Company on Tour, Bad Company's Simon Kirke interview, Fleetwood Mac: Where Did They Come From & Where are They Going?, Bay City Rollers, Starz: Moped Terror, Little River Band, Talking Heads, Styx, Kiss: A Complete History Part I, Linda Ronstadt's Men, Carole King, Elvis Presley: Ready for the Scrap Heap, Ruby Starr, Rex Smith $6–12

1979
May Kiss, Exclusive Interview With Ace Frehley, Bob Seger, A Decade With Black Sabbath Rock, Fleetwood Mac: Still Number One, Led Zeppelin, Ian Anderson: A New Life for Jethro Tull, Nektar, Rod Stewart, Billy Joel, The Real Bee Gees Story, Steve Miller's Book of Dreams, David Bowie, The Rolling Stones..$7–15

SUPER ROCK AWARDS
1979
Spring Special Kiss Diary Issue, Kiss War of the Worlds, The Kiss Caper, Meat Loaf, The Blues Brothers, Great Kiss Pix..$10–20

SUPER ROCK SPECTACULAR

1978/79

Winter Special Kiss Issue, Kiss: Modern-day Theatrics, Fleetwood Mac: Spreading Rumors, Led Zeppelin, Can Peter Frampton Survive?, Carly Simon is Back, The Bee Gees, Aerosmith Photo Gallery, Heart: Do it With Heart, Black Sabbath, Queen: Kings of Rock, Touring With Suzi Quatro, Ted Nugent, Linda Ronstadt $6–12

SUPERSTAR FACTS AND PIX MAGAZINE

1986

#10 Issue contains 23 awesome color pin-ups, Ozzy Osbourne, Motley Crue, Bon Jovi, David Lee Roth, Kiss, Black Sabbath, Lita Ford, Iron Maiden $2–4

1987

#12 U2, Ozzy Osborne's Tribute, Survivor, The Beastie Boys, Bon Jovi, Stryper, Cinderella, Europe, Poison, David Bowie, Huey Lewis, The Bangles $2–3

1989

#21 Axl Rose Color Spectacular & Other Fierce Frontmen Issue, Steven Tyler, Sebastian Bach, James Hetfield, Corey Glover, Phil Lewis $2–3

1990

#22 Summer Fun With New Kids on Block, Madonna Paper Doll Cut-outs, Janet Jackson's Recipe for World Peace, Fred Savage $2–3

SUPERSTARS

1989

Fall New Kids on the Block Diary, Johnny Depp, Corey Haim, Debbie Gibson, Bros, The Monkees, Tiffany, River Phoenix, Chad Allen, Menudo, Alyssa Milanno, Kirk Cameron, Ralph Macchio, Faustino $2–3

SUPERSTARS BOOK COVERS OR POSTERS MAGAZINE

1986

Michael J. Fox, Bruce Springsteen, Madonna, Whitney Houston, Bryan Adams, Malcolm Jamal Warner, Ralph Macchio $2–4

SUPERSTARS FACTS AND PIX PRESENTS
RAP MASTERS MAGAZINE

1987

#13 Featuring Run DMC & The Beastie Boys, pin-ups & centerfolds, On the Road With All Six Rappers $1–2

SUPERSTARS MAGAZINE/MICK JAGGER
AND THE ROLLING STONES SPECIAL

1970

#2 Issue includes over 100 great photos, An Intimate Close-up of the Stones-men & Their Music, Their Lives & Loves, Their Troubles & Triumphs, Their Millions & Their Antics, Plus Interviews $25–50

SUPERSTAR SPECIAL/HEAVY METAL
POSTERS MAGAZINE

1986

#18 Issue includes 10 awesome 16″ × 22″ color wall posters of Jon Bon Jovi, Kiss, Ozzy Osbourne, Vince Neil, Ratt, Judas Priest, Iron Maiden, W.A.S.P., Dio, Metallica, Stryper, Lita Ford $3–6

1987

#2 Issue contains 10 giant wall posters of Motley Crue, Europe, Ozzy Osbourne, Cinderella, Whitesnake, Poison, Kiss, Keel, Stryper, Ratt & Jon Bon Jovi $3–6

1988

#25 Issue includes 10 16″ × 22″ color wall posters, Backstage With Poison, Motley Crue, Whitesnake, Metallica, Def Leppard, Kiss, Dokken, Stryper, Cinderella, Gene Simmons, Aerosmith, Europe, Kiss Speaks Out $3–6

1989

June Heavy Metal Poster Issue containing 10 16″ × 22″ color wall posters, Bon Jovi, Metallica, Def Leppard, Skid Row, Poison, Kiss, Guns 'n' Roses, Vixen, Bulletboys, Kiss Talk $2–4
Oct. Issue contains 10 16″ × 22″ color wall posters, Metallica, Skid Row, Winger, Ozzy Osbourne & Lita Ford, Guns 'n' Roses, Bon Jovi, Black Sabbath, Motley Crue $2–4
Dec. Issue contains 10 16″ × 22″ color wall posters, Metallica, Skid Row, Winger, The Cult, White Lion, Poison, Blue Murder, Warrent, Aerosmith, Bon Jovi, Alice Cooper $2–4

SUPERSTAR SPECIAL'S THE BEST OF METAL EDGE

1989

Feb. Bon Jovi, Warrent, Motley Crue, Winger, Skid Row, Aerosmith, Bad English, Testament $2–3

SUPERTEEN

1986

Dec. Jon Bon Jovi, Kirk Cameron, John Stamos, Chad Allen, Michael J. Fox, Alyssa Milano, Lisa Bonet, issue includes pin-ups.....................................$2–3

1988

Feb. Kirk Cameron, John Stamos, Jon Bon Jovi, The New Monkees, Michael Jackson, Corey Haim $2–3

1989

Sept. The New Kids on the Block Concert Pix, Debbie Gibson on Tour, Jon Bon Jovi: One by One, Kirk Cameron, Alyssa Milano, Poison.....................................$2–3
Oct. The New Kids on the Block, Poison, Debbie Gibson, Bon Jovi, Kirk Cameron, Michael Damian, issue includes the 1990 Superteen Calendar featuring The New Kids on the Block.....................................$2–3
Dec. The New Kids on the Block feature & giant 16″ × 22″ color wall poster, Bros, Debbie Gibson: Top 10, Tommy Page, Bon Jovi.....................................$2–3

1990

Jan. The New Kids on the Block, Debbie Gibson's Dating Dilemma, Bros, Matt Dillon, Tommy Page, Kirk Cameron, Johnny Depp, Young Riders, Alyssa Milano, Chad Allen ..$2–3
All other issues $2–3

SUPERTEEN PHOTO ALBUM

1989

#15 Poison: Off Guard, issue includes 20 shocking double-sized color pin-ups & centerfolds, Bon Jovi, Guns 'n' Roses, Skid Row, Lita Ford, White Lion & others ...$2–3

SUPERTEEN'S LOUD MOUTH MAGAZINE

1989

#8 New Kids on the Block: Double Dynamite Issue, Debbie Gibson's Private Side, Bros, Outsiders, Grieco, with posters & pin-ups.....................................$2–3

SUPERTEEN SPECIAL'S ROCK RAP
1986
Jan. Paul Young, Huey Lewis, Spandau Ballet, Sting, Power Station, Stephanie Mills, A-ha, Kim Carnes, Van Halen, The Police, Duran Duran, Pat Benetar, AC/DC, Madonna, Wham, Billy Idol $2–4

July George Michael, Madonna, Pat Benatar, A-ha, Bruce Springsteen: Living Up to His Legend, Ted Nugent, King Kobra, Tina Turner, Sting, Tears for Fears, Van Halen, Huey Lewis, Billy Idol $2–4

Sept. Motley Crue, Billy Idol, David Lee Roth, Ratt, Krokus, Loverboy, A-ha, The Pet Shop Boys, Brian Seltzer, Falco Madonna, Mr. Mister...$2–4

SUPERTEEN SPECIAL'S THE BEST OF METAL EDGE
1987
Jan. Motley Crue, Lita Ford, Ozzy Osbourne, Dokken, Bon Jovi, Ratt, Iron Maiden, Quiet Riot, Stryper, Judas Priest, AC/DC $2–3

SUPERTEEN'S SUPER-SIZE PIN-UPS MAGAZINE
1989
#15 Issue includes 24 color centerfolds, Kirk Cameron, Johnny Depp, Debbie Gibson, Patrick Swayze, Jon Bon Jovi, Rick Astley $2–3

SUPERTEEN YEAR BOOK
1989
#14 Motley Crue Photo Album Special, Skid Row, Bulletboys, Winger, Leatherwolf, Victory, Dogs D'Amour, Bang Tango...$2–3

T

TEEN

1957

June #1 James Dean, "Pow Right in the Kisser": Elvis Presley vs. Harry Belafonte, Is Lawrence Welk Square? $100–200

June #2 Harry Belafonte: The Belafonte Secret, Tommy Sands, Calypso Luau $50–100

Aug. #3 Carol Parker & Dick Fallman, America's Next Voice Sensation—Dick Fallman $10–20

Oct. #5 Jerry Lewis as a cheerleader on cover & feature story $20–40

Nov. #6 Tommy Sands & Molly Bee: Two of a Kind, Two New Faces: Jerry Lee Lewis & Buddy Knox $30–60

Dec. #7 Dwayne Hickman & Uncle Bob Cummings cover & story: "Is Dwayne for Real? Lets Dance Mouseketeers—Doreen, Tracey & Bobby Burgess $20–40

1958

Jan. Pat Boone cover & feature story, Sandra Dee: "Dee Lightful & Dee Lovely"—Hollywood's Youngest Glamor Queen, The King of Rock-&-Roll Elvis Presley Speaks Up—"Rock-&-Roll is Here to Stay," The Tony Perkins Legend $30–60

Feb. Ronnie Burns cover & feature story: "Ronnie, A Real Regular Guy," "American Bandstand's" Dick Clark: Philadelphia's Pied Piper $20–40

Mar. Barry Cole, "Ricky Still Rocks 'Em": The Ricky Nelson Story, "Sing Boy Sing": A Story About Young Tommy Sands $30–60

Apr. The Story of Lili Gentle, How to Do the Stroll, Dick Clark $20–40

May Ricky Nelson cover & feature story: "Ricky's Red Hot," Johnny Mathis Threatens the Top Two Pop Kings...$30–60

June Elvis Presley cover & feature story: Will the Army Change Elvis?, Top Pop Poll Champions/Your Favorite Stars of the Year $30–60

July Johnny Saxon: Hollywood's Rebel With a Cause—A Revealing Profile of the Mystifying Johnny Saxon $15–30

Aug. Dick Clark: "American Bandstand"—America Loves It $20–40

Sept. Dolores Hart, How to Start a Fan Club $10–20

Oct. Carol Lynley: The Lonely Miss Lynley—How a Teenage Star Can be Lonely in a Crowd..$20–40

Nov. Elvis Presley, Ricky Nelson & Dick Clark: Today's Three Greatest Rockers, includes autographed color pin-up of Dick Clark $30–60

Dec. Sandra Dee cover & feature story: "The Secret of Sandra Dee"......................$20–40

1959

Jan. Millie Perkins: "Little Girl Lost"—What's Next for Millie? $10–20

Feb. Dick Clark, Surprise Success for Delores Hart...$10–20

Mar. Sal Mineo cover & feature story: "Sal Mineo on the War Path, A Day With Dwayne Hickman..$20–40

TEEN, 1958, Dec.

TEEN, 1959, Jan.

TEEN, 1959, Mar.

TEEN, 1959, Apr.

TEEN, 1959, May

TEEN, 1959, Aug.

TEEN, 1959, Sept.

TEEN, 1959, Nov.

TEEN, 1960, Feb.

Apr. Annette Funicello cover & feature story: "Annette's Success Story, Top Pop Poll: Elvis Presley Wins Again, A Date With Dwayne Hickman, Conway Twitty: The Newest Singing Sensation...$30–60

May Frankie Avalon cover & feature story: "Fired-up Frankie, Today's Surefire Sensation," We'll Remember Ritchie (Valenz), He Died Too Young..$30–60

June Pat Molittieri: "My Farewell to 'American Bandstand' ".............................$10–20

July Bill Gray cover & feature story: "The Double Life of Billy Gray," The Secret of Pink Shoe Laces: Dodie Stevens...$15–30

Aug. Annette Funicello & Roberta Shore cover, Annette's Swinging Slumber Party All Nite Bash $30–60

Sept. Edd Byrnes: Is He Trapped?, Pat Molittieri's Party Line/"American Bandstand," "Where are They Now?": The Mouseketeers Have a New Look $20–40

Oct. Pat, Kenny & Arlene of "American Bandstand": TV's Top Kids Live it Up at "Bandstand" Blast...$15–30

Nov. Roberta Shore: She Sees Her Future Through Rose-colored Glasses, What Happened to Delores Hart?...$10–20

Dec. Doreen Tracey & Brandon DeWilde: A Date With Doreen, Annette Funicello's Fun Diet: Diet Secrets Just for You...$20–40

1960

Jan. Frani Giordeno: "What Makes Frani Fun," Connie Francis: Meet the Gal Who Sells More Records Than Anyone Else in the Female World $20–40

Feb. The Lennon Sisters cover & feature story..$15–30

Apr. Annette Funicello cover & feature story: The Truth About Annette Funicello, Rod Lauren: New Singing Sensation, Tommy Dow's Treehouse....................................$25–50

May Frankie Avalon cover & feature story: Will Frankie's Flame Flicker?............$25–50

June Shelley Fabare cover & feature story: TV's Supergirl Shelley Fabare Will Shock You, Should Janet Lennon Grow Up?..$25–50

July Sandra Dee cover & feature story: "I Was Never a Teenager," Annette Funicello's Crazy Calendar, Annette's Private Life...$25–50

Aug. Bobby Rydell cover & feature story: "Keep Laughing"—Bobby Rydell's Success Story..$25–50

Sept. Fabian cover & feature story: "I'm Here to Stay," The Duane Eddy Story...$15–30

Nov. Janet Lennon & Patti McCormick Sound Off, "American Bandstand" $10–20

Dec. Annette Funicello, Dick Clark & Bobby Rydell cover & feature: The Big Three, Doddie Stevens: Is She Finished at 14?...$25–50

1961

Jan. Sandra Dee cover, Who Will Last: Sandra or Annette Funicello? $20–40

Feb. The Everly Brothers cover & feature story: Are the Everly Brothers Splitting Up? Brenda Lee: Little Miss Dynamite $20–40

Mar. Roberta Shore, Johnny Tillotson: New Singing Sensation................................$10–20

Apr. Annette Funicello cover & story: The New Annette, "Bandstand"...................$20–40

May Janet Lennon: Will Janet Always be Too Young? Is Elvis Presley All Shook Up? $15–30

July Miss Teen, The Return of Tommy Cole, My Crazy Life: Annette Funicello's Crazy Life..$15–30

Aug. Jessica Allbright, Brenda Lee Blasts Connie Francis....................................$10–20

Sept. The Truth About Pat Molittieri's Return to "American Bandstand".............$10–20

Oct. Fabian cover & story: Fabian's First Love..$10–20

Nov. Janet Lennon cover & story: Janet's Secret Life...$10–20

Dec. Natalie Wood cover & feature story: Her Hollywood Years, Annette Funicello's Holiday Surprise...$20–40

1962

Jan. Hayley Mills cover & feature story: Why She's Tops...$15–30

Feb. Janet Lennon & Don Grady: "Is it Wrong to be Different?," Shelley Fabare's Charm Tips, Dick & Deedie: New Recording Team...$15–30

Mar. Texas Teens, Deb Star Ball, Hollywood's New Stars $10–20

Apr. Is "American Bandstand" Finished?...$10–20

May De De Lind, Dancetime U.S.A.: More on "American Bandstand"...................$10–20
June Annette Funicello, Paul Anka, Tuesday Weld, Elvis Presley.............................$15–30
July Deborah Walley: Her Double Life...$10–20
Aug. Debbie Bryant, Shelley Fabare: Will Sudden Illness Stop Her Career?...........$10–20
Oct. Paul Petersen & De De Lind, Patty Duke...$10–20
Nov. Dick Chamberlain: Lucky or Lonely, "Bandstand" Still a Blast.....................$10–20
Dec. Roberta Shore: TV's Brightest Young Star, Janet Lennon cover, Annette Funicello:
Why She's Grown Up Now...$10–20

1963

Jan. Randy Boone, Meet the Gal Who Writes Hits for Elvis Presley & Bobby Rydell
....$10–20
Feb. Miss Teenage America Darla Banks, Lynn Loring.......................................$10–20
Apr. Sandra Dee: A Visit With Sandra..$10–20
June The Private Hours of Elvis Presley...$15–30
July Sue Lyon cover, Paul & Paula, Donna Loren...$10–20
Aug. The Sides of Anita Bryant...$10–20
Sept. Wendy Turner: The Elf from England...$10–20
Oct. Mr. Novak, TV's New Faces, "American Bandstand" Flashback....................$10–20
Nov. The New Noreen of "Bachelor Father"..$10–20
Dec. Hayley Mills: From Pigtails to Princess $10–20

1964

Jan. The Rise & Fall of Teenage Idols...$10–20
Feb. Miss Teenage America Contest Special...$10–20
Mar. Dianna Smith, Joey, Catherine & Chris: Hollywood Starlets......................$10–20
Apr. Annette Funicello & Janet Lennon, The Success & Struggle of De De Sharp.....$15–30
May Greg Ritter & Nancy Sphar on Cover With Beatle Haircuts, Jack Jones the Singer's
Singer, Everything's Coming Up Beatles...$10–20
June Hayley Mills cover & feature story: Hayley the Magnificent...........................$15–30
July Donna Loren, The Dave Clark Five...$10–20
Aug. Linda Feller: Junior Miss, "American Bandstand" 's Big Switch, Backstage Secrets of
the Beatles..$15–30
Sept. Debbie Watson, Will the Beatles Last?..$15–30
Oct. The Beach Boys, Why the Beatles Won't Last, Andy Williams.......................$15–30
Nov. Teen Beauty Queens, Special Section on the Beatles, The Beach Boys, Dave Clark
Five, Peter & Gordon & The Rolling Stones...$20–40
Dec. Colleen Corby: America's #1 Teen Model, The Beatles Closeup $10–20

1965

Jan. The Mods vs. the Rockers $10–20
Feb. Colleen Corby, Girls Who Date the Beatles...$10–20
Mar. Vicki George covergirl, Special Feature: "I Kissed Dave Clark 5 Times"......$10–20
Apr. Cathy McKay covergirl, Rare Photos of the Beatles....................................$10–20
May Special Liverpool Issue..$10–20
June Lynne Kimoto: Hawaiian Covergirl, England's Top Darlings..........................$7–15
July Preview of the Beatles' New Movie...$7–15
Aug. Barbara Parkins: "Peyton Place" 's Bad Girl..$7–15
Sept. Secrets Behind the Rock-&-Roll Revolution, Herman's Hermits, The Rolling Stones
& the Beatles Speak Out $15–30
Oct. Peggy Lipton: TV's New Sweetheart, England's Go-go Girl...........................$10–20
Nov. Donna Loren, Sonny & Cher: Pop of Pop, The Byrds Bomb Blast Britain....$15–30
Dec. Joanne Vitelli, *Harum Scarum*: Elvis Presley's Newest Movie, Bob Dylan's Folk
Rock, Bedlam in Beatledom $15–30

1966

Jan. Molly Corby covergirl, Herman's Hermits Orbit on Film, Who is James Bond?..$15–30
Feb. Kelly Harman covergirl, The Rolling Stones, David McCallum: Still Agent Runs
Deep..$15–30
Mar. Sally Mardick covergirl $5–10

Apr. Joanne Vitelli, The Tijuana Brass: Herb Albert & Other Delights, Gary Lewis: Playboys One...$7–15
May Batman vs. 007...$7–15
June A Day With the Beach Boys, Sidewalk Surfing With Jan & Dean, The Turtles.$15–30
July Kay Cambell covergirl, The Sounds of the Righteous Brothers, Noel Harrison.$10–20
Aug. Paul Revere & the Raiders, The Association, The Leaves, The Remains, The Bobby Fuller Four, The Byrds, The Young Rascals & The Beau Brummels.......................$20–40
Sept. Cheryl Tiegs & Noel Harrison cover, The Monkees, The Green Hornet, The Girl from U.N.C.L.E..$15–30
Oct. Dear Monkees, Why Do American Girls Like English Boys? Herman's Hermits, The Rolling Stones, The Beatles..$15–30
Nov. Cathy Fuller covergirl, The Beatles vs. God, Dear Monkees...........................$15–30
Dec. Sally Murdock covergirl, The Monkees on the Beatles Back, Dear Monkees.$15–30

1967

Jan. Cathy Fuller covergirl, The Mamas & the Papas Feud....................................$15–30
Feb. Brian Hyland & Pamela Clark, Jackie Deshannon, Petula Clark, Johnny Rivers, Chris Montez, Ravi Shankar...$7–15
Mar. Nancy Sinatra cover & feature story: On Her Way Up, Special Feature on Jackie Deshannon...$20–40
Apr. Sandy Roberts: Miss Teenager 1967, David McCallum.................................$7–15
May The Monkees: I'm Sorry...$7–15
June Peter Noone of Herman's Hermits & covergirl Patti O'Herlicky on the cover & feature story: Is Herman a Hermit?, Nitty Gritty Dirt Band..$25–50
July Cathy Fuller covergirl, Which Raider are You?...$7–15
Aug. Twiggy: "I'm Sick of Twiggy"...$7–15
Sept. Freddy Weller Newest Raider, The Doors, The Buckinghams, Spanky & Our Gang, The Grass Roots, *Harper's Bizarre*..$20–40
Oct. The Supremes...$10–20
Nov. Tracy Weed covergirl..$7–15
Dec. Cathy Fuller covergirl, The Monkees & The Mamas & the Papas: The Tree They Live In..$15–30

1968

Jan. Jay North & Madelyn Stevens cover, The Young Rascals...............................$15–30
Feb. Super Teen Underground...$5–10
Mar. Kathleen Kennedy, The Smothers Brothers..$5–10
Apr. Kathy Fuller covergirl, The Buckinghams Take a Bow..................................$15–30
May Kathy Fuller covergirl, How the Bee Gees Bug the Beatles.............................$15–30
June Judy Karn of "Laugh In": Will the Laugh Last?..$10–20
July Robin Milan & Glen Campbell..$5–10
Aug. Steve Barna & Cathy Fuller cover, The Cowsills...$10–20
Sept. Rowam & Martin: Daze of the "Laugh In"..$10–20
Oct. Gary Puckett & the Union Gap cover & feature story: The Union Gap's Beatle Plan, Chris Jones...$15–30
Nov. Jim Webb & Patsy Sullivan: The Real Jim Webb...$5–10
Dec. Peggy Flemming cover, How the Rascals Romp..$10–20

1969

Jan. Carla Beck covergirl, The Fifth Dimension..$5–10
Feb. Mark Lindsay: Super Raider...$7–15
Mar. Jill Twiddi covergirl, The Cowsills' Family-style Success Story, The Raiders Keep Coming...$10–20
Apr. Joanne Vitelli covergirl, The Association..$5–10
May Cathy Witt covergirl, Blood, Sweat & Tears..$5–10
June Cathy Davis covergirl, The Soul Explosion, James Taylor.............................$5–10
July Valerie Fitzgerald covergirl, Creedence Clearwater Revival............................$5–10
Aug. Elvis Presley in Memphis, Classics IV: Rock With Class...............................$7–15
Sept. Leslie Pagett covergirl, Billy Blue Grows Up, Crosby, Stills & Nash, Elvis Presley, Bobby Vinton...$7–15

Oct. "Dark Shadows," Creem, Bee Gees, Dusty Springfield, Wm. Puckett $7–15
Nov. Jill Twiddy covergirl, "Dark Shadows," Bobby Sherman, Peggy Lipton $7–15
Dec. Barbara Levene Covergirl, Three Dog Night $7–15

1970

Jan. Roe Roe Roe Your Rock, Spanky, Bobby Sherman $7–15
Feb. Cindy Copeland covergirl, Gary Puckett & the Union Gap, The Grass Roots, Mama Cass, Three Dog Night...$7–15
Mar. The Bobby Sherman Nobody Knows, Blood, Sweat & Tears Interview $10–20
Apr. Sue Rice covergirl, The Byrds, The Bee Gees, The Grass Roots.....................$7–15
May Bonnie Rupracht in bikini cover, Has Mark Lindsay Changed? $7–15
June Bonnie Rupracht covergirl, The Jackson Five..$10–20
July Cathy Davis covergirl, Bobby Sherman, Holy Rock-&-Rollers $7–15
Aug. Sue Rice covergirl, A House Call on Jim Brolin $5–10
Sept. Sherry Miles covergirl, The Real Name Game..$5–10
Oct. The World's Most Beautiful Teens Issue, The Temptations, Eric Clapton, Kurt Russell $7–15
Nov. Beth Bernette covergirl, The Next Bobby Sherman, The Guess Who, David Cassidy: Is He the Next Bobby Sherman?...$15–30
Dec. Paul Newman at Ease..$5–10

1971

Jan. Susan Dey of "The Partridge Family" cover & feature story, The Carpenters.$20–40
Feb. Hilarie Thompson covergirl, Emitt Roades...$5–10
Mar. Ryan O'Neil interview $5–10
Apr. Cathy Davis covergirl..$5–10
May Bikini-clad covergirls from Malibu U, The Carpenters.....................................$5–10
June Debbie & David Cassidy cover & feature story: A Day With David $20–40
July Spotlighting the New Seekers $5–10
Aug. Cheryl Tiegs covergirl, Jane Fonda: Mystery Militant or Myth?.....................$7–15
Sept. Return of the Raiders...$7–15
Oct. Miss U.S.A. Teen Princess Jana Keer, The Carpenters, Three Dog Night in Concert $7–15
Nov. Cheryl Tiegs: All-American Covergirl, The Mamas & the Papas Come Back Together: The Inside Story...$10–20
Dec. Dawn Thatcher covergirl $5–10

1972

Jan. Tommy James Hooked on Drugs...$5–10
Feb. Chicago, The Rolling Stones $3–6
Mar. ....
Apr. Neil Diamond: Not Interested in Success..$5–10
May Cheryl Tiegs covergirl, Bread: A Slice of Rock Life $5–10
June Love is on Location with B.J. Thomas...$5–10
July Ann Azama covergirl, Neil Young: Mystery Man $5–10
Aug. Joe Cocker: Is He Wiped Out?..$5–10
Sept. A Day With the New Seekers $5–10
Oct. Cathie Mann covergirl, Rick Springfield, Eagles, Linda Ronstadt $7–15
Nov. Cathy St. Johns covergirl, What is Alice Cooper: Satanic Symbol of Rock or World's Biggest Put-on?, The Rock 'n' Roll Revival..$15–30
Dec. Rick Springfield cover & feature story...$10–20

1973

Jan. Ricky Nelson $7–15
Feb. Stephanie Steele covergirl, Eric Clapton, Creem..$5–10
Mar. Karen Umphreys covergirl, The Heywoods $5–10
Apr. Elvis Presley, Who Will Win the Title of Rock King?..$7–15
May Pam West covergirl, The New Seekers: They're the Real Thing $7–15
June Cheryl covergirl, Slade: Return of the Goodtime Rockers...............................$10–20

July Jena Gibbs covergirl, Deep Purple: Rock World's New Sensation, Those So Sweet Boone Sisters, Albert Hammond $10–20
Aug. Cathy Davis covergirl, Three Dog Night: What Makes Them Run? $5–10
Sept. Deborah Raffin covergirl, "Jesus Christ Superstar"................................$5–10
Oct. Ann Joiner covergirl, Bo Donaldson & the Heywoods, Drugs & Rock............$5–10
Nov. Gena Gibbs covergirl, Elton John: Call Me Crazy, Seals & Crofts: Our Music/God's Music...$5–10
Dec. Gena Gibbs cover, The Grass Roots $5–10

1974

Jan. Linda Tonge covergirl...$3–6
Feb. The Life & Hard Times of Rod Stewart, Rock Star.....................................$7–15
Mar. Cheryl Garmley, Pete Townsend of the Who, John Lennon: Working-class Hero of Bel Aire $7–15
Apr. Gena Gibbs covergirl, Bob Dylan: Bringing it All Back Home $7–15
May Deborah Raffin covergirl, Linda Blair Talks of the Devil................................$7–15
June Gena Gibbs covergirl, Jim Croce: Birth of a Legend, Tanya Tucker: Teen Star.$7–15
July Leigh Tippit covergirl, Marie Osmond: Getting in the Act $10–20
Aug. Jenny Hillseth covergirl, The Zombies, Fleetwood Mac, Helen Reddy $7–15
Sept. Grand Funk Railroad: Shinin' On, Mac Davis $5–10
Oct. Cindy Harrell covergirl, The Osmonds & Their Fans, Mick Jagger: Devilish Enigma $10–20
Nov. Martha Longley covergirl, Crosby, Stills, Nash & Young $5–10
Dec. John Denver, Rod Stewart..$5–10

1975

Jan. $3–6
Feb. Deborah Raffin covergirl...$3–6
Mar. The Sensational Alex Harvey Band..$3–6
Apr. Nancy Fitzgerald covergirl $3–6
May Alison Bretch covergirl, Black Oak Arkansas: Hillbilly Boys Making it Good.$5–10
June The Beach Boys Trip Down Memory Lane $5–10
July Carina Haley covergirl, The Return of Alice Cooper.....................................$5–10
Aug. Three Dog Night: The Way They Are..$5–10
Sept. Deborah Raffin covergirl...$3–6
Oct. Lindsay Erwin covergirl, Tony Orlando & Dawn, The Rolling Stones Plus Ron.$5–10
Nov. Lindsay Erwin covergirl, Olivia Newton-John at Home in the Country $7–15
Dec. Cindy Peters covergirl, Rod Stewart, Alice Cooper.....................................$5–10

1976

Jan. Susan Keile covergirl, The Bay City Rollers, Leo Sayer, Linda Ronstadt $5–10
Feb. Cindi Peters covergirl, Elton John: A Star for a Star $5–10
Mar. Lindsay Erwin covergirl, Mac Davis: From Blue Jeans to Tuxedos, Barbra Streisand, The Kinks $5–10
Apr. Kathy Allen covergirl, KC & the Sunshine Band, Eric Carmen, Beyond the Raspberries...$5–10
May Nancy Fitzgerald covergirl, The Bay City Rollers $3–6
June Lisa Lindgren covergirl, Fleetwood Mac, Electric Light Orchestra.....................$3–6
July Linda Kamphus covergirl, Chicago, The Who, The Heywoods.........................$3–6
Aug. Jayne Madean covergirl, The Bay City Rollers, Captain & Tennille $3–6
Sept. Lindsay Erwin covergirl, The Beach Boys, Sailor, Bernie Taupin, Joan Jett & the Runaways...$5–10
Oct. Cindy Harrell covergirl, Bobby Goldsboro, Paul McCartney & Wings $3–6
Nov. Lisa Lindgren covergirl, Inside "The Donny & Marie Show" $5–10
Dec. Cindy Harrell covergirl, Jefferson Starship..$3–6

1977

Jan. Cindy Harrell covergirl, The Bay City Rollers Hit Philadelphbia, Kiss: Not Just a Kiss, Rick Derringer: Born to Rock-&-Roll..$3–6
Feb. Nancy Fitzgerald covergirl, Hall & Oates, Abba, The Eagles..............................$3–6

Mar. Lisa Lindgren covergirl, Eric Clapton: Caught in the Act.....................................$3–6
Apr. Laura Robinson covergirl, Lynyrd Skynyrd...$3–6
May Cindy Harrell covergirl, Shaun Cassidy: Making it on His Own, The Bee Gees, Maureen McCormick $3–6
June Cindy Harrell covergirl, Queen: Caught in the Act, Alice Cooper, The Babys, Robert Redford $3–6
July Janet Johnson covergirl, The Doobie Brothers...$3–6
Aug. Shelley Johnson covergirl, Lynda Carter...$3–6
Sept. Lindsay Erwin covergirl, Bad Company, ZZ Top.......................................$3–6
Oct. Maria Kelly covergirl, Jesus Rock, Parker Stevenson, KC & the Sunshine Band.....$3–6
Nov. Janet Johnson covergirl, Leif Garrett, Happy Days....................................$3–6
Dec. Lindsay Erwin covergirl, Electric Light Orchestra, Mink Deville.......................$3–6

1978

Jan. Cheryl Ladd, Kansas, Pamela Sue Martin $3–6
Feb. Suzanne Gregard covergirl, The Rubinoos $3–6
Mar. Lindsay Erwin covergirl, Charlie Rich, Barbara Mandrell, Jessi Colter, Ronnie Milsap $3–6
Apr. Janet Johnson covergirl, Debbie Boone, Cheap Trick, Erik Estrada $3–6
May Cindy Harrell covergirl, Scott Baio, Bob Welch $3–6
June Carynn Liten covergirl, Andy Gibb, Shaun Cassidy, Pablo Cruise, Olivia Newton-John, Jimmy Osmond $3–6
July Styx: Headed for High Tide, John Travolta, Donny & Marie $4–8
Aug. Janet Johnson covergirl, Foghat, Leo Sayer, The Bee Gees...........................$3–6
Sept. Cindy Adish covergirl, Mark Hamill, Paul McCartney, Rush, Firefall $3–6
Oct. Dara Sedaka covergirl, Rosetta Stone, Leif Garrett, Eddie Money $3–6
Nov. Pamela Hedges covergirl, Aerosmith, Donny & Marie, Gene Simmons $4–8
Dec. Janet Johnson covergirl, Foreigner, Brooke Shields, Van Halen...........................$3–6

1979

Jan. Barry Manilow, Michael Jackson, "Three's Company" $3–6
Feb. Linda Ronstadt, The Cars, John Travolta, Billy Joel...................................$3–6
Mar. Queen, Barbra Streisand & Neil Diamond, Andy Gibb, John Belushi $3–6
Apr. Burt Reynolds, Eric Carmen, Michael Jackson, Songwriters Issue $3–6
May Maria Kelly covergirl, Warren Beatty, Alan Alda $3–6
June Cindy Adiesh covergirl, Parker Stevenson, The Doobie Brothers $3–6
July Carynn Liton covergirl, Pablo Cruise, Joey Travolta.....................................$3–6
Aug. Tina Tyson covergirl, Robby Benson, Morgan Brittany.................................$3–6
Sept. Rex Smith, Erik Estrada..$3–6
Oct. Special Disco Issue—The Beat Goes On...$2–4
Nov. Rod Stewart, Bad Company, The Doobie Brothers $2–4
Dec. Mana Kelly covergirl, Dirk Benedick, Burt Bacharach, Charlene Tilton, Robert Wagner, Nancy Morgan $2–4

1980

to the present..$1–2

TEENAGE MAGAZINE

1981

Sept. Quiet Riot's Kevin Dubrow on Having Fun, Justine Bateman, Queen, Judas Priest, Accept $1–3

1984

Oct. Unmasking the New Heavy Metal: Motley Crue's Vince Neil & Others............$1–2
Nov. Rod Stewart: Giving Up the Glitter at 40, Steve Perry.......................................$1–2

1985

Jan./Feb. Inside the Making of *Dune*, Sting, Ratt, Missing Persons $1–2
Mar. Jerry Mathers & the Beaver, UB40, Stompers, Kool & the Gang......................$1–2

Oct. Bruce Springsteen: Rock's Legend—Two Decades of Bruce, Los Lobos: A Howl in the Wilderness, Simply Red..$1–2
Nov./Dec. John Cleese, Mel Gibson, Huey Lewis, Madonna...$1–2

1986

Feb. Sting, Midnight Oil, The Smiths, Kerri Green, Lea Thompson............................$1–2

TEEN BAG

1977

Feb. #1 John Travolta: "Women Want to Marry Me," Jimmy Osmond, Vince Van Patten, Henry Winkler, Donnie Osmond Will Love His Girl Forever, Peter Frampton Live, Marie Osmond's Secret, Diana Ross' Inspirations, Shaun Cassidy, Labelle, K.C. & the Sunshine Band..$5–10
June #5 David Soul, Farrah Fawcett is Leaving "Charlie's Angels," Vince Van Patten, Jodi Foster, Shaun Cassidy & Parker Stevenson, Abba, Tanya Tucker's Private Battle Against Loneliness, The Bay City Rollers, Donny Osmond, Leif Garrett.....................................$2–4

1978

June Shaun Cassidy Tells of His Near Fatal Accident, Valerie Bertinelli Confesses, Scott Baio: The Whole Truth, Leif Garrett, Kristy McNichol's Never-told Secrets, Andy Gibb, Cheryl Ladd, Rosetta Stone, Jimmy Osmond, Tony Defranco...$2–4

1979

Sept. Jimmy McNichol & Tatum O'Neil: Little Darlings, Andy Gibb Talks About the Girls in His Life, Shaun Cassidy, Leif Garrett, Scott Baio, The Village People, Rex Smith, The Bay City Rollers, Brooke Shields, Peter Frampton, K.C. & the Sunshine Band..........$2–4
Nov. Greg Evigan, How Leif Garrett Tried to Hide, Shaun Cassidy's Most Embarrassing Moment, The Village People, John Schneider, The Bay City Rollers, Kiss, Rex Smith, Kristy McNichol, Scott Baio...$2–4

1980

Mar. John Schneider, Tom Wopat, Barry Manilow: Is He Romantic?, Why Shaun Cassidy Married Ann, The Accident That Changed Leif Garrett's Life, Scott Baio poster, Rex Smith, Kristy McNichol...$2–4
Sept. Andy Gibb: Movie Star, Scott Baio, John Schneider, John Travolta: Cowboy, Melissa Gilbert, Rex Smith poster, Meat Loaf, Blondie, Olivia Newton-John, Shaun Cassidy, Pam Dawber...$2–4
Nov. Brooke Shields, Matt Dillon, Mark Hamill: The Empire Strikes Japan, Scott Baio, Leif Garrett, Kiss, Has Andy Gibb Found Love?, La Toya Jackson, The Village People, Carrie Fisher, Olivia Newton-John, Rex Smith..$2–4

1981

July Scott Baio: The Girl He Won't Talk About, Ralph Macchio, Valerie Bertinelli, John Schneider & Matt Dillon poster, Julian Lennon's Own Story About His Dad, Cheryl Tiegs, Harrison Ford $2–4
Sept. Ralph Macchio story & poster, How a Kiss Almost Killed Scott Baio, John Schneider, Beatlemania, Spend a Day With Brooke Shields, Matt Dillon, Peter Barton is Back, Billy Joel, Air Supply, The Village People...$2–4
Nov. The Things John Schneider Does for Love, What Scott Baio is Really Like, Peter Barton Poster, Ralph Macchio's Secret Thrills, The Truth About Brooke Shields & John Travolta, Sheena Easton, Kristy McNichol, Ralph Macchio $2–4

1982

July Scott Baio feature & poster, Ralph Macchio: Torn Between Two Loves, Matt Dillon, John Schneider, Kristy McNichol, Rick Springfield, Tom Cruise, Timothy Gibb, Andy Gibb, Solid Gold Dancers, Nancy McKeon $2–3
Sept. Scott Baio, The Truth About Gary Coleman, Rick Springfield, Hall & Oates, Leif Garrett, Tom Cruise, Olivia Newton-John, Eddie Van Halen & Valerie Bertinelli, John Schneider $2–3

1983

Oct. Scott Baio, Matt Dillon, Duran Duran: A Week With Them, Duran poster, Def Leppard, Adam Ant, Michael Jackson, Rob Lowe, John Stamos, Bruce Penhill, Rick Springfield, John Schneider, Brooke Shields $2–3

1984

Apr. Duran Duran in Concert, Rick Springfield, Rob Lowe, John Stamos, Tom Howell, Matt Dillon, The Outsiders, Tom Cruise Scrapbook, Def Leppard in London, Scott Baio $2–3
May Rick Springfield's Return, John Stamos, Quiet Riot, Duran Duran Meets the Press, Jason & Justine Bateman, The Real Ricky Schroder, The Jacksons: Making Musical Magic, Jump for Van Halen, Menudo, Def Leppard, Rob Lowe $2–3
Aug. Tom Howell, Tom Cruise, Menudo, Rob Lowe, Duran Duran: Touring Tales, Nancy McKeon Scrapbook, Michael Jackson Steps Out, Rick Springfield, Culture Club, Van Halen, Cindy Gibb, Ralph Macchio $2–3
Oct. Michael Jackson: His Public Women & His Private Love, John Stamos, The Go-go's Get Respect, Duran Duran: The Big Bust-up, Nancy McKeon, Matt Dillon, Tom Howell, Straight Talk from Boy George, Ricky Schroder, Van Halen $2–3
Nov. Duran Duran: The Temptation That Drives Them Wild, Menudo Scrapbook, Ricky Schroder, Ralph Macchio, Solving the Michael Jackson Mystery, John Stamos, Scott Baio, Cyndi Lauper, Van Halen, Rick Springfield $2–3
Dec. Michael Jackson: Those Mean Lies, John Stamos, Tom Howell, Boy George, Meet the New Menudo, Stray Cats, Ricky Schroder, Nancy McKeon, Ralph Macchio, Cyndi Lauper, Def Leppard $2–3

1985

Jan. Michael Jackson's Private Concert, John Stamos, Ricky Schroder, Duran Duran: Breaking Up, Cyndi Lauper, Boy George, "Fame" Special, Scott Baio, Ralph Macchio, Rob Lowe, Annie Lennox's Marriage $2–3
Feb. Duran Duran: An Inside Report on Their Women, Ralph Macchio, Michael Jackson's Bittersweet Victory, Tom Howell, Cyndi Lauper: Always the Outsider, John Stamos, Ricky Schroeder, Janet Jackson, Gene Simmons Gets Tough, Van Halen, Prince $2–3

TEEN BAG ANNUAL

1979

Fall Kiss feature story with Gene Simmons poster, Shaun Cassidy: By the Girl Who Knows Best, Rod Stewart: Still the Bad Boy of Rock, Leif Garrett Working Too Hard, Gene Simmons: The Demon Meets Walt Disney, Tony Danza, The Village People, Marie Osmond a Bride, Sha Na Na, John Travolta, Olivia Newton-John $5–10

1980

Fall The Brand-new Scott Baio, Meet Fleetwood Mac, Relaxing With Rex Smith, Matt Dillon, Andy Gibb is Back, Backstage with Kiss, Kristy & Jimmy McNichol, The Clash, Blondie, Leif Garrett, Kiss color wall poster, John Schneider, Barry Manilow $3–6

1982

Spring John Schneider, Hanging Out With Matt Dillon, The New Ralph Macchio, Rick Springfield, Scott Baio, Brooke Shields, Springfield, Air Supply, REO, Jimmy McNichol $2–4

TEEN BAG POSTER WHOPPERS

1979

#3 Scott Baio, Kiss, Andy Gibb, Leif Garrett, Shaun Cassidy, John Travolta, Rosetta Stone, Bay City Rollers, Dirk Benedict, Richard Hatch, Christopher Reeve, Jim & Kristy McNichol $3–6

TEEN BAG PRESENTS THE ELVIS STORY

1977

#1 Issue includes 300 exclusive pictures with feature stories, a wall poster, Elvis' private life & loves $3–6

TEEN BAG'S POP-TEEN
1984
Winter #2 Duran Duran Spectacular, Eurythmics' Annie Lennox: Man She's No Boy, X-rated Billy Idol, Huey Lewis, Thompson Twins, Fast Fax on Boy George, Van Halen: Will They Ever Grow Up?, The Scorpions, Madonna Breaks into the Movies, The Rolling Stones Stop Rolling, Bruce Springsteen, Menudo, Motley Crue, The Police, John Cougar Mellencamp, The Cars, INXS, Prince, Cyndi Lauper, Def Leppard, Billy Squier, Quiet Riot...$2–5

TEEN BEAT
All issues...$2–6

TEEN DATEBOOK (Young World Press)
All issues...$10–25

TEEN GREATS
1978
Mar. #1...$4–8
Apr. #2 John Travolta, Can Donny Osmond Handle the Pressure?, The Babys, Abba: Love & Money, Leif Garrett, Shaun Cassidy giant wall poster, Marie Osmond: Beauty, Sha Na Na, Dwight Twilley, Kiss, Bay City Rollers $4–8
May #3 The New Women in John Travolta's Life, Linda Thompson Talks About Life With Elvis Presley, Was Shaun Cassidy Born to Fame?, The Incredible Kiss Phenomenon, Where Donny Osmond Goes at Midnight, Fonzie poster, Fleetwood Mac: Five Stars Make One Big Mac, Stevie Nicks...$4–8
June #4 Gene Simmons: The Rock 'n' Roll Vampire—An Exclusive Interview, The Problem Leif Can't Solve, "Laverne & Shirley," Shaun & Parker, Parker Stevenson wall poster, Scott Baio, Kristy McNichol: Has She Gone Too Far?, Olivia Newton-John, Donny & Marie Osmond: To Be Normal $5–10
July #5 Shaun Cassidy: What His Mom Really Thinks of Him, Donny Osmond poster & story, Kiss: Gene Simmons Exclusive Fan-art, David Soul, Henry Winkler, John Travolta's Burning Ambition, Barry Manilow, Debby Boone, "Charlie's Angels," The Ramones, Valerie Bertinelli, Peter Frampton, Olivia Newton-John.......................................$3–6
Aug. #6 John Travolta Proving the Critics Wrong, Shaun Cassidy's Glittery Past Revealed, Gene Simmons poster, Top Secret Kiss Fact File, Andy Gibb's American Love Affair, Leif Garrett interview, Suzanne Somers, Angel: Creating Magical Rock, Queen, Donny & Marie: Screen Stars...$4–8
Oct. Shaun Cassidy Talks About Success & Loneliness, Peter Frampton & Lindsay Wagner, The Paul Stanley You've Never Seen, Leif Garrett's New Passion, The Off-screen John Travolta, Bee Gees wall poster, Donny & Marie: "We Lead Old-fashioned Lives," Susan Dey, Abba, Carly Simon $4–8
Nov. Gene Simmons' Horrifying Ambition, Leif Garrett wall poster, Mark Hamill: Following His Heart, Marie Osmond: "I Like Having Rules," Shaun & Parker, John Travolta Stays in Control, Kristy McNichol, Andy Gibb, Glynnis O'Connor, Tom Petty: "Elvis Presley Was My Idol," Rosetta Stone, Suzanne Somers $4–8
Dec. Shaun Cassidy Gets Back at His Critics, Kiss: The Mystique Behind the Super Group, John Travolta, Leif Garrett, Paul Stanley poster, Bruce Springsteen, Tatum O'Neal, Abba...$3–6

1979
Feb. The Long Tough Road for Peter Criss of Kiss, Shaun Cassidy, Donny & Marie Behind the Scenes, Robin Williams, What Andy Gibb Has Got to Stop, Scott Baio wall poster, Leif Garrett, Debby Boone...$5–10
Mar. Paul Stanley: "I Need a Challenge," The Day Shaun Cassidy Fell in Love, Jimmy &

Kristy McNichol wall poster, Gallactica, Leif Garrett, Why the Bay City Rollers are Unhappy, Barry Manilow's Changed Life, Bee Gees $5–10

Apr. Kiss Exclusive: The Real Reason Kiss Finally Broke Up, John Travolta, Scott Baio, Donny & Marie Osmond, Andy Gibb: His Secret Success, Debby Boone: Her Greatest Passion, Barry Manilow, Donny & Marie wall poster, Shaun Cassidy's Hideaway, David Cassidy: "Look Out I'm Coming Back," Dara Sedaka, Angels, Fleetwood Mac, Lindsay Wagner $5–10

May Kiss, issue includes giant color Kiss wall poster, Andy Gibb, Donny & Marie Osmond's Personal Lives Exposed, Scott Baio, Olivia Newton-John................................$4–8

June Andy Gibb: The Loner, Debby Boone, Donny & Marie Osmond: The Good Old Days, Kiss, Kate Jackson, Shaun Cassidy wall poster, The Lost Dream of John Travolta, Linda Ronstadt, Kristy McNichol, Farrah, Cheryl Tiegs $3–5

TEEN HEROES DYNAMIC ROCK FESTIVAL

1978

Dec. #1 Issue includes giant color Kiss Halloween card poster, Dark Cloud Over Led Zeppelin, Shaun Cassidy's Dream, Peter Frampton in Crisis, Leif Garrett, John Travolta's Needs, Angel, Van Halen, Paul McCartney, Journey, Meat Loaf, Bee Gees & Andy Gibb, Rosetta Stone, The Coming Kiss Explosion—Bigger Than The H-bomb, Virgin.....$10–20

TEEN IDOLS

1987

Feb. Michael J. Fox, Rob Lowe, Michael Jackson, Tom Cruise Speaks Out, Cyndi Lauper, Psychedelic Furs, The Monkees, Madonna...$1–2

Oct. Rob Lowe, Kirk Cameron, Madonna, The Monkees: Old & New, Bon Jovi $1–2

All other issues $1–2

TEEN IDOLS PRESENTS NEW KIDS ON THE BLOCK SPECTACULAR PERSONAL PHOTO ALBUM

1990

#1 The Real New Kids Story, issue includes 10 huge New Kids 16″ × 22″ pullout posters $3–5

TEEN LIFE (Publication House, Inc.)

All issues $10–25

TEEN LIFE (A.A.A. Magazines)

All issues $10–20

TEEN MACHINE

1986

May Michael J. Fox, Duran Duran Together Forever, A-ha, Ralph Macchio, Madonna ...$1–2

1987

May Michael J. Fox, A-ha, The New Monkees Talk to You, Cyndi Lauper $1–2

Sept. Jon Bon Jovi Special, The Beastie Boys, Michael J. Fox $1–2

1988

Jan. Kirk Cameron, Wil Wheaton, John Stamos, Jon Bon Jovi interview, Alyssa Milano $1–2

TEEN PIN-UPS

All issues 1962–1969 ....$10–20

All other issues $3–6

TEEN SCENE
1972
June David Cassidy: The Secrets About David Only Shirley Jones Knows, Donny Osmond's Dream Vacation, Susan Dey, The Jackson Five, Maureen McCormick, "The Brady Bunch," Bobby Sherman $6–12

TEEN SCOOP
1967
Feb./Mar. The Yardbirds, Inside the Outsiders, Dusty Springfield, The Lovin' Spoonful, Paul Revere & the Raiders, Mitch Ryder, Tommy Roe, The Rolling Stones: Will They or Won't They?, Chad & Jeremy $10–20

TEEN SCREEN
1966
May Batman & Robin, The Beatles, The Rolling Stones, Herman's Hermits $10–20
Aug. The Beatles, Exclusive John Lennon & Paul McCartney in the U.S.A., The Monkees, Peter Tork Spills All About the New Monkee Movie, Sajid Khan, The Cowsills, Jim Morrison Opens the Doors, Jefferson Airplane $10–20
All other issues $10–20

TEEN SET
1966
Feb. Herman's Hermits, Sonny & Cher, The Beatles, The Beach Boys, Bob Dylan, Soupy Sales, The 5th Beatle $15–30

1967
Mar. The Rolling Stones Exclusive With First-time Photos, Paul McCartney's New House, Personal Byrd Intervies, The Yardbirds, Eric Burdon, Ian Whitcomb, Chad & Jeremy, Jim Valley $15–30

1968
Feb. John Lennon: A New Career, Bob Dylan Exclusive, Jefferson Airplane, The Bee Gees, The Monkees: A Visit to the Set, Larry Ramos, The Seekers, Behind the Magical Mystery Tour, The Turtles' Turtle Soup, The Buckinghams, Aretha Franklin, Jackie Wilson, Micky Dolenz $15–30
Apr. Neil Young: His Past, Present & Future, The Association, The Monkees, The Beatles, The Young Rascals, Jim Morrison, Small Faces $15–30
June Jim Morrison: An Afternoon With Jim, Cream, The Who, The Beatles, The Association $20–40
Aug. The Cream, The Doors, The Association, Troggs, Rascals, Stones, Beatles, Tiny Tim, Iron Butterfly, Steve Miller, Paul Kanter & Jefferson Airplane, Micky Dolenz, John Lennon, Tim Hardin, Big Brother & Janis Joplin $15–30
Sept. Janis Joplin: Janis & The Boys in the Band, The Doors: A Little Myth Perpetuating, George Harrison, Frank Zappa, The Bee Gees, Big Brother, The Rolling Stones: Incredible Long-ago Photos, Paul McCartney, Brian Jones & Jimi Hendrix full-page color pin-ups, Jack Cassidy $35–70
Oct. Mick Jagger, Incredible Yellow Submarine, Are the Doors Bombing? $20–40

1969
Jan. Grack Slick: Slick is an Attention-Getting Device, Jimi Hendrix: Black Power & Money special feature story, Smothers Brothers, The Beatle Sessions, Henry Gibson, Iron Butterfly $30–60
Feb. John Lennon Feature Story, The Beatles, Hair & Nudity, Good Old Jefferson Airplane, Peter Sellers, Laura Nyro, Farewell to the Hippies, Dino Valente, Jimi Hendrix $20–40

1986
Aug. Remembering Duran Duran, Motley Crue, A-ha, Ratt $1–2
All other issues $1–2

TEEN SET PRESENTS PAULA AND JANET
1990
#4 Complete life stories with photos of Paula Abdul & Janet Jackson, The Truth Behind the Feud, Their Music, color pin-ups & Paula Abdul centerfold poster $3–5

TEEN SET'S PARTY PIN-UPS MAGAZINE
1989
Winter New Kids on the Block, Alyssa Milano, Kirk Cameron, Fred Savage, Debbie Gibson, Corey Haim, Jay Ferguson, Menudo, Chad Allen, Christina Nigra $2–3

TEEN SET SPECIAL KISS POSTER MAGAZINE
1978
Kiss Off & On Stage, A Complete Kisstory..$12–25

TEEN SET "YELLOW SUBMARINE" SPECIAL
1968
Issue contains dozens of full-page color photos from the film including a color wall poster, The Doors as Seen by Their Manager, Joni Mitchell, Steppenwolf, Newport Pop Festival, Elvis Presley: The King is Still Very Much Around, Canned Heat, Buffalo Springfield, John Lennon, Spencer Dryden: Jefferson Airplane, Jimi Hendrix $15–30

1989
Dec. Corey Haim, Kirk Cameron & Alyssa Milano, New Kids on the Block, The Outsiders, Debbie Gibson Getting Infatuated, Chad Allen, Menudo, Corey Feldman, Brian Green $2–3

TEENS NOW
1973
Jan. David Cassidy, What It's Like to Live With Chris Knight, Ben Murphy, The New Love in Susan Dey's Life, Osmond Brothers, Meet the Real Donny Osmond, Movin' With the Jackson Five $7–15
All other issues $7–15

TEEN SPECTACULAR
1978
Aug. #5 Andy Gibb's Secret Fears & Tears, Leif Garrett's Sister Tattles on Him, Shaun Cassidy, Bay City Rollers, Olivia Newton-John, John Travolta $3–6
Sept. #6 Shaun Cassidy, Leif Garrett, Kiss: "Meet Us Backstage," Kiss: The Kiss Army is on the March, Marie Osmond: Her Socko Stuff, Olivia Newton-John..........................$3–6
Oct. #7 Andy Gibb: My Secret Life & Loves, Shaun Cassidy Cries, Leif Garrett & Kristy McNichol, "Kiss Kissed Me," Gene Simmons..$3–6
All other issues $3–6

TEEN STARS
1983
Dec. #2 John Stamos: His Whole Life Story From A to Z, David Hasselhoff, Tom Howell, Bruce Penhill, Rick Springfield Fact File, Scott Baio, John Schneider, Matt Dillon, Michael Jackson, Duran Duran, Missing Persons $2–4

1984
Feb. Rick Springfield: Facts File, Chris Atkins, John Stamos, Matt Dillon, Def Leppard, Loverboy, Journey, Duran Duran..$2–4
Nov. John Stamos, Michael Jackson: Raid His Personal Fax File, Duran Duran: John Taylor's Deepest, Darkest Secrets, Tom Howell, Rick Springfield, Motley Crue, The Go-go's, Cyndi Lauper, Thompson Twins, Scott Baio...$2–4

1985

Jan. John Stamos, John Taylor to Wed?, In the Bedroom With Tom Howell, David Lee Roth, Ralph Macchio: 25 Secrets, Rob Lowe, Tom Cruise, Timothy Gibbs, Van Halen, Prince Night Ranger, Menudo, Wang Chung, Judas Priest, Huey Lewis & the News, Michael Jackson's Memory Lane Photo Album, Rick Springfield Hunky Pullout Poster.................$2–4

Apr. Tom Howell, Rob Lowe, Rick Springfield, Ralph Macchio, Duran Duran Fax File, John Stamos, Quiet Riot, Bryan Adams, Bruce Springsteen, Slade, Cyndi Lauper, Rob Lowe poster, Scott Baio, Ratt, Tony Danza, Matt Dillon $2–4

1986

Sept. Kirk Cameron Exclusive Kiss 'n' Tell Interview, Michael J. Fox: Has Fame Cost Him His Special Love?, Menudo's Ricky, Jack Wagner, Kirk Cameron poster, Duran Duran, A-ha, INXS, Rob Lowe, The Jets, Prince, Ralph Macchio...$2–4

TEEN STARS GIANT POSTERS MAGAZINE

1984

Fall Issue contains eight 16″ × 20″ color wall posters of Van Halen, Duran Duran, Rick Springfield, Michael Jackson, Chris Atkins, John Stamos, Scott Baio, Rex Smith, David Hasselhoff, Bruce Penhill $3–6

TEEN STARS MAGAZINE

1972

July #6 Donny Osmond: Horsin' Around in Yosemite, issue includes two giant Osmond in Concert superposters & 27 color pin-ups, David Cassidy: What He Thinks & Feels on Stage, The True David Cassidy, Butch Partrick: "The Girl I'm Looking For," Chris Knight, Donny Osmond's Life & Career Chapter Four, Michael & Jermaine Jackson: Super Soul Brothers, Rick Springfield: A Visit Home With Michael Jackson, Donny Osmond's Past Pet....$10–20

TEEN STARS 1985 POSTER CALENDAR MAGAZINE

1985

John Stamos, Boy George, Cyndi Lauper, Michael Jackson, Simon Le Bon, Matt Dillon, David Hasselhoff, Sting, Chris Atkins, Duran Duran, Bruce Penhill, Rick Springfield, Tom Howell, Mr. T, Kevin Bacon, Reno $2–4

TEEN STARS PHOTO ALBUM (Each issue includes 21 full-page color pin-ups)

1981

#6 Rick Springfield, Mark Hamill, Tom Wopat, Olivia Newton-John, Carrie Fisher, Brooke Shields, Scott Baio, Ralph Macchio, John Schneider, Cathy Bach, Leif Garrett, Andy Gibb, Kristy McNichol, Harrison Ford, Shaun Cassidy, Tom Selleck, Parker Stevenson, Valerie Bertinelli $3–6

1982

#8 Scott Baio, Rick Springfield, Ralph Macchio, Brooke Shields, John Stamos, Cathy Bach, Olivia Newton-John, Kristy McNichol, Tim Hutton, Victoria Principal, Heather Thomas, Valerie Bertinelli, Harrison Ford, Priscilla Barnes, Matt Dillon, Belinda Carlisle of the Go-go's, John Schneider, Genie Francis...$2–4

1985

Feb. Cyndi Lauper, Prince, Duran Duran, Culture Club, Huey Lewis, Motley Crue, Madonna, Hall & Oates, Bruce Springsteen, Lindsay Buckingham, Billy Idol, Thompson Twins, Spandau Ballet, Stevie Nicks, The Police, Tom Petty, Quiet Riot, Pat Benatar, Night Ranger, David Bowie, The Go-go's, Ratt, Van Halen, Michael Jackson, The Eurythmics, Adam Ant, The Alarm $2–4

Oct. Julian Lennon, The Rolling Stones, Madonna, Pet Shop Boys, The Bangles, Whitney Houston, Billy Idol, Eurythmics, Bruce Springsteen, U2 ....$2–4

Dec. Duran Duran, Madonna, Wham, Motley Crue, Hall & Oates, DeBarge, Rick Springfield, David Lee Roth, Sheila E., Twisted Sister, Bruce Springsteen, Tina Turner, Go West,

Cyndi Lauper, Sheena Easton, Prince, Frankie Goes to Hollywood, Ratt, Bon Jovi, Simon Le Bon, Billy Idol, Huey Lewis, Joan Jett, Sade, Heart, Phil Collins, Lita Ford, 'Til Tuesday, Billy Squier, Bob Geldof...$2–4

1986

Feb. Madonna, Cyndi Lauper, Wham, Duran Duran, Ratt, Prince, Bryan Adams, Lita Ford, David Lee Roth, Paul Young, Sheena Easton, Billy Idol, Tears for Fears, Tina Turner, Bruce Springsteen, Motley Crue, Rick Springfield, A-ha, Huey Lewis & the News, Sting, Spandau Ballet, Hall & Oates, Katrina & the Waves, Go West, Dio, Jon Bon Jovi, Mary Jane Girls, Vanity, Howard Jones, Air Supply, Sade $2–4

Apr. Madonna, Power Station, Arcadia, Eurythmics, Tears for Fears, Duran Duran, David Lee Roth, Cyndi Lauper, A-ha, Billy Idol, Pat Benatar, Grace Slick, Wham, Prince, Bruce Springsteen, Thompson Twins, Rick Springfield, Huey Lewis, John Taylor, Joan Jett, Van Halen, Hall & Oates, Culture Club, Go West, ABC, X, Whitney Houston, Air Supply, Platinum Blonde, Kool & the Gang...$2–4

June Madonna, Duran Duran, Wham, Bryan Adams, Corey Hart, Ratt, Rick Springfield, Prince, Bon Jovi, Hooters, Motley Crue, Huey Lewis, Billy Idol, Van Halen, Bruce Springsteen, Sting, Paul Young, Tears for Fears, John Cougar Mellencamp, Thompson Twins, Sheena Easton, Cyndi Lauper, Tina Turner, Boy George, Adam Ant, New Edition, Lindsay Buckingham, The Pointer Sisters, Joan Jett, Weird Al, Dire Straits, Sade $2–4

1987

Feb. Hard Rock's Metal Studs Issue—Motley Crue, Cinderella, Poison, Bon Jovi, Stryper, Rough Cut, Black 'n' Blue, Keel, Quiet Riot, Bruce Dickinson, Van Halen, Queenscryche, Kiss: Work Hard & Party Harty...$2–4

Apr. Kirk Cameron, Rob Lowe, Ralph Macchio, Michael Fox, Corey Hart, Glass Tiger, Tom Cruise, Jon Bon Jovi, Don Johnson, Madonna, Platinum Blonde, A-ha, Matt Dillon, Pet Shop Boys, Huey Lewis, David Lee Roth, Bruce Springsteen, Menudo, Nancy McKeon $2–4

July Exclusive interviews With Saxon, Raven, Ratt, Poison, Motley Crue, REO Speedwagon & Glass Tiger, Jon Bon Jovi, Cinderella, Joan Jett in the Spotlight, The Beastie Boys, Bruce Hornsby, Georgia Satellites..$2–4

Nov. Interviews with Poison, Stryper, Ace Frehley, Sheena Easton & Europe, U2: Their History, Bon Jovi, Motley Crue, Night Ranger, The Triumphant Return of Whitesnake, Whitney Houston, Beastie Boys, George Michael, Pseudo Echo, Crowded House, Psychbedelic Furs, Fuzzbox, Heart Roars With Bad Animals, U2 & Bon Jovi centerfolds $2–4

1988

Jan. Metal Studs Issue, issue includes special Kiss section: Killer Days/Crazy Nights, Kiss Bios on All Four Members, Exclusive Interviews With Gene Simmons & Paul Stanley, Def Leppard, Bon Jovi, Twisted Sister, Whitesnake, Stryper, Poison, Motley Crue on the Road, Keel, Loudness, Kiss & Motley Crue posters $2–5

Mar. Kirk Cameron Confesses, Jon Bon Jovi, Chad Allen, River Phoenix, John Stamos, Michael J. Fox, Wil Wheaton, Rob Lowe, Michael Jackson, Lisa Bonet, Charlie Sheen.......$2–4

TEEN STARS PHOTO ALBUM ROCK RAP

1986

Dec. Ozzy Osbourne: The Ultimate Master of Metal, Motley Crue on Stage, Stryper, Kiss' Eric Carr Unmasks the Future, David Lee Roth, Aerosmith, Black 'n' Blue, Paul Stanley, Rolling Stones $2–4

TEEN STARS ROCK SPECIAL

1985

Issue includes four color wall-size posters, Van Halen's Eddie & David: Playing Post Office, Simon Le Bon, The Cyndi Lauper Success Story, Special Bonus Section on Michael Jackson: Victory Rock With the Jacksons, Motley Crue, The Stray Cats, Loverboy, Boy George, Getting to Know the Go-go's, Billy Idol: Punk's Hunk of the Year...............$3–6

TEEN TALK (Scully Publishing)

1965

Mar. #4 The Animals: Just How Good are They?, The Rolling Stones: Fact or Fraud?, Can the Dave Clark Make it on Their Own?, The Beatles: A Brand-new Look at What Their Success Means, The Bachelors, Paul Petersen Profile, The Beach Boys..................$15–30
May #5 The Beach Boys: The Concert That Never Was, Peter & Gordon Interview, The Beatles...$15–30
All other issues $15–30

TEEN TALK (E-go Enterprises)

1976

Dec. Marie Osmond: Running from Love, Elvis Presley Searches for God, Elton John, The Friends, Guess Who, Bianca Jagger, The Tubes, Nils Lofgren, Jodie Foster, The Bay City Rollers, Diana Ross, "The Bionic Woman"...$3–6

1978

Jan. #1 Kiss: How Much Do You Really Know About Them?, Robby Benson, Shaun Cassidy Exclusive, The Bay City Rollers in Michigan, Farrah Fawcett, John Travolta, Parker Stevenson, Elvis Presley: A Living Tribute, Donny & Marie Osmond: Direct from Utah, Mark Hamill: Magnificent, *Grease* Preview, Leo Sayer, Cheryl Ladd, The Incredible K.C., Leif Garrett: How He Spends His Time, Kristy McNichol, "Charlie's Angels" poster $5–10
Mar. #3 Why Kiss Has Gone into Hiding, Leif Garrett, The Reason Shaun Cassidy is Leaving Home, What Marriage Means to Marie Osmond, John Travolta Speaks Out, giant color wall poster of Mark Hamill, Ron Howard, Tatum O'Neal, Behind Fleetwood Mack's Success, Tedd Wass, Emerson, Lake & Palmer, On Tour With the Osmonds, Mark Hamill: Down to Earth Star...$5–10
Aug. #8 Ace Frehley of Kiss: "I Was a Loser," Why Aerosmith Remains Humble, Cindy Williams, Parker Stevenson poster, Donny Osmond, Shaun Cassidy, John Travolta, Leif Garrett Talks of Marriage..$4–8
Sept. #9 Why Shaun Cassidy is Holding Back, Farrah's Agonizing Choice, John Travolta Stunned by Loss, giant K.C. wall poster, Why Kiss are Slaves, Henry Winkler, Parker Stevenson, Donny & Marie Tell the Truth About Love, Debby Boone, Linda Ronstadt, Leif Garrett, The Bay City Rollers Scrapbook, Olivia Newton-John's New Beginning, The Bee Gees, Bobby Carradine..$5–10
Dec. Gene Simmons & Cher: "The Odd Couple," Shaun Cassidy: Was He Changed?, Kristy McNichol Romances Leif Garrett, Andy Gibb life-size poster, Tatum O'Neal, Paul Stanley: "The Pain Will Go Away," Olivia Newton-John's Big Gamble, Mark Hamill, Elvis Costello: "I'm Not a Punk," Donny Osmond $4–8

1979

June Kiss: Paul Stanley's Secret Plan, Meet the Newest Bay City Roller, Why Andy Gibb Isn't Touring With the Bee Gees, Leif Garrett, Donny & Marie Osmond, Shaun Cassidy's Fears About Fame, Willie Ames, John Travolta wall poster, Peter Criss.....................$4–8

1980

Apr. Paul Stanley: A Strange Memory of the Past, Kristy McNichol, A Broken Crystal Gayle: The Biggest Night of Her Life, Leif Garrett: Why He is a Family Man, "Love Boat," "Mork & Mindy," Shaun Cassidy Special Super Pull-out Poster, Elton John, Michael Landon, "Charlie's Angels," Jethro Tull, Andy Gibb, Blondie: Deborah Harry, Adam Rich, Robert Urich, The Police $5–10

1982

Mar. Kristy McNichol: How She Feels About Making it Big, Scott Baio, John Schneider, Matt Dillon, Cathy Bach, Leif Garrett, Chris Atkins, Jimmy McNichol, Tom Wopat, Olivia Newton-John, Shaun Cassidy, Parker Stevenson, Barry Manilow, Peter Frampton, Gene Simmons, Andy Gibb, Queen, Linda Ronstadt, Debbie Harry $4–8

1984

June Michael Jackson: Unbeatable, Menudo, Duran Duran $2–4
Aug. Michael Jackson, Cyndi Lauper, Boy George...$2–4

Oct. Talking to Tommy Howell, Cyndi Lauper, The Go-go's, Menudo Mini-photo Album, Michael Jackson, Prince $2–4
Dec. Looking Back on the Jackson Five Tour, Duran Duran, Prince, Timothy Gibbs, Billy Joel, Steve Perry $2–4

TEEN TALK: BEST OF
1978

#1 Kiss: What is Your Kiss Quotient?, John Travolta: *Saturday Night Fever*, Leif Garrett, Carrie Fisher: Down to Earth, What Marriage Means to Marie Osmond, Barry Manilow, Elton John, Shaun Cassidy, The Strange Story of Fleetwood Mac's Success, Rod Stewart's Rocky Road from Soccer to Stardom, Bee Gees, Linda Ronstadt, Paul & Linda McCartney
....$5–10

TEEN TALK PRESENTS

#4 Scott Baio, Jimmy McNichol, John Schneider, Greg Evigan $2–4

TEEN TALK PRESENTS KISS AND OTHER TOP ROCK BANDS
1979

#2 Kiss: Super Group of the Century, Ride Along With Kiss on Tour, The Kiss Curse, Kiss in the Beginning, special features on each member of Kiss, The Secret of Kiss, Pablo Cruise, Starz, The Pointer Sisters, Aerosmith, Queen, The Tubes, UFO, AC/DC, Van Halen, Alice Cooper, The Runaways, Led Zeppelin, Patti Smith...$10–20

TEEN THROBS
1990

Mar. Bon Jovi: Raise the Flag, Cinderella, Motley Crue, Scorpions, Ozzy Osbourne, *Gorky Park*, Skid Row Exclusive Interviews...$2–4
All other issues $2–4

TEENS TOP TEN
1966

Aug. #4 The Animals at Play, The Dave Clark Five, Nancy Sinatra Hits the Top, Rick of the McCoys, Lou Christie, The Byrds, Fortunes, The Beatles: The Golden Touch, Ryan Twins, "Batman," The Mersey Beats: Dare to be Different, Kinks Have Klass, Sam the Sham: New Image, Sonny & Cher, Dionne Warwick, Etc. $10–20
All other issues $10–20

TEEN SUPER STAR
1976

Oct. #1 Donny & Marie Osmond: Do They Ever Stop Acting?, Leif Garrett, John Travolta, The Bay City Rollers: Rollermania, The High Cost of Loving Donny Osmond, The Beatles, Cher's Bundle of Joy...$6–12
Dec. #3 Donny & Marie: How They Grew, John Travolta: What His Friends Say About Him, The Captain & Tennille at Home, Leif Garrett, Meet the New Heywoods, Bay City Rollers..$4–8

TEEN TRENDS
1966

Jan. #2 The Dave Clark Five: A Close Friend of Theirs Tells All, The Day Herman Lost His Clothes, Cilla Black Talks About the Beatles, Ringo: All About His New Baby, John Andrea, Chad & Jeremy, The Animals, The Rolling Stones, Freddie & the Dreamers: An Intimate Visit, The Hondells, Dusty Springfield..$10–20
All other issues $10–20

TEENVILLE
1965
Nov. #1 More on the Beatles: A Complete Manual on Top Personalities, Dave Clark Five, Rolling Stones, Billy J. Kramer With the Dakotas, Peter & Gordon, Gerry & the Pacemakers, The Swinging Blue Jeans, The Rip Chords, Cliff Richard, Jimmy Clanton, Bobby Vinton, Tommy Regan, Etc. $15–30

TEEN WORLD
1962
June Bobby Rydell is Changing, Paul Anka, Troy Donahue, Fabian, Frankie Avalon, Bobby Vee, Chubby Checker, Hayley Mills, Annette Funicello, Brenda Lee, The Unbelievable True Life of Elvis Presley, Ricky Nelson $15–30

1964
Aug. The Beatles: They Snitch on Each Other, Secrets Paul Peterson Told Us, The Night Patty Duke Cried, Hayley Mills, Elvis Presley, Ricky Nelson, Lesley Gore, The Beach Boys $12–25
Sept. The Beatles, Their Secret Hideaway, A Beatles Special $12–25
Oct. The Beatles: Pictures for Your Eyes Only, The Rolling Stones, The Dave Clark Five, Hayley Mills, The Searchers, Elvis Presley, Patty Duke, The Beatles Love Letters .$12–25
Dec. The Beatles: They Will Never Return, Peter & Gordon, Elvis Presley, Hayley Mills, Bobby Rydell, DC5, Rolling Stones, The Searchers, Patty Duke $12–25

1965
Feb. The Beatles: Body & Soul, The Animals, The Rolling Stones, Elvis Presley .$12–25
Apr. The Beatles, Patty Duke's Datebook, Hayley's Scrapbook, Elvis' Lost Love, The Rolling Stones, The Animals, Peter & Gordon, DC5 ....$12–25
June The Beatles, Hayley Mills, Inside Look at "Shindig," Elvis Presley, The Rolling Stones, Bobby Vinton, Lesley Gore $12–25
July The Beatles: "Our Naughty Nights," Hayley Mills, Elvis Presley, The Rolling Stones $12–25
Aug. The Beatles: We Lose Everything, Will Soupy Sales Sell Out?, Elvis Anniversary Special, Gene Pitney, Tom Jones $12–25
Sept. The Beatles Exclusive: We're in Trouble, Soupy Sales' Wife Snitches, Elvis Presley, Hayley Mills, Patty Duke, Sean Connery $12–25
Oct. The Beatles: "Our Stormy Days & Nights," Herman & His Hide-out, Beach Boys, Elvis Presley, Hayley Mills, Tom Jones, The Rolling Stones $12–25
Dec. The Beatles: We Snoop on Each Other, Hayley Mills, Elvis Presley, The Kinks, Freddie & the Dreamers, The Animals, The Rolling Stones, The Beach Boys $12–25

1966
Feb. The Beatles: "Our Very Hot Secrets," David McCallum: The Threat to My Life," Herman & Hayley Mills, The Rolling Stones, Elvis Presley, Sonny & Cher, The Kinks, Pacemakers, The Animals, Patty Duke $12–25
Apr. The Beatles: "Our Very Intimate File," Herman: I Kiss & Tell, DC5, The Kinks, The Rolling Stones, Sonny & Cher, The Beach Boys, The Dreamers $12–25
June The Beatles & Hermits Gossip About Each Other, Byrds, The Beach Boys, Hayley Mills, Rolling Stones, DC5, The Kinks, The Animals, Sonny & Cher $12–25
July The Beatles: Their Sizzling Life Stories, Sonny & Cher, The Beach Boys, The Kinks, The Byrds, Hayley Mills, Patty Duke, Peter & Gordon...$12–25
Dec. The Beatles: Their Nervous Breakdown, Batman & Robin: Behind Their Masks, The Rolling Stones, The Byrds, Herman's Hermits, Sonny & Cher................................$12–25

1967
Feb. The Beatles: Why They Won't Sing Again, Rolling Stones, Herman's Hermits, The Raiders, Sonny & Cher $12–25
Apr. The Monkees Special, A Very Personal Monkee Business, Herman's Hermits, The Beatles Exclusive, Rolling Stones, Sonny & Cher, Lovin' Spoonful, Mamas & Papas, Yardbirds, DC5, David McCallum $15–30

1971

Apr. David Cassidy: His Secret Thrills, The Osmonds: The Danger They Face Every Day, The Bugaloos, Bobby Sherman: A Page from His Love Book, A Visit to Susan Dey's Home, The Cowsills $6–12

June David Cassidy's After-dark Confessions, The Osmonds' Private Hideaway, On Stage With the Partridge Family, "Brady Bunch," Bugaloos, Bobby Sherman $6–12

Aug. David Cassidy's Love Diary, Susan Dey: The Boy Who Changed Her Life, Spying on the Partridges, Maureen McCormick: A Day in Her Life, Donny Osmond Talks, Bobby Sherman $6–12

Oct. David Cassidy: His Deepest Secrets, Susan Dey: A Private Love Guide, The Jackson Five: Super Question Session, The Partridges: An Exclusive Peek into Their Future, The Osmonds: "The Story of Our Lives," plus a Donny special, Bobby Sherman $6–12

Dec. David Cassidy: "Kisses I Remember," Bobby Sherman's Best-kept Secrets, Donny Osmond's Love Schedule: Minute by Minute, The Jackson Five Love List, The Partridge Family Album..$6–12

1972

June Donny Osmond, 70 Super Facts About the Partridge Family, Bobby Sherman Sick of Show Biz, The Jackson Five Jealous of Each Other, Susan Dey..................................$6–12

Dec. Michael Jackson, Jermaine Jackson's Wedding, David Cassidy in Concert, Susan Dey: Headed for Heartbreak, Bobby Sherman: Is He Too Old?..$6–12

1973

Feb. Donny Osmond After Dark Confessions, Michael Jackson: Will He Kiss & Tell?, David Cassidy: His Special Love Needs, Susan Dey: The Secret She Hides, Cher.......$6–12

June Donny Osmond, Marie Osmond Confesses: "I'm the Loneliest Girl in the World," Elvis Presley, Exclusive Eve Plum Interview, David Cassidy, Susan Dey, Jan Michael...$5–10

1974

Aug. Donny Osmond: 21 Things That Tempt Him, Eve Plumb interview, David Cassidy: Workin' Hard, Elvis Presley, Susan Dey, Andy & David, Marie Osmond, Maureen McCormick $5–10

1975

Mar. Donny Osmond: His Minute-to-minute Love Story, Eve Plumb, David Cassidy Exclusive from Hawaii, Rick Springfield, Marie Osmond, Elvis Presley $4–8

1978

Dec. Shaun Cassidy, Andy Gibb, Parker's Battle, Leif Garrett, Scott Baio, Kiss, Bruce Springsteen...$2–4

1979

Apr. Shaun Cassidy: "I'm Not Getting Married," Andy Gibb, Parker Forced into Hiding, Marie Osmond, John Travolta, Leif Garrett, Kristy McNichol, Scott Baio, Beatlemania....$2–4

June Andy Gibb: From Front to Back, Kiss Tells All, Shaun Cassidy: Is it the End?, John Travolta, Peter Frampton, Parker Stevenson, Billy Joel, Leif Garrett, Rod Stewart, Queen....$2–4

Aug. Andy Gibb: The Truth About Him, Kiss, Paul Stanley Exclusive Interview, Shaun Cassidy...$2–4

TEEN WORLD AND TEEN LIFE

All issues...$2–4

TIGER BEAT

1965

Sept. #1 Annette Funicello: The Beach Party Gang, Rolling Stones Three-Page Special, The Righteous Brothers, Herman's Hermits, Around the World With the Beatles, Jan & Dean, The Love Life of the Beatles, Freddie & the Dreamers, Chuck Berry, David McCallum & the Men from U.N.C.L.E. $25–50

Oct. #2 Annette Funicello: The Beach Party Gang, The Rolling Stones Three-Page Special, Herman's Hermits, The Byrds $20–40

Rod Stewart

Collecting
ROD STEWART

To rock-and-roll music lovers, the word "enduring" conjures up an image of Rod Stewart. His unique and instantly recognizable voice, along with his undeniable songwriting talent, have combined to firmly establish him as one of the truly great rock-and-roll superstars of all time.

His 1971 breakthrough single "Maggie May" topped both the North American and British charts simultaneously and paved the pathway for the road to success. Critics of the '70s lavishly praised Rod Stewart's early works, citing him as a master story teller and genius of song, only to later accuse him of selling out in the latter years of the decade. They claimed that he no longer approached his music with the same deep conviction reflected in his releases of the early '70s. Critics relentlessly accused him of "going Hollywood" and adopting the spandex image of the stereotype rock-and-roll superstar. They justified their constant critique by reiterating the belief that Stewart had already passed his prime and his career was on the downward slide to oblivion.

Yet the one fact that the critics chose to overlook was that the soulful trademark possessed by this man was instantly recognizable by millions worldwide, and that this voice sold, and continues to sell, records by the millions. Ask any Rod Stewart fan why, and likely he or she will point out the exceptional gift Stewart possesses for magically transforming personal experiences and feelings into song.

Rod Stewart's music appeals to a wide range and diversity of ages, a factor ensuring the continued longevity of an established, albeit sometimes rocky, career. A quick survey of the audience in attendance at his live concert performances will confirm a variety of ages from the very young to the "forever young." A live Rod Stewart concert is an experience not to be missed. Here one will witness the man at his best—the metamorphosis of a finely crafted song into an emotional, sometimes raunchy, but always soulful stage performance, its contagious electricity guarantees that even the most stubborn skeptic will come away a converted fan.

The art of Rod Stewart collecting thrives today amongst the staunchest of his fans around the world. The recent renewed interest in his career was fueled by the astounding success of his 1988 album "Out of Order" and subsequent 14-month tour of the same name. This resurgence of his popularity has resulted in a new generation of Rod Stewart fans and collectors who will discover, upon closer investigation, a wealth of Stewart memorabilia available.

Because his popularity extends worldwide, the Stewart collector will discover both album and single sleeves released in a variety of formats, varying by country. Also, many releases and, in particular, compilation- or greatest hits-type albums are often released by only one country, complicating the search for the collector striving to acquire them all. As an example, the 1978 album "Blondes Have More Fun" is the only Rod Stewart picture disc released in North America. The other eight picture discs in existence, with two exceptions, are all British releases, and searching for them challenges even the most patient and persevering collector.

Other collectible Rod Stewart items in circulation include picture sleeve 45 singles, the majority of which are foreign releases (but well worth having for their glossy color sleeves featuring stunning photos). In particular, the Japanese sleeves are extremely attractive. Other Stewart collectibles in circulation include posters, sheet music, buttons, pins, scarves, tour programs, T-shirts, tour jackets, calendars, mirrors, stand-up displays, backstage passes, press kits, picture discs, colored vinyl, test pressing—the list is endless.

One of the most sought-after treasures to complete any memorabilia collection is an authentic autograph. There is a generous supply of bona fide Stewart autographs in circulation, owing in part to Rod Stewart's good-natured accommodation of his fans' requests. He rarely turns down a request for a signature, often stopping to chat with fans who intercept him in public. Rod is also notorious for kicking his trademark soccer balls into the audience during his concerts, and being lucky enough to catch one is a dream come true for an ardent Stewart fan. These balls, personally signed by Rod, are worth their weight in gold. Several such autographed soccer balls featured at charity auctions have fetched upwards of $750–800 and more over the past few years.

Other Rod Stewart items in circulation include picture sleeve 45 singles, the majority of which, again, are foreign releases.

MISCELLANEOUS COLLECTIBLES

"A Nod's as Good as a Wink" Sew & Stuff Pillow Kit, 1972, Warner Bros. Promo
....$25–50
Black trifold nylon wallet, "R.S." in "Blondes Have More Fun" writing $10–20
"Body Wishes" royal blue tour scarf, 1983...$20–40
"Body Wishes" album bin divider, 1983, Warner Bros. Promo $10–20
Brown ceramic mug, 1971 Mercury promo for "Every Picture Tells a Story" $75–100
"Camouflage 1984" green tour jacket, Canada Dry Gingerale $150–300
"Camouflage tour 1984" red cotton bandana, 22″ long.................................$15–30
Chrome butane lighter with Rod Stewart decal, c. 1975 ....$20–40
"Foolish Behavior" world tour scarf, polka dotted, 1980–81...........................$20–40
Framed mirror with photos of Rod on glass, c. 1975, from the United Kingdom.....$25–50
1986 European tour taffeta scarf, magenta with black fringed ends, reads "Rod Stewart
Special Guests ELO/Feargal/Blow Monkeys"...$20–40
1986 European tour white nylon headband, 39″ × 24½″, reads "R.S. European Tour
1986"...$10–20
1986 World tour wool scarf, 4′ long, red, reads "R.S. World Tour 1986" in white
....$20–40
Red styrofoam letters, rigid, spell R-O-D, 3′ long, 1984, Warner Bros., a "Camouflage" al-
bum promo item...$15–30
Rod Stewart 1985 coil-bound calendar, 12 color photos 12″ × 16″, made in the United
Kingdom $15–30
"Tonight I'm Yours" black tour logo jacket, red piping, 1981 ....$200–400
"Tonight I'm Yours" 5′ plaid tour scarf, 1981 ....$20–40
"Tonight I'm Yours" nylon tour scarf, 1981, 21″ long....................................$15–30
"Tonight I'm Yours" tour logo suspenders, 1981 ....$15–30
"Tonight I'm Yours" backpack with tour logo, 1981 ....$15–30
"Tonight I'm Yours" tour log frisbee, 1981 ....$15–30
"Tonight I'm Yours" press kit, 1981, includes custom folder with seven-page biography
& glossy black & white photo $10–20

TOUR PROGRAMS

"Blondes Have More Fun" world tour 1978–79, 96 pages................................$15–30
"Camouflage" tour 1984, 24 pages..$12–25
"Every Beat of My Heart" European tour 1986, 32 pages................................$15–30
"Foolish Behavior" world tour 1980–81, 96 pages $15–30
Le Grande Tour of America & Canada 1981–82, 96 pages $15–30
Levi's Cords Present Labour Day Live '84, an RKO radio concert, four-page fold-out
with poster..$10–20
"Lost in America" tour 1989, 20 pages..$9–18
"Out of Order" tour 1988, 20 pages...$9–18

STAND-UP CARDBOARD PROMOTIONAL DISPLAYS

"Atlantic Crossing", 1975, 66″ tall, Warner Bros......................................$40–80
"Blondes Have More Fun," 1978, 69″ tall, Warner Bros. $50–100
"Body Wishes," 1983, 17″ tall, Warner Bros. $10–20
"Downtown Train"/"Storyteller," 32″ tall, Warner Bros...............................$25–50
"Tonight I'm Yours," 1981, 28″ tall, Warner Bros. $12–25

OUT-OF-PRINT BOOKS

Rod Stewart, 1977, by Tony Jaspar (hardcover, 93 pages, U.S.A.) $10–20
Rod Stewart, 1981, by Paul Nelson and Lester Bangs (softcover, 159 pages)........$10–20
Rod Stewart: A Biography in Words and Pictures, 1976, by Richard Cromelin (softcover,
56 pages, U.S.A.)..$12–25
Rod Stewart and the Changing Faces, 1976, by John Pidgeon (paperback, 144 pages,
U.K.) $7–15
The Rod Stewart Story, 1976, by George Tremlett (paperback, 143 pages, U.K.)....$7–15

ALBUM AND SINGLE PROMO POSTERS (WARNER BROS.)

"Tonight I'm Yours," 1981, 36″ × 48″ $12–25
"Absolutely Live," 1982, 26″ × 38″ $12–25
"Body Wishes," 1983, 25″ × 38″...$7–15
"Camouflage," 1984, 48″ × 60″...$15–30
"Rod Stewart," 1986, 27″ × 38″..$7–15
"Out of Order," 1988, 23″ × 35″..$6–12
"Storyteller," 1989, 23″ × 35″...$6–12
"Downtown Train Anthology," 1989, 23″ × 35″...$6–12

"SMILER" FAN CLUB

The official, worldwide Rod Stewart fan club Smiler was originally founded in England in 1981 by its editor John Gray. What makes Smiler so outstanding in its field is that Smiler has Rod Stewart's 100% personal support and full cooperation. Smiler's staff devote themselves to Smiler for the love of good music. Their pledge is to treat each and every member with the same individual touch that they themselves have come to expect.

The basis and foundation of the fan club is the Rod Stewart quarterly magazine, *Smiler*. This 40-page publication features a wealth of excellent color and black and white photos of Rod dating back to 1964 and up to the present. *Smiler* also contains multiregular features such as news, editorials, readers' letters, and trivia puzzles, as well as a wealth of special articles, exclusive interviews and vintage press items. They're in frequent contact with Rod himself, which means any news from him is a direct and accurate preview. *Smiler* is a definite must for all Rod Stewart fans around the world. *Smiler* currently reaches more than 20 countries around the world. Their free classified ads will introduce you to the art of Rod Stewart collecting and worldwide pen pals. In addition, they provide members with regular newsletters which detail tour news, record releases, and periodic contests offering terrific Stewart-related prizes. Members are also offered spec sheets detailing numerous aspects of Rod Stewart collecting, with illustrated and pertinent information on books, picture discs, tour schedules, videos, sheet music, cover-story magazines, and much, much more.

Smiler is published in London, England, in the spring, summer, fall, and winter. The Rod Stewart worldwide fan club does not solicit membership fees; rather, members have the option of purchasing one or each quarterly issue of *Smiler* as it is published. An optional one-year subscription package for four issues is also available. Members are informed in advance by mail when each new issue becomes available. Your requests for information and assistance are always honored to the best of the club's ability.

The North American branch office of *Smiler*, centrally located in Winnipeg, Manitoba, Canada, was established in 1986 to efficiently process memberships and serve members both in the United States and Canada. All inquiries from within North America should be directed to their Canadian address. Feel free to write them for detailed information and current rates. In the United States please include one international reply coupon (IRC) or $.50 in coin; in Canada, a self-addressed stamped envelope. Write to: Smiler, Box 433, Postal Station A, Winnipeg, Manitoba, R3K 2C2, Canada.

Nov. #3 Sonny & Cher: The Sweetest Love Story of the Rock Age, Annette Funicello, Elvis Presley's Secret Love Life, Beach Boys, Rolling Stones, Beatles, Bob Dylan, Donovan, David McCallum, Groupies $20–40
Dec. #4 Lesley Gore: Stranger in the Music World, Sonny & Cher, John Lennon, Bob Dylan, Paul Revere & the Raiders, The Turtles, Donovan, The Animals, Elvis Presley, Beatles, Janis Ian, We Five, Dave Clark Five, Rolling Stones, The McCoys..........$20–40

1966

Jan. #5...$15–30
Feb. #6 ....$15–30
Mar. #7 ....$15–30
Apr. #8 George Harrison Talks, The Beatles, Bobby Vinton, The Beach Boys, Elvis Presley, Gary Lewis & the Playboys, The Kinks, Dino, Desi & Billy, Simon & Garfunkel: As Different as Their Names, Yardbirds, Sonny & Cher Battling Back, James Brown, Paul Revere & the Raiders, Ringo...$15–30
May #9 Mick Jagger & the Rolling Stones, The Beatles, Bob Dylan's High School Daze, Jan & Dean, Herman's Hermits Movie, Peter & Gordon $15–30
June #10 The Rolling Stones in Hollywood, Paul Revere & the Raiders, Sonny & Cher's New Glamour Look, Herman's Hermits, The Mamas & the Papas, Byrds, Petula Clark $15–30
July $15–30
Aug. John Lennon: Life With the Beatles, The Rolling Stones, The Beach Boys, Paul Revere & the Raiders, Cher's New Movie Wardrode, The Hollies..$15–30
Sept. The New Raiders Exclusive, Sonny & Cher, Herman's Hermits, Simon & Garfunkel, Lovin' Spoonful $12–25
Oct. The Beatles, Herman's Hermits, Stones, Sonny & Cher, Hollies $12–25
Nov. Dino, Desi & Billy, Herman's Hermits, Paul Revere & the Raiders, The Monkees' Personal Story, A Beach Boy Wedding, The Beatles, Sonny & Cher's Life Together, Rolling Stones, The Lovin' Spoonful $12–25
Dec. The Monkees: By Their Closest Friends, On Tour With the Raiders, Two Secret Hours With the Beatles...$12–25

1967

Jan. $12–25
Feb. $12–25
Mar. $12–25
Apr...$12–25
May..$12–25
June $12–25
July Davy Jones Exclusive, Peter Noone & Girls, The Monkees, Kurt Russell $12–25
Aug. Micky Dolenz: Micky's Days as Circus Boy, A Very Private Look at Davy Jones, Why Mike Nesmith Married Phyllis, Buffalo Springfield, Herman's Hermits, Paul Revere & the Raiders Whole Story, Dino, Desi & Billy...$12–25
Sept. $12–25
Oct. The Monkees: A Special Photo Report—The Private Lives of the Monkees, The Monkees Tour...$12–25
Nov...$12–15
Dec. The Monkees: At Home with the Monkees Exclusive $12–25

1968

Jan. The Monkees: Super Pix, Sally Field, Leonard Nimoy: The Man Behind Mr. Spock, Peter Tork Reveals His Inner Thoughts, The Bee Gees, Davy Jones Weekend........$12–25
Feb. The Monkees: The Secret Hideouts, Monkee Songs, Davy Jones, Sajid Khan, Sally Field, Mark Lindsay, Paul Revere $12–25
Mar. $12–25
Apr. Micky Dolenz & Sammy in Hawaii, Davy Jones' Secret Travels $12–25
May Davy Jones Remembers His Mother, Sajid Khan, Leonard Nimoy, The Cowsills, "I Live With Mark Lindsay," Walter Koenig, The Bee Gees...$12–25
June The Monkees: A Special Color Monkee Movie Issue, Cowsills, The Who, Sajid Khan, Dino, Desi & Billy, Paul Revere & the Raiders...$12–25

July Peter Tork's Divorce, The Bee Gees, The Monkees................................$12–25
Aug. The Monkees, Cher, Meet the Cast of "Dark Shadows" Photo Special $12–25
Sept. The Monkees: Special Scoops & Stories, Sajid Khan, Goldie Hawn, Tiny Tim, Davy Jones' Secret Sister, Mark Lindsay, Raiders..$12–25
Oct. Davy Jones: His Sister's Story, The Monkees Secret Struggle........................$12–25
Nov...$12–25
Dec...$12–25

1969
Jan.–Dec...$10–20

1970
Jan.–Dec...$10–20

1971
Jan. David Cassidy Quits, "The Story of My Life" by David Cassidy, Bobby Sherman, Susan Dey: Telling it Like it Is, "Dark Shadows," "The Partridge Family," Mark Lindsay
....$10–20
Feb...$10–20
Mar. David Cassidy: Where He Lives, His Secrets by His Roommate, Bobby Sherman: His Marriage Plans, The Osmonds, Jack Wild, Mike Nesmith: His Memory Book, "Dark Shadows," The Jackson Five, Kurt Russell, Susan Dey................................$10–20
Apr. David Cassidy's Secret Trip, Bobby Sherman Working With the Partridges, Susan Dey Exclusive..$10–20
May David Cassidy Finds a House, The Osmonds' Day of Terror, Bobby Sherman, The Jackson Five, "Dark Shadows," Susan Dey $10–20
June..$10–20
July David Cassidy's Birthday Exclusive, The Jackson Five Dream Marriage, Susan Dey's Love, David Cassidy Almost Drowns, Michael Jackson's Memory Book, Bobby Sherman
....$10–20
Aug. David Cassidy's Wild Wild Weekend, "My Brothers" by Marie Osmond, Bobby Sherman, Donny Osmond, Susan Dey, The Jackson Five Tell Secrets on Jermaine, Brian Foster, Rick Ely $10–20
Sept. David Cassidy's Best Kept Secret, The Jackson Five Nearly Killed, Bobby Sherman, Susan Dey, Donny Osmond $10–20
Oct. David Cassidy Asks "Can You Love me Enough?," Osmond Exclusive, The Jackson Five Meet the Brady Bunch, Bobby Sherman, Susan Dey, Peter Duel, Donny Osmond
....$10–20
Nov. David Cassidy's Heartbreak: The Girl Who Left Him Behind, Donny Osmond, The Jackson Five's Dad Tells All, Susan Dey's Secret Trip, Michael Jackson's Memory Book, Bobby Sherman, Partridges $10–20
Dec. David Cassidy: In His Dressing Room & at Home, David Cassidy Talks, Donny Osmond, Bobby Sherman, The Jackson Five: Life at Home, Susan Dey's Homelife, On "The Partridge Family" Set $10–20

1972
Jan. David Cassidy in Hawaii, Handwritten Notes from the Jackson Five, Susan Dey Exclusive, Donny Osmond's New Haircut, Bobby Sherman Heartbroken $10–20
Feb. David Cassidy's New Home, Bobby Sherman on Tour, Dinner With Donny Osmond, Michael Jackson Reveals All, Interview With Susan Dey $10–20
Mar. David Cassidy is in Danger, Bobby Sherman at the Crossroads, Making Music With Donny Osmond, The Jackson Five..$10–20
Apr. David Cassidy Talks, The Jackson Five, Osmond Wedding $7–15
May The New David Cassidy: The Trip That Changed Him, The Osmonds at Home, The Jackson Five: A Private Peak $7–15
June Behind Donny Osmond's Door, David Cassidy's New Romance: Follow Him on a Private Weekend, Marie Osmond Exclusive, Susan Dey, The DeFrancos....................$7–15
July David Cassidy's Secret Party, Donny & Marie Intimate Photos, Michael & Jermaine Jackson..$7–15

Aug. David Cassidy: Living With Him, The Osmonds in Hawaii, Bobby Sherman, The Jackson Five, Michael Jackson at Home $7–15

Sept. Why David Cassidy Cries & Cries & Cries, Donny Osmond's Day of Disaster, DeFrancos, Susan Dey's Wedding Plans...$7–15

Oct. David Cassidy Exclusive, Bobby Sherman's Secret Message, Donny Osmond & Fatherhood, Rick Springfield..$7–15

Nov. Why David Cassidy Must Leave You Forever, The Osmonds Off-guard, The Bradys, Rick Springfield $7–15

Dec. Donny Osmond's Tomorrow, Osmond History Exclusive, Bobby Sherman, David Cassidy's New Girls, Rick Springfield, Mark Hamill, Backstage on "General Hospital"
....$7–15

1973

Jan. David Cassidy's Midnight of Fun, Michael Gray, Donny Osmond, The Osmonds Leave Hollywood, Rick Springfield, DeFrancos, Marie Osmond $6–12

Feb. Donny Osmond's Private Journal, The Jackson Five are Different Now, The Bradys, David Cassidy $6–12

Mar. The Real Donny Osmond, David Cassidy: Do His Kisses Mean Danger?, Marie Osmond, DeFrancos, The Jackson Five, Rick Springfield, Andy & Dave, The Osmond Movie $6–12

Apr. Is Marie Osmond Jealous of Her Brothers?, Have All David Cassidy's Concerts Ended?, Rick Springfield, The Jackson Five: Another Wedding, Bobby Sherman.....$6–12

May Why David Cassidy & Donny Osmond are Both Afraid, Donny's Secret Room, The Jackson Five Admit They've Changed, Rick Springfield......................................$6–12

June Donny Osmond: The Night He Turned from God, Why David Cassidy is Leaving, DeFrancos, Rick Springfield, Andy & David...$6–12

July Super Osmond Annual, David Cassidy's 10 Mistakes, Michael Jackson: Over 1001 Secrets, Rick Springfield $6–12

Aug. Donny Osmond's Intimate Love Letters, Andy & Dave: Their Lonely Nights, David Cassidy's Secret Book, DeFrancos, Rick Springfield, The Heywoods, Jackson Five.$6–12

Sept. Donny in Hollywood, Andy & Dave Face Danger, The Osmonds, The DeFrancos, The Osmonds..$6–12

Oct. Donny Osmond, David Cassidy: The Child That Changed Him, Randy, Andy & Dave, Tony DeFranco's Secret Days, The Partridge Family,.....................................$6–12

Nov. Donny Osmond, Bradys, DeFrancos, Randy, Andy & Dave $6–12

Dec. Tony DeFranco: A Visit to His House, Donny Osmond: Did Merrill's Wedding Hurt Him?, David Cassidy: Bad Luck With Girls, Andy & Dave: Could They Fall for You?, The Osmonds $6–12

1974

Jan. DeFrancos, Chris Knight, David Cassidy, Andy & Dave, Osmonds $5–10

1975

Jan.–Dec..$4–8

1976

Jan.–Dec..$3–6

1977

Jan.–Dec..$3–6

1978

Jan.–Dec..$3–6

1979

Jan.–Dec..$3–6

1980

Jan.–Dec..$3–6

1981

Jan.–Dec..$3–6

1982–1985 ....$2–4

1986–1990 ....$1–3

TIGER BEAT ANNUAL

All issues $5–10

TIGER BEAT FAVE

1967

Sept. #1 Davy Jones: His Private Glads & Sads, Meeting the Monkees, The Beatles, Herman's Hermits $20–40
Oct. #2 Monkees' special featuring giant full-color pages $15–30
Nov. #3 Davy Jones, Monkee Special Issue..$15–30
Dec. #4 The Monkees $15–30

1968

Jan. The Monkees $15–30
Feb. Micky Dolenz & Davy Jones, Super Fab Love Issue, Micky's Heart, Paul Revere & the Raiders, Sajid Khan...$15–30
Mar. Davy Jones, The Monkees, Sally Field...$15–30
Apr.–Dec. All feature The Monkees & The Raiders.....................................$15–30

1969

Jan.–Dec...$15–30

1970

Jan.–Dec...$12–25

1971

Jan. $10–20
Feb...$10–20
Mar. David Cassidy: On TV With David, Bobby Sherman's Hidden House, Partridges' Private Photo Album Bonus, Susan Dey: Is She Too Pretty?, The Osmonds, Chris Stone, Shirley Jones $10–20
Apr...$10–20
May..$10–20
June Davidy Cassidy in Trouble: Who Frightens Him?, Why Bobby Sherman Cries, Donny Osmond Exclusive: Donny Tells All, Peter Duel, Wes Stone, Partridges, Ben Murphy, Osmonds..$10–20
July $10–20
Aug. David Cassidy is Lost: Where is He?, Bobby Sherman: His 5 Hidden Letters, A Week With the Osmonds, The Jackson Five: Love in Their Family, Partridges: Pix-Fax & Fan Club, Susan Dey, Donny Osmond..$10–20
Sept. David Cassidy's Confession: "I'm Hurting My Fans," Bobby Sherman: The Secret Letters He Hides, Jackson Five: Morning, Noon & Night With Them, Partridges' Lowdown Chart, Donny Osmond Answers All Your Questions, 50 Intimate Fax on Ben Murphy, Susan Dey..$10–20
Oct. David Cassidy's Secret Love: Who is She?, The Shocking Truth Behind Bobby Sherman's Return, The Osmonds in Trouble: Why They Need You, The Partridges at Home, at Work & at Play, Michael Jackson & the Jackson Five in Hollywood.................$10–20
Nov. David Cassidy, Bobby Sherman Talks, The Jackson Five Talk About Each Other, Susan Dey as Revealed by Her Handwriting, Danny Spills the Beans About David & Susan, Osmonds $10–20
Dec. $10–2

1972

Jan. David Cassidy, Bobby Sherman, Donny Osmond, The Osmonds.....................$10–20
Feb. David Cassidy Special Issue, Are You Hurting Him?, Bobby Sherman Needs Your Help, The Partridge Family..$10–20

Mar. Donny Osmond's Secrets, David Cassidy Scoop, Did You Fail Bobby Sherman?
....$10–20
Apr...$10–20
May Donny Osmond's Best Kept Secret, How to be a Jackson Five Girl, On the Set With Michael Gray, David Cassidy, Chris Knight: What He Hides, Mitch Vogel's 16th Birthday, Osmonds $10–20
July Donny Osmond: Be an Osmond Bride, David Cassidy's Secret Love Moments, Have You Lost Bobby Sherman Forever?, Michael Gray, Mark Hamill: A New Fave, Michael Jackson..$10–20
Aug. David Cassidy's Own Story: The Confessions of a Teen Idol, Donny Osmond, Another Osmond Wedding, Touring With Bobby Sherman, Memories With Little Jimmy Osmond, Michael Grey, Sonny & Cher, Jackson Five, The DeFrancos........................$10–20
Sept...$10–20
Oct...$10–20
Nov. Donny Osmond: Red Hot Lovers, David Cassidy: Accept His Love Challenge, Jackson Five: Is it All Over? Chris Knight, Three Dog Night, Bobby Sherman.............$10–20
Dec. Donny Osmond's Hidden Love, Chris Knight Tells: All Brady Secrets, Michael Gray, How Far Can David Cassidy be Trusted?, A Beach Date Osmond Style.................$10–20

1973
All issues..$10–20

TIGER BEAT OFFICIAL MONKEE SPECTACULAR
1967/68
#1–#16 ....$15–30
Reprint issues...$3–6

TIGER BEAT OFFICIAL PARTRIDGE FAMILY MAGAZINE
1970
Dec. #1 Come Home With David Cassidy, Susan Dey Exclusive Home Photos, Behind the Scenes With "The Partridge Family," Interviews, Secrets & Intimate Facts.............$20–40

1971
Mar. #2 Who is the Real David Cassidy?, Rapping With Shirley Jones, My Son Danny, Susan Dey Doing Commercials, At School With the Partridges $20–40
May #3 David Cassidy's New House, Everything You Ever Wanted to Know About the Partridges, Susan Dey Talks About Bobby Sherman, In Hollywood With "The Partridge Family" $20–40
Aug. #4 David Cassidy's Shocking Discovery, Rapping With Susan Dey, Come to David Cassidy's 21st Birthday Party $17–35
Oct. #5 David Cassidy's Lonely Days & Nights, On Location With the Partridges, David on Tour, Is David Ill?..$17–35
Nov. #6 David Cassidy Cries, Why Susan Dey is Special, David Cassidy: Then & Now, "Susan Dey" by Her Mother, Secrets $17–35
Dec. #7 The Truth About David Cassidy & Susan Dey: Why He Can't Love, Flashback With Shirley Jones, Danny's Private Homelife $17–35

1972
Jan. Exclusive: David Cassidy's Mother Tells Her Story, The Girls in Danny's Life, Shirley Jones Models..$15–30
Feb. David Cassidy Revealed by Those Who Love Him, David's Concerts: On Tour Secrets, Susan Dey's Hidden Home..$15–30
Mar. David Cassidy vs. Donny Osmond, The Partridges on Tour, At Home & on the Set, How Susan Dey Feels About Showbiz..$15–30
Apr. Secret Hours With David Cassidy, Susan Dey's Wedding Day, On Tour With David, Partridge Family Secrets..$15–30
May David Cassidy & How He Grew: His TV Life in Photos, His Secret Love, Why Susan Dey Said Goodbye, Tour News $15–30

June Special Giant Susan & David Issue, David Injured & How Susan Helped Him, Susan
Secrets $15–30
July $15–30
Aug. David Cassidy's Party, Shaun Cassidy, The Guys in Susan's Life, Susan Dey Ready
for Love, Fashions $15–30
Fall David Cassidy Exposed: The Lonely Life He Tries to Hides, Susan Dey: Small-town
Girl or Big City Swinger?, Tour Bonus, Special 114-page double issue...................$20–40

TIGER BEAT POSTER SPECIAL

1987
Includes Posters of Michael J. Fox, Davy Jones, Peter Tork, Jon Bon Jovi, Kirk Cameron,
Corey Haim, The Monkees, Alyssa Milano $2–4

TIGER BEAT PRESENTS DONNY AND MARIE

1977
#2 Never-before-seen Family Pix $2–4

TIGER BEAT PRESENTS GETTING TOGETHER
WITH BOBBY (SHERMAN) MAGAZINE

1972
All You Need to Know About Bobby Sherman, color pin-ups, Bobby's Sister, Wes Stern,
hundreds of photos..$6–12

TIGER BEAT PRESENTS GIANT, GIANT 1987
ROCK POSTER CALENDAR MAGAZINE

1987
Issue includes giant color wall posters of Madonna, Van Halen, A-ha & Bruce Springsteen
....$2–5

TIGER BEAT PRESENTS LOVE POSTER QUARTERLY

1972
Apr. David Cassidy, The Osmonds, Donny Osmond's Love Letters, issue includes 10 giant
all-color pullout posters $10–20

TIGER BEAT PRESENTS THE LOVEBOOK

1986
Sept. Madonna, Michael Fox, Duran Duran Together at Last, Wham, Prince, The Bangles
....$1–3

TIGER BEAT PRESENTS TV ALL-STAR SPECTACULAR

All issues..$4–8

TIGER BEAT SPECTACULAR

1970
Spring #1 Bobby Sherman Special Issue, All You Need to Know About Bobby, His Sister's
Intimate Story, Bobby's Special Secret, Here Come the Brides, Bobby's Concert Life, pin-
ups..$10–20
Fall #2 ....$10–20

1971
Feb. #3 David Cassidy Special Issue...$15–30
Apr. #4 David Cassidy: Spend a Lifetime With Him, The Girl Bobby Sherman Cares
About, The Jackson Five: How They Feel About You, Susan Dey & Popularity, The

Osmond Brothers: Why God Comes First, Boys & Maureen McCormick, Bobby Sherman's Own Story: How to Make a Marriage Work $10–20
June #5 Gigantic Summer Lovebook, David Cassidy, Bobby Sherman, Peter Duel, The Jackson Five, The Osmonds..$10–20
Aug. #6 David Cassidy: Can He Change Your Life?, The Osmonds: Live With Them, Bobby Sherman: How to be His Love, The Bradys, Michael Jackson, Jackson Five Flashback, Jack Wild $10–20
Oct. #7 David Cassidy: Is He Trapped by Love?, Michael Jackson: Can You Marry Him?, Bobby Sherman, Why Donny Osmond Can't Go Steady, The Jackson Five, Osmonds $10–20
Nov. David Cassidy: Who Broke His Heart?, The Jackson Five Love Photos, Bobby Sherman's Night of Faith, West Stern, At Home With Donny Osmond, David Cassidy's Special Friends, Susan Dey: Does She Hide From Love?, Michael Gray $10–20
Dec. Super Sweethearts Issue, David Cassidy Fights Back, Donny Osmond's Search for Love, The Tears David Hides, Bobby Sherman: The Girl Who Showed Him Love, The Osmonds: Family Fun, Susan Dey: Why She's Alone, Jackson Five: Be Their Girl...$10–20

1972

Jan. Donny Osmond's Brush With Death, David Cassidy's Love List, Is Bobby Sherman Quitting?, Jackson Five: Why Can't They Go Home?, Wes Stern: Christmas With Him $10–20
Feb. Donny Osmond: His Love Life, The Osmond's History: Birth Till Now, Marie Osmond Answers All Your Questions About Her Brothers, David Cassidy: Who Fills His Life With Love?, Special Osmond Issue..$10–20
Mar. Special Contest Issue, Donny Osmond, David Cassidy, Bobby Sherman, The Osmonds..$10–20
Apr. Donny Osmond to Quit, David Cassidy: Why He's Still Alone, Jimmy Osmond Disappears, 100 Osmond Secrets, Bobby Sherman $10–20
May Donny Osmond: Is He in Love?, Why David Cassidy is Crying Inside, Mrs. Osmond Tells All, Is the Jackson Five Splitting Up?, Bobby Sherman's Secret Holiday, Michael Gray $10–20
June The Osmonds: Their Private Confessions of Love, Special Everything Osmond Issue, Owning the Key to Donny's Heart $12–25
July A Peek into Mr. Osmond's Private File With Hidden Photos, David Cassidy: Will He be Alone Forever?, Chris Knight, Why Randy Joined the Jackson Five, Donny Begs Alan: Don't Leave..$10–20
Aug. Donny Osmond: How to Love Him, The Bradys, Chris Knight, The Jackson Five & The Osmonds Reveal Their Secret Kissing Places, David Cassidy: Please Love Me Again $10–20
Sept. Super Secrets Issue, The Osmonds: Jay Tells on Them, The Osmonds in London, David Cassidy: "Do You Know the Real Me?," Bradys' Secrets, Michael Jackson: Latest Whispers, Susan Dey, Maureen McCormick: The Girls Reveal All $10–20
Oct. Donny Osmond: The Day Donny Dreads, Cuddling Up With the Osmonds, Run Away With the Bradys, Can You Satisfy David Cassidy?, A Private Peek at the Jackson Five, Bobby Sherman, Michael Jackson, Mantooth & the DeFrancos.................................$10–20
Nov. David Cassidy/Donny Osmond/Chris Knight: Then & Now, David's Hidden Honeymoon, Can You Delight Donny Osmond?, Is Donny Tired of Success?, Michael Jackson, Rick Springfield $10–20
Dec. How to Date the Osmonds, Does Donny Tell You Lies?, The Jackson Five & Their Dreamhouse, Michael Gray, David Cassidy...$10–20

1973

Feb. Special Lover's Issue, 25 Private Messages from the Stars, Donny Osmond, David Cassidy, The Jackson Five, Michael Jackson, Michael Gray, The Bradys, Richard Thomas, Special Osmond Love Fiction Story & Osmond Secrets....................................$10–20
Apr. David Cassidy's Hidden Life, Party-line Whispers With Donny Osmond, Marie Osmond Shares Her 1st Love, Michael Gray: "Meet My Kids," The Things the Osmonds Say Behind Donny's Back, Rick Springfield, Andy & David, Richard Thomas, Bobby Sherman, Michael Jackson in Love, DeFrancos...$10–20
June Donny Osmond: The Dreams That Haunt Him, David's Last Song for You, Read

Michael Gray's Intimate Diary, Mike Ontkean, Rick Springfield Ambushed, Andy & David William's Mysterious Illness, The Jackson Five, DeFrancos, Heywoods, Bradys.....$10–20
Aug. Donny Osmond: Is it Wedding Bells?, Andy & David: Loving Them Both, Tony DeFranco: A Star is Born, David Cassidy's Last Year as a Partridge, The Secrets the Osmonds Hide From, Richard Thomas, The Devilish Side of Rick Springfield, Chris Knight Interview, The Wild Side of the Heywoods, Randy Mantooth...................................$10–20
Oct. $10–20
Dec. Donny Osmond: Is This Hello or Goodbye?, David Cassidy's True Feelings About Leaving "The Partridge Family," Special DeFranco Section, On Tour With Tony, Junior High School Pix of the Osmonds, The Carpenters, Michael Gray, Randy Mantooth, Bradys
....$10–20

TIGER BEAT'S ROCK

1988
Dec. White Lion, Cinderella, Europe, Megadeth, Kiss & Ace Frehley's Comet, issue includes four giant wall posters, Iron Maiden, Poison $2–4

1989
Sept. Skid Row, Motley Crue, L.A. Guns, Living Colour, The Who: 25 Years of Rock
....$2–4

TIGER BEAT'S STAR

1977
Apr. Bay City Rollers: What They Think of You, "The Hardy Boys": Shaun Cassidy & Parker Stevenson—Sweet, Sexy & Single, Leif Garrett's Movies, Donny & Marie: "We Don't Need Acting Lessons," Captain & Tennille..$3–6
Oct. Shaun Cassidy & Parker Stevenson: Meet the Hardy Boys Face to Face, Bay City Rollers: What Would You Do for Them?, Donny & Marie's Last TV Season, An Ex-Rollers' New Life, Mark Hamill...$3–6
Nov. Shaun Cassidy: His Biggest Heartbreak, Happiest Day & Greatest Love, Pamela Sue Martin Tells All, Donny & Marie: Hollywood Has Changed Them, Parker Stevenson, Bay City Rollers $3–6
Dec. Shaun Cassidy: A Private Visit to His New House, Leif Garrett's Back, Parker Stevenson, Donny & Marie: Have They Changed Too Much for You?, Bay City Rollers: The Secret Meaning Behind Their Songs, Kristy McNichol, Robby Benson.................$3–6

1978
Jan. Leif Garrett: Back in the Saddle Again, Shaun Cassidy, Has Marie Osmond Stolen the Show?, Bay City Rollers: What Will 1978 Bring Them?, Christmas Memories With Pamela Sue Martin, Scott Baio...$3–6
Apr. Shaun Cassidy: Danger on "The Hardy Boys" Set, Leif's Late Nights Out, Scott Baio: He Knows About Love, Donny's Favorite Place, Abba: The Movie, The Business of Being a Roller $3–6
May Shaun Cassidy's Shy Side, Leif Garrett: Could He Live Without Fame?, The New Nancy Drew, A Visit With Donny & Marie Backstage $3–6
June Shaun Cassidy: Is He Lonely at Home?, Scott Baio's Secrets, Leif in Concert, Marie Osmond: Wait Twenty Years, Rollers...$3–6
July Shaun Cassidy: Why His Kisses are Special, Leif Garrett: What & Who Upsets Him the Most, Parker Stevenson's Favorite Photos, Scott Baio, Rollers, John Travolta, Barry Manilow, Peter Frampton, Donny & Marie, Robby Benson $3–6
Sept. Shaun Cassidy: The Girl He'll Make Time For, Rollers: Can They Really Make a Comeback?, Scott Baio's New TV Show, Leif Garrett, Donny & Marie's Super Season, Kristy McNichol, Willie Aames, Debbie Boone, "Charlie's Angels"............................$3–6
Oct. Shaun Cassidy: Caught in a Fire, Scott Baio's Birthday, Leif Garrett Hysteria, Is Donny Different Now?, John Travolta, Rollers, Andy Gibb, Kristy McNichol $3–6
Dec. Shaun Cassidy: No More Concerts, Leif Garrett: Fighting for His Fans, A Love Letter From Scott Baio, Will the Rollers Keep Changing?, Tony Danza, Donny Osmond & Debbie in Danger, Andy Gibb, Kristy McNichol...$3–6

1979

Mar. Scott Baio: Foxy in so Many Ways, Erik Estrada, Leif Garrett, David Cassidy, Donnie & Marie, "Battlestar Galactica"...$3–6

Apr. Leif Garrett, Shaun Cassidy & Erik Estrada: Do They Dress Funky or Fancy?, Donny & Marie, John Travolta, Willie Aames, Rollers...$3–6

June Shaun Cassidy, Leif Garrett & Scott Baio: Which Guy is at the End of Your Rainbow?, Tony Danza: His Mother's Day Memories...$3–5

July Erik Estrada, Scott Baio, Tony Danza, Robby Benson: Why Tall, Dark & Handsome is In, Shaun Cassidy's New Look, Dirk Benedict & Marie Osmond: Are They Still Together?, Rollers...$3–5

Aug. Greg Evigan, Leif Garrett, John Schneider, Shaun Cassidy, Shaun Stevens, Erik Estrada, Tony Danza & Scott Baio: Those Young, Sexy & Single Guys, Bay City Rollers..$ 3–5

Sept. A Wedding for Marie Osmond, Rollers, Shaun Cassidy, Leif Garrett, Scott Baio, Rex Smith...$3–5

Oct. Scott Baio: Shaun Cassidy, Greg Evigan, Tony Danza, Erik & Leif: The Most Wanted Guys, The Village People: Disco's Sexy Six, Rollers: The Way They Were (With Les), Donny & Marie..$3–5

1980

Apr. Scott Baio, Teena Maria, Pablo Cruise, Rod Stewart, Rex Smith, Robby Benson, Kristy McNichol..$2–3

1981

Feb./Mar. Blondes vs. Dark Issue, Scott Baio, Shaun Cassidy, Matt Dillon, Michael Damian, Doobie Brothers, The Knack, issue includes 14 full-page color pin-ups $3–5

1985

July Wham Live from London, Madonna, Prince, Rick Springfield, Sting, Menudo, Corey Feldman...$2–3

1987

Sept. Cooking With the Monkees, Madonna, Ralph Macchio, A-ha, Simon Le Bon, Michael Fox, Annette Funicello: Back to the Beach...$2–3

Oct. Madonna's Ultimate Fantasy, Ralph Macchio, Menudo's Newest Member, Michael Fox, Rob Lowe, Peter Tork, The Monkees $2–3

1988

Mar. Kirk Cameron, River Phoenix Hitting the Road, Alyssa Milano, Corey Haim, Chad Allen..$2–3

All other issues $2–3

TIGER BEAT'S STAR POSTER SPECIAL

1987

Fall Issue includes 10 giant color wall posters of John Taylor, Rob Lowe, Michael J. Fox, Corey Haim, Petersen, Ricky Schroder, Madonna & Ralph Macchio.............................$2–4

TIGER BEAT'S STAR PRESENTS JOHN TAYLOR AND NICK RHODES

1986

#3 Issue also includes stories on Madonna, Duran Duran, A-ha......................$1–3

TIGER BEAT'S STAR PRESENTS THE DURAN DURAN SPECIAL

1987

Includes All the Dynamite Details & Photos, Madonna, Michael Fox.........................$1–3

TIGER BEAT'S STAR SUPER SPECIAL PRESENTS A-HA MAGAZINE

1987

Includes exclusive interviews & dozens of pin-ups, stories on The Monkees, Madonna, Michael J. Fox, John Stamos & Ralph Macchio...$1–3

TIGER BEAT SUPER ANNUAL

1971

Sept. #1 David Cassidy & the Partridge Family: Behind-the-scenes History, Bobby Sherman, The Jackson Five Special, The Osmonds Tell About Each Other, Susan Dey
.... $10–20

1972

May #2 Donny Osmond, issue includes a Donny Osmond game, Osmond's Hidden History Scrapbook, David Cassidy's Eight Lives: The Whole Untold Story, What Really Happened Behind the Camera on "The Partridge Family," Jackson 5: Over a Dozen-page Special, The Brady Bunch: A Behind-the-camera Look, Bobby Sherman......................................$10–20
Sept. David Cassidy's Secret Wish, The Dream Donny Osmond Fears, Susan Dey's Dream Marriage, Michael Jackson's Nightmare, The Brady Bunch, Bobby Sherman............$7–15

1973

Fall Special Donny Osmond Yearbook, issue includes 200 pullout pin-ups, David Cassidy, The DeFrancos & others $7–15

TIGER BEAT SUPER SPECIAL

1980

Apr./May #2 John Schneider, Scott Baio, Robby Benson, The First On-screen Kiss, Leif Garrett $2–4

TIGER BEAT SUPER SPECIAL PRESENTS CELEBRITY TRIVIA MAGAZINE

1986

John Taylor, Michael J. Fox, Madonna, Bruce Springsteen, Duran Duran, Kirk Cameron, A-ha, New Edition, The Monkees...$2–3

TIGER BEAT SUPER SPECIAL PRESENTS THE BOYS OF SUMMER

1986

#2 Thomas Howell, Kirk Cameron, Michael J. Fox, David Lee Roth $1–2

TIME

1979

Dec. 17 The Who cover & feature: Rock's Outer Limits..$3–7

1980

Dec. 22 John Lennon cover & feature: When the Music Died....................................$2–5

1983

July 18 David Bowie cover & feature: Dancing to the Music—David Bowie Rockets Onward $3–6

1985

May 27 Madonna: Why She's Hot..$2–3

1989

Sept. The Rolling Stones cover & feature: Rock Rolls On—Aging Stars Like the Rolling Stones Strut Their Staying Power...$2–4

TIME BARRIER: THE ROCK-AND-ROLL HISTORY MAGAZINE

All issues $2–4

TRAFFIC (New York Tabloid)

1989

June Jimi Hendrix: The Legacy of Jimi Hendrix, The 10 Most Important Guitarists in Rock History $3–6

TRAVOLTA ENCOUNTER

1977

John Travolta Teaches You to Disco, Experience All the Subtle Fires Which Burn Through John's Loves & Hates, Interviews With His Fans, A Special Look at *Grease*, Rare Photos...$2–4

TRAVOLTA FEVER

1977

Special John Travolta Magazine Filled With Color Posters, Life Story, His Tragic Love Affair, His Dancing Secrets...$2–4

TRAVOLTA FEVER 2

1977

Behind-the-scenes *Grease* Photos, Exclusive Interviews With the Bee Gees, Whose Music Moved John Travolta's Soul?, His Secret Diary $2–4

TRIAD

1976

Aug. Paul McCartney Exclusive, Jive With Journey..$2–4

TROUSER PRESS

1974

#1 The Who, Rory Gallagher, King Crimson, Beatle Bootlegs.............................$25–50
#3 The Who Special Including Who's English Discography, Mott the Hoople, Peter Frampton...$20–40
#4 Jeff Beck & the Yardbirds Part II, King Crimson Complete Discography, David Bowie vs. Powerman & the Moneyground...$15–30
#5 English Tour Summer '74, The Complete Yardbirds Part III, The Jimmy Page Era, Ron Wood—My Own Interview, Sparks, Frampton...$15–30

1975

#6 Robert Fripp interview, Robin Trower, Roy Wood's Wizard, The Complete Yardbirds: Part IV $12–25
#7 The Early Animals, Alan Price, Robert Fripp Chats Part II, The Strawbs, The Yardbirds, Rolling Stones...$10–20
#9 Mick Jagger: The Stones on Film—The Reel Stones, The Animals Part III, Curved Air: A Brief Blast, Sparks, John Entwistle...$15–30
#11 Alex Harvey, Fairport Convention, Pink Floyd, Be-bop Delux, Wings, Sweet, Mott $10–20

1976

#12 Roxy Music, Dave Edmunds, New York Rock, Al Stewart, Renaissance, Andy Ellison $10–20
#13 Ray Davies: The Kinks, John Cale, Gentle Giant, Pretty Things, Rory Gallagher, Flamin' Groovies...$10–20

#14 Keith Moon's Split Personality, Genesis, Free, Lou Reed, Michael Brown, Sutherland Brothers & Quiver $10–20
#15 The Feelgoods, Nazareth, Sailor, Boxer, Roy Harper $7–15
#16 Queen: Superband Analyzed, Kevin Ayers in the Bottle, Graham Parker/Rumour Questioned, Steve Hillage..$10–20
#17 ELO, Be-bop Deluxe: A Personal View, Tommy James $6–12

1977

#18 David Bowie: Cleaning Out Mr. Bowie's Closet, John Entwistle Blows His Own Horn, The Rods, The Sex Pistols, Damned, The Clash $6–12
#19 Thin Lizzy, David Bowie: You'll Never Hear, Gentle Giant, Steve Harley, Dave Stewart, Chris Spedding $6–12
#20 Peter Gabriel, Genesis, Eno, David Bowie Part 3, Rick Wakeman, The Babys, The Damned $10–20
#21 Jimmy Page Part I, British Heavy Metal, Kevin Ayers, Peter Hammill, Dave Edmunds, Deaf School..$10–20
#22 Sex Pistols, New Wave, R.I.P., Jimmy Page on the Yardbirds, Small Faces, Nick Lowe, Phil Manzanera...$10–20
#23 Bryan Ferry, Jimmy Page Part 3, Gentle Giant, AC/DC, Blondie, The Rolling Stones, Dwight Twilley...$10–20
#24 Elvis Costello: "I'm an Extraordinary Bitter Person," Boomtown Rats: Playing Music for 1978, Be-bop Deluxe, The Motors, Tom Petty: The Heartbreak Kid....................$5–10

1978

#25 Steve Winwood & Traffic, Graham Parker, The Jam, Iggy Pop, Eddie & the Hot Rods $5–10
#26 Paul McCartney, The Clash, Cheap Trick, Tom Robinson, Syd Barrett...............$5–10
#27 Pete Townshend Cops It: "I Am the Establishment," Hot Rods, Devo $5–10
#28 Pink Floyd: Moonmen Return to Earth, Rezillos, Pere Ubu, Pete Townshend: The Meaning of Life, ELP, Television...$5–10
#29 The Rolling Stones & Others Recalled, The Dictators, Judas Priest, Tom Robinson, The Kink's Dave Advies Talks, Steve Hackett, The Ruttles, Elvis Costello, X-ray Spex.$5–10
#30 Todd Rundgren: Everything You Ever Wanted to Know, David Bowie, Ritchie Blackmore Escapes the Purple Haze, Ian Dury, Buddy Holly, The Flamin' Groovies $5–10
#31 Cheap Trick, Dave Edmunds, Be-bop Deluxe $5–10
#32 Ray Davies/The Kinks, Peter Gabriel, Robert Fripp, Brian Eno, Blondie, The Troggs $5–10
#33 John Entwistle, The Ramones, Joe Perry, Talking Heads, The Cars, The Stranglers, The Sweet..$5–10
#34 Guitarists Special, Thin Lizzy, Kiss, Tom Petty...$5–10
#35 Devo, Guitarist Special, Part II, Buffalo Springfield, John Wetton, UFO, Paley Brothers...$5–10
#36 Mind Games With Lou Reed, Elton John: A Single Man Speaks, Clash: On the Offensive, Captain Beefheart, The Police, Debbie Harry, Pat Travers $5–10

1979

#37 The Who: *The Kids are Alright* Film Preview, The Stiffs in New York, Frank Zappa, 10CC: The Second Coming, Jim Morrison/The Doors: Personal Reminiscences........$5–10
#38 John Lennon: Come Back—John Lennon in Limboland, The Boomtown Rats, Badfinger, The Jam, Boston, Roxy Music, Johnny Rotten, Joe Jackson $5–10
#39 Elvis Costello: Who Pulls the Strings?, Bob Dylan Exclusive Interview, On Tour With Dire Straits, The Clash, Ian Hunter, .999, Sham 69, Ultravox, Siouxsie & The Banshees, Rubinoos $4–8
#40 The Rolling Stones: The New Barbarians—Stone-Free & Rolling: Ron Wood in New York & Keith Richards in Paris, The Ramones, Van Morrison, Stiff Little Fingers, Horslips, A Strange Interlude With Nico...$4–8
#41 The Cars: Ric Ocasek, The 80s' Beach Boys, The Police: Mick Taylor, The Pretenders, The Who, Penetration $4–8
#42 Blondie: Glass Heart Top Charts—Fighting the Sell-out Rumors, Wings, John Cale,

TROUSER PRESS,
1976, #13

TROUSER PRESS,
1976, #12

TROUSER PRESS,
1976, #16

TROUSER PRESS,
1977, #19

TROUSER PRESS,
1977, #24

TROUSER PRESS,
1978, #25

TROUSER PRESS,
1978, #27

TROUSER PRESS,
1978, #28

TROUSER PRESS,
1978, #30

Moon Martin, Devo, Robert Fripp, Rock in Japan Special, Kenny Jones: Facing Up to Life With the Stones..$5–10

#43 David Bowie: Rock 'n' Roll's Own Dashing Dan, Brian Jones: Ten Years After His Death, Ian Dury, Lene Lovich, Bay City Rollers, Rachel Sweet, Todd Rundgren.....$5–10

#44 David Byrne: Talking Heads Face Their Fears, The B-52s: Regressive Rock With a Southern Accent, Thin Lizzy. N.Y. Dolls, Dave Davies Talks About the Kinks..........$4–8

#45 The Police Carry On, Brand X, Joe Jackson, Abba: Invasion from the North, UBU $4–8

1980

#46 *Trouser Press* Remembers the 70s, Rock Deaths of the 70s—Janis Joplin, Jimi Hendrix, Bobby Darin, Etc., Best Albums of the 70s...$4–8

#47 Frank Zappa: The Man Behind the Moustache, Iggy Pop: From Stoogetown to Osterberg, Joe Perry/Aerosmith, Madness, Flying Lizards $4–8

#48 The Clash: Death or Glory?, Tom Petty: If You Really Care, Slits, The Beat, Boomtown Rats, Robin Lane, The Specials, Roy Wood $4–8

#49 Neil Young, Elvis Costello, Fleetwood Mac, Genesis, Inmates, The Searchers ..$5–10

#50 The Ramones Come Home, Marc Bolin Lives, The Jam, Pink Floyd, Gary Numan, Darryl Hall: What are We Fighting For?, Reggae, Cindy Bullens................................$4–8

#51 The Beatles: Have the Bill Wymans Gone Pffft?, The Romantics, Angel City: Martha Lost One of Her Vandellas, The Tourists, Squeeze, Public Image Ltd., Joan Armatrading, Ringo Starr $4–8

#52 Pete Townshend Talks, Alice Cooper: Turning the Kaleidoscope on Friendship, J. Geils, The Motors, The Motels, Telephone, Plastics: Japanese Know-how, The Cure.............$4–8

#53 Dave Davies & the Kinks: Facing the Future, Pete Townshend Interview, Gang of Four, Ian Hunter: Don't Follow the Leader, Blues Band, Women in Rock: Sex & Women & Rock-&-role-playing—Chrissie Hynde, Lene Lovich, Patti Smith, Debbie Harry, Marianne Faithful, Lydia Lunch & Others Speak Out $5–10

#54 The Rolling Stones: Second That Emotion, The Beat, Phil Lynott, Feelies, Undertones, Roxy Music, Residents...$4–8

#55 Bruce Springsteen: "Of Course I Remember You," X, Wreckless Eric, Peter Noone, Peter Gabriel, Devo, Tom Robinson...$4–8

#56 The Cars in Progress, David Bowie: A Good Glass, Joan Jett: Twenty-one Degrees, Dexy's Midnight Runners, Shaun Cassidy in the Devil's Seat, Split Enz, Dire Straits, Jeff Beck, Human League...$4–8

#57 Cheap Trick, The B-52s, Buzzcocks, John Hiatt, AC/DC, The Mo-dettes, Custom Labels $4–8

1981

#58 Gary Numan: Stylistic Synthesist at the Crossroads, Ultravox, Carlene Carter, Captain Beefheart, Stranglers, XTC, The Beat, Michael Des Barres..$4–8

#59 Rockpile: Is This the Last Rock 'n' Roll Band?, The Police at the Top of the Charts, Siouxsie and the Banshees, Try a Little Tenderness, Gang of Four's Revolution Rock, George Thorogood, Bad Manners..$4–8

#60 Send in the Clash: A 15-minute Conversation on Psychological Problems, The Vapors, Grace Slick, Martha & the Muffins, The Stiffs, The Female Teenage Audience Examined: Devils or Angels? $4–8

#61 Elvis Costello: A Look Inside, David Byrne & Brian Eno, The Who's Scrapbook, Steve Winwood, Motorhead, Garland Jeffreys, Shoes, Phil Seymour.......................................$4–8

#62 Debbie Harry/Blondie is Still a Group, Teardrop Explodes, Echo & the Bunnymen, Phil Collins, Squeeze, Utopia, Nazareth, The Yardbirds, Scrapbook, The Jam...................$5–10

#63 Sex Pistols, Adam & the Ants, U2, Heavy Metal $4–8

#64 Tom Petty Keeps His Promise, Lounge Lizards, Steve Marriot, Billy Idol, Rock Magazines Throughout the Years...$4–8

#65 Jim Morrison & the Doors: Why Now?—The Doors Revived, John Entwistle, Spandau Ballet, Adam Ant's Family Tree, Stiff Scrapbook, Southern Punk $4–8

#66 Alice Cooper, Wendy O'Williams: Sleaze in Rock, Sparks, Madness, Southside Johnny, Holly & the Italians, Squeeze, Malcolm McLaren...$4–8

#67 The Pretenders: The Wait is Over—Exclusive Interviews, Bill Nelson: Return of a

TROUSER PRESS,
1979, #37

TROUSER PRESS,
1979, #39

TROUSER PRESS,
1979, #42

TROUSER PRESS,
1979, #44

TROUSER PRESS,
1980, #46

TROUSER PRESS,
1980, #48

TROUSER PRESS,
1980, #50

TROUSER PRESS,
1980, #51

TROUSER PRESS,
1980, #52

Dreamer, The Tubes Take a New Turn, ELO, Kraftwerk, The Cure Talk, the Patti Smith Scrapbook, Ron Wood Remembers $4–8
#68 Bill Wyman, The Go-go's, Greg Kihn, Rock Videos..$4–8

1982

#69 Charm & Deliver: Adam Ant—How to Live on Nothing, The Who, Lene Lovich, Bow Wow Wow, Duran Duran, Tom Verlaine, Thomas Baker..$4–8
#70 Devo Gets Down, Blue Oyster Cult: From a Whisper to a Scream, Paul's Brother Mike McCartney Remembers the Beatles, Lulu, Orchestra Maneuvers $4–8
#71 Genesis Look at Themselves: An Autodiscography, King Crimson: Robert Fripp Starts it Up Again, U2's October Children, Joy Division..$4–8
#72 Talking Heads: He Was Born in the Bronx, Fleshtone's Jimmy Destri, Pete Shelley, Blasters, Led Zeppelin's Greatest Hits..$4–8
#73 The Police: What Next, Ultravox, Waitress, Alan Vega $4–8
#74 Joan Jett: The Ramones Autodiscography, Paul Weller $5–10
#75 Nick Lowe, Ultravox, Simple Minds, Skids Family Tree, John Hiatt, Larry Fast.$4–8
#76 The Squeeze on the Road & on the Way Up, Brian Eno, Human League, Hardcore Punk Across the U.S.A., Split Enz, Romeo Void, Human Switchboard.......................$4–8
#77 Debbie Harry/Blondie: In Their Own Words or Homicide at Home, Jim Morrison: Words & Photos, Dave Edmunds: 15 Years of Rock 'n' Roll, Haircut 100, The Beat.$5–10
#78 The Who: Maximum Rock 'n' Roll Band—The Pre-*Tommy* Years, Jethro Tull Autodiscography, Marshall Crenshaw, Laurie Anderson, Kim Wilde, Stray Cats, German Rock $4–8
#79 The Go-go's, The Motels, X, Sparks Autodiscography...................................$5–10
#80 Adam Ant: But of Mind, Bananarama, Gun Club: Through Another Dimension, Translator, Joe Jackson: A Journey into a Wonderous Land, English Beat, Black Uhuru....$4–8

1983

#81 Peter Gabriel, Iggy Pop, Lords of the New Church $4–8
#82 The Cars' Ric Ocasek Keeps Busy, The Jam: A Fond Farewell, Yaz, Soft Cell, ABC: British Blue-eyed Soul..$4–8
#83 The Jefferson Airplane/Starship, Missing Persons, John Cale, Altered Images $4–8
#84 The Four Sides of the Clash: A Listeners' Guide, Duran Duran, Trio, Rank & File, Doll by Doll, Swollen Monkey $4–8
#85 The Pretenders: Back to Work, Dexy's: The Gospel According to Kevin Rowland, Malcolm McLaren..$4–8
#86 Boy George & Culture Club: It Hurts So Good, Black Flag, Musical Youth, Simple Minds: The Miracle Men, British Pop 1955–1979 ....$4–8
#87 U2, Lene Lovich, Ultravox, The Stranglers, Autodiscography, Wall of Voodoo, INXS, Hot Chocolate...$4–8
#88 The Jam: The Greatest Hits They Won't Let You Buy, R.E.M., Violent Femmes, Pete Shelley: Ditching the Buzzcocks, Berlin: Kinky Sex on the Airwaves $4–8
#89 A Flock of Seagulls: Mersey's New Fab Four, Heaven 17, The Damned Autodiscography, Joe Carrasco, Human League Family Tree, Tears for Fears, Shriekback $4–8
#90 Duran Duran, Grandmaster Flash, Thomas Dolby, XTC, UB40, The Eurythmics, Joan Jett..$4–8

TUFF MAG (Pop & soul poster magazine)

1989
#51 Al B. Sure Exclusive $1–2

TV AND MOVIE SCREEN

1989
Dec. New Kids on the Block, Debbie Gibson, Jon Bon Jovi, Cyndi Lauper, Madonna, Bobby Brown, Bros, Prince, John Cougar, The Who, INXS, The Rolling Stones, The Doobie Brothers, Milli Vanilli, The Bangles, Paul McCartney, Paula Abdul.................$2–3

1990

Feb. New Kids on the Block Special Feature With Tons of Pin-ups, Darlin' Debbie Gibson $2–3

TV GUIDE

1956

#180 Elvis Presley $30–90

1960

#371 Elvis Presley $20–40

1967

#756 The Monkees: The Day the Monkees Rebelled.......................................$12–25

1969

#857 Johnny Cash..$3–6

1970

#892 Glen Campbell...$3–6
#898 Johnny Cash..$3–6
#916 David Cassidy & the Partridge Family $10–20

1971

#947 David Cassidy: David's Teenage World $10–20
#977 The Partridge Family cast cover and feature $10–20
#978 Bobby Sherman $5–10

1972

#507 The Partridge Family's David Cassidy cover and feature.............................$10–20
#530 The Partridge Family $10–20
#990 Sonny and Cher cover and feature $5–10

1973

#559 Sonny & Cher: Their Public & Private Life...$5–10

1974

#1105 Sonny & Cher: The Day it Ended for Sonny & Cher $5–10

1975

#1150 Cher: Without Sonny...$5–10

1976

#1210 Sonny & Cher: Their Love Lives, Donny & Marie Osmond $5–10
#1218 The Beach Boys..$4–8
#1219 Donny & Marie $4–8
#1224 Bob Dylan Today: A Rare Interview...$4–8

1977

#1240 John Travolta: Sweathog, Sex Object, Millionaire $3–6
#1280 Donny & Marie Osmond, "Hee Haw"..$4–8

1978

#1336 John Travolta: "Welcome Back Kotter" $3–6

1979

#1389 The Bee Gees: Coming to Television..$4–8

1981

#1481 Elvis Presley: The Day Elvis Died..$2–5
#1495 John Lennon: One Year Later, TV & the John Lennon Tragedy $2–5

TV GUIDE, 1967, #756

TV GUIDE, 1970, #916

TV GUIDE, 1971, #947

TV GUIDE, 1973, #359

TV GUIDE, 1975, #1150

TV GUIDE, 1976, #1210

TV GUIDE, 1976, #1219

TV GUIDE, 1985, #1665

TV GUIDE, 1990, #1925

1982

#1516 Cast of "Happy Days," Scott Baio: Daddy Dearest..$2–4
#1529 Rick Springfield..$2–4

1983

#1567 Elvis Presley: Judging His Music $2–4
#1569 Fonzie & Linda Purl of "Happy Days" $2–4

1985

#1665 Why Prince & Bruce Springsteen May Beat Michael Jackson.........................$3–6

1987

#1803 Dolly Parton Comes to TV $1–3

1988

#1818 Elvis Presley: "My Life With Elvis" by Priscilla Presley....................................$1–3

1990

#1925 Elvis Presley: Behind-the-scenes Look at the Hot New Series.........................$1–3
#1953 Janet Jackson/Paula Abdul/Madonna: Why Women Now Rule Rock $1–3

TV PICTURE LIFE/METAL EDGE

1989

Jan. Bon Jovi, Anthrax, Cinderella Backstage, Motley Crue Confidential, Poison, Bulletboys, Quiet Riot, includes 25 color pin-ups $2–3
May Bon Jovi: Live in Concert, Kiss, Accept, includes four posters $2–3
Oct. Special 116-page issue with two giant color wall posters, Alice Cooper, Warrent, Bon Jovi, Skid Row, Metallica, Kix, Tesla, White Lion..$2–4
Dec. Issue contains 25 full-page pin-ups, Bon Jovi, Metallica, Faster Pussycat, Warrent & Others..$2–4

1990

Jan. Issue contains 30 pin-ups, Winger, Extreme, Ace Fehley Studio Exclusive, Bon Jovi
....$2–4
Feb. Kiss Exclusive, Skid Row, Danger Danger & Great White Backstage, Bon Jovi $2–4
Mar. Issue contains 30 pin-ups, The Biggest Issue Ever, Warrent: Road Stories, Hurricane, Paul Stanley, Bon Jovi, Dangerous Toys, Metallica, Def Leppard................................$2–4

TV PICTURE LIFE/ROCK COLOR CENTERFOLDS

1984

Nov. Issue includes poster & pin-ups, Boy George & Culture Club Special Section, Boy George Biography & History, Duran Duran, Michael Jackson, Sting, Cyndi Lauper, David Bowie, Rick Springfield, The Go-go's, Madonna, Yes...$2–4

TV SUPERSTAR

1978

Oct. Special Kiss Pin-up Book Edition, Kiss Vital Statistics, The Truth About Gene's Tongue, Peter: The Wild Man Behind the Cat Mask, Ace: His Search for the Perfect Guitar, Paul: What Turns Him On?, Kiss Puzzle, The Komplete Kisstory: From Beginning to Forever, also includes—Peter Frampton, Shaun Cassidy, Leif Garrett, K.C., The Bee Gees, Andy Gibb & Abba...$15–30

1979

Dec. Kiss Mania Special, with 11 full-color pin-ups, Gene Simmons' Outrageous Scrapbook, 99 Fax & Fantasies About Kiss, Kiss Speaks: A Krazy Dictionary, Kiss History: Then & Now, Kiss Answers the Questions, Cheap Trick Mini-special.....................$10–20

U

UNIQUE
1990
Sept./Oct. Alice Cooper cover & feature story $2–4

UPBEAT (The Miami News Magazine)
1977
Feb. 4 Patti Smith: "Don't Wanna Be No Cult Star" $5–10
1989
Nov. Issue contains 10 giant color wall posters: 16″ × 22″, Ziggy Marley & the Melody Makers, Kool Moe Dee, Lisa Lisa & Cult Jam, Mica Paris, Prince, Cookie Crew, LL Cool J, Bobby Brown, Twin Hype, Summer Rae $2–4

US SPECIAL: A TRIBUTE TO JOHN LENNON
1980
John & Yoko's Last Photo Sessions, His Life Story $3–6

US SPECIAL REPORT ON THE ROLLING STONES: THE LAST TOUR
1981
Contains hundreds of photos including a special 16-page foldout, Exclusive Mick Jagger Interview, 19 Years of Explosive Rock-&-Roll $6–12

US WEEKLY
1978
Feb. 2 The Queens of Rock—Linda Ronstadt, Joni Mitchell, Carly Simon & Stevie Nicks $5–10
Oct. 3 Mick Jagger: Rock's Menace is Now Calmer, A Doting Dad and a One-woman Man $3–6
1979
June 29 The Village People $2–4
Oct. 16 Blondie/Debbie Harry: Ex-Playboy Bunny $4–8
1980
Dec. 9 Marie Osmond cover & feature story: Saucy & Sexy—Marie at 21, Family & Men Play Second Fiddle, David Bowie Tells Almost All, The Other Women in Kenny Rogers Life, Kim Carnes $3–6

US, 1978, 2–21

US, 1978, 10–3

US, 1979, 6–29

US, 1979, 10–16

US, 1981, 11–10

US, 1981, 12–8

US, 1984, 5–7

*US, ROLLING STONE
SPECIAL*, 1987

*US, TRIBUTE TO JOHN
LENNON*, 1980

1981

Nov. 10 Mick Jagger: Marriage Turns Him to Stone $2–4
Dec. 8 John Lennon & Yoko Ono: All They Needed Was Love..................................$3–6

1984

May 7 Michael Jackson's Women...$2–4

1989

June 12 Madonna: So Hot Exclusive $2–4

V

VANITY FAIR
1990
Apr. Madonna cover and photos: White Heat, Madonna Undresses $3–6
1992
Feb. Mick Jagger cover and feature: Jagger's Edge..$2–4

VIBRATIONS
1968
Mar. #7 Janis Joplin, Traffic, Jimi Hendrix, Bob Dylan Returns, The Kinks, Jim Morrison Arrested..$30–60
June Jimi Hendrix, Pete Townshend Six-Page Special With Rare Pix $30–60
1970
#32 Crosby, Stills, Nash & Young, Abbie Hoffman..$10–20

VIDEOGRAPHY
1977
Dec. Cafe Manhattan, Interview With Time, Inc. $1–2
1980
Jan. Rock Justice..$1–2
Apr. Todd Rundgren Opens His New Video Studio..$2–4

VIDEO ROCK STARS
1986
Summer #1 A-ha Takes on the World, A Heart to Heart Talk With Corey, Whan: Go-goes as George Michaels Solos, The Secret Life of Julian Lennon, Prince on Parade, Mr. Mister: Welcome to Their World, Duran Duran Reunite, Billy Idol, Madonna, INXS, Tears for Fears, Motley Crue, Howard Jones, Bryan Adams, Eurythmics, Heart $2–4
All other issues $2–4

W

WEIGHT WATCHERS MAGAZINE
1978
Apr. Marie Osmond cover & feature story: She Grows Up & Trims Down $4–8

WELCOME BACK BEATLES
Issues featuring mainly the Beatles...$3–6
Issues featuring covers & feature stories on Kiss..$10–20

WHAT'S HOT
1987
Aug. #1...$2–4
Sept. #2 Club Nouveau, The Disorderly Fat Boys, Grandmaster Flash, Teen Dream, The
System, Simply Red, Shirley Murdock $2–4

WHO PUT THE BOMP
All issues...$5–15

WHO'S WHO IN THE TEEN WORLD
1971
Sept. #3 Special Personal Life Stories Issue—David Cassidy, The Brady Bunch, The Par-
tridge Family, James Taylor, Bob Dylan, Dionne Warwick, Cass Elliot, Melanie, Jackie
DeShannon, Diana Ross, Tommy Roe, Billy Joe Royal, Tina Turner, John Lennon, Neil
Young, Donny Osmond, Susan Dey, Michael Jackson & the Jackson Five, Elvis Pres-
ley..$10–20

WINNER
1986
Oct. #1 Madonna: Can Her Celebrity Marriage Work?, Charlie Sexton $3–6
Nov. #2 David Lee Roth: Taking Off His Warpaint, Rock-&-Roll Censorship, Cyndi Lauper,
REM, Psychedelic Furs $2–4

WOMAN'S DAY
1978
June 14 Marie Osmond cover & feature: Marie Osmond's Summer Top & Five Other Items
to Knit & Crochet, Directions for Her Hairdo...$4–8

WORDS & MUSIC (Poppy Press)

1972

June In Defense of Paul & Linda McCartney/With Exclusive Photos, Charlie Waitts: Rolling Stones' Drummer, Kris Kristofferson, The Guess Who, Al Green..................$5–10

July B.B. King & Hot Tuna, David Bowie: Phallus in Pigtail & Cosmic Boogie, Gladys Knight & the Pips: Very Together..$5–10

Sept. Elvis Presley: The Greatest Money-making Performer the Pop World Has Ever Seen, Buffalo Springfield..$5–10

Nov. John Lennon & Yoko Ono Petition: Anti-Deportation, Elton John & Bernie Taupin: In Retrospect, Loggins & Messina, Argent: All Together Now, Woodstock: A Music Community, The Staple Singers, Special Portfolio of Rock Couples—June & Marc Bolan, John & Yoko, Bianca & Mick Jagger, Ringo, Todd Rundgren & Bebe Buel, Rod Stewart, Ike & Tina Turner...$7–15

1973

Jan. T. Rex: The Boogie Man Cometh, Rock 'n' Roll 1973, The Hollies: Quiet, Dedicated Energy, LaBelle: The Girls Keep on Keeping On, Roxy Music, Slade, Mother Earth $5–10

Feb. John Denver: A Man for All Seasons, Led Zeppelin: Zep Have Set Up Their Own Musical World, Johnny Nash is Here Again..$5–10

Mar. Matt the Hoople: Up & Raving, The Byrds: New Directions $4–8

WORDS & MUSIC (U.S. Publishing)

1987

Aug. #1 Bruce Springsteen: Writing His Way to the Top, Chuck Berry: Rock-&-Roll Hall of Fame, Bruce Hornsby $3–6

WORD UP

All issues..$1–3

WOW

1989

Holiday issue contains 18 huge color pin-ups—The New Kids on the Block, Bon Jovi $2–3

All other issues $2–3

Y & Z

YOUNG MISS
1979
Feb. A New Look at Donny & Marie Osmond $3–6

ZING
1989
Dec. Bon Jovi's Secret Identities, James Dean: The Legend Lives On, Debbie Gibson, New Kids on the Block, River Phoenix, Johnny Depp: The Legend Begins, Madonna.......$2–3
All other issues $2–3

ZOO WORLD (Tabloid)
1972
#7 Creedence Clearwater Revival, Billy Joel: The Kid from Spaghetti Drive............$6–12
Aug. 28 #15 Rod Stewart: Never a Dull Moment, Peter Frampton, Argent, Flo & Eddie, Blue Oyster Cult, Wishbone Ash $5–10
Sept. 11 #16 Chicago, Kim Foley, Sha Na Na, Argent, Bob Seger............................$5–10
Sept. 30 #17 T. Rex, Slade Alive, Jefferson Airplane's Long John Silver, Commander Cody, Ted Nugent, Rory Gallagher, Billy Squier, Fritz the Cat...$5–10
Oct. 14 #18 The Kinks, The Band, Martin Mull, ELP, Lorna Luft, Crazy Horse, Quicksilver, Fillmore Flicks..$5–10
Oct. 28 #19 Three Dog Night, Dr. Hook, Slade, Eagles, De Shannon $5–10
Nov. 11 #20 Marc Bolan, Jeff Beck, Yes, Buffy St. Marie, Grand Funk Railroad....$5–10
Nov. 25 #21 J. Geils Band, Black Sabbath, Michael Jackson, Pentangle, Paul Kantner, The Doobies, Harvey Mandel...$5–10
Dec. 9 #22 Cat Stevens, John Prine, Johnny Rivers, Dion, Bo Diddley, Ursa Major.....$5–10
Dec. 12 #23 War, David Bowie, Black Sabbath, Deep Purple, Nazareth, Fabian, Donna Fargo $5–10

1973
Jan. 6 #24 Rita Coolidge, Humble Pie, Delanie & Bonnie, Richie Havens, War, Elvis Presley on Tour..$5–10
Jan. 20 #25 The Grateful Dead's Europe '72, Lou Reed, Duane Allman, Grand Funk Railroad, Mott the Hoople, Janis Joplin Biography...$5–10
Feb. 3 #26 Rick Nelson's Garden Party, Roxy Music, John Entwistle, Pete Townshend Solo, Ten Years After, Glen Campbell...$5–10
Feb. 17 #27 The Rolling Stones: More Hot Rocks, Neil Diamond's Hot August Night, Captain Beefheart, Dr. John...$6–12
Mar. 29 #29 Elton John, Mick Jagger, Soupy Sales, Al Green, Frank Zappa, Edgar Winter, Melanie, Bonnie Raitt..$5–10

Apr. 12 #30 The Beach Boys in Holland, The Guess Who, Yoko Ono, Rita Coolidge, Dusty Springfield, Uriah Heep, Genesis, Nils Lofgren..$6–12
Apr. 26 #31 Three Dog Night, The Fifth Dimension, Frank Zappa, Mark Almond..$5–10
May 10 #32 Rory Gallagher, Rare Earth, Tom T. Hall, Mac Davis, Black Kangaroo, Capt. Beefheart..$5–10
May 24 #33 Around the World With Three Dog Night, The 5th Dimension, Black Oak Arkansas, Paul Anka $5–10
June 7 #34 Jefferson Airplane: Thirty Seconds Over Winterland, Alice Cooper: The Sicker You are the Sicker We'll Get, Engelbert Humperdinck, Seals & Crofts, Brownsville Station, Humble Pie..$6–12
June 21 #35 Paul McCartney & Wings, Chicago, John Fogerty, Sonny & Cher: The Beat Still Goes On, Flo & Eddie, David Bromberg, John Hammond, Argent, Elton John......$5–10
July 5 #36 Paul Simon: There Goes Simon, Jerry Lee Lewis, Stevie Wonder, The Sweet, Sandy Denny, Carole King, The Byrds..$5–10
#37 Curtis Mayfield: Back to the World, Linda Lovelace, The Incredible String Band, Alvin Lee & Led Zeppelin's Jimmy Page, Iggy Pop, Peter Frampton, Anne Murray, Earl Scruggs, The New York Dolls, David Bowie, Faces, The Eagles $6–12
Aug. 2 #38 The Carpenters, The Bee Gees, King Crimson, "Jesus Christ Superstar," The Hollies, Simon Turner May be Replacing David Cassidy on "The Partridge Family".....$6–12
Aug. 16 #39 Leon Russell Live, Dick Clark, Doobie Brothers, Status Quo $5–10
Aug. 30 #40 Cat Stevens, Rod Stewart: Cockerel-Haired Working Class Hero, Humble Pie, Lee Michaels, Manfred Mann's Earth Band..$5–10
Sept. 13 #41 Elvis Presley: How Does He Keep His Sanity?, Smokey Robinson & the Miracles, Rod McKuen, The Eagles Shoot it Out, The Newport Festival $6–12
Sept. 27 #42 Janis Joplin: The Drugs, the Sex & Everything, David Cassidy Asks: "What the Hell am I Doing?," Savoy Brown, The Allman Brothers: Pride of the South, Tanya Tucker, Herman & the Hermits $10–20
#43 Rick Nelson: Living With Himself, Janis Joplin: Buried Alive, Jethor Tull Calls it Quits, John Denver: "I'm Not David Bowie, Alice Cooper or Mick Jagger"..........$10–20
Oct. 25 #44 Bette Midler: "I Want to be the Most Desired Woman on Earth," Cass Elliot: "Don't Call Her Mama Anymore," Gene Vincent: A Be-Bop Tragedy, Marvin Gaye, Hawkwind..$6–12
#45 Mick Jagger: The Rolling Stones' Goats Head Soup, Alice Cooper...................$7–15
Nov. 22 #46 Mick Jagger: The Biography Part I, Judy Collins: The Last Folk Singer, Elton John: "Goodbye Yellow Brick Road," Roberta Flack...$7–15
Dec. 6 #47 Elton John: Dedicated to the New York Mets, The Who "Quadrophenia," Mick Jagger Biography Part II, Gilbert O'Sullivan, The Wailers.........................$6–12
Dec. 20 #48 The Who's Pete Townshend Explains Quadrophenia, The New York Dolls, Dave Mason, Tina Turner, Red Buddah $7–15

1974

Jan. 3 #49 Alice Cooper, Dolls, Todd Rundgren, Dick Clark, David Essex, J. Geils, The Jesus Christ Superstory, Moondog, Ringo & God..$6–12
Jan. 17 #50 Music Awards Issue, Bob Dylan, Elvis Presley, Dr. John, Rolling Stones, Elton John, John Mayall: The Jazz-blues Decade, ELO, Taj Mahal, Blackfoot Sue, Gregg Allman, Bryan Ferry, Gallagher $5–10
Jan. 31 #51 The Grateful Dead on Tour, Roy Clark, Johnny Rodrigues, Bobby Darin Dead at 37, Bob Dylan $6–12
Feb. 11 #52 Black Oak Arkansas to the Rescue, Steve Miller, James Gang, Alvin Lee, ELO, BTO $5–10
Feb. 23 #53 Bob Dylan Part I, Dylan & the Band, Boston, Lou Reed, Labelle, Dave Mason $5–10
Mar. 14 #54 Bob Dylan, Bill Graham: The Inside Story, Commander Cody, Todd Rundgren, Carly Simon, Joni Mitchell, Coryell, Phil Ochs $5–10
Mar. 28 #55 Rod Stewart: Rare Bird in California, Liza Minelli, Alice Cooper & Johnny Mathis, Marshall Tucker Band...$5–10
Apr. 11 #56 The Beatles: Reunion Spring of '75, Canned Heat, Grand Funk, Rolling Stones, Yes, Chick Corea, Sandy Denny, Mama Lion: She Don't Sing Through Her Nipples, Jackie DeShannon..$7–15

#57 The Grand Funk Phenomenon: Grand Funk at the Ole Opry, Crosby, Stills, Nash & Young Reunion, Janis Joplin Insurance Trial: Bored Alive, Little Richard, Lynyrd Skynyrd, NRBQ, Steve Miller, Three Dog Night, Lou Reed, Slade, Aerosmith, Barbra Streisand $7–15

#58 Chicago: Somehow Some Things Change, B.J. Thomas, Foghat, Johnny Winters— Much More Than Survival, Oregon, Argent, Queen, Pointer Sisters, Grace Slick, Hot Tuna $6–12

#59 Steely Dan Madness, Linda Ronstadt interview, The Eagles on the Border, Herb Alpert, Country Joe, John Stewart $5–10

#60 Ringo & His Flick, The Kinks, Manfred Mann, Moby Grape, The Rolling Stones Flick: What Really Happened, Renaissance, Freddy Fender, Melanie, Kiki Dee, Helen Reddy $6–12

#61 Isaac Hayes, The Secret Lives of Buffy Ste. Marie, Bob Dylan, Bob Seger, Arlo Guthrie, Hot Tuna, Susi Quatro, Janis Ian, The Carpenters...$5–10

#62 Leon Russell: Hank Wilson Never Left, Maria Muldaur: Cactus is Her Friend, At Home With Arlo Guthrie, Tanya Tucker, Farewell to Duke Ellington, Robin Trower $5–10

#63 Paul McCartney & Peggy Lee, Sly Stone, At Home With Harry Chapin, Willie Nelson, Chuck Mangione, Persuasions, Joe Cocker, The Who, Jerry Garcia...........................$5–10

#64 The Electric Flag, David Bowie in '74, Elvis Presley, Waylon Jennings, Elton John $5–10

#65 Al Green, Gordon Lightfoot, Marvin Gaye, Crosby, Stills, Nash & Young: The Second Coming, Asleep at the Wheel, The Grateful Dead, Steeleye Span, 10CC $4–8

#66 Howard Stein: Rock Promoter, Bad Company, Jimi Hendrix: Setting the Record Straight, Bobby Bare, Kiss Just for Fun, Kansas, Bob Dylan, Dana Gillespie.............$4–8

#67 Loggins & Messina, John Denver, ELP, Joni Mitchell, The Tommy James Story $4–8

#68 The Secret of the Beatles, Beatlemania: The Second Decade................................$4–8

#69 The Pointer Sisters: Ain't Gonna Stop Now, Traffic '74, The Band After Bob Dylan, Martha Reeves, Barbi Benton, The Andrew Sisters, Peter Noone $5–10

#70 Edgar Winter, Bachman-Turner Overdrive, Beach Boys: Another Endless Summer, Stevie Wonder, Wakeman, Keith Moon, Lou Reed, Motown's Number One Woman......$5–10

#71 Marvin Gaye Live: The End of the Road, Bonnie Raitt, Steppenwolf, Elton John: Hercules Unchained in Texas, John Lennon vs. the Fools on the Hill...............................$4–8

#72 Elton John & Billy Jean King, Cousin Brucie, Suzi Quatro & The Who, Tiny Tim, Randy Newman, T. Rex $4–8

#74 David Bowie: The Man Who Souled the World, Jefferson Starship Still Gets You There on Time, George Harrison & Ravi Shankar, The Allmans Hit the Road, The Rolling Stones: Ain't Too Proud to Rock 'n' Roll, Average White Band, Ron Wood......................$5–10

#75 Barry White, Touring With Frank Zappa, Sgt. Pepper on Broadway, John Enwistle..$4–8

ZYGOTE (Tabloid)

1970

#3 Creedence Clearwater Revival interview, John Mayall Live, String Band, Ray Charles, Felix Pappalardi, The Grateful Dead..$10–20

#4 Crosby, Stills, Nash & Young, Jefferson Airplane, The Grateful Dead, Jethro Tull interview..$10–20

#5 Miles Davis, The Band, Steppenwolf, Mick Jagger: Ned Kelly $10–20

#6 Chicago, Grand Funk Railroad, Procol Harum, Charles Manson, The Kinks......$10–20

ROCK CONCERT POSTERS

THE FAMILY DOG

BILL GRAHAM PRESENTS

THE NEW FILLMORE SERIES

RUSS GIBB PRESENTS

JIM SALZER PRESENTS

PHILIP CUSHWAY LITHOS

Introduction

Poster Art

BUYING AND SELLING ROCK POSTERS

Classic rock concert poster collecting is a small but growing specialty field. Originally used as an inexpensive method of advertising shows, these posters are now found at garage sales, flea markets, and record conventions. Other sources are fan clubs, fan conventions, and fanzines, many of which have a classified section offering items to buy, sell, or trade.

The widest selection can be found at mail order and retail poster companies specializing in rock concert posters. One such company is ArtRock (located at 115B Mission Street, San Francisco, CA 94103). They specialize in purchasing entire collections and also offer a considerable selection of posters for sale. They will send you a free full-color catalogue if you write to them and mention this book, *The Official Identification and Price Guide to Rock and Roll*.

Happy hunting!

DETERMINING POSTER VALUE

There are many factors that contribute to a poster's value. Of course, interest in the bands featured, quantities available, design, and condition all affect a poster's value as a collectible. Posters featuring bands with long-lasting appeal usually have more value. Hard-to-get posters, especially those that are part of a numbered set, are always more valuable. A beautiful poster done by a name artist would obviously have more value as well.

Many posters are very difficult to price since rare items tend to be traded rather than sold. Essentially, however, a poster is worth what someone is willing to pay for it. Consequently, the values listed here are benchmark prices only. As this is one of the first comprehensive price guides of its kind, response and feedback from poster dealers, private collectors, auctions, etc., will greatly refine the pricing in subsequent editions.

There were more posters published than are listed here. To inquire about these, or to acquire information regarding buying, selling, grading, etc., please call the **Poster Collector Hotline** at (415) 255-9238 10:00 AM to 6:00 PM Pacific Standard Time, Monday through Friday.

San Francisco

Poster Art

The classic rock music posters of the 1960s originated in psychedelic San Francisco. It all began with the music, of course. In 1965, as part of the English and American rock 'n' roll renaissance, the San Francisco rock bands emerged. With the increasing confidence and ambition of the musicians, and the advent of promoters, the San Francisco rock scene grew from informal sessions, advertised by word of mouth, to large-scale, nationally famous events. During the high years of 1966 and 1967 dances were presented at numerous halls and clubs, but the Fillmore and the Avalon were the first and most prominent venues.

Beginning in early 1966 dance concerts were held at these halls from two to five nights a week for several years. The Family Dog organization, directed by Chet Helms, produced dances at the old Avalon Ballroom until the end of 1968. During the latter months of 1967 there was also a Family Dog ballroom in Denver, Colorado. The other producer was Bill Graham, who first regularly presented dances at the Fillmore Auditorium, and later at a larger San Francisco hall, called Fillmore West, until July 1971. Graham also produced events at other Bay Area auditoriums, such as Winterland, and in New York City at the Fillmore East. It was through the patronage of these two producers that poster art developed into a unique, highly creative art form.

The uniqueness of these posters derives from two major cultural factors: the special conditions of its patronage, and the availability and usage of mind-expanding drugs, such as marijuana and LSD. The music was part of the local hippie culture, which provided its financial support. With such an audience everything was permitted, and the artists were given almost complete artistic freedom. These posters were thus liberated from the usual restrictions related to commercial advertising. And the first artists, and many others, emerged from the scene. They were mostly unschooled, and they were involved in the high times. Feeling free, they put their intensified vision, feelings, and enthusiasm into their art, and pushed it to the limit.

Suddenly the poster became a very popular art form, the first medium of psychedelic art (excepting light shows), and the leading edge of commercial art. Among the hippies the rock posters were appreciated for their art and also as a matter of identification with the new culture. People took them off the streets and hung them on their walls. The posters were instant art, and they were free—given away at the ballrooms, and at various locations around the Bay Area.

The Family Dog and Bill Graham Presents produced a total of about 150 and 300 posters, respectively; an average of about one per week each. This constitutes the main body of the San Francisco poster art. But the major artists also produced designs for other dance halls, and as art for sale as well. A conservative estimate of all the posters designed by the Fillmore and Avalon artists alone, up to 1971, would come to about 550. These two ballrooms printed editions ranging from 300 at first, then 1500, then 5000, and almost all the posters were reprinted for retail sales. An enormous quantity of high quality graphic art flowed out of San Francisco during the five and a half years of the poster movement.

Like the rock music it served, poster art remains as a record of the consciousness of some of the most perceptive, intelligent, and creative people of that generation. The viewer who cares to enter into this art, who is willing to invest something of the time, the openness, and the imagination that the artists have invested in their work will come away positively affected by these delightful, beautiful, and sometimes profound works of art.

With the closing of the Fillmore in July 1971, the golden era of rock poster art came to an end in the quiet depth of David Singer's art. But the early, visually intense, assertive poster style had long since made its mark. Local newspapers and journals began reporting on the art in late 1966, and national coverage soon followed. In the summer of 1967 *Life* magazine did a seven-page article on "The Great Poster Wave," which included photos of Wes Wilson, Stanley Mouse, Victor Moscoso, and Rick Griffin posed among their art. The article began, "Suddenly posters are the national hangup. They serve as low-cost paintings, do-it-yourself wallpaper, comic Valentines, or propaganda for such things as Batman and rye bread. Posters in every dimension and description, from playing card size to billboard blowups, are being plastered across the U.S. More than a million a week are gobbled up by avid visual maniacs who apparently abhor a void." Filling the void, indeed. The expansive hippie aesthetic of "MORE!" had already begun its surge over the clean norms of fashion and behavior, from costume and interior decoration to dropout lifestyles.

Personality posters, the enlarged photos of movie stars and other cultural heroes, had been popular for several years, but it was the San Francisco art that created the poster craze. The graphic style of rock posters became popular within and without the rock music culture. A lot of mediocre art was generated, but also some excellent poster artists developed around the music centers of America, some of whom modeled their art on one or another of the San Francisco artists. The most notable subcenters of poster art were Los

Angeles; Austin, Texas; and Detroit, Michigan. And like the local psyche-delic music, the art went overseas: London had a poster scene, and San Francisco posters were seen on walls in Europe and Australia. Even Cuban political posters were affected.

In straight commercial art it was primarily the brilliant patterns and dense lettering—derived from Wes Wilson's style—which were adopted. These el-ements became the stereotype of "turned on" graphic art. Bright pattern, di-luted from its psychedelic origin, was useful in projecting that happy, expansive mood which supposedly stimulates consumers. And the unreadable lettering was, of course, adjusted for non-psychedelicized eyes. It took a cou-ple of years, but eventually these stylistic devices were commonly seen in public print advertising. Such ads appeared mostly in newspapers and popular periodicals, often related to fashion-dominated products, such as the apparel, automotive, and music recording industries. But they also appeared in sober professional journals.

In the 1950s, the era of the gray flannel suit and the buttoned-down collar, commercial graphic art had become increasingly dominated by the use of photographs and a simple typeface selected from a printer's catalogue. The poster craze inspired a renewed interest in unique, handmade graphic art. Ev-ery graphic style since the 1890s, the first heyday of the poster, was revived, and scores of books, covering every significant artist and aspect of graphics, were published. Besides the retail poster outlets, art galleries specializing in turn-of-the-century posters flourished. Most important, it re-established graphic design as an art form. Handmade graphic art became the standard of the industry, exploiting other techniques, such as airbrush, and lending itself to later styles, such as Punk in the '70s, and the Neo-Deco of the '80s.

Walter Medeiros, 1991

Art historian Walter Medeiros began researching San Francisco rock poster art in 1971. In 1976 he organized a retrospective exhibition of San Francisco rock posters at the San Francisco Museum of Modern Art, and has served as consultant for other exhibitions and for several books, including The Art of Rock. *He is a lecturer and custodian of The Archive of Counterculture Art in Berkeley, California.*

The Family Dog

The Family Dog name originated in late 1965, when four "hippies" who shared a house, and a few dogs, put on the first San Francisco rock 'n' roll dances. They retired after three dances, and some acquaintances later put on a couple of events using that name before Chet Helms adopted it in February 1966. Helms put on four dances at the Fillmore Auditorium before settling into the old Avalon Ballroom, where he operated until December 1968. From September through December 1967, the Family Dog also presented dances in Denver, Colorado.

Wes Wilson produced the Family Dog posters for about the first four months, generally under the art direction of Helms. During the following year, while Wilson continued working for Bill Graham Presents, the Family Dog provided the opportunity for four other outstanding artists to develop. Alton Kelley and Stanley "Mouse" Miller, working together as Mouse Studios, used the attractive power of images to provide various graphic "hits"— comic, illicit, bizarre, heroic, beautiful, etc.—which their audience could relate to. Victor Moscoso exploited techniques with form and color to create engaging optical effects. Cartoonist Rick Griffin evolved a powerful graphic style involving commonplace imagery and various levels of symbolism. These "first five" artists established the standards of imagination and craftsmanship for subsequent artists. Among the many artists later commissioned by the Family Dog, Robert Fried and Robert Schnepf closely matched the artistic quality of the first five. All of these artists, except Schnepf, also produced a few posters for Bill Graham Presents (BGP).

FD1   "Tribal Stomp" by Wes Wilson. 2/19/66
           Jefferson Airplane, Big Brother & The Holding Co.
           1/c: Black (14" x 20.5")
           Black and outline lettering with illustration of Indians on horseback
           on white background
           Poster...$50-500 / Handbill...$50-100

FD2   "King Kong" by Wes Wilson and Chet Helms. 2/26/66
           Great Society, Grass Roots, Big Brother & The Holding Co.,
           Quicksilver Messenger Service
           2/c: Orange, Black (14" x 20")
           Duotone photo of gorilla on orange background;
           First appearance of Family Dog logo
           Poster...$30-300 / Handbill...$50-100

FD3   "Butterfield Man" by Wes Wilson. 3/25-27/66
           Paul Butterfield Blues Band, Quicksilver Messenger Service
           1/c: Black (14" x 20.5")
           White lettering with monochrome photo of man on black background
           with white border
           Poster...$30-300 / Handbill...$50-100

FD4   "Love Dancers" by Wes Wilson. 4/8-9/66
           Love, Sons Of Adam, Big Brother & Charlatans
           1/c: Black (14" x 20.5")
           Black lettering and illustration of dancing couple on
           white background
           Poster...$30-300 / Handbill...$50-100

FD5   "Baby Jesus" by Wes Wilson. 4/22-23/66
           Blues Project, Great Society
           3/c: Blue, Red, Black (14" x 20.5")
           Black lettering and Family Dog logo on stars and stripes background
           Poster...$30-300 / Handbill...$30-75

FD6   "Sin Dance" by Wes Wilson. 4/29-30/66
           Grass Roots, Sons Of Adam, Big Brother & The Holding Co.
           3/c: Green, Black, Red (14" x 20")
           Black "snake" lettering surrounding green woman on red background
           Poster...$200-400 / Handbill...$30-50

FD7   "Euphoria" by Wes Wilson. 5/6-7/66
           Daily Flash, Rising Sons, Big Brother & The Holding Co.,
           Charlatans
           2/c: Red, Black (14" x 20.5")
           Green and black design on white background
           Poster...$30-300 / Handbill...$30-50

FD8   "Laugh Cure" by Wes Wilson. 5/13-14/66
           Blues Project, Sons Of Adam, Quicksilver Messenger Service
           2/c: Red, Black (14" x 20.5")
           Red and black design on white background
           Poster...$30-300 / Handbill...$30-50

FD9   "Hupmobile 8" by Wes Wilson. 5/20-22/66
Love, Captain Beefheart & His Magic Band,
Big Brother & The Holding Co.
2/c: Green, Black (14" x 20.5")
Black lettering with monochrome photo of woman on green background
Poster...$30-300 / Handbill...$30-50

FD10   "Hayfever" by Wes Wilson. 5/27-28/66
Leaves, Grass Roots, Grateful Dead
2/c: Gold, Brown (14" x 20.5")
Gold and brown lettering on white background
Poster...$30-300 / Handbill...$75-100

FD11   "Stone Facade" by Victor Moscoso. 6/3-4/66
Grass Roots, Big Brother & The Holding Co., Buddha From Muir Beach
1/c: Black (13" x 20.5")
Black and white lettering on monochrome photo of gargoyle
Poster...$30-300 / Handbill...$50-100

FD12   "The Quick and the Dead" by Wes Wilson. 6/10-11/66
Grateful Dead, Quicksilver Messenger Service, New Tweedy Brothers
1/c: Black (14" x 20.5")
White lettering and illustration of skeleton on black background with
white border
Poster...$30-300 / Handbill...$50-100

FD13   "Red Bull" by Stanley Mouse. 6/17-18/66
Captain Beefheart & His Magic Band, Oxford Circle
2/c: Red, Black (14" x 20.5")
White lettering and illustration of ox on red background with white border
Poster...$30-300 / Handbill...$50-100

FD14   "Zig-Zag" by Mouse & Kelley. 6/24-25/66
Big Brother & The Holding Co., Quicksilver Messenger Service
2/c: Blue, Gold (14" x 20")
Gold lettering with illustration of blue Zig Zag Man on cream background
Poster...$40-400 / Handbill...$50-100

FD15   "Wonderland" by Wes Wilson. 7/1-3/66
Grass Roots, Daily Flash, Sopwith Camel
2/c: Pink, Magenta (14" x 20.5")
Magenta lettering and monochrome photo of figure
on pink op background
Poster...$30-300 / Handbill...$40-80

FD16   "Keep California Green" by Mouse & Kelley. 7/8-10/66
Sir Douglas Quintet, Everpresent Fullness
2/c: Green, Brown (14" x 20.5")
Green lettering with illustration of Smokey the Bear on white background
Poster...$30-300 / Handbill...$40-80

FD17A   "Odd One" by Mouse & Kelley / Franz Stuck. 7/15-16/66
           <u>Love, Big Brother & The Holding Company</u>
           1/c: Red (14" x 20")
           Magenta lettering and monochrome photo of woman on white background
           This dance was cancelled and most of the posters and handbills destroyed
           Poster...$200-300 / Handbill...$60-80

FD17   "Snake Lady" by Mouse & Kelley / Franz Stuck. 7/22-23/66
           <u>Jefferson Airplane, Great Society</u>
           2/c: Metallic Gold, Purple (14" x 20")
           Purple lettering and duotone photo of woman on
           metallic gold background
           Poster...$60-300 / Handbill...$60-80

FD18   "Voice of Music" by Mouse & Kelley. 7/28-30/66
           <u>Bo Diddley, Quicksilver Messenger Service</u>
           3/c: Red, Orange, Peach (14" x 19.5")
           Red lettering with illustration of Nipper, the RCA dog,
           on peach background
           Poster...$30-150 / Handbill...$60-80

FD19   "Dollar Bill" by Mouse & Kelley. 8/5–6/66
           <u>Bo Diddley, Sons Of Adam, Big Brother & The Holding Co., Oxford Circle</u>
           1/c: Black (20" x 8.5")
           Green lettering with Family Dog logo in Federal Reserve note format
           Poster...$30-150 / Handbill...$60-80

FD20   "Men in a Rowboat" by Mouse & Kelley. 8/5-7/66
           <u>Bo Diddley, Sons of Adam, Little Walter</u>
           Split fountain: Yellow, Red, Blue, Green (12.5" x 20")
           Blue and white lettering in configuration of yin yang with illustration
           of longshoremen in boat on split fountain background
           Poster...$200-400 / Handbill...$70-100

FD21   "Earthquake" by Mouse & Kelley. 8/12-13/66
           <u>Bo Diddley, Big Brother & The Holding Co.</u>
           2/c: Yellow, Black (14" x 20.5")
           Red lettering and monochrome photo of levelled building on blue
           background with red border
           Poster...$30-200 / Handbill...$70-100

FD22   "Grateful Dead" by Mouse & Kelley. 8/19-20/66
           <u>Grateful Dead, Sopwith Camel</u>
           2/c: Yellow, Black (14" x 20.5")
           Black lettering with illustration of Frankenstein on yellow background
           with white border
           Poster...$30-200 / Handbill...$70-100

FD23   "Merry Old Souls" by Mouse & Kelley. 8/26-27/66
           <u>Captain Beefheart & His Magic Band, Charlatans</u>
           3/c: Yellow, Green, Blue (14" x 20.5")
           Yellow lettering with illustration of minstrels on green background
           Poster...$30-125 / Handbill...$70-100

FD24   "Barnyard" by Mouse & Kelley. 9/2-3/66
13th Floor Elevators, Sir Douglas Quintet
2/c: Magenta, Green (14" x 20")
Red and brown lettering with illustration of house held in bird claw
on green background with white border
Poster...$30-150 / Handbill...$40-60

FD25   "Indian" by Mouse & Kelley. 9/9-10/66
Quicksilver Messenger Service, Great Society
2/c: Red, Brown (13.5" x 20")
Red lettering and monochrome photo of Indian in profile
on white background
Poster...$30-150 / Handbill...$40-60

FD26   "Skeleton and Roses" by Mouse & Kelley. 9/16-17/66
Grateful Dead, Oxford Circle
3/c: Blue, Red, Black (14" x 20")
Black, blue and white lettering with illustration of skeleton and roses
(by Edmund J. Sullivan) on blue background
Poster...$125-400 / Handbill...$100-150

FD27   "Wolf" by Mouse & Kelley. 9/23-24/66
Howlin' Wolf, Big Brother & The Holding Co.
3/c: Green, Red, Black (14" x 20")
Black lettering and illustration of wolf bearing its teeth
on green and white background
Poster...$125-400 / Handbill...$80-100

FD28   "Space Man" by Mouse & Kelley. 9/30/66 - 10/1/66
13th Floor Elevators, Quicksilver Messenger Service
2/c: Orange, Blue (14" x 20")
White lettering and orange striped man on blue background
with white border
Poster...$30-150 / Handbill...$40-60

FD29   "Girl with Green Hair" by Mouse & Kelley. 10/7-8/66
Jim Kweskin, Big Brother & The Holding Co., Electric Train
4/c: Magenta, Red, Black, Green (14" x 20")
Mouse & Kelley acknowledge their debt to art nouveau with a liberal
borrowing from Alphonse Mucha
Poster...$30-150 / Handbill...$40-60

FD30   "One Year Anniversary" by Mouse & Kelley. 10/15-16/66
Big Brother & The Holding Co, Sir Douglas Quintet
3/c: Purple, Red, Blue (14" x 20")
Purple and blue lettering on red insets;
Features a photo of Gloria Swanson by Edward Steichen
Poster...$30-150 / Handbill...$40-60

FD31   By Mouse & Kelley. 10/21-22/66
         Daily Flash, Country Joe & The Fish
         1/c: Black (14" x 20.5")
         White lettering and monochrome of man on black background;
         First printing was printed with the wrong dates
         Poster...$30-150 / Handbill...$40-60

FD32   By Victor Moscoso. 10/28-29/66
         Quicksilver Messenger Service, Blackburn & Snow, Sons Of Champlin
         2/c: Magenta, Black (14" x 20")
         White lettering with illustration of rooster riding unicycle
         on magenta background
         Poster...$100-200 / Handbill...$60-80

FD33   By Mouse & Kelley. 11/4-5/66
         Grateful Dead, Oxford Circle
         2/c: Green, Red (14" x 20")
         Green lettering and red Family Dog logo on star-spangled background
         Poster...$50-150 / Handbill...$40-60

FD34   By Steve Renick. 11/11-12/66
         13th Floor Elevators, Moby Grape
         2/c: Green, Magenta (14" x 20")
         Magenta and green op spiral with "eye in the pyramid" design
         Poster...$30-125 / Handbill...$25-50

FD35   By Mouse & Kelley. 11/18-19/66
         Daily Flash, Quicksilver Messenger Service, Country Joe & The Fish
         3/c: Red, Blue, Black (14" x 20")
         Blue and white lettering with illustration of hot air balloon
         on blue background
         Poster...$30-75 / Handbill...$30-40

FD36   By Victor Moscoso. 11/25-26/66
         Quicksilver Messenger Service, Big Brother & The Holding Co.,
         Country Joe & The Fish
         3/c: Yellow, Red, Blue (14" x 20")
         Red lettering with illustrated flowers on dark blue background
         with yellow border
         Poster...$30-100 / Handbill...$50-70

FD37   By Ned Lamont. 12/2-3/66
         Buffalo Springfield, Daily Flash, Congress Of Wonders
         2/c: Magenta, Green (14" x 20")
         Green and magenta lettering on pink background with white border
         Poster...$30-100 / Handbill...$40-60

FD38   By Victor Moscoso. 12/9-10/66
         Big Brother & The Holding Co., Oxford Circle, Lee Michaels
         3/c: Red, Blue, Black (14" x 20.5")
         Red lettering and Family Dog Indian on red and blue op art background
         with white border
         Poster...$30-100 / Handbill...$40-60

FD39   "Redskin" by Mouse & Kelley. 12/16-17/66
        Youngbloods, Sparrow, Sons Of Champlin
        3/c: Yellow, Red, Blue (14" x 20")
        Blue lettering and illustrated warrior on red background
        with blue chevron borders
        Poster...$30-100 / Handbill...$40-60

FD40   "Satyr" by Victor Moscoso. 12/23-24/66
        Grateful Dead, Steve Miller Blues Band, Moby Grape
        2/c: Red, Green (14" x 20")
        White lettering and illustrated Santa Claus with horns
        on red and green patterned background
        Poster...$30-100 / Handbill...$40-60

FD41   "New Year's" by Mouse & Kelley. 12/30-31/66
        Country Joe & The Fish, Moby Grape, Lee Michaels
        4/c: Yellow, Red, Blue, Black (14" x 20")
        Black lettering and illustrated clipper ship on yellow background
        Poster...$30-100 / Handbill...$40-60

FD42   "Swirl Dance" by Victor Moscoso. 1/6-7/67
        Quicksilver Messenger Service, Miller Blues Band, Other Half
        3/c: Magenta, Blue, Gold (13" x 19")
        Illustration of woman on swirling orange and olive green background
        Poster...$30-100 / Postcard...$20-30

FD43   "Movie Star" by Mouse & Kelley. 1/13-14/67
        Moby Grape, Sparrow, Charlatans
        2/c: Red, Blue (14" x 20")
        White lettering with monochrome photo of silent film actress
        on red background
        Poster...$45-100 / Postcard...$10-20

FD44   "Pouring Vessel" by Victor Moscoso. 1/20-21/67
        Miller Blues Band, Lee Michaels, Congress Of Wonders
        3/c: Purple, Red, Yellow (14" x 20")
        White lettering with illustration of man pouring water from urn
        Poster...$20-30 / Postcard...$4-6

FD45   "Girl with Long Hair" by Mouse & Kelley. 1/27-28/67
        Grateful Dead, Quicksilver Messenger Service
        3/c: Gold, Green, Red (14" x 20")
        Green lettering with "Art Nouveau" illustrated woman
        on red and gold background
        Poster...$50-100 / Postcard...$5-10

FD46   "Five Moons Dance" by Victor Moscoso. 2/3-4/67
        Country Joe & The Fish, Sparrow, Kaleidoscope
        3/c: Red, Green, Blue (14" x 20")
        Red lettering and five green "eclipses" on blue background
        Poster...$20-30 / Postcard...$4-6

FD47   "Sphinx Dance" by Victor Moscoso. 2/10–11/67
          Miller Blues Band, Lee Michaels, Peanut Butter Conspiracy
          3/c: Magenta, Red, Green (14" x 20")
          Green lettering and illustrated sphinx on red background
          Poster...$20-30 / Postcard...$4-6

FD48   "Tribal Stomp #2" by Mouse & Kelley. 2/17-18/67
          Big Brother & The Holding Co,
          Quicksilver Messenger Service, Oxford Circle
          2/c: Gold, Black (20" x 14")
          Gold lettering and monochrome photo of James Gurley
          on black background with gold border
          Poster...$20-30 / Postcard...$4-6

FD49   "Neptune's Notions" by Victor Moscoso. 2/24-25/67
          Moby Grape, Charlatans
          3/c: Orange, Magenta, Blue (14" x 20")
          Blue lettering with illustration of Neptune on blue, orange
          and magenta background
          Poster...$20-30 / Postcard...$4-6

FD50   "Break On Through" by Victor Moscoso. 3/3-4/67
          Country Joe & The Fish, Sparrow, Doors
          3/c: Blue, Red, Green (14" x 20")
          Red lettering with color wheel inset of woman and mandala design
          on green background
          Poster...$40-60 / Postcard...$4-6

FD51   "Peacock Ball" by Victor Moscoso. 3/10-11/67
          Quicksilver Messenger Service, Miller Blues Band, Daily Flash
          3/c: Yellow, Blue, Magenta (14" x 20")
          Illustrated peacock on black background with magenta border
          Poster...$20-30 / Postcard...$4-6

FD52   "Contact" by Rick Griffin. 3/17-18/67
          Big Brother & The Holding Co, Charles Lloyd, Sir Douglas Quintet
          3/c: Magenta, Green, Brown (20" x 14")
          Magenta and green lettering with "sepia" photo of Michelangelo's Adam
          Poster...$20-30 / Postcard...$4-6

FD53   "Plains of Quicksilver" by Victor Moscoso. 3/22-23/67
          Quicksilver Messenger Service, John Lee Hooker, Miller Blues Band
          3/c: Magenta, Yellow, Green (14" x 20")
          Multi-colored lettering in concentric circles with duotone photo of
          Quicksilver on magenta background
          Poster...$20-30 / Postcard...$4-6

FD54   "Three Indian Dudes" by Rick Griffin. 3/24-26/67
          Grateful Dead, Quicksilver Messenger Service,
          John Hammond & His Screaming Nighthawks, Robert Baker
          2/c: Red, Blue (14" x 20")
          Blue and red lettering with "sepia" photo of American Indians
          Poster...$20-30 / Postcard...$4-6

FD55   "Eye Ball" by Victor Moscoso. 3/31/67–4/1/67
        Big Brother & The Holding Co., Charlatans, Blue Cheer
        3/c: Magenta, Yellow, Blue (14" x 20")
        "God's Eye" lettering on green and brown background with blue border
        Poster...$20–30 / Postcard...$4-6

FD56   "Canned Heat" by Rick Griffin and George Hunter. 4/7-8/67
        Charlatans, Sparrow, Canned Heat
        4/c: Magenta, Yellow, Blue (14" x 20")
        Sepia photo of Charlatans with illustration of canned "sparrow"
        on white background
        Poster...$20-30 / Postcard...$4-6

FD57   "Psychedelic" by Victor Moscoso. 4/14-15/67
        The Doors, Miller Blues Band, Haji Baba
        3/c: Magenta, Yellow, Blue (14" x 20")
        Blue lettering with magenta and green color wheel design
        Poster...$50-75 / Postcard...$4-6

FD58   "Pot" by Rick Griffin. 4/21-22/67
        Quicksilver Messenger Service,
        John Hammond & His Screaming Nighthawks, Charles Lloyd
        4/c: Red, Yellow, Green, Black (14" x 20")
        Multi-colored lettering with illustration of Family Dog Indian
        sitting in large pot on red background
        Poster...$20-30 / Postcard...$4-6

FD59   "Bobbsey Twins" by Victor Moscoso. 4/28-29/67
        Chambers Brothers, Iron Butterfly
        3/c: Orange, Magenta, Blue (14" x 20")
        Blue lettering in configuration of two fans above duotone of
        two Renaissance women
        Poster...$20-30 / Postcard...$4-6

FD60   "Motherload" by Rick Griffin. 5/5-7/67
        Big Brother & The Holding Co, Sir Douglas Quintet,
        Orkustra
        4/c: Red, Blue, Brown, Black (14" x 20")
        Multi-colored lettering and sepia photo of Big Brother
        on blue background
        Poster...$20-30 / Postcard...$4-6

FD61   "Butterfly Lady" by Victor Moscoso. 5/12-13/67
        The Doors, Sparrow
        3/c: Magenta, Yellow, Blue (14" x 20")
        Blue lettering with color wheel inset of "Annabelle" on blue background
        Poster...$40-60 / Postcard...$4-6

FD62   "Sutter's Mill" by Rick Griffin. 5/19-21/67
        Quicksilver Messenger Service, Country Joe & The Fish
        4/c: Yellow, Red, Blue, Black (20" x 14")
        Red lettering with illustration of panning goldminer on green background
        Poster...$20-30 / Postcard...$4-6

FD63   "CHA" by Rick Griffin. Photo by Herb Greene. 5/26-28/67
Charlatans, Salvation Army Banned, Blue Cheer
3/c: Black, Brown, Red (14" x 22")
Black and red lettering with "sepia" photo of Charlatans;
FD63, FD67 and FD71 form a triptych
Poster...$30-40 / Postcard...$4-6

FD64   "Pink Panther" by Victor Moscoso. 6/1-4/67
Miller Blues Band, Daily Flash, The Doors, Miller Blues Band
3/c: Green, Magenta, Blue (14" x 20")
Multi-colored lettering with magenta and green color wheel
design of cat's eyes on blue background
Poster...$40-60 / Postcard...$4-6

FD65   "Aunt Jemima" by Rick Griffin. 6/8-11/67
Big Brother & The Holding Co, Canned Heat Blues Band
4/c: Yellow, Red, Blue, Black (14" x 20")
Multi-colored lettering and illustration of black gypsy
fortune teller on blue background with yellow border
Poster...$20-30 / Postcard...$4-6

FD66   "Strongman" by Victor Moscoso. 6/15-18/67
Youngbloods, Siegal Schwall Band
3/c: Yellow, Red, Blue (14" x 20")
Red lettering and color wheel inset of circus sideshow on red background
Poster...$20-30 / Postcard...$4-6

FD67   "RLAT" by Rick Griffin. 6/22-25/67
Charlatans, 13th Floor Elevators
3/c: Black, Blue, Red (13.5" x 21.5")
Black and blue lettering with "sepia" photo of Charlatans;
FD63, FD67 and FD71 form a triptych
Poster...$30-40 / Postcard...$4-6

FD68   "Horns of Plenty" by Victor Moscoso. 6/29/67 - 7/2/67
Quicksilver Messenger Service, Mount Rushmore,
Big Brother & The Holding Co, Blue Cheer
3/c: Blue, Green, Magenta (14" x 20")
Blue and green lettering in configuration of yin-yang
Poster...$20-30 / Postcard...$4-6

FD69   "Independence" by Rick Griffin. 7/4/67
Quicksilver Messenger Service, Siegal Schwall, Phoenix
2/c: Metallic Gold, Black (14.5" x 22")
Black lettering and metallic gold border on white background
Poster...$20-30 / Postcard...$4-6

FD70   "Chicago Fire" by Victor Moscoso. 7/6-9/67
Miller Blues Band, Siegal Schwall Band
3/c: Magenta, Blue, Yellow (14" x 20")
Magenta lettering and photo inset of Miller Blues Band
on magenta background
Poster...$20-30 / Postcard...$4-6

FD71   "ANS" by Robert Fried. Photo by Herb Greene. 7/13-16/67
            Charlatans, Youngbloods, Other Half
            3/c: Black, Brown, Yellow (14" x 21")
            Black and yellow lettering with "sepia" photo of Charlatans;
            FD63, FD67 and FD71 form a triptych
            Poster...$30-40 / Postcard...$4-6

FD72   "Family Portrait" by Dennis Nolan. 7/20-23/67
            Big Brother & The Holding Co., Mount Rushmore, Canned Heat,
            Mother Earth
            3/c: Gold, Red, Black (14" x 20")
            Black lettering and illustrated inset of James Gurley with child
            on gold background
            Poster...$20-30 / Postcard...$4-6

FD73   "Smiling Hun" by Ned Lamont. 7/27-30/67
            Blue Cheer, Captain Beefheart & His Magic Band, Youngbloods
            2/c: Red, Blue (12.5" x 21")
            Orange lettering and blue illustrations of Hun
            on orange and white background
            Poster...$20-30 / Postcard...$4-6

FD74   "Tripping" by Robert Fried. 8/3-6/67
            Charles Lloyd Quartet, West Coast Natural Gas Co.,
            Tripping West to East
            3/c: Magenta, Yellow, Blue (14" x 22")
            Family Dog Indian on background photo of Taj Mahal
            Poster...$20-30 / Postcard...$4-6

FD75   "Three Little Bares" by Victor Moscoso. 8/10-13/67
            Moby Grape, Canned Heat, Vanilla Fudge
            3/c: Yellow, Blue, Black (14" x 20")
            Blue lettering and photo inset of "angels" in underwear
            on blue background
            Poster...$20-30 / Postcard...$4-6

FD76   "High Yo Silver" by Jack Hatfield. 8/17-20/67
            Quicksilver Messenger Service, Other Half, Melvin Q
            3/c: Metallic Silver, Red, Blue (14" x 20")
            Blue "etching" on metallic silver background
            with red and blue border
            Poster...$20-30 / Postcard...$4-6

FD77   "War and Peace" by Robert Fried. 8/24-27/67
            Big Brother & The Holding Co., Bo Diddley,
            Bukka White, Salvation Army Banned
            4/c: Yellow, Orange, Blue, Metallic Silver (14" x 20")
            Orange lettering and photo of "soldier" on
            orange and metallic silver background
            Poster...$20-30 / Postcard...$4-6

FD78   "Angel" by Mouse & Kelley. 9/1-3/67
        <u>Miller Blues Band, Mother Earth, Bukka White</u>
        3/c: Magenta, Blue, Orange (14" x 20")
        Magenta and blue lettering with orange angel on blue background
        Poster...$20-30 / Postcard...$4-6

FD79   "Denver Opening" by Rick Griffin. 9/8-9/67
        <u>Big Brother & The Holding Co., Blue Cheer, Eighth Penny Matter</u>
        5/c: Yellow, Red, Blue, Black, Metallic Gold (20" x 14")
        Multi-colored lettering with black and white illustrated collage of
        advertising personalities on blue background
        Poster...$20-30 / Postcard...$4-6

FD80   "Tea Party" by Greg Irons. 9/8-10/67
        <u>South Side Sound System, Phoenix, Freedom Highway</u>
        4/c: Yellow, Red, Black, Metallic Silver (14" x 20.5")
        Flaming red lettering with illustration of revelling party "in costume"
        on metallic silver inset and black background
        Poster...$20-30 / Postcard...$4-6

FD81   "Mist Dance" by Victor Moscoso. 9/15-17/67
        <u>Youngbloods, Other Half, Mad River</u>
        4/c: Magenta, Blue, Green, Orange (14" x 20")
        Psychedelic silhouette of couple dancing on patterned background
        Poster...$20-30 / Postcard...$4-6

FD82   "The Head" by Dennis Nolan. 9/22-23/67
        <u>Grateful Dead, Mother Earth</u>
        4/c: Red, Blue, Yellow, Black (14" x 20")
        Illustration of skeleton on green background with red border
        Poster...$20-30 / Postcard...$4-6

FD83   "Sky Web" by Robert Fried. 9/22-24/67
        <u>Charlatans, Buddy Guy</u>
        4/c: Yellow, Magenta, Orange, Blue (14" x 20")
        Orange lettering with silhouette of skydiver on magenta and yellow
        patterned "sky" background
        Poster...$20-30 / Postcard...$4-6

FD84   "Flash" by Bob Schnepf. 9/29-30/67
        <u>Lothar & Hand People, The Doors</u>
        3/c: Yellow, Magenta, Blue (14" x 20")
        Green lettering with "etching" of minstrels on yellow and white
        orb background
        Poster...$75-150 / Postcard...$6-8

FD85   "Dian" by Alton Kelley. 9/29/67 - 10/1/67
        <u>Vanilla Fudge, Charles Lloyd Quartet</u>
        4/c: Orange, Red, Green, Black (14" x 20")
        Black lettering with green monochrome photo of 1920's woman
        on red background
        Poster...$20-30 / Postcard...$4-6

FD86   "Flower Pot" by Victor Moscoso. 10/6-8/67
        Blue Cheer, Lee Michaels, Clifton Chenier
        3/c: Magenta, Yellow, Blue (14" x 20")
        Red lettering in floral arrangement on red and navy blue background
        Poster...$20-30 / Postcard...$4-6

FD87   "King of Spades" by Jack Hatfield. 10/13-15/67
        Buddy Guy, Captain Beefheart, Blue Cheer
        4/c: Red, Yellow, Blue, Black (14" x 20")
        Illustration of "King of Spades" lion on white background
        Poster...$20-30 / Postcard...$4-6

FD88   "Burning" by Wes Wilson. 10/20-22/67
        Van Morrison, Daily Flash, Hair
        3/c: Red, Purple, Green (14" x 20")
        Purple "flame" lettering on green and red background
        Poster...$20-30 / Postcard...$4-6

FD89   "Morning Paper" by Rick Griffin. 10/27-29/67
        Quicksilver Messenger Service, Sons Of Champlin,
        Taj Mahal, Blue Flames
        4/c: Red, Yellow, Blue, Black (14" x 20")
        Black lettering and Zap style comic strip on white background
        Poster...$40-60 / Postcard...$4-6

FD90   "Super Ball" by Robert Fried. 11/3-5/67
        Canned Heat, Lothar & Hand People, Allmen Joy,
        Superball
        4/c: Yellow, Orange, Green, Blue (14" x 20")
        Inset of black cat embracing nude women on green background
        Poster...$20-30 / Postcard...$4-6

FD91   "Sunny Side In" by Chris Johnson. 11/10-12/67
        Youngbloods, Mad River
        4/c: Black, Tan, Yellow, Red (14" x 20")
        Illustration of John Lennon pulling sun out of his ribs
        on tan background with white border
        Poster...$20-30 / Postcard...$4-6

FD92   "Squiggly Trinity" by William Henry. 11/17-19/67
        Bo Diddley, Lee Michaels
        3/c: Red, Purple, Chartreuse (14" x 20")
        Illustration of three mystical women on ornate
        chartreuse and red background
        Poster...$20-30 / Postcard...$4-6

FD93   "Optical Occlusion" by Joe Gomez. 11/23-25/67
        Big Brother & The Holding Co, Mount Rushmore
        3/c: Blue, Magenta, Orange (14" x 20")
        Blue "eyeshadow" lettering on photo of orange woman
        on magenta and blue op background
        Poster...$20-30 / Postcard...$4-6

FD94   "Nashville Katz" by Doyle Phillips. 11/30/67 - 12/2/67
         Flatt & Scruggs, Lewis & Clarke Expedition
         4/c: Blue, Red, Yellow, Black (14" x 20")
         Illustration of Flatt & Scruggs and yellow "flower child"
         on multi-colored background
         Poster...$20-30 / Postcard...$4-6

FD95   "Avalon Splash" by Rick Griffin and Victor Moscoso. 12/8-10/67
         Jim Kweskin Jug Band, Sons Of Champlin
         3/c: Yellow, Magenta, Blue (14" x 20")
         Illustration of Jim Kweskin with white "cloud" lettering in
         rainbow landscape. Companion piece to FDD13
         Poster...$20-30 / Postcard...$4-6

FD96   "Dance Dance" by Mouse & Kellley. 12/15-17/67
         Quicksilver Messenger Service, Charlatans, Congress Of Wonders
         3/c: Magenta, Blue, Black (11" x 20.5")
         Magenta lettering and photo inset of embracing couple
         on lavender background
         Poster...$20-30 / Postcard...$4-6

FD97   "Collage" by Chris Johnson. 12/21-23/67
         Siegal Schwall, Blue Cheer, Soul Survivors
         3/c: Yellow, Red, Blue (14" x 20")
         Photo collage of Yosemite Valley in the jaws of a bear
         Poster...$20-30 / Postcard...$4-6

FD98   "Tree Frog" by Bob Schnepf. 12/28-30/67
         Jim Kweskin & His Jug Band, Country Joe & The Fish,
         Lee Michaels, Blue Cheer
         3/c: Yellow, Magenta, Blue (11" x 28")
         Duotone photo of woman with distorted arms on purple background
         Poster...$20-30 / Postcard...$4-6

FD99   "Sitting Pretty" by Bob Schnepf. 12/21/67
         Blue Cheer, Country Joe & The Fish, Lee Michaels, Flamin' Groovies,
         Mad River, Mount Rushmore
         3/c: Yellow, Magenta, Blue (28" x 11")
         Blue lettering and duotone photo of nude woman on green background
         Poster...$20-30 / Postcard...$4-6

FD100   "Rocking Cloud" by Charles Laurens Heald. 1/5-7/68
         Youngbloods, Ace Of Cups, John Bauer's Rocking Cloud
         4/c: Yellow, Magenta, Blue, Black (14" x 20")
         Monochrome photo of the Youngbloods with illustrated tree
         in stormy landscape
         Poster...$20-30 / Postcard...$4-6

FD101   "Eternal Reservoir" by Rick Griffin. 1/12-14/68
         Quicksilver Messenger Service, Kaleidoscope, Charley Musselwhite
         4/c: Red, Black, Blue, Yellow (14" x 20")
         Red lettering with illustration of "bleeding heart" on black background
         Poster...$30-40 / Postcard...$4-6

FD102   "Rocking Chair" by Robert Fried. 1/19-21/68
         Genesis, Siegal Schwall, Mother Earth
         3/c: Red, Yellow, Blue (14" x 21")
         Woman in rocking chair and Family Dog Indian on red patterned
         background with black border
         Poster...$20-30 / Postcard...$4-6

FD103   "Heavy" by Mouse & Kelley. 1/26-28/68
         Country Joe & The Fish, Charlatans,
         Dan Hicks & The Hot Licks
         3/c: Yellow, Red, Black (14" x 20")
         Yellow lettering and photo inset of writer on red and black background
         Poster...$20-30 / Postcard...$4-6

FD104   "The Finger" by Victor Moscoso. 2/2-4/68
         Electric Flag, Mad River, Fugs,
         13th Floor Elevators
         3/c: Yellow, Blue, Red (14" x 20")
         Red lettering with illustration of eagle, sun, and "finger"
         on blue background
         Poster...$20-30 / Postcard...$4-6

FD105   "Dinosaur" by Joel Beck. 2/9-11/68
         Siegal Schwall, Buddy Guy, Hour Glass,
         Mance Lipscomb
         4/c: Yellow, Blue, Red, Black (14" x 21")
         Multi-colored lettering and illustration of dinosaur in prehistoric,
         Tolkienesque setting
         Poster...$20-30 / Postcard...$4-6

FD106   "One Hundred Six" by William Henry. 2/16-18/68
         Youngbloods, Mount Rushmore, Phoenix
         3/c: Magenta, Red, Blue (14" x 20")
         Magenta lettering on magenta, blue and purple op background
         Poster...$20-30 / Postcard...$4-6

FD107   "The Circus Is Coming" by Paul Zavorskas. 2/23-25/68
         Quicksilver Messenger Service, Buddy Guy, Jon House
         4/c: Yellow, Blue, Magenta, Black (14" x 20")
         Illustrated collage of people
         Poster...$20-30 / Postcard...$4-6

FD108   "Peyote Bird" by Neon Park. 3/1-3/68
         Blues Project, Genesis, Taj Mahal, Blue Flames
         4/c: Yellow, Blue, Magenta, Black (14" x 20")
         Multi-colored lettering with illustrated green, blue and yellow "clouds"
         Poster...$20-30 / Postcard...$4-6

FD109   "Love Lady" by Stanley Mouse. 3/8-10/68
         Love, Congress Of Wonders, Sons Of Champlin
         2/c: Green, Magenta (12.5" x 20")
         Magenta drawing of woman covered in her own hair on green background
         Poster...$20-30 / Postcard...$4-6

FD110   "Liberty" by Stanley Mouse. 3/15-17/68
Blood, Sweat & Tears; John Handy; Son House
3/c: Red, Yellow, Black (14" x 20")
Orange lettering and illustration of Statue Of Liberty with tear in her eye
on red background
Poster...$20-30 / Postcard...$4-6

FD111   "Charlie Chaplin" by San Andreas Fault. 3/22-24/68
Siegal Schwall, Kaleidoscope, Savage Resurrection
3/c: Blue, Yellow, Magenta (14" x 20")
Metallic silver lettering with illustrated palm trees and women on
magenta and blue background with red border
Poster...$20-30 / Postcard...$4-6

FD112   "Triplets" by Bob Schnepf. 3/29-31/68
Jerry Steig & Satyrs, Sons Of Champlin, 4th Way,
Alexander's Timeless Bloozband
3/c: Red, Metallic Gold, Brown (13.5" x 20")
Metallic gold lettering in circular inset with illustration of three children
on peach background
Poster...$20-30 / Postcard...$4-6

FD113   "Rorschach Test" by Wes Wilson. 4/5-7/68
Blues Project, It's A Beautiful Day, Nazz Are Blues Band
3/c: Yellow, Red, Black (14" x 20.5")
Yellow and red "mandala" on black background
Poster...$20-30 / Postcard...$4-6

FD114   "Flip Flop" by Jaxon. 4/12-14/68
Fugs, Aces Of Cups, Allmen Joy
3/c: Yellow, Blue, Magenta (14" x 22")
Illustrated monster and martyr images on green and yellow background
Poster...$20-30 / Postcard...$4-6

FD115   "The Sorcerer" by Robert Fried. 4/19-21/68
Steppenwolf, Charley Musselwhite, 4th Way,
Indian Head Band
4/c: Magenta, Yellow, Blue, Black (14" x 21")
Illustrated "sorcerer" on green background
Poster...$20-30 / Postcard...$4-6

FD116   "It's a Gas" by Alton Kelley. 4/26-28/68
Quicksilver Messenger Service, Charlatans,
It's A Beautiful, Day
3/c: Yellow, Red, Blue (20" x 14")
Yellow and red lettering with duotone photo of men wearing gas masks
Poster...$20-30 / Postcard...$4-6

FD117   "Giddyap" by Carl Lundgren. 5/3-5/68
Junior Wells, Canned Heat, Crome Syrcus, Clover
4/c: Black, Magenta, Blue, Yellow (13.5" x 20")
Multi-colored lettering with illustration of nude woman riding
fantasy creature on gray background with black border
Poster...$20-30 / Postcard...$4-6

FD118   "Dancing Bear" by Bob Schnepf. 5/10-12/68
         Quicksilver Messenger Service, Ace Of Cups,
         Flamin' Groovies
         4/c: Blue, Yellow, Red, Black (14" x 19")
         Illustration of bear holding purple banner
         Poster...$20-30 / Postcard...$4-6

FD119   "245765" by William Henry. 5/17-19/68
         Junior Wells, Sons Of Champlin, Santana
         3/c: Blue, Magenta, Yellow (14" x 20")
         Magenta and brown design on blue background
         Poster...$20-30 / Postcard...$4-6

FD120   "Spaghetti Hair Lady" by John Thompson. 5/24-26/68
         Youngbloods, Kaleidoscope, Hour Glass
         4/c: Orange, Yellow, Blue, Purple (13.5" x 20")
         Illustration of woman and castle interior on multi-colored background
         Poster...$20-30 / Postcard...$4-6

FD121   "Mechanico Mandala" by David Smith. 5/31/68 - 6/2/68
         Taj Mahal, Dave Van Ronk, Family Tree, A.B. Skhy,
         Creedance Clearwater Revival
         4/c: Metallic Silver, Yellow, Aqua, Pink or Blue (13" x 22")
         Photo of couple in mirror image;
         First printing appears in two color variations
         Poster...$20-30 / Postcard...$4-6

FD122   "Iron Butterfly" by Bob Schnepf. 6/7-9/68
         Iron Butterfly, Velvet Underground, Chrome Cyrcus
         3/c: Magenta, Green, Metallic Silver (13" x 20")
         Illustration of "butterfly" on green and metallic silver background
         Poster...$30-50 / Postcard...$8-10

FD123   "Rorschach II" by Larry Stark. 6/14-16/68
         Frumius Bander Snatch, Clearlight, Buddy Guy
         1/c: Black (14" x 22")
         White lettering and nude woman on black background
         Poster...$20-30 / Postcard...$4-6

FD124   "Pop-up Poster" by Patrick Lofthouse. 6/21-23/68
         Kaleidoscope, Mother Earth, Country Weather
         3/c: Black, Blue, Magenta (14" x 22")
         Magenta lettering with illustrated cutout figures on black background
         Poster...$20-30 / Postcard...$4-6

FD125   "Alice Jaundice" by David Warren. 6/28-30/68
         Youngbloods, It's A Beautiful Day, Santana
         3/c: Magenta, Yellow, Blue (14" x 20")
         Magenta lettering with illustration of "Alice" in oval inset
         on red background
         Poster...$20-30 / Postcard...$4-6

FD126   "Alice Griffin" by Dottie. 7/4-7/68
        Iron Butterfly, Indian Head Band, Collectors
        3/c: Blue, Magenta, Yellow (14" x 20.5")
        Outline lettering with illustration of Alice in Wonderland and griffin
        on floral background
        Poster...$20-30 / Postcard...$4-6

FD127   "Forest" by Paul Kagan. 7/12-14/68
        Steve Miller Band, Howlin' Wolf, Conqueroo
        3/c: Magenta, Blue, Black (20" x 14")
        Magenta lettering and monochrome photo of couple on blue and black
        background photo of orchard
        Poster...$20-30 / Postcard...$4-6

FD128   "In a Woodpile" by Paul Kagan. 7/19-21/68
        Tim Buckley, Velvet Underground, Allmen Joy
        2/c: Magenta, Black (14" x 20")
        Black lettering with photo of couple and trees on magenta background
        Poster...$30-50 / Postcard...$8-10

FD129   "Rosebud" by San Andreas Fault. 7/23-25/68
        Country Joe & The Fish, Pacific Gas & Electric, Boogie
        1/c: Black (14" x 21")
        Outline lettering and monochrome photo of woman sitting in lotus position
        Poster...$20-30 / Postcard...$4-6

FD130   "Black and White Indian" by Casey Simpson. 7/26-28/68
        Quicksilver Messenger Service, Dan Hicks & His Hot Licks,
        Howlin' Wolf
        1/c: Black (14" x 21")
        White lettering and negative image of person in oval inset
        on black background
        Poster...$20-30 / Postcard...$4-6

FD131   "Cosmos" by Bob Schnepf. 8/2-4/68
        Chrome Syrcus, Holy Modal Rounders, Pink Floyd
        1/c: Black (14" x 21.5")
        Monochrome photo of hand with spiraling planets on black background
        Poster...$30-50 / Postcard...$4-6

FD132   "Aurora" by Billy Glover. 8/9-11/68
        Steppenwolf, Siegal Schwall, Santana
        1/c: Black (14" x 21.5")
        White lettering with monochrome photo of cemetery
        Poster...$20-30 / Postcard...$4-6

FD133   "Tom Donohue" by George Hunter. 8/16-18/68
        Bill Haley & The Comets, The Drifters, Flamin' Groovies
        1/c: Brown (14" x 22")
        Monochrome photo of radio personality, Tom Donohue,
        on cream background
        Poster...$20-30 / Postcard...$4-6

FD134   "Reach" by Stanley Mouse. 8/23-25/68
Spirit, Sir Douglas Quintet +2, Notes From The Underground
1/c: Brown (13" x 22")
Monochrome photo inset of woman holding "SPIRIT"
on beige background
Poster...$20-30 / Postcard...$4-6

FD135   "Alligator Bush" by Roger Weil. 8/29-31/68
Youngbloods, It's A Beautiful Day, Initial Shock
1/c: Black (14" x 21.5")
White lettering and photo collage on black background
Poster...$20-30 / Postcard...$4-6

FD136   "Garden of Eden" by Roger Weil. 9/6-8/68
James Cotton Blues Band, Sir Douglas Quintet +2,
Pulse, Womb
1/c: Black (14" x 22")
White lettering and circular photo collage on black background
Poster...$20-30 / Postcard...$4-6

FD137   "Train Trip" by Wes Wilson. 9/13-15/68
John Mayall, Big Mama Mae Thornton & Hound Dog Band
Featuring Harmonica George, Black Pearl
1/c: Black (22" x 14")
Black lettering and monochrome photo of train
Poster...$50-75 / Postcard...$8-10

FD138   "Distortion" by Wes Wilson. 9/20-22/68
Steve Miller Band, Muddy Waters, A.B. Skhy
1/c: Black (20" x 14")
Black lettering with distorted photo of man on white background
Poster...$20-30 / Postcard...$4-6

FD139   By Wes Wilson. 9/27-29/68
Flatt & Scruggs, Jack Elliott, Sons Of Champlin,
Country Weather
1/c: Black (22" x 14")
White lettering and monochrome photo of dilapidated gas station
Poster...$20-30 / Postcard...$4-6

FD140   By Wes Wilson. 10/4-6/68
Quicksilver Messenger Service, Black Pearl, Ace Of Cups
1/c: Black (22" x 14")
White lettering and monochrome photo of gutted television set
Poster...$20-30 / Postcard...$4-6

FD141   By Wes Wilson. 10/11-13/68
Grateful Dead, Lee Michaels, Linn County, Mance Lipscomb
1/c: Black (14" x 22")
Black lettering with photo inset of distorted man on white background
Poster...$20-30 / Postcard...$4-6

FD142   By Wes Wilson. Photo by Bellmer Wright. 10/18-20/68
         Velvet Underground, Charlie Musselwhite, Initial Shock
         1/c: Black (20" x 14")
         Monochrome photo of woman's face superimposed over tree branches
         Poster...$20-30 / Postcard...$4-6

FD143   By Wes Wilson. Photo by Jerry Uelsmann. 10/25-27/68
         Buddy Miles Express, Dino Valenti
         1/c: Black (20" x 14")
         Monochrome photo of bananas and nude women
         Poster...$20-30 / Postcard...$4-6

FD144   By Wes Wilson. Photo by Jerry Uelsmann. 11/1-3/68
         The Byrds, Taj Mahal, Genesis
         1/c: Black (14" x 20")
         Monochrome photo of hands superimposed over negative image of fields
         Poster...$20-30 / Postcard...$4-6

FD145   By San Andreas Fault. 11/8-10/68
         Mother Earth, Kaleidoscope, A.B. Skhy
         1/c: Black (14.5" x 21.5")
         Outline lettering with monochrome photo of Statue of Liberty souvenir
         and man in picture frame on white background
         Poster...$20-30 / Postcard...$4-6

FD146   By San Andreas Fault. 11/15-17/68
         Love, Lee Michaels, Saloom Sinclair & Mother Bear
         1/c: Black (22" x 14")
         Outline lettering and mezzotint photo of nude woman on black background
         Poster...$20-30 / Postcard...$4-6

FD147   By San Andreas Fault. 11/28-30/68
         Quicksilver Messenger Service, Sons Of Champlin, Initial Shock
         1/c: Black (22" x 14")
         White lettering with monochrome photo of Head Lights on screened
         background with black border
         Poster...$20-30 / Postcard...$4-6

FDD1   *See FD79*

FDD2   "Haw Haw" by Michael Ferguson and George Hunter. 9/15-16/67
         Quicksilver Messenger Service, Charlatans, Superband
         3/c: Blue, Yellow, Brown (15" x 23")
         Multi-colored lettering with illustration of musicians on yellow paper
         Poster...$20-30 / Postcard...$4-6

FDD3   *See FD82*

FDD4   *See FD84*

FDD5   "Kitty" by Robert Fried. 10/6-7/67
        Buffalo Springfield, Eighth Penny Matter
        4/c: Magenta, Gold, Blue, Black (14" x 19")
        White lettering bordering pink and purple photo inset of cat
        on gray background
        Poster...$20-30 / Postcard...$4-6

FDD6   "Apache" by Mouse & Kelley. 10/13-14/67
        Van Morrison, Daily Flash
        3/c: Red, Orange, Black (14" x 22")
        Black lettering with photo of American Indian on white background
        Poster...$20-30 / Postcard...$4-6

FDD7   "Celestial Moonchild" by Alton Kelley. 10/20-21/67
        Canned Heat, Allmen Joy
        3/c: Red, Yellow, Gold (14" x 22")
        Metallic gold lettering with portrait of woman on magenta background
        Poster...$20-30 / Postcard...$4-6

FDD8   "Incidental Inca" by Mouse & Kelley. 10/27-28/67
        Allmen Joy, Lothar & Hand People
        3/c: Gold, Black, Red (14" x 22")
        White lettering with ankh cross on tan background
        Poster...$20-30 / Postcard...$4-6

FDD9   "Fan Fare" by Alton Kelley. 11/7-8/67
        Jefferson Airplane, Other Half
        2/c: Red, Black (14" x 20")
        Outline lettering with monochrome photo of statue on black background
        Poster...$20-30 / Postcard...$4-6

FDD10   "Washday Detergent" by Robert Fried. 11/3-4/67
        Blue Cheer, Superfine Dandelion
        4/c: Blue, Yellow, Orange, Black (13.5" x 20")
        Photo collage of woman riding an owl on blue background
        Poster...$20-30 / Postcard...$4-6

FDD11   "Expansion" by Mouse & Kelley. 11/10-11/67
        Other Half, Sons Of Champlin
        4/c: Black, Lime Green, Forest Green, Gold (13" x 22.5")
        Illustration of Alfred E. Neuman on gold and green striped background
        with white border
        Poster...$20-30 / Postcard...$4-6

FDD12   "Chaotic License" by Victor Moscoso and Rick Griffin. 11/17-18/67
        Chuck Berry, Sons Of Champlin
        4/c: Yellow, Red, Blue, Black (14" x 20")
        Illustration of star-spangled man in oval inset on blue background
        Poster...$20-30 / Postcard...$4-6

FDD13   "Denver Splash" by Rick Griffin and Victor Moscoso. 12/1-2/67
Jim Kweskin, Solid Muldoon
3/c: Blue, Magenta, Yellow (14" x 20")
Illustrated portrait of Jim Kweskin with "cloud" lettering and
rainbow on blue background; Companion piece to FD95
Poster...$20-30 / Postcard...$4-6

FDD14   "Fireball" by Robert Fried. 12/8-9/67
Canned Heat, Siegal Schwall
3/c: Red, Yellow, Blue (14" x 20")
Illustration of women riding ocean "chariot" pulled by fish
Poster...$20-30 / Postcard...$4-6

FDD15   "Truth" by Alton Kelley. 12/15-16/67
Soul Survivors, Box Tops, Jimmerfield Legend
2/c: Blue, Black (20" x 14")
White lettering with duotone photo of custom motorcycle
on white background
Poster...$20-30 / Postcard...$4-6

FDD18   "Pay Attention" by Rick Griffin. 12/29-31/67
The Doors, Allmen Joy, Gingerbred Blu
4/c: Blue, Yellow, Magenta, Black (12.5" x 21.5")
Illustration of "alien" holding acid tab on purple background
Poster...$50-60 / Postcard...$8-10

Bill Graham Presents

The Fillmore Auditorium was the first venue for regular rock 'n' roll dances, which began in February 1966. For about two months the hall remained open for public rental, and several different promoters used it during that period. In late March 1966, Bill Graham acquired a lease, and it served as his primary venue for two and a half years. In July 1968, Bill Graham Presents (BGP) moved to the large Carousel Ballroom. It was briefly called "Fillmore-Carousel," then "Fillmore West." Beginning in the fall of 1967, BGP frequently produced events at Winterland, a very large San Francisco auditorium. Other occasional BGP venues include San Francisco's Cow Palace, the Oakland Coliseum, and the Hollywood Bowl. In New York City, the Fillmore East presented weekend events from March 1968 to June 1971. On July 4, 1971, the Fillmore West closed, ending Graham's five and a half years of weekly productions.

Among the many artists BGP commissioned during those years, about half a dozen are prominent for the quality and quantity of their work. Wes Wilson became the first poster artist through his reputation as an artist and a low-cost printer. He designed over fifty posters in the first year, and created the distinctive psychedelic style. Bonnie MacLean, who succeeded Wilson, often combined Gothic and medieval details with elements of Wilson's style. In all the poster art, Lee Conklin's bizarre drawings are the most direct examples of a hand, eye, and imagination informed by psychedelic experience. Randy Tuten, inspired by the art of Mouse Studios, old-fashioned product labels, and a sense of humor, developed his own versions of the traditional poster format. Norman Orr, an impressive draftsman, was also inspired by the first five poster artists, especially Griffin. David Singer brought the S.F. rock poster movement to a close with a cool, contemplative, pictorial style that sharply contrasts with the hot style that began the era.

BG0 By Bonnie MacLean. 4/22-23/66
Grass Roots, Quicksilver Messenger Service, Family Tree
1/c: Green (12.5" x 18.5")
Olive green design printed on orange paper
Poster...$75-100 / Handbill...$50-75

BG1 By Peter Bailey. 2/4-6/66
Jefferson Airplane
2/c: Yellow, Red (15" x 19")
Illustration of Pegasus with biplane "wings" on yellow background
Poster...$75-200 / Handbill...$75-100 / Postcard...$4-6

BG2 "Batman" by Wes Wilson. 3/18-20/66
Mystery Trend, Big Brother & The Holding Co, Family Tree,
Gentleman's Band, Great Society, Skins
1/c: Black (14" x 20")
Illustrated Batman and Robin printed on orange paper
Poster...$150-250 / Handbill...$75-100 / Postcard...$30-50

BG3 "Blues Rock Bash" by Wes Wilson. 4/15-17/66
Paul Butterfield Blues Band, Jefferson Airplane
2/c: Orange, Red (14" x 20")
Orange and red lettering in face configuration on red background
Poster...$35-150 / Handbill...$40-60 / Postcard...$4-6

BG4 By Wes Wilson. 4/29-30/66
Jefferson Airplane, Quicksilver Messenger Service,
Lightning Hopkins
3/c: Purple, Green, Black (14" x 20")
Black, white and green lettering on purple background
Poster...$150-250 / Handbill...$40-60

BG5 By Wes Wilson. 5/6-7/66
Jefferson Airplane, Jay Walkers
2/c: Green, Orange (14" x 20")
Green, orange and white lettering on white background
Poster...$150-300 / Handbill...$30-50 / Postcard...$4-6

BG6 By Wes Wilson. 5/13-14/66
New Generation, Jay Walkers, Charlatans
2/c: Magenta, Purple (14" x 20")
Magenta lettering on purple background with white border
Poster...$150-250 / Handbill...$30-50 / Postcard...$4-6

BG7 By Wes Wilson. 5/20-21/66
Quicksilver Messenger Service, Final Solution
3/c: Magenta, Black, Green (14" x 20")
Green and white lettering on red and green op background with
black and white border
Poster...$150-250 / Handbill...$30-50 / Postcard...$4-6

BG8   "Pop-Op Rock" by Wes Wilson. 5/27-29/66
Andy Warhol & His Plastic Inevitable, Velvet Underground & Nico, Mothers
2/c: Orange, Black (14" x 20")
Orange and white lettering on black background with white border
Poster...$250-450 / Handbill...$100-150 / Postcard...$15-20

BG9   By Wes Wilson. 6/3-4/66
Quicksilver Messenger Service, Grateful Dead, Mothers
2/c: Green, Blue (14" x 20")
Green, blue and white lettering on green and blue background with white border
Poster...$75-200 / Handbill...$40-60 / Postcard...$4-6

BG10   By Wes Wilson. 6/10-11/66
Jefferson Airplane, Great Society, Heavenly Blues Band
2/c: Red, Black (14" x 20")
White lettering in black "bubble" on red background with white border
Poster...$75-150 / Handbill...$30-50 / Postcard...$4-6

BG11   By Wes Wilson. 6/17-18/66
Wailers, Quicksilver Messenger Service
2/c: Red, Blue (14" x 20")
Red lettering on red and blue op background with white border
Poster...$40-150 / Handbill...$40-60 / Postcard...$4-6

BG12   By Wes Wilson. 6/23/66
Them, New Tweedy Brothers
2/c: Magenta, Green (14" x 20")
Magenta and green lettering on magenta and green background with white border
Poster...$50-150 / Handbill...$30-50 / Postcard...$4-6

BG13   By Wes Wilson. 6/24-25/66
Lenny Bruce, Mothers
2/c: Purple, Orange (14" x 20")
Purple lettering and portrait of Lenny Bruce on orange background with white border
Poster...$75-250 / Handbill...$60-80 / Postcard...$8-12

BG14   "Independence Ball" by Wes Wilson. 7/1-3/66
Quicksilver Messenger Service, Big Brother & The Holding Co, Jay Walkers, Great Society, Sopwith Camel, Charlatans, Love, Grateful Dead, Group B
2/c: Magenta, Purple (14" x 20")
Magenta lettering on purple background with white border
Poster...$125-200 / Handbill...$60-80

BG15   By Wes Wilson. 7/6/66
Turtles, Oxford Circle
3/c: Green, Yellow, Black (14" x 20")
Illustration of turtles with musical instruments on black background with yellow and white border
Poster...$40-100 / Handbill...$30-50 / Postcard...$4-6

BG16   By Wes Wilson. 7/8-9/66
         Mindbenders, Chocolate Watchband
         2/c: Purple, Chartreuse (14" x 20")
         Chartreuse and purple lettering on purple background with white border
         Poster...$40-150 / Handbill...$40-60 / Postcard...$4-6

BG17   By Wes Wilson. 7/15-17/66
         Jefferson Airplane, Grateful Dead
         2/c: Magenta, Black (14" x 20")
         Red lettering in white bubbles on black background with white border
         Poster...$60-150 / Handbill...$50-70

BG18   By Wes Wilson. 7/22-23/66
         **Association, Quicksilver Messenger Service, Grass Roots,
         Sopwith Camel**
         2/c: Red, Green (13.5" x 20")
         Red lettering on green background
         Poster...$50-125 / Handbill...$40-60 / Postcard...$4-6

BG19   By Wes Wilson. 7/24/66
         The American Theater performing "The Beard" by Michael McClure
         2/c: Red, Purple (14" x 20")
         Red outline illustration of couple on blue background with white border
         Poster...$200-300 / Handbill...$75-125

BG20   By Wes Wilson. 7/29-30/66
         Them, Sons Of Champlin
         2/c: Red, Blue (14" x 20")
         Black and red lettering on blue background
         Poster...$40-125 / Handbill...$30-50 / Postcard...$4-6

BG21   By Wes Wilson. 8/5-6/66
         Love, Everpresent Fullness
         2/c: Magenta, Green (14" x 20")
         Green lettering on magenta airbrushed background
         Poster...$40-75 / Handbill...$30-50

BG22   By Wes Wilson. 8/10/66
         Sam The Sham & The Pharaohs, The Sit-Ins
         2/c: Red, Blue (14" x 20")
         Blue lettering on red background with white border
         Poster...$40-100 / Handbill...$30-50 / Postcard...$4-6

BG23   By Wes Wilson. 8/12-13/66
         Jefferson Airplane, Grateful Dead
         2/c: Red, Purple (14" x 20")
         *Red lettering and photo insets of the Grateful Dead and Jefferson Airplane
         on purple background*
         Poster...$40-100 / Handbill...$60-80 / Postcard...$4-6

BG24   By Wes Wilson. 8/19-20/66
        <u>Young Rascals, Quicksilver Messenger Service</u>
        2/c: Red, Green (14" x 20")
        Green lettering and photo inset of the Young Rascals on red background
        with white border
        Poster...$30-125 / Handbill...$30-50 / Postcard...$4-6

BG25   By Wes Wilson. 8/26-27/66
        <u>13th Floor Elevators, Great Society, Sopwith Camel</u>
        2/c: Red, Blue (14" x 21")
        Blue lettering and photo inset of Grace Slick on white background
        with red border
        Poster...$75-125 / Handbill...$15-25 / Postcard...$4-6

BG26   By Wes Wilson. 9/2-5/66
        <u>Jefferson Airplane, PH Phactor, Jug Band, Andrew Staples,</u>
        <u>Grateful Dead, Quicksilver Messenger Service, Country Joe & The Fish,</u>
        <u>Martha & The Vandellas, Johnny Talbot, De Thangs</u>
        2/c: Black, Magenta (13.5" x 21")
        Magenta lettering and illustration of woman on black background
        Poster...$40-75 / Handbill...$15-25 / Postcard...$4-6

BG27   By John H. Myers. 9/9-10/66
        <u>The Mothers, Oxford Circle</u>
        2/c: Purple, Orange (14" x 20")
        Purple lettering and duotone photo of the Mothers on orange background
        with white border
        Poster...$60-125 / Handbill...$25-35 / Postcard...$4-8

BG28   By Wes Wilson. 9/16-17/66
        <u>Byrds, Wildflower, New Stage Company performing</u>
        <u>Le Roi Jones' "The Dutchman"</u>
        2/c: Orange, Blue (14" x 24.5")
        Blue and orange lettering and monochrome photo of the Byrds
        on white background with orange border
        Poster...$60-100 / Handbill...$10-20 / Postcard...$4-6

BG29   "The Sound" by Wes Wilson. 9/23-25/66 & 9/30/66 - 10/1-2/66
        <u>Jefferson Airplane, Butterfield Blues, Muddy Waters</u>
        3/c: Green, Orange, Purple (13" x 24")
        Orange lettering and illustration of woman on green background
        with orange border
        Poster...$60-125 / Handbill...$15-25 / Postcard...$4-6

BG30   By Wes Wilson. 10/7-8/66
        <u>Butterfield Blues Band, Jefferson Airplane, Grateful Dead</u>
        3/c: Red, Blue, Black (12" x 24")
        Black lettering and red and blue op art on white background
        with blue border
        Poster...$40-100 / Handbill...$10-15 / Postcard...$4-6

BG31   By Wes Wilson. 10/14-16/66
         Butterfield Blues Band, Jefferson Airplane, Big Mama Mae Thornton
         2/c: Metallic Gold, Black (13.5" x 23.5")
         Metallic gold lettering and photo of Big Mama Mae Thornton
         on gray background
         Poster...$30-100 / Handbill...$10-15 / Postcard...$4-6

BG32   By Wes Wilson. 10/21-23/66
         Grateful Dead, Lightning Hopkins, Loading Zone, Yardbirds,
         Country Joe & The Fish
         1/c: Black (14" x 22")
         Black lettering and photo of Jerry Garcia on white background
         Poster...$40-100 / Handbill...$10-15 / Postcard...$8-10

BG33   By John H. Myers. 10/23/66
         Yardbirds, Country Joe & The Fish
         2/c: Magenta, Black (14" x 20")
         Black lettering and duotone photo of the Yardbirds on magenta
         background with white border
         Poster...$40-100 / Handbill...$30-50 / Postcard...$4-6

BG34   By Wes Wilson. 10/28-30/66
         Captain Beefheart & His Magic Band, Chocolate Watchband,
         Great Pumpkin
         2/c: Red, Purple (14" x 19")
         Red lettering and illustration of woman on multi-colored background
         with red border
         Poster...$30-60 / Handbill...$10-15 / Postcard...$4-6

BG35   By Wes Wilson. 11/4-6/66
         Muddy Waters Blues Band, Quicksilver Messenger Service,
         Andrew Staples
         2/c: Green, Red (14" x 22.5")
         Duotone photo of Muddy Waters' face and red lettering on red background
         Poster...$30-75 / Handbill...$10-15 / Postcard...$4-6

BG36   By Wes Wilson. 11/11-13/66
         Bola Sete, Country Joe & The Fish, Buffalo Springfield
         2/c: Purple, Green (14" x 24.5")
         Green lettering and illustration of woman on purple background
         Poster...$60-100 / Handbill...$10-15 / Postcard...$4-6

BG37   By Wes Wilson. 12/30-31/66
         Jefferson Airplane, Grateful Dead, Quicksilver Messenger Service
         3/c: Red, Purple, Metallic Silver (14" x 24.5")
         Red and metallic silver lettering and illustration of person holding
         hourglass on dark blue and black background
         Poster...$75-150 / Handbill...$10-15 / Postcard...$4-6

BG38   By Wes Wilson. 11/18-20/66
        <u>Grateful Dead, James Cotton Chicago Blues Band, Lothar & Hand People</u>
        2/c: Yellow, Black (13.5" x 21")
        Illustration of woman holding peace symbol on gray background
        Poster...$40-80 / Handbill...$10-15 / Postcard...$4-6

BG39   By Wes Wilson. 11/25-27/66
        <u>Jefferson Airplane, James Cotton Chicago Blues Band, Moby Grape</u>
        4/c: Orange, Yellow, Magenta, Blue (13.5" x 22")
        Illustration of couple on multiple split fountain background
        Poster...$40-100 / Handbill...$10-15 / Postcard...$4-6

BG40   By Wes Wilson. 12/2-4/66
        <u>Love, Moby Grape, Lee Michaels</u>
        2/c: Yellow, Blue (14" x 23.5")
        Blue lettering and illustration of woman on yellow background
        Poster...$40-75 / Handbill...$10-15 / Postcard...$8-10

BG41   By Wes Wilson. 12/9-11/66
        <u>Grateful Dead, Big Mama Mae Thornton, Tim Rose</u>
        3/c: Yellow, Red, Purple (14" x 22")
        Red lettering and illustration of face on red, yellow and purple background
        Poster...$40-75 / Handbill...$10-15 / Postcard...$4-6

BG42   By Wes Wilson. 12/16-18/66
        <u>Jefferson Airplane, Junior Wells Chicago Blues Band, Tim Rose</u>
        3/c: Purple, Blue, Red (14" x 22")
        Blue lettering and monochrome photo of Jefferson Airplane on red,
        purple and blue background
        Poster...$40-75 / Handbill...$10-15 / Postcard...$4-6

BG43   By Wes Wilson. 12/20-22/66
        <u>Otis Redding & His Orchestra, Grateful Dead,</u>
        <u>Johnny Talbot & De Thangs, Country Joe & The Fish</u>
        2/c: Blue, Red (14" x 22.5")
        Magenta lettering and monochrome photo of Otis Redding
        Poster...$40-60 / Handbill...$10-15 / Postcard...$10-15

BG44   By Wes Wilson. 1/6-8/67
        <u>Young Rascals, Sopwith Camel, The Doors</u>
        2/c: Purple, Magenta (14" x 24")
        Purple lettering and illustration of woman on patterned
        magenta and purple background
        Poster...$40-75 / Handbill...$10-15 / Postcard...$8-10

BG45   By Wes Wilson. 1/13-15/67
        <u>Junior Wells Chicago Blues Band, The Doors, Grateful Dead</u>
        3/c: Red, Green, Purple (14" x 22")
        Purple lettering and illustration of face on green background
        Poster...$40-75 / Handbill...$10-15 / Postcard...$4-6

BG46   By Wes Wilson. 1/20-22/67
         Butterfield Blues Band, Charles Lloyd Quartet
         3/c: Metallic Gold, Purple, Black (14" x 22")
         Gold lettering and photo inset of the Butterfield Blues Band
         on purple and black background
         Poster...$40-60 / Postcard...$4-6

BG47   By Wes Wilson. 1/27-29/67
         Butterfield Blues Band, Charles Lloyd Quartet
         3/c: Black, Red, Yellow (14.5" x 23")
         Yellow lettering and photo of Charles Lloyd on red and black background
         Poster...$30-50 / Postcard...$4-6

BG48   By Wes Wilson. 2/3-5/67
         Jefferson Airplane, Quicksilver Messenger Service, Dino Valenti
         3/c: Green, Red, Purple (13.5" x 23")
         Purple lettering and illustration of faces on red background with
         green border
         Poster...$30-50 / Handbill...$10-15 / Postcard...$4-6

BG49   By John H. Myers. 2/10-12/67
         Blues Project, Mothers, Canned Heat Blues Band
         2/c: Green, Blue (13.5" x 22")
         White lettering and illustration of harmonica player on blue background
         Poster...$20-30 / Postcard...$4-6

BG50   By Wes Wilson. 2/17-19/67
         Blues Project, Mothers, Canned Heat Blues Band
         3/c: Magenta, Orange, Blue (13.5" x 21")
         Magenta lettering and illustration of figures on orange background
         with blue border
         Poster...$40-50 / Postcard...$8-10

BG51   By Wes Wilson. 2/24-26/67
         Otis Rush & His Chicago Blues Band, Grateful Dead,
         Canned Heat Blues Band
         3/c: Pink, Blue, Black (13.5" x 22")
         Pink and black lettering and illustration of face on multi-colored background
         Poster...$40-60 / Postcard...$4-6

BG52   By John H. Myers. 2/26/67
         B.B. King, Moby Grape, Steve Miller Blues Band
         3/c: Yellow, Red, Black (14" x 22")
         White lettering and illustration of figures on yellow and red background
         Poster...$25-35 / Postcard...$4-6

BG53   By Wes Wilson. 3/3-5/67
         Otis Rush & His Chicago Blues Band, Mothers, Morning Glory
         4/c: Yellow, Red, Blue, Black (13.5" x 22.5")
         White lettering and multi-colored illustration of faces with black border
         Poster...$20-40 / Postcard...$8-10

BG54   By Wes Wilson. 3/10-12/67
        Jefferson Airplane, Jimmy Reed, John Lee Hooker,
        Stu Gardner Trio
        3/c: Green, Purple, Red (13.5" x 20")
        Purple lettering and multi-colored illustration on red background
        Poster...$25-35 / Postcard...$8-10

BG55   By Wes Wilson. 2/17-19/67
        Chuck Berry, Grateful Dead, Johnny Talbot & De Thangs
        2/c: Chartreuse, Black (13.5" x 20.5")
        Outline lettering and illustration of woman with snake on
        chartreuse background
        Poster...$25-35 / Postcard...$4-6

BG56   By Wes Wilson. 3/24-26/67
        Moby Grape, Chambers Brothers, Charlatans
        4/c: Orange, Red, Blue, Black (14" x 21")
        Outline lettering and illustration of mask on split fountain background
        Poster...$25-35 / Postcard...$8-10

BG57   By Wes Wilson. 3/31/67 - 4/2/67
        The Byrds, Moby Grape, Andrew Staples
        3/c: Red, Blue, Black (14" x 22")
        Red lettering and b/w illustration of peacock on blue background
        with red and black border
        Poster...$40-60 / Postcard...$4-6

BG58   By Wes Wilson. 4/7-9/67
        Chambers Brothers, Quicksilver Messenger Service, Sandy Bull
        3/c: Green, Red, Purple (14" x 25")
        Outline lettering and illustration of woman on purple background
        Poster...$40-60 / Postcard...$8-10

BG59   By Peter Bailey. 4/14-16/67
        Howlin' Wolf, Country Joe & The Fish, Loading Zone
        3/c: Magenta, Purple, Gold (14" x 22")
        Illustration of woman on multi-colored background
        Poster...$25-35 / Postcard...$4-6

BG60   By Wes Wilson. 4/21-23/67
        Howlin' Wolf, Big Brother & The Holding Co, Hargbinger Complex
        3/c: Red, Yellow, Blue (14" x 24")
        Red lettering and orange illustration of woman on multi-colored background
        Poster...$25-35 / Postcard...$4-6

BG61   By Wes Wilson. 4/28-30/67
        Buffalo Springfield, Steve Miller Blues Band, Freedom Highway
        3/c: Yellow, Metallic Silver, Black (14" x 21.5")
        Yellow and metallic silver lettering with illustration
        of face on black background
        Poster...$25-35 / Postcard...$4-6

BG62   By Wes Wilson. 5/5-6/67
        Grateful Dead, Paupers, Collage
        3/c: Orange, Green, Black (14" x 24")
        Outline lettering and illustration on split fountain background
        Poster...$40-60 / Postcard...$6-8

BG63   By Bonnie MacLean. 5/12-14/67
        Jefferson Airplane, Paupers
        3/c: Red, Brown, Black (14" x 23")
        Red lettering with Gothic photo of Jorma Kaukonen on red background
        Poster...$30-40 / Postcard...$8-10

BG64   By Bonnie MacLean. 5/19-20/67
        Martha & The Vandellas, Paupers
        3/c: Blue, Chartreuse, Red (14" x 23")
        Red lettering and blue outline illustration of women
        on chartreuse background
        Poster...$25-35 / Postcard...$4-6

BG65   By Bonnie MacLean. 5/26-27/67
        Big Brother & The Holding Co, Steve Miller Blues Band
        3/c: Metallic Gold, Purple, Red (14" x 23")
        Red lettering with illustration of medieval figure
        on metallic gold background
        Poster...$30-40 / Postcard...$8-10

BG66   By Bonnie MacLean. 6/2-3/67
        Jim Kweskin Jug Band, Peanutbutter Conspiracy, Sparrow
        3/c: Yellow, Green, Blue (14" x 23")
        Yellow lettering with illustration of woman on blue and green background
        Poster...$30-40 / Postcard...$8-10

BG67   By Bonnie MacLean. 6/9-10/67
        The Doors, Jim Kweskin Jug Band
        3/c: Gold, Magenta, Black (14" x 23")
        Gold lettering and illustration of magenta griffin surrounding a collage
        of faces on gold background
        Poster...$60-80 / Postcard...$8-10

BG68   By Bonnie MacLean. 6/16-17/67
        The Who, Loading Zone
        2/c: Purple, Orange (14" x 22")
        Orange and purple lettering with illustrated collage of faces
        on orange background
        Poster...$100-150 / Postcard...$6-8

BG69   "Opening of the Summer Series" by Clifford Charles Seeley. 6/20-25/67
        Jefferson Airplane, Gabor Szabo, Jimi Hendrix
        2/c: Purple, Orange (14" x 22")
        Purple lettering and outline illustration of woman on orange background
        Poster...$100-150 / Postcard...$6-8

BG70   By Greg Irons. 6/27/67 - 7/2/67
Chuck Berry, Eric Burdon & The Animals, Steve Miller Blues Band
3/c: Magenta, Orange, Black (14" x 22")
Multi-colored lettering and illustration of man with modified derby hat
on orange and red background
Poster...$30-40 / Postcard...$8-10

BG71   By Bonnie MacLean. 7/4-9/67
Bo Diddley, Big Brother & The Holding Co,
Quicksilver Messenger Service, Big Joe Williams
3/c: Red, Green, Black (14" x 21")
Red and olive green lettering with illustration of "alien" people
on olive green and black background
Poster...$25-35 / Postcard...$6-8

BG72   By Bonnie MacLean. 7/11-16/67
Butterfield Blues Band, Roland Kirk Quartet, New Salvation Army,
Mount Rushmore
3/c: Blue, Pale Blue, Yellow (14" x 21")
Blue lettering with illustration of cosmic face
on blue and pale blue background
Poster...$25-35 / Postcard...$4-6

BG73   By Bonnie MacLean. 7/18-23/67
Sam & Dave, James Cotton Blues Band,
Country Joe & The Fish, Loading Zone
3/c: Magenta, Yellow, Blue (14" x 21")
Blue lettering and multi-colored illustration of totem on blue background
Poster...$25-35 / Postcard...$4-6

BG74   "The San Francisco Scene in Toronto" by James Gardner. 7/31/67 - 8/5/67
Jefferson Airplane, Grateful Dead
3/c: Orange, Green, Black (14" x 20.5")
Orange lettering with photo insets of Jefferson Airplane and
the Grateful Dead on green background
Poster...$300-500 / Postcard...$75-100

BG75   By Bonnie MacLean. 7/25-30/67
Yardbirds, Doors, James Cotton Blues Band,
Richie Havens
3/c: Blue, Orange, Green (14" x 21.5")
Blue lettering with illustration of peacock and face in green, orange and blue
Poster...$40-60 / Postcard...$4-6

BG76   By Bonnie MacLean. 8/1-6/67
Muddy Waters, Buffalo Springfield, Richie Havens
3/c: Green, Magenta, Blue (14" x 21.5")
Multi-colored lettering with illustration of face
on green and blue background
Poster...$25-35 / Postcard...$6-8

BG77   By Bonnie MacLean. 8/8-13/67
         Electric Flag American Music Band, Moby Grape,
         Steve Miller Blues Band, South Side Sound System
         3/c: Brown, Red, Black (14" x 21")
         Black lettering with duotone mezzotint photo of the Electric Flag Band
         on brown, red and black background
         Poster...$25-35 / Postcard...$6-8

BG78   By Jim Blashfield. 8/15-21/67
         Chuck Berry, Charles Lloyd Quartet, Steve Miller,
         Young Rascals, Hair, Count Basie & His Orchestra
         3/c: Brown, Red, Green (14" x 21")
         Red lettering with illustration of peering faces on red background
         Poster...$25-35 / Postcard...$6-8

BG79   By Bonnie MacLean. 8/22-27/67
         Paul Butterfield Blues Band, Cream, Southside Sound System
         3/c: Brown, Purple, Red (14" x 21")
         Beige lettering in orb configuration with illustration of magician
         in red robes on multi-colored background
         Poster...$30-40 / Postcard...$4-6

BG80   By Jim Blashfield. 8/29/67 - 9/3/67
         Cream, Electric Flag American Music Band, Gary Burton
         3/c: Magenta, Purple, Gold (14" x 21")
         Magenta lettering and illustration of man with bird puppet
         in magenta, purple and gold
         Poster...$35-45 / Postcard...$6-8

BG81   "The San Francisco Scene in Los Angeles" by Jim Blashfield.
         Photo by Herb Greene. 9/15/67
         Jefferson Airplane, Grateful Dead, Big Brother & The Holding Co
         4/c: Magenta, Blue, Green, Yellow (14" x 20.5")
         Red airbrushed lettering with duotone photo of Jefferson Airplane
         on green background
         Poster...$35-45 / Postcard...$4-6

BG82   By Jim Blashfield. 9/7-9/67
         The Byrds, Loading Zone, LDM Spiritual Band
         3/c: Green, Purple, Orange (14" x 21")
         Purple and green lettering and duotone photo of the Byrds
         embellished with drawings of leaves and pine cones
         Poster...$30-40 / Postcard...$6-8

BG83   By Jim Blashfield. 9/14-16/67
         Electric Flag American Music Band, Mother Earth, LDM Spiritual Band
         3/c: Orange, Green, Black (14" x 21")
         Green and orange lettering with illustration of birds
         on black and green background
         Poster...$25-35 / Postcard...$6-8

BG84   By Bonnie MacLean. 9/21-23/67
        Blue Cheer, Vanilla Fudge, Sunshine Company
        3/c: Magenta, Yellow, Black (14" x 21")
        Gray lettering and multi-colored "moon face" on black background
        Poster...$25-35 / Postcard...$8-10

BG85   By Greg Irons. 9/28-30/67
        Jefferson Airplane, Flamin' Groovies, Mother Earth
        4/c: Yellow, Green, Blue, Black (14" x 21")
        White, blue and black lettering with illustration of biplane flying around
        a green Mother Earth on black background
        Poster...$25-35 / Postcard...$8-10

BG86   By Bonnie MacLean. 9/22/67
        Donovan
        3/c: Brown, Yellow, Magenta (14" x 21.5")
        "Sepia" photo of Donovan in illustrated floral frame on red background
        Poster...$30-40 / Postcard...$4-6

BG87   By Bonnie MacLean. 10/5-7/67
        Quicksilver Messenger Service, Grass Roots, Mad River
        3/c: Yellow, Blue, Purple (14" x 21")
        Yellow lettering with illustration of Quicksilver flying over
        river and meadow
        Poster...$30-40 / Postcard...$8-10

BG88   By Bonnie MacLean. 10/11-14/67
        Jefferson Airplane, Charlatans, Blue Cheer
        2/c: Purple, Chartreuse (14" x 21")
        Chartreuse lettering with chartreuse and purple insets of
        all three bands on brown background
        Poster...$40-60 / Postcard...$6-8

BG89   By Bonnie MacLean. 10/19-21/67
        Eric Burdon & The Animals, Mother Earth, Hour Glass
        3/c: Pink, Red, Black (14" x 21")
        Illustration of woman with pink "headdress" lettering on black background
        Poster...$25-35 / Postcard...$8-10

BG90   By Bonnie MacLean. 10/26-28/67
        Pink Floyd, Lee Michaels, Clear Light
        3/c: Yellow, Red, Black (14" x 21")
        Red lettering with illustration of man in multi-colored brocade shirt
        on black background
        Poster...$60-80 / Postcard...$8-10

BG91   By Bonnie MacLean. 11/2-4/67
        Big Brother & The Holding Co., Pink Floyd, Richie Havens
        3/c: Burgundy, Olive Green, Black (14" x 21")
        Burgundy lettering with illustration of three women
        in corridor with vaulted ceiling
        Poster...$50-70 / Postcard...$8-10

BG92   By Nicholas Kouninos. 11/9-11/67
          Procol Harum, Pink Floyd, H.P. Lovecraft
          3/c: Gold, Red, Black (14" x 21")
          Multi-colored lettering and illustration of wizard on red background
          Poster...$40-60 / Postcard...$8-10

BG93   By Jim Blashfield. 11/16-18/67
          The Doors, Procol Harum, Mt. Rushmore
          4/c: Magenta, Blue, Yellow, Black (14" x 22")
          *Yellow lettering with illustration of two multi-colored figures
          bordered in blue and red*
          Poster...$50-70 / Postcard...$6-8

BG94   By Nicholas Kouninos. 11/9-11/67
          Donovan, H.P. Lovecraft, Mother Earth
          3/c: Gold, Purple, Magenta (14" x 21")
          *Illustration of Queen of Clubs "playing card"
          in purple, magenta and gold*
          Poster...$40-60 / Postcard...$4-6

BG95   By Bonnie MacLean. 11/30/67 - 12/2/67
          Nitty Gritty Dirt Band, Clear Light, Blue Cheer
          4/c: Yellow, Magenta, Blue, Black (14" x 21")
          *Magenta lettering with illustration of Renaissance man
          on blue and olive green background*
          Poster...$25-35 / Postcard...$8-10

BG96   By Bonnie MacLean. 12/7-9/67
          The Byrds, Electric Flag, B.B. King
          4/c: Magenta, Blue, Yellow, Black (14" x 21")
          *Black and white lettering with magenta and blue watercolor
          collage of faces on black background*
          Poster...$40-50 / Postcard...$6-8

BG97   By Stanley Mouse. 12/14-16/67
          Tim Buckley, Chambers Brothers, Mothers Of Invention
          4/c: Black, Blue, Red, Yellow (13" x 22")
          *Illustrations of sun, skeleton hand, flowers, and Earth in
          ornate black and white border on gray background*
          Poster...$50-70 / Postcard...$8-10

BG98   By Mouse & Kelley. 12/21-23/67
          Buffalo Springfield, Collectors, Hour Glass
          4/c: Magenta, Yellow, Black, Blue (11" x 21")
          *Multi-colored lettering and duotone photo of industrial machinery
          on diagonally striped magenta and yellow background*
          Poster...$35-50 / Postcard...$4-6

BG99   "Six Days of Sound" by Bonnie MacLean. 12/26-28/67
The Doors, Salvation, Chuck Berry, Big Brother & The Holding Co,
Quicksilver Messenger Service, Jefferson Airplane, Freedom Highway
4/c: Red, Yellow, Blue, Black (14" x 21")
Red lettering with illustration of hooded woman holding peace symbol
on blue background
Poster...$50-70 / Postcard...$6-8

BG100   "New Year's Eve" by Bonnie MacLean. 12/31/67
Jefferson Airplane, Big Brother & The Holding Co,
Quicksilver Messenger Service, Freedom Highway
4/c: Magenta, Yellow, Blue, Black (14" x 21")
Gold lettering with illustration of peace symbol and dove
on black background
Poster...$40-60 / Postcard...$6-8

BG101   By Lee Conklin. 1/4-6/68
Vanilla Fudge, Steve Miller Band, Sonny Terry & Bonnie McGhee
1/c: Black (14" x 21")
White lettering with "etching" of moon and hands on black background
Poster...$40-75 / Postcard...$6-8

BG102   By Bonnie MacLean. 1/11-13/68
Chambers Brothers, Sunshine Company, Siegal Schwall
2/c: Black, Red (14" x 21")
Red lettering on black and white op background
Poster...$25-35 / Postcard...$4-6

BG103   By Jack Hatfield. 1/18-20/68
Butterfield Blues Band, Charles Lloyd Quartet, Ultimate Spinach
3/c: Yellow, Blue, Red (14" x 21")
Red lettering and duotone photo of woman with cape
on green and yellow background
Poster...$30-40 / Postcard...$4-6

BG104   By Jack Hatfield. 1/25-27/68
Big Brother & The Holding Co, Electric Flag, Youngbloods,
Ultimate Spinach
3/c: Yellow, Magenta, Blue (14" x 21")
Purple lettering and duotone photo of woman on magenta background
Poster...$25-35 / Postcard...$4-6

BG105   "Flying Eyeball" by Rick Griffin. 2/1-4/68
Jimi Hendrix Experience, John Mayall & Blues Breakers, Albert King
5/c: Yellow, Red, Black, Blue, Gold (14" x 21.5")
Gold and black lettering with illustration of "flying eyeball"
on red background
Poster...$100-250 / Postcard...$25-35

BG106   By Stanley Mouse. 2/8-10/68
          John Mayall & Blues Breakers, Arlo Guthrie, Loading Zone
          4/c: Gold, Magenta, Blue, Orange (14" x 21.5")
          Gold and purple lettering on red background with green border
          Poster...$40-75 / Postcard...$4-6

BG107   By Lee Conklin. 2/15-17/68
          Butterfield Blues Band, James Cotton Blues Band, Albert King
          2/c: Magenta, Blue (14" x 21")
          Blue lettering with illustration of "hand person" on magenta background
          Poster...$30-50 / Postcard...$4-6

BG108   By Lee Conklin. 2/22-24/68
          The Who, Cannonball Adderly, Vagrants
          3/c: Red, Yellow, Blue (14" x 21")
          Green lettering and illustration of "flying ears" on yellow background
          with green border
          Poster...$60-100 / Postcard...$8-10

BG109   By Lee Conklin. 2/29/68 - 3/3/68
          Cream, Big Black, Loading Zone
          3/c: Blue, Magenta, Yellow (14" x 21")
          White and magenta lettering with illustration of Cream
          on red and yellow background with blue border
          Poster...$75-125 / Postcard...$8-10

BG110   By Stanley Mouse. 3/7-10/68
          Cream; James Cotton Blues Band; Jeremy & Satyrs;
          Blood, Sweat & Tears
          3/c: Yellow, Magenta, Blue (14" x 21")
          Black lettering and illustration of Cream on yellow background
          Poster...$75-150 / Postcard...$6-8

BG111   By Mouse & Kelley. 3/14-16/68
          Traffic, H.P. Lovecraft, Blue Cheer, Mother Earth, Penny Nichols
          2/c: Blue, Black (14" x 21")
          Blue lettering and duotone photo of imposter musicians (Rick Griffin,
          Stanley Mouse, Bob Seidemann, and two others) on white background
          Poster...$25-50 / Postcard...$4-6

BG112   By Lee Conklin. 3/21-23/68
          Moby Grape, Traffic, Lemon Pipers, Spirit
          2/c: Orange, Blue (14" x 21")
          Blue and white lettering with illustrated faces on orange background
          Poster...$30-40 / Postcard...$4-6

BG113   By Dana W. Johnson. 3/28-30/68
          Country Joe & The Fish, Steppenwolf, Flamin' Groovies
          4/c: Yellow, Magenta, Blue, Black (14" x 22")
          Yellow lettering with illustrated landscape and faces
          on multi-colored background
          Poster...$30-40 / Postcard...$4-6

BG114   By Dana W. Johnson. 4/4-6/68
         Eric Burdon & The Animals, Quicksilver Messenger Service,
         Sons Of Champlin
         4/c: Yellow, Black, Magenta, Blue (14" x 22")
         Companion piece to BG113
         Poster...$40-60 / Postcard...$8-10

BG115   By Patrick Lofthouse. 4/11-13/68
         Big Brother & The Holding Co, Iron Butterfly, Booker T & The MG's
         3/c: Burgundy, Blue, Gold (14" x 21")
         Burgundy and gold lettering with monochrome photo of Big Brother
         on blue background
         Poster...$40-50 / Postcard...$4-6

BG116   By Patrick Lofthouse. 4/18-20/68
         Love, Staple Singers, Roland Kirk
         2/c: Gold, Blue (14" x 21")
         Gold "insect" lettering on green, blue and white background
         Poster...$25-35 / Postcard...$6-8

BG117   By Mari Tepper. 4/25-27/68
         Albert King, Electric Flag American Music Band, Collectors
         3/c: Purple, Blue, Black (13.5" x 21")
         Blue lettering with illustration of couple on purple inset
         Poster...$25-35 / Postcard...$6-8

BG118   By Mari Tepper. 5/2-4/68
         Country Joe & The Fish, Moby Grape, Hour Glass,
         United States Of America
         3/c: Purple, Blue, Black (13.5" x 21")
         Multi-colored lettering and illustrated figures on white background
         Poster...$25-35 / Postcard...$4-6

BG119   By Weisser. 5/9-11/68
         Loading Zone, Crome Syrcus, H.P. Lovecraft, Tiny Tim
         3/c: Magenta, Yellow, Black (14" x 22")
         Multi-colored lettering and illustrated figure
         on yellow and black op background
         Poster...$30-40 / Postcard...$6-8

BG120   By Weisser. 5/16-18/68
         Country Joe & The Fish, Incredible String Band, Albert Collins
         3/c: Yellow, Magenta, Black (14" x 21")
         Magenta lettering with illustrated octopus on black background
         Poster...$30-40 / Postcard...$4-6

BG121   By Lee Conklin. 5/23-25/68
         Yardbirds, It's A Beautiful Day, Cecil Taylor
         3/c: Yellow, Blue, Black (14" x 21")
         Yellow lettering and illustration of mutated foot
         on blue and black background
         Poster...$30-40 / Postcard...$4-6

BG122   By Lee Conklin. 5/29/68 - 6/1/68
          Buffalo Springfield, Chambers Brothers, Richie Havens
          2/c: Purple, Black (14" x 21")
          White lettering and "etching" of reclining woman with singing
          toes on purple and black background
          Poster...$30-40 / Postcard...$4-6

BG123   By Bob Fried. 6/6-8/68
          Mothers Of Invention, B.B. King, Booker T & The MG's
          4/c: Yellow, Magenta, Blue, Black (14" x 22")
          Multi-colored lettering with illustration of cosmic figure
          on black background
          Poster...$25-35 / Postcard...$8-10

BG124   By Bob Fried. 6/13-15/68
          Big Brother & The Holding Co, Crazy World Of Arthur Brown,
          Foundations
          3/c: Magenta, Blue, Yellow (14" x 22")
          Red lettering with photo inset of mad scientist on black background
          Poster...$30-40 / Postcard...$6-8

BG125   By Lee Conklin. 6/18-23/68
          Chambers Brothers, Beautiful Day, Crazy World Of Arthur Brown,
          Quicksilver Messenger Service, Sly & The Family Stone
          3/c: Red, Blue, Black (14" x 21")
          Black and red figurative lettering on blue background
          Poster...$25-35 / Postcard...$4-6

BG126   By Lee Conklin. 6/25-30/68
          Albert King, Loading Zone, Rain, Ten Years After, Canned Heat,
          Dan Hicks & His Hot Licks
          3/c: Red, Blue, Black (14" x 21")
          Red and white lettering on illustrated white landscape with red sky
          Poster...$25-35 / Postcard...$6-8

BG127   By Lee Conklin. 7/2-7/68
          Creedance Clearwater Revival, Steppenwolf, It's A Beautiful Day,
          Butterfield Blues Band, Ten Years After, Truth
          3/c: Magenta, Yellow, Blue (14" x 21")
          Multi-colored lettering with illustration of mutated figure
          on green background
          Poster...$25-35 / Postcard...$6-8

BG128   "Blues Bash" by Lee Conklin. 7/9-14/68
          Electric Flag, Buddy Guy, Freddie King,
          Blue Cheer, Ike & Tina Turner, Freddie King
          3/c: Yellow, Magenta, Blue (14" x 21")
          Pink and yellow lettering with illustrated goat creatures
          on pink and peach background
          Poster...$25-35 / Postcard...$4-6

BG129　By Lee Conklin. 7/16-21/68
Big Brother & The Holding Co, Richie Havens, Illinois Speed Press,
Sly & The Family Stone, Jeff Beck Group, Siegal Schwall
3/c: Magenta, Yellow, Black (14" x 21")
Multi-colored lettering with illustrated pink "eggs"
on orange background
Poster...$25-35 / Postcard...$6-8

BG130　By Lee Conklin. 7/23-28/68
Moby Grape, Jeff Beck Group, Mint Tattoo, Charles Lloyd Quartet,
Herd, James Cotton Blues Band
2/c: Yellow, Blue (14" x 21")
Purple lettering with illustrated lizards on red background
Poster...$25-35 / Postcard...$6-8

BG131　By Lee Conklin. 7/30/68 - 8/4/68
Butterfield Blues Band, Santana, Hello People,
Iron Butterfly, Canned Heat, Initial Shock
3/c: Orange, Blue, Magenta (14" x 21")
Illustration of orange "hands" in blue and magenta landscape
Poster...$40-50 / Postcard...$6-8

BG132　By Lee Conklin. 8/6-11/68
Chambers Brothers; Charlatans; Queen Lily's Soap;
Eric Burdon & The Animals; Blood, Sweat & Tears;
Gypsy Wizard Band
3/c: Red, Blue, Orange (14" x 21")
Red and white lettering in figurative landscape on purple background
Poster...$30-40 / Postcard...$4-6

BG133　By Kelley & Griffin. 8/13-18/68, 8/20-25/68
Who, James Cotton, Magic Sam, Creedance Clearwater Revival,
It's A Beautiful Day, Albert Collins, Grateful Dead, Kaleidoscope,
Albert Collins, Quicksilver Messenger Service, Spooky Tooth, Cold Blood
4/c: Red, Yellow, Blue, Black (28.5" x 22")
Triptych of insets with yellow lettering and photo collage
including atomic mushroom cloud on black background
Poster...$75-100 / Postcard...$8-10

BG134　By Lee Conklin. 8/27/68 - 9/1/68
Steppenwolf, Staple Singers, Santana, Grateful Dead,
Preservation Hall Jazz Band, Sons Of Champlin
1/c: Black (14" x 21")
White lettering and illustration of lion's head on black background
Poster...$50-150 / Postcard...$6-8

BG135　By Lee Conklin. 9/5-7/68
Chuck Berry, Steve Miller Band, Kensington Market
1/c: Black (14" x 21")
Black lettering and illustration of moose with hand "antlers"
on black and white background
Poster...$30-40 / Postcard...$4-6

BG136   "Heart and Torch" by Rick Griffin. 9/12-14/68
         Big Brother & The Holding Co, Santana, Chicago Transit Authority
         4/c: Blue, Magenta, Yellow, Black (14" x 22")
         Multi-colored lettering with illustrated hand, heart, and torch
         on blue background
         Poster...$60-80 / Postcard...$4-6

BG137   "Bull's Eye" by Rick Griffin. 9/19-21/68
         Albert King, Creedance Clearwater Revival, Black Pearl
         4/c: Magenta, Yellow, Blue, Black (22" x 14")
         Multi-colored lettering with illustration of bull's head
         on green background
         Poster...$40-60 / Postcard...$8-10

BG138   By Lee Conklin. 9/26-28/68
         Super Session (Mike Bloomfield, Al Kooper & Friends),
         It's A Beautiful Day, Loading Zone
         3/c: Blue, Red, Yellow (14" x 21")
         Outline lettering and illustrated landscape of mutated figures
         on cream background with red border
         Poster...$25-35 / Postcard...$8-10

BG139   By Lee Conklin. 10/3-5/68
         Canned Heat, Gordon Lightfoot, Cold Blood
         3/c: Red, Yellow, Blue (14" x 21")
         Multi-colored lettering on background montage of swirling figures
         Poster...$25-35 / Postcard...$8-10

BG140   By Rick Griffin and Victor Moscoso. 10/10-12/68
         Jimi Hendrix Experience, Buddy Miles Express, Dino Valenti
         4/c: Blue, Yellow, Red, Black (14" x 21.5")
         Yellow lettering with illustrated beetle and dancing yin-yangs
         on black background
         Poster...$150-200 / Postcard...$10-15

BG140A   By Pat Hanks. 10/11-12/68
         Buck Owens & His Buckaroos
         1/c: Black (14" x 22")
         Black lettering and monochrome photo of Buck Owens
         in boxing style format
         Poster...$40-60 / Postcard...$10-15

BG141   By Rick Griffin and Victor Moscoso. 10/17-19/68
         Iron Butterfly, Sir Douglas Quintet, Sea Train
         4/c: Yellow, Red, Blue, Black (14" x 22")
         Companion piece to BG140
         Poster...$40-60 / Postcard...$6-8

BG142   By Lee Conklin. 10/24-26/68
         Jefferson Airplane, Ballet Afro-Haiti, A.B. Skhy
         3/c: Gold, Red, Black (14" x 21")
         Gold and orange lettering with elaborate montage of figures
         Poster...$25-35 / Postcard...$6-8

BG143   By Lee Conklin. 10/31/68 - 11/2/68
         <u>Procol Harum, Santana, Salloom Sinclair</u>
         2/c: Red, Black (14" x 21")
         Red and black lettering on red and black op background
         Poster...$25-35 / Postcard...$4-6

BG144   By Lee Conklin. 11/7-10/68
         <u>Quicksilver Messenger Service, Grateful Dead, Linn County</u>
         3/c: Metallic Silver, Blue, Red (14" x 21")
         Metallic silver and blue lettering with illustrated face
         on blue background
         Poster...$25-50 / Postcard...$6-8

BG145   By Lee Conklin. 11/14-17/68
         <u>Ten Years After, Country Weather, Sun Ra</u>
         3/c: Metallic Silver, Blue, Red (14" x 21")
         Metallic silver lettering with illustrated "tree" woman
         on red background
         Poster...$30-40 / Postcard...$4-6

BG146   By Griffin and Kelley. 10/21-24/68
         <u>Moody Blues, Chicago Transit Authority,</u>
         <u>Frumious Bandersnatch</u>
         3/c: Blue, Yellow, Black (14" x 22")
         Black lettering with cartoon figure
         on yellow and black background
         Poster...$40-60 / Postcard...$8-10

BG147   By Griffin and Kelley. 11/28/68 - 12/1/68
         <u>It's A Beautiful Day, Deep Purple, Cold Blood</u>
         2/c: Yellow, Black (14" x 22")
         Photo inset of ape on yellow and black checkered background
         Poster...$30-40 / Postcard...$4-6

BG148   By Lee Conklin. 12/5-8/68
         <u>Jeff Beck Group, Spirit, Linda Tillery, Sweet Linda Divine, Sweetwater</u>
         3/c: Red, Magenta, Black (14" x 21")
         White figurative lettering on red background with
         purple and black checkered border
         Poster...$25-35 / Postcard...$4-6

BG149   By Lee Conklin. 12/12-15/68
         <u>Country & The Fish, Terry Reid, Sea Train</u>
         4/c: Red, Purple, Orange, Black (21" x 14")
         White lettering and illustrated landscape of figures
         on orange and purple background with red border
         Poster...$30-40 / Postcard...$6-8

BG150   By Wes Wilson. 12/19-22/68
         <u>Santana, Grass Roots, Pacific Gas & Electric</u>
         3/c: Blue, Metallic Silver, Red (14" x 21")
         White lettering and silver abstract design on blue background
         Poster...$20-30 / Postcard...$4-6

BG151   By Wes Wilson. 12/26-29/68
<u>**Steve Miller Band, Sly & The Family Stone, Pogo**</u>
3/c: Gold, Red, Blue (14" x 21")
White lettering and illustration of gold sun
on red background
Poster...$20-30 / Postcard...$4-6

BG152   By Lee Conklin. 12/31/68
<u>**Grateful Dead, Quicksilver Messenger Service,**</u>
<u>**It's a Beautiful Day, Santana**</u>
4/c: Magenta, Yellow, Blue, Brown (14" x 21")
Multi-colored lettering with illustration of baby
breaking out of skull
Poster...$30-60 / Postcard...$4-6

BG153   By Lee Conklin. 12/31/68
<u>**Vanilla Fudge, Richie Havens, Youngbloods, Cold Blood**</u>
4/c: Magenta, Yellow, Blue, Brown (14" x 21")
Orange lettering and illustration of hourglass filled with people
on green background
Poster...$30-60 / Postcard...$4-6

BG154   By Randy Tuten. 1/2-4/69
<u>**Grateful Dead; Blood, Sweat & Tears; Spirit**</u>
3/c: Red, Black, Green (14" x 21.5")
White lettering, illustration of door, and monochrome photo
of the Queen Mary ship on green background
Poster...$30-40 / Postcard...$4-6

BG155   By Randy Tuten and D. Bread. 1/9-11/69
<u>**Country Joe & The Fish, Led Zeppelin, Taj Mahal**</u>
2/c: Red, Black (14" x 21.5")
Red and black lettering with monochrome photo of vintage car
on black background
Poster... $100-150 / Postcard...$6-8

BG156   By Lee Conklin. 1/16-19/69
<u>**Creedance Clearwater Revival, Fleetwood Mac, Albert Collins**</u>
3/c: Yellow, Magenta, Blue (14" x 21")
Yellow and white lettering on illustrated island of body parts
Poster...$25-35 / Postcard...$4-6

BG157   By Lee Conklin. 1/23-26/69
<u>**Chuck Berry, Jam (Mike Bloomfield, Nick Gravenites,**</u>
<u>**Mark Naftalin & Friends), Initial Shock**</u>
3/c: Magenta, Yellow, Blue (14" x 22")
Multi-colored lettering and illustrated portrait of woman
with "flying saucer" eyes
Poster...$25-35 / Postcard...$6-8

BG158   By Randy Tuten. 1/30/69 - 2/2/69
Chuck Berry, Jam (Mike Bloomfield, Nick Gravenites,
Mark Naftalin & Friends), Initial Shock
3/c: Magenta, Yellow, Blue (14" x 21")
Black lettering with illustration of hamburger on green background
Poster...$25-35 / Postcard...$4-6

BG159   By Randy Tuten. 2/6-9/69
Jam (Mike Bloomfield, Nick Gravenites, Mark Naftalin & Friends),
Byrds, Pacific Gas & Electric
2/c: Magenta, Black (14" x 22")
White lettering and monochrome photo of woman on magenta background
Poster...$25-35 / Postcard...$4-6

BG160   By Greg Irons. 2/13-16/69
Santana, Collectors, Melanie
3/c: Yellow, Red, Black (13" x 22")
Photo of Santana above illustrated urban scene on black background
with yellow border
Poster...$25-35 / Postcard...$4-6

BG161   By Greg Irons. 2/20-23/69
Move, Cold Blood, Albert King
3/c: Yellow, Red, Black (14" x 22")
Black and white lettering with circular illustration of four men
sharing a common mouth on magenta and yellow background
Poster...$25-35 / Postcard...$4-6

BG162   By Lee Conklin. Photo by Herb Greene. 2/27/69 - 3/2/69
Grateful Dead, Pentangle, Sir Douglas Quintet
2/c: Orange, Red (14" x 21")
Duotone photo of the Grateful Dead on variegated
magenta and orange background
Poster...$25-50 / Postcard...$6-8

BG163   By Lee Conklin. 3/6-9/69
Spirit, Ten Years After, Country Weather
2/c: Orange, Purple (14" x 21")
Multi-colored lettering and illustration of armchair with human limbs
on red background with purple border
Poster...$20-30 / Postcard...$4-6

BG164   By Randy Tuten. 3/13-16/69
Creedance Clearwater Revival, Jethro Tull, Sanpaku
4/c: Yellow, Blue, Red, Metallic Silver (14" x 21")
Diagonally slanted lettering and futuristic landscape
on red background
Poster...$30-40 / Postcard...$6-8

BG165   By Randy Tuten and D. Bread. 3/20-23/69
Janis Joplin & Her Band, Savoy Brown, Aum
4/c: Red, Yellow, Blue, Metallic Silver (14" x 21")
Green lettering and full color photo inset of Janis Joplin
with metallic silver border on black background
Poster...$30-75 / Postcard...$6-8

BG166   By Greg Irons. 3/27-30/69
Butterfield Blues Band, Bloomfield & Friends, Birth
3/c: Yellow, Red, Blue (13" x 22")
Mirror imaged guitars on black background with white border
Poster...$30-40 / Postcard...$4-6

BG167   By Greg Irons. 4/3-6/69
Procol Harum, Buddy Miles Express, Blues Image
3/c: Magenta, Yellow, Blue (14" x 21.5")
Illustration of magenta mountain pulling train out of its "mouth"
Poster...$30-40 / Postcard...$6-8

BG168   By Randy Tuten. 4/10-13/69
Jeff Beck Group, Aynsley Dunbar Retaliation, Zephyr
3/c: Black, Yellow, Red (13" x 21")
Red lettering with illustration of the Union Pacific train
on gray background
Poster...$25-35 / Postcard...$6-8

BG169   By Randy Tuten. 4/17-19/69
The Band, Sons Of Champlin, Ace Of Cups
3/c: Yellow, Red, Black (14" x 21")
Yellow and red lettering with monochrome photo of The Band
Poster...$25-60 / Postcard...$4-6

BG170   By Randy Tuten. 4/24-27/69
**Led Zeppelin, Julie Driscoll, Brian Auger, Trinity,
Colwell & Winfield**
3/c: Magenta, Yellow, Black (14" x 20.5")
White lettering with photo of avocado on green background
Poster...$50-70 / Postcard...$6-8

BG171   By Randy Tuten. 5/1-4/69
**Jefferson Airplain, Grateful Dead, Mongo Santamaria,
Elvin Bishop Group**
4/c: Blue, Red, Black, Yellow (14" x 21")
Black lettering with illustration by Edmund J. Sullivan
on blue background
Poster...$40-60 / Postcard...$4-6

BG172   By Lee Conklin. 5/8-11/69
Albert King, It's A Beautiful Day, Aum
3/c: Magenta, Gold, Blue (14" x 21")
Aqua lettering with illustration of "melting" person on red and purple
background with gold border
Poster...$25-35 / Postcard...$4-6

BG173 By Lee Conklin. 5/15-18/69
<u>**Santana, Youngbloods, Allmen Joy**</u>
3/c: Blue, Yellow, Magenta (21" x 14")
White lettering with illustrated sea of "hand" waves, magenta clouds,
and yellow sun on brown background
Poster...$25-35 / Postcard...$4-6

BG174 By Randy Tuten. 5/22-24/69
<u>**Creedance Clearwater Revival, Northern California State Youth Choir**</u>
 <u>**with Dorothy Morrison, Bangor Flying Circus**</u>
4/c: Red, Blue, Black, Yellow (14" x 21")
Red and blue lettering with photo inset of the sinking Titanic
on black background
Poster...$30-40 / Postcard...$8-10

BG175 By Randy Tuten. 5/29/69 - 6/1/69
<u>**Steve Miller Band, Chicago, Charlatans**</u>
3/c: Red, Yellow, Blue (14" x 21")
Black lettering surrounding duotone photo of Steve Miller on
red background with green sunset
Poster...$25-35 / Postcard...$8-10

BG176 By Randy Tuten. 6/5-8/69
<u>**Grateful Dead, Junior Walker & All Stars, Glass Family**</u>
3/c: Green, Black, Brown (14" x 21")
Green lettering with photo inset of "Cool Ade" baby
on brown background
Poster...$25-50 / Postcard...$8-10

BG177 By Randy Tuten. 6/12-15/69
<u>**The Byrds, Pacific Gas & Electric, Joe Cocker & Grease Band**</u>
3/c: Green, Black, Brown (14" x 21")
White lettering with oval photo inset of turn-of-the-century
St. Louis Bridge on striped beige and brown background
Poster...$30-40 / Postcard...$8-10

BG178 By David Singer. 6/17-22/69
<u>**The Who, Woody Herman & His Orchestra, A.B. Skhy**</u>
<u>**Santana, The Impressions, Ike & Tina Turner, Blues Image**</u>
4/c: Blue, Yellow, Black, Red (14" x 22")
White lettering with photo inset of Venus De Milo and arch
in desert landscape on black background
Poster...$40-60 / Postcard...$8-10

BG179 By David Singer. 6/24-29/69
<u>**Iron Butterfly, Cold Blood, Sanpaku, Spirit, Lee Michaels,**</u>
<u>**Pyewacket**</u>
4/c: Blue, Yellow, Red, Black (14" x 22")
White lettering with photo inset of tulip field and lips
on brown background
Poster...$30-40 / Postcard...$8-10

BG180   By David Singer. 7/1-3/69
          Johnny Winter, Lonnie Mack, Rockin' Foo, Eric Burdon & His Band,
          It's A Beautiful Day, Cat Mother & All Night Newsboys
          4/c: Black, Red, Blue, Yellow (14" x 22")
          White lettering with photo inset of demolished cars and crucifixion scene
          on blue background
          Poster...$30-40 / Postcard...$8-10

BG181   By David Singer. 7/8-13/69
          B.B. King, Aum, Frost, Santana, Taj Mahal, Flamin' Groovies
          4/c: Black, Yellow, Blue, Red (14" x 22")
          White lettering with photo inset of statue facing window where soldier
          runs from artillery fire
          Poster...$30-40 / Postcard...$8-10

BG182   By David Singer. 7/15-20/69
          B.B. King, Elvin Bishop Group, Love Sculpture, Country Joe & The Fish,
          Joe Cocker & Grease Band, Country Weather
          4/c: Blue, Yellow, Black, Red (14" x 22)
          Black lettering with photo inset of Indian in desert landscape
          on green background
          Poster...$30-40 / Postcard...$8-10

BG183   By David Singer. 7/22-27/69
          Ten Years After, Ike & Tina Turner, Flock, Steve Miller Band,
          Albert King, Mountain with Felix Pappalardi
          4/c: Blue, Black, Yellow, Red (14" x 22")
          Black lettering with photo inset of U.S. Capitol, statue of Christ, and
          Greek columns wrapped in hooded cloak on gray background
          Poster...$30-40 / Postcard...$8-10

BG184   By David Singer. 7/29-31/69
          Canned Heat, Preservation Hall Jazz Band, Southwind, Everly Brothers,
          Sons Of Champlin, Baby Huey & Baby Sitters
          4/c: Black, Blue, Red, Yellow (14" x 22")
          White lettering with photo inset of large stone hand in cosmic landscape
          on black background
          Poster...$30-40 / Postcard...$8-10

BG185   By David Singer. 8/5-10/69
          Fleetwood Mac, SRC, Jr. Walker & All Stars, Lee Michaels,
          Tony Joe White
          4/c: Red, Yellow, Blue, Black (14" x 22")
          White lettering with photo inset of arches and shadow of horseman
          on black background
          Poster...$30-40 / Postcard...$8-10

BG186   By Randy Tuten. 7/25/69
          The Doors, Lonnie Mack, Elvin Bishop
          2/c: Red, Black (14" x 21.5")
          Black and white lettering with duotone photo of the Doors
          on red background
          Poster...$40-100 / Postcard...$8-10

BG187   By David Singer. 8/12-17/69
<u>**Chuck Berry, Jethro Tull, Loading Zone, Chicago Transit Authority,**</u>
<u>**Youngbloods, Colosseum**</u>
4/c: Yellow, Black, Blue, Red (14" × 22")
Black lettering with photo inset eagle statue on cobblestoned street
Poster...$30-40 / Postcard...$8-10

BG188   By David Singer. 8/19-24/69
<u>**John Mayall, Mother Earth, New York Rock & Roll Ensemble**</u>
4/c: Red, Black, Yellow, Blue (14" x 22")
Black lettering with photo inset of staircase and planets in dark forest
on pink background
Poster...$40-60 / Postcard...$8-10

BG189   By David Singer. 8/26-31/69
<u>**Ten Years After, Terry Reid, Barkay's, Spirit, Savoy Brown, Womb**</u>
4/c: Yellow, Black, Blue, Red (14" x 22")
Black lettering with photo inset of Michelangelo's David on the moon
Poster...$40-50 / Postcard...$8-10

BG190   By David Singer. 9/4-7/69
<u>**Santana, Sea Train, Yusef Lateef**</u>
4/c: Black, Yellow, Red, Blue (14" x 22")
Black lettering with photo inset of hand holding orb over field of grass
on orange background
Poster...$30-40 / Postcard...$8-10

BG191   By Randy Tuten. 9/11-14/69
<u>**Steve Miller Band, James Cotton Blues Band, Keef Hartley**</u>
1/c: Black (14" x 21")
Black lettering and monochrome photo of gears on black background
Poster...$30-40 / Postcard...$8-10

BG192   By Randy Tuten. 9/18-21/69
<u>**Taj Mahal, Buddy Guy, Spooky Tooth**</u>
1/c: Black (14" x 21")
Black and white lettering with monochrome photo of man
in Mickey Mouse hat on white background
Poster...$30-40 / Postcard...$8-10

BG193   By Greg Irons. 9/25-28/69
<u>**Chuck Berry, Aum, Loading Zone**</u>
3/c: Magenta, Yellow, Blue (13" x 21")
Multi-colored lettering with illustration of Chuck Berry leaping
over cityscape on purple background
Poster...$30-40 / Postcard...$8-10

BG194   By Greg Irons. 10/2-4/69
<u>**Crosby, Stills, Nash & Young; Blues Image; John Sebastian**</u>
3/c: Red, Yellow, Blue (14" x 21")
Yellow lettering with illustration of couple kissing
on red and green background
Poster...$40-50 / Postcard...$8-10

BG195   By Randy Tuten. 10/9-12/69
         Country Joe & The Fish, Albert King, Blodwyn Pig
         3/c: Red, Black, Green (14" x 21")
         Black and white lettering with circular photo inset of
         Berkeley campus riot on green background
         Poster...$30-40 / Postcard...$8-10

BG196   By David Singer and Randy Tuten. 10/16-19/69
         Joe Cocker & Grease Band, Little Richard, Move
         2/c: Black, Red (21" x 14")
         Black, white and red lettering with photo inset of Greek statue
         and woman wearing "wreath" of hands
         Poster...$40-50 / Postcard...$8-10

BG197   By Bonnie MacLean Graham. 10/24-25/69
         Jefferson Airplane, Grateful Dead, Sons Of Champlin
         1/c: Black (14" x 21")
         White lettering with monochrome photo collage of Jerry Garcia,
         Jack Cassady, Sons Of Champlin on black background
         Poster...$30-40 / Postcard...$8-10

BG198   By Bonnie MacLean Graham. 10/30/69 - 11/2/69
         It's A Beautiful Day, Ike & Tina Turner, Alice Cooper
         1/c: Black (14" x 21")
         White lettering with monochrome photo of Kabuki actors
         on black background
         Poster...$50-60 / Postcard...$8-10

BG199   By Randy Tuten. 11/6-9/69
         Led Zeppelin, Bonzo Dog Band,
         Rahsaan Roland Kirk & His Vibration Society
         3/c: Blue, Red, Black (14" x 21.5")
         Gray lettering with duotone photo of a zeppelin on blue background
         Poster...$150-200 / Postcard...$20-30

BG200   By Randy Tuten. 11/13-16/69
         Crosby, Stills, Nash & Young; Cold Blood; Joy of Cooking; Lamb
         3/c: Red, Blue, Black (21.5" x 14")
         Purple lettering with monochrome photo insets of Crosby, Stills, Nash
         & Young on red background
         Poster...$60-80 / Postcard...$15-20

BG201   By Randy Tuten. Photo by Ron Raffaelli. 11/9/69
         Rolling Stones
         2/c: Black, Metallic Silver (14" x 22")
         Metallic silver lettering with monochrome photo of the Rolling Stones
         Poster...$50-75 / Postcard...$10-15

BG202   By Randy Tuten. Photo by Ron Raffaelli. 11/10-11/69
         Rolling Stones
         2/c: Black, Metallic Silver (14" x 22")
         Artwork identical to BG201
         Poster...$150-250 / Postcard...$25-40

BG203 By Randy Tuten. 11/20-23/69
Jethro Tull, MC5, Sanpaku
4/c: Blue, Yellow, Red, Black (14" x 21")
Blue lettering with photo inset of Victorian woman and bicycle
on red background with blue and purple striped border
Poster...$30-40 / Postcard...$8-10

BG204 By Randy Tuten. 11/27-30/69
The Kinks, Taj Mahal, Sha-Na-Na
4/c: Red, Blue, Yellow, Black (14" x 21")
Yellow lettering with duotone photos of Taj Mahal, the Kinks
and Sha-Na-Na on red and yellow background
Poster...$25-35 / Postcard...$8-10

BG205 By David Singer. 12/4-7/69
Grateful Dead, Flock, Humble Pie
3/c: Red, Blue, Black (14" x 22")
Black lettering with photo inset of pills and face of statue
on gray background
Poster...$40-50 / Postcard...$8-10

BG206 By David Singer. 12/11-14/69
Chambers Brothers, Nice, King Crimson
3/c: Yellow, Red, Blue (14" x 22")
Yellow lettering with photo inset of "tree" woman and sand dunes
on brown background
Poster...$30-40 / Postcard...$8-10

BG207 By David Singer. 12/18-21/69
Santana, Grand Funk Railroad, Fat Matress with Noel Redding
4/c: Black, Blue, Yellow, Red (14" x 22")
Black lettering with photo inset of horse hoof and waterfall
on blue background
Poster...$30-40 / Postcard...$8-10

BG208 By David Singer. 12/26-28/69
Sly & The Family Stone, Spirit, Southwind, Ballin' Jack
4/c: Yellow, Red, Blue, Black (14" x 22")
Black lettering with photo inset of planets and columns
on white background with black border
Poster...$40-60 / Postcard...$8-10

BG209 By Bonnie MacLean Graham. 12/31/69
Santana, It's A Beautiful Day, Elvin Bishop Group, Joy Of Cooking
4/c: Black, Blue, Yellow, Magenta (28" x 21")
White lettering with watercolor collage of faces, flowers, peace symbol,
Earth, and dove on black background with white border
Poster...$50-70 / Postcard...$8-10

BG210   By David Singer. 1/2-4/70
The Byrds, Fleetwood Mac, John Hammond
4/c: Brown, Yellow, Red, Blue (14" x 22")
*Gray lettering with photo inset of eagle holding American flag
in its beak on brown background*
Poster...$25-35 / Postcard...$8-10

BG211   By David Singer. 1/8-11/70
Chicago, Guess Who, Seals & Croft
3/c: Red, Yellow, Blue (14" x 22")
*Red lettering with photo inset of American flag and hand of child
holding a triple scoop ice cream cone on blue background*
Poster...$25-35 / Postcard...$8-10

BG212   By David Singer. 1/15-18/70
B.B. King, Buddy Guy, Allman Brothers
3/c: Metallic Gold, Black, Red (14" x 19.5")
*Red lettering on black background with "King of Spades"
metallic gold border*
Poster...$40-60 / Postcard...$8-10

BG213   By David Singer. 1/22-25/70
Albert King, Savoy Brown, Zephyr
3/c: Metallic Gold, Red, Black (14" x 19.5")
*Black lettering on red background with "King of Clubs"
metallic gold border*
Poster...$30-40 / Postcard...$8-10

BG214   By David Singer. 1/29/70 - 2/1/70
Steve Miller, Sha-Na-Na, Ten Wheel Drive with Genya Ravan
4/c: Yellow, Red, Blue, Black (14" x 22")
Black lettering with photo inset of hand holding Earth on gray background
Poster...$25-35 / Postcard...$8-10

BG215   By Bonnie MacLean Graham and Pat Hanks. 1/24/70 & 1/31/70
Laura Nyro, The Band
1/c: Black (22" x 14")
*Monochrome photo insets of Laura Nyro and The Band
on white background*
Poster...$75-90 / Postcard...$20-30

BG215A By Bonnie MacLean Graham and Pat Hanks. 4/2/70 & 4/11/70
Moody Blues, Tom Rush, Richie Havens, Turley Richards
1/c: Brown on off-white paper (22" x 14")
*Monochrome photo insets of the Moody Blues and Richie Havens
on cream background*
Poster...$75-90 / Postcard...$20-30

BG216   By David Singer. 2/5-8/70
Grateful Dead, Taj Mahal, Big Foot
4/c: Yellow, Red, Blue, Black (14" x 22")
Black lettering with photo inset of mushrooms on orange background
Poster...$75-90 / Postcard...$8-10

BG217   By David Singer. 2/12-15/70
         Country Joe & The Fish, Sons, Area Code 615
         3/c: Beige, Blue, Brown (14" x 21.5")
         Blue lettering with photo inset of man carrying shotgun
         on beige background with brown border
         Poster...$25-30 / Postcard...$8-10

BG218   By David Singer. 2/19-22/70
         Delaney & Bonnie & Friends with Eric Clapton,
         N.Y. Rock & Roll Ensemble, Golden Earrings
         3/c: Beige, Blue, Brown (14" x 22")
         Brown lettering with photo inset of large face and tombstones
         on blue background with cream border
         Poster...$30-40 / Postcard...$8-10

BG219   By Randy Tuten. 2/5-6/70
         The Doors, Cold Blood, Doug Kershaw, Commander Cody
         3/c: Yellow, Red, Black (14" x 21")
         Monochrome photo inset of the Doors on red background
         Poster...$100-150 / Postcard...$8-10

BG220   By David Singer. 2/26/70 - 3/1/70
         Jack Bruce & Friends, Johnny Winter, Mountain,
         Eric Mercury 'Birthrite'
         3/c: Magenta, Yellow, Blue (14" x 21")
         Green lettering with illustration of blue hand holding flower
         with "eye" petals on black background
         Poster...$20-30 / Postcard...$8-10

BG221   By David Singer. 3/5-8/70
         Butterfield Blues Band, Savoy Brown, Keith Relf's Renaissance
         3/c: Magenta, Yellow, Blue (14" x 22")
         Purple lettering and photo collage of Christ standing on water
         with atomic explosion in background
         Poster...$30-40 / Postcard...$8-10

BG222   By Randy Tuten. 2/23/70
         Jefferson Airplane, Quicksilver Messenger Service, Santana,
         It's A Beautiful Day, Dan Hicks & His Hot Licks
         3/c: Red, Orange, Brown (14" x 21")
         Brown lettering with illustration of skeleton "musketeer" on
         red and beige background of skulls
         Poster...$200-250 / Postcard...$20-30

BG223   By David Singer. 3/12-15/70
         Ten Years After, Buddy Rich & His Orchestra, Sea Train, Kimberley
         4/c: Yellow, Red, Blue, Black (14" x 22")
         Black lettering with illustration of muscle structure of arm
         on gold background
         Poster...$20-30 / Postcard...$8-10

BG224   By David Singer. 3/19-22/70
It's A Beautiful Day, Chuck Berry, Loading Zone
4/c: Yellow, Red, Blue, Black (14" x 22")
Black lettering with photo inset of Mona Lisa collage on white background
Poster...$30-40 / Postcard...$8-10

BG225   By David Singer. 3/26-29/70
Chicago, James Cotton Blues Band, Family Fritz
3/c: Gold, Blue, Black (14" x 22")
Black lettering with duotone photo of skeleton on blue background
Poster...$30-40 / Postcard...$8-10

BG226   By David Singer. 4/2-5/70
Jethro Tull, Manfred Mann 'Chapter Three',
Bessie Jones & Georgia Sea Island Singers, Clouds
3/c: Gold, Black, Blue (14" x 22")
Blue lettering with photo collage of Moses holding
the Ten Commandments tablets
Poster...$100-125 / Postcard...$8-10

BG227   By David Singer. 4/9-12/70
Grateful Dead, Miles Davis Quartet, Stone The Crows
3/c: Blue, Magenta, Black (14" x 21")
White lettering X-ray photo of hand and nautilus shell
on black background
Poster...$40-75 / Postcard...$8-10

BG228   By David Singer. 4/16-19/70
John Mayall, Larry Corryell, Argent
3/c: Red, Blue, Black (14" x 21")
Black lettering with photo inset of hand holding gun on red background
Poster...$30-40 / Postcard...$8-10

BG229   By David Singer. 4/23-26/70
Joe Cocker, Mad Dogs & Englishmen, Van Morrison, Stonemans
2/c: Gold, Brown (14" x 22")
Brown lettering with photo collage of Mt. Rushmore, apes, hummingbirds,
and nude bodies on orange background
Poster...$30-40 / Postcard...$8-10

BG230   By Pat Hanks. 4/29/70
Pink Floyd
1/c: Brown on yellow paper (14" x 22")
Brown lettering and illustration of American eagle with photo inset
of Pink Floyd on yellow background
Poster...$100-150 / Postcard...$20-30

BG230A   By Pat Hanks. 10/21/70
Pink Floyd
1/c: Brown on gold paper (14" x 22")
Artwork identical to BG230
Poster...$100-150 / Postcard...$20-30

BG231   By David Singer. 4/30/70 - 5/3/70
<u>Jethro Tull, Fairport Convention, Salt 'n Pepper, Cloudy</u>
2/c: Orange, Black (14" x 22")
Brown lettering and "engraving" of young girl sitting in marshland
on orange background
Poster...$40-50 / Postcard...$8-10

BG232   By David Singer. 5/7-10/70
<u>Lee Michaels, Small Faces with Rod Stewart, Catfish,</u>
<u>Shortly with George Fame</u>
3/c: Magenta, Blue, Black (14" x 21")
Blue lettering with illustration of the Pantheon on black background
Poster...$30-40 / Postcard...$8-10

BG232A By Pat Hanks. 5/11-13/70
<u>Incredible String Band</u>
1/c: Blue (14" x 21")
Blue lettering and monochrome photo inset of the Incredible String Band
on white background
Poster...$75-100 / Postcard...$20-30

BG233   By David Singer. 5/14-17/70
<u>Spirit, Poco, Gypsy</u>
3/c: Magenta, Blue, Brown (14" x 21")
Purple lettering and white kitten on magenta background with brown border
Poster...$25-35 / Postcard...$8-10

BG234   *No poster bearing this number was printed*

BG235   By David Singer and Satty. 5/21-24/70
<u>B.B. King, Albert King, Mendelbaum</u>
3/c: Magenta, Yellow, Black (14" x 22")
Black lettering and illustration of statuesque woman with children
sitting on large cat
Poster...$30-40 / Postcard...$8-10

BG236   By David Singer. 5/28-31/70
<u>Country Joe & The Fish, Blues Image, Silver Madre</u>
3/c: Blue, Yellow, Black (22" x 14")
Black lettering with illustration of harpist playing to forest animals
on yellow and blue split fountain background
Poster...$30-40 / Postcard...$8-10

BG237   By David Singer. 6/4-7/70
<u>Grateful Dead, New Riders Of The Purple Sage, Southern Comfort</u>
2/c: Olive Green, Black (14" x 21")
Black lettering with photo collage of troops, American eagle,
and sand dunes on olive green background
Poster...$30-40 / Postcard...$8-10

BG238   By David Singer. 6/11-14/70
         John Sebastian, Buddy Miles, Rig
         2/c: Olive Green, Black (14" x 21")
         Black lettering with photo inset of Statue of Liberty on olive green background
         Poster...$30-40 / Postcard...$8-10

BG239   By David Singer. 6/18-21/70
         Quicksilver Messenger Service, Don Ellis & His Orchestra, Rockwell
         2/c: Metallic Silver, Black (14" x 21")
         Metallic silver lettering with photo collage of cavalry scene and
         woman's legs holding a nickel coin on black background
         Poster...$30-40 / Postcard...$8-10

BG240   By David Singer. 6/25-28/70, 6/30/70 - 7/2/70
         Sha-Na-Na, Pacific Gas & Electric, Dan Hicks & His Hot Licks,
         Traffic, Leon Russell
         2/c: Metallic Silver, Black (14" x 21.5")
         Black lettering and photo collage on metallic silver background
         Poster...$30–40 / Postcard...$8–10

BG241   By David Singer. 6/30/70 - 7/2/70
         Traffic with Steve Winwood, Chris Wood, and Jim Capaldi;
         John Hammond; Lamb
         2/c: Blue, Black (14" x 21")
         Black lettering with photo collage of parachuting businessman
         on blue background with white border
         Poster...$30–40 / Postcard...$8–10

BG242   By David Singer. 7/9-12/70
         Quicksilver Messenger Service, Mott The Hoople, Silver Metre
         2/c: Blue, Black (14" x 21")
         Black lettering with photo collage of eclipse and figure jumping
         into liquid on blue background with white border
         Poster...$25–35 / Postcard...$8–10

BG243   By David Singer. 7/16-19/70
         Steve Miller Band, Bo Diddley, Crow
         3/c: Blue, Yellow, Red (14" x 21")
         Red lettering with illustrated lighthouse and yellow flower
         on white background
         Poster...$30-40 / Postcard...$8-10

BG244   By Satty and David Singer. 7/23-24/70 & 7/28-30/70
         Lee Michaels, Cold Blood, Brethren, Ten Years After,
         Cactus, Toe Fat
         3/c: Yellow, Red, Blue (14" x 21")
         Blue lettering with illustration of women carrying urns on white background
         Poster...$30-40 / Postcard...$8-10

BG245   By David Singer. 7/28/70 - 8/9/70
Ten Years After, Cactus, Toe Fat, It's A Beautiful Day, Elvin Bishop,
Boz Scaggs, Procol Harum, Leon Russell, Blodwyn Pig, Fleetwood Mac,
Buddy Miles, Albert Collins
2/c: Red, Blue (28" x 21")
Red lettering with statue of angel on triptych of insets
Poster...$75-100 / Postcard...$8-10

BG246   By David Singer. 8/13-16/70 & 8/20-26/70 & 8/30/70 & 9/2/70
The Byrds, Poco, Commander Cody, Van Morrison, John Lee Hooker,
Led Zeppelin, Albert King, Cold Blood, Mason Proffit, Iron Butterfly
with Pinera and Rhino, Aum, Black Oak Arkansas
3/c: Green, Brown, Black (28" x 21")
Black lettering and photo collage on triptych of insets
Poster...$75-100 / Postcard...$10-15

BG247   By Alton Kelley. 8/24/70 - 9/6/70
Iron Butterfly, Aum, Black Oak Arkansas, John Mayall, Elvin Bishop,
Herbie Hancock Sextet, Savoy Brown, Fairport Convention,
Chicken Shock, Johnny Winter, Boz Scaggs, Freddie King
3/c: Magenta, Yellow, Black (22" x 28")
Illustration of woman's face in circular inset on black and white
patterned background
Poster...$70-90 / Postcard...$8-10

BG248   By Norman Orr. 9/10-13/70
Santana, Dr. John, Luther Allison
3/c: Orange, Black, Metallic Silver (14" x 21")
Metallic silver, orange and black lettering with illustration
of African animals on black background
Poster...$25-35 / Postcard...$8-10

BG249   By Norman Orr. 9/17-20/70
Quicksilver Messenger Service, Buddy Miles, Robert Savage
3/c: Orange, Black, Metallic Silver (14" x 21")
Metallic silver, orange and black lettering with illustrated musicians
on black background
Poster...$30-40 / Postcard...$8-10

BG250   By David Singer. 9/24-27/70 & 10/1-4/70
Chuck Berry, Buddy Miles, Loading Zone,
Eric Burdon & War, Seals & Crofts, Clover
4/c: Yellow, Red, Blue, Black (28" x 21"), (9.25" x 7")
Black lettering with two full color, mirror image insets of a statue and
birds flying over a desert landscape
Poster...$75-100 / Postcard...$8-10

BG251   By Norman Orr. 10/8-11/70
Van Morrison, Captain Beefheart & His Magic Band,
Jerry Hahn Brotherhood
3/c: Red, Yellow, Black (14" x 21")
Red "ribbon" lettering with illustrated minstrels on yellow background
Poster...$25-35 / Postcard...$8-10

BG252　By Norman Orr.　10/15-18/70
Leon Russell, Miles Davis, Sea Train, Hammer
3/c: Black, Yellow, Magenta (14" x 21")
Magenta lettering with illustration of baby "Uncle Sam" on
yellow and black background
Poster...$25-35 / Postcard...$4-6

BG253　By David Singer.　10/22-25/70
Bo Diddley, Lightning Hopkins, New York Rock Ensemble
4/c: Yellow, Red, Blue, Black (14" x 21")
Yellow lettering with photo collage of man in nautilus shell
on black background
Poster...$30–40 / Postcard...$8–10

BG254　By David Singer.　10/29/70 - 11/1/70
Procol Harum, Poco, Mungo Jerry, Small Faces with Rod Stewart
4/c: Yellow, Red, Blue, Black (14" x 21")
Black lettering and photo collage of spaceman with monkey
on yellow background
Poster...$30–40 / Postcard...$8–10

BG255　By David Singer.　11/5-7/70
Frank Zappa & The Mothers of Invention; Boz Scaggs;
Ashton, Gardner & Dyke
2/c: Magenta, Black (14" x 21")
Black lettering with photo collage of woman and snake
on white background
Poster...$30-40 / Postcard...$8-10

BG256　By David Singer.　11/12-15/70
The Kinks, Elton John, Ballin' Jack, Juicy Lucy
2/c: Blue, Black (14" x 21")
Black lettering with photo collage of statue on white background
Poster...$30-40 / Postcard...$8-10

BG257/8　By Norman Orr.　11/19-22/70 & 11/26-29/70
Love with Arthur Lee, James Gang, Black Sabbath, Sha-Na-Na,
Elvin Bishop, Tower of Power
3/c: Yellow, Magenta, Black (28" x 21.5")
Yellow lettering and illustration of American Indian breaking an arrow
on black background
Poster...$60-80 / Postcard...$8-10

BG259　By David Singer.　12/3-6/70
Savoy Brown, Sea Train, Ry Cooder, Humble Pie
4/c: Blue, Red, Yellow, Black (14" x 22")
Black lettering with photo collage of statue of Christ raising arms to
U.S. silver dollar on gray background
Poster...$25-35 / Postcard...$8-10

BG260   By David Singer. 12/10-13/70
          Lee Michaels, Albert King, Atlee
          4/c: Orange, Black, Blue, Red (14" x 22")
          Black lettering with photo collage of man in the desert
          on orange background
          Poster...$30-40 / Postcard...$8-10

BG261   By Norman Orr. 12/14/70 & 12/16-20/70
          Butterfield Blues Band, Buddy Miles, Quartermass,
          Incredible String Band, Ravi Shankar
          2/c: Yellow, Brown (14" x 21")
          Yellow and brown lettering with illustrations of musicians
          on yellow background
          Poster...$25-35 / Postcard...$8-10

BG262   By Norman Orr. 12/26-29/70
          Delaney & Bonnie & Friends, Voices Of East Harlem,
          Jam and Factory
          2/c: Yellow, Brown (14" x 21")
          Yellow lettering with illustration of Jesus Christ
          on yellow and brown background
          Poster...$25-35 / Postcard...$8-10

BG263   By David Singer. 12/31/70
          Cold Blood, Elvin Bishop, Boz Scaggs, Voices Of East Harlem
          4/c: Yellow, Red, Blue, Black (21" x 28")
          Red lettering with photo inset of the San Francisco Ferry Building
          on blue background
          Poster...$60-80 / Postcard...$8-10

BG264   By Norman Orr. 12/31/70-1/3/71
          Cold Blood, Boz Scaggs, Voices Of East Harlem, Elvin Bishop,
          Stoneground
          2/c: Black, Red (14" x 21")
          White lettering with illustration of American Indians on black background
          Poster...$25-35 / Postcard...$8-10

BG265   By Norman Orr. 1/7-10/71
          Spirit, Elvin Bishop Group, Kwane & Kwan Ditos
          2/c: Red, Black (14" x 21")
          White lettering with illustrations of the Great Pyramids and American
          Indians on black background
          Poster...$25-35 / Postcard...$8-10

BG266/7   By David Singer. 1/14-17/71 & 1/21-24/71
          Free, Bloodrock, Edward's Hand, Spencer Davis, Taj Mahal, Fox
          3/c: Blue, Red, Metallic Silver (28" x 21")
          Diagonally slanted lettering with two circular insets of illustrated women
          on galactic background
          Poster...$60-80 / Postcard...$8-10

BG268   By Norman Orr. 1/28-31/71
         Hot Tuna -- Jack Casady & Jorma Kaukonen, Allman Brothers,
         24 Piece Trinidad Tripoli Steel Band
         3/c: Yellow, Magenta, Black (14" x 21")
         Yellow lettering with illustrated nude woman and guitarist
         on black background
         Poster...$40-60 / Postcard...$8-10

BG269   By Norman Orr. 2/4-7/71
         B.B. King, Ballin' Jack, Christian Rapid
         3/c: Yellow, Red, Black (14" x 21")
         Airbrushed lettering with illustration of B.B. King
         Poster...$60-80 / Postcard...$8-10

BG270   By Pierre. 2/11-14/71 & 2/18-21/71
         Fleetwood Mac, Tom Rush, Clover, Steppenwolf, Cold Blood,
         Shiva's Headband, Buddy Guy, Junior Wells Blues Band,
         It's A Beautiful Day, Blues Image, Tower of Power
         3/c: Yellow, Red, Black (28" x 21")
         Red lettering with illustrated castle turrets in medieval scene
         on black background
         Poster...$60-80 / Postcard...$8-10

BG271   By David Singer & Satty. 2/25-28/71
         New Riders of the Purple Sage, Boz Scaggs, James & Good Brothers
         4/c: Black, Yellow, Blue, Magenta (14" x 21")
         Yellow lettering with illustration of Uncle Sam on black background
         Poster...$25-35 / Postcard...$4-6

BG272   By David Singer. 3/5-7/71
         Aretha Franklin, King Curtis & The Kingpins, James Anderson,
         Tower Of Power
         4/c: Magenta, Black, Blue, Yellow (14" x 21")
         Magenta lettering and full color photo of Aretha Franklin on black background
         Poster...$25-35 / Postcard...$4-6

BG273/4 By Norman Orr. 3/11-14/71 & 3/18-21/71
         Poco, Siegal Schwall, Wishbone Ash,
         Sons Of Champlin, Mark Almond, Commander Cody
         3/c: Magenta, Yellow, Black (28" x 22")
         Illustration of nude woman holding pipe on split fountain and
         black background
         Poster..$60-80 / Postcard...$8-10

BG275   By David Singer. 3/25-28/71 & 3/26-27/71 & 4/1-4/71
         Eric Burdon & War, J. Geils Band, War, Santana, Buddy Miles,
         Wayne Cochran, C.C. Riders, Sugarloaf
         2/c: Red, Blue (21" x 28")
         Black lettering with illustration of Puss N' Boots on red background
         Poster...$60-80 / Postcard...$8-10

BG276A   By Willyum Rowe. 4/8-11/71 & 4/18/71 & 4/15-18/71
John Mayall, Sha-Na-Na, Randall's Island, Grand Funk Railroad, Blood Rock, Johnny Winter, J. Geils Band, Dreams, Dave Mason, Isley Brothers, Fanny
4/c: Blue, Yellow, Magenta, Black (28" x 21")
Black, magenta and green lettering on multi-colored background
Poster...$60-80 / Postcard...$8-10

BG277   By Randy Tuten & D. Bread. 4/22-25/71 & 4/30/71 - 5/1/71
Taj Mahal, Stoneground, Trapeze, Ten Years After, Cactus, Pot Liquor
3/c: Yellow, Magenta, Blue (14" x 22")
Black and green lettering with illustration of couple in green car pulling an Airstream trailer on cream background
Poster...$20-30 / Postcard...$8-10

BG278   By Randy Tuten. 4/29/71 - 5/2/71
Mike Bloomfield with Chicago Slim, Bola Sete, Mike Finnigan, Ten Years After, Cactus, Pot Liquor
3/c: Magenta, Blue, Yellow (22" x 14")
Green lettering with duotone photos of circus sideshow attractions on white background with brown border
Poster...$30-40 / Postcard...$8-10

BG279   By David Singer. 5/6-9/71
Miles Davis, Elvin Bishop Group, Mandrill
3/c: Magenta, Yellow, Black (14" x 21")
Black lettering and "deco" illustration on orange background
Poster...$20-30 / Postcard...$8-10

BG280   By David Singer. 5/13-16/71
Humble Pie, Swamp Dogg, Shanti
3/c: Yellow, Magenta, Black (14" x 21")
Black lettering and "deco" illustration on cream background
Poster...$25-35 / Postcard...$8-10

BG281   By Randy Tuten. 5/20-23/71
Rascals, Grootna, Grin
1/c: Black (14" x 21")
Black and white lettering with illustration of tomatoes on black background
Poster...$30-40 / Postcard...$8-10

BG282   By Randy Tuten. 5/27-29/71
Cold Blood, Joy Of Cooking, Sweat Hog with Frosty, Grateful Dead, New Riders Of The Purple Sage, R.J. Fox, James & Good Brothers
1/c: Black (14" x 22")
Black lettering and illustration of zebra on white background
Poster...$25-35 / Postcard...$8-10

BG283   By Willyum Rowe. 6/3-6/71
Albert King, Mott The Hoople, Freddie King
3/c: Magenta, Yellow, Blue (14" x 21")
Black lettering with illustration of soldier on floral background
Poster...$20-30 / Postcard...$8-10

BG284   By Willyum Rowe. 6/10-13/71
Cactus, Flamin' Groovies, Redeye
3/c: Yellow, Magenta, Blue (14" x 21")
Yellow lettering with illustration of man and dog
Poster...$20-30 / Postcard...$8-10

BG285   By David Singer. 6/17-20/71
Boz Scaggs, Tower Of Power, Mason Proffit
3/c: Red, Blue, Metallic Silver (14" x 21")
Blue lettering and illustration of fairies on metallic silver background
Poster...$20-30 / Postcard...$8-10

BG286   By David Singer. 6/24-27/71
Moby Grape, Spencer Davis & Peter Jameson,
Flash Cadillac & The Continental Kids
3/c: Red, Blue, Metallic Silver (14" x 21")
Red lettering with metallic silver and blue illustration of natives
on tropical island
Poster...$20-30 / Postcard...$8-10

BG287   By David Singer. 6/30/71-7/4/71
Boz Scaggs, Cold Blood, Flamin' Groovies, Stoneground,
It's A Beautiful Day, Elvin Bishop Group, Grootna, Lamb,
Grateful Dead, New Riders Of The Purple Sage, Rowan Brothers,
Quicksilver Messenger Service, Hot Tuna, Yogi Phlegm, Santana,
Creedance Clearwater Revival, Tower Of Power,
San Francisco Musician Jam
3/c: Black, Blue, Metallic Silver (28" x 22")
Black and white lettering with photo inset of cat's eyes on blue background
Poster...$200-300

The
New Fillmore
Series

NF1   By Kate Graham. 3/4/88
         Hot Tuna: Jorma Kaukonen, Jack Casady, Paul Kantner;
         Papa John Creach
         3/c: Red, Blue, Black (11" x 17")
         Black lettering on red and blue "painted" background
         Poster...$30-40

NF2   By Kate Graham. 4/17/88
         Midnight Oil, The Looters
         3/c: Yellow, Orange, Black (17" x 22")
         Yellow and black lettering on orange background
         Poster...$50-60

NF3   By Kate Graham. 3/13/88
         The Alarm, The 77's, House Of Freaks
         3/c: Blue, Orange, Black (17" x 22")
         Black and white lettering on "target" background
         Poster...$50-60

NF4   By Arlene Owseichik. 3/25/88
         The Gunslinger Tour: Bo Diddley and Ron Wood
         3/c: Red, Brown, Orange (12.5" x 20")
         Airbrushed western theme
         Poster...$30-40

NF5   By Arlene Owseichik. 4/9/88
         The Red Hot Chili Peppers, Slammin' Watusis, Primus
         3/c: Red, Green, Black (13" x 19")
         Socks pinned to clothesline on green background
         Poster...$25-35

NF6   By Arlene Owseichik. 4/13/88
         Robyn Hitchcock & The Egyptians,
         Timmie Hesla & The Converse All Stars
         2/c: Pink, Green (13" x 19")
         Fish and frog motif on green background
         Poster...$15-25

NF7   By Arlene Owseichik. 4/15/88
         Jerry Harrison: Casual Gods
         3/c: Black, Blue, Pink (13" x 19")
         Black and white photo insets of Marilyn Monroe,
         Elvis Presley, and James Dean on black background
         Poster...$15-25

NF8   By Arlene Owseichik. 4/16/88
         Joe Satriani
         3/c: Magenta, Orange, Yellow (13" x 19")
         Yellow alien surfing on magenta and orange moonscape
         Poster...$15-25

NF9   By Arlene Owseichik. 4/22/88
         Jesse Johnson, Freaky Executives
         2/c: Blue, Orange (13" x 19.5")
         Monochrome blue portrait of Jesse Johnson on spiral
         orange and blue background
         Poster...$15–25

NF10   By Arlene Owseichik. 5/1-2/88
         Terence Trent D'Arby, Warren Thomas
         3/c: Black, Blue, Magenta (13" x 19.5")
         Black silhouette of Terence Trent D'Arby on
         white and blue background
         Poster...$15-25

NF11   By Libbie Schock. 5/5/88
         3: Keith Emerson, Carl Palmer, Robert Berry
         3/c: Blue, Orange, Magenta (13" x 19.5")
         Geometric design with white and magenta lettering on
         blue and orange background
         Poster...$15-25

NF12   By Arlene Owseichick. 5/1-28/88
         Monthly Line-up Poster: Terence Trent D'Arby; 3: Keith Emerson,
         Carl Palmer, and Robert Berry; Jerry Garcia Electric Band;
         Ziggy Marley & The Melody Makers; Peter Murphy; Carlos Santana's
         Blues For Salvador; Neville Brothers; The Church;
         Camper Van Beethoven; Leon Russell & Edgar Winter;
         The Fall; Joy Of Cooking
         5/c: Black, Grey, Red, Blue, Green (12" x 19.5")
         Fillmore logo in op blue and red on gray background
         Poster...$15-25

NF13   By Arlene Owseichik & James P. Olness. 5/6/88
         Jerry's Back!: Jerry Garcia Electric Band
         2/c: Black, Yellow (13" x 19.5")
         Monochrome photo of Jerry's back on yellow and white op background
         Poster...$30-40

NF14   By Arlene Owseichik. 5/9/88
         Ziggy Marley, DV8, Ivory and Steel
         2/c: Red, Black (13" x 19.5")
         Black lettering and abstract "Z" on red and white background
         Poster...$15-25

NF15   By Arlene Owseichik. 5/10/88
         Peter Murphy, Passion Fodder, Penelope Houston
         2/c: Blue, Purple (13" x 19.5")
         Purple and blue illustration of Peter Murphy
         Poster...$15-25

NF16　　By Libbie Schock. 5/11/88
<u>**Carlos Santana's Blues For Salvador: Armando Peraza,**</u>
<u>**Chester Thompson , Alphonso Johnson, "Ndugu" Leon Chander,**</u>
<u>**The Caribbean All Stars**</u>
3/c: Brick Red, Mustard Yellow, Blue (13" x 19.5")
Profile of Carlos Santana and map outline of El Salvador
on brick red background
Poster...$15-25

NF17　　By Arlene Owseichik. 5/13/88
<u>**Neville Brothers, Zulu Spear, Hot Borscht**</u>
3/c: Navy Blue, Green, Pink (13" x 19.5")
Fluorescent orange lettering and abstract design of Zulu headdress
in green and purple
Poster...$15-25

NF18　　By Arlene Owseichik. 5/14/88
<u>**The Church, The Rave Ups**</u>
3/c: Navy Blue, Green, Pink (13" x 19.5")
"Starfish moon" on navy blue sky background
Poster...$15-25

NF19　　By Arlene Owseichik. 5/20/88
<u>**Camper Van Beethoven, Mojo Nixon & Skid Roper, Medna Usta**</u>
3/c: Black, Purple, Olive Green (13" x 19.5")
Modern hieroglyphics on beige background
Poster...$15-25

NF20　　By Libbie Schock. 5/21/88
<u>**Leon Russell & Edgar Winter, Thee Hellhounds**</u>
2/c: Blue, Orange (13" x 19.5")
White lettering on orange and blue background
Poster...$15-25

NF21　　By Arlene Owseichik. 5/24/88
<u>**The Fall, Luxuria**</u>
2/c: Black, Red (13" x 19.5")
Bold black, red and gray graphics
Poster...$15-25

NF22　　By Libbie Schock. 5/27/88
<u>**Yngwie J. Malmsteen's Rising Force, Lita Ford**</u>
3/c: Yellow, Orange, Black
Black lettering and "block print" griffin on yellow and red
split fountain background
Poster...$15-25

NF23　　By Arlene Owseichik. 5/28/88
<u>**Joy Of Cooking, Dan Hicks**</u>
3/c: Black, Pink, Blue (13" x 19.5")
50's style lettering and graphics
Poster...$15-25

NF24   By Arlene Owseichik. 6/2-3/88
        The Pogues, Luka Bloom, Darden Smith
        3/c: Purple, Blue, Green (13" x 19.5")
        Green Celtic lettering and monochrome photo of Pogues falling
        from Zeus' hands into purple sea
        Poster...$15-25

NF25   By Michael Shurtz. 6/11/88
        Graham Parker, Aslan
        3/c: Cream, Blue, Olive Green (13" x 19.5")
        "Picasso" violin and Mona Lisa collage on cream background
        Poster...$15-25

NF26   By Libbie Schock. 6/15/88
        Carlos Santana, Wayne Shorter
        3/c: Peach, Purple, Green (13" x 19.5")
        Guitar and saxophone on peach background
        Poster...$15-25

NF27   By Arlene Owseichik. 6/16/88
        Wire, Voice Farm
        2/c: Purple, Red (13" x 19.5")
        Red kidney beans on purple bingo card
        Poster...$15-25

NF28   By Arlene Owseichik. 6/17/88
        The Mission UK, The Zarkons
        2/c: Black, Metallic Silver (13" x 19.5")
        White and silver lettering with black and white photo
        on black background
        Poster...$15-25

NF29   By Gail Weissman and James Olness. 6/20/88
        Thomas Dolby & The Lost Toy People, The Prime Movers
        3/c: Black, Purple, Aqua (13" x 19.5")
        Black and white illustration on spiral purple and aqua background
        Poster...$15-25

NF30   By Arlene Owseichik. 6/30-7/1/88
        Ornette Coleman and Prime Time
        3/c: Brown, Blue, Pink (13" x 19.5")
        Brown lettering and primitive design on ornate Victorian background
        Poster...$15-25

NF31   By Michael Shurtz. 7/6/88
        Aswad, Thaddeus, D.J. Wendt & The Midnite Dread Sound System
        3/c: Purple, Brown, Aqua (13" x 19.5")
        Illustration of lion superimposed over image of Aswad on aqua background
        Poster...$15-25

X NF32   By Arlene Owseichik. 7/10/88
          Iggy Pop
          2/c: Red, Blue (13" x 19.5")
          Duotone photo of Iggy's torso in aqua and pink
          Poster...$15-25

NF33   By Arlene Owseichik. 7/9/88
          Gregg Allman, Doug Hamblin & Jan Fanucci
          2/c: Red, Blue (13" x 19")
          Blue lettering on Confederate background
          Poster...$15-25

NF34   By Richard Blakely. 7/15/88
          Little Charlie & The Nightcats, The Paladins, Katie Webster
          2/c: Black, Blue (13" x 19.5")
          Blue lettering and monochrome photo of Buick Eight grill
          Poster...$15-25

X NF35   By Arlene Owseichik. 7/11/88
          The Ramones, The Dickies, Snatches Of Pink
          3/c: Purple, Green, Beige (13" x 19")
          Tattooed man and woman on beige background
          Poster...$25-35

NF36   By 220Graphics. 7/16/88
          Buster Poindexter & His Banshees Of Blue, Beatnik Beatch
          3/c: Black, Blue, Pink (13" x 19.5")
          Modern deco illustration on pink background
          Poster...$15-25

NF37   By Arlene Owseichik. 7/23/88
          X, Thelonius Monster, The Hangmen
          3/c: Black, Green, Orange (13" x 19.5")
          "X" on neon orange and green background
          Poster...$15-25

NF38   By Arlene Owseichik. 7/27/88
          K.D. Lang & The Reclines, Darden Smith
          3/c: Yellow, Red, Green (13" x 19.5")
          Red maple leaf on white background with floral patterned border
          Poster...$15-25

NF39   By Richard Blakely. 8/1/88
          Erasure, Shona Laing
          2/c: Black, Magenta (13" x 19")
          Duotone portrait of band
          Poster...$15-25

NF40   By Arlene Owseichik. 8/7/88
Reggaefest '88: Judy Mowatt, The Itals, Oku Onoura
4/c: Green, Blue, Magenta, Orange (13" x 19.5")
Abstract palm tree on magenta and orange split fountain background
Poster...$15-25

NF41   By Michael Schurtz. 8/19-20/88
Laura Nyro
3/c: Red, Black, Cream (13" x 19.5")
Red lettering with photo of New York City skyline
Poster...$15-25

NF42   By Arlene Owseichik. 8/25-26/88
Jimmy Cliff, Caribbean All Stars, The Looters
3/c: Blue, Green, Orange (13" x 19.5")
Bird on floral print background
Poster...$15-25

NF43   By Libbie Schock. 8/29/88
Toni Childs
3/c: Blue, Peach, Green, Black (13" x 19.5")
Split fountain seascape with sepia photo inset of Toni Childs
Poster...$15-25

NF44   By Arlene Owseichik. 9/8/88
Little Feat, Robben Ford
3/c: Purple, Blue, Orange (13" x 19.5")
Multi-colored footprints on white background
Poster...$15-25

NF45   By Arlene Owseichik. 9/8/88
Robyn Hitchcock & The Egyptians, Game Theory, Monks Of Doom
2/c: Blue, Orange (13" x 19.5")
Illustration of sphinx with Robyn Hitchcock's head
Poster...$15-25

NF46   By Alton Kelley. 9/10/88
The Dinosaurs, Commander Cody, NRPS
3/c: Red, Blue, Black (19.5" x 13")
Red and blue lettering and vintage car on black background
Poster...$25-35

NF47   By Arlene Owseichik. 9/9/88
Miriam Makeba, Hugh Masekela
2/c: Purple, Aqua (19.5" x 13")
Purple and brown illustration of the African continent
Poster...$15-25

NF48   By Arlene Owseichik. 9/13/88
        Stray Cats, Beat Farmers
        2/c: Purple, Aqua (19.5" x 13")
        Repeated image of man combing his hair
        Poster...$15-25

NF49   By Richard Blakely. 9/16/88
        Joan Jett and the Blackhearts
        3/c: Black, Yellow, Red (12.5" x 19")
        Inset of Victorian woman on yellow background
        Poster...$15-25

NF50   By Arlene Owseichik. 9/20/88
        Djavan
        4/c: Blue, Magenta, Yellow, Green (13" x 19.5")
        Bird-of-paradise flowers on blue background with red border
        Poster...$15-25

NF51   By Elsa Bouman. 9/24/88
        David Lindley & El Rayo-X, The Bhundu Boys
        3/c: Brown, Yellow, Green (12.5" x 19")
        Tiki lettering on patterned background
        Poster...$15-25

NF52   By Arlene Owseichik. 9/30/88
        The Smithereens, Paul Kelly & The Messengers, Danny Phillips
        2/c: Yellow, Green (13" x 19")
        Collage on green background
        Poster...$15-25

NF53   By Libbie Schock. 10/1/88
        **Reggaefest '88: Dennis Brown with Lloyd Parks
        & We The People Band, Thaddeus & Santa Cruz Steel**
        4/c: Red, Blue, Green, Yellow (13" x 19.5")
        Green, red, and yellow flags on blue background
        Poster...$15-25

NF54   By Arlene Owseichik. 10/7/88
        Skinny Puppy, Sons Of Freedom
        3/c: Black, Red, Orange (13" x 19")
        Eyeball with red iris on black and orange background
        Poster...$15-25

NF55   By Arlene Owseichik. 10/12/88
        **Richard Thompson Band, Victoria Williams,
        Clive Greggson & Christine Collister**
        3/c: Brick Red, Yellow, Orange (13" x 19.5")
        Orange shawl and tambourine on brick red background
        Poster...$15-25

NF56 By Whit Clifton. 10/15/88
Reggaefest '88: The Wailers, Joe Higgs, C.K. Ladzekpo
5/c: Black, Red, Green, Blue, Metallic Gold (13" x 19.5")
Gold and black illustration of lion on black background
Poster...$15-25

NF57 By Marc D'Estout. 10/29/88
Leonard Cohen
3/c: Blue, Yellow, Magenta (13" x 19.5")
Portrait of Leonard Cohen on magenta and blue variegated background
Poster...$15-25

NF58 By Arlene Owseichik. 10/26/88
Devo
3/c: Chartreuse, Maroon, Orange
Neon orange lettering and duotone photo of man with sunglasses
Poster...$15-25

NF59 By Arlene Owseichik. 10/28/88
Blue Oyster Cult, Impellitteri Masi
2/c: Green, Blue (13" x 19.5")
Bauhaus style lettering on background photo of San Francisco's
turn-of-the-century Cliff House
Poster...$15-25

NF60 By Libbie Schock. 10/30/88
Warren Zevon
2/c: Green, Gold (13" x 19.5")
Skeleton with aviator sunglasses and cigarette on green and gold
background
Poster...$15-25

XNF61 By Arlene Owseichik. 10/31/88
The Cramps
5/c: Yellow, Orange, Green, Red, Black (13" x 19.5")
Portrait of the band on 3-D background in Halloween theme
Poster...$15-25

NF62 By Richard Blakely. 11/5/88
The Feelies, Downey Mildew, Call Me Bwana
2/c: Orange, Maroon (13.5" x 19.5")
Off-register duotone of the Feelies in orange and maroon
Poster...$15-25

XNF63 By Arlene Owseichik. 11/15/88
Sonic Youth, Die Kruezen, Mudhoney
3/c: Pink, Green, Orange (13" x 19.5")
Photo of mass wedding in neon pink, orange, and green
Poster...$20-30

NF64   By Michael Shurtz. 11/25/88
         Word To Word: Jim Carroll, Ray Manzarek, Michael McClure
         3/c: Black, Orange, Purple (13" x 19.5")
         Portrait of poets on purple background with orange border
         Poster...$20-30

NF65   By Whit Clifton. 12/2/88
         Johnny Winter, John Mayall's Blues Breakers, Chester D.
         4/c: Black, Red, Blue, Yellow (13" x 19.5")
         Space scene with "atomic" Earth in foreground
         Poster...$15-25

NF66   By Arlene Owseichik. 12/9/88
         Edie Brickell & New Bohemians, Show Of Hands, Genuine Diamelles
         3/c: Blue, Yellow, Magenta (13" x 19.5")
         Illustrations of telescope, stars, and planets on blue background
         Poster...$15-25

NF67   By Arlene Owseichik. 12/6/88
         The Gypsy Kings
         3/c: Black, Magenta, Yellow (13" x 19.5")
         Yellow, magenta, and gray "folk" design on black background
         Poster...$15-25

NF68   By Arlene Owseichik. 12/16/88
         Fishbone, Psychotic Pineapple
         2/c: Black, Green (13" x 19.5")
         *Photo inset of fisherman holding fish with Fishbone logo on a
         green and gray newsprint background*
         Poster...$15-25

NF69   By Arlene Owseichik. 12/17/88
         Tower of Power, Blazing Redheads, Wiley Roberts
         3/c: Red, Black, Metallic Gold (13" x 19.5")
         Red lettering and musical instruments on black background
         Poster...$15-25

NF70   By Marc D'Estout. 12/30/88
         Hot Tuna: Jorma Kaukonen & Jack Casady
         3/c: Black, Red, Yellow (13" x 19.5")
         Illustration of yellow fish above red and yellow flames on black background
         Poster...$20-30

NF71   By Arlene Owseichik. 12/22/88
         BGP Christmas Party
         4/c: Red, Green, Black, Metallic Gold (13" x 19.5")
         Fillmore logo in op green and red on black background
         Poster...$15-25

NF72   By Arlene Owseichik. 12/31/88
          K.D. Lang & The Reclines, Harry Dean Stanton & The Repo Men,
          Marga Gomez
          3/c: Black, Pink, Purple (13" x 19.5")
          White lettering in black inset on background of pink and purple cupids
          Poster...$15-25

NF73   By Dan Quarnstrom. 1/28/89
          Stray Cats
          3/c: Blue, Black, Red (13" x 19.5")
          Computer illustration of dogs on black background
          Poster...$15-25

NF74   By Libbie Schock. 2/3/89
          Toots & The Maytals, Joe Higgs & His Band, Thaddeus
          3/c: Purple, Green, Orange (13" x 19.5")
          Orange lettering on purple and green background
          Poster...$15-25

NF75   By Arlene Owseichik. 2/15/89
          Hothouse Flowers, Indigo Girls
          3/c: Red, Blue, Yellow (13" x 19")
          Blue lettering and illustration of sunflower on red background
          Poster...$15-25

NF76   By Arlene Owseichik. 2/16/89
          Neville Brothers, Crazy 8's, Doc Collins
          3/c: Brown, Peach, Black (12.5" x 19")
          Black and white photo of Rosa Parks on brown background
          with peach lettering
          Poster...$15-25

NF77   By Arlene Owseichik & Kathleen Ahern. 2/17/89
          The Pursuit Of Happiness, The Proclaimers, The Connells,
          Slammin' Watusis, Sidewinders
          5/c: Yellow, Magenta, Blue, Black, Orange (13" x 19")
          "Dog bone" lettering and full color photo of collie
          Poster...$15-25

NF78   By Arlene Owseichik. 2/28/89
          Nick Cave & The Bad Seeds, Wolfgang Press
          4/c: Black, Orange, Red, Green (13" x 19.5")
          Orange to red split fountain lettering and photo inset of Nick Cave
          on olive green background
          Poster...$15-25

NF79   By Elsa Bouman. 3/4/89
          Reggaefest '89: Sugar Minott & Abra Shanti, Pato Banton & His Band,
          The Sugarbeats
          4/c: Blue, Red, Yellow, Black (13" x 19")
          Black type on multi-colored "brick" background
          Poster...$15-25

NF80   By Arlene Owseichik: 3/8/89
The Jeff Healey Band, Doug Hamlin & Jan Fanucci, The Thieves
2/c: Violet, Black (19" x 13")
Illustration of Fender guitar with "braille" dots
on split gray and purple background
Poster...$15-25

NF81   By Whit Clifton & Dave Kenton. 3/10/89
That Petrol Emotion, Voice Of The Beehive, Swamp Zombies
4/c: Yellow, Magenta, Black, Blue (13" x 19.5")
Illustration of heart melts into honeycomb landscape
on magenta background
Poster...$15-25

NF82   By Arlene Owseichik. 3/17/89
David Grisman Quartet, New Grass Revival
3/c: Blue, Orange, Black (13" x 19.5")
Neon orange lettering and black and white photo
on black background
Poster...$15-25

NF83   By Michael Schurtz. 3/18/89
The Stephen Stills Band, Zero
2/c: Black, Metallic Silver (13" x 19.5")
Monochrome photo of cowboy on white background
with silver vignette
Poster...$15-25

NF84   By Libbie Schock. 3/30/89
Book Of Love, Legal Reins
3/c: Orange, Magenta, Green (13" x 19")
Illustration of couple in heart inset on peach background
Poster...$15-25

NF85   By Arlene Owseichik. 3/31/89
Graham Parker, Pierce Turner, Genuine Diamelles
4/c: Blue, Green, Purple, Orange (12.5" x 19.5")
Photo of person looking at the Statue of Liberty
on blue to green split fountain background
Poster...$15-25

NF86   By Arlene Owseichik. 4/1/89
Steve Earle & The Dukes
3/c: Red, Blue, Green (13" x 19.5")
Illustration of American eagle on red background
Poster...$15-25

NF87   By Arlene Owseichik. 4/7/89
Red Hot Chili Peppers, Thelonious Monster
3/c: Red, Black, Neon Green (13.5" x 18.5")
Illustration of chili pepper on Day-Glogreen background
Poster...$25-35

NF88   By Arlene Owseichik. 4/15/89
David Lindley & El Rayo X, The Henry Kaiser Band,
Tom Constanten
3/c: Magenta, Green, Brown (13" x 19")
Photo inset of David Lindley with illustration of madras shorts
and clashing patterned shirt on pink, beige, and brown background
Poster...$15-25

NF89   By Arlene Owseichik. 4/22/89
Midge Ure, Love Club
3/c: Purple, Blue, Green (13" x 19.5")
Photo of Rodin's "The Thinker" and grid pattern landscape
on purple to blue split fountain background
Poster...$15-25

NF90   By Mike "Art Abuse" Hazlett and Orin Green. 4/29/89
Dead Milkmen, MCM & The Monster
3/c: Green, Yellow, Magenta (13" x 19.5")
Photo of lizard in "Dead Milkmen" shirt on paisley background
Poster...$15-25

NF91   By Arlene Owseichik. 4/30/89
The Proclaimers, Penelope Houston, Cindy Lee Berryhill
3/c: Magenta, Yellow, Black (13" x 19.5")
White lettering and illustration of two pairs of orange sunglasses
on madras plaid background
Poster...$15-25

NF92   By Whit Clifton. 5/3/89
David Crosby, Michael Hedges
4/c: Yellow, Black, Blue, Red
Illustration of David Crosby's profile and airbrushed
lettering on yellow background
Poster...$15-25

NF93   By Marc D'Estout. 5/5/89
Shinehead & The A-Team Band, D.J. Doug Wendt &
The Midnight Dread Sound System, M.C. Tony Moses
3/c: Blue, Green, Black (13" x 19.5")
Green lettering on split blue and black background
Poster...$15-25

NF94   By Dan Quarnstrom. 5/6/89
Redd Kross, Christmas, Frightwig
3/c: Yellow, Magenta, Blue (13" x 19.5")
Cartoon illustration of guitarist on magenta, yellow,
and blue background
Poster...$15-25

NF95   By Dan Quartstrom. 5/7-8/89
        Jane's Addiction, Caterwaul, The Sextants, Gherkin
        Raucous, House Of Wheels
        3/c: Blue, Magenta, Orange (13" x 19.5")
        Magenta lettering and duotone photo of Jane's Addiction
        on orange background
        Poster...$20-30

NF96   By Elsa Bouman. 5/9/89
        The Fixx, Jimmy Wood & The Immortals
        3/c: Red, Brown, Yellow (13" x 19.5")
        Seascape with red sky and yellow beach
        Poster...$15-25

NF97   By Arlene Owseichik. 5/10/89
        Willy DeVille & The Mink DeVille Band, The Gospel Hummingbirds
        3/c: Purple, Brown, Orange (13" x 19")
        Illustration of playing card from a fleur-de-lis "suit" on orange background
        Poster...$15-25

NF98   By Richard Blakely. 5/12-13/89
        Reggaefest '89: Third World, The Wailers
        4/c: Red, Green, Yellow, Black (13" x 19.5")
        Black lettering on red and yellow background
        Poster...$15-25

NF99   By Arlene Owseichik. 5/17/89
        Front 242, Wayne Doba
        4/c: Red, Yellow, Brown, Black (13" x 19.5")
        Large "Front 242" lettering on marbleized brown and gold background
        Poster...$15-25

NF100   By Arlene Owseichik. 5/20/89
        Bob Mould, Peter Case, American Music Club
        2/c: Rust, Black (13" x 19")
        Duotone photo of bust in pile of maple leaves
        Poster...$15-25

NF101   By Arlene Owseichik. 5/21/89
        Indigo Girls, Pastiche
        2/c: Blue, Aqua (13" x 19.5")
        Illustrated tiger lilies on blue background
        Poster...$15-25

NF102   By Randy Tuten. 6/2/89
        The Radiators, Jason D. Williams
        3/c: Red, Green, Black (13" x 19.5")
        Airbrushed lettering and illustration of woman riding
        a fish in underwater scene
        Poster...$15-25

NF103 By Arlene Owseichik. 6/5-6/89
Cowboy Junkies, Lucinda Williams
3/c: Red, Brown, Black (13" x 19.5")
Red lettering on "sepia" photo of bench
Poster...$15-25

NF104 By Arlene Owseichik. 6/3/89
Buck Owens & The Buckaroos, Thee Hellhounds,
Jason D. Williams
1/c: Brown (13" x 19.5")
Brown lettering with brown and white "buckskin" above map of California
on beige background
Poster...$75-100

NF105 By Matthew Foster. 6/8/89
Guadalcanal Diary, Treat Her Right
3/c: Red, Blue, Silver (10.5" x 18.5")
Contemporary graphics on blue background
Poster...$25-35

NF106 By Bavi. 6/10/89
Ruben Blades Y Son Del Solar, Conjunto Cespedes
3/c: Purple, Red, Black (13" x 19.5")
Red lettering and duotone photo of child wearing Ruben Blades T-shirt
Poster...$25-35

NF107 By Arlene Owseichik. 6/23/89
The Untouchables, Limbomaniacs, Psychefunkapus
4/c: Blue, Neon Green, Neon Pink, Black (12.5" x 19.5")
Inset of the Untouchables on zebra and leopard print background
Poster...$25-35

NF108 By Arlene Owseichik. 7/5-6/89
Tom Tom Club, Polymorphia, Zulu Spear
3/c: Purple, Green, Black (13" x 19.5")
Purple lettering and black silhouette of children playing
Poster...$25-35

NF109 By Arlene Owseichik. 7/12/89
Todd Rundgren, Big Bamboo
3/c: Maroon, Blue, Brown (13" x 19.5")
Abstract design in blue, maroon, and brown
Poster...$25-35

NF110 By Arlene Owseichik. 7/14/89
Exodus, Forbidden
3/c: Red, Blue, Beige (13" x 19.5")
Illustration of angry mob and decapitated head on red background
Poster...$25-35

NF111   By Elsa Bouman. 7/24/89
          Pixies, Happy Mondays
          2/c: Purple, Green (13" x 19")
          Diagonally repeated green and purple fractiles
          Poster...$25-35

NF112   By Arlene Owseichik. 7/28-30/89
          The B52's, Royal Crescent Mob
          4/c: Yellow, Blue, Black, Red (13" x 19.5")
          Full color photo of Barbie and Ken dolls reclining in
          bowl of green gelatin
          Poster...$25-35

NF113   By Arlene Owseichik. 9/9/89
          Fela Anikulapo Kuti & Egypt '80, Ephat Mujuru &
          The Balafon Marimba Ensemble
          2/c: Rust, Gold (13" x 19.5")
          Illustration of African continent encircled by "Africa must unite"
          banner on gold and rust background
          Poster...$25-35

NF114   By The Flea Ranch/ Gary LaRochelle. 9/7/89
          A Benefit For KUSF 90.3: Love & Rockets,
          Maximillion's Motorcycle Club, Heaven Insects
          3/c: Peach, Red, Black (13" x 19.5")
          Phot inset of Love & Rockets on background of missiles
          Poster...$25-35

NF115   By Kozik. 9/15-16/89
          Red Hot Chili Peppers, Mary's Danish, Primus
          4/c: Pink, Purple, Blue, Black (13" x 19")
          Woman with skull and crossbones on op purple and pink background
          Poster...$25-35

NF116   By Arlene Owseichik. 9/10/89
          Natalie Cole, Warren Thomas
          3/c: Magenta, Green, Brown (13" x 19")
          Brown lettering on marbleized pink and mint green background
          Poster...$25-35

NF117   By Arlene Owseichik. 9/26-28/89
          Jefferson Airplane
          4/c: Blue, Green, Pink, Black (19.5" x 13")
          Blue and green lettering and illustration of biplane
          on black and white photo of the Golden Gate Bridge
          Poster...$25-35

NF118   By Arlene Owseichik. 10/4/89
          BoDeans, 54·40, The Sextants
          2/c: Maroon, Red (13" x 19")
          Maroon lettering and red heart on pink and white mezzotint background
          Poster...$25-35

NF119 By Elsa Bouman. 10/22/89
Deborah Harry
3/c: Red, Blue, Metallic Gold (13" x 19.5")
Red lettering and partial photo of woman behind lace
Poster...$25-35

NF120 By Arlene Owseichik. 10/20-21/89
George Clinton & The P-Funk Allstars, Smoking Section
3/c: Magenta, Orange, Dark Blue (13" x 19.5")
Photo inset of George Clinton on magenta and dark blue background
Poster...$25-35

Russ Gibb Presents

Detroit, Michigan, is one of several areas outside of San Francisco to produce quality rock poster art, largely due to the efforts of artists Gary Grimshaw and Carl Lundgren. From 1966 through 1969, the primary venue was the Grande Ballroom, booked by promoter Russ Gibb. This section includes posters, handbills, and postcards for shows presented by Russ Gibb, and uses RG as the item prefix.

While we have listed the handbills for the sake of completeness, we cannot encourage collectors to pursue them. Bootlegs of these pieces have appeared with increasing regularity since 1990, and it is virtually impossible for a novice to distinguish the genuine article from the facsimile.

RG1

RG2

RG0   Artist Unknown. 9/16/66
Grande Ballroom Opening:
Dancing Every Friday and Saturday!
2/c: Black, Yellow (21.5" x 27.5")
White letttering with illustration of trumpet on black background
Poster Price Undetermined

RG1   By Gary Grimshaw. 10/7-8/66
MC5, The Chosen Few
2/c: Red, Black (13" x 18")
Red and black letttering with illustration of seagull on white background
Poster...$200-300 / Handbill...$80-120

RG2   By Gary Grimshaw. 10/14-15/66
The Woolies, MC5
2/c: Magenta, Green (15.5" x 20")
Illustration of skeleton sporting hair and bandana on white background
Poster...$125-200

RG3   By Gary Grimshaw. 10/21-22/66
MC5, The Prime Movers Blues Band
2/c: Magenta, Blue (17.5" x 22.5")
Blue lettering and striped man (see FD28) on magenta background
Poster...$125-200

RG4   By Rob Tyner. 10/28-29/66
MC5, Southbound Freeway, Chosen Few
1/c: Black (8.5" x 11")
White lettering on black and white background
Handbill...$125-200

RG5   By Gary Grimshaw. 11/4-5/66
Southbound Freeway, MC5, Bossmen
2/c: Orange, Black (11.5" x 22")
White lettering with illustration of "mod man" reaching for sun
on orange background
Poster...$125-200

RG6   By Gary Grimshaw. 11/18-19/66
Walking Wounded, Whas?, Poor Souls, MC5
1/c: Black (8.5" x 14")
Illustrated hippie in circular sunglasses on white background
Handbill...$40-75

RG7   By Rob Tyner. 11/25-26/66
Jagged Edge, MC5, Black and Blues Band
1/c: Black (8.5" x 11")
Black lettering with illustration of "hip party"
borrowed from MAD magazine
Handbill...$40-75

RG10

RG15

RG24

RG42

RG8   By Rob Tyner. 12/9-10/66
Jagged Edge, Ourselves, MC5, The Kynde
1/c: Black (8.5" x 11")
Comic strip with hipster describing his first trip to the Grande Ballroom
Handbill...$40-75

RG9   By Rob Tyner. 12/16-17/66
The Landeers, The Plague, MC5, Wha?, The Badger, The Atomic Pile
1/c: Black (8.5" x 11")
Black lettering and cartoon faces on white background
Handbill...$40-75

RG10   By Gary Grimshaw. 12/22-23/66 & 12/29-31/66
MC5, Green Grass Blues, Urban Roots, Black and Blues Band, Taboos, Thyme, Cosmic Expanding, Poor Souls
2/c: Orange, Black (15" x 22.5")
Brown and white lettering surrounded by woman's hair on white background
Poster...$125-200

RG11   By Donnie Dope. 1/13-14/67
Unrelated Segments, Southbound Freeway, MC5
1/c: Black (8.5" x 11")
White lettering with illustration of hippie eating "ACID"
Handbill...$40-75

RG12   By Gary Grimshaw. 1/20-21/67 & 1/27-28/67
MC5, The Trees, Scotty's Group, The Passing Clouds, The Plague, C-Water Blues, Vernor Highway Band
2/c: Yellow, Blue (14.25" x 21")
White lettering and photo inset of Fred Smith on green background
Poster...$125-200

RG13   *"Guerilla Lovefare"* by Gary Grimshaw. 1/29/67
Spiked Rivers, MC5, Livonia Tool & Die Co., Detroit Edison White Light Band, Lyman Woodward Ensemble, Joseph Jarman, English Spangler Jazz Unit, Bugging Eyeballs of Guatama, Poets: Jim Semark. Jerry Younkins, John Sinclair, Art Rosch, Don Hoye
1/c: Black (17.5" x 22")
White lettering with illustration of man in profile
on black and white background
Poster...$150-200

RG14   By Gary Grimshaw. 2/3-4/67
MC5, Wha?, Little Sisters, The Raven
2/c: Purple, Green (6" x 10")
Split fountain design with photo of turn-of-the-century musicians
printed on blue paper
Handbill...$50-75

RG15   By Gary Grimshaw. 2/10-11/67
         Thyme, People, Rationals, Zymodics
         3/c: Blue, Magenta, Yellow (17" x 21.5")
         White lettering and split fountain design on blue background
         Poster...$125-200

RG16   By David Carlin. 2/17-18/67
         Barons Ashmollyan Quintet, Landeers Cosmic Expanding
         1/c: Magenta (8.5" x 11")
         Magenta design on green paper
         Handbill...$50-75

RG17   By Carlin and Grimshaw. 2/24-25/67
         Scot Richard Case & The Village Beaus, Jagged Edge, The D.S.R.
         3/c: Blue, Yellow, Black (16.5" x 22")
         Black lettering with illustration of Greta Garbo and silhouette of mob
         in yellow insets on blue background
         Poster...$125-200

RG18   By Carlin. 3/10-11/67
         Poor Souls, We Who Are, Frut Of The Loom, The Southbound Freeway,
         Passing Clouds
         2/c: Red, Purple (17" x 21.5")
         Purple lettering with illustration of "flapper" on mauve background
         Poster...$125-200

RG19   By David Carlin. 3/17-18/67
         MC5, Scot Richard Case, The Strange Fate, The Gang
         1/c: Black (8.5" x 11")
         Black lettering covers illustration of woman's face
         Handbill...$40-75

RG20   By Gary Grimshaw. 3/24-25/67
         Landeers, Henchmen, Born Blues, City Limits, MC5
         1/c: Black (8.5" x 14")
         Photo inset of woman with illustrated third eye
         Poster...$75-125

RG21   By David Carlin. 3/30-31/67 - 4/1/67
         Scot Richard Case, Somethin' Else, Thyme, Wild Cargo,
         Yesterdays Shadows, Detroit Blues Ball, Jagged Edge, Seventh Seal
         2/c: Red, Blue (17" x 21.5")
         White lettering with photo inset of American Indian on red background
         Poster...$100-175

RG22   By David Carlin. 4/2/67
         MC5, Water Blues, Seventh Seal, Billy C & The Sunshine
         1/c: Black (8.5" x 11")
         Profile of woman in ornate headdress bordered by white lettering
         Handbill...$40-75

RG23   By Gary Grimshaw. 4/7-8/67
        Poor Souls, Reason Why?, Restless Set, Hideaways
        1/c: Green (8.5" x 11")
        White lettering with illustration of couple dancing
        on green and white background
        Handbill...$40-75

RG24   By Gary Grimshaw. 4/14-15/67
        Changing Tymes, Weeds, Sum Guys, One Way Street, Thyme, Gang
        2/c: Orange, Green (16.5" x 21.5")
        Green lettering on orange background
        Poster...$100-175

RG25   By Gary Grimshaw. 4/21-22/67
        Jagged Edge, Sons Of Sound, Scot Richard Set, Manchild, New Spirit
        1/c: Black (8.5" x 11")
        Black lettering with illustration of young man on spiral op background;
        Show is "In Honor Of The Vanishing American: The American Barber"
        Handbill...$40-75

RG26   By Gary Grimshaw and John Ka. 5/5-6/67
        Billy C & The Sunshine, Primates, Harmon Street Blues,
        Panic & The Pack
        1/c: Black (8.5" x 11")
        Illustration of "flower child" with lettering in the configuration of leaves
        on white background
        Handbill...$40-75

RG27   By Gary Grimshaw. 5/12-13/67
        Earth Mother, Ourselves, Berry Patch, Apostles,
        Echoes From A Broken Mirror
        1/c: Brown (8.5" x 11")
        Monochrome illustration of Raphaelesque women printed on green paper
        Handbill...$40-75

RG28   By Gary Grimshaw. 5/19-20/67
        Scot Richard Case, Thyme, December's Children, Odds & Ends
        1/c: Purple (8.5" x 11")
        Outline lettering with illustrated Egyptian symbols on white background
        Handbill...$40-75

RG29   By Donnie Dope. 5/26-27/67
        Southbound Freeway, Cowardly Thangs, Harmon Street Blues,
        Vernor Highway
        2/c: Blue, Red (17" x 20.5")
        Illustrated dancer with flowers on red and blue background
        Poster...$100-150

RG30   By Donnie Forsyth. 6/2-3/67
        Rationals, C-Water Blues, Jagged Edge, Belshire
        1/c: Blue (8.5" x 11")
        Illustration of man in sunglasses printed on green paper
        Handbill...$40-75

RG46

RG47

RG48

RG49

RG31   By Donnie Dope. 6/9-10/67
       Morticians, Apostles, Thyme
       1/c: Black (8.5" x 11")
       Illustration of androgynous figure holding decapitated head
       on cream paper
       Handbill...$40-75

RG32   By Donnie Dope. 6/16-17/67
       Jagged Edge, Shifting Sands, Those Guys, MC5
       1/c: Red (8.5" x 11")
       Red lettering and illustration of thug with "dog" face on white background
       Handbill...$40-75

RG33   By Donnie Dope. 6/23-24/67
       MC5, Phogg, Scot Richard Case, Up, Set
       1/c: Black (8.5" x 11")
       Illustration of "Mother Goose" printed on green paper
       Handbill...$40-75

RG34   By Carlson. 6/30/67
       Jefferson Airplane, MC5, Rationals, Apostles, Ourselves
       2/c: Blue, Purple (16" x 21.5"), (8.5 x 11")
       Illustration of woman with blue hair on purple and white background
       Poster...$150-200 / Handbill...$60-100

RG35   By Donnie Dope. 7/7-8/67
       Hideaways, Ourselves, Primates
       2/c: Gold, Purple (8.5" x 11")
       Illustration of man in profile with Beatles hairstyle on purple background
       Handbill...$40-60

RG36   By Donnie Dope. 7/14-15/67
       Rationals, Bump, Jagged Edge, Craig Suterland Movement
       2/c: Green, Black (8.5" x 11")
       Green and gray lettering with illustrated octopus
       on green background
       Handbill...$40-60

RG37   By Donnie Dope. 7/21-22/67
       Tim Buckley, Ourselves, Shaggs
       2/c: Yellow, Red (10.5" x 16.5")
       Illustrated sun on yellow background
       Poster...$100-175

RG38   By Donnie Dope. 7/28-29/67
       Scot Richard Case, Euphonic Aggregation, Apostles, Upset
       1/c: Blue (7.5" x 10.75")
       Light blue lettering with illustration of smoking woman
       on blue background
       Handbill...$40-60

RG50

RG51

RG52

RG55

RG39   By Donnie Dope. 8/11-12/67
Grateful Dead, Rationals, Southbound Freeway, Bishops,
Ashmollyan Quintet
1/c: Red (8.5" x 12")
Illustration of naked woman with butterfly wings printed on green paper
Handbill...$50-75

RG40   By Donnie Dope. 8/18-19/67
Thyme, Uncalled Four, Troyes, Shaggs
2/c: Magenta, Blue (7.25" x 10.5")
Illustration of eye with claw on magenta and blue background
Handbill...$40-60

RG41   By Alice Cow and Donnie Dope. 8/25-26/67
Apostles, Our Mothers Children, Scot Richard Case,
Certified Chalk Cyrcle
2/c: Magenta, Orange (8.5" x 11")
Orange lettering with illustration of couple in purple inset
on white background
Handbill...$40-60

RG42   By Gary Grimshaw. 9/1-2/67
Chambers Brothers, MC5, Thyme
1/c: Brown (14" x 21.75"), (7" x 10.5")
Photo inset of the Chambers Brothers on brown background
Poster...$100-175 / Handbill...$40-60

RG43   By Donnie Dope. 9/8-9/67
Scot Richard Case, Buoys, Rationals, Jagged Edge, Up
1/c: Black (8.5" x 11")
Illustration of peacock on white background
Handbill...$40-60

RG44   By Donnie Dope. 9/15-16/67
MC5, Gang, Ourselves, Pack, Ashmollyan Quintet
1/c: Blue (8" x 10.25")
Photo of Paul McCartney with Mouseketeer ears on blue background
Handbill...$40-60

RG45   By Gary Grimshaw. 9/22-24/67
Southbound Freeway, Billy C & The Sunshine, MC5, Buoys,
Charles Moore Ensemble, Up, Poets: John Sinclair, Jim Semark
2/c: Red, Purple (12" x 22"), (3.5" x 7.5")
Red lettering and illustration of Shiva on red and purple background
Poster...$125-175 / Postcard...$30-50

RG46   By Gary Grimshaw. Photo by Leni Sinclair. 9/29-30/67
Apostles, MC5, East Side Orphans, Spike Drivers
2/c: Yellow, Black (14" x 22"), (4.25" x 7")
Yellow and black lettering with monochrome photo of Rob Tyner
Poster...$125-175 / Postcard...$30-50

RG56

RG57

RG58

RG59

RG47   By Gary Grimshaw. 10/6-7/67
<u>Scot Richard Case, Billy & The Sunshine, MC5, Gang, Odds and Ends</u>
2/c: Green, Purple (14" x 22"), (4.25" x 7.5")
Green lettering and oval photo inset of statue
on green and purple background
Poster...$75-150 / Postcard...$25-40

RG48   By Gary Grimshaw. 10/13-15/67
<u>Cream, MC5, Rationals, Apostles</u>
3/c: Magenta, Green, Orange (3.75" x 7"), (12" x 22")
Beige lettering with photo inset of Cream on orange background
Poster...$75-150 / Postcard...$25-40

RG49   By Gary Grimshaw. 10/20-21/67
<u>Pack, Gold, Our Mothers Children, MC5, Gang, Billy & The Sunshine</u>
2/c: Magenta, Blue (13" x 22"), (4.25" x 7.5")
Magenta lettering and illustrated inset of 18th century youth
on blue background
Poster...$75-150 / Postcard...$25-40

RG50   By Gary Grimshaw. 10/27-28/67
<u>James Gang, MC5, Rationals, Up</u>
2/c: Magenta, Blue (12.5" x 21"), (4" x 7")
Blue lettering and yin-yang symbol with nude figures
on magenta background
Poster...$75-150 / Postcard...$20-30

RG51   By Gary Grimshaw. 11/3-5/67
<u>Paupers, Gang, Thyme, MC5, Rationals</u>
2/c: Blue, Red (12.5" x 22"), (4" x 7")
Red lettering with 3-D photo inset of American Indian children
on blue background
Poster...$175-250 / Postcard...$25-40

RG52   By Carl Lundgren. 11/10-11/67
<u>MC5, James Cotton Blues Band, Billy C & The Sunshine</u>
2/c: Magenta, Green (14" x 24")
Magenta lettering and duotone photo of Vanessa Redgrave
on green background
Poster...$175-250 / Postcard...$20-30

RG53   By Gary Grimshaw. 11/17-18/67
<u>Scot Richard Case, Apostles, Lost Generation, Odds and Ends,</u>
<u>Epidemic, Our Mothers Children</u>
1/c: Purple (4" x 7")
Purple lettering with monochrome illustration of sultan
on white background
Postcard...$20-30

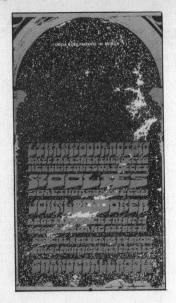

RG60

RG61

RG62

RG63

RG54   Artist Unknown. 11/23/67
MC5, Scot Richard Case
1/c: Red (8.5" x 11")
Illustration of peacock on white background
Handbill...$40-60

RG55   By Gary Grimshaw. 11/24-25/67
Fugs, Gang, Ashmollyan Quintet, MC5
3/c: Orange, Magenta, Black (15" x 22"), (5" x 7")
Monochrome photo inset of the Fugs on orange and magenta background
Poster...$75-150 / Postcard...$20-30

RG56   By Carl Lundgren. 12/1-2/67
Chambers Brothers, Children, Thyme, Up
3/c: Blue, Yellow, Red (14" x 23.5"), (4.5" x 7.5")
Photo collage and split fountain circular lettering on blue background
Poster...$75-125 / Postcard...$15-25

RG57   By Gary Grimshaw. 12/8-9/67
Moby Grape, Rationals, MC5
2/c: Blue, Magenta (3.75" x 7")
*Magenta lettering with illustration of the Goddess of Wine
on blue background*
Postcard...$10-20

RG58   By Carl Lundgren. 12/15-17/67
Vanilla Fudge, Thyme, Rationals, MC5
3/c: Red, Yellow, Blue (13" x 22"), (4.25" x 7.5")
Double split fountain design on white background
Poster...$75-125 / Postcard...$10-20

RG59   By Gary Grimshaw. 12/21-23/67
**Paul Butterfield Blues Band, Thyme, Rationals, Cream,
Billy C & The Sunshine, MC5, Soap**
3/c: Magenta, Gold, Black (13" x 22"), (4.5" x 7.5")
*Magenta and gold split fountain lettering with photo collage
on black background*
Poster...$75-125 / Postcard...$10-15

RG60   By Carl Lundgren. 12/26-30/67
**Lyman Woodward Trio, Billy C, Talismen, MC5, Up, Woolies, Soap,
John Lee Hooker, Apostles, Pack, Gang, Prime Movers**
3/c: Blue, Red, Green (13" x 22"), (4" x 7.5")
Green lettering with illustration of biplane on blue background
Poster...$75-100 / Postcard...$10-15

RG61   By Gary Grimshaw. 1/5-6/68
Clear Light, Gipsy Blue, Children
2/c: Purple, Yellow (4" x 7")
Gold lettering on purple background
Postcard...$10-15

RG68

RG62   By Carl Lundgren. 1/12-13/68
        Buddy Guy Blues Band, Gang, Soap
        3/c: Magenta, Yellow, Blue (4.25" x 7")
        Red lettering with illustrated angels on multi-colored sun background
        Postcard...$10-15

RG63   By Gary Grimshaw. 1/19-20/67 & 1/23/68
        Scot Richard Case, Amboy Dukes, Apple Pie Motherhood,
        John Mayall's Blues Breakers, Rationals
        2/c: Orange, Aqua (13" x 22"), (4" x 7")
        Circular photo inset of John Mayall on orange background
        Poster...$75-100 / Postcard...$10-15

RG64   By Carl Lundgren. 1/26-27/68
        Lyman Woodward Trio, Thyme, Jagged Edge
        3/c: Green, Blue, Magenta (7.5" x 5")
        White lettering with kaleidoscope design on split fountain background
        Postcard...$10-15

RG65   By Gary Grimshaw. 2/2-3/68
        Beacon Street Union, MC5, Charging Rhinocerous of Soul
        2/c: Green, Red (4" x 7")
        Red circle with mezzotint photo of Beacon Street Union
        on green background
        Postcard...$15-25

RG66   By Carl Lundgren. 2/9-10/68
        Frost, Children, Jagged Edge, Ashmollyan Quintet
        1/c: Black (4.5" x 7.5")
        Black lettering with "walking bed" cartoon inset on white background
        Postcard...$10-15

RG67   By Carl Lundgren. 2/16-18/68
        The Byrds, Canned Heat, Apostles, Thyme, Carousel, Up, Rationals,
        Wilson Mower Pursuit
        3/c: Magenta, Blue, Yellow (4" x 7")
        Split fountain mezzotint photos of the Byrds and Canned Heat
        Postcard...$15-25

RG68   By Gary Grimshaw. 2/23/68
        Jimi Hendrix Experience, Soft Machine, MC5, Rationals
        3/c: Red, Yellow, Blue (4.25" x 7")
        Red lettering and duotone photo of Hendrix playing guitar behind his head
        superimposed over green and white photo of magnified electron field
        Postcard...$75-100

RG69   By Gary Grimshaw. Photo by Leni Sinclair. 2/23-24/68
        Frut of the Loom, Scot Richard Case, Tiers, Born Blues
        1/c: Black (4" x 7")
        Black lettering with photo inset of Gary Grimshaw on white background
        Postcard...$15-25

RG65

RG67

RG70

RG71

RG70   By Gary Grimshaw. 2/24/68
       Jimi Hendrix Experience, Soft Machine, Paupers
       3/c: Yellow, Magenta, Blue (13" x 22"), (4.25" x 7.25")
       Yellow lettering and mezzotint photo of the Jimi Hendrix Experience
       on magenta and blue "lace" background with purple border
       Poster...$300-400 / Postcard...$100-125

RG71   By Gary Grimshaw. 3/1-2/68
       Big Brother & The Holding Co., MC5, Pink Peech Mob, Tiffany Shade,
       Family Dumptruck
       2/c: Red, Blue (13" x 22"), (4" x 7")
       Purple lettering and photo inset of Big Brother & The Holding Co.
       on blue background
       Poster...$125-150 / Postcard...$15-25

RG72   By Gary Grimshaw. 3/3/68
       Blood, Sweat & Tears; Carousel; Psychedelic Stooges
       2/c: Red, Green (13" x 22"), (4 x 7.25")
       Red lettering and photo inset of Blood, Sweat & Tears
       on green background
       Poster...$125-150 / Postcard...$15-25

RG73   By Gary Grimshaw. 3/8-9/68
       Electric Prunes, Thyme, Who, Soap
       2/c: Orange, Brown (3.75" x 7")
       Orange lettering with illustration of cave people on
       orange and brown background
       Postcard...$10-15

RG74   By Gary Grimshaw. 3/15-17/68
       Youngbloods, Rationals, Up, James Gang, MC5, Thyme
       2/c: Red, Brown (4" x 7")
       Tan lettering with photo inset of "Venus" on red background
       Postcard...$15-20

RG75   By Gary Grimshaw. 3/22-23/68
       Eric Burdon & The Animals, Grateful Dead, Aere Apparent, Apostles,
       Jagged Edge
       2/c: Magenta, Green (4" x 7")
       Green lettering with abstract yin-yang on magenta and purple background
       Postcard...$15-20

RG76   By Gary Grimshaw. 3/29-30/68
       Fugs, Sly & The Family Stone, MC5, Psychedelic Stooges
       1/c: Purple (4" x 7")
       Purple lettering with photo inset of the Fugs on screened background
       with purple border
       Postcard...$10-15

RG72

RG73

RG74

RG75

RG77   By Gary Grimshaw. 4/5-7/68
        Troggs, Tiffany Shade, MC5, Junior Wells, Psychedelic Stooges, Up,
        Apostles
        1/c: Purple (4" x 7")
        White lettering on purple background
        Postcard...$10-15

RG78   By Gary Grimshaw. 4/7/68
        The Who, Troggs, Raja
        2/c: Red, Blue (13" x 22"), (4" x 7")
        Red lettering with photo inset of the Who on blue background
        Poster...$20-30 / Postcard...$10-15

RG79   By Gary Grimshaw. 4/12-13/68
        Traffic, Jagged Edge, Ashmollyan Quintet, Panic & The Pack, Thyme
        2/c: Orange, Chartreuse (4" x 7")
        Orange lettering with illustrated flower on chartreuse background
        Postcard...$15-20

RG80   By Gary Grimshaw. 4/17-21/68
        Cream, Children, Poor Richard's Almanac, Rationals, Frost, James Gang,
        Psychedelic Stooges, MC5, Jagged Edge, Scot Richard Case, Thyme,
        Ashmollyan Quintet
        1/c: Brown (4" x 7")
        White lettering with photo inset of Cream on brown background
        Postcard...$20-30

RG81   By Gary Grimshaw. 4/26-28/68
        Rationals, Thyme, Apple Corps, Jagged Edge, Orange Fuzz, Mothers,
        Psychedelic Stooges, Charging Rhinocerous of Soul, MC5, Carousel
        2/c: Orange, Blue (4" x 7")
        Black lettering and blue design on orange background
        Postcard...$15-20

RG82   By Gary Grimshaw. 5/3-4/68
        Yardbirds, Frost, Stuart Avery Assemblage, MC5, Odds and Ends
        1/c: Purple (4" x 7")
        White lettering and photo of Jimmy Page on purple background
        Postcard...$20-30

RG83   By Gary Grimshaw. 5/10-12/68
        James Cotton Blues Band, MC5, Buffey Reed Phenomena, Up, Children,
        East Side Orphans
        1/c: Green (4" x 7")
        Green lettering and photo of James Cotton Blues Band with
        ornate green border
        Postcard...$15-20

RG76

RG77

RG78

RG79

RG84   By Gary Grimshaw. 5/11/68
The Doors, James Cotton Blues Band, Crazy World of Arthur Brown,
Jagged Edge
2/c: Brown, Blue (13" x 22"), (4" x 7")
Blue lettering and photo inset of the Doors on brown background
Poster...$200-300 / Postcard...$20-30

RG85   By Gary Grimshaw. 5/17-18/68
Procol Harum, Influence, Nirvana, The Nickel Plate Express,
Soul Remains, Muff
2/c: Red, Purple (4" x 7")
Purple lettering with illustration of skull superimposed over woman
on red background
Postcard...$15-20

RG86   By Gary Grimshaw. 5/24-26/68
Butterfield Blues Band, Frost, Buffy, Jagged Edge, Fox, MC5,
Psychedelic Stooges
2/c: Brown, Blue (4" x 7")
Blue lettering with duotone photo of the Butterfield Blues Band
on brown background
Postcard...$10-15

RG87   By Gary Grimshaw. 5/29/68 - 6/1/68
Crazy World of Arthur Brown, Toad, Carousel, Jagged Edge, Rhino of Soul,
Love, Wilson Mower Pursuit, Psychedelic Stooges
1/c: Maroon (4.25" x 7")
White lettering and abstract design on maroon background
Postcard...$10-15

RG88   By Gary Grimshaw. 6/7-9/68
Cream, MC5, Carousel, Nickel Plate Express, St. Louis Union,
James Gang, Thyme
2/c: Purple, Red (13" x 21"), (4.25" x 7")
Purple lettering with mezzotint photo of Cream on purple and red
"brocade" background
Poster...$150-200 / Postcard...$20-30

RG89   By Gary Grimshaw. 6/14-15/68
Soft Machine, Wilson Mower Pursuit, Oaesse, Pack, Up
3/c: Magenta, Green, Black (4" x 7")
Black lettering with photo of William S. Burroughs and illustration
of monster on magenta background with green border
Postcard...$15-20

RG90   By Gary Grimshaw. 6/21-23/68
Blue Cheer, Jagged Edge, Soul Remains, Nature's Children,
MC5, Psychedelic Stooges
3/c: Blue, Yellow, Red (4" x 7")
Red lettering with illustration of "moonscape" on blue background
Postcard...$10-15

RG82

RG84

RG86

RG88

RG91   By Gary Grimshaw. 6/28-30/68
Wayne Cochran, Odds and Ends, London Fog, Jameson Roberts,
Orange Fuzz, Rationals
3/c: Blue, Purple, Black (4" x 7")
Black lettering and abstract purple design on blue background
Postcard...$10-15

RG92   By Gary Grimshaw. 7/5-6/68
Jeff Beck Group, Faith, Charging Rhino of Soul, Gold, Frost
3/c: Gold, Blue, Red (4" x 7")
Red lettering with abstract eye in pyramid design on blue background
with gold border
Postcard...$10-15

RG93   By Carl Lundgren. 7/11-13/68
Fleetwood Mac, Pink Floyd, The Who, Thyme, Jagged Edge
Psychedelic Stooges
1/c: Black (4.25" x 7")
White lettering with illustration of "Goddess" in dark lagoon
Postcard...$15-20

RG94   By Carl Lundgren. 7/19-21/68
Spirit, Fever Tree, James Gang, Soul Remains, Stuart Avery Assembly
3/c: Magenta, Yellow, Blue (4.25" x 7")
Black lettering with photo inset of Spirit on blue background
Postcard...$10-15

RG95   Artist Unkown. 7/26-28/68
Steve Miller Blues Band, Odds and Ends, Carousel, Air Speed Indicator
1/c: Black (4.25" x 6.5")
White lettering with Art Nouveau style illustration of woman
on black background with white border
Postcard...$10-15

RG96   By Carl Lundgren. 8/2-4/68
Paupers, Rain, Hawk, Thyme
4/c: Blue, Yellow, Magenta, Black (4.25" x 7.25")
Black lettering with illustration of green winged creature
on "watercolor" background
Postcard...$10-15

RG97   Artist Unknown. 8/6-7/68
Frost, All the Lonely People, Third Power
1/c: Green (14.5" x 18.5"), (4.25" x 7")
Lettering superimposed over face of woman
Poster...$50-75 / Postcard...$10-15

RG98   By Carl Lundgren. 8/9-11/68
Canned Heat, Rationals, Jagged Edge, Children
2/c: Metallic Silver, Black (4.25" x 7.25")
Op lettering with photo of mushrooms on metallic silver background
Postcard...$10-15

RG89

RG90

RG92

RG93

RG99   By Carl Lundgren. 8/16-18/68
         Country Joe & The Fish, Muff, Pack, H.P. and Grass Route Movement
         4/c: Magenta, Yellow, Blue, Black (4.25" x 7.25")
         Green lettering with photo of Country Joe & The Fish
         on magenta background
         Postcard...$15-20

RG100   By Carl Lundgren. 8/23-25/68
         Albert King, Rationals, Toad, Dharma, Psychedelic Stooges, Jagged Edge,
         Blues Confederation, Wilson Mower Pursuit
         1/c: Black (4.25" x 7.25")
         Outline lettering and photo collage printed on different colors of paper
         Postcard...$10-15

RG101   By Carl Lundgren. 8/30-31/68
         Howlin' Wolf, Chrysalis, Thyme, Rhino
         4/c: Magenta, Yellow, Blue, Black (4" x 7")
         Orange lettering with op photo of Howlin' Wolf on chartreuse background
         Postcard...$15-20

RG102   By Carl Lundgren. 9/1/68
         Procol Harum, Pink Floyd, Howlin' Wolf, Chrysalis, Rationals,
         Scot Richard Case, Thyme, MC5, Jagged Edge, Psychedelic Stooges,
         Frost, Children
         4/c: Blue, Yellow, Red, Black (4.25" x 7")
         Gray lettering with photo collage of butterfly in galactic landscape
         Postcard...$15-25

RG103   By Morton. 9/6-8/68
         B.B. King, Jagged Edge, Frost, Psychedelic Stooges
         3/c: Yellow, Blue, Red (4.25" x 7.25")
         Black lettering with illustrated mushrooms on yellow background
         with blue border
         Postcard...$10-15

RG104   By Donnie Dope and Carl Lundgren. 9/13-15/68
         Procol Harum, Children, Third Power, H.P. &
         The Grass Route Movement, Thyme
         3/c: Yellow, Magenta, Blue (8.5" x 5.25")
         Illustration of "Earth face" on multi-colored background
         Postcard...$15-20

RG105   By Donnie Dope. 9/20-22/68
         Amboy Dukes, MC5, Up, McKenna Mendleson Mainline, Rodney Night,
         Psychedelic Stooges
         3/c: Magenta, Blue (4.25" x 8.5")
         Purple lettering with skeleton face in profile on magenta background
         Postcard...$15-20

RG94

RG96

RG98

RG99

RG106   By Carl Lundgren. 9/27-29/68
          Spooky Tooth, McCoys
          3/c: Yellow, Magenta, Blue (4" x 7")
          Duotone photo of ostriches on multi-colored background
          Postcard...$10-15

RG107   By Carl Lundgren. 10/4-6/68
          Ten Years After, Rationals, Dave Workman Band, Orange Fuzz,
          Stuart Avery Assembly
          3/c: Blue, Yellow, Magenta (4.25" x 7.5")
          Green lettering with photo of lemur on rainbow colored inset
          Postcard...$10-15

RG108   By Carl Lundgren. 10/11-13/68
          John Mayall, Psychedelic Stooges
          1/c: Black (4.25" x 7.5")
          Illustration of nude woman with horse on gray background
          Postcard...$10-15

RG109   By Carl Lundgren. 10/15/68
          Big Brother & The Holding Company with Janis Joplin, Thyme
          1/c: Black (4.25" x 7.5")
          White lettering with screened photo of Janis Joplin
          on gray background
          Postcard...$15-25

RG110   By Bonnie Green. 10/18-20/68
          Kensington Market, Pacific Gas & Electric Co., Renaissance Faire, MC5
          3/c: Magenta, Yellow, Blue (4.25" x 7.25")
          Green lettering and "rocket" in galactic landscape
          Postcard...$10-15

RG111   By Dr. Mabuse. 10/25-26/68
          Procol Harum, Wilson Mower Pursuit, Carousel
          3/c: Magenta, Yellow, Blue (4.25" x 7.5")
          Green lettering with illustrated "lettuce head" on blue background
          Postcard...$10-15

RG112   By Carl Lundgren. 10/29/68
          Quicksilver Messenger Service, Frost
          3/c: Magenta, Yellow, Blue (4" x 7.5")
          Photo collage on polka dot background
          Postcard...$100-150

RG113   By Matthew. 10/30-31/68
          MC5
          1/c: Brown (14" x 21.5")
          Brown lettering with photo inset of MC5 on beige background
          Poster...$40-75

RG100

RG101

RG106

RG107

RG114 Artist Unknown. 10/31/68 - 11/3/68
Deep Purple; Halloween Dance: Frost, Pack
1/c: Black (4" x 7.5")
Black lettering and photo collage with skeleton on gray background
Postcard...$10-15

RG115 By Carl Lundgren. 11/1-3/68
Jeff Beck, Toad, Joyful Wisdom, McKenna Mendleson Mainline
4/c: Yellow, Magenta, Blue, Metallic Silver (4.25" x 7.5")
Multi-colored lettering and photo inset of actor on metallic silver background
Postcard...$10-15

RG116 By Bonnie Green. 11/8-10/68
Buddy Guy, Charging Rhinocerous Of Soul, March Brothers,
The Case Of E.T. Hooley
1/c: Black (4.25" x 7")
Monochrome photo of Buddy Guy in collage of images
Postcard...$10-15

RG117 Artist Unknown. 11/15-17/68
Steve Miller, Move, Moody Blues
1/c: Black (4.25" x 7.5")
White lettering and photo collage on black background
Postcard...$10-15

RG118 By Carl Lundgren and Jerry Younkins. 11/21-24/68
Jefferson Airplane, Tim Buckley, Terry Reid, Blue Cheer, Frost,
Stooges, Wilson Mower Pursuit
3/c: Yellow, Magenta, Blue (4" x 7.5")
Photo collage with Grace Slick and cat on split fountain background
Postcard...$15-25

RG119 By Gary Grimshaw. 11/22-23/68 & 11/30/68
Jeff Beck; Blood, Sweat & Tears; MC5; Stooges
1/c: Blue (4.25" x 7")
Photo collage with casket of Tutankhamen on blue background
Postcard...$10-15

RG120 By Donnie Dope. 11/27/68 - 12/1/68
Grateful Dead; Blood, Sweat & Tears; Rationals; Stuart Avery Assemblage;
Dharma; Popcorn Blizzard; MC5; Frost; Stooges
2/c: Magenta, Brown (4.25" x 7.25")
Pink lettering and illustrated skull face with "KISS ME" appearing in
eye sockets on brown background
Postcard...$15-25

RG121 By Donnie Dope. 12/6-8/68
Canned Heat, Hamilton Face, Teagarden & Van Winkle
3/c: Magenta, Yellow, Blue (4.25" x 7.25")
Illustrated painted woman with pink hair on psychedelic landscape
Postcard...$10-15

RG115

RG122   By Carl Lundgren. 12/13-15/68
Deep Purple, Lee Michaels, James Cotton
1/c: Green (4.25" x 7")
Green lettering and monochrome photo of Deep Purple
on green polka-dotted background
Postcard...$10-15

RG123   By Carl Lundgren. 12/20-22/68
New York Rock & Roll Ensemble, Iron Butterfly, Scot Richard Case
1/c: Black (4.25" x 7.25")
Illustration of "buildings" playing instruments on white background
Postcard...$10-15

RG124   By Harry Pumpkins. 12/26-27/68
Fleetwood Mac, Rotary Connection, Stooges, Wicked
3/c: Yellow, Blue, Red (4" x 7.5")
Abstract face with red eyes on multi-colored background
Postcard...$10-15

RG125   By Chad Hines. 1/3-5/69
Amboy Dukes, Up, Pack, Dick Rabbit, Stooges, Frozen Sun
2/c: Blue, Black (4.25" x 7.5")
Blue lettering with illustration of full moon on white background
Postcard...$10-15

RG126   Artist Unknown. 1/10-12/69
Terry Reid, Mr. Stress Blues Band, Caste, Pavement, Paraphernalia,
James Gang
(6.25" x 7.25")
Close crop photo of Terry Reid in an unusual postcard format
Postcard...$25-40

RG127   By Forsyth. 1/23/69
Announcing The Marriage Of The Decade:
Sheila Ann Phillips and David Kermit Miller
1/c: Black (8" x 11.5")
Black lettering and illustrated inset of "fairy" in lush landscape
Handbill...$15-20

RG128   By Robin Sommers. 1/24-26/69
MC5, Taj Mahal, Train, March Brothers, Piers, Asian Flu
2/c: Red, Blue (4" x 7.25")
Blue lettering with monochrome photo of J.C. Crawford and
American flag on red background
Postcard...$10-15

RG129   By Melkus. 2/28/69 - 3/2/69
Steppenwolf, MC5, Three Dog Nite
1/c: Black (4" x 7.25")
Outline lettering with negative image of eye on black background
Postcard...$10-15

RG109

RG112

RG118

RG119

RG130   By Gary Grimshaw. 4/4-6/69
        MC5, Wicked Religion, The Maxx, PG & E, James Gang
        2/c: Red, Black (4" x 7")
        Illustrated "crest" of eagle and eye in television set
        on red and blue background
        Postcard...$10-15

RG131   By Gary Grimshaw. 4/11-13/69
        Side One: Velvet Underground, Nice, Earth Opera
        Side Two: Savoy Brown, Third Power, Commander Cody &
        His Swing Band, Jethro Tull, Sky, Caste
        2/c: Purple, Orange and 2/c: Black, Blue or Maroon (4" x 7")
        Side One: Purple lettering and photo collage of hands
                    on orange background
        Side Two: Black and outline lettering on blue or maroon background
        Postcard...$20-30

RG132   By Matthew. 4/18-19/69
        Chuck Berry, Julie Driscol, Brian Auger & The Trinity, Rare Earth
        3/c: Blue, Yellow, Magenta (4" x 6.5")
        Blue lettering on patterned split fountain background
        Postcard...$20-30

RG133   By Leni Sinclair. 4/25-27/69
        Canned Heat, Family, Red White & Blues, Caste, Stooges, Third Power,
        All The Lonely People
        3/c: Magenta, Blue, Black (4" x 7.25")
        Monochrome photo insets of Canned Heat and Iggy Pop
        on split fountain background
        Postcard...$20-30

RG134   By Leni Sinclair. 5/2-4/69
        Creedance Clearwater Revival, Taj Mahal, Churls & Litter
        2/c: Blue, Brown (4" x 7")
        Photo of Creedance Clearwater Revival superimposed over photo
        of Revival meeting
        Postcard...$15-25

RG135   By Carl Lundgren. 5/9-11/69
        Who, Joe Cocker & His Grease Band, Maend, Mixed Generation, Rush
        3/c: Magenta, Blue, Green (4" x 7")
        Cartoon strip illustration on split fountain background
        Postcard...$15-25

RG136   By Gary Grimshaw. 5/16-18/69
        Sun Ra & His Myth-Science Arkestra, Led Zeppelin,
        Golden Earrings, MC5
        2/c: Magenta, Yellow (4" x 7")
        Circular photo inset of Sun Ra on yellow and red photo
        of magnified electron field
        Postcard...$15-25

RG130

RG131

RG131

RG137

RG137   By Gary Grimshaw. 5/30-31/69
First Annual Detroit Rock & Roll Revival:
MC5; Chuck Berry; Sun Ra; Dr. John The Night Tripper; Johnny Winter;
Psychedelic Stooges; Terry Reid; Amboy Dukes; Scot Richard Case; Frost;
Rationals; Teegarden & Van Winkle; Lyman Woodward; Up;
Wilson Mower Pursuit; Third Power; N.Y. Rock & Roll Ensemble;
David Peel & The Lower East Side; Red, White & Blues; Sky; Train;
Savage Grace; James Gang; Cast; Gold Brothers; Dutch Elm
4/c: Yellow, Red, Blue, Black (17" x 22"), (5.25" x 7")
Green lettering with illustration of a "stairway to heaven"
on red background with blue and rainbow colored borders
Poster...$125-175 / Postcard...$25-40

RG138   By Linz. 10/31/69
Black Magic Rock & Roll: Arthur Brown, Tim Leary, Frost,
Ralph Adams (modern Houdini), Mystic Peter Hurkos, Amboy Dukes,
Bonzo Dog Band, Stooges, Coven, Pink Floyd, Savage Grace, Kim Fowley,
Alice Cooper, Sky, Teegarden & Van Winkle, Satan (himself), Scot
Richard Case, Frut, Bob Seger, All The Lonely People, Pleasure Seekers
5/c: Red, Yellow, Blue, Black, Metallic Silver (14.5" x 21.5"), (4.25" x 6.75")
Illustrated skeletons and demons on metallic silver and black background
Poster...$150-200 / Postcard...$30-40

RG139   By Al Shamie. 3/7/70
First St. Louis Pop Festival:
Country Joe & The Fish, Steam, Rotary Connection, Chuck Berry,
Blues Magoos, Amboy Dukes, Stooges, Frijid Pink, Frost,
Pleasure Seekers, Cradle, Touch, Murge, Pax, Aardvark, Spur,
Jay Barry, Alvin Pivil, Stop
2/c: Yellow, Blue (17" x 22"), (4.25" x 7.5")
Outline lettering and illustrated eye on green and yellow background
Poster...$125 / Postcard...$30-40

RG140   Artist Unknown. 3/26/70
Cincinnati Pop Festival:
Joe Cocker, Savoy Brown, Frijid Pink, Mountains, MC5, Amboy Dukes,
Pleasure Seekers, Stooges, Brownsville Station, Cradle, Bitterblood,
Balderdash, Glass Wall, Whale Feathers, East Orange Express
2/c: Magenta, Blue (17" x 22"), (4.5" x 7")
White lettering and illustration of "stairway to heaven" borrowed from
RG137 on magenta background
Poster...$125-175 / Postcard...$20-30

RG141   Artist Unknown. 6/13/70
Cincinnati Summer Pop Festival:
Traffic, Grand Funk Railroad, Ten Years After, Mountain,
Mott The Hoople, Stooges, Bob Seger, Alice Cooper, Blood Rock,
Zephyr, Savage Grace, Sky, Mighty Quick, Damnation Of Adam's Blessing,
Third Power, Brownsville Station, Cradle, Mike Quatro Band
1/c: Magenta (11" x 5.5")
Illustrated reclining woman on magenta and white background
Handbill...$75-100

Jim Salzer Presents

Some of the more memorable shows, circa 1968, were presented by concert promoter Jim Salzer, who first staged his events at the Starlight Ballroom and the Electric Flash in Oxnard and Santa Barbara, California, respectively. For larger concerts, the Santa Monica Civic Auditorium, and more often, the Earl Warren Showgrounds, were sites for such remarkable bills as the Doors and the Grateful Dead.

Additional illustrations of posters in the Jim Salzer Series can be found in the color section.

JS1

JS1   By J. Cushing. 4/29/67
Grateful Dead, The Doors, UFO, Captain Speed
2/c: Black, Yellow (17" x 22.5")
Yellow lettering with illustration of "psychedelic diver"
Poster...$15-25

JS2   By Rosie Haynes. 5/27/67
The Doors, Country Joe & The Fish, Andrew Staples,
Captain Speed
3/c: Purple, Green, Magenta (17" x 22.5")
Multi-colored lettering on white background
Poster...$15-25

JS3   Artist Unknown. 6/24/67
The Chambers Brothers, Steve Miller Blues Band,
Alexander's Timeless Blooz Band, Canned Heat
2/c: Brown, Black (13.5" x 20")
Illustration of woman with op eyes and pipe
printed on blue paper
Poster...$15-25

JS4   Artist Unknown. 7/1/67
The Jimi Hendrix Experience, Country Joe & The Fish,
Strawberry Alarm Clock, Captain Speed
3/c: Yellow, Magenta, Black (13.5" x 21")
Multi-colored lettering with photo inset
of the Strawberry Alarm Clock
Poster...$15-25

JS5   By R. Tolmach. 7/22/67
The Yardbirds, Moby Grape, Captain Beefheart & His Magic Band,
Heart, Iron Butterfly, West Coast Pop Art
3/c: Red, Yellow, Blue (14.75" x 23.5")
Illustration of the Yardbirds on multi-colored background
Poster...$15-25

JS6   By R. Tolmach. 8/5/67
The Doors, Lavendar Hill Mob, Joint Effort, Captain Speed
3/c: Orange, Green, Black (13.25" x 22.75")
Black lettering with illustrated corridor of green and orange arches
Poster...$15-25

JS7   By R. Tolmach. 8/19/67
Jimi Hendrix Experience, Moby Grape, Captain Speed,
Tim Buckley
2/c: Red, Green (17.25" x 23.25")
Red lettering with illustration of the Jimi Hendrix Experience
on red and green background
Poster...$15-25

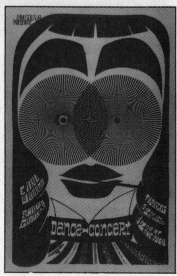

JS2   JS3

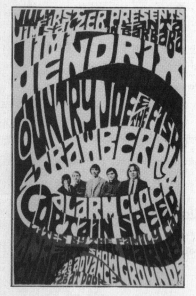

JS4   JS5

JS8

JS10

JS11

JS12

JS13

JS14

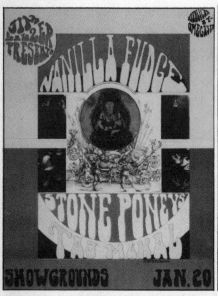

JS15

JS16

JS8   Artist Unknown. 9/2/67
Paul Butterfield Blues Band, Sunshine Company,
Peanut Butter Conspiracy, Alexander's Timeless Blooz Band
3/c: Red, Black, Tan (16.5" x 24")
Black lettering and photo collage in tan insets on red background
Poster...$15-25

JS9   Artist Unknown. 9/16/67
The Seeds, Thee Midnighters, Chocolate Watch Band,
West Coast Pop Art Experimental Band
2/c: Blue, Yellow (17" x 22.75")
Blue lettering with photo of the Seeds on yellow background
Poster...$15-25

JS10   Artist Unknown. 9/30/67
Quicksilver Messenger Service, Blue Cheer,
The Van Morrison Group
3/c: Yellow, Magenta, Black (15.75" x 23.25")
Red lettering and illustrated figure on multi-colored background
Poster...$15-25

JS11   By R. Tolmach. 10/7/67
Jefferson Airplane
2/c: Red, Blue (16.75" x 23")
Abstract design of plane wing on red and blue background
Poster...$15-25

JS12   By R. Tolmach. 11/4/67
Buffalo Springfield, Watts 103rd Street Band,
Lewis & Clark Expedition
3/c: Red, Yellow, Blue (16.25" x 22.25")
Blue lettering with illustration of ankh cross on red background
Poster...$15-25

JS13   By Frank Bettencourt. 11/25/67
The Youngbloods, Canned Heat, Merry Go Round
2/c: Orange, Blue (17.75" x 23.25")
Religious figure on orange and purple background
Poster...$15-25

JS14   By Frank Bettencourt. 1/6/68
Buffalo Springfield, Charles Lloyd, Turquoise
2/c: Red, Metallic Gold (16.25" x 22")
Illustration of young girl on red and metallic gold background
Poster...$15-25

JS15   By Frank Bettencourt. 1/20/68
Vanilla Fudge, Stone Poneys, Taj Mahal
3/c: Pink, Green, Black (16.5" x 21")
Illustration of Buddha on pink and green background
Poster...$15-25

JS17

JS18

JS19

JS20

JS16   Artist Unknown. 2/3/68
        Big Brother & The Holding Co., Electric Flag,
        Sweetwater
        3/c: Red, Blue, Black (16.5" x 21.5")
        Black lettering with photo inset of Big Brother and the Holding Co.
        on red, white, and blue background
        Poster...$15-25

JS17   By Frank Bettencourt. 2/11/68
        Eric Burdon & The Animals, The Fugs, Eire Apparent
        3/c: Blue, Yellow, Lavendar (17" x 22")
        Blue lettering with antique photo of woman
        on lavender background
        Poster...$15-25

JS18   By Frank Bettencourt. 2/24/68
        Cream, Taj Mahal, James Cotton Blues Band
        3/c: Yellow, Magenta, Blue (16.25" x 21.75")
        Photo inset of woman on multi-colored background
        Poster...$15-25

JS19   By Frank Bettencourt. 2/28/68
        Sweetwater, Evergreen Blues Band, Strange Brew
        2/c: Magenta, Green (11" x 16.5")
        Mouse "cartoon strip" in magenta and green
        Poster...$15-25

JS20   By Frank Bettencourt. 3/16/68
        Blue Cheer, Nitty Gritty Dirt Band, The Nazz
        2/c: Pink, Metallic Silver (15.75" x 21.25")
        "Alien" faces on metallic silver and neon pink background
        Poster...$15-25

JS21   Artist Unknown. 4/6/68
        Electric Flag, Traffic, Steppenwolf
        3/c: Orange, Green, Red (17" x 22.5")
        Abstract design in neon colors
        Poster...$15-25

JS22   By Frank Bettencourt. 5/10/68
        The Yardbirds; Dave Dee, Dozy, Beaky, Mich, Tich;
        Turquoise
        3/c: Magenta, Yellow, Blue (17.5" x 22.5")
        Couple under moonlit horizon illustrated in fluorescent colors
        Poster...$15-25

JS23   By Frank Bettencourt. 8/1/69
        Led Zeppelin, Jethro Tull, Fraternity Of Man
        3/c: Magenta, Yellow, Blue (17.5" x 22.5")
        Illustrated pilgrim, castle, and burning zeppelin
        Poster...$15-25 / Handbill...$15-20

JS21   JS22

JS24   JS25

JS24   By Frank Bettencourt. 8/16/69
         Blind Faith Festival: Eric Clapton; Steve Winwood; Ginger Baker;
         Rick Grech; Bonnie, Delaney & Friends
         3/c: Yellow, Blue, Black (17.5" x 22.5")
         Illustration of biblical figure sitting on rainbow
         Poster...$15-25 / Handbill...$15-20

JS25   By K. Wirebaugh. 3/21/71
         Blues Image, Redeye, Fanny
         1/c: Black (13" x 18")
         Black lettering and illustration of eye printed on tan paper
         Poster...$15-25

Philip Cushway Lithos

The Art Rock/Philip Cushway Series of lithographs and silkscreen prints continues the tradition of rock poster art, presenting new works by some of the top graphic artists working in the music industry.

Each limited edition poster is printed on heavy stock and individually numbered to ensure its value as a collectible. Additional illustrations of posters in the Philip Cushway Lithos (PCL) Series can be found in the color section. Missing numbers in the PCL sequence represent posters for which art was completed, but never published.

PCL2

PCL3

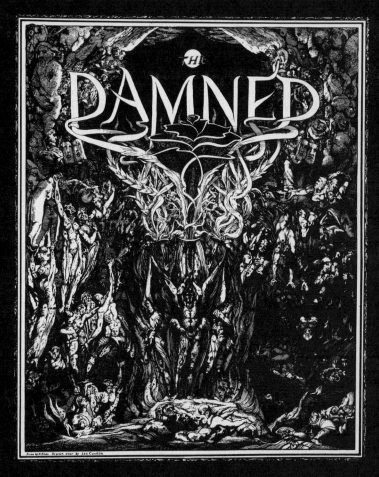

PCL4

PCL1   By Victor Moscoso. 6/6-7/86
        Siouxsie and the Banshees
        5/c: Blue, Magenta, Black, Orange,
        Green (22" x 30")
        Poster...$35

PCL2   By Stanley Mouse.
        Siouxsie and the Banshees
        4/c: Orange, Pink, Blue, Black
        (21.25" x 29.5")
        North American Tour 1986
        Poster...$15

PCL3   By R. Tuten and R. Griffin. 9/13/86
        R.E.M.
        4/c: Red, Yellow, Blue, Black
        (22" x 30")
        Poster...$50

PCL4   By Lee Conklin.
        The Damned
        2/c: Black, Red (22.25" x 28.5")
        Poster...$12

PCL4B   By Lee Conklin. 7/20/89
        The Damned
        2/c: Black, Metallic Silver
        (23" x 25.5")
        Poster...$12

PCL5A   By Hugh Brown.
        The Cult
        4/c: Magenta, Yellow, Green,
        Metallic Gold (23" x 25.5")
        Poster...$10

PCL5B   By Hugh Brown
        The Cult
        4/c: Blue, Green, Red,
        Metallic Gold (23" x 25.5")
        Poster...$10

PCL6   By Philip Cushway
        PiL
        3/c: Blue, Red, Black (20" x 28")
        Poster...$10

PCL5A   PCL5B

PCL9

PCL8

PCL11

PCL12

PCL7B By Hugh Brown. 12/31/87
Grateful Dead
4/c: Yellow, Red, Blue, Black
(19" x 27.5")
Poster...$15

PCL8 By Hugh Brown.
David Bowie
3/c: Magenta, Blue, White
(29.5" x 22.5")
Poster...$10

PCL9 By Philip Cushway. 9/13/87
New Order
2/c: Metallic Gold, Black
(17.5" x 23")
Poster...$125

PCL11 By Gary Grimshaw.
Iggy Pop, Reruns, Cadillac Kidz,
Retro, R.U.R., Mutants, Coldcock
3/c: Peach, Blue, Red (18.5" x 28.5")
Second printing
Poster...$10

PCL12 By Gary Grimshaw.
Jimi Hendrix Experience,
Soft Machine, The Paupers
3/c: Magenta, Yellow, Blue
(17" x 29")
Second printing
Poster...$10

PCL13 By Gary Grimshaw.
The Doors, Steppenwolf,
The Chambers Brothers
2/c:Blue, Black (19.5" x 29")
20th Anniversary Edition
Poster...$10

PCL14 By Gunther Keiser.
Jimi Hendrix Experience
4/c: Yellow, Red, Blue, Black
(25" x 26")
Signed and numbered lithograph
Poster...$175

PCL15 By Gary Grimshaw.
Led Zeppelin
4/c: Blue, Red, Yellow,
Metallic Silver (18" x 26")
Poster...$10

PCL16 By Gary Grimshaw.
R.E.M.
4/c: Green, Orange, Black, Blue
(16.25" x 27.5")
Poster...$10

PCL17 By Gary Grimshaw. 7/19/89
New Order, PiL, Sugar Cubes
4/c: Magenta, Blue, Yellow, Black
(18" x 26.5")
Poster...$10

PCL18 By Stanley Mouse.
The Beatles
1/c: Black (28.5" x 22.5")
Poster...$10

PCL19A By Gary Grimshaw. 8/10/89
The Pixies
2/c: Metallic Bronze, Black
(14.5" x 22")
Poster...$10

PCL19B By Gary Grimshaw. 8/15/89
The Pixies
2/c: Metallic Bronze, Black
(14.5" x 22")
Poster...$10

PCL20 By Gary Grimshaw.
The Who
4/c: Red, Blue, Black, Metallic Silver
(17.25" x 28.25")
Silver Anniversary Edition
Poster...$10

PCL21 By Gary Grimshaw. 10/23-24/89 &
10/26-27/89
The Who
4/c: Red, Blue, Black, Metallic Silver
(17.25" x 28.25")
Poster...$10

PCL23 By Gary Grimshaw.
The Who
4/c: Red, Yellow, Blue, Black
(17" x 28")
North America 1989
Poster...$10

PCL13

PCL17

PCL18

PCL19A

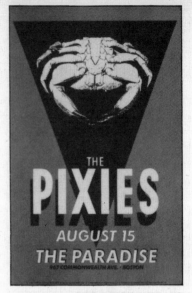

PCL19B

PCL21

PCL24

PCL24   By Gary Grimshaw and
Manhattan Design. 1/2-5/90
The B-52's
3/c: Yellow, Magenta, Blue
(17" x 28")
Poster...$10

PCL26   By Gary Grimshaw.
Depeche Mode
3/c: Red, Blue, Black (17" x 27")
North America 1990
Poster...$10

PCL28   By Gary Grimshaw.
Madonna
5/c: Yellow, Red, Blue, Black,
Metallic Gold (17" x 27.5")
Blond Ambition World Tour '90
Poster...$10

PCL29   By Gary Grimshaw.
The Doors
4/c: Magenta, Yellow, Blue, Black
(16.75" x 26.75")
Poster...$10

PCL30   By Gary Grimshaw.
The Beatles
5/c: Blue, Metallic Silver, Black,
Yellow, Red (16.75" x 27.5")
North America Tours
Poster...$10

PCL33   By Gary Grimshaw.
Eric Clapton
5/c: Blue, Yellow, Magenta, Black,
Metallic Gold (11.75" x 20.25")
Royal Albert Hall, 1991
Poster...$10

PCL34   By Gary Grimshaw.
Jim Morrison
4/c: Blue, Red, Yellow, Black
(17" x 27")
Poster...$10

PCL26

PCL34

APPENDIXES

APPENDIXES

Fan Clubs

Fan clubs have been around for as long as any of us can remember, dating back to the silent film days. Later, when film stars were under contract to the movie studios, their fan clubs were run by the studio, which controlled a big part of their lives. Sadly, there is no documented information about the earliest fan clubs, and very little has been written about them.

There are more fan clubs today than ever before, and they are more mature, more efficient. Whereas many of the early fan clubs were run by teenagers, today's fan clubs are mostly run by mature, educated people, both men and women, who find the work an enjoyable hobby. There is an added bonus of meeting many wonderful people and forming lasting friendships.

There are fan clubs for people in all types of music, TV, films, sports, and even for some animals! There are all types of people in fan clubs, from young school children to mothers, grandmothers, and professional people in all walks of life. Most everyone has a favorite entertainer, and a fan club is the best source of information on a celebrity.

Fan clubs publish regular newsletters with up-to-date news on the celebrity, giving the fans a source of current information on their favorite entertainer, and also provide a link to the fans for the celebrity. The person who runs the club assumes responsibility for both the star and the fans, working long hours with no thought of being paid for the work he/she has done. It is strictly a "labor of love" for an entertainer they respect and admire.

In 1977 the National Association of Fan Clubs was formed in cooperation with a group of long-term fan club presidents who saw a need for a guiding force in fan clubs, as well as a need to upgrade the fan club image, which had been badly damaged by irresponsible people, such as "groupies," who used the fan club name to serve their own purpose. One of NAFC's major goals has been to educate the public about what fan clubs are all about, and to let people know the good they do, such as donating thousands of dollars to charity each year, and the wonderful service they provide to the entertainer and his/her fans. NAFC also provides information to new fan clubs to help them better serve the celebrity. NAFC publishes an annual fan club directory, listing all fan clubs whose addresses and activities can be verified.

In 14 years NAFC has made great strides in accomplishing the goal it set

517

out to do, and many fan club articles have been published in prestigious publications throughout the United States. Still very active and still growing, the National Association of Fan Clubs can be reached at P.O. Box 4559, Pueblo, CO 81003.

Bryan Adams Fan Club
C/O Michele Booth
#406–68 Water Street
Vancouver, B.C.,
V6B 1A4 Canada

Aerosmith
C/O Aero Force One
P.O. Box 4668
San Francisco, CA 94101

A-ha
Viking Uprising
(A fanzine for A-ha)
P.O. Box 2578
Sepulveda, CA 91343-2578

Air Supply
P.O. Box 25909
Los Angeles, CA 90025

Alabama Fan Club
P.O. Box 529
Ft. Payne, AL 35967

The Alarm
Alarm Information Center
Box 1739 GPO
New York, NY 10116

Allman Brothers Band NL
C/O Joanne Zangrilli
742 S. Oak Park Avenue
Oak Park, IL 60304

American Bandstand Fan Club
David Frees
Box 131
Adamstown, PA 19501

Lynn Anderson Fan Club
P.O. Box 90454
Charleston, SC 29410

Paul Anka
Box 100
Carmel, CA 93921

Paul Anka Fan Club
124 Terryville Road
Port Jefferson Station, NY 11776

Adam Ant
P.O. Box 77505
San Francisco, CA 94107

Rick Astley Collector
C/O Meredith Peters
695 Weatherly Lane N.W.
Atlanta, GA 30328

Bobby Bare Fan Club
Greil Works Mgmt.
Box 120681
Nashville, TN 37272

Beach Boys
101 Mesa Lane
Santa Barbara, CA 93109

Beach Boys Fan Club
P.O. Box 84282
Los Angeles, CA 90073

Beach Boys Fan Club
P.O. Box 10405
Elmwood, CT 06110

Beatles
Liverpool Productions
C/O Charles F. Rosenay
397 Edgewood Avenue
New Haven, CT 06511

Beatles
The Working Class Hero
C/O Barb Whatmough
3311 Niagra Street
Pittsburgh, PA 15213

Beatles
C/O Yesterday & Today
The Secretary
161 Willowfield
Woodside
Telford
Shropshire
England

Beatles Unlimited
P.O. Box 602
3430 AP Nieusegen
The Netherlands

Bee Gees
P.O. Box 11359
Burbank, CA 91510

Bee Gees
The Gibb Family Friendship Club
C/O Brenda Cornwell
301 Mackie Lane
Louisville, KY 40214

Bee Gees
Gibb Style
C/O Nancy/Robyn/Jean/Renee
P.O. Box 10314
Pompano Beach, FL 33060

Bee Gees
Brothers Gibb Information
C/O Anneke Konemans
Haringubiestraat 61
3313 EA Dondrecht
The Netherlands

Bee Gees & Andy Gibb Fan Club
C/O Yuko Nishihara
Nakano Kito P.O. Box 38
Nakano-Ku, Tokyo 165
Japan

Bee Gees/Barry Gibb
Barry's Babes
C/O Nancy Bennett
99 Tindall Road
Middletown, NJ 07748

Bee Gees/Maurice Gibb
Mo Time C/O Julie Rae Richard
Olanta, PA 16863

Bee Gees News
C/O Andreas Anderegg
P.O. Box 7532
8500 Frauenfeld
Switzerland

Harry Belafonte
157 W. 57th Street
New York, NY 10019

The Belamy Brothers Fan Club
P.O. Box 801
San Antonio, FL 33576

Black Sabbath
P.O. Box 77505
San Francisco, CA 94107

Blue Oyster Cult Fan Club
1610 N. Martel, #8
West Hollywood, CA 90046

Bon Jovi Secret Society
P.O. Box 4843
San Francisco, CA 94101

Bon Jovi Fan Club
P.O. Box 326
Fords, NJ 08863

Debby Boone Fan Club
C/O Chris Bujnovsky
526 Boeing Avenue
Reading, PA 19601

Pat Boone
8899 Beverly Boulevard
Los Angeles, CA 90048

Pat Boone International Fan Club
C/O Chris Bujnovsky
526 Boeing Avenue
Reading, PA 19601

David Bowie Fan Club Information
P.O. Box 5242
FDR Station
New York, NY 10150

Teresa Brewer Fan Club
C/O Bill Munroe
584 Prospect Street
New Haven, CT 06511

Bros
Bros Front
P.O. Box 276
London E2 7BW
England

The Buckinghams Fan Club
2521 Ridge Road
Lansing, IL 60438

Kate Bush
P.O. Box 120
Welling
Kent K16 3DS
England

Belinda Carlisle
P.O. Box 22
Van Nuys, CA 96032

Carter Family Fan Club
P.O. Box 1371
Hendersonville, TN 37077-1371

**Johnny Cash/June Carter Cash
Fan Club**
Rte. 12, Box 350
Winston-Salem, NC 27107

David Cassidy
Cassidy Class
C/O Susan Stiward
825 Oak Grove Road, #20
Concord, CA 94518

David Cassidy
Box 188
Plantersville, TX 77363

David Cassidy Appreciation Society
C/O Katy Leuty
The Old Post House
The Street
Litlington, E. Essex
BN26 5RD, England

Friends of Shaun Cassidy
C/O Cheryl Corwin
859 Old Woods Road
Worthington, OH 43085

Cheap Trick
Cheap Trick Fan Newsletter
C/O Jessica Muse
191 Colabaugh Pond Road
Croton-on-Hudson, NY 10019

Cher
5807 Hornet Drive
Orlando, FL 32808

Chicago Fans International
C/O Nicole Greveche
Hammer Hof 16
2000 Hamburg, 26
West Germany

Lou Christie Fan Club
C/O Harry Young
#10-H, 1645 E. 50th Street
Chicago, IL 60615

Cinderella Fan Club
P.O. Box 543
Drexel Hill, PA 19026

Eric Clapton
5619 Bradley Boulevard
Bethesda, MD 20814

Roy Clark Fan Club
P.O. Box 470304
Tulsa, OK 74147

Patsy Cline Fan Club
P.O. Box 244
Dorchester, MA 02125

Eddie Cochran
10 Albert Edward Terrace
Bolden Colliery
Tyne & Wear
NE35 9HL
England

Phil Collins
P.O. Box 107
London N6 5RN
England

Phil Collins
Solo
55 Fulham High Street
London SW6
England

Phil Collins/Genesis News Exchange
C/O Cathy Brogg
418 W. Center, #10
Bountiful, UT 84010

Phil Collins/Genesis Newsletter
Connection
Box 660832
Miami Springs, FL 33266

Cowsills Fan Club
Box 83
Lexington, MA 39095

Billy "Crash" Craddock
P.O. Box 1585
Mt. Vernon, IL 62864

Tom Cruise Fan Club
14755 Ventura Boulevard
#1-710
Sherman Oaks, CA 91403

Culture Club
Dept. RB, Box 947
Hollywood, CA 90069

The Cure
Acme House
26-40 St. Andrews Street
Northampton, NM1 2HY
England

Vic Damone Appreciation Society of Great Britain
Victoria & Leslie Goodwin
7 Lakeview, Crouch Lane
Winkfield, Berkshire
SL4 4SA, England

Charlie Daniels Band Volunteers
P.O. Box 882
Mt. Juliet, TN 37122

Terence Trent D'Arby
The Hardline Society
P.O. Box 91OL
London NW1 9AQ
England

James Dean
We Remember James Dean
P.O. Box 5025
Fullerton, CA 92635

James Dean Memory Club
497 Atlantic Avenue
Brooklyn, NY 11217

Def Leppard Official Fan Club
P.O. Box 670
Old Chelsea Station
New York, NY 10113

John Denver
Partners in Harmony
C/O Nancy Mounts
Rte. 1, Box 584
Purcelville, VA 22132

John Denver
From Heart to Heart
C/O Carol Blevins
1213 River Road
Quarryville, PA 17566

John Denver
Spirit in the Wind
C/O Susie Baldwin
11026 32nd Drive S.E.
Everett, WA 98204

John Denver
Sunshine on My Shoulders
2-65-6 Itabshi
Itabshi-Ku
Tokyo, 173
Japan

John Denver
Music & Communication
Kirchenstrasse 9
6602 Dudweiler
West Germany

John Denver
Free Spirit
3 Almond Walk Hazelmere Near
High Wycombe
Buckinghamshire
HP 157RE, England

**John Denver Early Warning
Network**
C/O Lorrie Sjoquist
P.O. Box 1722
Bothel, WA 98041-1722

**John Denver Music Appreciation
Society**
C/O Alma Hansen
25 Mariners Crescent
West Lakes SA 5021
Australia

The World of John Denver
P.O. Box 262
8160 AG EPE
The Netherlands

Depeche Mode
P.O. Box 982
London SW19 3TW
England

Club Devo
9120 Sunset Boulevard
Los Angeles, CA 90046

Dokken
Bay Area Dokken Appreciators
P.O. Box 322
Mount Eden, CA 94557-0322

Thomas Dolby Fan Club
8335 Sunset Boulevard, #100
Los Angeles, CA 90069

The Doors Fan Club
AM Oelveback 5
1 Ranier Moddemann
D-4150 Krefeld-Stratum 12
West Germany

Peter Duel Remembrance Club
Melody Cecko
2091 Duluth Street
Maplewood, MN 55109

Duran Duran Fan Club
C/O Debbie Klam
118 N. Milwaukee Street
Waterford, WI 53185

Bob Dylan
9 Northampton Drive
Willingsboro, NJ 08046

Sheena Easton Fan Club
5300 Laurel Canyon Boulevard
Box 500
North Hollywood, CA 91607

Duane Eddy Circle
C/O Rich Gallagher
P.O. Box 620093
Littleton, CO 80162

**Gloria Estefan & the Miami Sound
Machine Fan Club**
P.O. Box 52-0907
Miami, FL 33152

Eurythmics
1710 Nichols Canyon Road
Los Angeles, CA 90046

Eurythmics
P.O. Box 245
53 Park Road
London, N8 8SY
England

Everly Brothers
Sharing & Caring
1501 N. 15th Street
Reading, PA 19604

Everly Brothers International
C/O Carla Parker
714 Kenny Way
Las Vegas, NV 89107

Everly Brothers International
15 Fischer Court
Brentwood, TN 37027

Sally Field Fan Club
P.O. Box 1029-115
Van Nuys, CA 91408

**Fleetwood Mac/Stevie Nicks
Newsletter**
106-A Farmwood Drive
Kernersville, NC 27284

Dan Fogelberg Newsletter
Box 3111
Olathe, KS 66062

Connie Francis Fan Club
C/O Michael Giambra
61 Westwood Drive
Rochester, NY 14616

Connie Francis Fan Club
1975 Howard Avenue
Pottsville, PA 17901

**Bobby Fuller Four Ever
International Fan Club**
720 Quinta Luz Circle
El Paso, TX 79922-2318

Annette Funicello Fan Club
C/O Sandi Kreml
P.O. Box 26610-313
Sacramento, CA 95826

Annette Funicello Fan Club
C/O Mary Lou Fitton
Box 134, Nestleton
Ontario, Canada L0B 1L0

Gerry & the Pacemakers
Mike Oestricher
Box 6063
Round Barn Station
Champaign, IL 61826

Debbie Gibson
P.O. Box 489
Merrick, NY 10028

Girls Groups of the 60s
C/O Louis Wendruck
P.O. Box 69A04
W. Hollywood, CA 90069

Giuffria
P.O. Box 77505
San Francisco, CA 94107

The Go-go's
P.O. Box 77505
San Francisco, CA 94107

Leslie Gore Fan Club
C/O Jack Natoli
141 Vernon Avenue
Paterson, NJ 07503

Guns 'n' Roses
Conspiracies, Inc.
P.O. Box 67279
Los Angeles, CA 90067

Daryl Hall & John Oates
P.O. Box 77505
San Francisco, CA 94107

Debbie Harry Appreciation Society
C/O Bob Hollings
547 Stapleton Road
Eastville, Bristol
BS5 6SQ England

Debbie Harry Fan Info Network
C/O Al Munroe
2558 Fifth Lane W.
Mississauga, Ontario
L5K 1W3 Canada

Heart
P.O. Box 77505
San Francisco, CA 94107

Helix
104 King Street S.
Waterloo, Ontario
N2J 1P5 Canada

Jimi Hendrix
ADA
2920 Avenue R
Suite 111
Brooklyn, NY 11229

Jimi Hendrix
Sky Church Music
C/O Joseph Selby
450 E. Tompkins Street
Columbus, OH 43202

Jimi Hendrix
Straight Ahead
P.O. Box 965
Novato, CA 94948

Jimi Hendrix
The Purple Haze Archives
C/O Ken Matesich
P.O. Box 41133
Tucson, AZ 85717

Jimi Hendrix Archives
C/O Tony Brown
28 Chadwick Square
Seabank, Kings Lynn
Norfolk, PE30 2LT
England

Jimi Hendrix Club One
4712 Avenue N, Apt. 109
Brooklyn, NY 11234

Jimi Hendrix Info
P.O. Box 374
Des Plains, IL 60016

Herman's Hermits Fan Club
C/O Janet & Stephanie Gorski,
Co-presidents
733 Valley Forge Avenue
Trenton, NJ 08648

Hollies
14 Buckly Drive
Rochester, NY 14624

Buddy Holly Memorial Society
C/O William Griggs
3022 56th Street
Lubbock, TX 79413

Engelbert Humperdinck
San Diegans for Engelbert
C/O Lavonne Simonides
3356 Landis Street
San Diego, CA 92104

Engelbert Humperdinck
Enges Joyous Notes
C/O Irene George
P.O. Box 782
Winters, CA 95694

Engelbert Humperdinck
Love is All for Enge
C/O Nathalie Ellington
4210 Norton Way
Sacramento, CA 94820

Engelbert Humperdinck
Engelbert's Aquarians
C/O Mary Jane Lamb
1400 S. Douglas Road, #220
Anaheim, CA 92806

Billy Idol
Vital Idol Star Fleet
P.O. Box 1450
New York, NY 10028

Julio Iglesias
The American Friends of Julio
Iglesias
P.O. Box 1425
La Mirada, CA 90637-1425

Julio Iglesias
Friends of Julio Iglesias
C/O Isabel Butterfield
28 Farmington
Longmeadow, MA 01106

Julio Iglesias Fan Club
C/O Chrintine Arren
P.O. Box 57
Wellesley, MA 02181

Iron Butterfly, Inc.
Box 1685
Fontana, CA 92334

Jackson Family Fan Club
W4490 Pope Road, Box 9-10
Merrill, WI 54452

Jan & Dean
Gotthelfweg 9
5036 Berentfelden
Switzerland

Jan & Dean/Surfun
C/O Lori Brown
1510 16th Street
Summer, WA 98390

Jefferson Starship
P.O. Box 77505
San Francisco, CA 94107

Joan Jett & the Blackhearts
P.O. Box 77505
San Francisco, CA 94107

Billy Joel Newsletter
Root Beer Rag
375 North Broadway
Suite 208
Jericho, NY 11753

David Jones Fan Club
P.O. Box 750491
Memphis, TN 38175-0491

Tom Jones
Tom's Arizona Gems
C/O Donna K. Berry
7114 E. Broadway
Mesa, AZ 85208

Tom Jones
Tom's Darlings
C/O Darlene Russo
P.O. Box 3542
Anaheim, CA 92803

Tom Jones
Body & Soul of Tom Jones
C/O Diana Davis
51 Greenbriar Road
Fairfield, CT 06430

Tom Jones
Tom Terrific
C/O Margaret Maritti
411 Coram
Shelton, CT 06484

Tom Jones
The World of Tom Jones
C/O Evelyn Borman
1231 W. 60th Terrace
Hialeah, FL 33012

Tom Jones
Tom's Memories of Chicago
C/O Dorothy Franczak
1259 W. Fry Street
Chicago, IL 60612

Tom Jones
Dynamic Tom
C/O Martha Pess
55 Trapper Lane
Levittown, NY 11756

Tom Jones
Tiger Tom Fan Club
C/O Ana D. Cruz
321 Rockaway Parkway
Valley Stream, NY 11580

Tom Jones
Tom's Darlins
C/O Mary Pascale
18 Cliftwood Place
Kings Park, NY 11754

Tom Jones
Tom's Vegas Luv's
C/O Cynthia Eliaers
1433 #D E. Reno
Las Vegas, NV 89119

Tom Jones
The New Jersey Jones Girls
C/O Pat Troiano
68 Beach Street
Kearney, NJ 07032

Tom Jones Atlanta Fan Club
C/O Carolyn Lyons
966 Dofwood Way
Norcross, GA 30093

Tom Jones' Darlins
C/O Eunice Shparago
7031 Carol Avenue
Niles, IL 60643

Tom Jones' Fans of Soul
C/O Marion Shannon
2191 N.W. 58th Street
Miami, FL 33142

Tom Jones Goldcoast Gals
C/O Sharon Mitchelson
7938 Woodvale Circle
Tampa, FL 33615

Tom Jones Love Circle
C/O Estelle Sirkin
917 W. Helena Drive
Phoenix, AZ 85023

Tom Jones Love Connection
C/O Caroline Theis
2212 N. 50th Street
Fort Smith, AR 72904

Tom Jones Prince of Luv
C/O Betty Porco
17 Cherrywood Drive
Goshen, NY 10924

Tom Jones Unlimited
C/O Donna Schwartz
19 Edgewood Road
Peekskill, NY 10566

Tom Jones Western Region
C/O Linda Bible
2344 N. 52nd Street
Phoenix, AZ 85008

Kingston Trio
Kingston Korner
6 S. 230 Cohasset Road
Naperville, IL 60540

Kiss
Black Diamond Magazine
11 Teak Court
Ringwood, NJ 07456

Kiss
The New England Kiss Collector's
Network
168 Oakland Avenue
Providence, RI 02908

Kiss
Mask
P.O. Box 381
Rancocas, NJ 08073

Kiss
Planet Kiss
1800 Fullerwiser #1410
Euless, TX 76039

Kiss
Potpourri/The Gene Scene
3221 Midway Drive #501
San Diego, CA 92110

Kiss
Strange Ways
P.O. Box 70
Vandalia, OH 45377

Kiss
Firehouse Magazine
66 7158 138th Street
Surrey, B.C. V3W 7V7
Canada

Kiss
Dark Light Magazine/Kiss Exciter
P.O. Box 409, Station B
London, Ontario N6A 4W1
Canada

Kiss
Dutch Firehouse Magazine
5923 AC Venlo
The Netherlands

Kiss
Destroyer Magazine
83 Cadillac Avenue
Victoria, B.C. V8Z 1T5
Canada

Kiss
Sure Know Somethin'
5 Draper Court
Kellor Downs
Victoria, 3038
Australia

Kiss
Animalize Kiss Fan Club
Jose De Alencar
486/108 Block B
POA RS
Brazil 90640

Kiss
P.O. Box 77505
San Francisco, CA 94107

Kiss Alive
P.O. Box 376
Hagerstown, MD 21741

Kiss Alliance
6 Prospect Street
Greenville, RI 02828

Kiss Army Asylum
P.O. Box 1305
Woodland Hills, CA 91365

Kiss Army International
Via A. Cialdi 5
00154 Rome
Italy

Kiss Army Sweden
Martensvo Gard
S-7191 Hellefors
Sweden

Kiss Army Worldwide
Marienddorfer Damm 399
1000 Berlin 42
Germany

Kiss Assault Force
1100 W. Jeffery Street, Apt. #79
Kankakee, IL 60901

Kiss Beat
RR. 2, Box 53
Beardstown, IL 62618

Kiss Crazy
Box A, 41 North Road
London N7 9DP
England

Kiss Crazy Knights
P.O. Box 408
Welland, 5007
SA, Adelaide
Australia

Kiss Desire
109-88 Swindon Way
Winnipeg, Manitoba R3P 1A7
Canada

Kiss Explosion
Mgr. Schrynen St., #10
6417 XZ Heerlen
The Netherlands

Kiss Express
2812 Oakdale Road
Modesto, CA 95355

Kiss Fan Club Japan
C/O Nippon Phonogram Co., Ltd.
Wako Bldg. 8-5
Roppongi 4 Chome
Minato-Ku, Tokyo 106
Japan

Kiss Fan Club Spain
C/Monasterio De Siresa, No 18 2B
50002 Zaragoza
Spain

Kiss Fever
San Jose De Calasanz 45 2-B
BS.AS CAP FED CP 1424
Argentina

Kiss Fire
P.O. Box 1461
Fairfield, CT 06432

Kiss Forum
85 Nimitz Drive
Dayton, OH 45431

Kiss Journal
119 Av. De St. Jerome
13013
Marseille
France

Kiss Klassics
P.O. Box 928
Woodbridge, NJ 07095

Kiss Konnection
P.O. Box 5626
San Angelo, TX 76902

Kiss Machine
519 25th Street
Niagara Falls, NY 14301

Kiss Reserve Asylum
Freilgrathstr. 6
Kothen 4370
German Democratic Republic

Kiss/Rock Legends
90 E. Main Street
Terryville, CT 06786

Kiss Rocks
P.O. Box 308-H
Scarsdale, NY 10583

Kiss Rocks/Grassroots Support Group
P.O. Box 1754
Springfield, IL 62705-1754

The Swiss Kiss Dynamite Fan Club
Pre-Grassey
Aurochs 1, 1610 Oron-La-Ville
Switzerland

Kiss Thunder
342 Kingsway Place
Milton, Ontario L9T 4C8
Canada

Kiss Underground
83 Vernon Place
Buffalo, NY 14214

Kris Kristofferson Fan Club
313 Lakeshore Drive
Marietta, GA 30067

Krokus
P.O. Box 77505
San Francisco, CA 94107

Nicollette Larson Fan Club
C/O Wanda Dorsey
67 Citadel Drive
Aiken, SC 29801

Led Zeppelin
Zoso
1390 Market Street
Suite 2623
San Francisco, CA

Huey Lewis
Newsline
P.O. Box 15702
Pittsburgh, PA 15244

Mark Lindsay Fan Organization
C/O Carolyn Wood
SE 1430 Arcadia Road
Shelton, WA 98584

Barry Manilow
Laurie Allen
Hogwild Over Barry
12 Buttermilk
Little Rock, AR 72207

Barry Manilow
San Francisco Baygels
C/O Debbie Theisen
530 Via Appia
Walnut Creek, CA 94598

Barry Manilow
No Other Love Barry Manilow Fan
Club
C/O Esther Acha
17400 Valley Boulevard, SP. 8
Fontana, CA 92335

Barry Manilow
Southern California Barry Manilow
Fan Club
C/O Jan Edwards & Debbie Riche
8389 Baker Avenue, SP. 52
Cucamonga, CA 91730

Barry Manilow
No Frills Barry Manilow Fan Club
C/O Candee Kennedy
1165 E. Carson, #5
Long Beach, CA 90803

Barry Manilow
Mile High for Manilow
C/O Pam Mena
13503 Hazel Place
Broomfield, CO 80020

Barry Manilow
Manilow Memories
C/O Beth Ballard
321 Abbe Road
Enfield, CT 06082

Barry Manilow Arizona Fan Club
Lori S. Mytnick
3740 N. Romero, #A-3
Tucson, AZ 85705

**Barry Manillow Fan Club of
South Africa**
C/O Shirley Ferrer
21 Glamorgan Road
Parkwood 2193
South Africa

Marillion
The Web Fan Club
P.O. Box 533
Richmond
Surrey TE9 2EX
England

Martika
947 Fairway Drive
Walnut, CA 91789

Johnny Mathis
Reflections of Mathis
C/O Melanie Slavia
P.O. Box 181
Jacksonville, NC 28541-0181

Johnny Mathis
Touch by Touch/Fan Club of New
Jersey
C/O Martha J. King
27 S. Hawthorne Lane
Newark, NJ 07107

Johnny Mathis
The Mythopoeic Society
P.O. Box 28427
San Jose, CA 95159

Johnny Mathis East Coast Fan Club
C/O Shirley Robinson
200 E. 33rd Street, #61
New York, NY 10016

**Johnny Mathis International Fan
Club**
P.O. Box 2066
Burbank, CA 91507

Johnny Mathis Society
P.O. Box 191
Santa Rosa, CA 95402

John Cougar Mellencamp Fan Club
Minutes to Memories
Box MTM/JCM
Latrobe, PA 15650

George Michael Showcase
Marlon Eckleben & Astrid Lubben
Blanhander Str. 24
D-2932 Zetel
West Germany

Monkees
Pool It
C/O Mary Daniel
3354 N. Baptiste Drive
Theodore, AL 36582

Monkees
Monkee Mates
C/O Janice Wyatt
P.O. Box 3188
Tuscaloosa, AL 35404-0408

Monkees
South West Beachwood Drive
Irregulars
C/O Teresa & Tracy Murray
1625 S. Avenida Sirio
Tucson, AZ 85730

Monkees
Band 6
C/O Heather French
P.O. Box 565414
Dallas, TX 75356-5414

Monkees
Davy Luvvers Fan Club
C/O Clara Castleschouldt
205 McMillian
Conroe, TX 77301

Monkees
Torkaholics Anonymous
C/O Alexa Perotti
5129 Silver Springs Road
Park City, UT 84060-5911

Monkees
Still Monkee'n Around
C/O Michele Brinkerhoff
7555 S. 1300 West
West Jordan, UT 84084

Monkees
The Monkees Info Center
C/O Debbie Campbell
P.O. Box 3786
Lacey, WA 98503-3786

Monkees
Monkee Fan for Life
C/O Theresa Clemons
137 N. Thomas
Olympia, WA 98502

Monkees
Idolenzatry Incorporated
C/O Kerri Cox
1906 W. Pacific, #7
Spokane, WA 99204

Monkees
I Surrender
C/O Dawn Pilarski
4957 Ridge O' Woods Drive
West Bend, WI 53095

Monkees
Monkee Ideas
C/O Tracy Potter
79 Waverly Road
Toronto, Ontario
M4L 3T2 Canada

Monkees
Papa Jeans Blues
C/O Kathy Connor
99 Coe Hill Drive, Apt. 101
Toronto, Ontario
M6S 3E4 Canada

Monkees
Dolenz Believers
C/O Beth Brinson
225 Cassandra Boulevard, #914
Toronto, Ontario
M3A 1V3 Canada

Monkees
The Monkeemaniacs Australian Club
C/O Ann O'Reilly
P.O. Box 9
Forest Hill, Victoria
3131 Australia

Monkees
David Jones Aussie Connection Club
C/O Rhonda Jones
7 Devereaux Court
Frankston, Victoria
3199 Australia

Monkees
Band 6
C/O Kirk White
44 Pembroke Road
Paighten, Devon
TQ3 3U2
England

Monkees
Feels So Good
C/O Yoko Inou
12-14 Bessho, 2 Chome
Urawa City
Saitama 336
Japan

Monkees
Tork Enthusiasts, Inc.
C/O Stephanie Rawson
14 Knollwood Drive
Livingston, NJ 07039

Monkees
Barrel Full of Monkees
K. Nardelli & L. Digise
1001 Arlington Drive
Toms River, NJ 08753

Monkees
Torkaholics Anonymous
C/O Patti Olson
1504 Rustic Drive, Apt. 7
Ocean Township, NJ 07712

Monkees
Monkee Headquarters
C/O Susan Starbrough
318 N. 4th
Lovington, NM 88860

Monkees
Monkeeshines Newsletter
C/O Charlotte Garfinkle
1625 Jackson Place
Reno, NV 89512

Monkees
Save the Texas Prairie Chicken
Denise Daily
285 Wellington Road
Webster, NY 14580-1441

Monkees
Monkee Love U.S.A.
C/O Barbara Wood
1144 Udall Road
Bay Shore, NY 11706

Monkees
Lovers of Davy Jones United
C/O Diane Mona
2690 Associated Road, #89
Fullerton, CA 92635

Monkees
Monkeemania Franchise
C/O Karyn Hazard
13358 Grant Street
Yucaipa, CA 92399

Monkees
The Monkees Press Club
C/O Randelyn Webster
1639 W. Washington Boulevard, #1
Venice, CA 90291

Monkees
Nice Kitty Konnection
C/O Lauri Kuster
14881 Hunter Lane
Midway City, CA 92655

Monkees
The Monkeeanian Fan Club
C/O Laura Hildebrand
P.O. Box 2355
Huntington, CT 06484

Monkees
Monkee Mania
C/O Caroline Savatore
18 Great Pond Road
Simsbury, CT 06070

Monkees
Nesmith United
C/O Ali Sharpe
65 E. Stephen Drive
Newark, DE 19713-1874

Monkees
Monkeemania Always
C/O Jennifer Oaks
12039 Turner Road, Rte. 2
Hampton, GA 30028

Monkees
The Purple Flower Gang
C/O Cindy Bryant
1015 ½ Hill Avenue
Muscatine, IA 52761

Monkees
Mostly Manchester Men
Sandie Slaughterbeck
2421 Butler Street
Lafayette, IN 47905

Monkees
Take a Giant Step into Micky's
World
C/O Mary Hogan
303 Jefferson, Apt. A
Evansville, IN 47713

Monkees
Mostly Monkees Fan Club
C/O Jennifer Goslowski
P.O. Box 3232
Aurora, IL 60504

Monkees
Headquarters Association
C/O Sabra Bean
P.O. Box 15442
Lenexa, KS 66215

Monkees
The Manchester Cowboy
C/O Rita Marciante
556 Sizeler
Jefferson, LA 70121

Monkees
Davy's Day Dream Believers
C/O Debbie Sunseri
206 Maple Ridge Drive
Metairie, LA 70001

Monkees
Nancy's Monkee Fan Club
C/O Nancy
P.O. Box 487
West Newberry, MA 01985

Monkees
Metal Micky
C/O Stephanie Tardo
92 Golden Avenue
Medford, MA 02155

Monkees
Ladies Aid Society of Massachusetts
C/O Susan Kenney
26 Utility Road
Scituate, MA 02066

Monkees
Head of the Monkees Fan Club
C/O Teresa Jones
262 Baltimore Avenue
Baltimore, MD 21220

Monkees
The Chesapeake Area Monkees Fan
Club
C/O Sheila Oertley
P.O. Box 415
Chesapeake Beach, MD 20732-0415

Monkees
Heart & Soul/Detroit
C/O Shelly Jarvis
2753 4th Street
Wyandotte, MI 48192

Monkees
Monkee Fun
C/O Aubrey Guilbault
1264 Dauner Road
Fenton, MI 48430

Monkees
The Fantasy Sequence
C/O Jeni Blom Rivken
3725 37th Avenue S.
Minneapolis, MN 55406

Monkees
Monkee Times Yearbook
C/O Cathy Greskovics
1709 207th Avenue N.E.
Cedar, MN 55011

Monkees
Shades of Gray
P.O. Box 4053
Hazelwood, MD 63042

Monkees
Peter Tork Fan Club
C/O Ruthann Matthews
310 Farmsworth Avenue, #2
Bordentown, NJ 08505

Monkees
Monkee Magic
C/O Susan Cruz
1427 Jefferson Avenue
West Islip, NY 11795

Monkees
Monkee Lovers United
C/O Rebecca Pastiner
84-59 Kneeland Avenue, #2-A
Elmhurst, NY 11373

Monkees
The Micky D. Show
C/O Valerie Lionel
69 Chestnut Road
Manhasset, NY 11030

Monkees
Ladies Air Society
C/O Vickie Barnhill
2801 Purdue Road
Dayton, OH 45420

Monkees
Listen to the Band
C/O Noel Carroll
640 Mahonig, #5
Warren, OH 44483

Monkees
Cuddly Toys
C/O Donna Rowan
12504 Millersberg Road S.W.
Massillon, OH 44616

Monkees
The Ohio Headquarters
C/O Erica Bendie
1444 N. Park Avenue
Warren, OH 47483

Monkees
Monkee Lovers Unlimited
C/O Traci Kishbaugh
633 E. 4th Street
Berwick, PA 18603

Monkees
Good Clean Fun
1152 S. Negley Avenue
Pittsburgh, PA 15217

Monkees
Amy Dolenz Fan Club
C/O Michael Shoefelt
RD. 31, Box 236A
Roaring Springs, PA 16673

Monkees
Monkee Mania Messenger
C/O B. McConnell & S. Schleir
2913 Meredith Place
Bensalem, PA 19020

Monkees
Operation Monkees
C/O Petera Doziotti
P.O. Box 10
Kutztown, PA 19530

Monkees
Manchester Marauders
C/O Heather Wilds
105 Charles Drive B4
Bryn Mawr, PA 19010-2307

Monkees
Nesmith News
C/O Ellen Puerzer
3209 S. Kennikennic
Milwaukee, WI 53207

Monkees
C/O Beth Warren
719 Marshall Avenue
S. Milwaukee, WI 53172

Monkees
Monkee Family Newsletter
C/O Ellen Puerzer
3209 S. Kennikennic
Milwaukee, WI 53207

Monkees
Good Clean Fun
C/O Linda Eiden
733 Johns Drive #3
Stevens Point, WI 54481

Monkees
As We Go Along
C/O Rachell Hawkins
P.O. Box 967
Pineville, WV 24874

Monkees
Monkee Madness Fan Club
C/O Debbie Hook
49 Winter Avenue
Scarborough, Ontario
M1K 4L9 Canada

Monkees
The Sana Neta
C/O Yoshiko Nishida
158 Kakuei
1321-144 Mutsuzaki
Sakura-Shi, Chiba 285
Japan

Monkees
The MRC in Japan
C/O Chie Hama
3-9-16 Kuramatsu
Sugito-Machi
Saitama, 345
Japan

Monkees
The Monkees/David Jones Fan Club
C/O Ella
Deventerstraat 158
732ICE Apeldoorn
The Netherlands

Monkees
The New Monkees Fan Club
C/O Julie Cote
15534 Mira Monte Drive
Houston, TX 77083

Monkees A La Mode
C/O Amy Childress
505 Carriage Road
Satellite Beach, FL 32927

Monkees Appreciation Society
C/O Diane M. Aull
28 Arcadia Cove
Columbia, SC 29206

*The Monkees/Boyce & Hart Photo
Fan Club*
C/O Jodi Hammrich
P.O. Box 411
Watertown, SD 57201-0411

Monkees Connection
C/O Jodie Maher
P.O. Box 6122
Terre Haute, IN 47802

Monkees Forever
C/O Jane Myhra
E. 715 Erickson Road
Iola, WI 54945

Monkees Greatest Hits
C/O Jessica Shapiro
12 Partridge Road
S. Weymouth, MA 02190

Monkees in Style
C/O Elizabeth Mary Freurk
6447 N. Range Line Road
Glendale, WI 53209

Monkees International
C/O Lee Kiviot
81 Lakeland Drive
Brick, NJ 08723

Monkees Manufactured Image Audio Club
C/O Kathleen Deleney & Chris Coyle
20 Mayer Road
Portland, ME 04102

Monkees Midwest
C/O Renee Luna
1206 27th Avenue S., #205
Moorhead, MN 56560

Monkees Network PMMD
C/O Donna Fay Hall
2755 Villa Drive
Toledo, OH 43617

Monkees Originals
C/O Kathy Tacoma
124 Nancy S.E.
Kentwood, MI 49508

Rick Nelson Fan Club
C/O Anita Young
P.O. Box 78
Pylesville, MD 21132

Willie Nelson Fan Club
C/O Jan Coney
P.O. Box 400
Wright, AR 72182

New Kids on the Block
P.O. Box 7001
Quincy, MA 02269

New Kids on the Block
52 Gover Court
Paradise Road
London SW4 6QT
England

New Kids on the Block Fan Club
C/O Melissa Natoli
576 Fritztown Road
Sinking Spring, PA 19608

Juice Newton Fan Club
P.O. Box 293323
Lewisville, TX 75020-3323

Wayne Newton Fan Club
P.O. Box 1554
Grand Rapids, MI 49501-1554

Peter Noone Fan Club
C/O Marlene Curson
58 Doncaster Avenue
Toronto, Ontario
M4C 1Y7 Canada

Peter Noone Fan Club
P.O. Box 661
Oceanside, CA 92054-0110

Oakridge Boys Fan Club
329 Rockland Road
Hebbersonville, TN 37075

Roy Orbison Newsletter
484 Lake Park Avenue, #80
Oakland, CA 94610

Osmonds
The Osmond Boys Fan Club
P.O. Box 1969
Provo, UT 84603

Osmonds
Merrill Osmond Fan Club
P.O. Box 1969
Provo, UT 84603

Osmonds
Alan, Wayne & Jay Osmond Fan
Club
P.O. Box 1969
Provo, UT 84603

Osmonds
Marie Osmond Fan Club
P.O. Box 6000
Provo, UT 84603

Osmonds
Donny Osmond International Network
P.O. Box 1448
Provo, UT 84603-1448

Osmonds
Osmonds Tape Exchange
C/O Kris Strejch
23156 Mt. Forest Drive
Burlington, Ontario
L7P 1J4 Canada

Elvis Fever Fan Club
C/O Anna Mae Meyers
4014 Keeners Road
Baltimore, MD 21220

Elvis Presley
Elvis Arkansas Style
C/O Beverly Rook
11300 Donnie Drive
Mabelvale, AR 72103

Elvis Presley
The Elvis Now Fan Club
C/O Sue McCasland
P.O. Box 6581
San Jose, CA 95150

Elvis Presley
King of Our Hearts
C/O Rosemary Luci
6117 Silberman Drive
San Jose, CA 95120

Elvis Presley
The Presley-Ites Fan Club
C/O Kathy Fergusson
1708 18th Street N.
Zephyrthills, FL 34248

Elvis Presley
Association of Elvis Presley Fan
Clubs
Joyce & Donna Gentry
5320 53rd Avenue E.
Lot Q 47
Bradenton, FL 34203

Elvis Presley
Elvis Always Fan Club
C/O Ann C. Morrison
Rte. 3, Box 1200
Folkston, GA 31537

Elvis Presley
TCB for Elvis Presley in Kentucky
C/O Linda Derositt
P.O. Box 21754
Lexington, KY 40522

Elvis Presley
If I Can Dream Elvis Presley Fan
Club
P.O. Box 1032
Cotuit, MA 02635

Elvis Presley
Memories of Elvis
C/O Betty Roloson
302 Whitman Court
Glen Burnie, MD 21061

Elvis Presley
True Fans for Elvis
C/O Carol Brocher
P.O. Box 681
Saco, ME 04072

Elvis Presley
All for the Love of Elvis
C/O Ilse Oulette
31 Sheppard Street
Fort Leonardwood, MD 25473

Elvis Presley
Taking Care of Business
C/O Gloria Johnson
P.O. Box 1158
Glen Allen, VA 23060

Elvis Presley
Elvis in Canada
C/O Fran Roberts
P.O. Box 6065
Station F
Hamilton, Ontario
L9C 5S2 Canada

Elvis Presley
The Exclusive Elvis Presley Fan Club
Tony & Pearl Cattemull
30 Addison Road
Teddington, Middlesex
TW11 9EX
England

Elvis Presley
Elvis Country Fan Club
P.O. Box 9113
Austin, TX 78766

Elvis Presley
Elvis Lives on Campaign
C/O Alice Schlichte
13658 S.E. 192nd
Renton, WA 98058

Elvis Presley
Elvisland
C/O Regina Cheung
P.O. Box 20720
Hennersy Road P.O.
Wanchai
Hong Kong

Elvis Presley Circle City Fan Club
C/O Velda Griner
2550 Mars Hill Street
Indianapolis, IN 46241

Elvis Presley Continentals of Florida
C/O Shirley Schwebs
P.O. Box 1371
Kissimmee, FL 32742

Elvis Presley Fan Club
25, Avenue Berchem
1231, Howald
Luxembourg
West Germany

Elvis Presley Fan Club of Australia
C/O Wayne Hawthorne
P.O. Box 82
Elsterwick
Victoria, 3185
Australia

Elvis Presley Fan Club of the
Capital District
Box 265, R.D. #3
Schenectady, NY 12306

Elvis Presley Fan Club of Great
Britain
C/O Todd Slaughter
P.O. Box 4
Leicester
England

Elvis Presley Fan Club of the
Hudson Valley
C/O Betty Stokes
260 Elvis Presley Boulevard
Stone Ridge, NY 12482

Elvis Presley Fan Club of Rochester,
New York
127 Duxbury Road
Rochester, NY 14626

Elvis Presley Memorial Center of
Texas
P.O. Box 3194
Waco, TX 76707

Elvis Presley Memorial Society of
Syracuse, New York
C/O Sue Fetcho
411 Mallard Drive
Camillus, NY 13031

Charley Pride Fan Club
P.O. Box 670507
Dallas, TX 75367-0507

Judas Priest
P.O. Box 6600
Macon, GA 31208

Prince
The New Breed
P.O. Box 858
Old Chelsea Station
New York, NY 10113

Prince
The New Power Generation
Office 4/5/6 Westgate Arcade
Otley
West Yorkshire
Leeds LS21 3AT
England

Prince
Controversy
P.O. Box 310
Croydon
CR9 6AP
England

Gary Puckett Newsletter
P.O. Box 1709
Redlands, CA 92373

Queen Official Fan Club
46 Pembridge Road
London W11 3HR
England

Queensryche Fan Club
P.O. Box 70503
Bellvue, WA 98007

Eddie Rabbitt Fan Club
P.O. Box 125
Lewiston, OH 43333

Ratt Fan Club
P.O. Box 93519
Los Angeles, CA 90093

R.E.M.
P.O. Box 8032
Athens, GA 30603

Cliff Richards Fan Club of America
8916 N. Skokie Boulevard, #3
Skokie, IL 60077

Kenny Rogers Fan Club
C/O Shannon Waggoner
1516 16th Avenue S.
Nashville, TN 37212

John Schneider #1 Fan Club
C/O Trails End Productions
P.O. Box 1726
Mechanicsburg, PA 17055

Rick Springfield Images Support Club
C/O Gail Plaskiewicz
214 Johnson Street
Torrington, CT 06790

Bruce Springsteen
Bruce Springsteen Monthly Fanzine
3850 Thisle Down
Florissant, MO 63033

Bruce Springsteen
The Fever: Bruce Springsteen
Monthly
Box 67261-RI
Los Angeles, CA 90067

Bruce Springsteen
Back Streets
P.O. Box 51225
Seattle, WA 98115

Statler Brothers Newsletter
P.O. Box 2703
Stauton, VA 24401

Connie Stevens Fan Club
C/O Betty Moran
2500 Gaither Street
Hillcrest Heights, MD 20748

Rod Stewart
Worldwide Rod Stewart Fan Club
Postal Station A
Winnipeg, Manitoba
R3K 2C2 Canada

Rolling Stones
Beggars Banquet Newsletter
P.O. Box 6152
New York, NY 10128

Donna Summer Fan Club
P.O. Box 10538
Detroit, MI 48210

Donna Summer Fan Club
C/O Maneo
1224 Vine Street
Los Angeles, CA 90038

B.J. Thomas Fan Club
P.O. Box 1682
Hendersonville, TN 37077-1682

Toto Legend Fan Club
C/O Laura Stine
18651 Clark Street, Apt. 11
Tarzana, CA 91356

T'Pau Fan Club
P.O. Box 1915
London W11 3HR
England

Tanya Tucker Fan Club
200 Chapple Bldg.
Brentwood, TN 37027

U2
Sing No More (No War No More)
P.O. Box 536
Franklin, MA 02088

U2 Info
P.O. Box 156
Princeton Junction, NJ 08550

Velvet Underground Appreciation Society
5721 S.E. Laguna Avenue
Stuart, FL 34997-7828

Bobby Vinton Fan Club
C/O Julie Walker
153 Washington Street
Mt. Vernon, NY 10550

Dionne Warwick Fan Club
P.O. Box 343
Wind Gap, PA 18091

W.A.S.P. Fan Club
P.O. Box 10
London SW19 3TW
England

Jody Watley
C/O Loot Unlimited
8439 Sunset Boulevard
Suite 103
Los Angeles, CA 90069

The Who
Who's News
C/O Mark Cohen
34 Beulah Street, #6
Framingham, MA 01701

The Who Club
P.O. Box 17A
London N6 5RV
England

Hank Williams Jr. Fan Club
P.O. Box 1350
Paris, TN 38242

Tammy Wynette Fan Club
P.O. Box 753
Richboro, PA 18954

Neil Young Appreciation Society
C/O Alan Jenkins
2A Llynfi Street
Mid Glamorgan
CF31 1SY
Wales
United Kingdom

The Rock-and-Roll Hall of Fame

THE HOME OF THE ROCK-AND-ROLL HALL OF FAME AND MUSEUM

The concept of a Hall of Fame for rock-and-roll began in late 1983 when a group of influential figures in the music industry created the Rock-and-Roll Hall of Fame Foundation. Their objective was to recognize and honor the musicians and industry professionals who were the true pioneers of rock-and-roll. After its formation, the Foundation began a search for an appropriate location to establish a permanent museum and archives to educate people about rock-and-roll.

The Hall of Fame Foundation examined a number of competing cities across the country to be the location for the Rock-and-Roll Hall of Fame and Museum—including Cleveland, Memphis, Philadelphia, Detroit, and San Francisco. Cleveland was considered one of the strongest cities because of its place in rock-and-roll history and the enormous enthusiasm shown the project by Clevelanders. A petition bearing more than 660,000 signatures was presented to the Foundation, asking that the Hall of Fame be located in Cleveland. And, when *USA Today* sponsored a national telephone poll to determine where the Hall of Fame should be, 110,315 votes were tabulated for Cleveland, 15 times that of the next highest city. The decision was made in 1986 and Cleveland was selected as the site for the Rock-and-Roll Hall of Fame and Museum. On November 15, 1989, the formal agreement legally designating Cleveland as the official site for the Hall of Fame was solidified.

Cleveland is historically recognized as the city where the term "rock-and-roll" was coined. The legendary Cleveland disc jockey, Alan Freed, began using this term to describe this new form of music and popularized it on his "Moondog" radio broadcasts on Cleveland radio station WJW in 1951. Freed's show is recognized as one of the nation's first—if not the first—rock-

and-roll program. In 1952, Freed and local record retailer Leo Mintz produced and promoted the nation's first rock-and-roll concert known as the "Moondog Coronation Ball" at the Cleveland Arena.

Just as it was in the 1950s and 1960s when Leo's Casino and other area night clubs headlined the Temptations and the Four Tops, the Cleveland of today remains an important part of the national and international contemporary music scene. Cleveland is the city that introduced David Bowie to American audiences and brought Bruce Springsteen's music to the mainstream. The region also spawned several rock legends including The Raspberrys, Eric Carmen, The James Gang, Chrissie Hynde and the Pretenders, Devo, and, in the 1990s, The Nine Inch Nails.

In both a historic and contemporary sense, Cleveland is the home of rock-and-roll and appropriately the home of the Rock-and-Roll Hall of Fame and Museum. Groundbreaking for the facility is scheduled for the second half of 1991, and the facility is to open in 1994.

A DESTINATION TOURIST AREA

With its power to both entertain and educate, the Rock-and-Roll Hall of Fame and Museum is conservatively estimated to attract at least 600,000 visitors a year to America's North Coast on the shore of Lake Erie. The Hall of Fame will be the first major attraction at North Coast Harbor, the new harbor development in the hub of downtown Cleveland. The lakefront site for the Hall of Fame is the perfect setting for this unique destination tourist attraction. Designed by world-renowned architect, I. M. Pei, the 120,000 square foot building will stand as a jewel on the lakeshore and become an architectural gem in the growing urban landscape of the city. This major facility will add to Cleveland's growing skyline and serve as a tribute to those individuals— past and present—who have influenced American culture through rock-and-roll music.

A LOOK AT THE HALL OF FAME AND MUSEUM

The Rock-and-Roll Hall of Fame and Museum will bring to life the sights, sounds, and emotions of the artists, songwriters, producers, and radio broadcasters of rock-and-roll music throughout its lifetime. The museum will serve as a window on American culture and history, reflecting the attitudes and beliefs over the years as expressed through the music itself and the composers and artists involved in its development.

The interior of the museum is being designed by a consortium of three of the country's leading interior and graphics firms: The Burdick Group of San Francisco, Herb Rosenthal of Los Angeles, and Lou Dorfsman of New York City. Their concepts are innovative and creative in design, immense in scope, and powerful in vision. Visitors will be captivated as they explore the Hall of Fame and allow themselves to be educated about, entertained by, and immersed in the world of rock-and-roll.

Throughout the facility, the story of rock-and-roll will unfold with exhibits punctuated by carefully selected artifacts and memorabilia of the artists who made it all possible. Visitors will not be passive observers; they will become involved in the events that shaped musical history. Interactive exhibits using state-of-the-art sound and video systems will chronicle the evolution of the music in the context of the sociology of the times. The performer's experience, the listener's experience, and the experience that all society felt will be presented in videos, displays, and oral histories. The rapid development of electronic technology and how those changes have revised the delivery of the music will be examined. A radio studio will be located in the museum, enabling radio personalities from across the country to conduct live broadcasts from the Hall of Fame. Because of the substantive depth of what will be presented in this facility, visitors will not be able to fully absorb the many exhibits in just one visit. Different temporary and rotating exhibits, as well as on-going programs and events, will make the Hall of Fame a living museum, encouraging visitors to return over and over again.

The interior design team is working in conjunction with museum architect I. M. Pei to create one of the most innovative and exciting attractions available anywhere. But the Hall of Fame is more than a museum and attraction; it will also be a scholarly repository and archives for the music itself, where students and educators can research and write, recognized internationally as a place for people of all ages to learn about rock-and-roll music, history, sociology, technology, and the impact that the music has had on our culture and society.

ROCK-AND-ROLL HALL OF FAME AND MUSEUM, INC.

INDUCTEES

1986

ROCK-AND-ROLL ARTISTS
1. Chuck Berry
2. James Brown
3. Ray Charles
4. Sam Cooke
5. Fats Domino
6. The Everly Brothers
7. Buddy Holly
8. Jerry Lee Lewis
9. Elvis Presley
10. Little Richard

NON-PERFORMERS
11. Alan Freed
12. Sam Phillips

EARLY INFLUENCES
13. John Hammond

14. Robert Johnson
15. Jimmie Rodgers
16. Jimmy Yancey

1987

ROCK-AND-ROLL ARTISTS
1. The Coasters
2. Eddie Cochran
3. Bo Diddley
4. Aretha Franklin
5. Marvin Gaye
6. Bill Haley
7. B. B. King
8. Clyde McPhatter
9. Ricky Nelson
10. Roy Orbison
11. Carl Perkins

12. Smokey Robinson
13. Big Joe Turner
14. Muddy Waters
15. Jackie Wilson

NON-PERFORMERS
16. Leonard Chess
17. Ahmet Ertegun
18. Jerome Leiber
19. Michael Stroller
20. Jerry Wexler

EARLY INFLUENCES
21. Louis Jordan
22. T-Bone Walker
23. Hank Williams

1988

ROCK-AND-ROLL ARTISTS
1. The Beach Boys
2. The Beatles
3. The Drifters
4. Bob Dylan
5. The Supremes

NON-PERFORMERS
6. Berry Gordy, Jr.

EARLY INFLUENCES
7. Woody Guthrie
8. Leadbelly
9. Les Paul

1989

ROCK-AND-ROLL ARTISTS
1. Dion
2. Otis Redding
3. The Rolling Stones
4. The Temptations
5. Stevie Wonder

NON-PERFORMERS
6. Phil Spector

EARLY INFLUENCES
7. The Ink Spots
8. Bessie Smith
9. The Soul Stirrers

1990

ROCK-AND-ROLL ARTISTS
1. Hank Ballard
2. Bobby Darin
3. The Four Seasons
4. The Four Tops
5. The Kinks
6. The Platters
7. Simon and Garfunkel
8. The Who

NON-PERFORMERS
9. Gerry Goffin and Carole King
10. Lamont Dozier, Brian Holland, and Eddie Holland

EARLY INFLUENCES
11. Louis Armstrong
12. Charlie Christian
13. Ma Rainey

1991

ROCK-AND-ROLL ARTISTS
1. LaVern Baker
2. The Byrds
3. John Lee Hooker
4. The Impressions
5. Wilson Pickett
6. Jimmy Reed
7. Ike and Tina Turner

NON-PERFORMERS
8. Dave Bartholomew
9. Ralph Bass

EARLY INFLUENCE
10. Howlin' Wolf

The co-chairmen of the Rock-and-Roll Hall of Fame and Museum, Inc., are: Mr. Ahmet Ertegun, Co-Chairman, Atlantic Records, and Mr. William Hulett, President, Stouffer Hotels and Resorts.

The executive director of the Rock-and-Roll Hall of Fame and Museum, Inc., is: Larry R. Thompson, Esq.

MAGAZINE INDEX

GENERAL INDEX

Aames, Willie, 353–54
Aardvark, 495
Abba, 9, 12–13, 45, 47, 50, 73, 75, 77, 80,
    111, 208, 211, 232, 242–43, 247,
    258, 263, 290, 318, 328, 330, 332,
    353, 359, 364
Abbattoir, 30, 246
ABC, 16–17, 50, 80–81, 83, 211, 235, 244,
    315–17, 337, 361
Abdul, Paula, 28, 34, 93, 234, 270, 289–90,
    304–05, 310, 317–18, 335, 361, 364
Abercrombie, John, 137
Abrian Belew, 80
AC/DC, 10, 14–15, 17, 19, 30–33, 47–52,
    79, 81, 84–86, 90, 93, 109, 136, 141,
    153–54, 156–58, 165–66, 188, 220,
    222, 232, 236, 240, 243, 245–46,
    252, 262–63, 286, 292–93, 308, 321,
    339, 357, 359
Accept, 51, 82, 85, 92, 109–10, 147,
    156–58, 165, 214, 234–35, 243–45,
    247, 292–93, 329, 364
Ace, 41, 43
Ace, Johnny, 131
Ace of Cups, 394, 396–97, 399, 426
Ackles, David, 36, 146
Adam & the Ants, 49, 79, 129, 153, 286,
    290, 359
Adams, Brooke, 265
Adams, Bryan, 81–83, 93, 99, 109, 188, 234,
    248, 267–68, 292–93, 319, 336–37,
    368

Adams, Ralph, 495
Adderly, Cannonball, 418
Adish, Cindy, 329
Adler, Lou, 252
Adler, Steven, 33
Aere Apparent, 477
Aerosmith, 11, 16, 30–33, 41–45, 47–48, 50,
    52, 54–56, 59, 71–73, 75, 77, 83–87,
    90, 96, 100, 109–11, 140–41,
    149–51, 153–54, 156–58, 164–67,
    169, 184, 186, 189–90, 194, 207,
    209, 212, 220, 222, 226–27, 232,
    235–37, 241–48, 251, 260, 262–63,
    266, 269–70, 284, 305, 310, 312,
    314, 317, 319–20, 329, 337–39, 359,
    373
Africa, 187
Agnostic Front, 220
A-Ha, 33, 93, 227, 246, 287–89, 293, 299,
    315–17, 321, 333–34, 336–37, 351,
    354–55, 368
Air Speed Indicator, 483
Air Supply, 286, 290, 292–93, 330–31, 337
Akkerman, Jan, 14, 56
Akroyd, Dan, 261–62
Al B., 218
Alabama, 15, 304, 308–09
Alan, Buddy, 306
Alan Parsons Project, 308
Alarm, 17, 19, 82–84, 188, 190, 251, 268,
    315–16, 336, 444
Albert, Herb, 326

552

Area Code 615, 433
Argent, 8, 66, 173, 225, 241, 370–73, 434
Argent, Keith, 56
Armatrading, Joan, 13, 69, 81, 98, 170, 187, 308, 359
Armed Forces, 227
Armored Saint, 30, 52, 54, 156, 220, 246
Arms Benefit, 214
Armstrong, Louis, 129, 543
Arnaz, Desi, Jr., 282, 296–97
Arnaz, Lucie, 281
Arquette, Rosanna, 265–66
Asbury Jukes, 9–10
Asher, Jane, 279–80
Asher, Peter, 130
Ashford & Simpson, 193, 204, 216, 219, 240, 308
Ashion, 438
Ashkenasy, Vladimir, 175
Ashmollyan Quintet, 469, 473, 475, 479
Asia, 19, 50, 52, 80–81, 109, 154, 211, 236, 264, 308
Asian Flu, 491
Aslan, 447
Asleep at the Wheel, 59, 68, 70, 129, 170, 226, 261, 307, 310, 373
Assembly, 188
Association, 94, 112, 129–30, 143–44, 306, 326, 334, 406
Astin, Mack, 288
Astin, Sean, 27, 287–88
Astley, Rick, 316, 321
Aswad, Thaddeus, D. J. Wendt & The Midnite Dread Sound System, 447
Atkins, Chet, 133, 135–36, 190
Atkins, Chris, 13, 15, 285–87, 294, 335–36, 338
Atlanta Rhythm Section, 45, 73, 170
Atlantic Record Party, 101
Atlantic Starr, 239
Atlantics, 9
Atlee, 439
Atomic Pile, 463
Atomic Playboys, 87
Au Paris, 80
Auger, Brian, 175, 426, 493
Aum, 426, 428–29, 437
Australian Rock, 131, 187
Autograph, 30, 85, 156–57, 244
Autry, Gene, 258
Avalon, Frankie, 128, 236, 275–77, 294, 299, 324, 340
Avedon, 182
Average White Band, 56, 59, 66, 68, 72, 149, 259, 261, 373
AWB, 41–42, 44–45

Axe Victims, 59
Axis, Jon Butcher, 211
Ayers, Bill, 100
Ayers, Kevin, 41, 357
Aykroyd, Dan, 47, 68–69, 109
Aynsley Dunbar Retaliation, 426
Azama, Ann, 327
Aztec Camera, 17–18, 82, 187

B-52's, 12, 77, 79–81, 92, 99, 151, 153, 167, 192, 220, 243, 263, 270, 312, 314–16, 359, 458, 513
B.A.D., 316
B Boys, 253
Baby Huey & Baby Sitters, 428
Babyface, 28
Babylon A.D., 55
Babys, 48, 68, 73, 77, 150–51, 167, 226, 284, 290, 329, 332, 357
Bach, Barbara, 14, 203
Bach, Catherine, 285–86, 294, 336, 338
Bach, J. S., 177
Bach, Sebastian, 31–33, 55, 110, 166, 222, 232, 319
Bacharach, Burt, 174, 329
"Bachelor Father," 325
Bachelors, 338
Bachman-Turner Overdrive, 26, 40–41, 56, 66, 71, 167, 259, 373
Bacon, Kevin, 240, 287, 294, 336
Bad Brains, 86–87
Bad Company, 10, 40–44, 47–48, 56, 59, 66, 71–73, 77, 80, 84, 86, 141, 147, 149–51, 154, 166, 208, 212, 226, 241–42, 246, 259, 262, 309, 318, 329, 373
Bad English, 111, 158, 178, 232, 320
Bad Manners, 359
Bad News Bears, 285
Badfinger, 8, 13, 39, 96, 146–47, 206, 262, 357
Badger, 463
Badlands, 55, 87, 92, 110–11, 141, 158, 164–65, 222
Baez, Joan, 8, 10, 35, 38–39, 63, 65, 72, 108, 131, 174, 203, 223–24, 236, 253, 255, 258–61, 265, 268
Bailey, Tom, 177
Baio, Scott, 203, 284–87, 294, 329–33, 335–36, 338–39, 341, 353–55, 364
Baird, Dan, 99
Baker, Anita, 193, 240, 267
Baker, Ginger, 17, 130, 146, 189, 211, 269, 310, 505
Baker Gurvitz Army, 59
Baker, LaVern, 543

ABOUT THE AUTHOR

DAVID HENKEL has been an active collector and dealer of rock and roll magazines and memorabilia for over thirty years. His personal collection is among the most comprehensive in the world. He has added to the music collections of the Chicago Public Library, the Library at Lincoln Center, and other institutes of learning, as well as servicing the personal collections of many rock stars.

Henkel has been instrumental in the acquisition of rare rock and roll posters for the Rock and Roll Hall of Fame in Cleveland, Ohio, and is the founder of the Rock and Roll Collectors' Hotline (201-641-7212), established in 1979, which provides collectors and researchers with information on the values of rock memorabilia, sources for buying and selling, and resources for photocopies and facsimiles of magazine articles from rare and long out-of-print rock or teen magazines.

Henkel continues to add to his collection with unrelenting enthusiasm and actively seeks examples of the thousands of rock and teen magazines and rock posters published throughout the world since 1957. He lives in New Jersey.